DAW 02/03   19.99   Ⓐ

KU-516-372

CLASS No. ....

ACCESSION 061425

LOCATION .... MW

ALISON
READER

English Legal System

Marton LRC
Middlesbrough College
Marton Road
Middlesbrough
TS4 3RZ

Middlesbrough College

00061425

We work with leading authors to develop the strongest educational materials in law, bringing cutting-edge thinking and best learning practice to a global market.

Under a range of well-known imprints, including Longman, we craft high quality print and electronic publications which help readers to understand and apply their content, whether studying or at work.

To find out more about the complete range of our publishing please visit us on the World Wide Web at: **www.pearsoneduc.com**

Middlesbrough College

Learning Resources Centre

Class No

Accession   061425

Location   MW

English
Legal System

Fourth Edition

Catherine Elliott
and Frances Quinn

An imprint of **Pearson Education**

Harlow, England · London · New York · Reading, Massachusetts · San Francisco
Toronto · Don Mills, Ontario · Sydney · Tokyo · Singapore · Hong Kong · Seoul
Taipei · Cape Town · Madrid · Mexico City · Amsterdam · Munich · Paris · Milan

Pearson Education Limited

Edinburgh Gate
Harlow
Essex CM20 2JE
England

and Associated Companies throughout the world

Visit us on the World Wide Web at:
http://www.pearsoneduc.com

First published 1996
Second edition 1998
Third edition 2000
Fourth edition 2002

© Pearson Education Limited 1996, 1998, 2000, 2002

The rights of Catherine Elliott and Frances Quinn to be identified as
authors of this Work have been asserted by them in accordance with
the Copyright, Designs and Patents Act 1988.

All rights reserved; no part of this publication may be reproduced, stored
in a retrieval system, or transmitted in any form or by any means, electronic,
mechanical, photocopying, recording, or otherwise without either the prior
written permission of the Publishers or a licence permitting restricted copying
in the United Kingdom issued by the Copyright Licensing Agency Ltd.,
90 Tottenham Court Road, London W1P 0LP.

ISBN 0 582 47313 6

British Library Cataloguing-in-Publication Data
A catalogue record for this book is available from the British Library

10 9 8 7 6 5 4 3 2 1
06 05 04 03 02

Typeset by 35 in 10.5/12pt Baskerville
Printed in Great Britain by Henry Ling Ltd., at the Dorset Press, Dorchester, Dorset

Contents

Preface

This book is designed to provide a clear explanation of the English legal system and how it works in practice today. As ever, the legal system and its operation are currently the subject of heated public debate, and we hope that the material here will allow you to enter into some of that debate and develop your own views as to how the system should develop. A new feature that has been added to this edition is 'Reading on the Internet' sections at the end of each chapter. These provide references to interesting material that has been referred to in the chapter and which is available free on the Internet.

One of our priorities in writing this book has been to explain the material clearly, so that it is easy to understand, without lowering the quality of the content. Too often, law is avoided as a difficult subject, when the real difficulty is the vocabulary and style of legal textbooks. For that reason, we have aimed to use 'plain English' as far as possible, and explain the more complex legal terminology where it arises. There is also a glossary of difficult words at the back of the book. In addition, chapters are structured so that material is in a systematic order for the purposes of both learning and revision, and clear subheadings make specific points easy to locate.

Although we hope that many readers will use this book to satisfy a general interest in law and the legal system, we recognize that the majority will be those who have to sit an examination on the subject. Therefore, each chapter features typical examination questions, with detailed guidance on answering them, using the material in the book. This is obviously useful at revision time, but we recommend that when first reading the book, you take the opportunity offered by the questions sections to think through the material that you have just read and look at it from different angles. This will help you both understand and remember it. You will also find a section at the end of the book which gives useful general advice on answering examination questions on the English legal system.

This book is part of a series that has been written by the same authors. The other books in the series are *Criminal Law, Contract Law* and *Tort Law*. We have endeavoured to state the law as at 1 January 2002.

Catherine Elliott
and Frances Quinn
London, 2002

A Companion Website accompanies *English Legal System*, Fourth Edition by Catherine Elliott and Frances Quinn

Visit the *English Legal System* Companion Website at *www.booksites.net/elliottquinn* to find valuable teaching and learning material including:

For Students and Lecturers:
- Updates from the author to make sure your knowledge of the subject is up-to-date
- A guide to cases, law reports and case references
- Guidelines for answering exam, essay and problem questions
- Web links to sites of interest

Also: This regularly maintained and updated site has a syllabus manager and search functions.

Acknowledgements

We are grateful to the following for permission to reproduce copyright material:

Tables 6.1 and 6.2, from *The Judiciary in the Magistrates' Courts*, (Morgan, R. and Russell, N. 2000), Home Office RDS Occasional Paper No. 66, being Crown Copyright reproduced with permission of the Controller of Her Majesty's Stationery Office; Figures 10.1, 10.2 and 11.1, from *Criminal Statistics England and Wales 1999*, being Crown Copyright published for the Home Office and reproduced with permission of the Controller of Her Majesty's Stationery Office; Figures 12.2, 13.1, 14.1 and 14.2, from *Judicial Statistics 1999*, being Crown Copyright published for the Lord Chancellor's Department and reproduced with permission of the Controller of Her Majesty's Stationery Office.

We are indebted to the following examination boards for permission to reproduce questions which have appeared in their examination papers:

The Associated Examination Board (*AEB* now *AQA*)
Northern Examinations and Assessment Board (*NEAB* now *AQA*)
Oxford Cambridge and RSA Examinations Board (*OCR*)
Edexcel
Welsh Joint Education Committee (*WJEC*)

AQA examination questions are reproduced by permission of the Assessment and Qualifications Alliance.

The examination boards are not responsible for the suggested answers to the questions. Full responsibility for these is accepted by the authors.

In some instances we have been unable to trace the owners of copyright material and we would appreciate any information that would enable us to do so.

Table of Cases

Table of Statutes

Table of Statutory Instruments

Cases, Law Reports and Case References: A Guide

In order to understand the table of cases and the reference to cases in this book generally, you need to know about the naming of cases, law reports and case references.

Case names

Each legal case that is taken to court is given a name. The name of the case is usually based on the family name of the parties involved. Where there are more than two parties on each side, the case name tends to be shortened to just include one name for each side. In essays, the name of the case should normally be put into italics or underlined, though in this book we have chosen to put them in bold. The exact case names in civil law and criminal law are slightly different so we will consider each in turn.

Criminal law case names

If Ms Smith steals Mr Brown's car then a criminal action is likely to be brought by the state against her. The written name of the case would then be **R** *v* **Smith**. The letter 'R' stands for the latin *Rex* (King) or *Regina* (Queen) depending on whether there was a king or queen in office at the time of the decision. Sometimes the full latin terms are used rather than the simple abbreviation R, so that the case **R** *v* **Smith** if brought in 1998 while Queen Elizabeth is in office could also be called **Regina** *v* **Smith**. The idea is that the action is ultimately being brought by the state against Ms Smith.

The 'v' separating the two parties names is short for 'versus', in the same way as one might write Nottingham Forest Football Club v Arsenal Football Club when the two teams are going to play a match against each other. When speaking, instead of saying 'R versus Smith' one should really say 'The Crown against Smith'.

If Ms Smith is only 13, and therefore still a minor, the courts cannot reveal the identity of the child to the public and therefore the case will be referred to by her initial rather than her full name: **R** *v* **S**.

Occasionally criminal prosecutions are brought by the Government's law officers. If an action was brought by the Attorney-General against

Ms Smith it would be called **A-G** *v* **Smith**. If it was brought by the Director of Public Prosecutions it would be called **DPP** *v* **Smith**. Should the state fail to bring an action at all, Mr Brown might choose to bring a private prosecution himself and the case would then be called **Brown** *v* **Smith**.

Civil law case names

In civil law if Mr Brown is in a neighbour dispute with Ms Smith and decides to bring an action against Ms Smith the name of the case will be **Brown** *v* **Smith**. This is orally expressed as 'Brown and Smith', rather than 'Brown versus Smith'. At the original trial, the first name used is the name of the person bringing the action (the claimant) and the second name used is that of the defendant. If there is an appeal against the original decision, then the first name will usually be the name of the appellant and the second name that of the respondent, though there are some exceptions to this.

In civil law the state can have an interest in what are described as judicial review cases. For example, Mr Brown may be unhappy with his local council, Hardfordshire City Council, for failing to take action against his neighbour. He may bring an action against the Council and the action would be called **R** *v* **Hardfordshire City Council ex parte Brown**.

In certain family and property actions a slightly different format may be used. For example, if Ms Smith's child, James Smith is out of control and needs to be taken into care, a resulting legal action might be called **Re Smith** or **In re Smith**. 'Re' is latin and simply means 'in the matter of' or 'concerning'. So the name **Re Smith** really means in the matter of James Smith.

As with civil cases there is sometimes a need to prevent the public from knowing the name of the parties, particularly where children are involved. The initials of the child are then used rather than their full name. So the above case might be called **Re S** rather than **Re Smith** to protect James.

The Law Reports

Because some cases lay down important legal principles, over 2,000 each year are published in law reports. Some of these law reports date back over 700 years. Perhaps the most respected series of law reports are those called *The Law Reports*, because before publication the report of each case included in them is checked for accuracy by the judge who tried it. It is this series that should be cited before a court in preference to any other. The series is divided into several sub-series depending on the court which heard the case, as follows:

Appeal Cases (containing decisions of the Court of Appeal, the House of Lords and the Privy Council)

Chancery Division (decisions of the Chancery Division of the High Court and their appeals to the Court of Appeal)

Family Division (decisions of the Family Division of the High Court and their appeals to the Court of Appeal)

Queen's Bench (decisions of the Queen's Bench Division of the High Court and their appeals to the Court of Appeal)

Neutral citation

Following the Practice Direction (Supreme Court Judgments: Format and Citation), a form of neutral citation was introduced in 2001 in the Court of Appeal and Administrative Court. At some stage in the future, the neutral citation will be extended to all judgments of the High Court. This form of citation was introduced to facilitate reference to cases reported on the Internet and in CD-ROMs. Unlike reports in books, these reports do not have fixed page numbers and volumes. A unique number is now given to each approved judgment and the paragraphs in each judgment are numbered. The three forms of the neutral citation are as follows:

Civil Division of the Court of Appeal: [2000] EWCA Civ 1, 2, 3, etc.
Criminal Division of the Court of
    Appeal: [2000] EWCA Crim 1, 2, 3, etc.
Administrative Court: [2000] EWHC Admin 1, 2, 3, etc.

The letters 'EW' stand for England and Wales. For example, if **Brown** *v* **Smith** is the fifth numbered judgment of 2002 in the Civil Division of the Court of Appeal, it would be cited: **Brown** *v* **Smith** [2002] EWCA Civ 5. If you wished to refer to the fourth paragraph of the judgment, the correct citation is [2002] EWCA Civ 5 at [4]. The neutral citation must always be used on at least one occasion when the judgment is cited before a court.

Case reference

Each case is given a reference(s) to explain exactly where it can be found in a law report(s). This reference consists of a series of letters and numbers that follow the case name. The pattern of this reference varies depending on the law report being referred to. The usual format is to follow the name of the case by:

A year. Where the date reference tells you the year in which the case was decided, the date is normally enclosed in round brackets. If the date is the year in which the case is reported, it is given in square brackets. The most common law reports tend to use square brackets.

A volume number. Not all law reports have a volume number, sometimes they simply identify their volumes by year.

The law report abbreviation. Each series of law reports have an abbreviation for their title so that the whole name does not need to be written out in full. The main law reports and their abbreviations are as follows:

All England Law Reports	(All ER)
Appeal Cases	(AC)
Chancery Division	(Ch D)
Criminal Appeal Reports	(Cr App R)
Family Division	(Fam)
King's Bench	(KB)
Queen's Bench Division	(QB)
Weekly Law Reports	(WLR)

A page number. This is the page at which the report of the case commences.

For example, **Cozens** *v* **Brutus** [1973] AC 854 means that the case was reported in the Appeal Cases law report in 1973 at page 854; **DPP** *v* **Hawkins** [1988] 1 WLR 1166 means that the case was reported in the first volume of the Weekly Law Reports of 1988 at page 1166; and **R** *v* **Angel** (1968) 52 Cr App R 280 means that the case was reported in the 52nd volume of the Criminal Appeal Reports at page 280.

These references can be used to go and find and read the case in a law library which stocks the relevant law reports. This is important as a textbook can only provide a summary of the case and has no legal status in itself, it is the actual case which contains the law.

Where a case has been decided after the Practice Direction of 2001 introducing neutral citations for the Court of Appeal and Administrative Court, the neutral citation will appear in front of the law report citation. For example: **Brown** *v* **Smith** [2002] EWCA Civ 5, [2002] QB 432, [2002] 3 All ER 21.

Introduction

This book examines the legal system of England and Wales, looking at how our law is made and applied. To understand the legal system, however, you first need to know something about the context in which this legal system is operating: the constitution. A constitution is a set of rules which details a country's system of government; in most cases it will be a written document, but in some countries, including Britain, the constitution cannot be found written down in one document, and is known as an unwritten constitution.

Constitutions essentially set out broad principles concerning who makes law and how, and allocate power between the main institutions of the state – government, Parliament and the judiciary. They may also indicate the basic values on which the country should expect to be governed, such as the idea that citizens should not be punished unless they have broken the law, or that certain rights and freedoms should be guaranteed, and the state prevented from overriding them.

The unwritten constitution

Britain is very unusual in not having a written constitution – every other Western democracy has one. In many cases, the document was written after a major political change, such as a revolution or securing independence from a colonial power. The fact that the British constitution is not to be found in a specific document does not mean that we do not have a constitution: if a country has rules about who holds the power to govern, what they can and cannot do with that power, and how that power is to be passed on or transferred, it has a constitution, even though there is no single constitutional document. In our constitution, for example, it is established that the Government is formed by the political party which wins a general election, and that power is transferred from that party when they lose an election.

Having said that, the exact details of some areas of our constitution are subject to debate. This is because its sources include not only Acts of Parliament and judicial decisions, which are of course written down (although not together in one document), but also what are known as conventions. Conventions are not law, but are long-established traditions which tend to be followed, not because there would be any legal sanction if they were not, but because they have simply become the right way to behave. In this respect they are a bit like the kind of social rules that most people follow – for example, it is not against the law to pick your nose in public, but doing so usually invites social disapproval, so we generally avoid it. In the same way, failing to observe a constitutional convention is not against the law, but provokes so much political disapproval that conventions generally are followed, and most people concerned would see them as binding. Some well-established examples of conventions are that the Queen does not refuse to give her consent to Acts of Parliament; judges do not undertake activities associated with a political party; and the Speaker of the House of Commons does his or her job impartially, despite being a member of one of the parties represented in the House.

Because conventions are not law, they are not enforced by the courts; but, someone who has broken a convention may end up being forced to resign from their post as a result of the disapproval it causes.

Three basic principles underlying the British constitution are the separation of powers, the supremacy of Parliament and the rule of law.

The separation of powers

One of the fundamental principles underlying our constitution is that of the separation of powers. According to this principle, developed by the eighteenth-century French philosopher Montesquieu, all state power can be divided into three types: executive, legislative and judicial. The executive represents what we would call the Government and its servants, such as the police and civil servants; the legislative power is Parliament; and judicial authority is exercised by the judges.

The basis of Montesquieu's theory was that these three types of power should not be concentrated in the hands of one person or group, since this would give them absolute control, with no one to check that the power was exercised for the good of the country. Instead, Montesquieu argued, each type of power should be exercised by a different body, so that they can each keep an eye on the activities of the other and make sure that they do not behave unacceptably.

Montesquieu believed that England, at the time when he was writing, was an excellent example of this principle being applied in practice. Whether that was true even then is debatable, and there are certainly areas of weakness now, as we shall see in later chapters.

The supremacy of Parliament

A second fundamental principle of our constitution has traditionally been the supremacy of Parliament. This means that Parliament is the highest source of English law; so long as a law has been passed according to the rules of parliamentary procedure, it must be applied by the courts. So if, for example, Parliament had passed a law stating that all newborn boys had to be killed, or that all dog owners had to keep a cat as well, there might well be an enormous public outcry, but the laws would still be valid and the courts would, in theory at least, be obliged to uphold them. The reasoning behind this approach is that Parliament, unlike the judiciary, is democratically elected, and therefore ought to have the upper hand when making the laws that every citizen has to live by.

This approach is unusual in democratic countries. Most comparable nations have what is known as a Bill of Rights. This is a statement of the basic rights which citizens can expect to have protected from state interference; it may form part of a written constitution, or be a separate document. In many countries, the job of a Bill of Rights is done by incorporating into national law the European Convention on Human Rights, an international Treaty which was agreed after the Second World War, and seeks to protect basic human rights such as freedom of expression, of religion and of movement. A Bill of Rights takes precedence over other laws and the courts are able to refuse to apply legislation which infringes any of the rights protected by it.

Although Britain is one of the original signatories of the European Convention on Human Rights, for many years it was not incorporated into English law. Parliament has now passed the Human Rights Act 1998, which came into force in October 2000. This Act at last incorporates the Convention into domestic law, but it does not give the convention superiority over English law. It requires that wherever possible, legislation should be interpreted in line with the principles of the Convention, but it does not allow the courts to override statutes that are incompatible with it, nor does it prevent Parliament from making laws that are in conflict with it.

Section 19 of the Act requires that when new legislation is made, a Government Minister must make a statement before the second reading of the Bill in Parliament, saying either that in their view the provisions of the Bill are compatible with the Convention, or that even if they are not, the Government wishes to proceed with the Bill anyway. Although the implication is obviously that, in most cases, Ministers will be able to say that a Bill conforms with the Convention, the Act's provision for the alternative statement confirms that parliamentary supremacy is not intended to be overridden. The Act does make one impact on parliamentary supremacy, though a small one: s. 10 allows a Minister of the Crown to amend by order any Act which has been found by the courts to be incompatible with the Convention, whereas normally an Act of Parliament could only be changed by another Act. However, there is no obligation to do this and a piece of legislation which has been found to be incompatible with the Convention would remain valid if the Government chose not to amend it.

By contrast, a definite erosion of parliamentary supremacy has been brought about by Britain's membership of the European Union (EU).

The EU can only make laws concerning particular subject areas, but in those areas, its law must take precedence over laws made by Parliament, and in this respect Parliament is no longer, strictly speaking, the supreme source of law in the UK. In areas of law not covered by the EU, however, Parliament remains supreme.

An interesting and unusual view of the present constitutional position has been put forward by Laws J, writing in the academic journal *Public Law*. He suggests that even without a Bill of Rights, it can be argued that Parliament is not quite so all-powerful as traditional constitutional doctrine would suggest. His point is that Parliament draws its power from the fact that it is democratically elected: we accept its authority to make law because we all have a say in who makes up Parliament. Therefore, says Laws J, it must follow that Parliament's power is restricted to making laws which are consistent with democracy, and with the idea that if we are all entitled to a vote, we must also be entitled to a certain minimum level of treatment. That would mean that our example of a law that all newborn babies had to be killed, which would clearly conflict with this entitlement, might actually be beyond Parliament's law-making powers and, according to Laws J, the courts would therefore be constitutionally entitled to refuse to uphold it. This view has not been tested by the courts, but it certainly provides an interesting contribution to the debate.

In 1998 some important constitutional changes were made which passed some of the powers of the Westminster Parliament to new bodies in Scotland and Northern Ireland. The new Scottish Parliament, created by the Scotland Act 1998, can make laws affecting Scotland only, on many important areas, including health, education, local government, criminal justice, food standards and agriculture, though legislation on foreign affairs, defence, national security, trade and industry and a number of other areas will still be made for the whole of the UK by the Westminster Parliament. The Northern Ireland Act 1998 similarly gives the Northern Ireland Assembly power to make legislation for Northern Ireland in some areas, though again, foreign policy, defence and certain other areas are still to be covered by Westminster.

In the same year, the Government of Wales Act established a new body for Wales, the Welsh Assembly, but unlike the other two bodies, the Welsh Assembly does not have the power to make primary legislation; legislation made in Westminster will continue to cover Wales. However, the Welsh Assembly is able to make what is called delegated legislation (discussed at p. 51).

The rule of law

The third basic principle of our constitution is known as the rule of law. It is developed from the writings of the nineteenth-century writer Dicey. According to Dicey, the rule of law had three elements. First, that there should be no sanction without breach, meaning that nobody should be punished by the state unless they had broken a law. Secondly, that one law should govern everyone, including both ordinary citizens and state officials. Thirdly, that the rights of the individual were not secured by a written constitution, but by the decisions of judges in ordinary law.

The real importance of the rule of law today lies in the basic idea underlying all three of Dicey's points (but especially the first) that the state should use its power according to agreed rules, and not arbitrarily. The issue has arisen frequently in the context of the troubles in Northern Ireland. For example, opposition to an alleged shoot to kill policy by the armed forces against suspected terrorists was based on the principle that suspected criminals should be fairly tried, according to the law, and punished only if convicted.

A written constitution?

There has been much debate in recent years about whether the UK should have a written constitution. The main reasons put forward in favour of this are that it would clear up some of the grey areas concerning conventions, make the constitution accessible to citizens, and, some argue, provide greater protection of basic rights and liberties, such as freedom of speech.

Written constitutions can be changed, but usually only by means of a special procedure, more difficult than that for changing ordinary law. Thus, it might be necessary to hold a referendum on the proposed change, or gain a larger than usual majority in Parliament, or both. This contrasts with our unwritten constitution, which can be altered by an ordinary piece of legislation. So, some people have argued that the right of people suspected of committing a crime to remain silent when questioned, without this being taken as evidence of guilt, was part of our constitution; nevertheless, that right was essentially abolished by the Criminal Justice and Public Order Act 1994. If the UK had had a written constitution then this right would probably have been contained in it and a special procedure would have had to be followed to amend the constitution to remove that right. The integration of the European Convention on Human Rights into domestic law may prove to be the first step towards a fully fledged written constitution.

Those in favour of our unwritten constitution argue that it is the product of centuries of gradual development, forming part of our cultural heritage which it would be wrong to destroy. They also point out that the lack of any special procedural requirements for changing it allows flexibility, so that the constitution develops along with the changing needs of society.

1 Sources of law

The word source can mean several different things with regard to law, but for our purposes it primarily describes the means by which the law comes into existence.

English law stems from seven main sources, though these vary a great deal in importance. The basis of our law today is case law, a mass of judge-made decisions which lays down rules to be followed in future cases. For many centuries it was the main form of law and it is still very important today. However, the most important form of law, in the sense that it prevails over most of the others, is statute, or Act of Parliament, which today is the source of most major changes in the law. As well as being a source of law in their own right, statutes contribute to case law, since the courts occasionally have to interpret statutory provisions, and such decisions lay down new precedents. Delegated legislation is a related source, laying down detailed rules made to implement the broader provisions of statutes.

An increasingly important source of law is the legislation of the European union, which is the only type of law that can take precedence over statutes in the UK, and is increasingly influencing the decisions of the courts in interpreting statutes. Finally, custom, equity and obligations relating to international treaties are minor sources of law, though Britain's obligations under the European Convention on Human Rights have produced notable contributions to law reform.

▶ CASE LAW

Before the Norman conquest, different areas of England were governed by different systems of law, often adapted from those of the various invaders who had settled there; roughly speaking, Dane law applied in the north, Mercian law around the midlands, and Wessex law in the south and west. Each was based largely on local custom, and even within the larger areas, these customs, and hence the law, varied from place to place. The king had little control over the country as a whole, and there was no effective central government.

When William the Conqueror gained the English throne in 1066, he established a strong central government and began, among other things, to standardize the law. Representatives of the king were sent out to the countryside to check local administration, and were given the job of adjudicating in local disputes, according to local law.

When these 'itinerant justices' returned to Westminster, they were able to discuss the various customs of different parts of the country and, by a process of sifting, reject unreasonable ones and accept those that seemed rational, to form a consistent body of rules. During this process – which went on for around two centuries – the principle of *stare decisis* ('let the decision stand') grew up. Whenever a new problem of law came to be decided, the decision formed a rule to be followed in all similar cases, making the law more predictable.

The result of all this was that by about 1250, a 'common law' had been produced, that ruled the whole country, would be applied consistently and could be used to predict what the courts might decide in a particular case. It contained many of what are now basic points of English law – the fact that murder is a crime, for example.

The principles behind this 'common law' are still used today in creating case law (which is in fact often known as common law). From the basic idea of *stare decisis*, a hierarchy of precedent grew up, in line with the hierarchy of the modern court system, so that, in general, a judge must follow decisions made in courts which are higher up the hierarchy than his or her own (the detailed rules on precedent are discussed later in this section). This process was made easier by the establishment of a regular system of publication of reports of cases in the higher courts. The body of decisions made by the higher courts, which the lower ones must respect, is known as case law.

Making case law

Case law comes from the decisions made by judges in the cases before them (the decisions of juries do not make case law). In deciding a case, there are two basic tasks: first, establishing what the facts are, meaning what actually happened; and secondly, how the law applies to those facts. It is the second task that can make case law, and the idea is that once a decision has been made on how the law applies to a particular set of facts, similar facts in later cases should be treated in the same way, following the principle of *stare decisis* described above. This is obviously fairer than allowing each judge to interpret the law differently, and also provides predictability, which makes it easier for people to live within the law.

The judges listen to the evidence and the legal argument and then prepare a written decision as to which party wins, based on what they believe the facts were, and how the law applies to them. This decision is known as the judgment, and is usually long, containing quite a lot of comment which is not strictly relevant to the case, as well as an explanation of the legal principles on which the judge has made a decision. The explanation of the legal principles on which the decision is made is called the *ratio decidendi* – Latin for the 'reason for deciding'. It is this part of the judgment, known as binding precedent, which forms case law.

All the parts of the judgment which do not form part of the *ratio decidendi* of the case are called *obiter dicta* – which is Latin for 'things said by the way'. These are often discussions of hypothetical situations: for example, the judge might say 'Jones did this, but if she had done that, my decision would have been . . .'. None of the *obiter dicta* forms part of the case law, though judges in later cases may be influenced by it, and it is said to be a persuasive precedent.

Judicial precedent

In deciding a case, a judge must follow any decision that has been made by a higher court in a case with similar facts. The rules concerning which courts are bound by which are known as the rules of judicial precedent, or *stare decisis*. As well as being bound by the decisions of courts above them, some courts must also follow their own previous decisions; they are said to be bound by themselves.

The hierarchy of the courts

The European Court of Justice

Decisions of the European Court of Justice (ECJ) on interpretation of the European Treaties, validity of the acts of Community institutions and interpretation of the statutes of Council bodies are binding on all English courts. It appears not to be bound by its own decisions.

The House of Lords

Apart from cases concerning European law, this is the highest appeal court on civil and criminal matters, and all other English courts are bound by it. It was traditionally bound by its own decisions, but in 1966 the Lord Chancellor issued a practice statement saying that the House of Lords was no longer bound by its previous decisions. However, it over-rules previous decisions only rarely. An example was the decision in **R** *v* **R** (1991) that rape within marriage is a crime, which overturned a legal principle that had stood for centuries.

In **Re Pinochet Ugarte** (1999), the House of Lords stated that it had the power to reopen an appeal where, through no fault of his or her own, one of the parties has been subjected to an unfair procedure. The case was part of the litigation concerning General Auguste Pinochet, the former Chilean head of state. The Lords reopened the appeal because one of the Law Lords who heard the original appeal, Lord Hoffmann, was connected with the human rights organization Amnesty International, which had been a party to the appeal. This meant that there was a possibility of bias and so the proceedings could be viewed as unfair. The Lords stressed, however, that there was no question of them being able to reopen an appeal because the decision made originally was thought to be wrong; the Pinochet appeal was reopened because it could be said that there had not been a fair hearing, and not because the decision reached was wrong (although at the second hearing of the appeal, the Lords did in fact come to a slightly different decision).

The Court of Appeal

This is split into Civil and Criminal Divisions; they do not bind each other. Both are bound by the House of Lords.

In **Young** *v* **Bristol Aeroplane Co Ltd** (1944), it was held that the Civil Division is usually bound by its own decisions, but that there were three exceptions:

1 Where the previous decision was made in ignorance of a relevant law (it is said to have been made *per incuriam*).
2 Where there are two previous conflicting decisions.
3 Where there is a later, conflicting House of Lords' decision.

In the Criminal Division, the results of cases heard may decide whether or not an individual goes to prison, so the Criminal Division takes a more flexible approach to its previous decisions and does not follow them where doing so could cause injustice.

The High Court

This court is divided between the Divisional Courts and the ordinary High Court. All are bound by the Court of Appeal and the House of Lords.

The Divisional Courts are the Queen's Bench Division, which deals with criminal appeals and judicial review, and the Chancery Division and the Family Division, which both deal with civil appeals. The two civil Divisional Courts are bound by their previous decisions, but the Divisional Court of the Queen's Bench is more flexible about this, for the same reason as the criminal division of the Court of Appeal. The Divisional Courts bind the ordinary High Court.

The ordinary High Court is not bound by its own previous decisions. It can produce precedents for courts below it, but these are of a lower status than those produced by the Court of Appeal or the House of Lords.

The Crown Court

The Crown Court is bound by all the courts above it. Its decisions do not form binding precedents, though when High Court judges sit in the Crown Court, their judgments form persuasive precedents, which must be given serious consideration in successive cases, though it is not obligatory to follow them. When a circuit or district judge is sitting no precedents are formed. Since the Crown Court cannot form binding precedents, it is obviously not bound by its own decisions.

Magistrates' and county courts

These are called the inferior courts. They are bound by the High Court, Court of Appeal and House of Lords. Their own decisions are not reported, and cannot produce binding precedents, or even persuasive ones; like the Crown Court, they are therefore not bound by their own decisions.

How judicial precedent works

When faced with a case on which there appears to be a relevant earlier decision, either by that court (if bound by itself), or a higher one, the judges can do any of the following:

Follow. If the facts are sufficiently similar, the precedent set by the earlier case is followed, and the law applied in the same way to produce a decision.

Distinguish. Where the facts of the case before the judge are significantly different from those of the earlier one, then the judge distinguishes the two cases and need not follow the earlier one.

Overrule. Where the earlier decision was made in a lower court, the judges can overrule that earlier decision if they disagree with the lower court's statement of the law. The outcome of the earlier decision remains the same, but will not be followed. The power to overrule cases is only used sparingly because it weakens the authority and respect of the lower courts.

Reverse. If the decision of a lower court is appealed to a higher one, the higher court may change it if they feel the lower court has wrongly interpreted the law. Clearly when a decision is reversed, the higher court is usually also overruling the lower court's statement of the law.

In practice the process is rather more complicated than this, since decisions are not always made on the basis of only one previous case; there are usually several different cases offered in support of each side's view of the question.

How do judges really decide cases?

The independence of the judiciary was ensured by the Act of Settlement 1700, which transferred the power to sack judges from the Crown to Parliament. Consequently, judges should theoretically make their decisions based purely on the logical deductions of precedent, uninfluenced by political or career considerations.

The eighteenth-century legal commentator, William Blackstone, introduced the declaratory theory of law, stating that judges do not make law, but merely, by the rules of precedent, discover and declare the law that has always been: '[the judge] being sworn to determine, not according to his private sentiments . . . not according to his own private judgment, but according to the known laws and customs of the land: not delegated to pronounce a new law, but to maintain and expound the old one'. Blackstone does not accept that precedent ever offers a choice between two or more interpretations of the law: where a bad decision is made, he states, the new one that reverses or overrules it is not a new law, nor a statement that the old decision was bad law, but a declaration that the previous decision was 'not law', in other words that it was the wrong answer. His view presupposes that there is always one right answer, to be deduced from an objective study of precedent.

Today, however, this position is considered somewhat unrealistic. If the operation of precedent is the precise science Blackstone suggests, a large majority of cases in the higher courts would never come to court at all. The lawyers concerned could simply look up the relevant case law and predict what the decision would be, then advise whichever of the clients would be bound to lose not to bother bringing or fighting the case. In a civil case, or any appeal case, no good lawyer would advise a client to bring or defend a case that they had no chance of winning. Therefore, where such a case is contested, it can be assumed that unless one of the lawyers has made a mistake, it could go either way, and still be in accordance with the law. Further evidence of this is provided by the fact that one can read a judgment of the Court of Appeal, argued as though it were the only possible decision in the light of the cases that had gone before, and then discover that this apparently inevitable decision has promptly been reversed by the House of Lords.

In practice, then, judges' decisions may not be as neutral as Blackstone's declaratory theory suggests: they have to make choices which are by no means spelt out by precedents. Yet, rather than openly stating that they are choosing between two or more equally relevant precedents, the courts find ways to avoid awkward ones, which give the impression that the precedents they do choose to follow are the only ones that could possibly apply. In theory, only the House of Lords, which can overrule its own decisions as well as those of other courts, can depart from precedent: all the other courts must follow the precedent that applies in a particular case, however much they dislike it. In fact, there are a number of ways in which judges may avoid awkward precedents that at first sight might appear binding:

- By distinguishing the awkward precedent on its facts – arguing that the facts of the case under consideration are different in some important way from those of the previous case, and therefore the rule laid down does not apply to them. Since the facts are unlikely to be identical, this is the simplest way to avoid an awkward precedent, and the courts have made some extremely narrow distinctions in this way.
- By distinguishing the point of law – arguing that the legal question answered by the precedent is not the same as that asked in the present case.
- By stating that the precedent has been superseded by more recent decisions, and is therefore outdated.
- By giving the precedent a very narrow *ratio decidendi*. The only part of a decision that forms binding precedent is the *ratio*, the legal principle on which the decision is based. Since judges never state 'this is the *ratio decidendi*', it is possible to argue at some length about which bits of the judgment actually form the *ratio* and therefore bind courts in later cases. Judges wishing to avoid an awkward precedent may reason that those parts of the judgment which seem to apply to their case are not part of the *ratio*, and are only *obiter dicta*, which they are not obliged to follow.
- By arguing that the precedent has no clear *ratio decidendi*. There are usually three judges sitting in Court of Appeal cases, and five in the House of Lords. Where each judge in the former case has given a different reason for coming to the same decision, or where, for example, two judges of the House of Lords take one view, two more another, and the fifth agrees with none of them, it can be argued that there is no one clear *ratio decidendi* for the decision.
- By claiming that the precedent is inconsistent with a later decision of a higher court, and has been overruled by implication.
- By stating that the previous decision was made *per incuriam*, meaning that the court failed to consider some relevant statute or precedent. This method is used only rarely, since it clearly undermines the status of the court below.
- By arguing that the precedent is outdated, and no longer in step with modern thinking. The best-known example of this approach (which is not frequently used) is the case of **R** *v* **R** (1991), when the House of Lords overturned a centuries-old common law rule that rape within marriage was not a crime (see p. 84).

We can see that there is considerable room for manoeuvre within the doctrine of precedent, so what factors guide judicial decisions, and to what extent? The following are some of the answers that have been suggested.

Dworkin: a seamless web of principles

Ronald Dworkin argues that judges have no real discretion in making case law. He sees law as a seamless web of principles, which supply a right answer – and only one – to every possible problem. Dworkin reasons that although stated legal rules may 'run out' (in the sense of not being directly applicable to a new case) legal principles never do, and therefore judges never need to use their own discretion.

In his book *Law's Empire*, Professor Dworkin claims that judges first look at previous cases, and from those deduce which principles could be said to apply to the case before them. Then they consult their own sense of justice as to which apply, and also consider what the community's view of justice dictates. Where the judge's view and that of the community coincide, there is no problem, but if they conflict, the judges then ask themselves whether or not it would be fair to impose their own sense of justice over that of the community. Dworkin calls this the interpretive approach, and although it may appear to involve a series of choices, he considers that the legal principles underlying the decisions mean that in the end only one result could possibly surface from any one case.

Dworkin's approach has been heavily criticized as being unrealistic: opponents believe that judges do not consider principles of justice but take a much more pragmatic approach, looking at the facts of the case, not the principles.

Critical theorists: precedent as legitimation

Critical legal theorists, such as David Kairys, take a quite different view. They argue that judges have considerable freedom within the doctrine of precedent. Kairys suggests that there is no such thing as legal reasoning, in the sense of a logical, neutral method of determining rules and results from what has gone before. He states that judicial decisions are actually based on 'a complex mixture of social, political, institutional, experiential and personal factors', and are simply legitimated, or justified, by reference to previous cases. The law provides 'a wide and conflicting variety' of such justifications 'from which courts pick and choose'.

The process is not necessarily as cynical as it sounds. Kairys points out that he is not saying that judges actually make the decision and then consider which precedents they can pick to justify it; rather their own beliefs and prejudices naturally lead them to give more weight to pre-cedents which support those views. Nevertheless, for critical legal theorists, all such decisions can be seen as reflecting social and political judge-ments, rather than objective, purely logical deductions.

Critical theory argues that the neutral appearance of so-called 'legal reasoning' disguises the true nature of legal decisions which, by the choices made, uphold existing power relations within society, tending to favour, for example, employers over employees, property owners over those without, women over men, and rich developed countries over poor undeveloped ones.

Griffith: political choices

In similar vein, Griffith argues that judges make their decisions based on what they see as the public interest, but that their view of this interest is coloured by their background and their position in society. He suggests that the narrow social background – usually public school and Oxbridge – of the highest judges (see p. 104), combined with their position as part of established authority, leads them to believe that it is in the public interest that the established order should be maintained: in other words, that those who are in charge – whether of the country or, for example, in the workplace – should stay in charge, and that traditional values should be maintained. This leads them to 'a tenderness for private property and dislike of trade unions, strong adherence to the maintenance of order, distaste for minority opinions, demonstrations and protests, the avoidance of conflict with Government policy even where it is manifestly oppressive of the most vulnerable, support of governmental secrecy, concern for the preservation of the moral and social behaviour [to which they are] accustomed'.

As Griffith points out, the judges' view of public interest assumes that the interests of all the members of society are roughly the same, ignoring the fact that within society, different groups – employers and employees, men and women, rich and poor – may have interests which are diametrically opposed. What appears to be acting in the public interest will usually mean in the interest of one group over another, and therefore cannot be seen as neutral.

Waldron: political choices, but why not?

In his book, *The Law*, Waldron agrees that judges do exercise discretion, and that they are influenced in those choices by political and ideological considerations, but argues that this is not necessarily a bad thing. He contends that while it would be wrong for judges to be biased towards one side in a case, or to make decisions based on political factors in the hope of promotion, it is unrealistic to expect a judge to be 'a political neuter – emasculated of all values and principled commitments'.

Waldron points out that to be a judge at all means a commitment to the values surrounding the legal system: recognition of Parliament as supreme, the importance of precedent, fairness, certainty, the public interest. He argues that this itself is a political choice, and further choices are made when judges have to balance these values against one another where they conflict. The responsible thing to do, according to Waldron, is to think through such conflicts in advance, and to decide which might generally be expected to give way to which. These will inevitably be political and ideological decisions. Waldron argues that since such decisions have to be made 'the thing to do is not to try to hide them, but to be as explicit as possible'. Rather than hiding such judgments behind 'smokescreens of legal mystery. . . if judges have developed particular theories of morals, politics and society, they should say so up front, and incorporate them explicitly into their decision-making'.

Waldron suggests that where judges feel uncomfortable about doing this, it may be a useful indication that they should re-examine their bias, and see whether it is an appropriate consideration by which they are to be influenced. In addition, if the public know the reasoning behind judicial decisions 'we can evaluate them and see whether we want to rely on reasons like that for the future'.

The judiciary: neutral decision-making

Judges themselves still cling to the image of themselves as neutral decision-makers, even though they admit that there are choices to be made. In a 1972 lecture Lord Reid agreed that the declaratory theory was something of a 'fairytale', but argued that:

> Everyone agrees that impartiality is the first essential in any judge. And that means not only that he must not appear to favour either party. It also means that he must not take sides on political issues. When public opinion is sharply divided on any question – whether or not the division is on party lines – no judge ought in my view to lean to one side or the other if that can possibly be avoided. But sometimes we get a case where that is very difficult to avoid. Then I think we must play safe. We must decide the case on the preponderance of existing authority.

The caution extended even where there was 'some freedom to go in one or other direction'; in these cases 'we should have regard to common sense, legal principle and public policy in that order'.

Lord Reid made it clear that the first two criteria were unlikely to leave much room for the application of the third, but his reasoning fails to take into account the fact that common sense is by no means a fixed quality – it may be common sense to an employer, for example, that pickets should not be allowed to disturb those employees who want to work, and equally common sense to those pickets that they should be able to protect their jobs in any peaceful way possible. Common sense may be as much a value judgement as public interest.

Do judges make law?

Although judges have traditionally seen themselves as declaring or finding rather than creating law, and frequently state that making law is the prerogative of Parliament, there are several areas in which they clearly do make law.

In the first place, historically, a great deal of our law is and always has been case law, made by judicial decisions. Contract and tort law are still largely judge-made, and many of the most important developments – for example, the development of negligence as a tort – have had profound effects. Even though statutes have later been passed on these subjects, and occasionally Parliament has attempted to embody whole areas of common law in statutory form, these still embody the original principles created by the judges.

Secondly, the application of law, whether case law or statute, to a particular case is not usually an automatic matter. Terminology may be vague or ambiguous, new developments in social life have to be accommodated, and the procedure requires interpretation as well as application. As we have suggested, judicial precedent does not always make a particular decision obvious and obligatory – there may be conflicting precedents, their implications may be unclear, and there are ways of getting round a precedent that would otherwise produce an undesirable decision. If it is accepted that Blackstone's declaratory theory does not apply in practice, then clearly the judges do make law, rather than explaining the law that is already there. The theories advanced by Kairys, Griffith and Waldron all accept that judges do have discretion, and therefore they do to some extent make law.

Where precedents do not spell out what should be done in a case before them, judges nevertheless have to make a decision. They cannot simply say that the law is not clear and refer it back to Parliament, even though in some cases they point out that the decision before them would be more appropriately decided by those who have been elected to make decisions on changes in the law. This was the case in **Airedale NHS** *v* **Bland** (1993), where the House of Lords considered the fate of Tony Bland, the football supporter left in a coma after the Hillsborough stadium disaster. The court had to decide whether it was lawful to stop supplying the drugs and artificial feeding that were keeping Mr Bland alive, even though it was known that doing so would mean his death soon afterwards. Several Law Lords made it plain that they felt that cases raising 'wholly new moral and social issues' should be decided by Parliament, the judges' role being to 'apply the principles which society, through the democratic process, adopts, not to impose their standards on society'. Nevertheless, the courts had no option but to make a decision one way or the other, and they decided that the action was lawful in the circumstances, because it was in the patient's best interests.

Thirdly, our judges have been left to define their own role, and the role of the courts generally in the political system, more or less as they please. They have, for example, given themselves the power to review decisions of any public body, even when Parliament has said those decisions are not to be reviewed. And despite their frequent pronouncements that it is not for them to interfere in Parliament's law-making role, the judges have made it plain that they will not, unless forced by very explicit wording, interpret statutes as encroaching on common law rights or judge-made law (see p. 36). They also control the operation of case law without reference to Parliament: an obvious example is that the 1966 Practice Direction announcing that the House of Lords would no longer be bound by its own decisions, which made case law more flexible and thereby gave the judges more power, was made on the court's own authority, without needing permission from Parliament.

▶ When should judges make law?

Again, this is a subject about which there are different views, not least among the judiciary and the following are some of the approaches which have been suggested.

Adapting to social change

In 1952, Lord Denning gave a lecture called 'The Need for a New Equity', arguing that judges had become too timid about adapting the law to the changing conditions of society. They were, he felt, leaving this role too much to Parliament, which was too slow and cumbersome to do the job well (by 1984, he felt that judges had taken up the task again).

Lord Scarman, in **McLoughlin** v **O'Brian** (1982), stated that the courts' function is to adjudicate according to principle, and if the results are socially unacceptable Parliament can legislate to overrule them. He felt that the risk was not that case law might develop too far, but that it stood still and did not therefore adapt to the changing needs of society.

Paterson's survey of 19 Law Lords active between 1967 and 1973 found that at least twelve thought that the Law Lords had a duty to develop the common law in response to changing social conditions. A case where the judges did eventually show themselves willing to change the law in the light of social change is **Fitzpatrick** v **Sterling Housing Association Ltd** (2000). The case concerned a homosexual man, Mr Fitzpatrick, who had lived with his partner, Mr Thompson, for 18 years, nursing and caring for him after Mr Thompson suffered an accident which caused irreversible brain damage and severe paralysis. Mr Thompson was the tenant of the flat in which they lived and, when he died in 1994, Mr Fitzpatrick applied to take over the tenancy, which gave the tenant certain protections under the Rent Acts. The landlords refused. The Rent Act 1977 states that when a statutory tenant dies, the tenancy can be taken over by a spouse, a person living with the ex-tenant as wife or husband, or a member of the family who was living with the tenant. Mr

Fitzpatrick's case sought to establish that he was a member of Mr Thompson's family, by virtue of their close and loving relationship.

The Court of Appeal agreed that 'if endurance, stability, interdependence and devotion were the sole hallmarks of family membership', there could be no doubt that the couple were a family. They also pointed out that discriminating against stable same-sex relationships was out of step with the values of modern society. However, they recognized that the law on succession to statutory tenancies was firmly rooted in the idea that families were based on marriage or kinship, and this had only ever been relaxed in terms of heterosexual couples living together, who were treated as if married. As a result, the Court concluded that it would be wrong to change the law by interpreting the word family to include same-sex couples; all three judges agreed that such a change should be made, in order to reflect modern values, but it should be made by Parliament. The House of Lords, however, overturned the Court of Appeal's decision. It ruled that the appellant could not be treated as the spouse of the deceased tenant, but as a matter of law a same-sex partner could establish the necessary familial link for the purposes of the legislation.

Types of law

Lord Reid has suggested that the basic areas of common law are appropriate for judge-made law, but that the judges should respect the need for certainty in property and contract law, and that criminal law, except for the issue of *mens rea*, was best left to Parliament.

Consensus law-making

Lord Devlin has distinguished between activist law-making and dynamic law-making. He saw new ideas within society as going through a long process of acceptance. At first society will be divided about them, and there will be controversy, but eventually such ideas may come to be accepted by most members of society, or most members will at least become prepared to put up with them. At this second stage we can say there is a consensus. We can see this process in the way that views have changed in this century on subjects such as homosexuality and sex before marriage.

Law-making which takes one side or another while an issue is still controversial is what Devlin called dynamic law-making, and he believed judges should not take part in it because it endangered their reputation for independence and impartiality. Their role is in activist law-making, concerning areas where there is a consensus. The problem with Devlin's view is that in practice the judges sometimes have no choice but to embark on dynamic law-making. In **Gillick *v* West Norfolk and Wisbech Area Health Authority** (1985), the House of Lords was asked to consider whether a girl under 16 needed her parents' consent before she could be given contraceptive services. It was an issue on which there was by no means a consensus, with one side claiming that teenage pregnancies would increase if the courts ruled that parental consent was necessary, and the other claiming that the judges would be encouraging under-age sex if they did not. The House of Lords held, by a majority of three to two, that a girl under 16 did not have to have parental consent if she was mature enough to make up her own mind. But the decision did not end the controversy, and it was widely suggested that the judges were not the right people to make the choice. However, since Parliament had given no lead, they had no option but to make a decision one way or the other, and were therefore forced to indulge in what Devlin would call dynamic law-making.

Respecting parliamentary opinion

It is often stated that judges should not make law where there is reason to believe Parliament does not support such changes. In **President of India** *v* **La Pintada Compania Navigacion S.A.** (1984), the House of Lords felt that there was a strong case for overruling a nineteenth-century decision that a party could receive no interest on a contract debt, but they noted that the Law Commission had recommended that this rule should be abolished and the legislators specifically decided not to do so. Lord Brandon said that to make new law in these circumstances would be an 'unjustifiable usurpation of the function which properly belongs to Parliament'.

Similarly, it is sometimes argued that judges should avoid making law in areas of public interest which Parliament is considering at the time. Lord Radcliffe suggested that in such areas, judges should be cautious 'not because the principles adopted by Parliament are more satisfactory or more enlightened, but because it is unacceptable constitutionally that there should be two independent sources of law-making at work at the same time'.

Protecting individual rights

In a 1992 lecture, Anthony Lester QC argued that while judges must have regard to precedent, they could still use their discretion within the system of precedent more effectively. He argued that in the past, judges have abdicated responsibility for law-making by surrounding themselves with self-made rules (such as the pre-1966 rule that the House of Lords was bound by its own decisions). Since the 1960s, however, he feels that this tendency has gradually been reduced, with judges taking on more responsibility for developing the common law in accordance with contemporary values, and being more willing to arbitrate fairly between the citizen and the state. Lester praises this development, arguing that the judges can establish protection for the individual against misuse of power, where Parliament refuses to do so.

The House of Lords' current approach

The House of Lords has explained its approach to judicial law-making in the case of **C v DPP** (1995) which raised the issue of children's liability for crime. The common law defence of *doli incapax* provided that a defendant aged between ten and fourteen could be liable for a crime only if the prosecution could prove that the child knew that what he or she did was seriously wrong. On appeal from the magistrates' court, the Divisional Court held that the defence was outdated and should no longer exist in law. An appeal was brought before the House of Lords, arguing that the Divisional Court was bound by precedent and not able to change the law in this way. The House of Lords agreed, and went on to consider whether it should change the law itself (as the 1966 Practice Direction clearly allowed it to do), but decided that this was not an appropriate case for judicial law-making. Explaining this decision, Lord Lowry suggested five factors were important:

- where the solution to a dilemma was doubtful, judges should be wary of imposing their own answer;
- judges should be cautious about addressing areas where Parliament had rejected opportunities of clearing up a known difficulty, or had passed legislation without doing so;
- areas of social policy over which there was dispute were least likely to be suitable for judicial law-making;
- fundamental legal doctrines should not be lightly set aside;
- judges should not change the law unless they can be sure that doing so is likely to achieve finality and certainty on the issue.

Despite this fairly cautious-sounding view, some commentators feel that the judiciary's current approach is tending to go too far, and straying outside its constitutional place. Writing in the *New Law Journal* in 1999, Francis Bennion, a former parliamentary counsel, criticized what he called the 'growing appetite of some judges for changing the law themselves, rather than waiting for Parliament to do it'. Bennion cites two cases as examples of this. The first, **Kleinwort Benson Ltd v Lincoln City Council** (1998), concerns contract law, and in particular, a long-standing rule, originating from case law, that where someone made a payment as a result of a mistake about the law, they did not have the right to get the money back. The rule had existed for nearly two centuries, and been much criticized in recent years – so much so that a previous Lord Chancellor had asked the Law Commission to consider whether it should be amended by legislation, and they had concluded that it should. This would normally be taken by the courts as a signal that they should leave the issue alone and wait for Parliament to act, but in this case the Lords decided to change the rule. In doing so, Lord Keith expressed the view that 'a robust view of judicial development of the law' was desirable.

Bennion argues that in making this decision, the Lords were usurping the authority which constitutionally belongs to Parliament. He also points out that judicial, rather than parliamentary, change of the law in this kind of area causes practical difficulties, because it has retrospective effect; a large number of transactions which were thought to be settled under the previous rule can now be reopened. This would not usually be the case if Parliament changed the law.

The second case Bennion criticizes is **DPP** *v* **Jones** (1999), which concerned a demonstration on the road near Stonehenge. In that case the Lords looked at another long-held rule, that the public have a right to use the highway for 'passing and repassing' (in other words, walking along the road), and for uses which are related to that, but that there is no right to use the highway in other ways, such as demonstrating or picketing. In **Jones**, the House of Lords stated that this rule placed unrealistic and unwarranted restrictions on everyday activities, and that the highway is a public place that the public has a right to enjoy for any reasonable purpose. This decision clearly has major implications for the powers of the police to break up demonstrations and pickets.

Bennion argues that in making decisions like these, the judiciary are taking powers to which they are not constitutionally entitled, and that they should not extend their law-making role into such controversial areas.

Should judges behave like law-makers?

Bearing in mind that, despite their protests, judges clearly do make law, some scholars have suggested that judges should decide hard cases on policy grounds – weighing social consequences and choosing the best option for the future, in the way we expect a legislator to do. Hart, for example, thinks it an advantage of the open texture of legal language that it leaves room for the flexible adaptation of policy in this way. Lord Hoffmann appeared to take this approach in **Arthur JS Hall** *v* **Simons** (2000), where the House of Lords dramatically removed the established immunity of barristers from liability in negligence for court work. In reaching his decision Lord Hoffmann stated:

> I hope that I will not be thought ungrateful if I do not encumber this speech with citations. The question of what the public interest now requires depends upon the strength of the arguments rather than the weight of authority.

Some academics, however, have expressed doubts about whether judges are the right people to produce policy-based legislation, even in hard cases. There are obvious reasons for caution: judges have neither the competence nor the accountability to deal adequately with considerations of policy; and the adversarial environment of the courtroom may not be the best forum for addressing the needs of society as a whole.

▶ Advantages of case law and judicial precedent

Certainty

Judicial precedent means litigants can assume that like cases will be treated alike, rather than judges making their own random decisions, which nobody could predict. This helps people plan their affairs.

Detailed practical rules

Case law is a response to real situations, as opposed to statutes, which may be more heavily based on theory and logic. Case law shows the detailed application of the law to various circumstances, and this gives more information than statute.

Free market in legal ideas

The right-wing philosopher Hayek has argued that there should be as little legislation as possible, with case law becoming the main source of law. He sees case law as developing in line with market forces; if the *ratio* of a case is seen not to work, it will be abandoned, if it works it will be followed. In this way the law can develop in response to demand. Hayek sees statute law as imposed by social planners, forcing their views on society whether they like it or not, and threatening the liberty of the individual.

Flexibility

Law needs to be flexible to meet the needs of a changing society, and case law can make changes far more quickly than Parliament. The most obvious signs of this are the radical changes the House of Lords has made in the field of criminal law, since announcing in 1966 that they would no longer be bound by their own decisions.

▶ Disadvantages of case law

Complexity and volume

There are hundreds of thousands of decided cases, comprising several thousand volumes of law reports, and more are added all the time. Judgments themselves are long, with many judges making no attempts at readability, and the *ratio decidendi* of a case may be buried in a sea of irrelevant material. This can make it very difficult to pinpoint appropriate principles.

Rigidity

The rules of judicial precedent mean that judges should follow a binding precedent even where they think it is bad law, or inappropriate. This can mean that bad judicial decisions are perpetuated for a long time before they come before a court high enough to have the power to overrule them.

Illogical distinctions

The fact that binding precedents must be followed unless the facts of the case are significantly different can lead to judges making minute distinctions between the facts of a previous case and the case before them, so that they can distinguish a precedent which they consider inappropriate. This in turn leads to a mass of cases all establishing different precedents in very similar circumstances, and further complicates the law.

Unpredictability

The advantages of certainty can be lost if too many of the kind of illogical distinctions referred to above are made, and it may be impossible to work out which precedents will be applied to a new case.

Dependence on chance

Case law changes only in response to those cases brought before it, so important changes may not be made unless someone has the money and determination to push a case far enough through the appeal system to allow a new precedent to be created.

Unsystematic progression

Case law develops according to the facts of each case and so does not provide a comprehensive code. A whole series of rules can be built on one case, and if this is overruled the whole structure can collapse.

Lack of research

When making case law the judges are only presented with the facts of the case and the legal arguments, and their task is to decide on the outcome of that particular dispute. Technically, they are not concerned with the social and economic implications of their decisions, and so they cannot commission research or consult experts as to these implications, as Parliament can when changing the law. In the US litigants are allowed to present written arguments containing socio-economic material, and Lord Simon has recommended that a law officer should be sent to the court in certain cases to present such arguments objectively. However, Lord Devlin considered that allowing such information would encourage the judges to go too far in making law.

Retrospective effect

Changes made by case law apply to events which happened before the case came to court, unlike legislation, which usually only applies to events after it comes into force. This may be considered unfair, since if a case changes the law, the parties concerned in that case could not have known what the law was before they acted. US courts sometimes get round the problems by deciding the case before them according to the old law, while declaring that in future the new law will prevail: or they may determine with what degree of retroactivity a new rule is to be enforced.

In **SW v United Kingdom** (1995), two men, who had been convicted of the rape and attempted rape of their wives, brought a case before the European Court of Human Rights, alleging that their convictions violated Art. 7 of the European Convention on Human Rights, which provides that criminal laws should not have retrospective effect. The men argued that when the incidents which gave rise to their convictions happened, it was not a crime for a man to force his wife to have sex; it only became a crime after the decision in **R v R** (1991) (see p. 84). The court dismissed the men's argument: Art. 7 did not prevent the courts from clarifying the principles of criminal liability, providing the developments could be clearly foreseen. In this case, there had been mounting criticism of the previous law, and a series of cases which had chipped away at the marital rape exemption, before the **R v R** decision.

Undemocratic

Lord Scarman pointed out in **Stock v Jones** (1978) that the judge cannot match the experience and vision of the legislator; and that unlike the legislator the judge is not answerable to the people. Theories, like Griffith's, which suggest that precedent can actually give judges a good deal of discretion, and allow them to decide cases on grounds of political and social policy, raise the question of whether judges, who are unelected, should have such freedom.

▶ ANSWERING QUESTIONS

1 To what extent does the doctrine of precedent curb judicial creativity? *WJEC*

The first thing to note here is that the words 'judicial creativity' really mean the judges' ability to create or make law. Your introduction should briefly describe what precedent is. A summary of the material contained under the headings 'judicial precedent' and 'how judicial precedent works' would be sufficient here.

Your essay should essentially put forward two opposing sets of arguments: on the one hand, the ways in which precedent curbs judges' freedom to make law; and on the other hand, the arguments that have been put forward that judges do actually have quite a bit of freedom. To illustrate the first set of arguments, you could discuss the role of the *ratio decidendi*, and the need for consistency and certainty in the law. When dealing with the opposing argument, you might discuss the three main points under the heading 'Do judges make law' in this chapter: the sheer amount of case law in our system (especially in contract and tort); the point that applying the law is not usually an automatic matter; and the fact that judges have been left to define their own role in the system. You should finish with a conclusion, drawing on the points you have made, that states how far you think precedent does curb judicial creativity.

2 **In what ways does legal reasoning both bind and free the judiciary in deciding particular cases?** *WJEC*

In this context 'legal reasoning' simply means the process by which judges work out how the rules laid down in previous cases apply to later ones – in other words, the creation of case law. You could tackle this question in two sections: how does this legal reasoning bind the judiciary; and in what circumstances does it allow freedom in making decisions?

For the first part, you need to explain the principle of judicial precedent, and outline the situations in which judges are bound by previous decisions. You could bring in here the declaratory theory of law.

In the second part, you can describe the ways in which judges can avoid awkward precedents, and bring in some of the theories about how judges really decide cases. You could also discuss the effects of the 1966 House of Lords Practice Direction.

Your conclusion might state whether you think that legal reasoning strikes the right balance between binding the judges and allowing them freedom, giving reasons for your view.

3 **What would be the effect on English law of the abolition of the doctrine of binding precedent?** *Edexcel*

You first need to describe the doctrine of binding precedent, but do not spend too much time on this, as pure description is not what the question is asking for.

You should then consider what the law would lose if precedent were abandoned – the material on the advantages of precedent is relevant here. Then talk about the disadvantages of the system of precedent, and what might be gained by abolishing it. You could bring in the effects of the 1966 House of Lords Practice Direction as an example of the relaxation of precedent, and talk about whether you feel it has benefited the law or not, mentioning appropriate cases.

You might mention innovations which would lessen the role of precedent, such as codification, and say whether you feel they would be desirable and why.

Your conclusion could state whether or not you feel precedent serves a useful role, and outline any changes which you feel should be made to its operation.

4 **To what extent does the doctrine of precedent allow judges to make law?** *WJEC*

Here again, you need to start by defining judicial precedent. You can then go on to describe the ways in which it prevents judges from making new law, and the declaratory theory. Follow this with a discussion of the ways in which judges can avoid awkward precedents, and whether this means that they make law. You might use some examples of judges making law, such as **R** v **R**. You can use the material on how judges really decide cases, and on whether judges make law, to debate how far judges are allowed by precedent to make law. You should make the point that theorists such as Kairys and Griffith who argue that precedent allows a great deal of discretion are arguing that judges do make law.

You might also introduce some of the ideas about when judges ought to make law, pointing out that some argue that they should actually be more active law-makers than they are – Anthony Lester's arguments are relevant here.

As a conclusion, you could suggest whether the present system strikes the right balance in the extent to which it allows judges to make law, giving reasons for your views and suggesting any changes you think should be made.

▶ STATUTE LAW

Statutes are made by Parliament, which consists of the House of Commons, the House of Lords and the Monarch. Following the House of Lords Act 1999, membership of the House of Lords is currently undergoing a major reform to remove the role of the hereditary peers. The Royal Commission for the Reform of the House of Lords, which was chaired by Lord Wakeham, published its report in January 2000. It has recommended that there should be a chamber of about 550 members. Only a minority would be elected and their role would be to represent the regions, the remainder would be appointed by an independent Appointments Commission. It would be responsible for selecting members who were broadly representative of British society. Approximately 20 per cent of its members would be politically independent and the others would reflect the political balance as expressed by the last general election. A modest payment would be made for attending the House. It would be under a statutory duty to ensure that at least 30 per cent of new members were women and that minorities were represented in numbers at least proportionate to their representation in the total population. The powers of the new chamber would be broadly comparable with the present Lords. The Government announced in the Queen's speech in 2001 that it intended to proceed with the reform of the House of Lords.

In Britain, Parliament is sovereign, which has traditionally meant that the law it makes takes precedence over law originating from any other source, though as we shall see, membership of the European Union (EU) has compromised this principle. EU law aside, Parliament can make or cancel any law it chooses, and the courts must enforce it. In other countries, such as the US, the courts can declare such legislation unconstitutional, but our courts may not do that. (This view has been challenged by Laws J – see p. 4).

Making an Act of Parliament

Bills

All statutes begin as a Bill, which is a proposal for a piece of legislation. There are three types of Bill:

Public Bills. These are prepared by the Cabinet and change the general law of the whole country. They are often preceded by a Green Paper, a consultation document putting forward tentative proposals, which interested parties may consult and give their views on.

Private Members' Bills. These are prepared by an individual back bench MP (someone who is not a member of the Cabinet). MPs wanting to put forward a Bill have to enter a ballot to win the right to do so, and then persuade the Government to allow enough parliamentary time for the Bill to go through. Consequently very few such Bills become Acts, and they tend to function more as a way of drawing attention to particular issues. Some, however, have made important contributions to legislation, an example being the Abortion Act 1967 which stemmed from a Private Member's Bill put forward by David Steele.

Private Bills. These are usually proposed by a local authority, public corporation or large public company, and usually only affect that sponsor. An example might be a local authority seeking the right to build a bridge or road.

The actual preparation of Bills is done by expert draftsmen known as Parliamentary Counsel.

First reading

The title of the prepared Bill is read to the House of Commons. This is called the first reading, and acts as a notification of the proposed measure.

Second reading

At the second reading, the proposals are debated fully, and may be amended, and members vote on whether the legislation should proceed.

In practice, the whip system (party officials whose job is to make sure MPs vote with their party) means that a Government with a reasonable majority can almost always get its legislation through at this and subsequent stages.

Committee stage

The Bill is then referred to a committee of the House of Commons for detailed examination, bearing in mind the points made during the debate. At this point further amendments to the Bill may be made.

Report stage

The committee then reports back to the House, and any proposed amendments are debated and voted upon.

Third reading

The Bill is re-presented to the House. There may be a short debate, and a vote on whether to accept or reject the legislation as it stands.

House of Lords

The Bill then goes to the House of Lords, where it goes through a similar process of three readings. If the House of Lords alters anything, the Bill returns to the Commons for further consideration. The Commons then responds with agreement, reasons for disagreement, or proposals for alternative changes.

At one time legislation could not be passed without the agreement of both houses, which meant that the unelected House of Lords could block legislation put forward by the elected House of Commons. The Parliament Acts of 1911–1949 lay down special procedures by which proposed legislation can go for Royal Assent without the approval of the House of Lords after specified periods of time. In fact these procedures are almost never used, as the House of Lords usually drops objections that are resisted by the Commons.

Royal Assent

In the vast majority of cases, agreement between Lords and Commons is reached, and the Bill is then presented for Royal Assent. Technically, the Queen must give her consent to all legislation before it can become law, but in practice that consent is never refused.

The Bill is then an Act of Parliament, and becomes law, though most do not take effect from the moment the Queen gives her consent, but on a specified date in the near future.

In the case of legislation about which there is no controversy, the procedure may be simplified, with the first three readings in the Lords, then three in the Commons, with the Bill passing back to the Lords only if there is disagreement. Private Bills technically go through the above procedure, and are examined to make sure that adequate warning has been given to anyone affected by the provisions, but there is little debate on them. Consolidating Acts, which simply bring together all the existing law on one topic also go through an accelerated procedure, with no debate, because they do not change the law; codification bills on the other hand, go through the normal process (see p. 86).

Statutory interpretation

Although Parliament makes legislation, it is left to the courts to apply it. The general public imagine that this is simply a case of looking up the relevant law and ruling accordingly, but the reality is not so simple. Despite the fact that Acts of Parliament are carefully drawn up by expert draftsmen, there are many occasions in which the courts find that the implications of a statute for the case before them are not at all clear.

Bennion (1990) has identified a number of factors that may cause this uncertainty:

- A word is left out because the draftsman thought it was automatically implied. For example, a draftsman writing a statute banning men with facial hair from parks might write that 'men with beards or moustaches are prohibited from parks'. Does this mean that a man who has a beard **and** a moustache would be allowed in? If the words and/or were used it would be clear, but the draftsman may have thought this was automatically implied.
- A broad term was used, leaving it to the user to decide what it includes. Where a statute bans vehicles from the park, this obviously includes cars and lorries, but the courts would have to decide whether it also prohibited skateboards, bikes, or roller skates, for example.
- An ambiguous word or phrase was used on purpose, perhaps because the provision is politically contentious. The European Communities Act 1972 was ambiguous about the position of UK legislation.
- The wording is inadequate because of a printing, drafting or other error.
- The events of the case before the court were not foreseen when the legislation was produced. In the example given above regarding vehicles, skateboards might not have been invented when the statute was drafted, so it would be impossible for Parliament to say whether they should be included in the term 'vehicles'.

In any of these cases, the job of the courts – in theory at least – is to discover how Parliament intended the law to apply and put that into practice. This is because, as you know, in our constitution, Parliament is the supreme source of law (excluding EU law, which will be discussed later), and therefore the judiciary's constitutional role is to put into practice what they think Parliament actually intended when it made a particular law, rather than simply what the judges themselves might think is the best interpretation in the case before them. However, as we shall see, the practice is not always as straightforward as the constitutional theory suggests.

What is parliamentary intention?

The idea of parliamentary intention is a very slippery concept in practice. The last example above is one illustration of this: how could Parliament have had any intention at all of how skateboards should be treated under the legislation, if skateboards were not invented when the legislation was passed?

More problems are revealed if we try to pin down precisely what parliamentary intention means. Is it the intention of every individual Member of Parliament at the time the law was passed? Obviously not, since not every member will have voted for the legislation or even necessarily been present when it was passed. The intention of all those who did support a particular piece of legislation is no easier to define either, since some of those are likely to be acting from loyalty to their party, and will not necessarily have detailed knowledge of the provisions, much less have thought hard about how they might apply in as yet unseen circumstances. Even among those MPs who have considered the detailed provisions, there may be many different opinions as to how they should apply in different situations. And even if one of these groups was taken to represent true parliamentary intention, how are their views to be assessed? It is hardly feasible to conduct a poll every time a legislative provision is found to be unclear.

In fact, the people who will have paid most attention to the wording of a statute are the Ministers who seek to get them through Parliament, the civil servants who advise the Ministers and the draftsmen who draw up the legislation. None of these can really be said to amount to Parliament.

As Glanville Williams has pointed out, the fact is that if the courts are having trouble deciding how a statutory provision applies in a particular situation, the chances are that Parliament never envisaged that situation in the first place, and so can hardly be said to have had any intention as to how the statute should apply to it. In view of this, Lord Reid has pointed out that when judges say they are looking for the intention of Parliament, what they really mean is that they are looking for 'the meaning of the words that parliament used. We are seeking not what parliament meant, but the true meaning of the words they used.'

Statutory interpretation and case law

Once the courts have interpreted a statute, or part of one, that interpretation becomes part of case law in just the same way as any other judicial decision, and subject to the same rules of precedent. A higher court may decide that the interpretation is wrong, and reverse the decision if it is appealed, or overrule it in a later case, but unless and until this happens, lower courts must interpret the statute in the same way.

How are statutes interpreted?

Parliament has given the courts some sources of guidance on statutory interpretation. The Interpretation Act 1978 provides certain standard definitions of common provisions, such as the rule that the singular includes the plural and 'he' includes 'she', while interpretation sections at the end of most modern Acts define some of the words used within them – the Police and Criminal Evidence Act 1984 contains such a section. A further source of help has been provided since the beginning of 1999: all Bills passed since that date are the subject of special explanatory notes, which are made public. These detail the background to the legislation and explain the effects particular provisions are intended to have.

Apart from this assistance, it has been left to the courts to decide what method to use to interpret statutes, and three basic approaches have developed, in conjunction with certain aids to interpretation.

Rules of interpretation

The literal rule
This rule gives all the words in a statute their ordinary and natural meaning, on the principle that the best way to interpret the will of Parliament is to follow the literal meaning of the words they have used. Under this rule, the literal meaning must be followed, even if the result is silly; for example, Lord Esher stated, in **R** *v* **Judge of the City of London Court** (1892): 'If the words of an Act are clear, you must follow them, even though they lead to a manifest absurdity. The court has nothing to do with the question of whether the legislature has committed an absurdity.'

Examples of the literal rule in use are:

Whitely *v* **Chapell** (1868). A statute aimed at preventing electoral malpractice made it an offence to impersonate 'any person entitled to vote' at an election. The accused was acquitted because he impersonated a dead person and a dead person was clearly not entitled to vote!

London and North Eastern Railway Co *v* **Berriman** (1946). A railway worker was knocked down and killed by a train, and his widow attempted to claim damages. The relevant statute provided that this was available to employees killed while engaging in 'relaying or repairing' tracks; the dead man had been doing routine maintenance and oiling, which the court held did not come within the meaning of 'relaying and repairing'.

Fisher *v* **Bell** (1961). After several violent incidents in which the weapon used was a flick-knife, Parliament decided that these knives should be banned. The Restriction of Offensive Weapons Act 1959 consequently made it an offence to 'sell or offer for sale' any flick-knife. The defendant had flick-knives in his shop window and was charged with offering these for sale. The courts held that 'offers for sale' must be given its ordinary meaning in law, and that in contract law this was not an offer for sale but only an invitation to people to make an offer to buy. The defendant was therefore not guilty of a crime under the Act, despite the fact that this was obviously just the sort of behaviour that Act was set up to prevent.

Advantages of the literal rule It respects parliamentary sovereignty, giving the courts a restricted role and leaving law-making to those elected for the job.

Disadvantages of the literal rule Where use of the literal rule does lead to an absurd or obviously unjust conclusion, it can hardly be said to be enacting the will of Parliament, since Parliament is unlikely to have intended absurdity and injustice. The case of **London and North Eastern Railway Co** *v* **Berriman** (above) is an example of literal interpretation creating injustice where Parliament probably never intended any – the difference in the type of work being done does not change the degree of danger to which the workers were exposed.

In addition, the literal rule is useless where the answer to a problem simply cannot be found in the words of the statute. As Hart has pointed out, some terms have a core of very clear meaning, but it may still be unclear how far that word stretches: the example above of an imaginary law banning 'vehicles' from the park clearly illustrates this. Where such a broad term is used, the answer is simply not there in the words of the statute, and the courts have to use some other method.

The Law Commission in 1969 pointed out that interpretation based only on literal meanings 'assumes unattainable perfection in draftsmanship'; even the most talented and experienced draftsmen cannot predict every situation to which legislation may have to be applied. As Ingman notes, it also expects too much of words in general, which are at best 'an imperfect means of communication'. The same word may mean different things to different people, and words also shift their meanings over time.

Zander, in his book *The Law-Making Process*, describes the literal approach as 'mechanical, divorced both from the realities of the use of language and from the expectations and aspirations of the human beings concerned . . . in that sense it is irresponsible'.

The golden rule
This provides that if the literal rule gives an absurd result, which Parliament could not have intended, then (and only then) the judge can substitute a reasonable meaning in the light of the statute as a whole. It was defined

by Lord Wensleydale in **Grey** *v* **Pearson** (1857): 'The grammatical and ordinary sense of the word is to be adhered to, unless that would lead to some absurdity, or some repugnance or inconsistency with the rest of the instrument, in which case the grammatical and ordinary sense of the words may be modified so as to avoid that absurdity and inconsistency, but no further.'

Examples of the golden rule in use are:

R *v* **Allen** (1872). Section 57 of the Offences Against the Person Act 1861 stated that 'Whosoever being married shall marry any other person during the life of the former husband or wife . . . shall be guilty of bigamy'. It was pointed out that it was impossible for a person already married to 'marry' someone else – they might go through a marriage ceremony, but would not actually be married; using the literal rule would make the statute useless. The courts therefore held that 'shall marry' should be interpreted to mean 'shall go through a marriage ceremony'.

Maddox *v* **Storer** (1963). Under the Road Traffic Act 1960, it was an offence to drive at more than 30 mph in a vehicle 'adapted to carry more than seven passengers'. The vehicle in the case was a minibus made to carry 11 passengers, rather than altered to do so, and the court held that 'adapted to' could be taken to mean 'suitable for'.

Adler *v* **George** (1964). The defendant was charged under s. 3 of the Official Secrets Act 1920, with obstructing a member of the armed forces 'in the vicinity of any prohibited place'. He argued that the natural meaning of 'in the vicinity of' meant near to, whereas the obstruction had actually occurred in the prohibited place itself, an air force station. The court held that while in many circumstances 'in the vicinity' could indeed only be interpreted as meaning near to, in this context it was reasonable to construe it as including being within the prohibited place.

Inco Europe Ltd *v* **First Choice Distribution** (2000): the House of Lords stated that words could be added to a statute by a judge to give effect to Parliament's intention where an obvious error had been made in drafting a statute.

Advantages of the golden rule The golden rule can prevent the absurdity and injustice caused by the literal rule, and help the courts put into practice what Parliament really means.

Disadvantages of the golden rule The Law Commission noted in 1969 that the 'rule' provided no clear meaning of an 'absurd result'. As in practice that was judged by reference to whether a particular interpretation was irreconcilable with the general policy of the legislature, the golden rule turns out to be a less explicit form of the mischief rule (discussed below).

The mischief rule
This rule was laid down in **Heydon's case** in the sixteenth century, and provides that judges should consider three factors:

- what the law was before the statute was passed;
- what problem, or 'mischief', the statute was trying to remedy;
- what remedy Parliament was trying to provide.

The judge should then interpret the statute in such a way as to put a stop to the problem that Parliament was addressing.

Examples of the mischief rule in use are:

Smith *v* **Hughes** (1960). The Street Offences Act 1958 made it a criminal offence for a prostitute to solicit potential customers in a street or public place. In this case, the prostitute was not actually in the street, but was sitting in a house, on the first floor, and tapping on the window to attract the attention of the men walking by. The judge decided that the aim of the Act was to enable people to walk along the streets without being solicited, and since the soliciting in question was aimed at people in the street, even though the prostitute was not in the street herself, the Act should be interpreted to include this activity.

Elliott *v* **Grey** (1960). The Road Traffic Act 1930 provided that it was an offence for an uninsured car to be 'used on the road'. The car in this case was on the road, but jacked up, with its battery removed, but the court held that as it was nevertheless a hazard of the type which the statute was designed to prevent, it was covered by the phrase 'used on the road'.

Royal College of Nursing *v* **DHSS** (1981). The Abortion Act 1967 stated that terminations of pregnancy were legal only if performed by a 'registered medical practitioner'. By 1972, surgical abortions were largely being replaced by drug-induced ones, in which the second stage of the process (attaching the patient to a drip), was carried out by nurses, under the instructions of a doctor. The House of Lords ruled that the mischief which the Act sought to remedy was the uncertain state of the previous law, which drove many women to dangerous back-street abortionists. It sought to do this by widening the grounds on which abortions could be obtained, and ensuring that they were carried out with proper skill in hygienic conditions, and the procedure in question promoted this aim, and was not unlawful. It was a controversial decision, with Lords Wilberforce and Edmund Davies claiming that the House was not interpreting legislation but rewriting it.

Advantages of the mischief rule The mischief rule helps avoid absurdity and injustice, and promotes flexibility. It was described by the Law Commission in 1969 as a 'rather more satisfactory approach' than the other two established rules.

Disadvantages of the mischief rule **Heydon's case** was the product of a time when statutes were a minor source of law, compared to the common law. Drafting was by no means as exact a process as it is today, and the supremacy of Parliament was not really established. At that time too, what statutes there were tended to include a lengthy preamble, which more or less spelt out the 'mischief' with which the Act was intended to deal. Judges of the time were very well qualified to decide what the previous law was and what problems a statute was intended to remedy, since they had usually drafted statutes on behalf of the king, and Parliament only rubberstamped them. Such a rule may be less appropriate now that the legislative situation is so different.

Aids to interpretation

Whichever approach the judges take to statutory interpretation, they have at their disposal a range of material to help. Some of these aids may be found within the piece of legislation itself, or in certain rules of language commonly applied in statutory texts – these are called internal aids. Others, outside the piece of legislation, are called external aids. Since 1995, a very important new external aid has been added in the form of the Human Rights Act 1998.

Internal aids
The literary rule and the golden rule both direct the judge to internal aids, though they are taken into account whatever the approach.

The statute itself To decide what a provision of the Act means the judge may draw a comparison with provisions elsewhere in the statute. Clues may also be provided by the long title of the Act or the subheadings within it.

Explanatory notes Acts passed since the beginning of 1999 are provided with explanatory notes, published at the same time as the Act.

Rules of language Developed by lawyers over time, these rules are really little more than common sense, despite their intimidating names. As with the rules of interpretation, they are not always precisely applied. Examples include:

Ejusdem generis General words which follow specific ones are taken to include only things of the same kind. For example, if an Act used the phrase 'dogs, cats and other animals' the phrase 'and other animals' would probably include other domestic animals, but not wild ones.
Expressio unius est exclusio alterius Express mention of one thing implies the exclusion of another. If an Act specifically mentioned 'Persian cats', the term would not include other breeds of cat.

Noscitur a sociis A word draws meaning from the other words around it. If a statute mentioned 'cat baskets, toy mice and food', it would be reasonable to assume that 'food' meant cat food, and dog food was not covered by the relevant provision.

Presumptions The courts assume that certain points are implied in all legislation. These presumptions include the following:

- statutes do not change the common law;
- the legislature does not intend to remove any matters from the juris-diction of the courts;
- existing rights are not to be interfered with;
- laws which create crimes should be interpreted in favour of the citizen where there is ambiguity;
- legislation does not operate retrospectively: its provisions operate from the day it comes into force, and are not backdated;
- statutes do not affect the monarch.

It is always open to Parliament to go against these presumptions if it sees fit – for example, the European Communities Act 1972 makes it clear that some of its provisions are to be applied retrospectively. But unless the wording of a statute makes it absolutely clear that Parliament has chosen to go against one or more of the presumptions, the courts can assume that the presumptions apply.

Some indication of the weight which judges feel should be attached to presumptions can be seen in the case of **L'Office Cherifien des Phosphates** *v* **Yamashita-Shinnihon Steamship Co Ltd** (1994), which concerned the presumption against retrospective effect. The House of Lords stated that the important issue was 'simple fairness': if they read the relevant statute as imposing the suggested degree of retrospective effect, would the result be so unfair that Parliament could not have intended it, even though their words might suggest retrospective effect. This could be judged by balancing a number of factors, including the nature of the rights affected, the clarity of the words used, and the background to the legislation.

What remains unclear is how judges decide between different presumptions if they conflict, and why certain values are selected for protection by presumptions, and not others. For example, the presumption that existing rights are not to be interfered with serves to protect the existing property or money of individuals, but there is no presumption in favour of people claiming state benefits.

External aids

The mischief rule directs the judge to external aids, including the following:

Historical setting A judge may consider the historical setting of the provision that is being interpreted, as well as other statutes dealing with the same subjects.

Dictionaries and textbooks These may be consulted to find the meaning of a word, or to gather information about the views of legal academics on a point of law.

Reports Legislation may be preceded by a report of a Royal Commission, the Law Commission or some other official advisory committee (see p. 88). The House of Lords stated in **Black-Clawson International Ltd** (1975) that official reports may be considered as evidence of the pre-existing state of the law and the mischief that the legislation was intended to deal with.

Treaties Treaties and international conventions can be considered when following the presumption that Parliament does not legislate in such a way that the UK would be in breach of its international obligations.

Previous practice General practice and commercial usage in the field covered by the legislation may shed light on the meaning of a statutory term.

The Human Rights Act 1998 This Act incorporates into UK law the European Convention on Human Rights, which is an international treaty signed by most democratic countries, and designed to protect basic human rights. In many countries, the Convention has been incorporated into national law as a Bill of Rights, which means that the courts can overrule domestic legislation which is in conflict with it. This is not the case in the UK. Instead, s. 3(1) of the Human Rights Act requires that: 'So far as it is possible to do so, primary and subordinate legislation must be read and given effect in a way which is compatible with the Convention rights.' This means essentially that where a statutory provision can be interpreted in more than one way, the interpretation which is compatible with the European Convention should be the one chosen. Section 2 further requires that in deciding any question which arises in connection with a right protected by the Convention, the courts should take into account any relevant judgments made by the European Court of Human Rights. If it is impossible to find an interpretation which is compatible with the Convention, the court concerned can make a declaration of incompatibility. This does not affect the validity of the statute in question, but it is designed to draw attention to the conflict so that the Government can change the law to bring it in line with the Convention (although the Act does not oblige the Government to do this). There is a special 'fast track' procedure by which a Minister can make the necessary changes.

To clarify interpretation, when new legislation is made, the relevant Bill must carry a statement from the relevant Minister, saying either that its provisions are compatible with the Convention, or that even if they are not, the Government wishes to go ahead with the legislation anyway. In the latter case, the Government would be specifically saying that the legislation must override Convention rights if there is a clash, but clearly any government intent on passing such legislation would be likely to face considerable opposition and so would have to have a very good reason, in the eyes of the public, for doing so.

Hansard This is the official daily report of parliamentary debates, and therefore a record of what was said during the introduction of legislation. For over 100 years, the judiciary held that such documents could not be consulted for the purpose of statutory interpretation. During his career, Lord Denning made strenuous efforts to do away with this rule, and in **Davis** *v* **Johnson** (1978), justified his interpretation of the Domestic Violence Act 1976 by reference to the parliamentary debates during its introduction. The House of Lords however rebuked him for doing so, and maintained that the rule should stand.

In 1993, the case of **Pepper** *v* **Hart** overturned the rule against consulting Hansard, and such consultation is clearly now allowed. The case was between teachers at a fee-paying school (Malvern College) and the Inland Revenue, and concerned the tax which employees should have to pay on perks (benefits related to their job). Malvern College allowed its teachers to send their sons there for one-fifth of the usual fee, if places were available. Tax law requires employees to pay tax on perks, and the amount of tax is based on the cost to the employer of providing the benefit, which is usually taken to mean any extra cost that the employer would not otherwise incur. The amount paid by Malvern teachers for their sons' places covered the extra cost to the school of having the child there (in books, food and so on), but did not cover the school's fixed costs, for paying teachers, maintaining buildings and so on, which would have been the same whether the teachers' children were there or not. Therefore the perk cost the school little or nothing, and so the teachers maintained that they should not have to pay tax on it. The Inland Revenue disagreed, arguing that the perk should be taxed on the basis of the amount it saved the teachers on the real cost of sending their children to the school.

The reason why the issue of consulting parliamentary debates arose was that during the passing of the Finance Act which laid down the tax rules in question, the then Secretary to the Treasury, Robert Sheldon, had specifically mentioned the kind of situation that arose in **Pepper** *v* **Hart**. He had stated that where the cost to an employer of a perk was minimal, employees should not have to pay tax on the full cost of it. The question was, could the judges take into account what the Minister had said? The House of Lords convened a special court of seven judges, which decided that they could look at Hansard to see what the Minister had said, and that his remarks could be used to decide what Parliament had intended.

The decision in **Pepper** *v* **Hart** was confirmed in **Three Rivers District Council** *v* **Bank of England (No. 2)** (1996), which concerned the correct interpretation of legislation passed in order to fulfil obligations arising from an EC directive. Although the legislation was not itself ambiguous, the claimants claimed that, if interpreted in the light of the information contained in Hansard, the legislation imposed certain duties on the defendants, which were not obvious from the legislation itself. The defendants argued that Hansard could only be consulted where legislation contained ambiguity, but the court disagreed, stating that where legislation was passed in order to give effect to international obligations, it was important to make sure that it did so, and consulting legislative materials was one way of helping to ensure this. The result would appear to be that Hansard can be consulted not just to explain ambiguous phrases, but to throw light on the general purpose of legislation.

In order to clarify the procedure for using Hansard in court cases, a Practice Direction was issued in 1995. It states that the relevant extract from Hansard, along with a summary of the argument concerning it, must be supplied to the court and the other parties at least five working days before the hearing.

Although it is now clear that parliamentary debates can be used as evidence of parliamentary intention, there is still much debate as to how useful they can be, and whether they really can be considered to be good evidence of what Parliament intended. The following are some of the arguments for use of these sources:

Usefulness. Lord Denning's argument, advanced in **Davis** *v* **Johnson** (1978), was that to ignore them would be to 'grope in the dark for the meaning of an Act without switching on the light'. When such an obvious source of enlightenment was available, it was ridiculous to ignore it – in fact Lord Denning said after the case that he intended to continue to consult Hansard, but simply not say he was doing so.

Other jurisdictions. Legislative materials are used in many foreign jurisdictions, including the US and many other European countries. In such countries, these materials tend to be more accessible and concise than Hansard – it is difficult to judge whether they are consulted because of this quality, or whether the fact that they are consulted has encouraged those who produce them to make them more readable. It is argued that the latter might be a useful side-effect of allowing the judges to consult parliamentary materials.

Media reports. Parliamentary proceedings are reported in newspapers and on radio and television. Since judges are as exposed to these as anyone else, it seems ridiculous to blinker themselves in court, or to pretend that they are blinkered.

The arguments against the use of these sources are:

Lack of clarity. The House of Lords, admonishing Lord Denning for his behaviour in **Davis** *v* **Johnson**, and directing that parliamentary debates were not to be consulted, stated that the evidence provided by the parliamentary debates might not be reliable; what was said in the cut and thrust of public debate was not 'conducive to a clear and unbiased explanation of the meaning of statutory language'.

Time and expense. Their Lordships also suggested that if debates were to be used, there was a danger that the lawyers arguing a case would devote too much time and attention to ministerial statements and so on, at the expense of considering the language used in the Act itself.

> It would add greatly to the time and expense involved in preparing cases involving the construction of a statute if counsel were expected to read all the debates in Hansard, and it would often be impracticable for counsel to get access to at least the older reports of debates in select committees in the House of Commons; moreover, in a very large proportion of cases such a search, even if practicable would throw no light on the question before the court . . .

Parliamentary intention. The nature of parliamentary intention is difficult, if not impossible, to pin down. Parliamentary debates usually reveal the views of only a few members, and even then, those words may need interpretation too.

How do judges really interpret statutes?

This question has much in common with the discussion of case law and the operation of precedent (p. 10); in both cases, discussion of rules conceals a certain amount of flexibility. The so-called 'rules of interpretation' are not rules at all, but different approaches. Judges do not methodically apply these rules to every case, and in any case, the fact that they can conflict with each other and produce different results necessarily implies some choice as to which is used. There is choice too in the relative weight given to internal and external aids, and rules of language, and approaches have varied over the years.

Just as with judicial precedent, the idea that statutory interpretation is an almost scientific process that can be used to produce a single right answer is simply nonsense. There is frequently room for more than one interpretation (otherwise the question would never reach the courts) and judges must choose between them. For clear evidence of this, there is no better example than the recent litigation concerning Auguste Pinochet, the former head of state of Chile. He had long been accused of crimes against humanity, including torture and murder and conspiracy to torture and to murder. When he made a visit to the UK, the Spanish Government requested that he should be extradited to Spain so that they could put him on trial. This led to a protracted series of litigation concerning whether it was legal for Britain to extradite him to Spain, and eventually the question came before the House of Lords. Pinochet's defence argued on the basis of the State Immunity Act 1978, which provides other states with immunity from prosecution in English courts; the Act provides that 'states' includes heads of state. The Lords were therefore asked to decide whether this immunity extended to Pinochet's involvement in the acts he was accused of and by a majority of three to two, they decided that it did not. Yet when the appeal was reopened (because one of the judges, Lord Hoffmann, was found to have links with Amnesty International, who were a party to the case), this time with seven Law Lords sitting, a different decision was reached. Although the Lords still stated that the General did not have complete immunity, by a majority of six to one, they restricted his liability to those acts which were committed after 1978, when torture committed outside the UK became a crime in the UK. This gave General Pinochet immunity for the vast majority of the torture allegations, and complete immunity for the allegations of murder and conspiracy to murder.

The reasoning behind both the decisions is complex and does not really need to concern us here; the important point to note is that in both hearings, the Lords were interpreting the same statutory provisions, yet they came up with significantly different verdicts. Because of the way it was reopened, the case gives us a rare insight into just how imprecise and unpredictable statutory interpretation can be, and it is hard to resist the implication that if you put any other case involving statutory interpretation before two separate panels of judges, they might well come up with different judgments too.

Given then that judges do have some freedom over questions of statutory interpretation, what influences the decisions they make? As with case law, there are a number of theories.

Dworkin: fitting in with principles
Dworkin (1986) claims that in approaching a case, the job of judges is to develop a theory about how the particular measure they are dealing with fits with the rest of the law as a whole. If there are two possible interpretations of a word or phrase, the judge should favour the one that allows the provision to sit most comfortably with the purpose of the rest of the law and with the principles and ideals of law and legality in general. This should be done, not for any mechanical reason, but because a body of law which is coherent and unified is, just for that reason, a body of law more entitled to the respect and allegiance of its citizens.

Cross: a contextual approach
Cross suggests that the courts take a 'contextual' approach in which, rather than choosing between different rules, they conduct a progressive analysis, considering first the ordinary meaning of the words in the context of the statute (taking a broad view of context), and then moving on to consider other possibilities if this provides an absurd result. Cross suggests that the courts can read in words that are necessarily implied, and have a limited power to add to, alter or ignore words that would

otherwise make a provision unintelligible, absurd, totally unreasonable, unworkable or completely inconsistent with the rest of the Act.

Willis: the just result

John Willis's influential article 'Statute Interpretation in a Nutshell' was cynical about the use of the three 'rules'. He points out that a statute is often capable of several different interpretations, each in line with one of the rules. Despite the emphasis placed on literal interpretation, Willis suggests that the courts view all three rules as equally valid. He claims they use whichever rule will produce the result that they themselves believe to be just.

Griffith: political choices

As with case law (see p. 14), Griffith claims that where there is ambiguity, the judiciary choose the interpretation that best suits their view of policy. An example of this was the 'Fares Fair' case, **Bromley London Borough Council *v* Greater London Council** (1983). The Labour-controlled GLC had enacted a policy – which was part of their election manifesto – to lower the cost of public transport in London, by subsidizing it from the money paid in rates (what we now call Council Tax). This meant higher rates. Conservative-controlled Bromley Council challenged the GLC's right to do this.

The powers of local authorities (which then included the GLC) are defined entirely by statute, and there is an assumption that if a power has not been granted to a local authority by Parliament, then it is not a power the authority is entitled to exercise. The judges' job then was to discover what powers Parliament had granted the GLC, and to determine whether their action on fares and rates was within those powers.

Section 1 of the Transport (London) Act 1969 stated: 'It shall be the general duty of the Greater London Council to develop policies, and to encourage, organize and where appropriate, carry out measures which will promote the provision of integrated, efficient and economic transport facilities and services in Greater London.' The key word here was 'economic', with each side taking a different view of its meaning.

The GLC said 'economic' meant 'cost-effective', in other words, giving good value for money. They stated that good value covered any of the policy goals that transport services could promote: efficient movement of passengers, reduction of pollution and congestion, possibly even social redistribution. Bromley Council, on the other hand, said that 'economic' meant 'breaking even': covering the expenses of its operation out of the fares charged to the passengers and not requiring a subsidy.

It is not difficult to see that both sides had a point – the word 'economic' could cover either meaning, making the literal rule more or less useless. Because of this, Lord Scarman refused to consult a dictionary, stating that: 'The dictionary may tell us the several meanings the word can have but the word will always take its specific meaning (or meanings) from its surroundings.' Lord Scarman stressed that those surroundings meant not just the statute as a whole, but also the general duties of the GLC to ratepayers; that duty must co-exist with the duty to the users of public transport.

Lord Scarman concluded:

'Economic' in s. 1 must, therefore, be construed widely enough to embrace both duties. Accordingly, I conclude that in s. 1(1) of the Act 'economic' covers not only the requirement that transport services be cost-effective but also the requirement that they be provided so as to avoid or diminish the burden on the ratepayers so far as it is practicable to do so.

Griffith has argued that the idea of a 'duty' to ratepayers as explained in the case is entirely judge-made, and that the Law Lords ruling that the interests of transport users had been preferred over those of ratepayers is interfering with the role of elected authorities. He suggests that 'public expenditure can always be criticised on the ground that it is excessive or wrongly directed', but that it is the role of elected bodies to make such decisions, and if the public does not like them 'the remedy lies in their hands at the next election'.

It is certainly odd that when the judges make so much play of the fact that Parliament should legislate because it is elected and accountable, they do not consider themselves bound to respect decisions made in fulfilment of an elected body's manifesto. What the Lords were doing, argues Griffith, was making a choice between two interpretations, based not on any real sense of what Parliament intended, but 'primarily [on] the Law Lords' strong preference for the principles of the market economy with a dislike of heavy subsidisation for social purposes' – in other words a political choice.

The judiciary would argue against this proposition, but it is certainly difficult to see where any of the 'rules of interpretation' fitted into this case: none of the rules of interpretation or the aids to interpretation forced the judges to favour Bromley Council's interpretation of the law over that of the GLC. They could have chosen either interpretation and still been within the law, so that choice must have been based on something other than the law.

Judicial attitudes to statutory interpretation

Over the past three decades, the judiciary have come to acknowledge that they do have some degree of discretion in interpreting statutes, but there is still considerable debate as to how far they can, and should, take this.

During his judicial career, Lord Denning was in the forefront of moves to establish a more purposive approach, aiming to produce decisions that put into practice the spirit of the law, even if that meant paying less than usual regard to the letter of the law, the actual words of the statute. He felt that the mischief rule could be interpreted broadly, so that it would not just allow the court to look at the history of the case, but it would also allow the court to carry out the intention of Parliament, however imperfectly this might have been expressed in the words used. The court in **Heydon's case** suggested that the mischief rule could be used in this broader sense.

Denning stated his view in **Magor and St Mellors** *v* **Newport Corporation** (1952): 'We do not sit here to pull the language of Parliament to pieces and make nonsense of it . . . we sit here to find out the intention of Parliament and carry it out, and we do this better by filling in the gaps and making sense of the enactment than by opening it up to destructive analysis.'

This approach was roundly criticized by the House of Lords, with Lord Simonds describing 'filling in the gaps' as 'a naked usurpation of the judicial function, under the guise of interpretation . . . If a gap is disclosed, the remedy lies in an amending Act.'

Denning's views nevertheless contributed to the growth of a more purposive approach which has gained ground in the last 20 years, with courts seeking to interpret statutes in ways which will promote the general purpose of the legislation. However, the courts still maintain that this cannot be taken too far. Lord Diplock stated in **Duport Steels Ltd** *v* **Sirs** (1980) that there was no place for the mischief rule where a statute was not ambiguous, even if a literal interpretation would give an absurd result:

> Where the meaning of the statutory words is plain and unambiguous, it is not for the judges to invent fancied ambiguities as an excuse for failing to give effect to its plain meaning because they themselves consider that the consequences of doing so would be inexpedient, or even unjust or immoral. In controversial matters . . . there is room for differences of opinion as to what is expedient, what is just, and what is morally justifiable. Under our constitution it is Parliament's opinion on these matters that is paramount.

Even where there was ambiguity, Lord Diplock felt that the mischief rule could only be used within tightly limited circumstances, which he defined in **Jones** *v* **Wrotham Park Settled Estates** (1980), stating that the mischief rule should only be applied where:

- it was possible to determine from consideration of the Act alone the precise mischief that the Act was to remedy; and
- it was an accident that the mischief had not been resolved by the Act's literal meaning; and
- it was possible to state with certainty what were the additional words that would have been inserted by the draftsman, and approved by Parliament, had the omission been drawn to their attention.

This approach clearly contrasts with that of Denning, who felt that the mischief rule should be used even where the wording was clear, if following that wording would lead to an absurd or obviously unjust result, and did not need to be used as tightly as suggested by Lord Diplock.

The introduction of the Human Rights Act 1998 is likely to prompt a shift towards more purposive interpretation, as the courts weigh up important issues concerning the rights of the individual against the state, and take into account the judgments of the European Court of Human Rights, which itself takes a purposive approach to interpretation. Some experts have predicted that the House of Lords role will become increasingly like that of the US Supreme Court, dealing with vital questions for society and the individual, rather than the detailed and technical commercial and taxation matters which form the bulk of its current work.

As with case law, there are various theories about the way in which judges use the discretion they have in statutory interpretation.

Interpretation of European legislation

Under Art. 234 of the Treaty of Rome, the European Court is the supreme tribunal for the interpretation of European Union law. Section 3(1) of the European Communities Act 1972 states that questions as to the validity, meaning or effect of European legislation are to be decided in accordance with the principles laid down by the European Court.

In the light of these provisions, Lord Denning stated that when interpreting European law, English courts should take the same approach as the European Court would:

> No longer must they examine the words in meticulous detail. No longer must they argue about the precise grammatical sense. They must look to the purpose or intent. To quote the words of the European Court in the **Da Costa** case they must deduce from the wording and the spirit of the Treaty the meaning of the Community rules . . . They must divine the spirit of the Treaty and gain inspiration from it. If they find a gap, they must fill it as best they can. They must do what the framers of the instrument would have done if they had thought about it. So we must do the same. (**Bulmer** *v* **Bollinger** (1974))

In other words, he was saying that rather than using the literal rule, the courts should apply a broadly interpreted mischief rule – which was of course, the same approach that he felt should be applied to domestic legislation.

If the English courts are uncertain as to how a piece of European legislation should be interpreted they can, and sometimes must, refer it to the European Court of Justice for interpretation (see p. 63). In such circumstances the case is adjourned, until the European Court directs the English one on how to interpret the European legislation. The English court then reopens the case in England and applies this interpretation.

Effect of EU membership on the interpretation of UK law

Section 2(4) of the European Communities Act 1972 provides that all parliamentary legislation (whether passed before or after the European Communities Act) must be construed and applied in accordance with Union law. The case of **R** *v* **Secretary of State for Transport, ex parte Factortame** (1990) makes it clear that the English courts must apply European law which is directly effective even if it conflicts with English law, including statute law (these issues are discussed more fully in the section on European law).

Reform of statutory interpretation

The problems with statutory interpretation have been recognized for decades, but despite several important reports, little has changed. The Law Commission examined the interpretation of statutes in 1967 and had 'little hesitation in suggesting that this is a field not suitable for codification'. Instead, it proposed certain improvements within the present system.

- More liberal use should be made of internal and external aids.
- In the event of ambiguity, the construction which best promoted the 'general legislative purpose' should be adopted. This could be seen as supporting Denning's approach.

The Renton Committee on the Preparation of Legislation produced its report in 1975, making many proposals for improving the procedure for making and drafting statutes, including the following:

- Acts could begin with a statement of purpose in the same way that older statutes used to have preambles.
- There should be a move towards including less detail in the legislation, introducing the simpler style used in countries such as France.
- More use could be made in statutes of examples showing the courts how an Act was intended to work in particular situations.
- Long, un-paragraphed sentences should be avoided.
- Statutes should be arranged to suit the convenience of the ultimate users.
- There should be more consolidation of legislation.

In 1978, Sir David Renton, in a speech entitled 'Failure to Implement the Renton Report' noted that there had been a small increase in the number of draftsmen and increased momentum in the consolidation process, but that Parliament had continued to pass a huge amount of legislation, with no reduction in the amount of detail and scarcely any use of statements of purpose. Fifteen years later, in 1993, a Commission appointed by the Hansard Society for Parliamentary Government reported that little had changed. Having consulted widely, it concluded that there was widespread dissatisfaction with the situation, and suggested that the drafting style adopted should be appropriate for the main end users of legislation, with the emphasis on clarity, simplicity and certainty. There should be some means of informing citizens, lawyers and the courts about the general purpose behind a particular piece of legislation, and unnecessary detail should be avoided. The Commission suggested that an increase in the number of draftsmen might be necessary to achieve these aims: since its report, four more draftsmen have been recruited, but otherwise there was little response from the previous Government. The current Government, however, has placed a high priority on making the workings of law and government accessible to ordinary people, and the introduction of explanatory notes to Bills passed from 1999 is an important step forward.

▶ ANSWERING QUESTIONS

1 A statute states that 'It is an offence to loiter or solicit in a street for the purposes of prostitution.'

Mary, a known prostitute, sits in a large bay window on the first floor of a house overlooking a busy street. She taps the window to attract the attention of men on the pavement. She invites John upstairs by beckoning and pointing to the door. He accepts her invitation.

Jane, a known prostitute, who is unable to speak, stands on a street corner and waits for men in cars to stop. She is observed getting into a car and handing Peter, the driver, a card which he reads. He then drives off immediately, without Jane.

Have any offences been committed? Discuss the rules of statutory interpretation which guide you to your answer. *WJEC*

You might start your answer by briefly describing the three rules of interpretation, and pointing out that there is no strict procedure dictating which should be applied, even though they can lead to different interpretations of the same statute.

You then need to take each person in turn, starting with Mary. The first thing to note is that it appears the offence can be committed in two ways: by either loitering in the street, or soliciting in the street, each for the purposes of prostitution. Taking a literal approach first, can Mary be said to be loitering in the street or soliciting in the street? Since she is not physically in the street, it seems unlikely that she could be described as loitering there. She is clearly soliciting, but can she be said to be doing so 'in the street'? She may not be in the street, but her soliciting appears to be taking effect in the street, so do you think the term can be interpreted to cover her behaviour? You could then point out that since there appears to be some ambiguity, the golden rule should be applied, allowing you to modify the sense of the words in order to resolve the ambiguity – point out that in a real case, you would want to look at the rest of the statute to help you do this.

If the golden rule is unhelpful, you could apply the mischief rule – again, in real life, you would want to consult the rest of the statute, and probably other materials too, to establish the purpose of the statute, so that you could interpret the provision in line with that purpose. Using this rule, whether Mary had committed an offence would depend on what the purpose of the statute was: if it was to stop men in the street being harassed by prostitutes, you might feel that the provision should be interpreted to make Mary guilty of an offence; alternatively, if, for example, the purpose was to keep prostitution within brothels, you might find that Mary had not committed an offence.

You also need to consider the issue of whether Mary's behaviour is 'for the purposes of prostitution': there does seem to be evidence of this, but on the facts as we have them here, it is only evidence which the jury or magistrates will consider, rather than definite proof.

Moving on to Jane, you can see that on a literal interpretation she is loitering in the street, but is she doing so for the purposes of prostitution? Here again, you might point out that you would need to know more about the facts (particularly what is on the card), but if there is evidence that she is acting for the purposes of prostitution, an offence may have been committed since she is clearly loitering in the street. The statute appears not to require that the accused should both loiter and solicit, so even though soliciting in the normal sense of the word would seem to require some sort of verbal communication, the fact that she has not spoken to the man does not mean she cannot have committed the offence. Since the literal rule does not give rise to ambiguity or absurdity, it appears not to be necessary to apply the golden or mischief rules.

You should conclude by pointing out that to make a firm decision on whether an offence has been committed, you would need to consider both internal and external aids to interpretation. You might also point out that there is a presumption that statutes which impose a criminal penalty should be interpreted in favour of the citizen where there is ambiguity, which might mean that in Mary's case the ambiguity could mean that she has committed no offence.

2 **Explain the methods used by judges in interpreting statutes and consider how far judges are concerned to discover the true intentions of Parliament.** *AQA (AEB)*

A good introduction would explain briefly why judges might need to interpret statutes (see p. 29), and then go on to talk about the importance of parliamentary intention. You need to show you understand why the courts are supposed to look for the intention of Parliament, by discussing the constitutional issue of parliamentary sovereignty, and the fact that judges are not elected. You should also examine the problems of deciding what parliamentary intention actually is, as discussed on p. 40. Having set the issue in its context, you can go on to look at the methods used by judges to attempt to find and apply parliamentary intention: the rules and presumptions, and the internal and external aids. Give examples of these in use if you can, as this shows you understand how they work. Don't forget to discuss the change made by **Pepper v Hart**, and the usefulness or otherwise of consulting Hansard.

You then need to answer the second part of the question, which essentially asks how far judicial interpretation of statutes is really concerned with applying parliamentary intention, and how far judges can make decisions on other grounds. You need to discuss the idea that a more purposive approach seems to be becoming the norm, mentioning the influence that European Community law has had in this area; and it would be a good idea to talk about the views of writers such as Cross, Griffith, Willis and Dworkin (see pp. 41–42).

Your conclusion might state whether you feel judges currently pay the right degree of attention to what Parliament intends, and why; if not, what reforms could change this?

3 Read the following extract and answer parts (a) to (c) which follow.

Exercise on Statutory Interpretation

Pepper v Hart [1993] 1 All ER 42

In this case, heard by seven Law Lords, the House of Lords (the Lord Chancellor dissenting) held that judges could consult Hansard to assist them in interpreting a statutory provision. Lord Browne-Wilkinson, who gave the leading judgment, said:

'Statute law consists of the words that Parliament has enacted. It is for the courts to construe those words and it is the court's duty in so doing to give effect to the intention of Parliament in using those words. It is an inescapable fact that, despite all the care taken in passing legislation, some statutory provisions when applied to the circumstances under consideration in any specific case are found to be ambiguous . . . In many, I suspect most, case references to parliamentary materials will not throw any light on the matter. But in a few cases it may emerge that the very question was considered by Parliament in passing the legislation. Why in such a case should the courts blind themselves to a clear indication of what Parliament intended in using those words? . . .

I therefore reach the conclusion . . . that the exclusionary rule should be relaxed so as to permit reference to parliamentary materials where (a) legislation is ambiguous or obscure, or leads to an absurdity; (b) the material relied on consists of one or more statements by a minister or other promoter of the Bill . . . (c) the statements relied on are clear. Further than this, I would not at present go.'

(a) What difficulties are faced by judges in finding the 'intention of Parliament'? With reference to the second paragraph of the extract, critically examine the arguments for and against the use of Hansard by judges when interpreting statutes.

(b) Briefly explain and evaluate the rules of statutory interpretation.

(c) With reference to the extract, and using the rules set out in your answers to (b), discuss the situation below.

In 1999 the (fictitious) Vehicles in Parks Act was passed in response to a Royal Commission recommendation that vehicles should be banned from public parks in order to ensure safe and unpolluted spaces within towns. In the course of the debate, an opposition MP said, 'It is not the intention of Parliament to ban all vehicles from parks – obviously motorcars and motorcycles may be a danger to children playing in the park, but there is no evidence that other vehicles are likely to cause either accidents or pollution'.

The Act provides that 'any person who knowingly brings any vehicle into a public park shall be guilty of an offence', and the interpretation section defines 'vehicle' as 'any wheeled conveyance designed for the carriage of people or goods'.

Adam, who went into Hightown Park in his motorized wheelchair, was charged under the Act. *OCR*

(a) Relevant material to answer the first part of this question can be found at p. 30 under the heading 'What is parliamentary intention'. To answer the second part of the question, look at p. 39. Make sure that in discussing this material you make reference to the extract as requested to do by the examiner.

(b) The material to answer this question can be found at pp. 31–40. In particular you needed to discuss the literal rule, the golden rule and the mischief rule, intrinsic aids (with particular reference to the language rules and the presumptions) and extrinsic aids (placing the Hansard reports as an extrinsic aid). In evaluating these rules you could refer to the specific criticism contained in the aforementioned pages, but also the alternative arguments on how judges really interpret statutes discussed at p. 40. You could also discuss the effect that membership of the EU has had on statutory interpretation (see p. 46).

(c) The literal rule would lead to a conviction as under its ordinary and natural meaning a motorized wheelchair is a 'vehicle'. There is no ambiguity in the Act so it would not be appropriate to rely on the golden rule. Adam would want the courts to apply the mischief rule in interpreting the statute. In applying this, use of Hansard is unlikely to be possible because the words referred to were those of an opposition MP; Lord Browne-Wilkinson stated in **Pepper** v **Hart** that the material relied on 'must consist of one or more statements by a minister or other promoter of the Bill'. However, the Royal Commission Report could be looked at as an external aid to interpretation and reference could be made to the case of **Black-Clawson International Ltd** (1975). As this report aimed to create 'safe' spaces in towns it could be argued that the motorized wheelchair should not be included within the statute's provisions as, at the speed it travels, it creates very little danger. It is also likely that the wheelchair has an electric motor which would not add to the problem of pollution.

DELEGATED LEGISLATION

In many cases, the statutes passed by Parliament lay down a basic framework of the law, with creation of the detailed rules delegated to Government departments, local authorities, or public or nationalized bodies; the statute is known as the enabling Act. There are three main forms of delegated legislation:

Statutory instruments. These are made by government departments.

Bye-laws. These are made by local authorities, public and nationalized bodies. Bye-laws have to be approved by central Government.

Orders in Council. These are made by Government in times of emergency. They are drafted by the relevant Government department, approved by the Privy Council and signed by the Queen.

On an everyday basis, delegated legislation is an extremely important source of law. The output of delegated legislation far exceeds that of Acts of Parliament, and its provisions include rules that can substantially affect the day-to-day lives of huge numbers of people – safety laws for industry, road traffic regulations, and rules relating to state education, for example.

Why is delegated legislation necessary?

Delegated legislation is necessary for a number of reasons:

Insufficient parliamentary time. Parliament does not have the time to debate every detailed rule necessary for efficient government.

Speed. It allows rules to be made more quickly than they could by Parliament. Parliament does not sit all the time, and its procedure is slow and cumbersome; delegated legislation often has to be made in response to emergencies and urgent problems.

Technicality of the subject matter. Modern legislation often needs to include detailed, technical provisions – those in building regulations or safety at work rules for example. MPs do not usually have the technical knowledge required, whereas delegated legislation can use experts who are familiar with the relevant areas.

Need for local knowledge. Local bye-laws in particular can only be made effectively with awareness of the locality. Recognition of the importance of local knowledge can be found with the new devolved assemblies for Scotland, Wales and Northern Ireland (see p. 4). These new democratic bodies have important powers to make delegated legislation.

Flexibility. Statutes require cumbersome procedures for enactment, and can only be revoked or amended by another statute. Delegated legislation, however, can be put into action quickly, and easily revoked if it proves problematic.

Future needs. Parliament cannot hope to foresee every problem that might arise as a result of a statute, especially concerning areas such as health provision or welfare benefits. Delegated legislation can be put in place as and when such problems arise.

Control of delegated legislation

Because it is not directly made by elected representatives, delegated legislation is subject to the following range of controls, designed to ensure that the power delegated is not abused.

Consultation

Those who make delegated legislation often consult experts within the relevant field, and those bodies who are likely to be affected by it. In the case of road traffic regulations for example, Ministers are likely to seek the advice of police, motoring organizations, vehicle manufacturers and local authorities before making the rules. Often the relevant statute makes such consultation obligatory and names the bodies who should be consulted. Under the National Insurance Act 1946, for example, draft regulations must be submitted to the National Insurance Advisory Committee, and any Minister proposing to make rules of procedure for a tribunal within a department is required by the Tribunals and Inquiries Act 1971 to consult the Council on Tribunals. In other cases there may be a general statutory requirement for 'such consultation as the minister thinks appropriate with such organizations as appear to him to represent the interest concerned'.

Publication

All delegated legislation is published, and therefore available for public scrutiny.

Supervision by Parliament

There are a number of ways in which Parliament can oversee delegated legislation.

Revocation
Parliamentary sovereignty means that Parliament can at any time revoke a piece of delegated legislation itself, or pass legislation on the same subject as the delegated legislation.

The affirmative resolution procedure
Enabling Acts dealing with subjects of special, often constitutional, importance may require Parliament to vote its approval of the delegated legislation. This is called the affirmative resolution procedure, whereby delegated legislation is laid before one or both Houses (sometimes in draft), and becomes law only if a motion approving it is passed within a specified time (usually 28 or 40 days). Since a vote has to be taken, the procedure means that the Government must find parliamentary time for debate, and opposition parties have an opportunity to raise any objections. In practice, though, it is very rare for the Government not to achieve a majority when such votes are taken.

The negative resolution procedure
Much delegated legislation is put before Parliament for MPs under the negative resolution procedure. Within a specified time (usually 40 days), any member may put down a motion to annul it. An annulment motion put down by a backbencher is not guaranteed to be dealt with, but one put down by the Official Opposition (the party with the second largest number of MPs) usually will be. If, after debate, either House passes an annulment motion, the delegated legislation is cancelled.

Committee supervision
A parliamentary committee watches over the making of delegated legislation, and reports to each House on any delegated legislation which requires special consideration, including any regulations made under an Act that prohibits challenge by the courts, or which seem to make unusual or unexpected use of the powers granted by the enabling Act. However, the Committee may not consider the merits of any piece of delegated legislation.

Questions from MPs
MPs can ask Ministers' questions about delegated legislation at question time, or raise them in debates.

The House of Lords
Although the House of Lords cannot veto proposed Acts, the same does not apply to delegated legislation. In 1968 the House of Lords rejected an order imposing sanctions against the Rhodesian Government made under the Southern Rhodesia Act 1965.

Control by the courts: judicial review

While the validity of a statute can never be challenged by the courts because of parliamentary sovereignty, delegated legislation can. It may be challenged on any of the following grounds under the procedure for judicial review.

Procedural *ultra vires*. Here the complainant claims that the procedures laid down in the enabling Act for producing delegated legislation have not been followed. In **Agricultural, Horticultural and Forestry Training Board *v* Aylesbury Mushrooms Ltd** (1972), an order was declared invalid because the requirement to consult with interested parties before making it had not been properly complied with.

Substantive *ultra vires*. This is usually based on a claim that the measure under review goes beyond the powers Parliament granted under the enabling Act. In **Commissioners of Customs and Excise *v* Cure and Deeley Ltd** (1962), the powers of the Commissioners to make delegated legislation under the Finance (No. 2) Act 1940 was challenged. The Act empowered them to produce regulations 'for any matter for which provision appears to them necessary for the purpose of giving effect to the Act'. The Commissioners held that this included allowing them to make a regulation giving them the power to determine the amount of tax due where a tax return was submitted late. The High Court invalidated the regulation on the ground that the Commissioners had given themselves powers far beyond what Parliament had intended; they were empowered only to collect such tax as was due by law, not to decide what amount they thought fit.

    R *v* Secretary of State for Social Security, ex parte Joint Council for the Welfare of Immigrants (1996) concerned the Asylum and Immigration Appeals Act 1993 which provided a framework for determining applications for asylum, and for appeals after unsuccessful applications. It allowed asylum seekers to apply for social security benefits while they were waiting for their applications or appeals to be decided, at a cost of over £200 million per year to British taxpayers. This led to concern from some quarters that the provisions might attract those who were simply seeking a better lifestyle than that available in their own countries (often called economic migrants), as opposed to those fleeing persecution, who the provisions were actually designed to help.

    In order to discourage economic migrants, the then Secretary of State for Social Security exercised his powers to make delegated legislation under the Social Security (Contributions and Benefits) Act 1992, and produced regulations which stated that social security benefits would no longer be available to those who sought asylum after they had entered the UK, rather than immediately on entry, or those who had been refused leave to stay here and were awaiting the outcome of appeals against the decision.

    The Joint Council for the Welfare of Immigrants challenged the regulations, claiming that they fell outside the powers granted by the

1992 Act. The Court of Appeal upheld their claim, stating that the 1993 Act was clearly intended to give asylum seekers rights which they did not have previously. The effect of the regulations was effectively to take those rights away again, since without access to social security benefits, most asylum seekers would either have to return to the countries from which they had fled, or live on nothing while their claims were processed. The Court ruled that Parliament could not have intended to give the Secretary of State powers to take away the rights it had given in the 1993 Act: this could only be done by a new statute, and therefore the regulations were *ultra vires.*

The decision was a controversial one, because the regulations had themselves been approved by Parliament, and overturning them could be seen as a challenge to the power of the legislature, despite the decision being explained by the Court as upholding that power.

Unreasonableness. If rules are manifestly unjust, have been made in bad faith (for example by someone with a financial interest in their operation) or are otherwise so perverse that no reasonable official could have made them, the courts can declare them invalid.

Criticism of delegated legislation

Lack of democratic involvement

This argument is put forward because delegated legislation is usually made by civil servants, rather than elected politicians. This is not seen as a particular problem where the delegated legislation takes the form of detailed administrative rules, since these would clearly take up impossible amounts of parliamentary time otherwise. However, in the latter years of the last Conservative Government there was increasing concern that delegated legislation was being used to implement important policies.

Overuse

Critics argue that there is too much delegated legislation; this is linked to the point above, as there would be little problem with increasing amounts of delegated legislation if its purpose was merely to flesh out technical detail.

Sub-delegation

Delegated legislation is sometimes made by people other than those who were given the original power to do so.

Lack of control

Despite the above list of controls over delegated legislation, the reality is that effective supervision is difficult. First, publication has only limited benefits, given that the general public are frequently unaware of the existence of delegated legislation, let alone on what grounds it can be challenged and how to go about doing so. This is turn has an effect on the ability of the courts to control delegated legislation, since judicial review relies on individual challenges being brought before the courts. This may not happen until years after a provision is enacted, when it finally affects someone who is prepared and able to challenge it. The obvious result is that legislation which largely affects a class of individuals who are not given to questioning official rules, are unaware of their rights, or who lack the financial resources to go to court, will rarely be challenged.

A further problem is that some enabling Acts confer extremely wide discretionary powers on Ministers; a phrase such as 'the Minister may make such regulations as he sees fit for the purpose of bringing the Act into operation' would not be unusual. This means that there is very little room for anything to be considered *ultra vires*, so judicial review is effectively frustrated.

The main method of control over delegated legislation is therefore parliamentary, but this too has its drawbacks. Although the affirmative resolution procedure usually ensures that parliamentary attention is drawn to important delegated legislation, it is rarely possible to prevent such legislation being passed. The Select Committee on the Scrutiny of Delegated Powers makes an important contribution, and has been able to secure changes to a number of important pieces of legislation. However, it too lacks real power, as it is unable to consider the merits of delegated legislation (as opposed to whether the delegated powers have been correctly used) and its reports have no binding effect.

▶ ANSWERING QUESTIONS

1 Why is it necessary to have controls over delegated legislation? Are the present controls satisfactory? *OCR*

Your introduction should explain what delegated legislation is. You should then go on to explain why it needs to be controlled – the main reason being the fact that it is not made by Parliament. Describe the controls that exist, and then go through the problems with those controls (the section on judicial review, p. 422, provides extra material which will be useful here). Your conclusion should state whether you feel the controls are adequate, and if not, whether you feel anything could be done to improve them.

2 Read the source material below and answer parts (a), (b) and (c) which follow.

Exercise on Delegated Legislation

Source A

Police and Criminal Evidence Act 1984
(1984 c.60)
Section 60
Tape-recording of Interviews

(1) It shall be the duty of the Secretary of State –

. . .

 (b) to make an order requiring the tape-recording of interviews of persons suspected of the commission of criminal offences, or of such descriptions of criminal offences as may be specified in the order . . .
(2) An order under subsection (1) above shall be made by statutory instrument and shall be subject to annulment in pursuance of a resolution of either House of Parliament.

Source B

Statutory Instrument
1991 No. 2687
The Police and Criminal Evidence Act 1984
(Tape-recording of Interview) (No. 1) Order 1991

Made	29th November 1991
Laid before Parliament	6th December 1991
Coming into force	1st January 1992

Now, therefore, in pursuance of the said section 60(1)(b), the Secretary of State hereby orders as follows:

. . .

2. This Order shall apply to interviews of persons suspected of the commission of indictable offences which are held by police officers at police stations in the police areas specified in the schedule to this Order and which commence after midnight on 31st December 1991.

3(1) Subject to paragraph (2) below, interviews to which this Order applies shall be tape-recorded in accordance with the requirements of the code of practice on tape-recording which came into operation on 29th July 1988 . . .

3(2) The duty to tape-record interviews under paragraph (1) above shall not apply to interviews –

(a) where the offence of which a person is suspected is one in respect of which he has been arrested or detained under section 14(1)(a) of the Prevention of Terrorism (Temporary Provisions) Act 1989; . . .

(a) Using Sources A and B to illustrate your answer, compare the legislative process in relation to an Act of Parliament on the one hand and delegated legislation on the other.

(b) What are the advantages and disadvantages of delegated legislation?

(c) Each of the following interviews was conducted by police officers and took place at a police station covered by SI 1991/2687, but none of the interviews was tape-recorded.

  (i)   On the 30th November 1991 Alice was charged with an indictable offence and interviewed;

  (ii) Bertie, who was suspected of an indictable offence, was interviewed on the 1st April 1998;

  (iii) Cedric, detained under s. 14(1)(a) of the Prevention of Terrorism (Temporary Provisions) Act 1989 was interviewed in April 1998.

Discuss interviews (i), (ii) and (iii) with reference to Source B.

(a)   For material on the legislative process in relation to an Act of Parliament see p. 27 and for delegated legislation pp. 51–53. You could point out that the Police and Criminal Evidence Act 1984 was an enabling Act which allowed the Secretary of State to make the Statutory Instrument 1991 No. 2687. You could mention that statutory instruments are made by government departments and contrast this with bye-laws and Orders in Council (p. 51). When explaining the negative resolution procedure (p. 53) you could refer to the fact that the statutory instrument on tape-recording interviews was laid before Parliament on 6 December 1991 and that s. 60(2) of PACE refers to this process.

(b)   Material on the advantages of delegated legislation can be found on p. 51 under the heading 'Why is delegated legislation necessary'. Criticisms can be found on pp. 55–56.

(c)(i) As Statutory Instrument 1991/2687 provides that its provisions only apply to interviews that take place after midnight of the 31 December 1991, the police were under no obligation to tape-record Alice's interview.

(ii) Bertie's interview should have been tape-recorded as he was suspected of committing an indictable offence and the interview took place after the provisions of the statutory instrument came into force. You could look at possible remedies, particularly the exclusion of the evidence obtained, which is discussed at p. 262.

(iii) There was no obligation to tape-record Cedric's interview as he had been detained under the Prevention of Terrorism (Temporary Provisions) Act 1989.

▶ EUROPEAN LAW

The European Union (EU) currently comprises 15 western European countries. The original members – France, West Germany, Belgium,

Luxembourg, Italy and The Netherlands – laid the foundations in 1951, when they created the European Coal and Steel Community (ECSC). Six years later, they signed the Treaties of Rome, creating the European Economic Community (EEC) and the European Atomic Energy Community (Euratom). The original six were joined by the UK, Ireland and Denmark in 1973, Greece in 1981 and Spain and Portugal in 1986, and in the same year, the member countries signed the Single European Act, which developed free movement of goods and people within the Community (the single market), and greater political unity. Finland, Austria and Sweden joined in 1995. Following the Nice summit, the EU is preparing to increase from the present 15 member states to a total of 27 by 2004. The next six countries likely to be allowed to join are Poland, the Czech Republic, Hungary, Slovenia, Estonia and Cyprus.

In 1993 the Maastricht Treaty renamed the European Economic Community the European Community and the European Economic Treaty was renamed the European Treaty. It also created the European Union (EU), which is likely to become the most important body in Europe and so will be the label that we will refer to in this book.

The aims of the European Union

The original aim of the first treaty signed, the Treaty of Paris, was to create political unity within Europe and prevent another world war. The ECSC placed the production of steel and coal in all the member states under the authority of a single community organization, with the object of indirectly controlling the manufacture of arms and therefore helping to prevent war between member states. Euratom was designed to produce cooperative nuclear research, and the EEC to improve Europe's economic strength.

Though all three communities still exist, it is the EEC (now known as the EU) that has the most significance, particularly for law. Its object now is to weld Europe into a single prosperous area by abolishing all restrictions affecting the movement of people, of goods and money between member states, producing a single market of over 370 million people, available to all producers in the member states. This, it is hoped, will help Europe to compete economically with Japan and the US, the member states being stronger as a block than they could possibly be on their own. The Single European Act 1986 was a major step towards this goal, setting a target of 1992 for the abolition of trade barriers between member states. The practical effect of this is that, for example, a company manufacturing rivets in Leeds, with an order from a company in Barcelona, can send the rivets all the way there by lorry without the driver having to fill in customs forms as he or she crosses every border. The rivets will be made to a common EU standard, so the Spanish firm will know exactly what they are going to receive, while any trademarks or other rights over the design of the rivets will be protected throughout the member states. Just as goods can now move freely throughout the EU, so can workers: for example, a designer from Paris can go and work in London, or Milan, or Dublin, with no need for a work permit and no problem with immigration controls.

Along with these closer economic ties, it is intended that there should be increasing political unity, though there is some disagreement – particularly, though not exclusively, in Britain – as to how far this should go. Nevertheless, progress is being made: the Treaty on European Union (TEU, also known as the Maastricht Treaty), signed in 1992, was the first major move in this direction, establishing the aims of a single currency, joint defence and foreign policies, and inter-governmental cooperation on justice and home affairs. The introduction of the single currency began in 1999 (though not in the UK, which had negotiated the right to opt out of the programme), and the Amsterdam Treaty, signed in 1997, has now given more precise definition to the common foreign and security policy and cooperation in justice and home affairs. These matters now fall within the scope of the EU.

The institutions of the European Union

There are four key European institutions: the Commission, the Council, the European Parliament and the European Court of Justice. Of less importance is the European Court of First Instance. Each of these institutions will be considered in turn.

The Commission

The Commission is composed of 20 members, called Commissioners, who are each appointed by the member states, subject to approval by the European Parliament, for five years. They must be nationals of a member state, and in practice there tend to be two each from the largest states – France, Germany, Italy, Spain and the UK – and one each from the rest. However, the Commissioners do not represent their own countries: they are independent, and their role is to represent the interests of the EU overall. The idea is that the Commission's commitment to furthering EU interests balances the role of the Council, whose members represent national interests.

In addition to its part in making EU legislation (see p. 61), the Commission is responsible for ensuring that member states uphold EU law, and has powers to investigate breaches by member states and, where necessary, bring them before the Court of Justice. It also plays an important role in the relationship of the EU with the rest of the world, negotiating trade agreements and the accession of new members, and draws up the annual draft budget for the EU. It is assisted in all these functions by an administrative staff, which has a similar role to that of the civil service in the UK.

The reputation of the Commission was seriously damaged in 1999 when an independent report found evidence of fraud, mismanagement and nepotism, forcing all the Commissioners to resign.

The Council

The Council represents the interests of individual member states. It is the most powerful body in Europe and plays an important role in the passing of legislation. It does not have a permanent membership – in each meeting, the members, one from each country, are chosen according to the subject under discussion (so, for example, a discussion of matters relating to farming would usually be attended by the Minister of Agriculture of each country). Presidency of the Council rotates among the member states every six months.

The Council may be questioned by the European Parliament, but the chief control is exercised by the national Governments controlling their Ministers who attend the Council.

A related institution is the European Council, which grew from the fact that heads of State or Government and Foreign Ministers of member states evolved an informal convention of twice-yearly summit meetings to discuss important issues. Much of the high-profile EEC business tended to be done at these meetings, which have now been recognized and formalized as the European Council by Art. 2 of the Single European Act 1986. They are now required to take place twice a year and, when discussing EU matters, have the same powers as the Council of Ministers, though the two are technically separate.

The European Parliament

The Parliament is composed of 626 members (MEPs), who are directly elected in their own countries. In Britain they are elected in the same way as MPs, and each represent a geographical area, though these are much larger than those of MPs, since there are only 87 MEPs for the whole country. Elections are held every five years.

The individual member countries are each allocated a number of seats, roughly according to population, though on this basis the smaller countries are over-represented. Members sit in political groupings rather than with others from their own country.

As well as taking part in the legislative process (discussed below) the Parliament has a variety of roles to play in connection with the other institutions. Over the Commission, it exercises a supervisory power. It has a right of veto over the appointment of the Commission as a whole, and can also dismiss the whole Commission by a vote of censure. In 1999 the entire

Commission resigned during a crisis over fraud and mismanagement within the Commission, to avoid a vote of censure. The Commission must make an annual report to Parliament, and Parliament can also require Commissioners to answer written or oral questions.

The Council is not accountable to Parliament in the same way, but the Parliament reports on it three times a year, and the President of the Council is obliged to address the Parliament once a year, followed by a debate. It has a right of veto over proposals for the annual budget, which are placed before it by the Council. The Parliament can also bring actions against other EU institutions for failure to implement EU law.

The Parliament appoints an Ombudsman, who investigates complaints of maladministration by EU institutions from individuals and MEPs. It can also be petitioned by any natural or legal person living or having an office within a member state, on any issue within the EU field which affects that person directly.

The European Court of Justice (ECJ)

The ECJ has the task of supervising the uniform application of EU law throughout the member states, and in so doing it can create case law. It is important not to confuse it with the European Court of Human Rights, which deals with alleged breaches of human rights by countries who are signatories to the European Convention on Human Rights. That court is completely separate, and not an institution of the EU.

The ECJ, which sits in Luxembourg, has 15 judges, appointed by agreement among member states, for a period of six years (which may be renewed). The judges are assisted by eight Advocates General, who produce opinions on the cases assigned to them, indicating the issues raised and suggesting conclusions. These are not binding, but are nevertheless usually followed by the court. Both judges and Advocates General are chosen from those who are eligible for the highest judicial posts in their own countries.

Most cases are heard in plenary session, that is with all the judges sitting together. Only one judgment will be delivered, giving no indication of the extent of agreement between the judges, and these often consist of fairly brief propositions, from which it can be difficult to discern any *ratio decidendi*. Consequently, lawyers seeking precedents often turn to the opinions written by the Advocates General. Since September 1989 the full ECJ has been assisted by a new Court of First Instance to deal with specialist economic law cases. Parties in such cases may appeal to the full ECJ on a point of law.

The majority of cases heard by the ECJ are brought by member states and institutions of the Community, or are referred to it by national courts. It has only limited power to deal with cases brought by individual citizens, and such cases are rarely heard.

The ECJ has two separate functions: a judicial role, deciding cases of dispute; and a supervisory role.

The judicial role of the ECJ

The ECJ hears cases of dispute between parties, which fall into two categories: proceedings against member states, and proceedings against European institutions.

Proceedings against member states may be brought by the Commission, or by other member states, and involve alleged breaches of European law by the country in question. For example, in **Re Tachographs: EC Commission** *v* **UK** (1979), the ECJ upheld a complaint against the UK for failing to implement a European regulation making it compulsory for lorries used to carry dangerous goods to be fitted with tachographs (devices used to record the speed and distance travelled, with the aim of preventing lorry drivers from speeding, or from driving for longer than the permitted number of hours). The Commission usually gives the member state the opportunity to put things right before bringing the case to the ECJ.

Proceedings against EU institutions may be brought by member states, other EU institutions and in certain circumstances, by individual citizens or organizations. The procedure can be used to review the legality of EU regulations, directives or decisions, on the grounds that proper procedures have not been followed, the provisions infringe a European Treaty or any rule relating to its application, or powers have been misused. In **United Kingdom** *v* **Council of the European Union** (1996) the UK sought to have the Directive on the 48-hour working week annulled on the basis that it had been unlawfully adopted by the Council. The application was unsuccessful.

In the past there was no machinery for enforcing judgments against states. Following the Maastricht Treaty, there is now provision for member states to be fined.

Decisions made in these kinds of cases cannot be questioned in UK courts.

The supervisory role of the ECJ

Article 234 (known as Art. 177 before the Treaty of Amsterdam) of the Treaty of Rome provides that any court or tribunal in a member state may refer a question on EU law to the ECJ if it considers that 'a decision on that question is necessary to enable it to give judgment'. The object of this referral system is to make sure that the law is interpreted in the same way throughout Europe.

A reference must be made if the national court is one from which there is no further appeal – so in Britain, the House of Lords must refer such questions, while the lower courts usually have some discretion about whether or not to do so; the Art. 234 procedure is expensive and time consuming, often delaying a decision on the case for a long time, and so lower courts have been discouraged from using it. Consequently attempts have been made to set down guidelines by which a court could determine when a decision would or would not be necessary.

In **Bulmer** *v* **Bollinger** (1974), the Court of Appeal was asked to review a judge's exercise of discretion to refer a question under what is now Art. 234. They pointed out that the European Court could not interfere with the exercise of a judge's discretion to refer, and Lord Denning set down guidelines on the points which should be taken into account in considering whether a reference was necessary. He emphasized the cost and delay that a reference could cause, and stated that no reference should be made:

- where it would not be conclusive of the case, and other matters would remain to be decided;
- where there had been a previous ruling on the same point;
- where the court considers that point to be reasonably clear and free from doubt;
- where the facts of the case had not yet been decided.

Unless the point to be decided could be considered 'really difficult and important', said Lord Denning, the court should save the expense and delay of a reference and decide the issue itself.

Denning's view has since been criticized by academics, who point out that it can be cheaper and quicker to refer a point at an early stage, than to drag the case up through the English courts first. In addition, the clear and consistent interpretation of EU law can come to depend on whether individual litigants have the resources to take their cases all the way up to the House of Lords. Critics also note that the apparent importance of the case should not be decisive, as many important decisions of the ECJ have arisen from cases where the parties actually had little at stake.

Although the judiciary still use Denning's **Bulmer** guidelines, there now appears to be a greater willingness to refer cases under the Art. 234 procedure. In **Customs and Excise** *v* **APS Samex** (1983), Bingham J pointed out that in interpreting European law, the Court of Justice has certain advantages over national courts: it can take a panoramic view of the whole of European law, compare the legislation as it is written in different member states' languages, and it is experienced in the purposive approach to interpretation for which European legislation was designed. In addition, it has the facility to allow member states to make their views on an issue known. As a result, it is better placed than a national court to decide issues of interpretation. In a later case, **R** *v* **International Stock Exchange, ex parte Else** (1993), the same judge (by then Master of the

Rolls), said that if, once the facts have been found, it is clear that an issue of European law is vital to a court's final decision, that court should normally make an Art. 177 referral (now Art. 234): English courts should only decide such issues without referral if they have real confidence that they can do so correctly, without the help of the ECJ.

Where a case is submitted, proceedings will be suspended in the national court until the ECJ has given its verdict. This verdict does not tell the national court how to decide the case, but simply explains what EU law on the matter is. The national court then has the duty of making its decision in the light of this.

Regardless of which national court submitted the point for consideration, a ruling from the ECJ should be followed by all other courts in the EU – so theoretically, a point raised by a county court in England may result in a ruling that the highest courts in all the member states have to follow. Where a ruling reveals that national legislation conflicts with EU law, the national Government usually enacts new legislation to put the matter right.

The court's decisions can be changed only by its own subsequent decision or by an amendment of the Treaty, which would require the unanimous approval of member states through their own Parliaments. Decisions of the European Court cannot be questioned in English courts. This principle has limited the jurisdiction of the House of Lords as a final appellate court.

An illustration of the use of Art. 234 is the case of **Marshall** v **Southampton Area Health Authority** (1986). Miss Marshall, a dietician, was compulsorily retired by the Authority from her job when she was 62, although she wished to continue to 65. It was the Authority's policy that the normal retiring age for its employees was the age at which state retirement pensions became payable: for women this was 60, though the Authority had waived the rule for two years in Miss Marshall's case. She claimed that the Authority was discriminating against women by adopting a policy that employees should retire at state pension age, hence requiring women to retire before men. This policy appeared to be legal under the relevant English legislation but was argued to be contrary to a Council directive providing for equal treatment of men and women. The national court made a reference to the ECJ asking for directions on the meaning of the directive. The ECJ found that there was a conflict with UK law, and the UK later changed its legislation to conform.

It is important to note that the ECJ is **not** an appeal court from decisions made in the member states. It does not substitute its own decisions for those of a lower court (except those of its own Court of First Instance, discussed below). It will assist a national court at any level in reaching a decision, but the actual decision remains the responsibility of the national court. When parties in an English case talk of taking the case to Europe, the only way they can do this is to get an English court to make a referral for an Art. 234 ruling, and they may have to take their case all the way to the House of Lords to ensure this.

European Court of First Instance

A European Court of First Instance was established in 1988 by the Single European Act inserting Art. 225 into the EC Treaty. The aim was to reduce the workload of the ECJ. It has a very limited jurisdiction, handling primarily internal staff litigation, and appeals on points of law are heard by the ECJ.

Making EU legislation

The Council, the Commission and the European Parliament all play a role in making EU legislation. A complicated range of different procedures has been developed to make these laws. All legislation starts with a proposal from the Commission and the Council enjoys the most power in the legislative process.

Parliament's legislative role was historically purely advisory, with the Commission and the Council having a much more powerful role in the legislative process. This led to concern over the lack of democracy within Europe, for while Parliament was directly elected by the citizens of Europe, the Commission and Council members were not. In addition many countries have experienced difficulties in holding Council members to account to national Parliaments for decisions made in Council – the UK Government does not, for example, always consult Parliament before it agrees on an EU matter in Council.

The role of the European Parliament in the passing of European legislation has gradually been increased by the Single European Act, the Maastricht Treaty and the Amsterdam Treaty. But problems still remain. There are still areas of law on which Parliament does not even have the right to be consulted. Where Parliament is consulted by the Council, it normally has no power to block the legislation, but can merely delay it, and the success of its amendments is largely dependent on them being adopted by the Commission, which is under no obligation to do so.

The Council plays an important role in the passing of European legislation. There are three systems of voting in the Council:

- **unanimity**, where proposals are only passed if all members vote for them;
- **simple majority**, where proposals only require more votes for than against; and
- **qualified majority**, which allows each state a specified number of votes (the larger the state, the more votes it has), and provides that a proposal can only be agreed if there are a specified number of votes in its favour. The number is calculated to ensure that larger states cannot force decisions on the smaller ones.

These voting procedures have been controversial, because where unanimity is not required a member state can be forced to abide by legislation for which it has not voted, and which it believes is against its interests. This is seen as compromising national sovereignty. However requiring unanimity makes it difficult to get things done quickly (or sometimes at all) and, as a result, initial progress towards the single market was very slow. The need to speed progress up led to both the Single European Act and the Maastricht Treaty requiring only qualified majority voting more often. The Amsterdam Treaty extended its use a little more, and it is now – officially at least – the norm for many areas. It remains politically sensitive, however, and controversial subjects are often still decided unanimously.

Where there is majority voting, no member state has a veto in the Council under the legal framework prescribed by the EC Treaty. None the less, the UK claims that it can exercise a veto where its vital national interests are at stake, even where the Treaty provides for simple or qualified majority voting.

Types of European legislation

There are a range of different forms of European legislation: treaties, regulations, directives and decisions. In considering the impact of this legislation on UK law a distinction has to be drawn between direct applicability and direct effect. Direct applicability refers to the fact that treaty articles, regulations and some decisions immediately become part of the law of each member state. Directives are not directly applicable.

Where European legislation has direct effect, it creates individual rights which national courts must protect without any need for implementing legislation in that member state. In the UK the national courts were given this power under s. 2(1) of the European Communities Act 1972.

There are two types of direct effect: vertical direct effect gives individuals rights against governments; and horizontal direct effect gives rights against other people and organizations.

Provisions of treaties, regulations and directives only have direct effect if they are clear, unconditional and their implementation requires no further legislation in member states. These conditions were first laid down in the context of treaties in **Van Gend en Loos** (1963).

The ability of individuals to rely on Community law before their national courts greatly enhances its effectiveness. National courts can quickly apply directly effective legislation and can draw on a wide range of remedies. Where legislation does not have direct effect, the only method of enforcement available in the past was an action brought by the Commission or a member state against a member state before the ECJ. This process can be slow and provides no direct remedy for the individual.

However, in the 1990s the ECJ recognized the right of individuals to be awarded damages by their national courts for breach of European legislation by a member state, even where the legislation did not have direct effect. Originally, in **Francovich v Italian Republic** (1992), this right was applied where directives had not been implemented but it has been developed to extend to any violation of European law. In **Francovich**, an Italian company went into liquidation, leaving its employees, including Francovich, unpaid arrears of salary. Italy had not set up a compensation scheme for employees in such circumstances as was required by a European directive. Francovich sued in the Italian courts. The court held that although the directive was not sufficiently precise to have direct effect it gave a right to damages.

Liability will be imposed on a member state if:

- the legislation was intended to confer rights on individuals;
- the content of those rights are clear from the provisions of the legislation;
- there is a direct causal link between the breach of the member state's obligation and the damage sustained by the individual.

In addition, a fourth condition was added by **Brasserie du Pecheur v Germany and R v Secretary of State, ex parte Factortame** (1996):

- there was a serious breach of European law.

The four different types of EU law will now be examined in turn.

Treaties

These are the highest source of EU law, and as well as laying down the general aims of the European Union, they themselves create some rights and obligations. The existing treaties are the three Treaties of Rome that established the framework for Europe (the European Coal and Steel Community Treaty, the Euratom Treaty and the European Community Treaty), the Single European Act, the Treaty on European Union (known as the Maastricht Treaty) and the Treaty of Amsterdam. The article numbers of the European Community Treaty were changed by the Treaty of Amsterdam, as old articles had been repealed and new articles added since it had been originally drafted. The case of **Van Gend en Loos** (1963) decided that a treaty provision has direct effect if it is unconditional, clear and precise as to the rights or obligations it creates, and leaves member states no discretion on implementing it. Treaty provisions which are unconditional, clear and precise, and allow no discretion on implementation have both horizontal and vertical direct effect. An example of a directly effective treaty provision is Art. 139 (known as Art. 119 before the Amsterdam Treaty) of the EC Treaty. This provides that 'men and women shall receive equal pay for equal work'. In **Macarthys v Smith** (1979), Art. 139 was held to give a woman in the UK the right to claim the same wages as were paid to the male predecessor in her job, even though she had no such right under the UK equal pay legislation passed in 1970, before the UK joined Europe.

Treaty provisions which are merely statements of intent or policy, rather than establishing clear rights or duties, require detailed legislation to be made before they can be enforced in the member states.

Regulations

A regulation is the nearest Community law comes to an English Act of Parliament. Regulations apply throughout the EU, usually to people in general, and they become part of the law of each member nation as soon as they come into force, without the need for each country to make its own legislation.

Regulations must be applied even if the member state has already passed legislation which conflicts with them. In **Leonesio** v **Italian Ministry of Agriculture** (1973), a regulation to encourage reduced dairy production stated that a cash premium should be payable to farmers who slaughtered cows and agreed not to produce milk for five years. Leonesio had fulfilled this requirement, but was refused payment because the Italian constitution required legislation to authorize government expenditure. The ECJ said that once Leonesio had satisfied the conditions, he was entitled to the payment; the Italian Government could not use its own laws to block that right.

Directives

Directives are less precisely worded than regulations, because they aim to set out broad objectives, leaving the member states to create their own detailed legislation in order to put those objectives into practice (within specified time limits). As a result, it was originally assumed by most member states that directives could not have direct effect, and would not create individual rights until they had been translated into domestic legislation. However, the ECJ has consistently refused to accept this view, arguing that direct effect is an essential weapon if the EU is to ensure that member states implement directives.

The case which initially established direct effect for directives was **Van Duyn** v **Home Office** (1974). The Home Office had refused Van Duyn permission to enter the UK, because she was a member of a religious group, the Scientologists, which the Government wanted to exclude from the country at the time. Van Duyn argued that her exclusion was contrary to provisions in the Treaty of Rome on freedom of movement. The Government responded by pointing out that the Treaty allowed exceptions on public policy grounds, but Van Duyn then relied on a later directive which said that public policy could only be invoked on the basis of personal conduct, and Van Duyn herself had done nothing to justify exclusion. The case was referred to the ECJ, which found that the obligation conferred on the Government was clear and unconditional, and so created enforceable rights.

The reasoning behind this approach was explained in **Publico Ministerio** *v* **Ratti** (1980), where the ECJ pointed out that member states could not be allowed to rely on their own wrongful failure to implement directives as a means of denying individual rights.

Directives have vertical direct effect but not horizontal direct effect. This means that they impose obligations on the state and not individuals. Thus, they have direct effect in proceedings against a member state (vertical) but not in proceedings between individuals (horizontal). A directive with direct effect can be utilized by an individual against the state when the state has failed to implement the directive properly or on time. However, the ECJ has found a number of ways to reduce the limiting effect of this principle, and that of the criteria on precision and clarity. First, it has defined 'the state' very broadly to include all public bodies, including local authorities and nationalized industries. This meant, for example, that in **Marshall** *v* **Southampton Area Health Authority** (1986), discussed at p. 65, Miss Marshall was able to take advantage of the relevant directive even though she was not suing the Government itself, because her employer was a health authority and therefore considered a public body.

Secondly, in **Von Colson** *v* **Land Nordrhein-Westfalen** (1984), the court introduced the principle of indirect effect, stating that national courts should interpret national law in accordance with relevant directives, whether the national law was designed to implement a directive or not. The principle was confirmed in **Marleasing SA** *v* **La Comercial Internacional de Alimentacion SA** (1990). Here, Marleasing alleged that La Comercial, a Spanish company, had been formed with the express purpose of defrauding creditors (of which they were one) and sought to have its articles of association (the document under which a company is formed) declared void. Spanish contract law allowed this, but the EU had passed a directive which did not. Which should the member state court follow? The ECJ held that where a provision of domestic law was 'to any extent open to interpretation', national courts had to interpret that law 'as far as possible' in line with the wording and purpose of any relevant directive. This would apply whether the domestic law was passed before or after the directive, except that domestic law passed before a directive would only be affected once the time limit for implementation of the directive had expired.

Marleasing has been much discussed by academics, but it is still unclear quite how far national courts are expected to go in implementing directives having indirect effect. EU law experts Craig and de Burca suggest, however, that the principle of indirect effect probably only applies where national law is sufficiently ambiguous to allow it to be interpreted in line with directives; where there is a conflict, but the national law is clear, member state courts are unlikely to be required to override that law.

Decisions

A decision may be addressed to a state, a person or a company and is binding only on the recipient. Examples include granting, or refusing, export licences to companies from outside the EU.

Recommendations and opinions

The Council and the Commission may issue recommendations and opinions which, although not to be disregarded, are not binding law.

How does EU law affect the UK?

Membership of the EU has had a number of effects on UK law and our legal system.

New sources of law

Joining the original EEC created new and very important sources of law for the UK. Section 2(4) of the European Communities Act 1972 provides that English law should be interpreted and have effect subject to the principle that EU law is supreme; this means that EU law now takes precedence over all domestic sources of law. As a result, it has had a profound effect on the rights of citizens in this country, and in particular, on the rights of employees, especially female workers. For example, in **R v Secretary of State for Employment, ex parte Equal Opportunities Commission** (1994), the House of Lords found that parts of the Employment Protection (Consolidation) Act 1978 were incompatible with European law on equal treatment for male and female employees, because the Act gave part-time workers fewer rights than full-timers. Since most part-time workers were women, this was held to discriminate on the basis of sex, and the UK Government was forced to change the law, and greatly improve the rights of part-time workers.

The role of the courts

Because EU law takes precedence over domestic legislation, the role of the courts has changed as a result of membership of the Community. Before the UK joined the EEC, statutes were the highest form of law, and judges had no power to refuse to apply them. Now, however, they can – in fact they should – refuse to apply statutes which are in conflict with directly effective EU law.

The leading case in this area is **R v Secretary of State for Transport, ex parte Factortame** (1990). It arose from the fishing policy decided by member states in 1983, which allowed member states to limit fishing within 12 miles of their own shores to boats from their own country, and left the remainder of the seas around the Community open to fishing boats from any member state. In addition, to preserve stocks of fish, each state was allocated a quota of fish, and required not to exceed it. Soon after the new rules were in place, the UK Government became concerned that Spanish fishing boats were registering as British vessels, so that their catches counted against the British quota rather than the Spanish, and genuine British fishermen were therefore getting a smaller share. The Government therefore passed the Merchant Shipping Act 1988, which contained provisions to prevent the Spanish trawlers taking advantage of the British quota.

Spanish boat owners challenged the Act, claiming it was in conflict with EU law on the freedom to set up business anywhere in the Community, and the House of Lords agreed. They stated that s. 2(4) of the European Communities Act 'has precisely the same effect as if a section were incorporated in . . . [the 1988 Act, saying] that the provisions with respect to registration of British fishing vessels were to be without prejudice to the directly enforceable Community rights of nationals of any member state . . .'.

The decision was criticized as compromising the rights of the UK Parliament to make law for this country, as the House of Lords rendered effectively unenforceable the Merchant Shipping Act. But the House of Lords was firm in dismissing such complaints, pointing out that it was very clear before the UK joined the Community that doing so would mean giving up some degree of sovereignty over our own law, and that this was accepted voluntarily when the UK joined the Community. 'Under . . . the Act of 1972, it has always been clear that it was the duty of a United Kingdom court, when delivering final judgment, to override any rule of national law found to be in conflict with any directly enforceable rule of Community law . . .'.

The role of the courts is also affected by the principle stated in **Marleasing** (see p. 70), which effectively means that the courts now have a new external aid to consider when interpreting statutes, and should take notice of it wherever they can do so without straining the words of the statute.

The UK courts are subjected to the supervisory jurisdiction of the ECJ, as explained (on p. 63), and this gives a further source of law, since the courts of all member states are bound by ECJ decisions on the interpretation and application of EU law.

The future

One view of the influence of UK membership of Europe on our national law was given by Lord Denning, in poetic mood, in **Bulmer** v **Bollinger**: 'The Treaty is like an incoming tide. It flows into the estuaries and up the rivers. It cannot be held back.' Lord Scarman, obviously in an equally lyrical frame of mind, commented:

For the moment, to adopt Lord Denning's imagery, the incoming tide has not yet mingled with the home waters of the common law: but it is inconceivable that, like the Rhone and the Arve where those two streams meet at Geneva, they should move on, side by side, one grey with the melted snows and ice of the distant mountains of our legal history, the other clear blue and clean, reflecting modern opinion. If we stay in the Common Market, I would expect to see its principles of legislation and statutory interpretation, and its conception of an activist court whose role is to strengthen and fulfil the purpose of statute law, replace the traditional attitudes of English judges and lawyers to statute law and the current complex style of statutory drafting.

What Lord Scarman was referring to was the difference in approach between the English legal system and those in mainland Europe. When drafting statutes, for example, English law has tended towards tightly written, very precise rules, whereas the continental style is looser, setting out broad principles to be followed. As a result, the continental style of statutory interpretation takes a very purposive approach, paying most attention to putting into practice the spirit of the legislation, and filling in any gaps in the wording if necessary, as opposed to the more literal style traditionally associated with English judges. The ECJ tends to take the continental approach, and it has been suggested that as time goes on, this will influence our own judges more and more, leading to more creative judicial decision-making, with corresponding changes in the drafting of statutes.

Following the **Factortame** litigation there was concern that Europe was threatening the sovereignty of the UK Parliament, as the ECJ ruling had caused an Act of Parliament to be set aside. Lord Denning revised his description of European law as like an 'incoming tide' and stated:

No longer is European law an incoming tide flowing up the estuaries of England. It is now like a tidal wave bringing down our sea walls and flowing inland over our fields and houses – to the dismay of all. (The *Independent*, 16 July 1996)

In **R** *v* **Secretary of State for Foreign and Commonwealth Affairs, ex parte Rees-Mogg** (1994) an unsuccessful attempt was made to demonstrate that the UK could not legally ratify the Maastricht Treaty. In rejecting this claim, the court pointed out that the Treaty did not involve the abandoning or transferring of powers, so that a government could choose to later denounce the Treaty, or fail to honour its obligations under it.

► ANSWERING QUESTIONS

1 Describe the composition and role of the European Court of Justice, and evaluate its importance with regard to the English legal system. *OCR*

The first part of this question requires a factual description of the ECJ and what it does. You need to talk about the judges, how they are appointed, how they deal with cases and then talk about the two roles of the ECJ, explaining its supervisory and its judicial roles.

For the second part of the question, you need more than just description as the question requires you to 'evaluate' its importance. You should obviously talk about the Art. 234 procedure, and the fact that decisions of the court in these cases provide precedents which the English courts must follow, which effectively means that the House of Lords no longer has the final say on those areas of law in which the EU is involved (but remember to explain that the ECJ is not an appellate court; it does not decide the cases referred to it under Art. 234, but explains the law so that the national court can do so). Point out that as a result of Art. 234 rulings, the Government have often had to change statute law – you could talk about **Marshall** as an example of this.

You could also discuss the way in which the ECJ has been instrumental in ensuring that member states abide by EU legislation. An example of this is its approach to directives: the ruling in **Van Duyn** that they could have direct effect; the broad interpretation of 'government' so as to extend vertical direct effect in **Marshall**; the creation of indirect effect in **Von Colson**; and the principles of compensation introduced in **Francovich**.

You might also discuss the fact that the ECJ uses a much more purposive style when interpreting legislation than has been traditional in the English legal system, and the suggestions that this may eventually influence English judges to move in a similar direction.

▶ CUSTOM

As we have seen, the basis of the common law was custom. The itinerant justices sent out by William the Conqueror (see p. 7) examined the different local practices of dealing with disputes and crime, filtered out the less practical and reasonable ones, and ended up with a set of laws that were to be applied uniformly throughout the country. As Sir Henry Maine, a nineteenth-century scholar who studied the evolution of legal systems has pointed out, this did not mean that custom itself was ever law – the law was created by the decisions of judges in recognizing some customs and not others.

Custom still plays a part in modern law, but a very small one. Its main use is in cases where a traditional local practice – such as fishermen being allowed to dry their nets on a particular piece of land, or villagers holding a fair in a certain place – is being challenged. Custom was defined in the **Tanistry Case** (1608) as 'such usage as has obtained the force of law', and in these cases, those whose practices are being challenged assert that the custom has existed for so long that it should be given the force of law, even though it may conflict with the general common law.

> ## When can custom be a source of law?

To be regarded as conferring legally enforceable rights, a custom must fulfil several criteria.

'Time immemorial'

It must have existed since 'time immemorial'. This was fixed by a statute in 1275 as meaning 'since at least 1189'. In practice today claimants usually seek to prove the custom has existed as far back as living memory can go, often by calling the oldest local inhabitant as a witness. However, this may not always be sufficient. In a dispute over a right to use local land in some way, for example, if the other side could prove that the land in question was under water until the seventeenth or eighteenth century, the right could therefore not have existed since 1189. In **Simpson** *v* **Wells** (1872), a charge of obstructing the public footway by setting up a refreshment stall was challenged by a claim that there was a customary right to do so derived from 'statute sessions', ancient fairs held for the purpose of hiring servants. It was then proved that statute sessions were first authorized by the Statutes of Labourers in the fourteenth century, so the right could not have existed since 1189.

Reasonableness

A legally enforceable custom cannot conflict with fundamental principles of right and wrong, so a customary right to commit a crime, for example, could never be accepted. In **Wolstanton Ltd** *v* **Newcastle-under-Lyme Borough Council** (1940) the lord of a manor claimed a customary right to take minerals from under a tenant's land, without paying compensation for any damage caused to buildings on the land. It was held that this was unreasonable.

Certainty and clarity

It must be certain and clear. The locality in which the custom operates must be defined, along with the people to whom rights are granted (local fishermen, for example, or tenants of a particular estate) and the extent of those rights. In **Wilson** *v* **Willes** (1806) the tenants of a manor claimed the customary right to take as much turf as they needed for their lawns from the manorial commons. This was held to be too vague, since there appeared to be no limit to the amount of turf which could be taken.

Locality

It must be specific to a particular geographic area. Where a custom is recognized as granting a right, it grants that right only to those specified

– a custom giving fishermen in Lowestoft the right to dry their nets on someone else's land would not give the same right to fishermen in Grimsby. Custom is only ever a source of local law.

Continuity

It must have existed continuously. The rights granted by custom do not have to have been exercised continuously since 1189, but it must have been possible to exercise them at all times since then. In **Wyld** *v* **Silver** (1963), a landowner wishing to build on land where the local inhabitants claimed a customary right to hold an annual fair, argued that the right had not been exercised within living memory. The court nevertheless granted an injunction preventing the building.

Exercised as of right

It must have been exercised peaceably, openly and as of right. Customs cannot create legal rights if they are exercised only by permission of someone else. In **Mills** *v* **Corporation of Colchester** (1867) it was held that a customary right to fish had no legal force where the right had always depended on the granting of a licence, even though such licences had traditionally been granted to local people on request.

Consistency

It must be consistent with other local customs. For example, if a custom is alleged to give the inhabitants of one farm the right to fish in a lake, it cannot also give the inhabitants of another the right to drain the lake. The usual course where a conflict arises is to deny that the opposing custom has any force, though this is not possible if it has already been recognized by a court.

Obligatory

Where a custom imposes a specific duty, that duty must be obligatory – a custom cannot provide that the lord of a manor grants villagers a right of way over his land only if he likes them, or happens not to mind people on his land that day.

Conformity with statute

A custom which is in conflict with a statute will not be held to give rise to law.

ANSWERING QUESTIONS

It is extremely rare for an examination question to be devoted to custom alone; however, you should revise it if you are thinking of answering a question on sources of law generally.

EQUITY

In ordinary language, equity simply means fairness, but in law it applies to a specific set of legal principles, which add to those provided in the common law. It was originally inspired by ideas of fairness and natural justice, but is now no more than a particular branch of English law. Lawyers often contrast 'law' and equity, but it is important to know that when they do this, they are using 'law' to mean common law. Equity and common law may be different, but both are law. Equity is an area of law which can only be understood in the light of its historical development.

How equity began

As we have seen, the common law was developed after the Norman Conquest through the 'itinerant justices' travelling around the country and sorting out disputes. By about the twelfth century, common law courts had developed which applied this common law. Civil actions in these courts had to be started by a writ, which set out the cause of the action or the grounds for the claim made, and there grew up different types of writ. Early on, new writs were created to suit new circumstances, but in the thirteenth century this was stopped. Litigants had to fit their circumstances to one of the available types of writ: if the case did not fall within one of those types, there was no way of bringing the case to the common law court. At the same time, the common law was itself becoming increasingly rigid, and offered only one remedy, damages, which was not always an adequate solution to every problem – if a litigant had been promised the chance to buy a particular piece of land, for example, and the seller then went back on the agreement, damages might not be an adequate remedy since the buyer really wanted the land, and may have made arrangements on the basis that it would be acquired.

Consequently, many people were unable to seek redress for wrongs through the common law courts. Many of these dissatisfied parties petitioned the king, who was thought of as the 'fountain of justice'. These petitions were commonly passed to the Chancellor, the king's chief minister, as the king did not want to spend time considering them. The Chancellor was usually a member of the clergy, and was thought of as 'keeper of the king's conscience'. Soon litigants began to petition the

Chancellor himself, and by 1474, the Chancellor had begun to make decisions on the cases on his own authority, rather than as a substitute for the king. This was the beginning of the Court of Chancery.

Litigants appeared before the Chancellor, who would question them, and then deliver a verdict based on his own moral view of the question. The court could insist that relevant documents be disclosed, as well as questioning the parties in person, unlike the common law courts which did not admit oral evidence until the sixteenth century, and had no way of extracting the truth from litigants. Because the court followed no binding rules, relying entirely on the Chancellor's view of right and wrong, it could enforce rights not recognized by the common law, which, restricted by precedent, was failing to adapt to new circumstances. The Court of Chancery could provide whatever remedy best suited the case – the decree of specific performance, for example, would have meant that the seller of land referred to above could be forced to honour the promise. This type of justice came to be known as equity.

Common law and equity

Not surprisingly, the Court of Chancery became popular, and caused some resentment among common lawyers, who argued that the quality of decisions varied with the length of the Chancellor's foot – in other words, that it depended on the qualities of the individual Chancellor. Because precedents were not followed and each case was considered purely on its merits, justice could appear arbitrary, and nobody could predict what a decision might be.

On the other hand this very flexibility was seen as the great advantage of equity – where any rules are laid down, there will always be situations in which those rules produce injustice. The more general the rule, the more likely this is, yet it is impossible to foresee and lay down all the specific exceptions in which it should not apply. Equity dealt with these situations by applying notions of good sense and fairness, but in doing so laid itself open to the charge that fairness is a subjective quality.

The common lawyers particularly resented the way in which equity could be used to restrict their own jurisdiction. Where the common law gave a litigant a right which, in the circumstances, it would be unjust to exercise, the Court of Chancery could issue a common injunction, preventing the exercise of the common law right. An example might be where a litigant had made a mistake in drawing up a document. Under common law the other party could enforce the document anyway, even if they were aware of the mistake but failed to draw attention to it. This was considered inequitable, and a common injunction would prevent the document being enforced.

Matters came to a head in 1615 in the **The Earl of Oxford's Case**, where conflicting judgments of the common law courts and the Court of

Chancery were referred to the king for a decision; he advised that where there was conflict, equity should prevail. Had this decision not been made, equity would have been worthless – it could not fulfil its role of filling in the gaps of the common law unless it was dominant.

Nevertheless, the rivalry continued for some time, but gradually abated as equity too began to be ruled by precedent and standard principles, a development related to the fact that it was becoming established practice to appoint lawyers rather than clergy to the office of Lord Chancellor. By the nineteenth century, equity had a developed case law and recognizable principles, and was no less rigid than the common law.

The Judicature Acts

Once equity became a body of law, rather than an arbitrary exercise of conscience, there was no reason why it needed its own courts. Consequently the Judicature Acts of 1873–75, which established the basis of the court structure we have today, provided that equity and common law could both be administered by all courts, and that there would no longer be different procedures for seeking equitable and common law remedies. Although the Court of Chancery remained as a division of the High Court, like all other courts it can now apply both common law and equity.

Equity today

It is important to note that the Judicature Acts did not fuse common law and equity, only their administration. There is still a body of rules of equity which is distinct from common law rules, and acts as an addition to it. Although they are implemented by the same courts, the two branches of the law are separate. Where there is conflict, equity still prevails.

Equitable maxims

Although both the common law and equity lay down rules developed from precedents, equity also created maxims which had to be satisfied before equitable rules could be applied. These maxims were designed to ensure that decisions were morally fair. The following are some of them.

'He who comes to equity must come with clean hands'
This means that claimants who have themselves been in the wrong in some way will not be granted an equitable remedy. In **D & C Builders** *v* **Rees** (1966) a small building firm did some work on the house of a couple named Rees. The bill came to £732, of which the Rees' had already paid £250. When the builders asked for the balance of £482, the Rees' announced that the work was defective, and they were only prepared to pay £300. As the builders were in serious financial difficulties (as the

Rees' knew), they reluctantly accepted the £300 'in completion of the account'. The decision to accept the money would not normally be binding in contract law, and afterwards the builders sued the Rees' for the outstanding amount. The Rees claimed that the court should apply the doctrine of equitable estoppel, which can make promises binding when they would normally not be. However, Lord Denning refused to apply the doctrine, on the grounds that the Rees' had taken unfair advantage of the builders' financial difficulties, and therefore had not come 'with clean hands'.

'He who seeks equity must do equity'

Anyone who seeks equitable relief must be prepared to act fairly towards their opponent. In **Chappell** *v* **Times Newspapers Ltd** (1975), newspaper employees who had been threatened that they would be sacked unless they stopped their strike action applied for an injunction to prevent their employers from carrying out the threat. The court held that in order to be awarded the remedy, the strikers should undertake that they would withdraw their strike action if the injunction was granted. Since they refused to do this, the injunction was refused.

'Delay defeats equities'

Where a claimant takes an unreasonably long time to bring an action, equitable remedies will not be available. The unreasonableness of any delay will be a matter of fact to be assessed in view of the circumstances in each case. In **Leaf** *v* **International Galleries** (1950) the claimant bought a painting of Salisbury Cathedral described (innocently) by the seller as a genuine Constable. Five years later, the buyer discovered that it was nothing of the sort, and claimed the equitable remedy of rescission, but the court held that the delay had been too long.

These maxims (there are several others) mean that where a claimant's case relies on a rule of equity, rather than a rule of common law, that rule can only be applied if the maxims are satisfied – unlike common law rules which have no such limitations.

Equitable remedies

Equity substantially increased the number of remedies available to a wronged party. The following are the most important:

Injunction. This orders the defendants to do or not to do something.
Specific performance. This compels a party to fulfil a previous agreement.
Rectification. This order alters the words of a document which does not express the true intentions of the parties to it.
Rescission. This restores parties to a contract to the position they were in before the contract was signed.

Equitable remedies are discretionary. A claimant who wins the case is awarded the common law remedy of damages as of right, but the courts may choose whether or not to award equitable remedies. They are very much an addition to common law remedies, and usually only available if common law remedies are plainly inadequate.

Equitable principles have had their greatest impact in the development of the law of property and contract, and remain important in these areas today. The two best-known contributions come from property law, and are the developments of the law of trusts, and the basis of the rules which today govern mortgages. The creation of alternative remedies has also been extremely important.

Equity tomorrow

Equity has shown itself capable of adapting and expanding to meet new needs, and so creating law reform. During the 1950s and 1960s, it responded to increasing marital breakdown by stating that a deserted wife could acquire an equitable interest in the family home, providing an interim solution to a growing problem until legislation could be passed in the form of the Matrimonial Homes Act 1967. And in the 1970s, two important new remedies were created by extending the scope of injunctions: the Anton Piller order, by which the court can order defendants to allow their premises to be searched and relevant documents to be removed, and the Mareva injunction, a court order to a third party, such as a bank, to freeze the assets of a party to a dispute where there is a danger that they may be removed from the court's jurisdiction (by being taken out of the country, for example, and therefore made unavailable if damages were ordered by the court).

However, more recent attempts to extend equitable jurisdiction, notably in **Scandinavian Trading Tanker Co AB** *v* **Flota Petrolera Ecuatoriana** (1983) and **Sport International Bussum BV** *v* **Inter-Footwear Ltd** (1984), have been firmly resisted by the House of Lords.

The availability of discretionary remedies means that equity still fulfils the traditional function of supplementing the common law, providing just and practical remedies where the common law alone is not enough, but restricting itself to cases where those remedies are felt to be genuinely and justly deserved.

ANSWERING QUESTIONS

1 'Equity was, and in many ways still is, common law's safety valve.' (Denham) Does this accurately describe the role of equity, both past and present?
OCR

It would be a good idea to divide this essay into two parts, dealing first with the role of equity in the past, and then in the present. On the historical side, you can start by explaining how it was that common law came to need a 'safety valve', and whether equity fulfilled this role, explaining both its initial success, and then the way in which equity too became rigid, limiting its success as a 'safety valve'.

Then move on to equity's present day role, pointing out the extra remedies which equity provides, which might be seen as a safety valve where common law remedies are insufficient. You could point out that the equitable maxims may act as a check on the role of a safety valve, since they limit the cases in which equity will intervene. You should discuss some of the cases referred to above, and the areas of law in which equity is important today. You might finish with some of the material under the heading of 'equity tomorrow'.

TREATIES

When the UK enters into treaties with other countries, it undertakes to implement domestic laws that are in accordance with the provisions of those treaties. For the purposes of the legal system, probably the most important treaties signed by the UK Government are those setting up and developing the European Union, and the European Convention on Human Rights (discussed on p. 456).

Implementation of treaties

In many countries, treaties automatically become part of domestic law when the country signs them. However, in the UK, the position is that signing treaties usually does not instantly make them law, so citizens cannot rely on them in proceedings brought in UK courts. Only when Parliament produces legislation to enact its treaty commitments do those commitments become law – the Taking of Hostages Act 1982 is an example of legislation incorporating the provisions of international treaties. Until such legislation is produced, individuals cannot usually take advantage of the protections envisaged by treaties.

However, there are some treaties which do not precisely follow this rule. Parts of the treaties setting up the European Communities are directly applicable in British courts, and can be relied on to create rights and duties just like an English statute (this subject is discussed in the section on European law).

ANSWERING QUESTIONS

An examination question on the European Convention on Human Rights can be found at the end of the section on civil liberties.

Reading on the Internet

Copies of recent legislation can be found at:

http://www.hmso.gov.uk/acts.htm

Useful explanatory notes prepared by the Government to explain the implications of recent legislation can be found at:

http://www.legislation.hmso.gov.uk/legislation/uk-expa.htm

The House of Lords recent judgments are available on the House of Lords judicial business website at:

http://www.publications.parliament.uk/pa/ld/ldjudinf.htm

2 Law reform

An effective legal system cannot stand still. Both legal procedures and the law itself must adapt to social change if they are to retain the respect of at least most of society, without which they cannot survive. Many laws which were made even as short a time ago as the nineteenth century simply do not fit the way we see society today – until the early part of this century, for example, married women were legally considered the property of their husbands, while, not much earlier, employees could be imprisoned for breaking their employment contracts.

Most legislation in this country stands until it is repealed – the fact that it may be completely out-of-date does not mean it technically ceases to apply. The offences of challenging to fight, eavesdropping and being a common scold for example, which long ago dropped out of use, nevertheless remained on the statute book until they were abolished by the Criminal Law Act 1967. In practice, of course, many such provisions simply cease to be used, but where it becomes clear that the law may be out of step with social conditions, or simply ineffective, there are a range of ways of bringing about change.

Judicial change

Case law can bring about some reform – one of the most notable recent examples was the decision in **R** *v* **R** (1991), in which the House of Lords declared that a husband who has sexual intercourse with his wife without her consent may be guilty of rape. Before this decision, the law on rape within marriage was based on an assertion by the eighteenth century jurist Sir Matthew Hale, that 'by marrying a man, a women consents to sexual intercourse with him, and may not retract that consent'. This position had been found offensive for many years before **R** *v* **R**. In 1976, Parliament considered it during a debate on the Sexual Offences Act, but decided not to make changes at that time, and it was not until 1991 that the Court of Appeal and then the House of Lords held that rape within marriage should be considered an offence.

Lord Keith stated that Hale's assertion reflected the status of women within marriage in his time, but since then both the status of women, and the marriage relationship had completely changed. The modern view of husband and wife as equal partners meant that a wife could no longer be considered to have given irrevocable consent to sex with her husband; the common law was capable of evolving to reflect such changes in society, and it was the duty of the court to help it do so.

In practice, however, major reforms like this are rarely produced by the courts, and would not be adequate as the sole agency of reform. Norman Marsh's book *Law Reform in the United Kingdom* puts forward a number of reasons for this.

First, as we saw in the chapter on case law, there is no systematic, state-funded process for bringing points of law in need of reform to the higher courts. The courts can only deal with such points as they arise in the cases before them, and this depends on the parties involved having sufficient finance, determination and interest to take their case up through the courts. Consequently, judge-made reform proceeds not on the basis of which areas of law need changes most, but on a haphazard presentation of cases.

Secondly, judges have to decide cases on the basis of the way the issues are presented to them by the parties concerned. They cannot commission research, or consult with interested bodies to find out the possible effects of a decision on individuals and organizations other than those in the case before them – yet their decision will apply to future cases.

Thirdly, judges have to recognize the doctrine of precedent, and for much of the time this prohibits any really radical reforms.

Marsh's fourth point is that reforming decisions by judges have the potential to be unjust to the losing party. Law reforms made by Parliament are prospective – they come into force on a specified date, and we are not usually expected to abide by them until after that date. Judicial decisions, on the other hand, are retrospective, affecting something that happened before the judges decided what the law was. The more reformatory such a decision is, the less the likelihood that the losing party could have abided by the law, even if they wanted to.

Finally, Marsh argues, judges are not elected, and therefore feel they should not make decisions which change the law in areas of great social or moral controversy. They themselves impose limits on their ability to make major changes and will often point out to Parliament the need for it to make reforms, as happened in the **Bland** case concerning the Hillsborough stadium disaster victim (see p. 16).

▶ REFORM BY PARLIAMENT

The majority of law reform is therefore carried out by Parliament. It is done in four ways:

- **Repeal** of old and/or obsolete laws.
- **Creation** of completely new law, or adaptation of existing provisions, to meet new needs. The creation of the offence of insider dealing (where company officials make money by using information gained by virtue of a privileged position) in the Companies Act 1980 was a response to public concern about 'sharp practice' in the city.
- **Consolidation**. When a new statute is created, problems with it may become apparent over time, in which case further legislation may be enacted to amend it. Consolidation brings together successive statutes on a particular subject and puts them into one statute. For example, the legislation in relation to companies was consolidated in 1985.
- **Codification**. Where a particular area of the law has developed over time to produce a large body of both case law and statute, a new statute may be created to bring together all the rules on that subject (case law and statute) in one place. That statute then becomes the starting point for cases concerning that area of the law, and case law, in time, builds up around it. The Criminal Attempts Act 1981 and the Police and Criminal Evidence Act 1984 are examples of codifying statutes. Codification is thought to be most suitable for areas of law where the principles are well worked out; areas that are still developing, such as tort, are less suitable for codifying.

These types of reform often happen together – the Public Order Act 1986, for example, created new public order offences designed to deal with specific problems of the time, such as football hooliganism, and at the same time, repealed out of date public order offences.

Some significant law reforms have come about as a result of Private Members' Bills (see p. 27) – an example is the Abortion Act 1967 which resulted from a Private Members' Bill put forward by David Steele.

Pressures for reform

The inspiration for reform may come from a variety of sources, alone or in combination. As well as encouraging Parliament to consider particular issues in the first place, they may have an influence during the consultation stage of legislation.

Pressure groups

Groups concerned with particular subjects may press for law reform in those areas – examples include charities such as Shelter, Help the Aged and the Child Poverty Action Group; professional organizations such as the Law Society and the British Medical Association; business representatives such as the Confederation of British Industry. JUSTICE is a pressure group specifically concerned with promoting law reform in general.

Pressure groups use a variety of tactics, including lobbying MPs, gaining as much publicity as possible for their cause, organizing petitions, and encouraging people to write to their own MP and/or relevant Ministers. Some groups are more effective than others: size obviously helps, but sheer persistence and a knack for grabbing headlines can be just as productive – the anti-porn campaigner Mary Whitehouse almost single-handedly pressurized the Government to create the Protection of Children Act 1978, which sought to prevent child pornography. The amount of power wielded by the members of a pressure group is also extremely important – organizations involved with big business tend to be particularly effective in influencing legislation, and there is a growing industry set up purely to help them lobby effectively, for a price. On the other hand, pressure groups made up of ordinary individuals can be very successful, particularly if the issue on which they are campaigning is one which stirs up strong emotion in the general public. A recent example was the Snowdrop Petition, organized after the shooting of 16 young children and their teacher in Dunblane, Scotland. Despite enormous opposition from shooting clubs, it managed to persuade the then Government to ban most types of handguns.

Political parties

Some of the most high-profile legislation is that passed in order to implement the Government party's election manifesto, or its general ideology – examples include the privatizations of gas and water and the creation of the Poll Tax by the Conservative Government which began in 1979.

The civil service

Although technically neutral, the civil service nevertheless has a great effect on legislation in general. It may not have party political goals, but various departments will have their own views as to what type of legislation enables them to achieve departmental goals most efficiently – which strategies might help the Home Office control the prison population, for example, or the Department of Health make the NHS more efficient. Ministers rely heavily on senior civil servants for advice and information on the issues of the day, and few would consistently turn down their suggestions.

Treaty obligations

The UK's obligations under the treaties establishing the EU and the European Convention on Human Rights both influence changes in British law (see pp. 59 and 456).

Public opinion and media pressure

As well as taking part in campaigns organized by pressure groups, members of the public make their feelings known by writing to their MPs, to Ministers and to newspapers. This is most likely to lead to reform where the ruling party has a small majority. The media can also be a very powerful force for law reform, by highlighting issues of concern. In 1997, media pressure helped secure a judicial inquiry into the racially motivated killing of South London teenager Stephen Lawrence. The inquiry was authorized to look not only at the Lawrence case itself, but at the general issue of how racially motivated killings are investigated.

Public opinion and media pressure interact; the media often claims to reflect public opinion, but it can also whip it up. What appears to be a major epidemic of a particular crime may in fact be no more than a reflection of the fact that once one interesting example of it hits the news, newspapers and broadcasting organizations are more likely to report others. An example of this is the rash of stories during 1993 about parents going on holiday and leaving their children alone, which caught the headlines largely because of a popular film about just such a situation, *Home Alone*. Leaving children alone like this may have been common practice for years, or it may be something done by a tiny minority of parents, but the media's selection of stories gave the impression of a sudden epidemic of parental negligence. In 2000 there was a high profile campaign by the *News of the World* to 'name and shame' paedophiles. The Government subsequently introduced a limited reform of the law.

Agencies of law reform

Much law reform happens as a direct response to pressure from one or more of the above sources, but there are also a number of agencies set up to consider the need for reform in areas referred to them by the Government. Often problems are referred to them as a result of the kind of pressures listed above – the Royal Commission on Criminal Justice 1993 was set up as a result of public concern and media pressure about high-profile miscarriages of justice, such as the Birmingham Six and the Guildford Four.

The Law Commission

Established in 1965 (along with another for Scotland), the Law Commission is a permanent body, comprising five people drawn from the judiciary, the legal profession and legal academics. In practice, the chairman tends to be a High Court judge, and the other four members to include a QC experienced in criminal law, a solicitor with experience of land law and equity, and two legal academics. They are assisted by legally qualified civil servants.

Under the Law Commission Act 1965 the Law Commission's task is to:

- codify the law
- remove anomalies in the law
- repeal obsolete and unnecessary legislation
- consolidate the law
- simplify and modernize the law

The Commission works on reform projects referred to it by the Lord Chancellor or a Government department, or on projects which the Commission itself has decided would be suitable for its consideration. At any one time the Commission will be engaged on between 20 and 30 projects of law reform.

A typical project will begin with a study of the area of law in question, and an attempt to identify its defects. Foreign legal systems will be examined to see how they deal with similar problems. The Commission normally publishes a consultation paper inviting comments on the subject. The consultation paper describes the present law and its shortcomings and sets out possible options for reform. The Commission's final recommendations are set out in a report which contains a draft Bill where legislation is proposed. It is then essentially for the Government to decide whether it accepts the recommendations and to introduce any necessary Bill in Parliament.

The Criminal Law Revision Committee

The CLRC considers reforms to the criminal law. It is responsible to the Home Secretary and its members include the Director of Public Prosecutions (DPP) as well as judges and academics. The CLRC has not been convened since 1985, though it has never been formally abolished.

Royal Commissions

These are set up to study particular areas of law reform, usually as a result of criticism and concern about the area concerned. They are made up of a wide cross-section of people: most have some expertise in the area concerned, but usually only a minority are legally qualified. The Commissions are supposed to be independent and non-political.

A Royal Commission can commission research, and also take submissions from interested parties. It produces a final report detailing its recommendations, which the Government can then choose to act upon or not. Usually a majority of proposals are acted upon, sometimes in amended form.

Important recent Royal Commissions include the 1981 Royal Commission on Criminal Procedure, the Royal Commission on Criminal Justice, which reported in 1993, and the Royal Commission on Reform of the House of Lords, which reported in 2000.

Public inquiries

Where a particular problem or incident is causing social concern, the Government may set up a one-off, temporary committee to examine possible options for dealing with it. Major disasters, such as the Hillsborough football stadium disaster, the sinking of the ferry *Herald of Free Enterprise* and the Paddington railway disaster; events such as the Brixton Riots during the 1980s; and advances in technology, especially medical technology (such as the ability to fertilize human eggs outside the body and produce 'test tube babies') may all be investigated by bodies set up especially for the job. These usually comprise individuals who are independent of Government, often with expertise in the particular area. Academics are frequent choices, as are judges – Lord Scarman headed the inquiry into the Brixton riots and Lord Cullen headed the inquiry into the Paddington railway disaster.

Public inquiries consult interested groups, and attempt to reach a consensus between them, conducting their investigation as far as possible in a non-political way. In the case of disasters and other events, they may try to discover the causes, as well as making recommendations on legislation to avoid a repeat.

Other temporary inquiries

From time to time, various Government departments set up temporary projects to investigate specific areas of law. One of the most important recent examples is the inquiry by Lord Woolf into the Civil Justice System (p. 357).

Performance of the law reform bodies

The Law Commission

One of the principal tasks of the Commission at its inception was codification, and this programme has not on the whole been a success. The Commission's programme was ambitious: in 1965 it announced that it would begin codifying family law, contract, landlord and tenant, and evidence. Attempts in the first three were abandoned – family in 1970, contract in 1973 and landlord and tenant in 1978. Evidence was never begun.

Zander (1988) suggests the reasons for the failure are 'a mixture of conservatism and a realisation on the part of draftsmen, legislators and even judges that [codification] simply did not fit the English style of lawmaking'. The draftsmen were not keen on the idea that codes would have to be drawn up in a broader manner than was normal for traditional statutes. Legislators were doubtful of the concept of a huge Bill which would attempt to state the law in a vast area such as landlord and tenant. The judges objected to the vision promoted by Lord Scarman, the Commission's first chairman, of the code coming down like an iron curtain making all pre-code law irrelevant. As Zander explains, this appeared to the judges like 'throwing the baby out with the bathwater – losing the priceless heritage of the past and wasting the fruits of legislation and litigation on numerous points which would still be relevant to interpret the new code'.

The Law Commission is particularly concerned with the Government's failure to codify the criminal law. From 1968–74 the Commission produced a series of working papers, but in 1980 announced that its shortage of resources would not allow it to continue, and appealed for help with the task. The Society of Public Teachers of Law responded, and set up a four-person committee, which by 1985 had produced a draft code. But this has never been legislated as law. In most countries criminal law is contained in a single code so that it is accessible to the people against whom it will be applied. The Commission has now embarked upon a programme to produce a series of draft Bills, based on the Code but incorporating appropriate law reform proposals, which will in themselves make substantial improvements in the law. If enacted, these Bills will form a criminal code. But at the moment there is no tangible sign of progress in implementation of any of their major reports dating back to 1993. Decisions of the courts continue to draw attention to defects in the substantive law in areas on which they have already reported. One ray of hope has been the passing of legislation consolidating the sentencing regime, and further impetus for codification has been given by the review of criminal procedure under Lord Justice Auld. In the Government's White Paper, *Criminal Justice: the Way Ahead* (2001) it stated that it did intend to codify the criminal law as part of its modernization process.

However, opinions are mixed on whether codification would prove to be of very great value even if it ever becomes possible. Supporters say it would provide accessibility, comprehensibility, consistency and certainty. A code allows people to see their rights and liabilities more clearly than a mixture of case law and separate statutes could, and should encourage judges and others who use it to look for and expect to find answers within it. Lord Hailsham has said that a good codification would save a great deal of judicial time and so reduce costs, and the academic Glanville Williams makes the point that criminal law is not like the law of procedure, meant for lawyers only, but is addressed to all classes of society, and so the greater accessibility and clarity of a code should be particularly welcomed in this area.

Critics say a very detailed codification could make the law too rigid, losing the flexibility of the common law. And if it were insufficiently detailed, as Zander points out, it would need to be interpreted by the courts, so creating a new body of case law around it, which would defeat the object of codification and make the law neither more accessible nor more certain. It may be that the Law Commission's failure to codify the law signifies a problem with codification, not with the Law Commission.

Instead of proceeding with large-scale codification, the Law Commission has chosen to clarify areas of law piece by piece, with the aim of eventual codification if possible. Family law in particular has been significantly reformed in this way, even if the results are, as Zander points out, a 'jumble of disconnected statutes rather than a spanking new code'.

As far as general law reform is concerned, as well as the major family law reforms, the Commission has radically changed contract law by recommending control of exclusion clauses which led to the passing of the Unfair Contract Terms Act 1977. Its report, *Conspiracy and Criminal Law Reform*, helped shape the Criminal Law Act 1977 and its working paper, *Offences Against Public Order*, was instrumental in creating the Public Order Act 1986. Following its recommendations, the Computer Misuse Act 1990 introduced new criminal offences relating to the misuse of computers; and the Family Law Act 1996 changed the law on domestic violence and divorce.

In recent years, however, there has been a major problem with lack of implementation of Law Commission proposals. By 1999, 102 law reform reports had been implemented, which represented two-thirds of their final reports. There is a better chance of proposals from the Law Commission becoming legislation if the subject concerned comes within the jurisdiction of the Lord Chancellor's Department; there is less chance if they concern other departments, particularly the Home Office. In any case, it has been pointed out that implementation of proposals is not the only benefit of a permanent law reform body. Stephen Cretney, a legal academic who has been a Law Commissioner, suggests that one of its most important contributions has simply been getting law reform under discussion and examination, and drawing attention to the needs of various areas of law.

Criminal Law Revision Committee

The Theft Acts 1968 and 1978 are generally thought of as the CLRC's greatest achievement. The legislation effectively codified the previous law in this area, aiming for a fundamental reconsideration of the principles underlying this branch of the law, to be embodied in a modern statute. Unfortunately this was not a complete success; as Smith and Hogan point out, one offence (that of obtaining a pecuniary advantage by deception) proved so troublesome that it had to be completely reviewed in the 1978 Act, and 'in some other respects cracks are beginning to show through . . . The legislation would benefit from a review.' Reported appeals in the first ten years of the Theft Act were more than double the number made in the ten years before.

The CLRC was also responsible for a report into the criminal justice system, which stated that the system had shifted much too far in favour of defendants' rights. It recommended a string of measures designed to tip the balance back in favour of the prosecution, including abolishing the right to silence, on the grounds that 'it is as much in the public interest that a guilty person should be convicted as that an innocent person should be acquitted'. As Zander points out, this contravenes the traditional belief that it is better that ten guilty people go free than that one innocent one is convicted – the reasoning behind our system's insistence on a suspect being innocent until proven guilty.

The report caused a storm of opposition, not only from civil liberties campaigners but from members of both Houses of Parliament, lawyers and judges, and none of it was implemented. History seems to suggest that the Committee's assessment was badly mistaken. The report was delivered in 1972; two years later, the Birmingham Six were wrongly convicted, followed in 1975 by the Guildford Four and in 1976 by the Maguire Seven. A whole string of other miscarriages of justice also date from this period. It is difficult to see these as the work of a system too heavily weighted towards defendants' rights.

Royal Commissions

These have had mixed success. The 1978 Royal Commission on Civil Liability and Compensation for Personal Injury produced a report that won neither public nor Government support, and few of its proposals were implemented.

The Royal Commission on Criminal Procedure has most of its recommendations implemented by the Police and Criminal Evidence Act 1984 (PACE), but subsequent criticisms of PACE mean this is less of a success than it appears. The Royal Commission stated that the aim behind its proposals was to secure a balance between the rights of individuals suspected of crime, and the need to bring guilty people to justice. PACE has however been criticized by the police as leaning too far towards suspects' rights, and by civil liberties campaigners as not leaning far enough.

Perhaps the most successful Royal Commission in recent years has been the Royal Commission on Assizes and Quarter Sessions, which reported in 1969. Its proposals for the reorganization of criminal courts were speedily implemented.

As regards the 1993 Royal Commission on Criminal Justice, this has met with mixed results. Some of its recommendations were introduced in the Criminal Justice and Public Order Act 1994 and the Criminal Appeals Act 1995, which created the Criminal Cases Review Commission (see p. 412) in response to the Commission's criticism of the criminal appeals system. On the other hand, the Government has ignored some of its proposals and has proceeded to introduce changes that the Royal Commission was specifically opposed to, for example the abolition of the right to silence.

Public inquiries and other temporary committees

These rely to a great extent on political will, and the best committees in the world may be ineffective if they propose changes that a Government dislikes. Lord Scarman's investigation into the Brixton riots is seen as a particularly effective public inquiry, getting to the root of the problem by going out to ask the people involved what caused it (his Lordship, then retired, shocked his previous colleagues by taking to the streets of Brixton and being shown on television chatting to residents and cuddling their babies). His proposals produced some of the steps towards police account-ability in PACE. But the subsequent inquiry into the case of Stephen Lawrence shows that the progress made was not sufficient. The Civil Justice Review was also instrumental in bringing about reform, though views on the success of the changes are mixed and the area has been tackled again recently by Lord Woolf.

Problems with law reform agencies

Lack of power

There is no obligation for Government to consult the permanent law reform bodies, or to set up Royal Commissions or other committees when considering major law reforms. Mrs Thatcher set up no Royal Commissions during her terms of office, despite the fact that important and controversial legislation – such as that abolishing the GLC – was being passed.

Political difficulties

Governments also have no obligation to follow recommendations, and perfectly well thought out proposals may be rejected on the grounds that they do not fit in with a Government's political position. An example was the recommendation of the Law Commission in 1978 that changes be made to the rule that interest is not payable on a contract debt unless the parties agreed otherwise. The idea was supported by the House of Lords in **President of India** (1984), but the Government was persuaded not to implement the proposals after lobbying from the CBI and consumer organizations.

Even where general suggestions for areas of new legislation are imple-mented, the detailed proposals may be radically altered. The recommenda-tions of law reform agencies may act as justification for introducing new legislation yet, as Zander points out, often when the Bill is published it becomes clear that the carefully constructed proposal put together by the law reform agency 'has been unstitched and a new and different package has been constructed'.

Lack of influence on results

Where proposals are implemented, ideas that are effective in themselves may be weakened if they are insufficiently funded when put into practice – a matter on which law reform bodies can have little or no influence. The 1981 Royal Commission on Criminal Procedure's recommendations were largely implemented in the Police and Criminal Evidence Act 1984, and one of them was that suspects questioned in a police station should have the right to free legal advice, leading to the setting up of the duty solicitor scheme. While the idea of the scheme was seen as a good one, underfunding has brought it close to collapse, and meant that in practice relatively small numbers of suspects actually get advice from qualified, experienced solicitors within a reasonable waiting time. This has clearly frustrated the aims of the Royal Commission's recommendation.

Too much compromise

Royal Commissions and temporary committees have the advantage of drawing members from wide backgrounds, with a good spread of experience and expertise. However, in some cases this can result in proposals that try too hard to represent a compromise. The result can be a lack of political support and little chance of implementation. It is generally agreed that this was the problem with the Pearson Report, the report of the Royal Commission on Civil Liability and Compensation for Personal Injury.

Influence of the legal profession

Where temporary law reform committees have a high proportion of non-lawyers, the result can be more innovative, imaginative ideas than might come from legally trained people who, however open-minded, are within 'the system' and accustomed to seeing the problems in a particular framework. However, this benefit is heavily diluted by the fact that the strong influence of the legal profession on any type of reform can defeat such proposals even before they reach an official report.

An example was the suggestion of the Civil Justice Review in its consultation paper that the county courts and High Court might merge, with some High Court judges being stationed in the provinces to deal with the more complex cases there. Despite a warm welcome from consumer groups and the National Association of Citizens' Advice Bureaux, the proposals were effectively shot down by the outcry from senior judges who were concerned that their status and way of life might be adversely affected, and the Bar, which was worried that it might lose too much work to solicitors. In the event the proposal was not included in the final report.

Waste of expertise

Royal Commissions and temporary committees are disbanded after producing their report, and take no part in the rest of the law-making process. This is in many ways a waste of the expertise they have built up.

Lack of ministerial involvement

There is no single ministry responsible for law reform so that often no Minister makes it their priority.

▶ ANSWERING QUESTIONS

1 'It shall be the duty of the Commissions to take and keep under review all the law with which they are respectively concerned, with a view to its systematic development and reform, including in particular the codification of such law . . .' (section 3, Law Commissions Act 1965). Should the Law Commission concentrate on codification, or are there more suitable ways of reforming the law? *OCR*

You could start by defining what codification is, and mention the plans for codification which the Law Commission had when it was created, and what happened to them. Then go on to discuss the advantages and disadvantages of codification, and whether you feel that the Law Commission should still concentrate on it.

You could then move on to look at the other ways of reforming the law. As well as examining the successful work which the Law Commission has done, you could look at other ways of law reform – such as the way in which public inquiries and temporary committees examine specific problems, using advisers who are not necessarily lawyers, but may have experience in the relevant field. Do you think this is an approach the Law Commission should consider?

Your conclusion should sum up what you think the Commission's priorities should be and why.

2 'The Law Commission has provided an important impetus to the process of law reform in England and Wales.' Discuss. *WJEC*

Here you are basically being asked how well the Law Commission has done its job. Your introduction might state what the Commission was set up to do, and then the rest of your essay can consider whether it has fulfilled that function and thereby given an important impetus to law reform.

You might want to consider the successes of the Law Commission first, and then go on to talk about codification, pointing out that the Commission has not provided much of an impetus in this area, but discussing the arguments on whether codification would actually be beneficial anyway. Finish by summing up what you think the Commission's contribution has been.

3 Critically evaluate the role of the law reform bodies. *OCR*

Note that this question can apply not only to the official bodies such as the Law Commission, but also to informal ones such as pressure groups, and you need to discuss both types. It may be a good idea to divide your answer into official and unofficial law reform bodies: taking each in turn, you can describe how they operate and assess their effectiveness, pointing out any problems in the way they work. Don't forget that what is needed is a critical account – just listing the bodies and what they do will get you very few marks. What the examiners want to know is not just what the bodies do, but how well they do it. Your conclusion might generally sum up the effect of these multiple bodies, saying whether, taken together, you feel they do an adequate job in reforming the law.

Reading on the Internet

The Law Commission's website is:

http://www.lawcom.gov.uk/

3 The judiciary

The judicial hierarchy

Just as the English court system is arranged in a hierarchy, so are its judges. At the top is the Lord Chancellor (see below), and then the 12 Lords of Appeal in Ordinary, more commonly known as the Law Lords. They sit in the House of Lords and the Privy Council.

At the next level down, the Court of Appeal, are 35 Lords Justices of Appeal. The criminal division of the Court of Appeal is presided over by the Lord Chief Justice, and the civil division by the Master of the Rolls. Following Lord Woolf's recommendations for reform of the civil justice system, a senior judge, Sir Richard Scott, has been appointed to head the whole of the civil justice system.

In the High Court, there are around 106 full-time judges. As well as sitting in the High Court itself, they hear the most serious criminal cases in the Crown Court. Although – like judges in the Court of Appeal and the House of Lords – High Court judges receive a knighthood, they are referred to as Mr or Mrs Justice Smith (or whatever their surname is), which is written as Smith J.

The next rank down are the circuit judges, who travel around the country, sitting in the county court and hearing the middle-ranking Crown Court cases. The Criminal Justice and Public Order Act 1994 added a further role, allowing them occasionally to sit in the criminal division of the Court of Appeal.

The slightly less serious Crown Court criminal cases are heard by district judges, and then there are recorders, who are part-time judges dealing with the least serious Crown Court criminal cases. Recorders are usually still working as barristers or solicitors, and the role is often used as a kind of apprenticeship before becoming a circuit judge. Because of the number of minor cases coming before the Crown Court, there are now assistant recorders as well, and at times retired circuit judges have been called upon to help out. Finally, in larger cities there are district judges (magistrates' courts), who were previously known as stipendiary judges, and are full-time, legally qualified judges working in magistrates' courts.

Tribunals are not served by members of the judiciary; cases there are heard by a panel of people who are not legally qualified but have experience in the relevant areas. The chairperson may be a practising lawyer, but this is not always the case.

The Lord Chancellor

The head of the whole judiciary is the Lord Chancellor, currently Lord Irvine, who effectively appoints all the other judges. He earns £167,000 a year. He (or she, though there has been no female Lord Chancellor yet) is President of the Supreme Court (comprising the High Court, the Crown Court and the Court of Appeal), and officially President of the Chancery Division of the High Court, although in practice the Vice-Chancellor usually performs this role. When the Lord Chancellor sits as a judge, it is in the House of Lords or the Privy Council, but few Lord Chancellors do so very often: in recent years the only Lord Chancellors to sit at all regularly have been Lords Hailsham and McKay.

The appointment is a political one: the Lord Chancellor is usually a Cabinet Minister and speaker of the House of Lords. Although technically appointed by the Queen, the Lord Chancellor is actually chosen by the Prime Minister and goes out of office when that party loses an election, as well as being eligible for removal by the Prime Minister, just like any other Minister.

As well as controlling judicial appointments, the Lord Chancellor has powers to give directions about the business of the courts, and responsibility for the Law Commission and the statutory legal aid and advice scheme. There are no formal qualifications for the post, but all previous Lord Chancellors have been barristers.

▶ Appointments to the judiciary

The selection process for judges in the High Court and above is explained in a booklet called 'Judicial Appointment', the latest edition of which was published by the Lord Chancellor's Department in 1999. The Courts and Legal Services Act 1990 has widened entry to the judiciary, reflecting the changes in rights of audience (see pp. 142–143), and (at least in theory) opening up the higher reaches of the profession to solicitors as well as barristers. To be appointed to the House of Lords a person must either have held judicial office for two years or have a right of audience in the Supreme Court; most will already have been judges in the Court of Appeal. The qualification for appointment to the Court of Appeal is either experience as a judge in the High Court or a right of audience in the High Court for ten years. To be appointed as a High Court judge it is also necessary to have had a right of audience for ten years in the High Court. Circuit judges, recorders or assistant recorders can now be appointed from anyone who has had general rights of audience in the Crown Court or county courts for ten years. Anyone who has been a district judge for at least three years is also eligible for appointment as a circuit judge, and the requirement that solicitors serve three years as a recorder before appointment as a circuit judge has been removed.

The Lord Chancellor, the Lords of Appeal in Ordinary and the Lord Justices of Appeal are appointed by the Queen on the advice of the Prime Minister who in turn is advised by the Lord Chancellor. High Court judges, circuit judges and recorders are all appointed by the Queen on the advice of the Lord Chancellor.

Over the years there has been considerable criticism of the method by which judges were appointed and, as a result, since 1995 some changes to the appointment process have been made. The selection process for judges in the High Court involves the Lord Chancellor's Department gathering information about potential candidates over a period of time by making informal inquiries (known as 'secret soundings') from leading barristers and judges. No single person's view about the suitability of a particular candidate should be decisive. Although facts obtained about potential candidates are normally available to the candidates on request so that they can ensure they are correct, opinions given in confidence will not be revealed on the grounds that this would make people less willing to assist the Lord Chancellor by giving their frank opinions.

The normal procedure for recruiting for a job is to place an advertisement in a newspaper and to allow people to apply. By contrast, until recently, there were no advertisements for judicial office, you simply waited to be invited to the post. Advertisements are now being placed for junior and High Court judges, but still not for positions in the Court of Appeal and the House of Lords. Some individuals will still be invited to become judges without having to apply. Selected candidates are interviewed and the final decision is formally taken by the Lord Chancellor.

The Lord Chancellor has said that appointments are to be made regardless of gender, race, religion and sexual orientation – in the past homosexuality could act as a bar to judicial office.

At the Government's request, an inquiry into the system for judicial appointments was undertaken by Sir Leonard Peach, a senior civil servant. His report was published in December 1999. Sir Leonard was generally happy with the quality of the work and the professionalism of the civil servants involved in the appointments' process. Feedback to unsuccessful candidates was impressive and not matched elsewhere in scale or take-up to his knowledge. One of the key recommendations of the report was that a Commissioner for Judicial Appointments should be appointed to provide independent monitoring of the procedures for appointing judges and Queen's Counsel (for an explanation of Queen's Counsel, see p. 131).

This recommendation was accepted by the Lord Chancellor and the first Commissioner was appointed in 2001. Sir Leonard Peach did not recommend any changes to the system of secret soundings.

Judicial selection in other countries

In civil law systems, such as France, there is normally a career judiciary. Individuals opt to become judges at an early stage, and are specifically trained for the job, rather than becoming lawyers first as they do here. The judiciary is organized on a hierarchical basis, and judges start in junior posts, dealing with least serious cases, and work up through the system as they gain experience. One drawback is that they can be viewed as part of the civil service, rather than as independent of Government.

In the US there are two basic methods of selection, appointment and election, although a compromise between the two methods is often made. All federal judges are appointed by the President, subject to confirmation by the Senate, which may include examining a prospective judge's character and past life, as the confirmation of Clarence Thomas, the judge accused of sexual harassment, did recently. Most state and local judges are elected, although genuine competition for a post is rare. In a number of states elections are used to confirm in office judges who have been in their posts for a limited period.

The Bill of Rights leads Americans to favour single-issue pressure groups which mount legal campaigns – most famously in the case of the 1954 decision to end racial segregation in schools – to achieve political aims. These groups realize the vital importance of the person who decides such cases and therefore spend a lot of time and money researching potential candidates to see if their views fit, and if not, whether there is any damaging information which could be used to prevent their appointment. There are also associations which are interested simply in enhancing the reputation of the court, so that the American Bar Association, in particular, launches extensive inquiries of every nominee involving hundreds of interviews with judges and academics, and commissioning studies of a candidate's opinions.

Although most US judicial nominations are confirmed, 20 per cent of nominees are rejected and, more importantly, presidents are discouraged from proposing people who might fall at this hurdle. The knowledge that one will have to submit oneself to such public examination might affect the way in which judges behave earlier in their careers.

Training

Although new judges have the benefit of many years' experience as barristers or solicitors, they have traditionally received a surprisingly small amount of training for their new role, limited until recently to a brief training period, organized by the Judicial Studies Board. In the last few years, this has been supplemented in several ways: the advent of the Children Act 1989 has meant that social workers, psychiatrists and paediatricians have shared their expertise with new judges, while concern about the perception of judges as racist, or at best racially unaware, has led to the introduction of training on race issues. The reforms to the civil justice system and the passing of the Human Rights Act 1998 have led to the provision of special training to prepare for these legal reforms.

The attention given to training has increased with the separation of the Judicial Studies Board from the Lord Chancellor's Department. Commenting on the increase in training provision, the head of the Judicial Studies Board, Henry J, has stated that it should be seen as a gradual response to obvious needs, rather than the beginning of some kind of judicial training college, as seen in other legal systems.

Pay

Judges are paid large salaries – £123,000 at High Court level – which are not subject to an annual vote in Parliament. The official justification for this is the need to attract an adequate supply of candidates of sufficient calibre for appointment to judicial office, and in fact top barristers can earn more by staying in practice. In the past, for many the security of a pensionable position after years of self-employment made up for a slight cut in salary, but the Judicial Pensions and Retirement Act 1993 requires 20 years of judicial service rather than 15 before full pension rights are obtained. With the earlier retirement age (see below), few judges will currently satisfy this requirement and the change has been very unpopular, being described as the equivalent of a 7.5 per cent cut in salary. The Bar Council is urging the Government to pay salaries at different rates depending on the area of law, for example tax and commercial law judges would receive more.

Promotion

The traditional view has been that there is no system of promotion of judges, on the ground that holders of judicial office might allow their promotion prospects to affect their decision-making. In practice, judges are promoted from lower courts to higher courts: potential recorders generally have to have proved themselves as assistant recorders; circuit judges as recorders. Those appointed to the High Court have usually served as a recorder or deputy High Court judge. The process appears to be much the same as that for initial appointments, being based on confidential soundings from those within the system.

▶ Termination of appointment

There are four ways in which a judge may leave office:

Dismissal. Apart from the Lord Chancellor, judges of the High Court and above are covered by the Act of Settlement 1700, which provides that they may only be removed from office by the Queen on the petition of both Houses of Parliament. The machinery for dismissal has been used successfully only once, when in 1830 Sir Jonah Barrington, a judge of the High Court of Admiralty in Ireland, was charged with appropriating £922 to his own use. Proceedings against the judge were conducted in each House and each passed a resolution against the judge calling for his dismissal, which was then confirmed by the king. No judge has been removed by petition of Parliament this century.

   Under the Courts Act 1971, circuit judges, district judges and stipendiary magistrates can be dismissed by the Lord Chancellor for 'inability or misbehaviour'. In fact this has occurred only once since the passing of the Act: Judge Bruce Campbell (a circuit judge) was sacked in 1983 after being convicted of smuggling spirits, cigarettes and tobacco into England in his yacht. In July 1994 the Lord Chancellor made it clear that 'misbehaviour' could include a conviction for drink-driving or any offence involving violence, dishonesty or moral turpitude. It would also include any behaviour likely to cause offence, particularly on religious or racial grounds or behaviour that amounted to sexual harassment.

   In addition to dismissal, there is of course, also the power not to re-appoint those who have been appointed for a limited period only.

Resignation. In practice, serious misbehaviour is dealt with not by dismissal, but by the Lord Chancellor suggesting to the judge that he or she should resign.

Retirement. The Lord Chancellor has recently reduced the retirement age to 70.

Removal due to infirmity. The Lord Chancellor has powers to remove a judge who is disabled by permanent infirmity from the performance of his or her duties and who is incapacitated from resigning his or her post.

▶ Discipline and criticism

In practice the mechanisms for disciplining judges who misbehave are more significant than those for removal, which is generally a last resort. Judges may be criticized in Parliament, or rebuked in the appellate courts, and are often censured in the press. There may be complaints from barristers, solicitors or litigants, made either in court or in private to the judge personally. 'Scurrilous abuse' of a judge may, however, be punished as contempt of court.

Independence of the judiciary

In our legal system great importance is attached to the idea that judges should be independent. In addition to the common sense view that they should be independent of pressure from the Government and political and other groups, and therefore able to decide cases impartially, judicial independence is required by the constitutional doctrine known as the separation of powers. First put forward by the eighteenth-century French political theorist Montesquieu, this doctrine states that the only way to safeguard individual liberties is to ensure that the power of the state is divided between three separate and independent arms: the judiciary, comprising the judges; the legislature who make the laws, in our case Parliament; and the executive, the Government of the day. The idea is that each arm of the state should operate independently, so that each one is checked and balanced by the other two, and none becomes all-powerful; Montesquieu stated that if all the powers were concentrated in the hands of one group, the result would be tyranny.

Therefore the doctrine requires that individuals should not occupy a position in more than one of the three arms of the state – judiciary, legislature and executive; that each should exercise its functions independently of any control or interference from the others; and that one arm of the state should not exercise the functions of either of the others.

The way in which the separation of powers works can be seen, for example, in judicial review, where the courts can scrutinize the behaviour of the executive, and in some cases declare it illegal. Other safeguards include the security of tenure given to judges, which ensures they cannot be removed at the whim of one of the other branches; the fact that their salaries are not subject to a parliamentary vote; and the rule that they cannot be sued for anything done while acting in their judicial capacity. Independence in decision-making is provided through the fact that judges are only accountable to higher judges in appellate courts.

However, there are a number of problems with the idea of the judiciary as independent (see p. 108). In addition, litigation that raises the question of judicial bias is discussed on p. 395.

Criticisms of the judiciary

Background, ethnic origin, sex and age

Judges are overwhelmingly white, male and middle to upper class, and frequently elderly, leading to accusations that they are unrepresentative of, and distanced from the majority of society. In 1995, 80 per cent of Lords of Appeal, Heads of Division, Lord Justices of Appeal and High Court judges were educated at Oxford or Cambridge. Over 50 per cent of the middle-ranking circuit judges went to Oxbridge but only 12 per cent of the lower-ranking district judges did. In a study carried out in 1994 by Labour Research it was found that of 641 judges, 80 per cent had been to public school. The appointments made under new Labour have not broken this mould. The narrow background of the judges does mean that they can be frighteningly out of touch with the world in which they are working. Mr Justice Harman, who resigned in 1998, said in three different cases, that he had not heard of the footballer Paul Gascoigne, the rock band Oasis and the singer Bruce Springsteen.

There are still no women sitting as judges in the European Court of Justice or the House of Lords, and Chris Mullin, a Labour MP, has commented that the only woman judge in the Court of Appeal happened to be the sister of a previous Lord Chancellor and the daughter of a Lord of Appeal. There are only eight females among the 97 High Court judges and just 36 of the 558 circuit judges are women. Law Society research conducted in 1991 suggested that male barristers were nearly twice as likely to obtain judicial appointment as women in practice for the same length of time. Ethnic minorities are even more scarcely represented; no members of the ethnic minorities have been appointed to the higher courts, and only 1 per cent are from ethnic minorities. Lord Lane, the 76-year-old former Lord Chief Justice, said after his retirement that his regret at being forced off the bench was due, at least partly, to the fact that his colleagues were 'a jolly nice bunch of chaps'. This remark reinforces the view of many that the judiciary is actually a sort of rarefied gentlemen's club.

The age of the full-time judiciary has remained constant over many years: the average on appointment is about 52 or 53. Inevitably, given the system of promotion, the average age is higher in the higher courts, thus the average age of a district judge was 54.3 and that of a Law Lord was 66.5 in 1995. Even the recently reduced retirement age is still five years older than that for most other occupations: before it was elected, the Labour Party suggested that the retirement age should be 65 though no action has so far been taken to implement this. David Pannick has written in his book, *Judges*, that 'a judiciary composed predominantly of senior citizens cannot hope to apply contemporary standards or to understand contemporary concerns'.

Before the Courts and Legal Services Act 1990, judges were almost exclusively selected from practising barristers. Since it is difficult for anyone without a private income to survive the first years of practice, successful barristers have tended to come from reasonably well-to-do families, who are of course more likely to send their sons or daughters to public schools and then to Oxford or Cambridge. Although the background of the Bar is gradually changing, the age at which judges are appointed means that it will be some years before this is reflected in the ranks of the judiciary.

The new opportunities provided for solicitors to join the judiciary, provided by the Courts and Legal Services Act 1990 may in time alter the traditional judicial background, since this branch of the profession provides wider opportunities for women, members of the ethnic minorities and those from less privileged backgrounds.

Selection and appointment

Despite the changes that have been made to the appointment process, criticisms still remain. The three main criticisms of the current mode of selecting judges is that it is dominated by politicians, secretive and discriminatory. On the first issue, the Lord Chancellor and the Prime Minister play central roles in this process but they are politicians and could be swayed by political factors in the selection of judges. The Lord Chancellor usually presents the Prime Minister with a shortlist of two or three names listing them in the order of his or her own preference. Mrs Thatcher is known to have selected Lord Hailsham's second choice on one occasion.

On the second issue, the constitutional reform organization Charter 88, among others, has criticized the selection process for being secretive and lacking clearly defined selection criteria. The process is handled by a small group of civil servants who, although they consult widely with judges and senior barristers, nevertheless wield a great deal of power. The danger is that too much reliance is placed on a collection of anecdotal reports from fellow lawyers, with candidates given no opportunity to challenge damning things said about them.

The process of 'secret soundings' gives real scope for discrimination, with lawyers instinctively falling back on gender and racial stereotypes in concluding whether someone is appropriate for judicial office. For example, individuals are asked whether they think candidates show 'decisiveness' and 'authority'. But these are very subjective concepts and Kamlesh Bahl has argued (*The Guardian*, 10 April 1995) that as the judiciary is seen as a male profession, perceptions of judicial characteristics, such as 'authority', are also seen as male characteristics. 'Authority' is dependent more on what others think than on the person's own qualities. Indeed, research published by the Bar Council in 1992 concluded:

> It is unlikely that the judicial appointment system offers equal access to women or fair access to promotion to women judges . . . The system depends on patronage, being noticed and being known. (*Without Prejudice? Sex Equality at the Bar and in the Judiciary*, 1992, para. 48(1))

The Law Society has added to the controversy surrounding the 'secret soundings' system by announcing in September 1999 that it would no longer participate in the process. The president of the Law Society, Bob Sayer, described the system as having 'all the elements of an old boys' network', and being inconsistent with an open and objective recruitment process. 'We suspect we were being used to legitimise a system where other peoples' views were more important than ours. It didn't really matter what we thought, it was the views of the senior judiciary and the Bar which counted.' The highest ranking solicitor among the judiciary is a solitary High Court judge.

A 1997 study commissioned by the Association of Women Barristers found that there was a strong tendency for judges to recommend candidates from their own former chambers. The study looked at appointments to the High Court over a ten-year period (1986–96) and found that of the 104 judges appointed, 70 (67.3 per cent) came from a set of chambers which had at least one ex-member among the judges likely to be consulted. In addition, a strikingly high percentage of appointments came from the same handful of chambers: 28.8 per cent of new judges from chambers which represented 1.8 per cent of the total number of chambers in England and Wales. The fact that those who advise on appointments are already well established within the system could make it unlikely that they will encourage appointment from a wider base: Lord Bridge, the retired Law Lord, commented in a 1992 television programme that they tend to look for 'chaps like ourselves'. As Helena Kennedy QC has put it 'the potential for cloning is overwhelming', and the outlook for potential female judges and those from the ethnic minorities not promising. The reforms introduced in 1995 seem to be merely window dressing as the Lord Chancellor has admitted that the process of obtaining 'soundings' will remain important.

The fact that appointments are effectively in the hands of a Government Minister is also seen as a problem, and although in theory the Lord Chancellor is accountable through Parliament for his appointments, in practice this means very little. The same arguments apply to the system of promotion. The new Judicial Appointments Commissioner has inadequate powers to make any real impact on the selection process.

However, in his book *The Judge*, Lord Devlin says that, while it would be good to open up the legal profession, so that it could get the very best candidates from all walks of life, the nature of the job means that judges will still be the same type of people whether they come from public schools and Oxbridge or not, namely those 'who do not seriously question the status quo'.

Training

Considering the importance of their work, judges receive very little training, even with recent changes. They may be experienced as lawyers, but the skills needed by a good lawyer are not identical to those required by a good judge. Unlike the career judge system seen on the continent, where judges cut their judicial teeth in the lower courts, and gain experience as they move up to more serious cases, our judges often begin their judicial careers with cases that may involve substantial loss of liberty for the individual. Nor are they required to have shown expertise in the areas of law they will be required to consider: it is perfectly possible for a High Court judge to try a serious criminal case, and possibly pass a sentence of a long term of imprisonment, without ever having done a criminal case as a lawyer in practice.

The most serious cases of all in the civil courts are not being heard by High Court judges but by deputy High Court judges. These deputies are circuit judges spending a few days in London or, more likely, barristers filling time between cases. The only thing to be said about this system is that it is cheaper for the Treasury.

Procedures for criticism and dismissal

Over the years there have been a few judges whose conduct has been frequently criticized, but who have nevertheless remained on the Bench, and the lack of a formal machinery for complaints is seen as protecting incompetent judges. However, this has to be balanced against the protection that security of tenure gives to judicial independence.

Problems with judicial independence

Despite the emphasis placed on the independence of the English judiciary, a number of factors compromise it.

Supremacy of Parliament

Apart from where European law is involved, it is never possible for the courts to question the validity of existing Acts of Parliament. In the UK all Acts of Parliament are treated as absolutely binding by the courts, until such time as any particular Act is repealed or altered by Parliament itself in another statute or by a Minister under the special fast-track procedure provided for under the Human Rights Act 1998. The judiciary are therefore ultimately subordinate to the will of Parliament – unlike, for example, judges in the US, who may declare legislation unconstitutional. Dworkin has argued that if judges had the power to set aside legislation as unconstitutional, judicial appointments would become undesirably political, and judges would be seen as politicians themselves. He points to the political character of high judicial appointments in the US.

The Lord Chancellor

The position of the Lord Chancellor as a member of the judiciary, the executive and the legislature clearly goes against the idea that no individual should be part of all three arms of the state, and his role ultimately means that all judicial appointments are made by the Government. Politically, the most important judicial appointment is that of Master of the Rolls: as president of the Court of Appeal his or her view on the proper relationship between the executive government and the individual is crucial. The appointment of Lord Donaldson, successor to Lord Denning, in 1982, was seen as a strongly political appointment and one which the then Prime Minister favoured: he had been a Conservative councillor, and was not promoted during the years of the previous Labour Government, 1974–79. There was some publicity concerning Lord Donaldson's political views at the time of the GCHQ case, and as a result, his Lordship declined to preside over the Court of Appeal when it considered the Government's appeal in that case.

The conflicting roles of the Lord Chancellor were highlighted in 2001 when the media drew attention to the fact that the Lord Chancellor had been involved in political fundraising. Guests to a dinner he had organized were invited to make donations to the Labour Party and there were concerns that lawyers might seek promotion by giving substantial donations. Legal Action Group, a pressure group, have argued that the various roles of the Lord Chancellor put him in breach of the European Convention on Human Rights.

Treasury counsel
Those barristers retained to represent the Government in court actions in which the Government are involved – called Treasury counsel – are very likely to be offered High Court judgeships in due course.

The House of Lords
Lords of Appeal in Ordinary are also members of more than one arm of the state, since they take part in the legislative business in the House of Lords. However, they tend not to get involved in political controversy or ally themselves with a particular party, confining their contributions to technical questions of a legal nature. They rarely sit in legislative debates and by the same token, the political members of the Lords do not participate in judicial hearings. In its evidence to the Royal Commission on reform of the House of Lords, the pressure group JUSTICE recommended that all serving judges should cease to sit in the House of Lords. It argued that the expansion of public law, including judicial review, and the Human Rights Act 1998 called for a clearer separation of powers between the judiciary and other branches of government. The Royal Commission simply recommended that the basic conventions that restricted the role of the Law Lords should be put down in writing.

Non-judicial work
Judges also get involved in non-judicial areas with political implications, such as chairing inquiries into events such as Bloody Sunday in

Londonderry, the Brixton riots or the Zeebrugge ferry disaster. Thus, Lord Justice Scott chaired the high profile inquiry into the arms-to-Iraq affair and the High Court Judge, Sir William Macpherson, headed the inquiry into the handling of the police investigation of the death of the black teenager Stephen Lawrence, who was murdered in South London. This function can often be seen to undermine the political neutrality of the judiciary – in the early 1970s, for example, Lord Diplock headed an inquiry into the administration of justice in the region, the report of which led to the abolition of jury trials for terrorist offences in the region. To this day such hearings are known as Diplock courts, which does nothing to uphold the reputation for independence of the judiciary.

The promotion system

In his book *Straight from the Bench*, the retired circuit judge James Pickles alleges that judges who are ambitious cannot be truly independent because they have to be careful not to offend the Lord Chancellor or his officials – this leads, he says, to 'cringing conformity'. The fact that the Lord Chancellor is a Government Minister lends further weight to the idea that the system of appointment and promotion compromises judicial independence. A recent illustration of this may be the case of Mr Justice Wood. He was president of the Employment Appeal Tribunal who had refused to deal with some cases in the more economical way that the last Conservative Lord Chancellor wanted. He received a letter from the Lord Chancellor asking him to 'consider his position' as president of the tribunal. When questioned about this by legal peers in the House of Lords, Lord McKay denied that he was suggesting that Wood should resign. Mr Justice Wood did in fact retire shortly afterwards though he said that he had planned to do so even before the incident occurred. The legal peers accused the Lord Chancellor, Lord McKay, of acting unconstitutionally in apparently pressuring a judge to adopt cost-cutting procedures or resign. The incident reflected general concern that pressures from the Treasury to contain the costs of the legal system were threatening judicial independence.

Part-time judges

In a Scottish case, **Starrs** *v* **Procurator Fiscal, Linlithgow** (1999) the court held that a judge who had no security of tenure was not 'independent' within the meaning of Art. 6 of the European Convention on Human Rights (discussed at p. 456). The Lord Chancellor subsequently announced in April 2000 new arrangements to guarantee the independence of part-time judges. From now on, part-time appointments will be for a minimum of five years. There will be five grounds on which a part-time judge can be removed from office:

- misbehaviour
- incapacity
- persistent failure to comply with sitting requirements, without good reason
- failure to comply with training requirements
- sustained failure to observe standards reasonably expected from a judge

The Lord Chief Justice will nominate a judge to investigate the case and must approve any decision to remove which the Lord Chancellor takes. The judge's contract will normally be renewed automatically every five years, though it need not be renewed if the number of judges is being reduced due to changes in operational requirements or due to a structural change to enable recruitment of new people. A decision not to renew will then be on a 'first in, first out' principle.

Cases with political implications

Although judges generally refrain from airing their political views, they are sometimes forced to make political decisions, affecting the balance between individuals and the state, the allocation of resources, and the relative powers of local and national government. Despite the official view of judges as apolitical, the fact that these decisions have political ramifications cannot be avoided; judges do not have the option of refusing to decide a case because it has political implications, and have to make a choice one way or the other.

However, concerns have been expressed that too often such decisions defend the interests of the Government of the day, sometimes at the expense of individual liberties. In the wartime case of **Liversidge v Anderson** (1942), Lord Atkin voiced concern about the decision by a majority of judges in the House of Lords that the Home Secretary was not required to give reasons to justify the detention of a citizen, commenting that the judges had shown themselves 'more executive minded than the executive'.

Certain cases have borne out this concern. In **McIlkenny v Chief Constable West Midlands** (1980), Lord Denning dismissed allegations of police brutality against the six men accused of the Birmingham pub bombings with the words:

> Just consider the course of events if this action were to go to trial . . . If the six men fail, it will mean that much time and money and worry will have been expended by many people for no good purpose. If the six men win, it will mean that the police were guilty of perjury, that they were guilty of violence and threats, that the confessions were involuntary and were improperly admitted in evidence: and that the convictions were erroneous. That would mean that the Home Secretary would have either to recommend they be pardoned or he would have to remit the case to the Court of

Appeal under section 17 of the Criminal Appeal Act 1968. This is such an appalling vista that every sensible person in the land would say: it cannot be right that these actions should go any further. They should be struck out.

In other words, Lord Denning was saying, the allegations should not be addressed, because if proved true, the result would be to bring the legal system into disrepute.

In **R** *v* **Ponting** (1985), the civil servant Clive Ponting was accused of leaking documents revealing that the Government had covered up the circumstances in which the Argentine ship the *General Belgrano* was sunk during the Falklands war. Ponting argued that he had acted 'in the interests of the state' (a defence laid down in the Official Secrets Act at the time), but Mr Justice McGowan directed the jury that 'interests of the state' meant nothing more or less than the policies of the government of the day. Nevertheless the jury acquitted Ponting (see p. 170).

The danger of political bias will be increased as a result of the Human Rights Act 1998 coming into force. While judges already decided some politically sensitive cases, the number is likely to increase, with litigation directly accusing Government actions and legislation of breaching fundamental human rights. The journalist Hugo Young argues that we will see the emergence of the 'political judge'. He observes:

> The Convention will require domestic judges to involve themselves in matters of principle, as Irvine was the first to understand. Not long ago, he lucidly described the emergence of what sounds like the 'political judge'. The presence of the Convention, he said, would sometimes require judges to give a decision on the morality of the conduct, and not simply its compliance with the bare letter of the law. (*The Guardian*, 18 July 1998)

The changing role of the judiciary will be particularly visible in the House of Lords. At the moment they decide about 100 cases a year which are usually on technical commercial and tax matters. With the implementation of the Human Rights Act 1998 the House of Lords will move closer to the US Supreme Court, deciding fundamental issues on the rights of the individual against the state.

Right-wing bias

In addition to their alleged readiness to support the Government of the day, the judiciary have been accused of being particularly biased towards the interests traditionally represented by the right wing of the political spectrum. In his influential book *The Politics of the Judiciary*, Griffith states that: 'in every major social issue which has come before the courts in the last thirty years – concerning industrial relations, political protest, race relations, government secrecy, police powers, moral behaviour – the judges have supported the conventional, settled and established interests.'

Among the cases he cites in support of this theory is **London Borough of Bromley *v* Greater London Council** (1982). In this case the Labour-run GLC had won an election with a promise to cut bus and tube fares by 25 per cent. The move necessitated an increase in the rates, levied on the London boroughs, and one of those boroughs, Conservative-controlled Bromley, challenged the GLC's right to do this. The challenge failed in the High Court, but succeeded on appeal. The Court of Appeal judges condemned the fare reduction as 'a crude abuse of power', and quashed the supplementary rate that the GLC had levied on the London boroughs to pay for it. The House of Lords agreed, the Law Lords holding unanimously that the GLC was bound by a statute requiring it to 'promote the provision of integrated, efficient and economic transport facilities and services in Greater London', which they interpreted to mean that the bus and tube system must be run according to 'ordinary business principles' of cost-effectiveness. The decision represented a political defeat for the Labour leaders of the GLC and a victory for the Conservative councillors of Bromley.

Other cases cited by Griffith include **Council of Civil Service Unions *v* Minister for the Civil Service** (1984) – the 'GCHQ' case in which the House of Lords supported the withdrawal of certain civil servants' rights to belong to a trade union; **Attorney-General *v* Guardian Newspapers Ltd** (1987), which banned publication of *Spycatcher*, a book on the security services, even though it was generally available in America and Australia; and several cases arising out of the 1984 miners' strike, such as **Thomas *v* NUM (South Wales Area)** (1985), in which injunctions were sought to prevent protesters collecting at pit gates and shouting abuse at those going to work. The judge in that case, according to Griffith, had some difficulty in finding the conduct illegal, but eventually decided that it amounted to 'a species of private nuisance, namely unreasonable interference with the victim's right to use the highway'; Griffith describes the decision as 'judicial creativity at its most blatant'.

Commentators have also noted that the great advances in judicial review in the 1960s and 1970s came almost entirely at the expense of Labour policies, and that judicial reluctance to review Government decisions of the executive is most likely to be decisive in cases where the Government in question is a Conservative one. However, the past few years have seen a shift; the last Conservative Home Secretary Michael Howard's decisions were several times found illegal by the courts. Legal journalist and writer Joshua Rozenberg argued that the bias at least in favour of the establishment has broken down. He has written:

> Much of the responsibility for the rift between judiciary and government must fall on the shoulders of the Lord Chancellor. By shaking up the legal profession and paving the way for solicitors – and probably, before long, Crown Prosecution Service lawyers – to appear in the higher courts, and by

his lack of support for judges on the key issues of pay, hours and pensions, Lord Mckay has fashioned a fundamental shift in the natural order: a judiciary which can no longer be relied on to support the establishment. (*Guardian*, Tuesday 12 April 1994)

Whether and how far this will change now that we have a change of government remains to be seen: political bias apart, the rift Rozenberg refers to may well have been the result of one party keeping power for so long that it felt able to risk alienating even its traditional supporters.

Bias against women

In her book *Eve was Framed*, Helena Kennedy argues that the attitude of many judges to women is outdated, and sometimes prejudiced. The problems are particularly apparent in cases involving sexual offences: Kennedy cites the comments of Cassell J in 1990, that a man who had unlawful intercourse with his twelve-year-old stepdaughter was understandably driven to it by his pregnant wife's loss of interest in sex; and the direction of Wild J in a 1982 rape case: 'women who say no do not always mean no . . . if she doesn't want it, she only has to keep her legs shut and she will not get it without force'.

Kennedy alleges that women are judged according to how well they fit traditional female stereotypes. Because crime is seen as stepping outside the feminine role, women are more severely punished than men, and women who do not fit traditional stereotypes are treated most harshly. She points out that three times as many women as men go to prison for a first offence (though this may be affected by their lack of financial resources, making financial penalties unsuitable). According to a report by the National Association for the Care and Resettlement of Offenders (NACRO) in 1990, 53 per cent of women have two or fewer convictions when they first go to prison compared with 22 per cent of men.

Research by the sociologist Pat Carlen into what affects the decision to send a woman to prison received the following answers from members of the judiciary:

- 'Women who live more ordered lives don't commit crime because with a husband and children to look after, they don't have time.'
- 'If they have left their husbands and their children are in care it may seem a very good idea to send them to prison for three months.'
- 'If she's a good mother, we don't want to take her away. If she's not a good mother it doesn't really matter.'

Influence of Freemasonry

Freemasonry is a secret society, which does not allow women to join. Among its stated aims is the mutual self-advancement of members and there has long been concern about the extent of membership among the police as well as the judiciary, on the basis that loyalty to other masons – who might be parties in a case, or colleagues seeking promotion or other favours – could have a corrupting influence. Josephine Hayes, chair of the Association of Women Barristers, told newspapers that anecdotal evidence suggested that there was public concern about the influence that masonic membership might have on judges: clients whose opponents were Freemasons had been known to express worries that the judge might also be one. She pointed out that although fears of actual influence might be unfounded, the concern that it might exist weakened confidence in the legal system.

The Association of Women Barristers also suggests that Freemasonry may have a discriminatory effect on women lawyers' chances of appointment to the Bench. It points out that because the current system of appointment depends on recommendation by existing judges, men benefited by the opportunities which Freemasonry provides to meet senior judges. Such opportunities, it points out, have become even more valuable now that the practising Bar has grown to over 8,000, so that judges no longer necessarily know all candidates for the judiciary personally. The Association has argued that judges should be obliged to resign from the Freemasons on appointment to the Bench. The previous Lord Chancellor, Lord McKay opposed such a rule, arguing that as a matter of principle individuals should be free to join any lawful organization they wished. He pointed out that the judicial oath requires all judges to swear 'to do right to all manner of people . . . without fear or favour, affection or ill will'. He suggested that this meant there was no conflict of interest between membership of the Freemasons and judicial office.

The current Lord Chancellor, Lord Irvine, in an attempt to introduce greater transparency, sent a questionnaire in 1998 to all members of the judiciary asking them to declare their 'Masonic status'. Five per cent of those who responded admitted to being Freemasons.

Lack of specialization

A very distinctive feature of the English system is that judges tend not to specialize: instead, they are organized in terms of the hierarchy of the courts in which they work. In France, for example, every region has its own court structure, and there will be hundreds of judges of equal status, instead of the elite group that form the pinnacle of our judiciary. It has been argued that this arrangement prevents our judiciary from developing the kind of expertise that, in France, has contributed to the development of specialist courts such as the *Conseil d'Etat*, which deals with administrative law; the development of our administrative law is said to have suffered as a result. However, it can also be argued that the English model gives the highest judges an overview of the whole system, which helps ensure that different branches of law remain fundamentally consistent with each other.

In any case, there are some signs that the system is changing. First, the growth of tribunals has removed many specialist areas from the ordinary courts: most tribunals are presided over by people with specialist knowledge of the relevant areas. The growth of mediation systems as an alternative method of dispute resolution (see chapter 16) has also contributed to this. Secondly, Lord Woolf's report on the civil justice system recommends that High Court and circuit judges should concentrate on fewer areas of work, though he did not suggest that they actually became specialists in particular subjects.

Shortage of time

There is a growing concern that judges currently have insufficient time allocated for them to read the papers for a case. Court of Appeal judges are only allocated four reading days a month when they can do legal research. The rest of the time they are expected to be sitting hearing court cases. This is in striking contrast with some appellate judges in the US who only hear cases four days per month.

Reform of the judiciary

Appointments and promotion

The appointment process needs to be radically overhauled. Several suggestions have been made for broadening the social, racial and gender base of the judiciary and making the selection process more open. Moving it away from the secretive, self-reproducing process run by the existing judiciary is widely seen as a priority and several interested organizations have recommended the creation of some kind of Judicial Appointments Commission. The law reform group JUSTICE, for example, recommends a committee comprised of representatives from the Bar, the Law Society, academic lawyers, the judiciary and possibly some lay members with experience in selection procedures. Under the JUSTICE model, interested bodies could propose names to the committee and individuals wishing to be considered could put their own names forward. The Lord Chancellor would also be able to make suggestions to the committee – and would work with it – but would not have the power to make appointments without the committee's agreement. A similar plan has been suggested by the constitutional reform group Charter 88, which recommends that the committee should be appointed by a Parliamentary Select Committee and be answerable to Parliament.

The Law Society, the Association of Women Barristers and other law reform bodies also recommended the creation of some kind of selection board when the issue was addressed by the House of Commons Select Committee on Home Affairs in 1996. The Select Committee divided along party lines, with the Conservative majority rejecting these proposals and concluding that there was no need for any major changes to the appointment system. However, the Labour Party had long recommended reform, and shortly after the 1997 election it was announced that the Government was considering creating a Judicial Appointments Commission, including lay members as well as lawyers and judges. The Commission would draw up a shortlist of names; the final decision would remain with the Lord Chancellor, but his or her powers would be curtailed by the fact that the choice would have to be made from candidates recommended by the Commission. The Commission would, of course, considerably dilute the influence of the existing judiciary, and senior judges immediately criticized the proposal, suggesting that it would bring politics into the process. The late Lord Chief Justice, Lord Taylor, said rather melodramatically that he 'could not imagine anything more horrific'. Unfortunately, since coming into office the Lord Chancellor has announced that a Judicial Appointments Commission is 'not a priority'.

Other reforms aimed at creating a judiciary with a more diverse background have also been suggested by Charter 88. It considers that it is vital to improve access to the legal profession as a whole, including better funding, so that students of all backgrounds can join the professions and eventually filter into the judiciary. In the shorter term, appointments should be opened up to younger lawyers, academics, and a higher proportion of solicitors. This would mean reducing the required amount of court experience, but it can be argued that experience in fighting cases as a lawyer does not in any case require or provide the same skills needed to hear them as a judge. Charter 88 is also in favour of positive discrimination for women and ethnic minority applicants, the introduction of more part-time appointments, and a career structure that could take into account the needs of women having children. This has been done in both the Netherlands and France, with the result that their judiciaries are made up of almost equal numbers of men and women. However, a report into judicial appointments by the House of Commons Home Affairs Committee in 1996 rejected the idea of positive discrimination.

The Law Society, the professional body representing solicitors, has greeted the limited reforms made following Sir Leonard Peach's report in 1999 as 'inadequate', particularly as the new Commissioner is merely responsible for monitoring the existing system, rather than having any direct involvement in the appointment process itself.

Dismissal and discipline

From time to time the suggestion has been made that the system of dismissal would be improved if there were some form of fair hearing for judges before they were dismissed and if the allegations against them were sifted by some form of tribunal or special commission. JUSTICE, in its 1972 report on the judiciary, recommended that there should be a three-person judicial commission to which the Lord Chancellor should have to refer any case in which he or she thought there were grounds for dismissing a judge of the High Court or above. The commission would inquire into the matter and recommend whether the question should be referred to the Judicial Committee of the Privy Council, which would then advise the Queen whether the judge should be dismissed. Any other judge dismissed by the Lord Chancellor should have the right of appeal to the judicial committee, which would appoint a judicial commission to apply the same procedure. A similar mechanism already exists in Scotland.

The Labour Party produced a policy document in 1995 suggesting that complaints against judges could be made to a commission and details of such complaints could be published in the form of league tables with judges being named. League tables would show the number of times a particular judge had been referred to the commission and the number of complaints upheld. A party spokesperson is reported to have said that if a judge had been complained about six times, and five of the complaints had been upheld 'it would be inconceivable' that the judge would continue to work in the same field.

Training

It has been widely suggested that judges should receive more training, not just at the beginning of their careers, but at frequent intervals throughout. Helena Kennedy suggests that judges might also benefit from sabbaticals, in which they could study the practices of other jurisdictions, and the work of social agencies and reform groups.

Judge Pickles has put forward the view that the judiciary needs more training in sociology, psychology, penology and criminology, and to learn more about how criminals are dealt with in other systems. Lord Scarman has put forward similar views. Lord Woolf has proposed that judges should receive training in information technology so that they can make greater use of computers in their work.

Organization

The Court Service issued a consultation document entitled *Transforming the Crown Court* (1999). This document proposes that judges should have planned work which begins at 9 am and finishes not before 5 pm, including an increase of their daily court sittings from five to six hours. It also suggests that it would be more efficient for some High Court judges to be based permanently outside London, rather than occasionally going on circuit in the provinces. These recommendations have already been made by Lord Woolf's Civil Justice Review and appear to have the Lord Chancellor's support.

▶ ANSWERING QUESTIONS

Questions about the judiciary generally focus on their independence, but as this is closely related to appointments, background and selection, you need to know more than just the information under the heading of independence of the judiciary, as the following example shows.

1 Can true judicial independence ever be achieved under the present method of appointment? *OCR*

Your introduction should explain why judicial independence is important. Then look at each aspect of judicial appointment and consider how it affects the independence of the judiciary; points to raise are the position of the Lord Chancellor, the secretive nature of the appointment procedure, the risk of discrimination and the role of the civil servants. You might then consider the background of the judges, as a result of the selection procedure, and whether this affects independence, giving examples (the material on right-wing and executive bias is relevant here). You might want to compare our system with those of other countries, and the independence of the judiciary there. Then look at suggested reforms, and finally conclude with your view on whether the judiciary can be sufficiently independent under our system, and if not, which reforms should be made.

2 Critically consider the possible effect of recent reforms to the appointment and training of judges. *OCR*

A good introduction here would explain that there have been for many years a number of perceived problems with the appointment and training of the English judiciary, including the lack of openness about the selection process, the narrow background of the resulting appointees and their perceived biases, and lack of training. Direct reference should be made to Sir Leonard Peach's report which is discussed at p. 100. Explain that a variety of recent reforms have taken place with the aim of addressing these problems. You could then briefly list some of the relevant reforms at this point: the creation of a Commissioner for Judicial Appointments; increased training; open advertising for some posts; openness about the selection process; and of course increased access to the judiciary for solicitors. Do not forget that any reform in the training of solicitors or barristers which widens access to those professions will also eventually have an effect on the composition of the judiciary, just as any limits on access to the professions can be a reason for problems with the narrow background of judges.

The main part of your essay should look at how these changes will address the problems with appointment and training. You could do this by taking each reform in turn and explaining what effect it is likely to have, or alternatively take each problem in turn, and describe how it might be addressed by the reforms – the approach you choose is up to you, but the important thing is to have a visible structure.

Finally, you could discuss some of the proposals for further reform in this area, such as the idea of a Judicial Appointments Commission with independent powers to select the judge and positive discrimination for some applicants. You might sum up by saying whether you think these further reforms are necessary or not, and why.

3 'For nearly 300 years, the English judge has been guaranteed his independence.' How far is this true? In your opinion, can the decisions of our judges be regarded as satisfactory to all members of society?

Your introduction should place the reference to 300 years by mentioning the provisions of the Act of Settlement (p. 11). After that the question seems to need answering in two parts: has the English judge been guaranteed independence, and in the light of the answer, can his or her judgments properly be regarded as satisfactory to all members of society?

In the first part, you should look at the factors that are supposed to guarantee the independence of the judiciary: security of tenure, separation of powers, salaries not subject to a parliamentary vote and so on (see p. 104). Then go on to examine the problems with independence that suggest it is not guaranteed.

In the second part of your answer, you can give examples of cases where the lack of judicial independence has resulted in decisions that are not satisfactory to certain members of society – again, the material on right-wing and executive bias is useful here.

If you have time you could add that the lack of independence is not the only reason that their decisions are not satisfactory to all members of society, and bring in the material about the background of judges and their alleged bias against women. Also, if you have time, you could add suggestions for reform, perhaps briefly in your conclusion.

NB If you happen to have swotted up on judges, you will naturally be looking for a question in which you can show off this knowledge, but beware: questions which at first sight look as though they concern the judiciary may actually be about statutory interpretation and the law-making role of judges – the following are examples:
Explain and critically examine the approaches adopted by judges to the interpretation of statutes. AQA (AEB)
and
Explain and illustrate the following statement: 'There was never a more sterile controversy than that upon the question of whether a judge makes law. Of course he does. How can he help it?' (Radcliffe) Edexcel

The material for answering this kind of question can be found in chapter 1: Sources of law.

Reading on the Internet

Sir Leonard Peach's report into judicial appointments is available on the Lord Chancellor's Department website:

http://www.lcd.gov.uk/judicial/peach/indexfr.htm

General information on the judiciary is available on the Lord Chancellor's Department website:

http://www.lcd.gov.uk/judicial/judgesfr.htm

Chapter 9 of the *Judicial Statistics for 1999* is dedicated to the subject of the judiciary:

http://www.lcd.gov.uk/jsar99/chapter9.pdf

The website of the Judicial Studies Board can be found at:

http://www.cix.co.uk/~jsb

4 Barristers and solicitors

The British legal profession, unlike that of most other countries, includes two separate branches: barristers and solicitors (the term 'lawyer' is a general one which covers both branches). They each do the same type of work – advocacy, which means representing clients in court, and paperwork, including drafting legal documents and giving written advice – but the proportions differ, with barristers generally spending a higher proportion of their time in court.

In addition, some types of work have traditionally been available to only one branch (conveyancing to solicitors, and advocacy in the higher courts to barristers, for example), and barristers cannot usually be hired directly by clients – their first point of contact will usually be a solicitor, who then engages a barrister on their behalf if it proves necessary. As we shall see though, these divisions are beginning to break down.

In the past, the two branches of the profession have been fairly free to arrange their own affairs, but over the past ten years, this situation has changed significantly. The Courts and Legal Services Act 1990 (CLSA) established the Lord Chancellor's Advisory Committee on Legal Education and Conduct (ACLEC), which had a general duty to help maintain and develop standards in education, training and performance, and was also the body which regulated new applications for rights of audience in the higher courts (see p. 142). ACLEC was abolished and replaced in January 2000 by the Legal Services Consultation Panel, set up by the Access to Justice Act 1999. This is a smaller and less powerful body than its predecessor.

Solicitors

There are around 80,000 solicitors. Their governing body is the Law Society, which supervises training and discipline, as well as acting on behalf of the profession as a whole.

Work

Solicitors have traditionally been able to do advocacy work in the magistrates' court and the county court, but not generally in the higher courts.

This situation was changed by the Courts and Legal Services Act 1990 and the Access to Justice Act 1999. These Acts put in place the mechanics for equalizing rights of audience between barristers and solicitors. Now all barristers and solicitors acquire full rights of audience when they are admitted to the roll, though they will only be able to exercise these rights on completion of the necessary training. There are currently 1,000 solicitor advocates. Many firms are sending their solicitors on courses, making advocacy training compulsory and designating individuals as in-house advocates. Thus, solicitors are increasingly doing the advocacy work themselves rather than sending it to a barrister. Where Government funding has established fixed fees for work, solicitors are faced with a simple choice: keep the money or give it away. Even those solicitors who do not have full rights of audience can appear in the High Court in bankruptcy proceedings, or to read out a formal, unchallenged statement; and in the Crown Court if the case is an appeal from the magistrates' court, or has been committed to the Crown Court for sentence, and they appeared in the same case in the magistrates' court. They can also appear before a single judge of the Court of Appeal, and in High Court proceedings held in chambers.

Traditionally, an individual solicitor did much less advocacy work than a barrister, but as more solicitors gain the necessary training, this is changing. In any case, solicitors as a group do more advocacy than barristers, simply because 98 per cent of criminal cases are tried in the magistrates' court, where the advocate is usually a solicitor. The amount of advocacy done by solicitors is also growing as a result of the removal of many contract and tort cases from the High Court to the county court, following the Courts and Legal Services Act 1990.

For most solicitors, paperwork takes up much of their time. It includes conveyancing (legal aspects of the buying and selling of houses and other property) and drawing up wills and contracts, as well as giving written and oral legal advice. Until 1985, solicitors were the only people allowed to do conveyancing work, but this is no longer the case – people from different occupations can qualify as licensed conveyancers, and the service is often offered by banks and building societies. Probate work (which concerns wills) can now also be done by banks, building societies, insurance companies and legal executives, and consequently the proportions of work done by solicitors are changing.

Solicitors can, and usually do, form partnerships, with other solicitors. Alternatively, since 2001, they can form a Limited Liability Partnership. Under an ordinary partnership a solicitor can be personally liable (even after retirement) for a claim in negligence against the solicitor firm, even if he or she was not involved in the transaction giving rise to the claim. Under the Limited Liability Partnership a partner's liability is limited to negligence for which he or she was personally responsible. This form of partnership already exists in the US and Germany.

Solicitors work in ordinary offices, with, in general, the same support staff as any office-based business, and have offices all over England and

Wales and in all towns. Practices range from huge London-based firms dealing only with large corporations, to small partnerships or individual solicitors, dealing with the conveyancing, wills, divorces and minor crime of a country town. Some solicitors work in Law Centres and other advice agencies, government departments, private industry and education rather than in private practice.

Figures published in the journal *Commercial Lawyer* in September 2000 show that an elite group of 100 city solicitors working in central London are earning more than £1 million per year. But this figure has to be seen in the context of a profession that has over 80,000 members.

Qualifications and training

Almost all solicitors begin with a degree, though not necessarily in law. Although no minimum degree classification is laid down, increased competition for entry to the profession means that most successful applicants now have an upper second class degree, and very few get in with less than a lower second.

Students whose degree is not in law have to take the one-year course leading to the Common Professional Examination (CPE). It is possible for non-graduate mature students, who have demonstrated some professional or business achievements, to enter the profession with a two-year, wider CPE course, but only a handful do so, and it is not a route the Law Society encourages – they suggest that for most people, it is worth putting in the extra year to do a law degree and enter in the conventional manner, especially bearing in mind that many universities and colleges now offer mature students law degrees which can be studied part-time, so that students do not have to give up paid employment.

The next step, for law graduates and those who have passed the CPE, is a one-year Legal Practice Course, designed to provide practical skills, including advocacy, as well as legal and procedural knowledge. Fees are around £5,000, yet both the CPE and the Legal Practice Course are eligible only for discretionary LEA grants, and are not covered by the Government's student loan scheme. The Law Society provides a very small number of bursaries, and has also negotiated a loans scheme with certain high street banks, which offers up to £5,000, which students do not begin paying back until they have finished studying; a few large London firms also offer assistance to those students they wish to attract into employment. The vast majority of students, however, are obliged to fund themselves or rely on loans.

After passing the Legal Practice exams, the prospective solicitor must find a place, usually in a firm, to serve a two-year apprenticeship. There can be intense competition for these places, especially in times of economic difficulty when firms are reluctant to invest in training; in 1995–96, there were only 4,170 traineeships on offer, for the almost 7,000 LPC students. Formally known as articles, the two-year period is now called a training contract, and includes a 20-day practical skills course, building on subjects studied during the Legal Practice Course. Trainee solicitors (or articled clerks as they were traditionally known) are paid, and the Law Society currently lays down a minimum wage of £12,150 in inner London, and £10,850 in the provinces, although firms can pay less by applying to the Law Society for a waiver, if the trainee agrees. For several years there has been pressure to abolish the minimum wage, as law firms have suffered from both a tougher economic climate and increased competition in areas such as conveyancing. The level has been frozen since 1993, and for a while, in the mid-1990s, it was widely thought that the minimum could be abolished altogether. The Law Society Council decided against this after being presented with evidence from the Trainee Solicitors Group. This group argued that abolishing the minimum wage would increase the difficulties of the many trainees who start their careers already in debt due to the lack of financial support for LPC courses: 25 per cent had debts of at least £7,000. They also pointed out that even without abolition, large numbers of firms were obtaining waivers and paying salaries as low as £6,510: trainees were agreeing to this because of the difficulty of finding alternative employment. The work of a trainee solicitor can be very demanding, and a survey carried out for the Law Society found that a third work more than 50 hours a week.

It is possible to become a solicitor without a degree, by completing the one-year Solicitors First Examination Course, and the Legal Practice Course, and having a five year training contract. Legal executives (see p. 150) sometimes go on to qualify this way.

Both stages of solicitors' training have been changed recently, with more emphasis being placed on practical skills in general, and advocacy in particular.

The majority of solicitors qualifying each year are still law graduates – in 1993–94, 64 per cent of those admitted to the Law Society Roll had a law degree, with only 19 per cent being graduates in subjects other than law. However, the Law Society say that the non-law degree and CPE route is becoming more popular, with a third of places on Legal Practice Courses currently being taken by people aiming to qualify this way. Legal academics have expressed some concern about this, but the Law Society point out that in some years, pass rates for non-law graduates in Solicitors' Finals have been higher than those for law graduates. Making up the remaining 17 per cent are Fellows of the Institute of Legal Executives, lawyers from overseas, solicitors transferring from Scotland or Northern Ireland and ex-barristers.

All solicitors are required to participate in continuing education throughout their careers. They are required to do 16 hours a year, with the subjects covered depending on each individual's areas of interest or need. Records must be kept of courses attended.

Lord Woolf has observed that the solicitor profession is becoming 'increasingly polarized' depending on the nature of the work carried out, with lawyers working in City firms earning significantly more than those in high street practices. Eight of the biggest City law firms established in 2001 a tailor-made course for their future trainees. Lord Woolf has criticized this development, as he fears it could undermine the concept of a single-solicitor profession with a single professional qualification. The course may, over time, create a barrier which prevents students from other colleges from entering a big commercial practice. Lord Woolf has observed that, given the quality of the trainees attracted by the City firms, it should be possible for them to provide any enhanced training they required after the end of the Legal Practice Course.

Complaints

Complaints can be made to the Office for the Supervision of Solicitors, to the Legal Services Ombudsman and/or by an action in negligence.

Office for the Supervision of Solicitors

Until 1996, complaints about solicitors were handled by the Solicitors Complaints Bureau (SCB). The Bureau was widely criticized for delay and inefficiency, and a report by the National Consumer Council in 1994 suggested that its policy of attempting to conciliate the parties favoured solicitors over complainants, tending in many cases to impose a settlement or dismiss the complaint. The maximum compensation available to complainants was £1,000, and this was criticized as being too low. Another frequent complaint was that the SCB was not sufficiently independent of the profession, as its powers were merely delegated to it by the Law Society.

Concerned at these criticisms, the Law Society looked into the problems and in 1995 produced a report entitled *Supervision of Solicitors; the Next Decade.* Its main recommendation was acted upon in 1996, when the SCB was replaced by a new organization, the Office for the Supervision of Solicitors (OSS). The new body was designed to be more efficient and customer-friendly, and has given non-lawyers a greater role in order to increase its independence from the profession. Complaints are initially handled by a seven-strong team of solicitors, who sift them into those which can be quickly dealt with on the telephone, those which involve serious allegations of shoddy work, and those which concern serious breaches of professional rules. The aim is to make early, direct contact with complainants, and ensure they are kept informed.

Minor complaints are sent to the firms concerned to deal with, as part of the OSS's aim to encourage law firms to develop better customer care practices: in 1996 it found that at least one in four had no in-house complaints procedure. Where complaints remain in the OSS's hands, they are directed to its network of local conciliation points, so that where possible, complainants can be seen face to face.

However, the problems associated with the SCB do not seem to have been solved by the new body. The first official verdict on its performance was delivered after its first year of operation, by the then Legal Services Ombudsman, Michael Barnes. He criticized it for backlogs in handling complaints, which were taking months to process. He stressed that the new body was more user-friendly than its predecessor, but warned that it was going to have to take a tough line on enforcing professional standards of conduct rather than interpreting the rules of the profession in favour of solicitors, as the SCB had been prone to do. He also suggested that the SCB's habit of looking for reasons to reject complaints had to an extent spilled over into the OSS too, and had to be stopped.

The OSS has also been criticized by the Consumers' Association magazine *Which?* for not being sufficiently independent of the profession: like the SCB, it is run by the Law Society, and its main decision-making committee comprises ten members of the public, and 15 solicitors, including ten who are members of the Law Society Council. The OSS's director also sits on the Law Society's management board. *Which?* suggests that complaints about solicitors should be handled by a completely independent organization, and this recommendation has been taken up by a group of back-bench MPs, who have been calling for an independent regulator with powers defined by statute. This view was echoed by the new Legal Services Ombudsman, Ann Abraham, when she took over the post: she has told newspapers that the OSS needs to demonstrate that things have improved a good deal by comparison with the SCB, or statutory regulation might be necessary.

By the time Ms Abraham delivered her second annual report in 1999, it was clear that the required improvements had not been made. The report stated that complaints handling at the OSS was spiralling out of control, that the OSS had failed to deliver service to its own published standards and targets and the Law Society's ability to protect the public was in jeopardy.

The Law Society commissioned a study by management consultants Ernst and Young, with the aim of coming up with a blueprint for delivering the necessary standards of service. In June 1999 the Law Society announced that it would be putting into practice the Ernst and Young recommendations and that Ernst and Young had advised that if this was done, the backlog – by now consisting of 17,000 complaints – could be cleared. The Law Society is seeking to increase the size of the compensation awards it can make to clients receiving inadequate service from solicitors, from £1,000 to £5,000. The Legal Services Ombudsman welcomed the plan, but criticized the Law Society for allowing the situation to deteriorate so badly before taking action.

The Lord Chancellor's Department has also indicated its dissatisfaction with the performance of the OSS, and the statutory regulation threatened by Ann Abraham in her first report almost came a step nearer during the process of the Access to Justice Bill, when the Government introduced an amendment creating an independent Legal Complaints Commissioner who could set targets for complaints handling, rather than allowing the professions to do this themselves. This was put on hold, while the Government waits to see whether the Law Society can improve its handling of complaints.

Legal Services Ombudsman

The Office of the Legal Services Ombudsman was established in 1990. Its role is to oversee the handling of complaints by the professional regulatory bodies, and offers the final appeal regarding complaints against lawyers. Complainants who are dissatisfied with the way their grievances are handled by the OSS can ask the Legal Services Ombudsman to investigate. The number of cases being accepted for investigation by the Ombudsman is at an all-time high. Between January 1998 and March 1999, the Ombudsman conducted 1,658 investigations, concerning solicitors, barristers and licensed conveyancers. If he or she is dissatisfied with the way the relevant professional body has handled the complaint, the Ombudsman can recommend that the relevant professional body reconsiders the complaint and/or order compensation to be paid. In 1998 one or both of these measures occurred in 33 per cent of cases, an increase of 3 per cent on the 1997 figure. According to the Ombudsman's annual report, this increase is almost entirely due to the deteriorating performance of the OSS.

In 1998 the performance of the Ombudsman's office itself came under scrutiny in a study commissioned by the Ombudsman, and the OSS might perhaps have been forgiven for indulging in a wry smile at the results. Although most members of the public seeking information and advice were happy with the service, and so were most lawyers who had professional contact with the Ombudsman's office, the majority of complainants who had their cases formally investigated were dissatisfied. They complained that they were not kept informed, that the processes of dealing with cases were complex and over-lengthy, and the role of the Ombudsman's service was unclear.

The Ombudsman promised that improvements would be made, and has already produced clearer information leaflets explaining the role of the service, and established new systems to keep complainants informed of the progress of their cases. However, she suggested part of the blame must lie with the professions themselves, in that lawyers' failure to resolve complaints more effectively in the first place naturally led to delay and dissatisfaction once complainants reached the Ombudsman's service.

Action for negligence
Solicitors can also be sued for negligent work like most other professionals. Following the House of Lords judgment of **Arthur JS Hall & Co** *v* **Simons** (2000) solicitors no longer enjoy any immunity from liability for work connected to the conduct of a case in court.

Promotion to the judiciary

In the past, solicitors were only eligible to become circuit judges, but the Courts and Legal Services Act 1990 has opened the way for them to become judges in the higher courts (see chapter 3: The judiciary).

▌ Barristers

There are around 9,000 barristers in independent practice, known collectively as the Bar. Their governing body is the Bar Council, which, like the Law Society, acts as a kind of trade union, safeguarding the interests of barristers, and also as a watchdog, regulating barristers' training and activities.

Work

Advocacy is the main function of barristers, and much of their time will be spent in court or preparing for it. Until the changes made under the Courts and Legal Services Act in 1990, barristers were, with a few exceptions, the only people allowed to advocate in the superior courts – the House of Lords, the Court of Appeal, the High Court, the Crown Court and the Employment Appeal Tribunal. We have seen that this has now changed, and they are increasingly having to compete with solicitors for this work. Barristers also do some paperwork, drafting legal documents and giving written opinions on legal problems.

Barristers are usually engaged by a solicitor on behalf of a client, and work on what is called the 'cab rank' rule – technically, this means that if they are not already committed for the time in question, they must accept any case which falls within their claimed area of specialization and for which a reasonable fee is offered (in practice, barristers' clerks, who take their bookings, may manipulate the rule to ensure that barristers are able to avoid cases they do not want to take). Barristers may also be directly hired by certain professionals, such as accountants and, since 1996, by members of the public whose cases have been prepared by suitably trained Citizens' Advice Bureaux staff.

Barristers must be self-employed and, under Bar rules, cannot form partnerships, but they usually share offices, called chambers, with other barristers. All the barristers in a particular chambers share a clerk, who is a type of business manager, arranging meetings with the client and the solicitor and also negotiating the barristers' fees. Around 70 per cent of practising barristers are based in London chambers, though they may travel to courts in the provinces; the rest are based in the other big cities.

Not all qualified barristers work as advocates at the Bar. Like solicitors, some are employed by law centres and other advice agencies, Government departments or private industry, and some teach. Some go into these jobs after practising at the Bar for a time, others never practise at the Bar.

Qualifications and training

The starting point is (at least) an upper second class degree. If this degree is not in law, applicants must do the one-year course leading to the Common Professional Examination (the same course taken by would-be solicitors with degrees in subjects other than law). Mature students may be accepted without a degree, but applications are subject to very stringent consideration, and this is not a likely route to the Bar.

All students then have to join one of the four Inns of Court: Inner Temple; Middle Temple; Gray's Inn; and Lincoln's Inn, all of which are in London. The Inns of Court first emerged in the thirteenth century and their role has evolved over time. Their main functions now cover the provision of professional accommodation for barristers' chambers and residential accommodation for judges, discipline, the provision of law libraries and the promotion of collegiate activities.

Students take the year-long Bar Vocational Course: until 1996, this was only available at the Inns of Court School of Law in London, but can now be taken at seven different institutions around the country. The course includes oral exercises, and tuition in interviewing skills and nego-tiating skills, and, as with solicitors' training, more emphasis has been laid on these practical aspects in recent years. Only discretionary Local Education Authority grants are available for this year and the Common Professional Examination, and neither are covered by the Student Loan Scheme. The Inns of Court between them provide around £2 million in sponsorship. Approximately 25 per cent of students will receive assistance from their Inn, with about half of these obtaining a sum of between £3,000 and £6,000. Around 1,600 people take the Bar Vocational Course each year, and each one has to pay approximately £7,000 for the course alone, and then find living expenses on top.

Until recently, students also had to dine at their Inn 18 times (previ-ously 24 times). This rather old-fashioned and much-criticized custom stemmed from the idea that students would benefit from the wisdom and experience of their elders if they sat among them at mealtimes. In 1997, the Bar Council announced that the dining requirement would be re-duced to 12 occasions, and the dinners would be linked to seminars, lectures and training weekends, in order to provide genuine educational benefit.

After this, the applicant is called to the Bar, and must then find a place in a chambers to serve his or her pupillage. This is a one-year apprenticeship in which pupils assist a qualified barrister, who is known as their pupil master. Competition for pupillage places can be fierce, with each graduate from the Bar Vocational Course having only a 50 per cent chance of finding a pupillage, and this is aggravated by the fact that pupillage is usually done in two six-month blocks, with different pupil masters and usually in different chambers, so there are in effect two places to be found. Since 1992, pupils have been required to take a further advocacy course before the end of pupillage, as part of the increased emphasis on practical skills.

Around half the 900 pupils each year receive funding of £6,000 (sometimes more) for their 12-month pupillage from their chambers, but for the rest, finance can be a big problem unless their parents (or partners in the case of mature students) are able to help out. The Bar Council Scholarship Trust provides interest-free loans for pupils of up to £4,000, but this does not go far considering that as well as general living expenses, pupils need to find money for a wig and gown (costing in the region of £550), smart work clothes, books and travelling expenses. Pupils may take on cases in their second six months, but the fees for that work are generally not high, and are not paid until some time after the work is done. In **Edmonds** *v* **Lawson** (2000) the Court of Appeal ruled that pupils did not have a contract of employment, and that therefore they were not entitled to the minimum wage. The Bar Council recommends that pupils should earn at least £10,000 a year.

Pupillage completed, the newly qualified barrister must find a permanent place in a chambers, known as a tenancy. This can be the most difficult part, and some are forced to 'squat' – remaining in their pupillage chambers for as long as they are allowed, without becoming a full member – until they find a permanent place. There are only around 300 tenancies available each year – one to every three pupils.

After ten years in practice, a barrister may apply to become a Queen's Counsel, or QC (sometimes called a silk, as they wear gowns made of silk). This usually means they will be offered higher-paid cases, and need do less preliminary paperwork. They may apply several times before being accepted. Not all barristers attempt or manage to become QCs – those that do not are called juniors, even up to retirement age. Juniors may assist QCs in big cases, as well as working alone. Since 1995, solicitors can also be appointed as QCs, but in 2001, of the 77 new QCs only one was a solicitor and there are currently only five QCs who come from the solicitor profession.

In 1993, the Royal Commission on Criminal Justice recommended that barristers should have to undertake further training during the course of their careers, after noting that both preparation of cases and advocacy were failing to reach acceptable standards. In response, the Bar Council introduced the New Practitioners' Programme on 1 October 1997 for barristers in their first three years of independent practice. This was extended on 1 October 1998 to barristers entering employed practice with the intention of exercising rights of audience. These practitioners must complete a minimum of 42 hours of continuing education in the prescribed subjects by the end of their first three years of practice. The Programme is comprised of four components:

- Case Preparation and Procedure;
- Substantive Law or Training relating to Practice;
- Ethics; and
- Advocacy Training.

The Bar Council has also introduced in 2001 a continuing professional development scheme for established practitioners.

Complaints

Until recently barristers enjoyed an immunity from liability for negligent work in court. This immunity had been recognized by the courts in the case of **Rondel** *v* **Worsley** (1969). The main justification for the immunity was that a negligence action would effectively result in a retrial of the case that gave rise to the allegation of negligence, which would damage the certainty and finality of the original verdict. In other words, clients would seek to use litigation against their barrister to reopen indirectly litigation that had already been lost. This immunity was dramatically abolished by the House of Lords in **Arthur JS Hall & Co** *v* **Simons** (2000). There was no longer any good reason to treat barristers any differently from other professionals – their negligence could give rise to liability in tort.

In the past the only avenue for complaints was the Bar Council but, if upheld, these only resulted in disciplinary action against the barrister, giving no redress to the client. This situation was criticized by the Bar's own Standards Review Body in 1994. It recommended the establishment of a complaints body along the lines of the Solicitors Complaints Bureau, to be directed by a non-lawyer and to include non-lawyers among its staff. Its jurisdiction would include work done in court.

The proposal was rejected by the Bar Council, as being too expensive, too far removed from the Council and unlikely to command the respect of barristers. Instead, in April 1997, the Bar Council appointed its first Complaints Commissioner, who can require barristers to reduce, refund or waive fees and order compensation of up to £2,000. However, work done in court is not covered by the new system. In his 1997 annual report, the Legal Services Ombudsman Michael Barnes then praised the new system as a 'big step forward', but criticized the fact that work in court is not covered. However, in her 1999 annual report, the current

Legal Services Ombudsman, Ann Abraham, praises the Bar's complaints handling, commenting that 'a more modern and consumerist mentality is starting to prevail'.

The Ombudsman oversees the Bar's handling of complaints in the same way as with complaints about solicitors (see p. 126).

Promotion to the judiciary

Suitably experienced barristers are eligible for appointment to all judicial posts, and the majority of current judges have practised at the Bar (for details of appointments, see chapter 3: The judiciary).

Background of barristers and solicitors

The legal profession as a whole has traditionally come from a very narrow social background, in terms of class, race and sex; there are also significant barriers to entrants with disabilities. This is of course a problem in several other areas of professional life in Britain and, in the law as elsewhere, the main disadvantage of these barriers is that they prevent the profession from attracting the best minds that the country has to offer, many of whom will be found outside the ranks of middle-class, white, able-bodied males. However, there are further problems for the legal profession in this situation. First, the narrow social background of many lawyers means that the professions are seen as unapproachable and elitist, which can put off some people from using lawyers and thereby benefiting from their legal rights (this issue is examined in chapter 8). Secondly, the English judiciary is drawn from the legal professions and, if their background is narrow, that of the judiciary will be too (this issue is examined in chapter 3).

So how narrow is the background of the professions? As far as class is concerned, both law students and lawyers remain largely middle-class. A 1989 Law Society Survey found that over a third of solicitors had come from fee-paying schools, despite the fact that only 7 per cent of the population attend such schools.

Part of the reason for this has been the lack of funding for legal training, which has made it very difficult for students without well-off parents to qualify, especially as barristers. In recent years the difficulties have worsened, as shortage of funds has meant that Local Education Authorities (LEAs) have become more reluctant to award discretionary grants even to cover fees, let alone for living expenses. A survey by the Law Society in 1992 found that of the 102 LEAs who replied, only six would consider giving discretionary grants to students on the CPE course, and 57 to students on the Legal Practice Course. Even these did not undertake to give grants to everyone who applied, and where grants were given, they rarely covered more than a percentage of tuition fees – a grant of

£749 towards tuition fees of £3,500 was typical. Maintenance grants were given in exceptional circumstances, but again, would usually only cover a percentage of living expenses.

One possible source of change for the future is the number of part-time law courses now available to mature students, who tend to come from a much broader range of backgrounds than those who attend university straight from school, and can support themselves by continuing to work while they study in the evenings and at weekends. Several universities around the country offer part-time law degrees, and the Legal Practice Course can also be studied part-time, over two years. In 1997, the Open University announced it would be offering a law degree, a development welcomed by the Lord Chancellor, who said it would help the profession attract a wider variety of people.

When it comes to race, the picture is not particularly bright. In 1989, ethnic minorities formed 5 per cent of the Bar, which it believes compares favourably with other professions, but were badly represented at the upper end of the profession, with only a handful of QCs. The proportions are slightly better among solicitors, yet white Europeans still comprised 81 per cent of the students enrolling with the Law Society in 1989–90.

Both the Law Society and the Bar Council have announced they are taking steps to prevent racial discrimination, but the success or otherwise of this may be seen by the regular news stories of black candidates doing less well in legal examinations than whites, particularly at the Bar, where it is suggested that oral examinations may be particularly vulnerable to subjective marking. There are also reports that black candidates find it very difficult to obtain training contracts, pupillage places and tenancies.

The area showing most change is that of sex. Although women still make up just 24 per cent of practising barristers and 31 per cent of practising solicitors, their presence is rapidly growing. The number of women solicitors has increased by 188 per cent since 1986; the number of women barristers by 49 per cent in the past four years; and among new entrants, there are now approximately equal numbers of men and women: in 1998 51 per cent of new solicitors were women, and 46 per cent of new barristers. But these figures do not tell the whole story. First, despite the fact that there are more women achieving first and upper second class law degrees than men, in 1998 the Law Society's Annual Statistical Survey found that new female entrants were earning on average 4.4 per cent less then new male entrants. Secondly, when it comes to the numbers of women staying in the professions, and the careers they make there, an even bigger divide between the sexes opens up. As of July 1998, only 33 per cent of practising solicitors were women, and 25 per cent of practising barristers, suggesting that a significant proportion of women entrants leave the profession early, either because they find it impossible to combine the demands of motherhood with a legal career or because they are frustrated at the 'glass ceiling' which seems to prevent women lawyers from achieving the same success as their male counterparts. Those that stay behind are significantly less likely to rise to high positions, and will, on average, earn less than male lawyers. A 1994 report by the Lord Chancellor's Department, called (presumably ironically) *Without Prejudice*, found that women lawyers were discriminated against at every stage of their careers. In both branches, women tended to earn less than men, and men tended to reach higher positions within their field than women. A 1996 survey by the Law Society found that differences in pay ranged from an average of £3,000 between male and female assistant solicitors, to as much as £15,000 between men and women at partner level in solicitors' firms. Only 25 per cent of women solicitors are at partner level, a proportion that has remained static for the last decade, despite an enormous rise in the number of women joining the profession. At the Bar, only five out of the 68 new QCs in 1997 were women.

In 1993, the Association of Women Solicitors set up a helpline for women who have been discriminated against for becoming pregnant. Judith Willis, who runs it, has told newspapers that some law firms force out women who become pregnant, by making them redundant, suggesting that their work is no longer up to standard, or merely making life very difficult for those who try to return to work after having a baby, despite the fact that such discrimination is illegal. The helpline has even been told of four cases in which firms suggested pregnant employees should have abortions, including one where the firm offered to pay for the termination. The legal professions are of course not alone in these practices and attitudes; women face discrimination in all kinds of professions and businesses. It is however particularly alarming to discover that those involved in administering the law should be so willing to flout it.

In recent years, both branches of the profession have taken steps to remedy this problem. The Law Society requires all solicitors' firms to have an anti-discrimination policy, and rules with which to implement it, while the Bar's Code of Conduct contains provisions designed to prevent sex discrimination by barristers, particularly in relation to pupillage. However, a major difficulty with such provisions is that women may be reluctant to bring complaints, and possibly harm their career prospects by being seen to 'rock the boat' – not a particularly surprising attitude given, for example, the comments made in 1997 by the then President of the Law Society Martin Mears, that prejudice against women was a 'fiction', and that it was men who needed protection from complaining 'zealots'.

Much attention has been paid to the under-representation of working-class people, ethnic minorities and women in the legal profession – though often with little effect – but disabled people are less often discussed. Skill as a lawyer requires brains, not physical strength or dexterity, yet it seems there are still significant barriers to entry for disabled students, particularly to the Bar. Part of the problem is simply practical: a quarter of court buildings are over 100 years old and were never designed to offer disabled access. Most now have rooms adapted for disabled people, but need notice if they are to be used, which is hardly feasible for junior barristers who often get cases at very short notice. The other main barrier is effectively the same as that for ethnic minorities, working-class people and women: with fierce competition for places, 'traditional' applicants have the advantage.

However, steps are being taken to address the problems of disabled applicants to the Bar. In 1992, Recorder Gary Flather QC set up the Bar's Disability Panel, which helps people with illnesses of all kinds. Help is offered both to those already within the profession and those hoping to enter it, by matching them to people who have overcome or managed to accommodate similar problems. The Inner Temple also gives grants for reading devices, special furniture and other aids, with the aim of creating a level playing field for disabled and able-bodied people.

Performance of the legal professions

Over the past 20 years, the performance of lawyers has come in for a great deal of criticism. The last good report was given by the 1979 Royal Commission on Legal Services, which found that 84 per cent of clients were satisfied with the work done by their lawyers, and only 13 per cent were actually dissatisfied. The Commission interpreted this as a vote of confidence for the profession, but as Zander (1988) pointed out, the research was not entirely reliable, since ordinary individuals are unlikely to have sufficient knowledge or experience to make informed judgments about the service they received – they might recognize very bad legal work, but were unlikely to know whether they had received the best advice or help for their situation. Significantly, a similar survey among corporate clients, who use lawyers more frequently, reported a higher level of dissatisfaction.

Since the 1979 Royal Commission, many different criticisms of the profession have been made, from many different quarters. In 1984, solicitor Michael Joseph wrote a book called *Lawyers Can Seriously Damage your Health*, describing in detail three personal injury cases, and revealing gross incompetence on the part of both solicitors and barristers. The book was a follow-up to an earlier work by Mr Joseph, which denounced conveyancing as a racket in which solicitors are paid hefty fees for work which housebuyers could do as well, and often better, themselves. Twelve years later, little seemed to have changed in that area: a 1996 report from the Council of Mortgage Lenders said that slapdash solicitors were responsible for the majority of compensation claims made for poor conveyancing work, and that most of the mistakes were caused by simple carelessness rather than misunderstanding complex issues.

Barristers and solicitors involved in criminal work were criticized by the 1993 Royal Commission on Criminal Justice, which found that defence cases were frequently inadequately prepared, often because the work was delegated to clerks and not properly supervised. Advocacy standards were also low, on the part of both barristers and solicitors, and the Commission suggested that inadequate training might be the reason for this; they particularly criticized the practice of allowing pupil barristers to take on cases during their second six months, and the lack of detailed assessment of pupils' experience during this time. They recognized that both branches of the profession were already increasing advocacy training, but suggested that more work might be needed.

The Commission also noted that lawyers frequently failed to advise convicted defendants about their appeal rights. Some 9 per cent of defendants surveyed had not been visited by their lawyer after the end of the case, while 23 per cent had had a visit, but no mention was made of the possibility of appeal. Of those lawyers who did mention appeal rights to their clients, many seriously misunderstood the powers of the Court of Appeal. These problems were partly felt to be due to defects in the guidance documents provided by the Court of Appeal, the Law Society and the Bar Council, but the Commission stated that bad practice by lawyers had also played a part.

In 1995, the Consumers' Association magazine *Which?* caused a stir with a survey of the standards of advice provided by solicitors. Its researchers phoned a number of solicitors, posing as members of the public seeking advice about simple consumer problems, and the advice given was assessed by the Association's own legal team. The verdict was not good, with much of the advice given being assessed as inadequate or simply wrong. Two years later, the magazine repeated the test and, once again, the results were bad: of the 79 solicitors approached by researchers, the majority gave advice which was incomplete, or in some cases incorrect. In several cases, researchers were incorrectly told that their situation gave them no claim in law; the magazine points out that real-life clients told this would probably not pursue the matter further and would therefore not take advantage of their full legal rights. *Which?* accepted that lawyers cannot be expected to be experts in every area of law, but argued that if asked something outside their area of expertise, they should admit that and either find out the answer or refer the client to someone else. The Law Society criticized both surveys, arguing that the methods employed were not realistic; and after complaints about the first survey, *Which?* admitted that its allegations against one firm had proved to be wrong.

The number of complaints made about lawyers continues to rise, according to the 1999 annual report from the Legal Services Ombudsman. It says that during 1998, one complaint was made for every 18 practising barristers, and a staggering one complaint for every 2.4 solicitors. Figures from the OSS seem to suggest that the problem is not spread throughout its branch of the profession however; it claims 80 per cent of complaints made to the OSS concern the same 950 firms, out of the 8,500 in practice.

Further criticism of solicitors' performance was made in a *Dispatches* television programme shown in December 1998, which revealed that many solicitors were being allowed to continue in practice after serious breaches of the professional rules. The programme analysed the findings of 200 cases before the Solicitors' Disciplinary Tribunal: 39 per cent of the cases involved misuse of clients' money, yet less than half the solicitors were struck off as a result of the breach.

A survey undertaken for the Law Society in 2001 found that the public perceive lawyers as formal, expensive and predatory. It may be that they are now being accused of being predatory because of the intensive television advertising by companies who pass work on to solicitors.

One of the most common areas for complaint is costs. The Law Society's Written Practice Standard requires solicitors to give clients written information about all aspects of financing their case, including how the fee is calculated, arrangements for payment and liability for the other side's costs. However, a 1995 report by the National Association of Citizens' Advice Bureaux (NACAB), *Barriers to Justice*, concluded that few clients actually received clear information about costs, and that this was part of the reason why fees were so often the cause of complaints. NACAB recommended that solicitors should have to agree with clients a timetable for regular updates on costs, confirm the arrangement in writing and provide leaflets giving information about costs.

Costs at the Bar have also been the subject of considerable criticism and, in particular, the fees charged by what the press have called 'super silks' – QCs whose annual earnings can top £1 million. As a result of this criticism, the House of Lords looked into the issue, and reported in October 1998 that the fees being charged in some cases were excessive. The report accused barristers' clerks of 'deliberately pitching fees at a very high level' (a conclusion which was not all that surprising since securing the best possible fee for his or her barrister is part of a clerk's job). The report called on the Lord Chancellor to give clear guidance on what should be considered a reasonable fee for a QC. The report was welcomed by the Legal Action Group, which said that the excessively high fees charged by some QCs were undermining public confidence in the legal system. It claimed that the QC system had only one function: to ensure that senior barristers could increase their earnings substantially. As such, it said, the system was a restrictive practice, of the kind which the Government had promised to wipe out in its general shake-up of the legal system, and it should be abolished. In 1999, the Law Society called for the abolition of QCs. However, in his address to the annual QC ceremony in 1999, the Lord Chancellor defended the QC system as a mark of quality and a means for customers to make informed choices about the lawyers who act for them.

Anti-competitive practices

The Office of Fair Trading (OFT) has issued a report *Competition in the Professions* (2001) which looks primarily at the restrictive practices in the legal profession. Barristers and solicitors are criticized as imposing unjustified restrictions on competition in the legal profession. The report makes wide-ranging criticisms and recommendations. It proposes that the rules of the different professional bodies preventing or hindering the establishment of multi-disciplinary partnerships should be relaxed to bring together accountants, lawyers and other professionals such as surveyors and estate agents. It questions whether the professional regulations preventing barristers forming partnerships with each other is necessary. The OFT believes that restrictions on barristers having direct access to clients restricts their ability to compete with each other and solicitors and 'requires customers to employ two types of lawyer where one might do'. At the moment solicitors in private employment are only allowed to represent their employers. The OFT suggests that this restriction should be removed 'to allow solicitors working in different business structures to compete on a broader front'. It considers that the position of Queen's Counsel should be abolished as it questions the operation of the system as a quality mark, and thought it offered no benefits to the consumer.

Most of these anti-competitive practices are the product of professional regulations rather than legislation. The OFT urges the professions to take prompt action to remove those anti-competitive practices which do not have a proper justification. Failing readiness to take such action within 12 months, the OFT warns that it will 'use its available powers with a view to removal of those restrictions'. The Secretary of State for Trade and Industry has stated that the Government accepts the recommendation that the professions should be subject to competition law.

Professor Zander (2001) has criticized the report, stating:

> What is deplorable about these developments is the simplistic belief that equating the work done by professional people to business will necessarily improve the position of the consumer, when the reality is that sometimes it may rather worsen it. Certainly one wants competition to ensure that professional fees are no higher than they need to be and that the professional rules did not unnecessarily inhibit efficiency. But what one looks for from the professions even more is standards, integrity and concern for the client of a higher order than that offered in the business world. To damage those even more important values in the name of value for the consumer in purely economic terms may be to throw out the baby with the bath water.

Do we need legal professionals?

In many areas, non-legally qualified people do the work of lawyers as well as professionals could, and sometimes more effectively – an obvious example is the large number of volunteer and employed lay advisers in the Citizens' Advice Bureaux who provide an accessible, economic and uncomplicated service to deal with legal and other queries. Legal executives often become so well-experienced in particular areas that they need no supervision from their legally qualified colleagues, and take on much of the work that the general public assumes only solicitors can do. Some work may even be better done by clients themselves, as Joseph's study of conveyancing seemed to show. So why should we need a profession (or two), and why should that profession be allowed sole access to certain types of work?

There are many reasons why a legal profession might be considered desirable, but two broad theories shed some interesting light on the reasons why we maintain it. The first, functionalism, emphasizes the importance of keeping society together, and it sees one important way of doing this as maintaining the status quo, keeping the structure of society the same.

Functionalists believe professions in general contribute to this process. They say those within a profession will share certain values, put public service before profit, and use expert knowledge for the good of society – the implication is that professionals have higher moral standards than ordinary people. They are supposed to believe in 'public service' and 'shared professional ethics', while plumbers, car manufacturers and shopkeepers, for example, are only interested in money. This is used to justify the fact that they are the only people to have access to certain types of work. It is difficult to reconcile this view with the fact that many lawyers compete to work for the big legal firms, working for the most powerful members of society – not because the work is interesting or socially useful, but because it pays so well.

A second theory, that of market control, has a very different view of the role played by professionals. It takes as its starting point the market place, where different suppliers compete with each other to get consumers to buy their goods and services. Economic theory reasons that at any given level of quality, consumers will choose the cheapest goods or services, so those offering good quality services cheaply will sell a lot, and the rest will go bust.

This may be good news for consumers, but tough for producers, who must be constantly striving to provide a better product for less money, while looking over their shoulder to make sure that someone else is not providing it cheaper or better than they can. Consequently, producers try to get round this competitive situation, and they can do so in a number of different ways – by forming monopolies and cartels, or by controlling the raw materials or the patents to a manufacturing process, for example.

Market control theory suggests that having professions is just one of those ways of escaping uncontrolled competition. Professions restrict access to their market by controlling who enters the profession, saying that only those with complicated qualifications can offer services in this area;

they control the way in which professionals offer their services, for example by stopping members of the profession using aggressive advertising to compete with each other; and they keep their own special area of expertise as complex and as obscure as they can.

One of the leading proponents of this point of view is Richard Abel, Professor of Law at the University of California. His book on the legal profession in England and Wales describes in great detail how solicitors and barristers have controlled who become lawyers, how they operate and what they sell. He suggests that they have done this in their own interests, to keep the price of legal services high. A recent example of this process is that during the difficult economic situation at the end of the 1980s, when there was increased competition for jobs, the Bar Council raised its entry requirement for initial training from a second class to an upper second class degree. Similarly, Abel has shown that the pass rate in Law Society exams goes up when there is a shortage of jobs, and down when there is a shortage of recruits.

Moves towards fusion?

The divided legal profession dates from the nineteenth century, when the Bar agreed to give all conveyancing work and all direct access to clients to the solicitors, in return for sole rights of audience in the higher courts and the sole rights to become senior judges for barristers. However, since the late 1960s, there have been a series of moves towards breaking down the division.

1969. In its submission to the Royal Commission on Assizes and Quarter Sessions, the Law Society argued for rights of audience in the Crown Court, but the Commission's report (the Beeching report) recommended only that solicitors should be allowed to advocate in areas where there were insufficient numbers of barristers. The Lord Chancellor was given powers to allow solicitors extended rights of audience in such circumstances.

1972. A Practice Direction from the Lord Chancellor's Department stated that solicitors could appear in appeals or committals for sentencing from the magistrates' to the Crown Court, where they had appeared for that client in the magistrates' court.

1979. The Law Society lobbied the Royal Commission on Legal Services for Crown Court rights of audience in either way offences, and for limited rights in the High Court. The Bar Council opposed the proposals, and the Commission recommended no change in rights of audience – though its decision was made only by an eight to seven majority. Complete fusion was unanimously rejected.

1985. In **Abse** v **Smith**, the then MP Cyril Smith challenged a judge's ruling that his solicitor could not read out a seven-line statement in the

High Court. The judge's ruling was upheld, but later a Practice Direction from the Lord Chancellor's Department permitted solicitors to appear in the Supreme Court in formal or unopposed proceedings, and when judgment is given in open court.

1986. The Law Society document *Lawyers and the Courts: Time for Some Changes* proposed that all lawyers should undergo the same training, work two or three years in 'general practice', and then choose to go on to train as barristers if they wanted to and were competent – rather as doctors choose, after preliminary training, to become GPs or to specialize and train further. While in 'general practice', lawyers would have rights of audience in the lower courts and tribunals; after that three years, they would be under no restrictions other than to act within their competence, and the Bar would therefore become a body of specialist advocates. The Bar Council's response to the document rejected this idea.

In the same year, the Legal Aid Scrutiny Report suggested allowing solicitors to appear for guilty pleas in the Crown Court. It estimated that this would save the Legal Aid fund around £1 million a year.

1987. The Government's White Paper on Legal Aid rejected the Scrutiny Report's proposal.

1988. The Marre Committee was set up by the Bar Council and the Law Society to look, among other things, at whether any changes were needed in the structure of the profession. It largely advocated maintaining the status quo, but did recommend that rights of audience in the Crown Court be extended to solicitors recommended by a Rights of Audience Board, and that barristers should be allowed to take instructions directly from professions other than solicitors.

1990. The Courts and Legal Services Act made the following provisions.

- Direct access to barristers by certain professional clients.
- Access to the higher levels of the judiciary for solicitors.
- Multi-disciplinary partnerships to be allowed, subject to the agreement of the professions' ruling bodies. Traditionally neither solicitors nor barristers were allowed to form partnerships with members of other professions; the Act provides that there should be no legal obstacle to them doing so, but that there was equally nothing to stop the Law Society and/or the Bar Council making their own rules to prevent such partnerships. So far neither branch has relaxed its rules, and multi-disciplinary partnerships are still not allowed – the Bar is particularly opposed to the idea.
- Rights of audience in all courts should be extended to 'suitably qualified' persons, not necessarily barristers or solicitors. The Act did not itself define 'suitably qualified'; applications by professional groups to be recognized as such were considered by the Lord Chancellor's Advisory Committee, and then had to be approved by the Lord Chancellor and four judges. The Act stated that the general objective

was that there should be a wider choice of people providing legal services, and that rights of audience and litigation should only be determined by reference to education, training and membership of a professional body with an effective set of rules.

1992. The Committee recommended that experienced solicitors should be given extended rights of audience after a short training course. They would then be given an advocacy certificate, allowing them to appear for either party in the High Court, and for the defence in the Crown Court. The certificate would be renewed each year, providing a specified number of hours had been spent in court. Solicitors holding advocacy certificates would be required to work on an equivalent basis to the Bar's cab rank rule. The recommendations excluded solicitors employed in industry and other organizations, on the ground that they were not sufficiently independent, and members of the Crown Prosecution Service, partly because its performance suggested it was not ready for added responsibility, and partly to avoid the danger of creating a 'monolithic' state prosecution service taking all prosecution work.

1996. The Bar Council announced a relaxation of the rules on access to barristers, allowing suitably trained Citizens' Advice Bureaux staff to prepare a case for a barrister on behalf of a member of the public, without involving a solicitor. The new rules apply to both legally aided and privately funded clients.

1997. The Lord Chancellor's Advisory Committee extended the opportunity to apply for rights of audience in the higher courts to solicitors employed in industry and other organizations (as opposed to law firms), subject to a number of restrictions. These are that employed solicitors will not be allowed to appear for the prosecution in criminal proceedings committed for trial in the Crown Court (though they can appear in Plea and Directions hearings and other preliminary procedures), nor in any civil proceedings in the higher courts (meaning above the county courts) where the hearing is intended to dispose partly or completely of the merits of the case, nor for local authorities in care proceedings.

1998. The Lord Chancellor presented his report, *Modernising Justice*, to Parliament. In it he said that the rules on rights of audience were still too restrictive, and pointed out that the CLSA had failed to deliver a sufficiently wide choice of legal service providers. He announced plans to ensure that, in principle, all barristers and solicitors should be able to appear in any court.

1999. These plans were put into practice in the Access to Justice Act, which replaces the Lord Chancellor's Advisory Committee on legal education and conduct with the new Legal Services Consultative Panel, which takes over the role of regulating rights of audience. The procedure for approving changes to the rules on rights of audience is simplified and the Lord Chancellor has a new power, subject to parliamentary approval, to change rules which are unduly restrictive. This last power is designed to ensure that the legal professions themselves cannot cling on to restrictive rules and prevent reform. All barristers and solicitors now acquire full rights of audience on call to the Bar or admission to the roll, though they are only able to exercise them by successfully completing the necessary training.

By December 1998, around 600 solicitors had qualified to gain rights of audience in the higher courts. Considering the size of the profession, this is a surprisingly small number, and many of these qualified because they had previously been barristers, rather than through the course run by the Law Society. There seems to be several reasons for this. The failure rate for the qualifying exams is high – only 29 per cent of 1995 candidates for the civil evidence and procedure test passed. In addition, going through the three-stage qualification procedure costs around £3,000, and it is difficult for many commercial solicitors to fulfil the requirement for two years' advocacy experience in the magistrates' and county courts. Following the Access to Justice Act 1999, solicitors automatically have rights of audience, but they still have to undertake training in order to exercise these rights. It is likely that an increasing number of solicitors will undertake this training.

Even for those who do qualify to exercise their rights of audience, winning acceptance appears to be a different story. In one case, when an unrepresented defendant appeared at Sheffield Crown Court, the circuit judge attempted to find a barrister to take on the case, but on being informed that a solicitor advocate was present in court, commented 'We don't need to stoop that low, do we?' After a complaint to the presiding circuit judge, he apologized in open court. Some solicitors who have gained rights of audience have said they are unwilling to use them, particularly in the High Court, for fear that judges' bias against solicitor advocates may prejudice the chances of the clients they represent.

The future

The moves described above, and especially the changes made by the CLSA, led to much discussion about whether the professions would eventually fuse. At the time when the CLSA was passed, it was thought that it might be the first step in Government plans to fuse the two professions by legislation. Until 1985, the two branches had been largely left alone to divide work between themselves, and had made their own arrangements for this; the abolition of solicitors' monopoly on conveyancing was the first major Government interference in this situation, and the CLSA was obviously a much bigger step towards regulation by Government rather than the professions themselves. Even if the Government did not force fusion, it was suggested, it could happen anyway if large numbers of solicitors took up rights of audience. Since solicitors have sole rights to initial contact with most clients, those who had advocacy certificates would be unlikely to pass cases on to barristers, and so the Bar would eventually wither and die.

Alternatively, it was suggested, the Bar might survive, but in a much reduced form, and there was much debate about which areas would suffer most. Barristers generally fall into two groups: those who specialize in commercial fields, such as company law, tax and patents; and those who have what is called a common law practice, which means that they deal with a fairly wide range of common legal issues, such as crime, housing and family law. Some legal experts believed that commercial lawyers would be most likely to survive, since they have a specialist knowledge that solicitors cannot provide. However, for several years now, solicitors in city firms have been becoming more specialist themselves, and if able to combine specialist knowledge with rights of audience, they would clearly be a threat to the commercial Bar. In addition, such firms offer high incomes, without the insecurity of self-employment at the Bar, and therefore they are able to attract first-rate students who once would have automatically been attracted to the more prestigious Bar. As these entrants work their way up through law firms, the Bar's traditional claim to offer the best expertise in high-level legal analysis will be difficult to sustain.

Others suggested that common law barristers had a better chance of surviving competition from solicitors. They cater for the needs of the ordinary high street solicitor, who generally has a wide-ranging practice, and spends much of his or her time seeing clients and gathering case information. This leaves little opportunity to swot up on the finer details of every area of law with which clients need help, so where specialist legal analysis is needed, they refer the client to a barrister with experience in the relevant area.

In practice, these fears have not been confirmed. Over the last ten years, the size of the Bar has increased from around 5,500 to around 8,500. The commercial Bar is unlikely to be seriously threatened in the near future, given the difficulty of city solicitors gaining sufficient advocacy experience. As far as common law barristers are concerned, even if the high street solicitors who refer most of their clients were to take up the opportunity to advocate in the higher courts in greater numbers, they would still be likely to use barristers to advocate in cases requiring detailed legal argument and specialized knowledge. In addition to advocacy, high street solicitors often use common law barristers as a source of specialized legal advice, and there seems to be no reason why extending rights of audience should alter this practice.

The Inns of Court (discussed on p. 127) set up a Working Party on the future of the Inns of Court which reported in 2000. The aim of the

Working Party was to review the impact of the Access to Justice Act 1999, which has made it easier for more solicitors and employed barristers to qualify to appear in the higher courts. It recommended that membership of the Inns should be offered to solicitors entitled to appear in the higher courts, on payment of an entrance fee of £1,000. The report warns that if the Inns cease to be of relevance to the profession they run the risk of decline. The Inns are financially dependent on rents from their properties, which are priced at the very top of the market. If the Bar does decline in numbers – as many predict – they could well find themselves left with property they cannot let at rents no one wants to pay. One of the greatest threats to the future of the Bar is the fact that employed lawyers rights of audience have increased. Much of the work that the Bar currently gets from the Crown Prosecution Service in particular is likely to disappear as the advocacy will be done 'in-house'.

The President of the Law Society, Mr Robert Sayer, tried to rekindle the debate over fusion in his speech at the annual solicitor's conference in 1999 that was held at Disneyland. He suggested that within 5 years there would be an all-embracing, unified profession which would include the current professions of solicitors, legal executives, licensed conveyancers and barristers. They would form part of the single profession of 'lawyers' who would be represented and regulated by the Law Society. The Bar Council immediately condemned this idea as a 'Mickey Mouse policy dreamt up in Disneyland'. Fusion is, thus, still possible, and below we look at some of the arguments for and against.

Arguments for fusion of the professions

Expense

With the divided profession a client often has to pay both a solicitor and a barrister, sometimes a solicitor and two barristers, and as Michael Zander puts it 'To have one taxi meter running is less expensive than to have two or three.' However, the Bar Council prepared a report called *The economic case for the Bar. A comparison of the costs of barristers and solicitors* (2000). This paper claimed that it was generally more economical to employ the services of a barrister, particularly a junior, for work within his or her area of expertise than to use a solicitor. In broad terms it stated that the differences in charge-out rates make it from 25 per cent to 50 per cent cheaper to employ the services of a junior barrister than an assistant solicitor in London. A major factor is that barristers' overheads are approximately half those of solicitors. However, the paper is misleading, as without direct access to clients for barristers it is not an either/or situation. The reality is that a client does not pay for either a solicitor or a barrister, but if they employ a barrister they must pay for both, along with the cost of the solicitor preparing the papers for the barrister.

Inefficiency

A two-tier system means work may be duplicated unnecessarily, and the solicitor prepares the case with little or no input from the barrister who will have to argue it in court. Barristers are often selected and instructed at the last moment – research by Bottoms and McLean in Sheffield revealed that in 96 per cent of cases where the plea was guilty, and 79 per cent where it was not guilty, clients saw their barrister for the first time on the morning of the trial. In this situation important points may be passed over or misunderstood.

Waste of talent

Prospective lawyers must decide very early on which branch of the profession they wish to enter, and if, having chosen to be a solicitor, the lawyer later discovers a talent for advocacy, they may be denied the chance to use it to the full.

Other countries

All common law countries have bodies of specialist advocates, and possibly need them, but no other country divides its legal profession in two as England does.

Arguments against fusion

Specialization

Two professions can each do their different jobs better than one profession doing both.

Independence

The Bar has traditionally argued that its cab rank principle guarantees this, ensuring that no defendant, however heinous the charges, goes undefended; and that no individual should lack representation because of the wealth or power of the opponent. The fact that barristers operate independently, rather than in partnerships, also contributes. However, the Courts and Legal Services Act does provide for solicitors with advocacy certificates to operate on a cab rank basis, which has somewhat weakened the Bar's argument. In addition, successful barristers do get round the cab rank rule in practice.

Importance of good advocacy

Our adversarial system means that the presentation of oral evidence is important; judges have no investigative powers and must rely on the lawyers to present the case properly.

The 1979 Royal Commission suggested that fusion would lead to a fall in the quality of the advocacy, arguing that although many solicitors were competent to advocate in the magistrates' and county courts, arguing before a jury required different skills and greater expertise, and if rights were extended it was unlikely that many solicitors would get sufficient practice to develop these.

The Bar Council's submission to the Lord Chancellor's Advisory Committee recommended that solicitors would need several months of training to appear in the Crown Court; this too was rejected.

Access to the Bar

Critics of moves towards fusion argued that it may result in many leading barristers joining the large firms of commercial solicitors, so making their specialist skills less accessible to the average person. Smaller practices might generate insufficient business to justify partnership with a barrister and find it difficult to secure a barrister of equal standing to the opponent's; they would be reluctant to refer a client to a large firm, for fear of losing them permanently. A major drift towards large firms could worsen the already uneven distribution of solicitors throughout the country.

The judiciary

A reduction in the number of specialist advocates might make it more difficult for the Lord Chancellor to make suitable appointments to the Bench; although the potential candidates would increase, they would not be as well known to the Lord Chancellor and his senior advisers. On the other hand this might eventually mean appointments would have to be made on a more open, regulated system, and from a wider social base.

Use of court time

Court cases are not given a fixed time, only a date; depending on the progress of previous cases they may appear at any time during a morning or afternoon session, or be held over until another day – the idea behind this is that the clients and their lawyers should wait for courts, rather than the other way round. It has been suggested that barristers are best organized for this, though there seems no reason why, within a united profession, those lawyers who specialize in court work could not organize themselves accordingly.

Other proposals for reform

Wider opportunities

The Charter 88 constitutional reform pressure group has argued that students should be funded throughout their legal training, so helping to open up the profession to the most able candidates, from a wide variety of backgrounds, regardless of means.

The Law Society and the Bar have established a working group studying funding pressures, and representations have been made to the Department of Education, pointing out that training for other professions such as medicine and teaching is paid, and that limiting funding is likely to further narrow the social background of the profession, but so far with no success. One interesting way round the problem is the four-year law degree offered by the University of Northumbria, which incorporates the Legal Practice Course within it: as an undergraduate course, it is eligible for the mandatory grant. However the Law Society do not see widespread adoption of this plan as either likely, or an adequate answer to the problem.

In her book *Eve was Framed*, Helena Kennedy QC argues that selection for the Bar in particular has always been based too much on 'connections' and financial resources rather than on ability, with both pupillages and scholarships too often given to a narrow class of applicant. As well as recommending public funding for legal education, she suggests that grants for pupillage should be centrally distributed by the Bar, rather than the Inns and chambers, and there should be incentives for chambers to take on less conventional candidates. Selection and scholarship-awarding committees throughout both professions should include women and members of the ethnic minorities.

Better training

Michael Zander argues that both the academic and the vocational stages of training could be improved, with a consequent rise in professional standards. Law degrees should include at least preliminary training in areas such as drafting documents and developing interviewing skills. Both pupillage and training contracts can be 'infinitely variable' in quality, according to Zander, 'ranging from excellent to deplorable' depending on where they are undertaken. He suggests a more integrated training is needed, like that undertaken by medical students, with better links between academic and vocational stages, and cites the Ormrod Committee's suggestion that articles be abolished and replaced with a fully developed practical skills course, followed by three years' supervised practice after qualification. The Lord Chancellor's Advisory Committee on Legal Education (ACLEC) examined the whole issue of legal training. Its 1996 report suggested that the two branches should no longer have completely separate training programmes at the post-graduate stage. Instead, after either a law degree or a degree in another subject plus the CPE, all students would take a Professional Legal Studies course, lasting around 18 weeks. Only then would they decide which branch of the profession to choose, going on to a Legal Practice Course (for solicitors) or Bar Vocational Course (for barristers) which would be 15–18 weeks long. This, ACLEC suggested, would prevent the problem of students having to specialize too early. ACLEC also recommends that funding should be made available for the

CPE course and the vocational stage of training, and that all lawyers should be obliged to take part in further training throughout their careers.

The Law Society has suggested a form of 'general practice' training (see p. 142).

Other legal personnel

Legal executives

Most firms of solicitors employ legal executives, who do much of the same basic work as solicitors (except advocacy). Their qualifications are supervised by the Institute of Legal Executives. Only about 600 people qualify each year as legal executives, with many people failing to complete their education. Although technically they are under the supervision of their employers, in practice many experienced executives specialize in particular areas – such as conveyancing – and take almost sole charge of that area. From the firm's point of view, they are obviously a cheaper option than solicitors for getting this work done, and in many cases will be more experienced in their particular area than a solicitor. However, clients are usually unaware that when they pay for a solicitor, they may be receiving the services of a legal executive.

Following the Courts and Legal Services Act 1990 and the Access to Justice Act 1999, the Institute of Legal Executives is now able to grant its members the rights to conduct litigation on the completion of suitable training. The first six legal executives qualified as advocates in the year 2000 and now have extended rights of audience in civil and matrimonial proceedings in the county court and magistrates' courts.

Legal executives are generally less well paid than solicitors. A survey carried out by the Institute of Legal Executives in 2001 found that a third of legal executives earned between £15,000 and £21,000, while 11 per cent earned over £27,000.

Licensed conveyancers

The Courts and Legal Services Act 1990 abolished the solicitor's monopoly of conveyancing and paved the way for a new profession, licensed conveyancers. As their name suggests, these professionals are purely involved in conveyancing and are increasingly being used by people buying and selling a home.

ANSWERING QUESTIONS

1 Do you consider that the current system of legal education and training can provide the lawyers that this country needs?

The first thing to note about this question is that it is not asking what the present system of legal eduction and training is; it wants to know how well that system performs. You do need to show that you are aware of the system, but a detailed description of it will waste time and gain few marks.

Your introduction should point out what you understand by the term lawyers – we suggest that you concentrate on barristers and solicitors in your answer, even though technically judges are also lawyers. Then you need to state what you think are the qualities this country needs in its lawyers – you might mention legal knowledge and practical skills, efficiency, cost-effectiveness, and an ability to use its skills for the benefit of all the members of society, for example.

You can then go on to outline the system of legal education and training but **keep it brief**! There is no point in writing pages of detailed description, because that is not what the question asks for. You need to point out that training for barristers and solicitors is different, and then just mention the stages for each.

The main part of your essay should be concerned with assessing whether the system provides the qualities you have mentioned in your introduction, and we suggest you consider them in turn. The following are points you might like to make:

- the need for legal knowledge and practical skills. You could mention the various criticisms of lawyers' performances, and point out that both professions are moving towards a more practical approach.
- the need for a cost-effective, efficient service. Here you might mention some of the disadvantages of the fact that we train two different types of lawyers to play two different roles – the criticisms of the divided profession in terms of cost and inefficiency are relevant here. You could also put forward the argument that a divided profession is wasteful of talent, especially as it divides so early on.
- the need for lawyers to be accessible to all members of the community. Here you will need to use some of the material on unmet legal need from chapter 8, pointing out that the middle-class image of solicitors puts many people off using them, especially for problems such as social security and employment. You can then point out that the system of training contributes directly to this problem, because it is so difficult for a student without well-off parents to survive financially during training, and so the profession continues its middle-class base.

You might want to bring in the issue of whether we need professional lawyers at all, mentioning the work done by unqualified legal advisers in agencies such as the Citizens' Advice Bureaux. You could also discuss here the market control theory which suggests that professions exist not to provide the best services, but as a way of controlling competition – so the emphasis on high academic qualifications can be seen as a way of limiting entry to the market.

It would be a good idea to point out that one of the reasons why this question is so important is that legal education and training provides not only lawyers, but eventually the judiciary – point out for example, that only when the legal profession becomes more mixed in terms of race, class and sex will the judiciary follow suit.

If you have time, you could include any reforms which you feel would improve legal education and training.

Your conclusion should sum up whether you feel legal education does provide the lawyers we need.

2 **How satisfactory are the current systems for clients to complain about their lawyers?** *Edexcel*

Your essay might start by explaining that this is an area of the legal system which has very recently undergone major changes, as a result of enormous criticism of the previous arrangements. You can then go on to explain what the complaints systems are: the Bar's Complaints Commissioner; the Office for the Supervision of Solicitors; and the Legal Services Ombudsman. Do not however spend too much time simply describing these systems – the main part of your answer should focus on how satisfactory they are. For this part, you need to point out how the new systems are an improvement over the old ones, and then go on to point out that even so, they have themselves been the subject of criticisms. In order to give your essay a coherent structure, deal with each system in turn, discussing its good and bad points before moving on to the next.

Finally, you should look at what might be done to meet some of the criticisms and, in particular, the idea that there should be an independent, statutory regulator.

▶ Reading on the Internet

The report of the Office of Fair Trading, *Competition in the Professions* (2001), is available on their website:
http://www.oft.gov.uk/html/rsearch/reports/oft328.htm

The Bar Council website can be found at:
http://www.barcouncil.org.uk/index.asp

The Law Society's website can be found at:
http://www.lawsociety.org.uk/

5 The jury system

History

The jury system was imported to Britain after the Norman conquest, though its early functions were quite different from those it fulfils today. The first jurors acted as witnesses, providing information about local matters, and were largely used for administrative business – gathering information for the Domesday Book for example. Later, under Henry II, the jury began to take on an important judicial function, moving from reporting on events they knew about, to deliberating on evidence produced by the parties involved in a dispute. Gradually it became accepted that a juror should know as little as possible about the facts of the case before the trial, and this is the case today.

A major milestone in the history of the jury was in **Bushell's Case** (1670). Before this, judges would try to bully juries into convicting the defendant, particularly where the crime had political overtones, but in **Bushell's Case** it was established that the jury were the sole judges of fact, with the right to give a verdict according to their conscience, and could not be penalized for taking a view of the facts opposed to that of the judge. The importance of this power now is that juries may acquit a defendant, even when the law demands a guilty verdict.

Today the jury is considered a fundamental part of the English legal system, though as we shall see, only a minority of cases are tried by jury. The main Act that now governs jury trial is the Juries Act 1974.

The function of the jury

The jury have to weigh up the evidence and decide what are the true facts of the case – in other words, what actually happened. The judge directs them as to what is the relevant law, and the jury then have to apply the law to the facts that they have found and thereby reach a verdict. If it is a criminal case and the jury have given a verdict of guilty, the judge will then decide on the appropriate sentence. In civil cases the jury decide on how much money should be awarded in damages.

When are juries used?

Criminal cases

Despite the symbolic importance of juries in the criminal justice system, they actually only operate in a minority of cases. Criminal offences are classified into three groups: summary only offences, which are tried in the magistrates' courts; indictable offences, which are tried in the Crown Court; and either way offences, which, as the name suggests, may be tried in either the magistrates' courts or the Crown Court. The majority of criminal offences are summary only, and because these are, in general, the least serious offences, they are also the ones most commonly committed (most road traffic offences, for example, are summary only). As a result, 95 per cent of criminal cases are heard in the magistrates' courts, where juries have no role (this proportion also includes cases involving either way offences where the defendant chooses to be tried by magistrates). Juries only decide cases heard in the Crown Court. Even among the 5 per cent of cases heard there, in a high proportion of these the defendant will plead guilty, which means there is no need for a jury and, on top of that, there are cases where the judge directs the jury that the law demands that they acquit the defendant, so that the jury effectively makes no decision here either. The result is that juries actually decide only around 1 per cent of criminal cases.

On the other hand, it is important to realize that even this 1 per cent amounts to 30,000 trials, and that these are usually the most serious ones to come before the courts – though here too the picture can be misleading, since some serious offences, such as assaulting a police officer or drink-driving, are dealt with only by magistrates, while even the most trivial theft can be tried in the Crown Court if the defendant wishes.

In the past 30 years there have been several attempts to reduce the proportion of jury trials still further, and when this book went to press, the Home Secretary had stated a definite intention to remove a defendant's right to choose jury trial for an either way offence.

Civil cases

In the past most civil cases were tried by juries, but trial by jury in the civil system is now almost obsolete. The erosion of the use of juries in civil cases was very gradual and appears to have started in the middle of the nineteenth century, when judges were given the right, in certain situations, to refuse to let a case be heard before a jury and insist that it be heard in front of a sole judge instead. Now less than 1 per cent of civil cases are tried by a jury. Today the Supreme Court Act 1981 gives a qualified right to jury trial of civil cases in four types of cases:

- libel and slander;
- malicious prosecution;
- false imprisonment; and
- fraud.

In these cases jury trial is to be granted, unless the court is of the opinion that the trial requires any prolonged examination of documents or accounts, or any scientific or local investigation which cannot conveniently be made with a jury. This right is exercised most frequently in defamation actions, although its use may be more limited now that the Defamation Act 1996 has introduced a new summary procedure for claims of less than £10,000, which can be heard by a judge alone.

In all other cases the right to jury trial is at the discretion of the court. In **Ward** *v* **James** (1966) the Court of Appeal stated that in personal injury cases (which constitute the majority of civil actions), trial should be by judge alone unless there were special considerations. In **Singh** *v* **London Underground** (1990) an application for trial by jury of a personal injury claim arising from the King's Cross underground fire of November 1987 was refused on the ground that a case involving such wide issues and technical topics was unsuitable for a jury.

There has been criticism of the distinction drawn between the four types of case which carry a qualified right to trial by jury and other civil cases. The Faulks Committee on Defamation 1975 rejected arguments for the complete abolition of juries in defamation cases, but recommended that in such cases the court should have the same discretion to order jury trial as it does in other civil cases, and that the function of the jury should be limited to deciding issues of liability, leaving the assessment of damages to the judge.

Qualifications for jury service

Before 1972, only those who owned a home which was over a prescribed rateable value were eligible for jury service. The Morris Committee in 1965 estimated that 78 per cent of the names on the electoral register did not qualify for jury service under this criteria, and 95 per cent of women were ineligible. This was either because they lived in rented accommodation or because they were wives or other relatives of the person in whose name the property was held. The Committee recommended that the right to do jury service should correspond with the right to vote. This reform was introduced by the Criminal Justice Act 1972 and the relevant law can now be found in the Juries Act 1974 (as amended). This Act now provides that potential jury members must be:

- aged 18 to 70;
- on the electoral register; and

- resident in the UK, Channel Islands or Isle of Man for at least five years since the age of 13.

From this group, certain categories are excluded or excused.

Disqualification

People who have been sentenced to prison or a young offenders' institute or its equivalent may be disqualified from jury service, depending on how long the sentence was for and how recently it was made. Someone who has received a community rehabilitation order, for example, is disqualified for ten years.

Ineligibility

Five categories of people are ineligible for jury service:

1 the judiciary;
2 those concerned with the administration of justice, such as barristers, solicitors, prison officers, and police officers and even secretaries working for the Crown Prosecution Service;
3 the clergy. The Runciman Commission saw no logical reason for the existence of this exception and recommended its abolition, but it still exists;
4 people with mental ill-health;
5 people on bail in criminal proceedings. This disqualification was introduced by s. 40 of the Criminal Justice and Public Order Act 1994 following a recommendation made by the Runciman Commission.

Excusal as of right

People who have duties that are considered more important than jury service may choose whether or not they wish to serve. These include MPs, members of the House of Lords, members of the armed forces and doctors and nurses. People over 65 can also be excused as of right. Following an extension of the law by s. 42 of the Criminal Justice and Public Order Act 1994 practising members of a religious society or order whose beliefs are incompatible with jury service are excused from performing such service.

Discretionary excusal

Others may be excused at the discretion of the judge if they show good reason, such as childcare problems, holidays booked which would clash with the jury service, personal involvement with the facts of the case, or conscientious objection. Where appropriate, jury service may be deferred rather than excused completely.

Discharge

Where there is some doubt about a potential juror's capacity to serve – because of deafness, language problems or infirmity, for example – the judge will decide whether to discharge the person concerned. Section 41 of the Criminal Justice and Public Order Act 1994 provides that the judge can discharge a juror if, in his or her opinion, the person is incapable of acting effectively as a juror on account of a physical disability. Media attention was drawn to this issue in 1999 when a deaf person, Mr McWhinney, was summoned for jury service and then subsequently prevented from sitting as a juror by a trial judge. Mr McWhinney wished to fulfil his role as a citizen by sitting on the jury and following the proceedings with the help of a signer, that is to say a person who would translate the proceedings into sign language. On appeal the decision of the trial judge was approved because while there was no practical reason why Mr McWhinney could not serve on a jury, the law prevented more than 12 people retiring into the jury room to deliberate their decision – the signer would be one person too many. The Lord Chancellor has announced that he is reviewing the situation.

Summoning the jury

In 2001 a Central Juror Summoning Bureau was established to administer the juror summoning process for the whole of the country. Computers are used to produce a random list of potential jurors from the electoral register. Summons are sent out (with a form to return confirming that the person does not fall into any of the disqualified or ineligible groups), and from the resulting list the jury panel is produced. This is made public for both sides in forthcoming cases to inspect, though only names and addresses are shown (before 1977 the occupation of the juror was also stated). It is at this stage that jury vetting may take place (see below). Jurors also receive a set of notes which explain a little of the procedure of the jury service and the functions of the juror.

Jury service is compulsory for all those not disqualified, ineligible or excused, and failure to attend on the specified date, or unfitness for service through drink or drugs is contempt of court and can result in a fine.

The jury for a particular case is chosen by random ballot in open court – the clerk has each panel member's name on a card, the cards are shuffled and the first 12 names called out. Unless there are any challenges (see p. 159), these 12 people will be sworn in. In a criminal case there are usually 12 jurors and there must never be fewer than nine. In civil cases in the county court there are eight jurors.

Jury vetting

Jury vetting consists of checking that the potential juror does not hold 'extremist' views which some feel would make them unsuitable for hearing a case. It is done by checking police, Special Branch and security service records.

This controversial practice first came to light in the 1978 'ABC Trial', in which two journalists and a soldier were accused of collecting secret information, in breach of the Official Secrets Act. During the trial it became known that the jury had been vetted to check their 'loyalty', under guidelines laid down by the Attorney-General, and a new trial was ordered.

The ensuing publicity eventually led to the publication of the Attorney-General's guidelines, which it was admitted had been in use since 1974. These guidelines were revised in 1988. They confirm that as a rule, juries should be chosen at random, with people being excluded only under the statutory exceptions, and that the proper way for the prosecution to exclude a juror was challenge for cause in open court (see below). But it was also stated that vetting might be necessary in certain special cases: those involving terrorism, where it was felt a juror's political beliefs might prevent him or her being impartial or lead to undue pressure on other jurors; and those concerning national security, where in addition to the problem of strong political beliefs there was the danger that some jurors might reveal evidence given *in camera* (i.e. heard in private and not in open court). Jurors could only be 'stood by' (see below) if the vetting revealed a very strong reason for doing so. In order to vet a jury in these cases authorization from the Attorney-General is required, who will be acting on the advice of the Director of Public Prosecutions. Checking whether a person has a criminal record is permissible in a much wider range of cases without special permission.

The legality of vetting was considered by the Court of Appeal in two cases during 1980. In **R** *v* **Sheffield Crown Court, ex parte Brownlow**, the defendants were police officers, and the defence wanted the jury vetted for previous convictions. The prosecution opposed it, but the Crown Court judge ordered that vetting should take place, and this decision was upheld by the Court of Appeal. Lords Denning and Shaw, *obiter dicta*, vigorously condemned vetting in security and terrorist cases as unconstitutional (because it was not provided for in the Juries Act 1974), and an invasion of privacy.

In **R** *v* **Mason** (1980), a convicted burglar appealed on the ground that the jury had been vetted for previous convictions, a common practice in the particular court at the time. The Court of Appeal decreed that vetting for previous convictions was necessary in order to ensure that disqualified persons could not serve. In such situations Lord Lawton described vetting as 'just common sense', though it should not be used to gain tactical advantage in minor cases.

The limits on vetting for previous convictions were, however, stressed again in **R _v_ Obellim and Others** (1996). The case concerned a criminal trial in which the judge had received a written question from the jury, which displayed a lot of knowledge about police powers and led him to suspect that one of the jurors might have such previous convictions as should have disqualified him or her. The judge ordered a security check on the jury, without telling the defence counsel, who only discovered the check had taken place when the jury complained about it after delivering their verdict.

The defendant, who was convicted, appealed on the grounds that the check on jury members might have prejudiced them. The Court of Appeal agreed, and quashed the conviction, stating that it was questionable whether the check should have been ordered at all on such grounds, and it certainly should not have been without informing defence counsel.

Vetting for any purpose remains controversial. Supporters claim that it can promote impartiality by excluding those whose views might bias the other members of the jury, and make them put pressure on others, as well as protecting national security and preventing disqualified persons from serving. Opponents say it infringes the individual's right to privacy, and gives the prosecution an unfair advantage, since it is too expensive for most defendants to undertake, and they do not have access to the same sources of information as the prosecution. Only on very rare occasions has the defence been granted legal aid to make its inquiries into the panel.

The whole process is still not sanctioned by legislation, and despite the publication of the Attorney-General's guidelines, it is impossible to know whether they are being followed – 60 potential jurors were vetted by MI5 for the Clive Ponting case (see p. 170), despite the fact that there was no apparent threat to national security.

Challenges

As members of the jury panel are called, and before they are sworn in, they may be challenged in one of two ways:

Challenge for cause. Either side may challenge for cause, on the grounds of privilege of peerage, disqualification, ineligibility or assumed bias. Jurors cannot be questioned before being challenged to ascertain whether there are grounds for a challenge. A successful challenge for cause is therefore only likely to succeed if the juror is personally known, or if jury vetting has been undertaken. If a challenge for cause is made it is tried by the trial judge.

Stand by. Only the prosecution may ask jurors to stand by for the Crown. Although there are specified grounds for this, in practice no reason need be given, and this is generally how the information supplied by jury vetting is used. The use of the power to stand by has been limited by guidelines issued by the Attorney-General which specifically state that the abolition of the peremptory challenge (see below) means that the power to stand by should only be used in connection with jury vetting or where the juror is manifestly unsuitable and the defence agrees with the exercise of the power.

Until 1988 there was a third type of challenge, peremptory challenge, available only to the defence. This meant that the defence could challenge up to three jurors without showing cause, which was equivalent to the prosecution's power to 'stand by' a juror. This was abolished, amid much opposition, on the recommendation of the Roskill Committee on fraud trials, on the grounds that it interfered with the random selection process and allowed defence lawyers to 'pack' the jury with those they thought were likely to be sympathetic. This was felt to be a particular problem when there were several defendants as (theoretically) they could combine their rights to peremptory challenge.

This limited process of challenging the jury should be contrasted with the system in the US where it can take days to empanel a jury, particularly where the case has received a lot of pre-trial media coverage. Potential jury members can be asked a wide range of questions about their attitudes to the issues raised by a case, and a great deal of money may be spent employing special consultants who claim to be able to judge which way people are likely to vote, based on their age, sex, politics, religion and other personal information.

In a high-profile 1998 case, **R** *v* **Andrews**, the defence wanted to use the American approach to establish whether members of the jury panel were likely to be biased against the defendant. She was accused of murdering her boyfriend, and the case had received an enormous amount of publicity since Ms Andrew had initially told police that her boyfriend was killed by an unknown assailant in a 'road rage' incident, sparking off a media hunt for the killer. Her lawyers wanted to issue questionnaires to the jury panel to check whether any of them showed a prejudice against her. The trial judge refused the request and when Ms Andrews was convicted, she appealed, arguing that the failure to allow questioning of the jury meant her conviction was unsafe. The argument was rejected by the Court of Appeal, which stated that questioning of the jury panel, whether orally or by written questionnaire should be avoided in all but the most exceptional cases, such as where potential jurors might have a direct or indirect connection to the facts of the trial (for example, if they were related to someone involved in the trial, or had lost money as a result of the defendant's actions).

Discharging the jury

The judge may discharge any juror, or even the whole jury, to prevent scandal or the perversion of justice. In one case the fact that a juror was giving the accused a lift in his car to the court each morning was found to be a reason to discharge that juror. In **R** *v* **Bansal** (1985) a case involved an Anti-National Front demonstration and the trial judge ordered that the jury should be drawn from an area with a large Asian population. However this approach was rejected as wrong in **R** *v* **Ford** (1989). The Court of Appeal held that race could not be taken into account when selecting jurors, and that a judge could not discharge jurors in order to achieve a racially representative jury.

The rules on discharging juries were challenged in the European Court of Human Rights in **Gregory** *v* **United Kingdom** (1997). Gregory was a black defendant accused of robbery. During his trial the jury had handed the judge a note asking that one juror be excused because of racial bias. The judge did not excuse the juror, but instead issued a strong direction to the jury to decide the case on the evidence alone. Gregory was convicted on a majority verdict and brought a case before the European Court of Human Rights, claiming that the judge should have discharged the whole jury, and that failure to do so infringed his right to a fair trial under the European Convention on Human Rights. The Court of Human Rights, however, held that in the circumstances, issuing a clear and carefully worded warning to the jury was sufficient to ensure a fair trial.

This case was distinguished in **Sander** *v* **United Kingdom** (2000). The applicant was an Asian man, who had been tried in the Crown Court with another Asian man on a charge of conspiracy to defraud. During the trial, a juror passed a note to the judge alleging that certain of his fellow jurors had made racist remarks and jokes. The juror who made the complaint was initially segregated from the rest of the jury while the court considered representations made by the lawyers. The judge then asked the complainant to rejoin the other jurors and instructed them to consider whether they were able to put aside any prejudices which they had and to try the case solely on the evidence. All of the jurors signed a letter to the judge stating:

> We utterly refute the allegation of possible racial bias. We are deeply offended by the allegation. We assure the Court that we intend to reach a verdict solely according to the evidence and without racial bias.

One juror, who believed that the allegations were directed at him, wrote a separate letter to confirm that he was not racially biased. The judge concluded that there was no real risk of bias and allowed the trial to continue with the same jury, and rejected the defence request to discharge the jury. At first instance, the applicant was convicted and his co-accused was acquitted.

The applicant appealed against his conviction up to the European Court of Human Rights. He complained that he had been denied the right to a fair trial before an impartial court, guaranteed by Art. 6(1) of the European Convention on Human Rights. The European Court held that it was not possible to state whether some of the jurors were actually biased as the matter had not been investigated. The fact that at least one juror had made comments that could be construed as jokes about Asians was not evidence of actual bias. But it was also important for the jurors to be viewed as objectively impartial, in other words that they were not just as a matter of fact impartial, but also that they would appear to an observer to be impartial. There was doubt as to the credibility of the letter which denied the allegations because the juror who had made the allegations also signed the letter. The identity of the juror who had made the allegations was revealed by his separation from the other jurors and this must have compromised his position with his fellow jurors, and inhibited him in the further discussion of the case. An admonition by a judge 'however clear, detailed and forceful would not change racist views overnight'. Even though it was not established that the jurors had such views, the judge's direction could not dispel the reasonable impression and fear of a lack of impartiality based on the original note. The fact that the jury had acquitted one Asian defendant was irrelevant since the case against him was much weaker. The judge should have discharged the jury. Thus, the court concluded that the appellant had not received a fair trial and Art. 6(1) had been breached.

The court distinguished its earlier decision of **Gregory v United Kingdom** (1997), mainly on the ground that in that case there was no admission by a juror that he had made racist comments, nor an indication as to which juror had made the complaint and the complaint was vague and imprecise.

Professor Zander has criticized the decision in **Sander v United Kingdom**. He controversially argues that:

> The decision in **Sander** is disturbing since it suggests that the Strasbourg court does not sufficiently understand or value the jury system. The great strength of the system is that generally the verdict of twelve ordinary citizens is felt to be understandable in terms either of the evidence or of the jury's sense of equity. This is despite the fact that most jurors probably have prejudices, which will often include racial prejudice. To pretend otherwise is naïve. But the process of deliberation in the jury room tends to neutralise individual prejudices. The possibility of a majority verdict provides an additional safeguard against the effect of prejudice but in fact in the great majority of cases the verdict is unanimous.

Are juries representative?

The basis of the use of juries in serious criminal cases is that the 12 people are randomly selected, and should therefore comprise a representative sample of the population as a whole. This ideal has come closer with the abolition of the property qualification and with the use of computers for the random selection process. Before computers were used an official would pick out names from the electoral list. Research by Baldwin and McConville (*Jury Trials* 1979) suggested that this could lead to discrimination. They found that only 1 per cent of jurors in Birmingham at the time were of Asian or West Indian origin, and 3.6 per cent were of Irish origin, while their proportion in the population as a whole was 12 per cent and 10 per cent respectively. This could only partly be explained by language difficulties. They also found that there was a lack of women on the juries. This may be partly accounted for by excusal due to childcare problems, and to the local practice, now discontinued, of summoning twice as many men as women.

In fact, random selection may make a jury less likely to be representative – if, for example, many women are found to be excused through childcare difficulties, summoning twice as many women as men might be a better way to achieve a representative section of the community.

Since Baldwin and McConville's research the gender and racial balance appears to have improved. Research carried out by Zander and Henderson in 1993 found that women were only slightly underrepresented and that non-white jurors constituted 5 per cent of jurors while they made up 5.9 per cent of the national population.

While this is encouraging, it has been argued by the Commission for Racial Equality that consideration needs to be given to the racial balance in particular cases. They suggest that where a case has a racial dimension and the defendant reasonably believes that he or she cannot receive a fair trial from an all white jury, then the judge should have the power to order that three of the jurors come from the same ethnic minority as the defendant or the victim. Both the Runciman Commission (1993) and the *Review of the Criminal Courts* (2001) have given their endorsement to this proposal but it has never been implemented.

The Society of Black Lawyers had, in addition, submitted to the Runciman Commission that there should always be a right to a multi-racial trial, that peremptory challenges should be reinstated and that certain cases with a black defendant should be tried by courts in areas with high black populations, and panels of black jurors who would be available at short notice should be set up. These proposals have not been implemented either.

The problems caused by lack of racial representation on juries can be seen in the high-profile Rodney King case in Los Angeles, where a policeman was found not guilty of assaulting a black motorist despite a videotape of the incident showing brutal conduct. The case was tried in an area with a very high white population, while the incident itself had occurred in an area with a high black population. However, the decision in **R** v **Ford** (1989), that there is no principle that a jury should be racially balanced, still holds.

Peremptory challenge was abolished because it was said to have interfered with the principle of random selection, especially in multi-defendant trials. However, Vennard and Riley's study found that the peremptory challenge was only used in 22 per cent of cases, with no evidence of widespread pooling of challenges, and research for the Crown Prosecution Service in 1987 showed that the use of peremptory challenge had no significant effect on the rate of acquittals.

Peremptory challenge could in fact be used to make juries more balanced in terms of race and sex, and it seems rather unjust that while the defence have had their right to a peremptory challenge removed, the prosecution is still allowed to stand by for the Crown.

Research carried out for the Home Office (*Jury Excusal and Deferral* (2000)) found that only two-thirds of the people summoned for jury service made themselves available to do it each year. About 15 per cent of summoned jurors fail to attend court on the day or have their summonses returned as 'undelivered'. Because enforcement has been poor, it has become widely known that a jury summons can be ignored with impunity. In his *Review of the Criminal Courts* (2001) Robin Auld argues that the many exclusions and excusals from jury service deprive juries of the experience and skills of a wide range of professional and successful people. Their absence creates the impression that jury service is only for those not important or clever enough to get out of it.

The secrecy of the jury

Once they retire to consider their verdict, jurors are not allowed to communicate with anyone other than the judge and an assigned court official, until after the verdict is delivered. Afterwards they are forbidden by the Contempt of Court Act 1981 from revealing anything that was said or done during their deliberations.

The arguments in favour of secrecy have been stated by McHugh J as:

- it ensures freedom of discussion in the jury room;
- it protects jurors from outside influences, and from harassment;
- if the public knew how juries reached their verdict they might respect the decision less;
- without secrecy citizens would be reluctant to serve as jurors;
- it ensures the finality of the verdict;
- it enables jurors to bring in unpopular verdicts;
- it prevents unreliable disclosures by jurors and misunderstanding of verdicts.

The arguments against secrecy and in favour of disclosure have been stated by the same author as:

- making juries more accountable;
- making it easier to inquire into the reliability of convictions and rectify injustices;
- showing where reform is required;
- educating the public;
- ensuring each juror's freedom of expression.

Research into the work of juries has always been made difficult by the requirement for secrecy. The Runciman Commission has recommended that the Contempt of Court Act 1981 should be amended so that valid research can be carried out into the way juries reach their verdicts.

The verdict

Ideally juries should produce a unanimous verdict, but in 1967 majority verdicts were introduced of ten to two (or nine to one if the jury has been reduced during the trial). This is now provided for in the Juries Act 1974. When the jury withdraw to consider their verdict they must be told by the judge to reach a unanimous verdict. If, however, the jury have failed to reach a unanimous verdict after what the judge considers a reasonable period of deliberation, given the complexity of the case (not less than two hours), the judge can direct them that they may reach a majority verdict. The foreman of the jury must state in open court the numbers of the jurors agreeing and disagreeing with the verdict. Majority verdicts were intended to help prevent jury 'nobbling' (where someone involved in the trial puts pressure on jurors to vote in a particular way, by bribes or threats). It also avoids the problem of one juror with extreme or intractable views holding out against the rest, and should lessen the need for expensive and time-consuming retrials. However, Brown and Neal's 1988 research found that the introduction of majority verdicts has not substantially affected the number of hung juries and consequent retrials. Freeman (1981) has suggested that majority verdicts dilute the concept of proof beyond reasonable doubt – on the grounds that if one juror is not satisfied, a doubt must exist – and give less protection against the risk of convicting the innocent. This in turn weakens public confidence in the system.

In Scotland the jury consists of 15 people and a conviction can be based on a simple majority verdict.

The future of the jury system

Despite its historical role in the English legal system, and the almost sacred place it occupies in the public imagination, the jury system has come under increasing attack in recent years. As we have seen, it is now used in no more than a handful of civil cases, and successive Governments have attempted to limit further its use in criminal cases as well. The 1977 Criminal Law Act removed the right to jury trial in a significant number of offences, by making most driving offences and cases of criminal damage involving property worth less than £2,000 summary only offences. At the same time, the then Government attempted to limit its use in criminal cases by making thefts involving property worth less than £20 into summary only offences, but the proposal was defeated in Parliament (the fact that the change in respect of criminal damage was accepted suggests that the majority felt that any offence which reflects on a person's honesty should be considered serious, regardless of the amount of money it involves). Since 1977, more and more offences have been removed from the realm of jury trial by being made summary only – criminal damage, for example, is now summary only unless it concerns property worth over £5,000.

Further and more drastic moves to limit the use of juries in criminal cases have been on the political agenda in the past few years, and now look likely to take place. The Royal Commission on Criminal Justice recommended in 1993 that for either way offences, defendants should no longer have the right to insist on trial by a jury. In 1997, a Home Office report, *Review of Delay in the Criminal Justice System* (known generally as the Narey Report), recommended that defendants charged with either way offences should no longer have the right to decide whether to be tried by magistrates or in the Crown Court. The decision should be left to magistrates instead.

The Conservative Government announced that these measures would be adopted, a decision which was fiercely opposed by the Labour Party; the then Shadow Home Secretary Jack Straw described the plan as 'not only wrong, but short-sighted, and likely to prove ineffective'. In the event the Conservative Government was defeated in the election before it had time to put the changes into practice, but it now appears that they will happen anyway, since the current Government has decided that the idea is not wrong, short-sighted or likely to prove ineffective after all.

In 1998 they published a consultation paper, *Determining Mode of Trial in Either Way Cases*, putting forward four possible options: maintaining the current position; reclassifying certain offences, such as minor theft and indecent assault, so that they became summary only; completely abolishing the defendant's right to choose jury trial in either way offences, leaving the choice to magistrates; or abolishing the defendant's right to choose jury trial in either way offences for everyone except first offenders (in this context meaning people who have not previously been convicted for an offence similar to the one before the court). In a speech to the 1999 Police Federation conference, Jack Straw – by then Home Secretary – said that the Government was committed to the third, and most severe, of the options listed above, namely ending a defendant's right to choose jury trial when charged with an either way offence. Magistrates will decide where such trials should take place taking into account whether the defendant has previous convictions and the effect of a conviction on a defendant's reputation and livelihood, though defendants would be given a right to appeal against their decision to the Crown Court. The two Government Bills seeking to introduce these reforms have both been rejected by the House of Lords.

The recommendations of Sir Robin Auld

The Government commissioned a major review of the criminal courts by Sir Robin Auld. The Review was primarily focused on the practices and procedures of the criminal courts and a wide range of recommendations were made. The central recommendation of the report was that a new criminal court should be created, which would be called the District Division. Cases before the District Division would be heard by a judge and two lay magistrates. The District Division would deal with a middle range of either-way cases which were unlikely to attract a sentence of more than two years' imprisonment. This would include most burglaries and thefts as well as some assault cases.

Only the judge would be able to determine questions of law, but the judge and lay magistrates would together be judges of fact. The order of proceedings would be broadly the same as in the Crown Division. The judge would rule on matters of law, procedure and inadmissibility of evidence, in the absence of the magistrates where it would be potentially unfair to the defendant to do so in their presence. The judge would not sum up the case to the magistrates, but would retire with them to consider the court's decision. They would reach their verdicts together, each having an equal vote. The judge would give a reasoned judgment and he or she would have sole responsibility for determining the sentence.

The judge would usually be a District judge, but could be a Recorder, a Circuit Judge or even a High Court judge depending on the complexity of the case.

Instead of having a separate Crown Court and magistrates' court there would be a single unified criminal court containing three divisions. The three divisions would be the Crown Division (currently the Crown Court), the Magistrates' Division (currently the magistrates' court) and the new, intermediate District Division.

Defendants would lose their right to insist on a jury trial. Instead, cases would be allocated by magistrates to the relevant Division according to their seriousness. Any disputes on the allocation of the case would be heard by a District judge on hearing representations from the parties and there would be a right of appeal to a Circuit Judge.

Defendants charged with an indictable offence would be able to request a trial by a judge alone, though the consent of the court would be required.

These recommendations of Sir Robin Auld represent a major attack on jury trial and if introduced would significantly reduce the number of cases heard by a jury. The proposals go further than the ill-fated Government Bills on the subject, and have been heavily criticized by supporters of the jury system. It is also questionable whether they would offer any financial savings. The Law Society has expressed its concern that 'an intermediate court would add an unnecessary level of bureaucracy'.

Serious fraud trials

The Government has also proposed restricting the use of juries in trials for serious fraud. Its 1998 consultation paper on this subject suggested four possible options: abolishing use of juries in fraud trials completely and replacing them with a specially trained single judge and two lay people with expertise in commercial affairs; replacing juries with a specially trained single judge or panel of judges, possibly with access to advisers on commercial matters; retaining jury trial but restricting the jury's role to deciding questions of dishonesty, with the judge deciding other matters; or replacing the traditional, randomly selected jury with a special jury, selected on the basis of qualifications or tests, or drawn from those who can demonstrate specialist knowledge of business and finance. No action has yet been taken on these proposals.

Sir Robin Auld favoured the first option of a specially trained single judge and two lay people with expertise on the subject. Under his recommendations a panel of experts would be established by the Lord Chancellor and the trial judge would select the lay members after giving the parties the opportunity to make written representations as to their suitability. The judge would be the sole judge of law, procedure, admissibility of evidence and sentence. All three would be judges of fact and they would therefore decide the verdict together. A majority of any two would suffice for a conviction. The defendant would always have the option of opting, with the consent of the court, for a trial by judge alone.

There are weaknesses in this proposal. The selection process and powers of the lay members risk undermining their stature in the eyes of the public. The power to convict on a majority of two to one could be seen as undermining the usual requirement in criminal law that, in order to convict, a defendant should be found guilty beyond reasonable doubt.

Arguments in favour of the jury system

Public participation

Juries allow the ordinary citizen to take part in the administration of justice, so that verdicts are seen to be those of society rather than of the judicial system, and satisfies the constitutional tradition of judgment by one's peers. Lord Denning described jury service as giving 'ordinary folk their finest lesson in citizenship'. This has particular importance when one considers the background of magistrates, which continues to be largely white and middle class. A defendant who does not come from this sector of society may well prefer to be judged by a jury, which is more likely to include members of his or her own race and/or class: a 1990 study by the Runnymede Trust found that black defendants charged with either way offences were more likely to opt for jury trial than white defendants in the same position. This is not to say that magistrates are biased against those from outside their race and/or class, and so unable to give them a fair trial, merely that if defendants believe this to be the case, trust in the legal system is reduced, and reduced even more if the option to choose a mode of trial which looks fairer is taken away.

However, it is important to realize that despite the symbolic importance of juries, the system remains dominated by judges and magistrates. Only a small proportion of cases are tried by juries, and even in these, judges can exert considerable influence.

Certainty

The jury adds certainty to the law, since it gives a general verdict which cannot give rise to misinterpretation. In a criminal case the jury simply states that the accused is guilty or not guilty, and gives no reasons. Consequently, the decision is not open to dispute.

Ability to judge according to conscience

Because juries have the ultimate right to find defendants innocent or guilty, they have been seen as a vital protection against oppressive or politically motivated prosecutions, and as a kind of safety valve for those cases where the law demands a guilty verdict, but it can be argued that genuine justice does not. For example, in the early nineteenth century, all felonies (a classification of crimes used at the time, marking out those considered most serious) were in theory punishable by death. Theft of goods or money above the value of a shilling was a felony, but juries were frequently reluctant to allow the death penalty to be imposed in what seemed to them trivial cases, so they would often find that the defendant was guilty, but the property stolen was worth less than a shilling.

There are several well-known recent cases of juries using their right to find according to their consciences, often concerning issues of political and moral controversy, such as **R** *v* **Kronlid and Others** (1996). The defendants here were three women who broke into a British Aerospace factory and caused damage costing over £1.5 million to a Hawk fighter plane. The women admitted doing this – they had left a video explaining their actions in the plane's cockpit – but claimed that they had a defence under s. 3 of the Criminal Law Act 1967, which provides that it is lawful to commit a crime in order to prevent another (usually more serious) crime being committed, and that this may involve using 'such force as is reasonable in all the circumstances'.

The defendants pointed out that the plane was part of a consignment due to be sold to the Government of Indonesia, which was involved in oppressive measures against the population of East Timor, a region forcibly annexed by Indonesia in 1975. They further explained that Amnesty International had estimated that the Indonesians have killed at least a third of the population of East Timor, and that the jet was likely to be used in a genocidal attack against the survivors. Genocide is a crime and therefore, they argued, their criminal damage was done in order to prevent a crime. However, the prosecution gave evidence that the Indonesian Government had given assurances that the planes would not be used against the East Timorese, and the British Government had accepted this and granted an export licence. Acquitting the women was therefore a criticism of the British Government's position on the issue, as well as the actions of the Indonesian Government, and in the face of the clear evidence that they had caused the damage, they were widely expected to be convicted. However, the jury found them all not guilty.

Other cases have involved what were seen to be oppressive prosecutions in matters involving the Government, such as **R** *v* **Ponting** (1985), where the defendant, a civil servant, was prosecuted for breaking the Official Secrets Act after passing confidential information to a journalist – even though doing so exposed a matter of public interest, namely the fact that the then Government had lied to Parliament. Ponting was acquitted.

Not all cases in which juries exercise this right are overtly political. In **R** *v* **Owen** (1992), the defendant was a man whose son had been knocked down and killed by a lorry driver who had never taken a driving test, and had a long criminal record for drink-driving and violence. The driver, who apparently showed no remorse for killing the boy, was convicted of a driving offence, sentenced to 18 months in prison and released after a year. He then resumed driving his lorry unlawfully. After contacting a number of different authorities to try to secure what he considered to be some sort of justice for his son's death, Mr Owen eventually took a shotgun and injured the lorry driver. He was charged with a number of offences, including attempted murder, but despite a great deal of evidence against him, the jury acquitted.

The importance of this aspect of the jury's involvement in criminal justice is very difficult to assess. In high-profile cases such as **Ponting** and **Kronlid**, it can be a valuable statement of public feeling to those in authority, but even in this kind of case, it cannot be relied on. Shortly after Ponting's acquittal, a similar case, **R** *v* **Tisdall** (1986) came to trial. As in **Ponting**, the information Ms Tisdall leaked exposed government wrongdoing, and it was admitted that the leak was no threat to national security, yet she was convicted.

Juries are never actually told that they can acquit if their consciences suggest they should: their instructions are quite the opposite, and before the case begins, they must swear to try the case according to the evidence. Nor do they give reasons for their decisions, so there is no way of knowing how often juries acquit defendants out of a sense of justice, even though they know that the law demands a guilty verdict. Where the verdict does clearly seem perverse in the face of the evidence, there may be other reasons for an acquittal, such as not understanding the evidence or the law.

However, there is one modern example of law reform being brought about at least partly in response to the actions of juries. This is the creation of the offence of causing death by dangerous driving, which was introduced after juries proved reluctant to convict of manslaughter those who had killed people by dangerous driving. It can be argued however, that this example shows that allowing the jury such freedom is not always a good thing, since the reason for the reluctance was thought to be that many jurors who were motorists could see how easily they could have found themselves in the dock: Sir Robin Auld (2001) appears to consider perverse verdicts by juries an affront to the criminal justice system, and has recommended reforms which would seek to prevent juries handing down such verdicts.

Criticisms of the jury system

Lack of competence

Lord Denning argued in *What Next in the Law?* that the selection of jurors is too wide, resulting in jurors that are not competent to perform their task. Praising the 'Golden Age' of jury service when only 'responsible heads of household from a select band of the middle classes' were eligible to serve, he claimed that the 1972 changes have led to jurors being summoned who are not sufficiently intelligent or educated to perform their task properly. Denning suggested that jurors should be selected in much the same way as magistrates are, with interviews and references required. This throws up several obvious problems: a more complicated selection process would be more time-consuming and costly; finding sufficient people willing to take part might prove difficult; and a jury that is intelligent and educated can still be biased, and may be more likely to be so if drawn from a narrow social group.

Particular concern has been expressed about the average jury's understanding of complex fraud cases. The Roskill Committee concluded that trial by random jury was not a satisfactory way of achieving justice in such cases, with many jurors 'out of their depth'. However, the Roskill Committee was unable to find accurate evidence of a higher proportion of acquittals in complex fraud cases than in any other kind – many of their conclusions were based on research by Baldwin and McConville, yet none of the questionable acquittals reported there was in a complex fraud case. Smith and Bailey point out that the research on the decision-making abilities of juries suggests that they are capable of coming to reasoned and fair verdicts in even complex cases. Evidence of the police to the Runciman Commission stated that the conviction rates for serious fraud, when compared with the overall conviction rate for cases that are considered by a jury, show that in serious fraud trials the jury are actually convicting a slightly higher percentage.

The 'perverse verdicts' problem

It is a matter of fact that juries acquit proportionately more defendants than magistrates do; research from the Home Office Planning Unit suggests that an acquittal is approximately twice as likely in a jury trial. Many critics of the jury system argue that this is a major failing on the part of juries, arising either from their inability to perform their role properly, as discussed above, or from their sympathy with defendants, or both.

This is a difficult area to research, as the Contempt of Court Act 1981 prohibits asking jurors about the basis on which they reached their decision. What research there is generally involves comparing actual jury decisions with those reached by legal professionals, or by shadow juries, who sit in on the case and reach their own decision just as the official jurors are asked to do.

A piece of research commissioned by the Roskill Committee on fraud trials concluded that jurors who found difficulty in comprehending the complex issues involved in fraud prosecution were more likely to acquit. They suggested that the jurors characterized their own confusions as a form of 'reasonable doubt' leading them to a decision to acquit.

A study by McCabe and Purves, *The Jury at Work* (1972), looked at 173 acquittals, and concluded that 15 (9 per cent) defied the evidence, the rest being attributable to weakness of the prosecution case or failure of their witnesses, or the credibility of the accused's explanation. McCabe and Purves viewed the proportion of apparently perverse verdicts as quite small, and from their observations of shadow juries, concluded that jurors did work methodically and rationally through the evidence, and try to put aside their own prejudices.

However, Baldwin and McConville's 1979 study (*Jury Trials*) examined 500 cases, both convictions and acquittals, and found up to 25 per cent of acquittals were questionable (as well as 5 per cent of convictions), and concluded that given the serious nature of the cases concerned, this was a problem. They describe trial by jury as 'an arbitrary and unpredictable business'.

Zander (1988) points out that the high rate of acquittals must be seen in the light of the high number of guilty pleas in the Crown Court. It must also be noted that many acquittals are directed or ordered by the judge: according to evidence from the Lord Chancellor's Department to the Runciman Commission, in 1990–91 40 per cent of all acquittals were ordered by the judge because the prosecution offered no evidence at the start of the trial. A further 16 per cent of the acquittals were directed by the judge after the prosecution had made their case as there was insufficient evidence to leave to the jury. Thus the jury were only responsible for 41 per cent of the acquittals, which was merely 7 per cent of all cases in the Crown Court. Bearing in mind the pressures on defendants to plead guilty, it is not surprising that those who resist tend to be those with the strongest cases – and of course the standard of proof required is very high. Nor is it beyond the bounds of possibility that part of the difference in conviction rates between magistrates and juries is due to magistrates convicting the innocent rather than juries acquitting the guilty.

In a high-profile case the Court of Appeal overturned a jury decision in civil proceedings on the basis that the jury decision had been perverse. In **Grobbelaar** *v* **News Group Newspapers Ltd** (2001) a jury had awarded the former goalkeeper for Liverpool FC, Bruce Grobbelaar, £85,000 on the basis that he had been defamed in the *Sun* newspaper. The *Sun* had published a story claiming that Bruce Grobbelaar had received cash to fix football matches. They had obtained secretly taped video footage of Grobbelaar where he apparently admitted receiving money in the past to lose matches, and appeared to accept cash following a proposal to fix matches in the future. A criminal prosecution of Grobbelaar had failed and he had sued in the civil courts for defamation. Grobbelaar accepted that he had made the confessions and accepted cash, but claimed that he had done so as a trick in order to bring the other person to justice. Despite the videotape evidence and some significant changes in Mr Grobbelaar's evidence, the jury accepted his claim and awarded damages. The *Sun*'s appeal was allowed on the basis that the jury's decision had been perverse. The Court of Appeal found Grobbelaar's story 'incredible'. In practice, it is extremely rare for a Court of Appeal to overturn a jury decision on this basis.

Bias

Ingman suggests that jurors may be biased for or against certain groups – for example, they may favour attractive members of the opposite sex, or be prejudiced against the police in cases of malicious prosecution or false imprisonment (and of course, some jurors may also be biased towards the police, and other figures of authority such as customs officers).

Bias appears to be a particular problem in libel cases, where juries prejudiced against newspapers award huge damages, apparently using them punitively rather than as compensation for the victim. Examples include the £500,000 awarded to Jeffrey Archer in 1987, and the £300,000 to Koo Stark a year later, as well as **Sutcliffe** *v* **Pressdram Ltd** (1990), in which *Private Eye* was ordered to pay £600,000 to the wife of the Yorkshire Ripper. In the latter case Lord Donaldson described the award as irrational, and suggested that judges should give more guidance on the amounts to be awarded – not by referring to previous cases or specific amounts, but by asking juries to think about the real value of money (such as what income the capital would produce, or what could be bought with it). The Courts and Legal Services Act 1990 now allows the Court of Appeal to reduce damages considered excessive.

For a discussion of cases concerned with potentially racist jurors see p. 161.

Manipulation by defendants

The Government's consultation paper, *Determining Mode of Trial in Either Way Cases*, suggests that manipulation of the right to jury trial by defendants is a major problem. It claims that many guilty defendants choose jury trial in a bid to make use of the delay such a choice provides. The report puts forward three reasons why guilty defendants want to do this. First, delay may put pressure on the Crown Prosecution Service to reduce the charge in exchange for the defendant pleading guilty and so speeding up the process. Secondly, it may make it more likely that prosecution witnesses will fail to attend the eventual trial, or at least weaken their recollections if they do attend, so making an acquittal more likely. Thirdly, if a defendant is being held on remand, they are kept at a local prison, and allowed additional visits and other privileges not given to convicted prisoners; time spent on remand is deducted from any eventual prison sentence, so for a defendant on remand who calculates that he or she is likely to be found guilty and sentenced to imprisonment, putting off the trial for as long as possible will maximize the amount of the sentence that can be spent under the more favourable conditions. Such manipulation is obviously undesirable from the point of view of justice, and it also wastes a great deal of time and money, since many defendants who manipulate the system in this way end up pleading guilty at the last minute (resulting in what is known as a 'cracked trial'), so that the time and money spent preparing the prosecution's case is wasted; in most cases, state funding will also have been spent on the defence case.

However, critics of the Government's plans to restrict further jury trials argue that this is a declining problem, as a result of the decision in **R** *v* **Hollington and Emmens** (1986). Where a defendant has pleaded guilty to an offence, the courts generally impose a lesser sentence than they otherwise would, but in this case, the Court of Appeal stated that a defendant charged with an either way offence who opts for Crown Court trial in an attempt to benefit by the subsequent delay cannot expect to receive the same reduction in sentence as someone who pleads guilty in the magistrates' courts (this decision has now been incorporated into s. 48 of the Criminal Justice and Public Order Act, which allows courts to take account of the stage at which a guilty plea was made when deciding how far to reduce the sentence). Lawyers were obviously bound to warn their clients that if they chose Crown Court trial and then pleaded guilty, they would receive heavier sentences than if they simply pleaded guilty in the magistrates' court. The Government's own consultation paper points out that since 1986, there has been a steady decline in the number of defendants in either way cases choosing jury trial. In 1987, defendants choosing jury trial accounted for 53 per cent of either way cases sent to the Crown Court, but by 1997, the proportion had fallen to 28 per cent.

Jury nobbling

This problem led to the suspension of jury trials for terrorist offences in Northern Ireland, and has caused problems in some English trials. In 1982 several Old Bailey trials had to be stopped because of attempted 'nobbling', one after seven months, and the problem became so serious that juries had to sit out of sight of the public gallery, brown paper was stuck over the windows in court doors, and jurors were warned to avoid local pubs and cafes and eat only in their own canteen. In 1984, jurors in the Brinks-Mat trial had to have police protection to and from the court, and their telephone calls intercepted, while in August 1994 a four-month fraud trial at Southwark Crown Court had to be abandoned after the jury had already delivered their verdict on one of the charges.

A new criminal offence was created under the Criminal Justice and Public Order Act 1994 to try to give additional protection to the jury. This provides under s. 51 that it is an offence to intimidate or threaten to harm, either physically or financially, certain people involved in a trial including jurors. Any offence that would have been committed under common law is still retained.

A more radical reform was introduced in the Criminal Procedure and Investigation Act 1996. Section 54 of the Act provides that where a person has been acquitted of an offence and someone is subsequently convicted of interfering with or intimidating jurors or witnesses in the case, then the High Court can quash the acquittal and the person can be retried. This is a wholly exceptional development in the law since traditionally acquittals were considered final, and subsequent retrial a breach of fundamental human rights. An argument in favour of the change is that it might reduce the chance of jury nobbling taking place in the first place.

Absence of reasons

When judges sit alone their judgment consists of a detailed and explicit finding of fact. When there is a jury it returns an unexplained verdict which simply finds in favour of one party or another. The former is more easily reviewed by appellate courts because the findings and the inferences of the trial judge can be examined. But when the appellate court is faced with a jury's verdict, it must support that verdict if there is any reasonable view of the evidence which leads to it.

Article 6 of the European Convention on Human Rights requires courts to give reasons for their judgments. In his review of the criminal courts Sir Robin Auld considered this matter in relation to the unreasoned jury verdicts. However, he concluded that the European Court of Human Rights would take into account the way the British jury trial works as a whole, and not find a violation of Art. 6.

Problems with compulsory jury service

Jury service is often unpopular but a refusal to act as a juror amounts to a contempt of court. Resentful jurors might make unsatisfactory decisions: in particular, jurors keen to get away as soon as possible are likely to simply go along with what the majority say, whether they agree or not.

Excessive damages

In the past juries in civil cases have awarded very high damages. The Court of Appeal now has the power either to order a new trial on the ground that damages awarded by a jury are excessive or, without the agreement of the parties, to substitute for the sum awarded by the jury such sum as appears to the court to be proper.

Cost and time

A Crown Court trial currently costs the taxpayer around £7,400 per day, as opposed to £1,000 per day for trial by magistrates. The jury process is time-consuming for all involved, with juries spending much of their time waiting around to be summoned into court.

Distress to jury members

Juries trying cases involving serious crimes of violence, particularly rape, murder or child abuse may have to listen to deeply distressing evidence, and in some cases, to inspect graphic photographs of injuries. One juror in a particularly gruesome murder case told a newspaper how he felt on hearing a tape of the last words of the victim as, fatally injured, she struggled to make herself understood on the phone to the emergency services:

> It was your worst nightmare. I've watched American police programmes where you have a murder every 15 seconds, pools of blood, chalk lines where the bodies were . . . that's nothing compared to the sound of this tape. You cannot believe the shock that runs through you, the fear when you know this is what happened. (*Sunday Times*, 13 April 1997)

At the end of the case, most members of the jury were in tears, and after delivering their verdict, it was over an hour before they could compose themselves sufficiently to leave the jury room. The problem is made worse by the fact that jurors are told not to discuss the case with anyone else.

The potential for distress to jurors was recognized in the recent trials of Rosemary West and the killers of James Bulger, where the jurors were offered counselling afterwards, and since these cases, the Lord Chancellor's Department has provided that court-appointed welfare officers should be made available. However, these are provided only in cases judges deem to be exceptional, and only if jurors request their help.

Other criticisms

See also the notes on jury vetting, the non-representative nature of juries, and the termination of peremptory challenges. The material on mode of trial discussed at p. 278 is also relevant.

Reform of the jury

A wide range of proposals have been put forward for the reform of the jury system.

Abolishing juries

It can be argued that since juries have already been abolished in all but a handful of civil cases with no apparent ill effects, and that they decide only 1 per cent of criminal cases anyway, the system really no longer needs them at all and they should be abolished. The pros and cons of this argument naturally depend on what would be put in their place.

One option would be to use a single judge, as happens in most civil cases. This has the advantages of making trials quicker, reducing the likelihood of 'perverse' verdicts, and defeating the problem of jury nobbling (in Northern Ireland single judges are already used in some cases because of the problem of jury nobbling). However, the benefits of public participation in the legal system would be lost, and all the problems associated with judicial bias and the restricted social background of judges (described in chapter 3) would be let loose on cases which involve vital questions for both the individuals concerned and society as a whole. Using a bench of perhaps three or five judges would give a little more protection against individual bias, but would still not give the benefit of community participation that the jury offers (and would also require massive investment to train the increased number of judges that would be required).

Lay participation and increased speed (and lower costs) could be achieved by allowing magistrates to decide all criminal cases, but it is highly unlikely that society would ever wish to trust decisions on the most serious crimes to non-legally qualified judges. Of course, it could be argued that that is exactly what the jury system does, but in that case the number of jurors, and the advantages of random selection in terms of representing society as a whole is thought by supporters to outweigh the amateur status of jurors – and in jury trials, the judge is always there to offer guidance on matters of law, and to decide the sentence in criminal cases.

Recommendations of Sir Robin Auld

Sir Robin Auld has undertaken a major review of the criminal courts and produced his final report in 2001. As well as favouring a reduction in the role of the jury (discussed at p. 166), Sir Robin Auld made a range of specific recommendations to improve the performance of the jury.

Help the jury to work effectively
The Auld Review recommended that in order to assist a jury in their work, the prosecution and defence advocates should prepare a written summary of the case and the issues that needed to be decided. This 'case and issues' summary would be agreed by the judge and distributed to the jurors at the start of the trial.

The judge would sum up the case at the end of the trial by forming questions which needed to be considered by the jurors. Juries would reach verdicts by answering these questions during their deliberations. Where the judge thought it appropriate he or she would be able to require the jury publicly to answer each of the questions and to declare a verdict in accordance with those answers. Sir Robin Auld argues that this would strengthen the jury as a tribunal of fact, provide a reasoned basis for jury verdicts and reduce the risk of perverse verdicts. While there can only be benefits from presenting the case more clearly to the jury, the use of questions which the jury may be forced to answer publicly seems to be an unnecessary restriction on the jury's freedom to reach a decision in accordance with their conscience as well as in accordance with the law.

Research was carried out for the Law Commission in New Zealand. This research included watching juries deliberate their verdict, a process that would be illegal in the UK. In the light of this research the New Zealand Law Commission has recommended in its *Report on the Jury in Criminal Trials* that reforms should be introduced to assist the work of a criminal jury. These reforms include changing the ways in which evidence is put before the jury. Evidence should be put before a jury in the same way that other information is given to them in their everyday lives. For example, clear explanations of legal terms ought to be given in writing. The court should make notes of the evidence and give these to the jury. If appropriate, visual aids should be supplied. Where possible, the court should set out briefly in writing what decisions the jury need to make, and in what order – a 'decision tree'. The court should tell the jury what the key issues are between the parties. Sir Robin Auld seems to have been attracted to this approach.

Prevent perverse verdicts

The Auld Review was concerned by the risk of juries reaching perverse verdicts. Rather than seeing these as a potential safeguard of civil liberties the Review seems to consider these as an insult to the law. It has therefore recommended that legislation should declare that juries have no right to acquit defendants in defiance of the law or in disregard of the evidence. The prosecution would be given a right to appeal against what it considered to be a perverse acquittal by a jury.

Sir Robin Auld recommended that where appropriate, the trial judge and the Court of Appeal should be allowed to investigate any alleged impropriety or failure in the way the jury reached their verdict, even where this is supposed to have happened during the traditionally secret deliberations of the jury. Such an investigation might look at accusations that some jurors ignored or slept through the deliberation or that the jury reached their verdict because of an irrational prejudice or whim, deliberately ignoring the evidence.

These recommendations show insufficient respect for the jurors and are unlikely to be acted upon by the Government.

Reserve jurors

One recommendation of the *Review of the Criminal Courts* was that where appropriate for long cases judges should be able to swear in extra jurors. These reserve jurors would be able to replace jurors who are unable to continue to hear a case, for example, because of illness.

Membership of the jury

Sir Robin Auld was keen to make juries more representative of the general population. He wanted jury service to become a compulsory public duty for all, to stop middle-class professionals opting out. He proposed that everyone should be eligible for jury service, save for the mentally ill. Apart from those who have recently undertaken, or been excused by a court from jury service, he recommended that no one should be excusable from jury service as of right, only on showing good reason for excusal. This would be backed up with rigorous and well-publicized enforcement of the obligation to undertake jury service with the use of fixed penalties.

He recommended that potential jurors should no longer only be selected from the electoral register. Many people are not registered to vote in elections, even though they are entitled to do so. To reach as many people as possible he therefore proposed that a range of publicly maintained lists and directories should be used.

As regards ethnic minority representation on juries, Sir Robin Auld suggested that a scheme should be devised, for cases in which the court considers that race is likely to be relevant to an issue of importance in the case, for the selection of a jury consisting of up to three people from any ethnic minority group. The Government already appears to have rejected this last recommendation.

► ANSWERING QUESTIONS

The majority of questions on the jury system require roughly the same basic material, and the main focus tends to be on a critical appraisal of the advantages and disadvantages of the system. We will look first at the simplest type of essay.

1 **Evaluate the importance of the jury system.** *Edexcel*

Your introduction should **briefly** outline what the jury is, what it does and when, and how it is selected. You should discuss the fact that in terms of the number of cases juries decide, the importance of the jury has declined over time, and mention that this process is continuing with the current plans to limit defendants' opportunities to choose jury trial. You can then go on to discuss how important the jury is in the areas where it does still operate. Work through the advantages of the jury, pointing out how these make the jury important in the legal system. Follow this with a look at the disadvantages of the system, again linking these points to the issue of the jury's importance. If you have time, run through the alternatives to juries and state whether (and why) you think any of these could provide a partial or complete replacement for juries.

Since the question asks you to **evaluate** the jury system, you should conclude by saying whether you think the advantages outweigh the disadvantages, and perhaps giving your opinion on whether the jury should be abolished, or still has a valuable role to play. If you feel it should be abolished, you might suggest which of the alternatives should replace it, while if you feel it should be retained, you could point out any reforms that you feel should be made.

2 **'We believe that twelve persons selected at random are likely to be a cross-selection of the people as a whole and thus represent the views of the common man.' (Lord Denning MR in R v Sheffield Crown Court ex parte Brownlow (1980)). Do you consider that this statement justifies the use of juries in criminal cases? Is there any other satisfactory justification?**

Here you first need to discuss to what extent juries are representative, mentioning the limitations on random selection imposed by the rules on eligibility, disqualification, jury vetting and so on, and using the material on the representativeness of juries found on p. 156. Having outlined this you should say whether in your opinion this alone justifies trial by jury in criminal cases, and why, using the material on public participation as an advantage of the jury system (p. 168).

Then move on to the other justifications for jury trials in criminal cases, which are of course the advantages listed on pp. 168–71. You should make it clear whether you feel these are alternative justifications to the principle of representing society, or complementary ones. You can then point out that despite these justifications, there are problems with the jury system, and work through the disadvantages we have listed (remember that this question deals with juries in criminal trials only, and leave out irrelevant material such as the problems with damages for libel). Go through the alternatives to the jury system as well if you have time.

Your conclusion should sum up whether you think that the principle of random selection and representativeness and/or any of the other advantages you have discussed outweigh the disadvantages strongly enough to justify the use of juries in criminal trials. If you conclude that the justifications are not sufficient, you should say what you feel should replace the jury system and why.

3 Bill Sykes is charged with manslaughter.
(a) Explain to him the sequence of events that will occur after he is charged, up to and including his trial.
(b) Critically examine the process of selection of the jury for the trial. *OCR*

The information for answering part (a) will be found in chapter 9: Criminal justice system. For part (b) you should first of all explain what the process of jury selection is, detailing the qualification for jury service, the process of summoning the jury, jury vetting and challenges. As the question asks you to 'critically examine' this process you also need to highlight the strengths and the weaknesses of this process.

Looking first at the strengths, the main point would be that the process of selection allows ordinary people from throughout the community to take part in the administration of justice and this is seen as promoting fairness and acceptance of the criminal legal process in general – the idea of judgment by one's peers.

As regards the weaknesses of the system, you could mention such issues as the problems associated with jury vetting and challenges and discuss the issue of whether juries are truly representative of the community as a whole, as examined in this chapter.

4 **(a) What part is played by juries and lay magistrates in the resolution of civil and criminal cases?** *(10 marks)*
(b) Examine critically the arguments for and against the use of either juries or lay magistrates in the English legal system. *(15 marks) AQA (AEB)*

For part (a), you need to talk about what juries do, and where they do it, addressing these questions in first the civil and then the criminal system. In your discussion of the civil system you should mention the restrictions on entitlement to jury trial, and the areas where there is discretion to allow it, and the fact that juries not only decide who wins, but assess damages. In the criminal area, point out what cases they deal with (and the proportion of criminal cases to which these amount), and their role as finders of fact, mentioning that sentencing is the preserve of the judge. You might include the rules on unanimity and majority verdicts.

You also need to go through the same steps for magistrates (the relevant information for this is found in chapter 6). Do not forget that you need to mention their responsibilities in the civil courts as well as their role in criminal cases, and do not limit your answer to the criminal part to trying cases – remember bail applications, search warrants, committal proceedings and legal aid. Matters such as selection of juries and appointment of magistrates are not relevant here.

Part (b) offers more marks, and so you should spend more time on it. The question makes it clear that you should choose to discuss either juries or magistrates, so do not cover both in this section – choose the one for which you have the most interesting and relevant material. The arguments for and against both magistrates and juries are clearly set out in this chapter and chapter 6, but as always the examiners want a critical discussion of them. It is not enough to list the advantages and disadvantages of anything – to get a good mark you need to be able to weigh them up against each other and come to a conclusion. For example, if you were discussing juries, you might point out that although issues like cost are important, it may be worth paying more for a system that promotes public involvement. You could also contrast the idea that juries lack skills and experience with the problems that would be associated with giving judges a greater role in criminal cases. Throughout your answer, show that you are addressing the issue from both sides, and that you can support whatever conclusion you reach.

NB If you are aiming to revise juries for your exam, you should also be prepared for a combined question on the role of lay people in the English legal system – in recent years examination questions have tended to incorporate the jury within such a question, rather than examining it as a single topic, and if you do not have at least some grasp of this additional material, you run a serious risk of wasting your revision on juries. We consider a question on lay participation in chapter 7.

▶ Reading on the Internet

The *Report on the Jury in Criminal Trials* published by the New Zealand Law Commission is available on their website on:

http://www.lawcom.govt.nz/

Leaflets on jury service are published on the court service website at:

http://www.courtservice.gov.uk/fandl/menu_jury.htm

6 Magistrates

▶ THE MAGISTRATES' COURTS

The magistrates' courts used to be run by the Home Office but this function was given to the Lord Chancellor's Department in 1992. The organization of the magistrates' courts was reformed by the Police and Magistrates' Courts Act 1994 which amended the Justices of the Peace Act 1979. These two Acts have now been consolidated in the Justices of the Peace Act 1997.

The country is divided geographically into 105 commissions which are then subdivided into what are known as petty sessional areas or benches of which there are around 600, though they vary considerably in size. Each petty sessional area has its own courthouse and justices' clerk. In the past the courthouses were essentially run by local committees for each commission area, with a maximum membership of 35 magistrates. But this approach was criticized by a Scrutiny Report carried out for the Home Office in 1989. The study concluded that at the time there was no coherent management structure; the justices' clerks were semi-autonomous but their exact managerial role was not clearly defined; there was an inadequate link between the distribution of resources and the actual work being carried out; performance and efficiency were not being monitored; the service was not giving value for money; trials in magistrates' courts were becoming more expensive and there was a backlog of cases to be heard. The Report proposed that some of these problems could be remedied by the establishment of a centralized 'Magistrates' Court Agency' which would be responsible for running the magistrates' courts service, and directly answerable to the relevant Minister.

These proposals were rejected by the Magistrates' Association, an influential body representing the magistrates themselves. The Association was concerned that the independence of the magistrates would be undermined and they would cease to have a role in the administration of the courts if the proposals were introduced. These criticisms were taken into account when the Government drew up its White Paper on the topic and the 1994 Police and Magistrates' Courts Act which followed. A national service was not created, instead the Lord Chancellor was given the power to reduce by about half the number of commission areas in order to streamline the system. Each commission area is administered by a Magistrates' Courts Committee (MCC). These committees are much smaller than their predecessors, with a maximum of 12 members of which up to two are not magistrates. The original proposal was that the chair of the MCC would be a nominee of the Lord Chancellor but this was rejected by Parliament as it was feared it might expose the committee to political pressure. The MCC appoints justices' clerks and the other court staff and provides the courtrooms, equipment, and training for magistrates under the supervision of the Judicial Studies Board. The Access to Justice Act 1999 replaced all the 22 Greater London area MCCs with the single Greater London Magistrates' Courts Authority. The aim of this reform is to achieve an efficient and effective administration of the magistrates' courts in the Greater London area.

Each commission area has a justices' chief executive. Their role is to carry out the day-to-day administration of the commission area. They are appointed by their MCC with the approval of the Lord Chancellor, and have performance-related and fixed-term contracts of employment. They can, with the Lord Chancellor's approval, be both a justices' clerk and a justices' chief executive at the same time.

If the MCC is failing in its duties without reasonable cause its members can be removed by the Lord Chancellor and replaced for up to three months with the Lord Chancellor's own appointees.

As regards the financial arrangements for the magistrates' courts, 60 per cent of their funding is now allocated on the basis of their workload, 25 per cent according to their efficiency in fine enforcement, 10 per cent depends on the time taken to deal with cases and the remaining 5 per cent for 'quality of service'. Performance targets have also been introduced. These arrangements have led to fears that the independence of the courts is threatened. Magistrates' courts' accounts can be reviewed by the Audit Commission.

The Police and Magistrates' Courts Act 1994 established an inspectorate of the magistrates' courts, known as 'Her Majesty's Magistrates' Courts Service Inspectorate'. It inspects the organization and administration of the courts and reports back to the Lord Chancellor. In its report for 1995 the inspectorate noted that the court organization was improving with the listing of cases for pre-set times having become an established practice, reducing the problem of people having to wait a long time in the court building before their case is heard. On the other hand, the average time in the hearing of cases in magistrates' courts has risen to an average of 132 days. Concern has also been expressed at the closure in London of the small local courts which have been rehoused in large new complexes. While this may create a pleasant environment for the court staff to work in, it takes the cases further away from the community that is affected by them.

THE JUSTICES OF THE PEACE

History

Like juries, lay magistrates have a long history in the English legal system, dating back to the Justices of the Peace Act 1361, which, probably in response to a crime wave, gave judicial powers to appointed lay people. Their main role then, as now, was dealing with criminals, but they also exercised certain administrative functions, and until the nineteenth century the business of local government was largely entrusted to them. A few of these administrative powers remain today.

There are over 30,000 lay magistrates (also called justices of the peace, or JPs), hearing over one million criminal cases a year – 95 per cent of all criminal trials, with the remaining being heard in the Crown Court. They are therefore often described as the backbone of the English criminal justice system.

There are also 96 professional judges who sit in the magistrates' courts. These are now called 'district judges (magistrates' courts)' following a reform introduced by the Access to Justice Act 1999. They had previously been known as stipendiary magistrates. They receive a salary of over £74,000. On top of the permanent district judges (magistrates' courts) there are also acting district judges who work part-time usually with a view to establishing their competence in order to get a full-time position in the future. These professional judges are appointed by the Queen on the recommendation of the Lord Chancellor, and must have a seven-year general advocacy qualification, meaning that they have had a right of audience in at least the lower courts for a minimum of seven years. Following the Access to Justice Act 1999, they are appointed to a single bench with national jurisdiction. They act as sole judge in their particular court, mostly in the large cities and London in particular, where 46 are based. Despite their name, they are really part of the professional judiciary, and most of the comments about magistrates in this chapter do not apply to them.

Selection and appointment

Lay magistrates are appointed by the Lord Chancellor in the name of the Crown, on the advice of local Advisory Committees (for historical reasons, magistrates in Lancashire, Greater Manchester and Merseyside are appointed by the Chancellor of the Duchy of Lancaster in the name of the Crown). Candidates are interviewed by the Committee, who then make a recommendation to the Lord Chancellor, who usually follows the recommendation.

Members of the local Advisory Committees are appointed by the Lord Chancellor. Two-thirds of them are magistrates, and the Lord Chancellor is supposed to ensure that they have good local knowledge, and represent a balance of political opinion. Their identity was at one time kept secret, but names are now available to the public.

Candidates are usually put forward to the committee by local political parties, voluntary groups, trade unions and other organizations, though individuals may apply in person. The only qualifications laid down for appointment to the magistracy are that the applicants must be under 65 and live within 15 miles of the commission area for which they are appointed. These qualifications may be dispensed with if the Lord Chancellor considers it to be in the public interest to do so. In practice they must also be able to devote an average of half a day a week to the task, for which usually only expenses and a small loss of earnings allowance are paid. Legal knowledge or experience is not required; nor is any level of academic qualification.

Certain people are excluded from appointment including: police officers, traffic wardens and members of the armed forces; anyone whose work is considered incompatible with the duties of a magistrate; anyone who due to a disability could not carry out all the duties of a magistrate; people with certain criminal convictions; undischarged bankrupts and those who have a close relative who is already a magistrate on the same Bench.

In 1998 the Lord Chancellor, Lord Irvine, revised the procedures for appointing lay magistrates. The reforms aimed to make the appointment criteria open and clear. Thus a job description for magistrates was introduced which declares that the six key qualities defining the personal suitability of candidates are: having good character, understanding and communication, social awareness, maturity and sound temperament, sound judgement and commitment and reliability. Positions are now advertised widely, including publications such as 'Inside Soaps' to attract a wider range of people.

Removal and retirement

Magistrates usually have to retire at 70, but they may indirectly be compulsorily retired before this, by being moved to the supplemental list, if, because of age or infirmity, they cannot do their job, or if they neglect to do so.

Lay magistrates can also be removed by the Lord Chancellor at any time without being given reasons, but in fact this is really only done where a magistrate is deemed to have misbehaved, or acted in a way that is inconsistent with the office – in 1985, magistrate Kathleen Cripps was dismissed by the Lord Chancellor for taking part in a CND demonstration outside the court where she normally sat because of a case being heard there. Her application to the High Court for judicial review of the decision was unsuccessful. The Lord Chancellor made it clear in 1994 that 'misbehaviour' justifying removal included conviction of a drink-driving offence or any offence involving violence, dishonesty or immoral conduct;

and any behaviour that could cause offence (particularly on racial or religious grounds) or that amounted to sexual harassment.

Background

Class

The 1948 Report of the Royal Commission on Justices of the Peace showed that approximately three-quarters of all magistrates came from professional or middle-class occupations. Little seems to have changed since: research carried out by Rod Morgan and Neil Russell (2000) found that more than two-thirds of lay magistrates were, or had been until retirement, employed in a professional or managerial position. Their social backgrounds were not representative of the community in which they served. For example, in a deprived metropolitan area, 79 per cent of the bench members were professionals or managers compared with only 20 per cent of the local population.

One of the reasons for this may be financial; while employers are required to give an employee who is appointed as a magistrate reasonable time off work, not all employers are able or willing to pay wages during their absence. To meet this difficulty, in 1968 a loss of earnings allowance was introduced, but this is not overly generous and will usually be less than the employee would have earned.

A further problem is that employees who take up the appointment against the wishes of their employer may find their promotion prospects jeopardized. This means that only those who are self-employed, or sufficiently far up the career ladder to have some power of their own, can serve as magistrates without risking damage to their own employment prospects. The outcome is that those outside the professional and managerial classes are proportionately underrepresented on the bench which is still predominantly drawn from the more middle-class occupations. The minimum age for appointment has been raised to 65 in the hope that working-class people, who were prevented from serving during their working lives, will do so in retirement, though so far the change has had little impact.

Only 4 per cent of magistrates are under the age of 40, and almost a third are in their 60s.

Age

There are few young magistrates – most are middle-aged or older. The problems concerning employment are likely to have an effect on the age as well as the social class of magistrates; people at the beginning of their careers are most dependent on the goodwill of employers for promotion, and least likely to be able to take regular time off without damaging their career prospects. They are also more likely to be busy bringing up families.

While a certain maturity is obviously a necessity for magistrates, younger justices would bring some understanding of the lifestyles of a younger generation.

Politics

Government figures released in 1995 showed that a high proportion of magistrates were Conservative supporters, and few voted Labour. A sample survey of 218 new appointments as magistrates in England and Wales showed that 91 were Conservative voters, 56 Labour, 41 Liberal Democrat, 24 had no political affiliation, and four voted for the Welsh party, Plaid Cymru. A report analysing the figures for 1992 compared the proportion of Conservative voters among magistrates to the proportion in their local area: in two Oldham constituencies, 52 per cent of the local people voted Labour, but only 27 per cent of magistrates, and slightly more magistrates than constituents in general voted Conservative. In Bristol, Labour had won 40 per cent of the votes, slightly more than the Tories; of the magistrates, 142 said they were Tory, and only 85 described themselves as Labour supporters.

Race

The Lord Chancellor's Department reported in 1987 that the proportion of black magistrates was almost 2 per cent, as against the proportion of black people in the general population of 4.69 per cent. The figures for 2001 show that lay magistrates increasingly reflect the ethnic diversity of contemporary Britain. Ninety-four per cent of the population in England and Wales is white, 2 per cent is black, 3 per cent is of Indian sub-continent or Asian origin and a further 1 per cent is drawn from other groups. The composition of the lay magistracy is now 2 per cent black, 2 per cent of Indian sub-continent or Asian origin and 1 per cent other.

Table 6.1 Ethnicity: lay magistrates and population generally

	White	Black Caribbean, Black African, Black other	Indian, Pakistani, Bangladeshi Chinese	Other	Not known	Total
Magistrates England and Wales						
Number	21,950	430	541	186	2,825	25,932[1]
Percentage	85%	2%	2%	1%	10%	100%
General population for England and Wales (1991 census)	94%	2%	3%	1%	–	100%

[1] Figures exclude magistrates in the Duchy of Lancaster

Source: Morgan and Russell (2000) *The Judiciary in the Magistrates' Courts*

But there is a considerable variation locally and the fit between the local benches and the local communities they serve is in several instances very wide.

Sex

The sexes are fairly evenly balanced among lay magistrates with 51 per cent men and 49 per cent women. However, district judges (magistrates' courts) are primarily male, with only 13 women holding this position.

Training

The Magistrates' Commission Committees are responsible for providing training under the supervision of the Judicial Studies Board. Magistrates are not expected to be experts on the law, and the aim of their training is mainly to familiarize them with court procedure, the techniques of chairing, and the theory and practice of sentencing. They undergo a short induction course on appointment, and have to undergo basic continuous training comprising 12 hours every three years. Magistrates who sit in juvenile courts or on domestic court panels receive additional training. In order to chair a court hearing a magistrate must, since 1996, take a Chairmanship Course the syllabus of which is set by the Judicial Studies Board. Since 1998 the training has included more 'hands on' practical experience, sessions in equality awareness and experienced magistrates act as monitors of more junior members of the Bench.

Sir Thomas Skyrme argued in 1983 that the money spent on the training and continuing education of magistrates was 'negligible'. He found that the amount and quality of the instruction varied according to the interest and energy of the particular individuals responsible in the area and, in general, fell far short of what was needed. Since the time of his research some improvements have been introduced.

Criminal jurisdiction

Magistrates have four main functions in criminal cases:

- Hearing applications for bail.
- Committal proceedings (see p. 280).
- Trial. Magistrates mainly try the least serious criminal cases. They are advised on matters of law by a justices' clerk, but they alone decide the facts, the law and the sentence.
- Appeals. In ordinary appeals from the magistrates' court to the Crown Court, magistrates sit with a judge. But, following a reform by the Access to Justice Act 1999, they no longer have this role in relation to appeals against sentence.

Magistrates also exercise some control over the investigation of crime, since they deal with applications for bail and requests by the police for arrest and search warrants.

Lay magistrates generally sit in groups of three. However, s. 49 of the Crime and Disorder Act 1998 provides that certain pre-trial judicial powers may be exercised by a single justice of the peace sitting alone. These include decisions to extend or vary the conditions of bail, to remit an offender to another court for sentence and to give directions as to the timetable for proceedings, the attendance of the parties, the service of documents and the manner in which evidence is to be given. These powers of single justices were tested in six pilot studies and, having proved to be successful, were applied nationally in November 1999.

The role of magistrates in the criminal justice system has been effect-ively increased in recent years. Some offences which were previously triable either way have been made summary only, notably in the Criminal Law Act 1977, where most motoring offences, and criminal damage worth less than £2,000 were made summary only (since raised to £5,000 in the Criminal Justice and Public Order Act 1994). The Government proposed at the time that thefts involving small amounts of money should also be made summary offences, but there was great opposition to the idea of removing the right to jury trial for offences which reflected on the accused's honesty. The proposal was dropped, but is still suggested from time to time.

The vast majority of new offences are summary only – there was con-troversy over the fact that the first offence created to deal with so-called 'joy-riding' was summary, given that the problem appeared to be a seri-ous one, and critics assume that it was made a summary offence in the interests of keeping costs down. Since then, the more serious joyriding offence, known as aggravated vehicle-taking, which occurs when joyriding causes serious personal injury or death, has been reduced to a summary offence by the Criminal Justice and Public Order Act 1994. Other serious offences which are summary only include assaulting a police officer, and many of the offences under the Public Order Act 1986.

New moves to increase the role of magistrates are discussed on pp. 165–67.

Civil jurisdiction

Magistrates' courts are responsible for granting licences to pubs and bet-ting shops, and have jurisdiction over domestic matters such as adoption. When hearing such cases they are known as family proceedings courts. The Child Support Agency has taken over most of their work in relation to fixing child maintenance payments.

The courts' domestic functions overlap considerably with the jurisdic-tion of the county court and the High Court, though some uniformity of approach is encouraged by the fact that appeals arising from these cases are all heard by the Family Division of the High Court.

The fact that for domestic matters different procedures and law are applied in the different courts, and cases are generally assigned to the magistrates' court because they fall within certain financial limits, has led to the criticism that there is a second class system of domestic courts for the poor, with the better off using the High Court and county courts where cases are heard by professional and highly qualified judges. Because of this, magistrates sitting in domestic cases must receive special training and the bench must contain both male and female magistrates.

The justices' clerk

There are about 250 justices' clerks who are employed by the Magistrates' Courts Committee for their area subject to the approval of the Lord Chancellor. Most must have a five year magistrates' court qualification, that is to say they must be qualified as barristers or solicitors with a right of audience in relation to all proceedings in the magistrates' courts for at least five years, though some hold office by reason of their length of service. In the past there have been problems with recruiting suitably qualified people, partly because the local organization of the courts meant there was no clear career structure. This led many clerks to leave for the Crown Prosecution Service where pay and promotion prospects were better.

The justices' clerks delegate many of their powers in practice to deputy justices' clerks and court clerks. This wide delegation has caused concerns about the qualifications of the people to whom these powers are being delegated. In an effort to raise standards, since 1 January 1999 all newly appointed court clerks must be qualified solicitors or barristers. Court clerks in post prior to this date who have a specialist diploma in magisterial law have ten years in which to requalify. There is an exemption for court clerks aged 40 or over on 1 January 1999. Not surprisingly, this reform has been angrily received by court clerks who do not yet have the requisite qualification. A union representing these individuals has brought a series of test cases to the employment tribunals arguing that the qualification change discriminates against women and people with disabilities.

A Practice Direction was issued by the High Court in 2000 clarifying the powers of the magistrates' clerk – Practice Direction (Justices: Clerk to Court) (2000). This was issued to make it clear that their powers conform with the European Convention on Human Rights following the passing of the Human Rights Act 1998.

The primary function of the court clerks is to advise the lay magistrates on law and procedure. They are not supposed to take any part in the actual decision of the bench; legal and procedural advice should be given in open court, and the clerk should not accompany the magistrates if they retire to consider their decision. Section 49(2) of the Crime and Disorder Act 1998 provides that many of the pre-trial judicial powers that are exercisable by a single justice of the peace can be delegated to a justices' clerk. Their independence is guaranteed by s. 48 of the Justices of the Peace Act 1997 which provides that when advising magistrates they are not to be subject to directions from any person or organization, including the Justices' Chief Executive and the Magistrates' Courts Committee. In the past the justices' clerk also had considerable administrative functions, but these are increasingly being passed to the Justices' Chief Executive.

Lay magistrates versus professional judges

In recent years there has been some discussion as to whether lay magistrates should be replaced by professional judges. There have been suspicions that this may be on the Government's political agenda. These suspicions have been fuelled by the increasing role of justices' clerks and the commission of research in the field by Rod Morgan and Neil Russell. Their report *The Judiciary in the Magistrates' Courts* (2000) has provided some useful up-to-date information to support the debate on the future role of lay magistrates in the criminal justice system. That research concluded:

> At no stage during the study was it suggested that . . . the magistrates' courts do not work well or fail to command general confidence. It is our view, therefore, that eliminating or greatly diminishing the role of lay magistrates would not be widely understood or supported.

Advantages of lay magistrates

Cost
It has traditionally been assumed that because lay magistrates are unpaid volunteers, they are necessarily cheaper than their stipendiary colleagues. However, it is not clear that this is the case. The research by Rod Morgan and Neil Russell (2000) found that a simple analysis of the direct costs for the Magistrates' Courts Service of using the two types of magistrates shows that lay magistrates are extraordinarily cheap compared with professional judges. The direct average cost of a lay justice is £495 per annum, that of a stipendiary £90,000. However, lay magistrates incur more indirect costs than professional judges. They are much slower than professional judges in hearing cases, as one professional judge handles as much work as 30 lay magistrates. Lay magistrates therefore make greater proportionate use of the court buildings. They need the support of legally qualified clerks to advise them. Administrative support is required for their recruitment, training and rota arrangements. When all the overheads are brought into the equation the cost per appearance for lay and professional magistrates becomes £52.10 and £61.78 respectively. These figures have to be seen in

Table 6.2 The cost of appearing before lay and stipendiary magistrates (per appearance)

	Lay Magistrates	Stipendiary Magistrates
	£	£
Direct costs (salary, expenses, training)	3.59	20.96
Indirect costs (premises, administration staff etc.)	48.51	40.82
Direct & indirect costs	52.10	61.78

Source: Morgan and Russell (2000) *The Judiciary in the Magistrates' Courts*

the context that professional judges are currently more likely to send someone to prison which is more expensive than the alternative sentences frequently imposed by lay magistrates. They are almost twice as likely to remand defendants in custody and they are also twice as likely to sentence defendants to immediate custody, a finding that may be partly attributable to their hearing the most serious cases.

Switching to Crown Court trials would be extremely expensive. The Home Office Research and Planning Unit has estimated that the average cost of a contested trial in the Crown Court is around £13,500, with guilty pleas costing about £2,500. By contrast, the costs of trial by lay magistrates are £1,500 and £500 respectively. This is partly a reflection of the more serious nature of cases tried in the Crown Court, but clearly Crown Court trials are a great deal more expensive overall.

Lay involvement

This is the same point as that cited in favour of the jury (see pp. 168–69). Lay magistrates are an ancient and important tradition of voluntary public service. They can also be seen as an example of participatory democracy. Lay involvement in judicial decision-making ensures that the courts are aware of community concerns. However, given the restricted social background of magistrates, and their alleged bias towards the police, the true value of this may be doubtful. Magistrates do not have the option, as juries do, of delivering a verdict according to their conscience.

Weight of numbers

The simple fact that magistrates must usually sit in threes may make a balanced view more likely.

Local knowledge

Magistrates must live within a reasonable distance of the court in which they sit, and therefore may have a more informed picture of local life than professional judges.

Disadvantages of lay magistrates

Inconsistent

There is considerable inconsistency in the decision-making of different benches. This is noticeable in the differences in awards of legal aid and the types of sentences ordered. To achieve the fundamental goal of a fair trial similar crimes committed in similar circumstances by offenders with similar backgrounds should receive a similar punishment. In the Crown Court, such consistency is promoted through the use of professional judges whose conduct is closely controlled by the Court of Appeal.

By contrast, magistrates receive little guidance on consistent sentencing – apart from their basic training, all they have is a booklet on the subject and advice from their clerk. In 1985, the Home Office noted in *Managing Criminal Justice*, that though benches tried to ensure their own decisions were consistent, they did not strive to achieve consistency with other benches. The National Association of Probation Officers found that magistrates in urban areas imposed lighter sentences than those in rural areas. The researchers Flood-Page and Mackie found in 1998 that district judges (magistrates' courts) sentenced a higher proportion of offenders to custody than lay magistrates after allowing for other factors. There are also marked variations in the granting of bail applications: in 1985, magistrates' courts in Hampshire granted 89 per cent of bail applications, while in Dorset only 63 per cent were allowed.

Inefficient

Most of the public sampled in the research by Rod Morgan and Neil Russell (2000) was largely unaware that there were two types of magistrate. When enlightened and questioned, a majority considered that magistrates' court work should be divided equally between the two types of magistrate or that the type of magistrate did not matter. However, professional court users have significantly greater levels of confidence in the district judges (magistrates' courts). They regard these judges as quicker than lay justices, more efficient and consistent in their decision-making, better able to control unruly defendants and better at questioning CPS and defence lawyers appropriately. In practice, straightforward guilty pleas to minor matters are normally dealt with by panels of lay magistrates whereas serious contested matters are increasingly dealt with by a single, professional judge who decides questions of both guilt and sentence. Rod Morgan and Neil Russell question whether the work should be distributed in the opposite way.

Bias towards the police

Police officers are frequent witnesses, and become well known to members of the Bench, and it is alleged that this results in an almost automatic tendency to believe police evidence. One magistrate was incautious enough to admit this: in **R** *v* **Bingham JJ, ex parte Jowitt** (1974), a speeding case where the only evidence was that of the motorist and a police constable, the chairman of the Bench said 'Quite the most unpleasant cases that we have to decide are those where the evidence is a direct conflict between a police officer and a member of the public. My principle in such cases has always been to believe the evidence of the police officer, and therefore we find the case proved.' The conviction was quashed on appeal because of this remark.

Magistrates were particularly criticized in this respect during the 1984 miners' strike for imposing wide bail conditions which prevented attendance on picket lines, and dispensing what appeared to be conveyor-belt justice.

Background

Despite the recommendations of two Royal Commissions (1910 and 1948) and the *Review of Criminal Courts* (2001), that magistrates should come from varied social backgrounds, magistrates still appear to be predominantly white, middle-class and middle-aged, with a strong Conservative bias.

The lack of representation of ethnic minorities has in the past been a particular problem: respondents to a 1988 study by the National Association for the Care and Resettlement of Offenders emphasized their view of courts as a white institution sitting in judgment upon black people, and their consequent lack of confidence in the system. King and May's research in 1985 found evidence of racial prejudice among some members of Advisory Committees, and concluded that both the selection procedure itself and the criteria applied by the committees discriminated, directly or indirectly, against ethnic minorities. No Afro-Caribbean people and few Asians were members of advisory committees, and while in some areas there had been a significant increase in the number of black magistrates appointed, the proportion on the bench in many areas still fell far short of the proportion of black people in the local community.

The selection process has also been blamed for the general narrowness of magistrates' backgrounds: Elizabeth Burney's 1979 study into selection methods concluded that the process was almost entirely dominated by existing magistrates who over and over again simply appointed people with similar backgrounds to their own.

The effect of their narrow background on the quality and fairness of magistrates' decisions is unclear. A survey of 160 magistrates by Bond and Lemon (1979) found no real evidence of significant differences in approach between those of different classes, but they did conclude that political affiliation had a noticeable effect on magistrates' attitudes to sentencing, with Conservatives tending to take a harder line. The research did not reveal whether these differences actually influenced the way magistrates carried out their duties in practice, but there is obviously a risk that they would do so.

In 1997, there was a slight controversy when, on winning the general election, the Labour Lord Chancellor called for more Labour voting candidates to be recommended for appointment as magistrates by Advisory Committees. His reasoning was that the political make up of the magistrates needed to reflect that of the general population which had shifted towards Labour. A consultation paper was subsequently issued in which it appeared that the Lord Chancellor had changed his mind, having concluded that it was no longer necessary to seek a political balance among magistrates because people no longer voted along class lines.

Some feel that the background of the Bench is not a particular problem: in *The Machinery of Justice in England* (1989) Jackson points out that 'Benches do tend to be largely middle to upper class, but that is a characteristic of those set in authority over us, whether in the town hall, Whitehall, hospitals and all manner of institutions'.

However, a narrow social and ethnic background does make the Bench unrepresentative of the general public and may weaken confidence in its decisions, on the part of society in general as well as the defendants before them. Jackson's argument that those 'set in authority over us' always tend to be middle to upper class is not a good reason for not trying to change things.

Suggested reforms

Professional judges

Professional judges could either replace lay magistrates, or sit together with them. In no other jurisdiction do lay judges alone or in panels deal with offences of the seriousness dealt with in the English and Welsh magistrates' courts by lay magistrates. But putting a professional judge in all magistrates' courts would be very expensive, and is unlikely to happen, though the Royal Commission on Criminal Justice did recommend in 1993 that more use should be made of professional judges. It is understood that the previous Home Secretary, Jack Straw, favoured replacing all lay magistrates with professional judges. The position of the current Home Secretary is not yet known. Rod Morgan and Neil Russell (2000) calculated that if the work of lay magistrates was transferred to professional judges, one professional judge would be needed for every 30 magistrates replaced.

The clerks' role

The current Government seems to be moving in the direction of allowing justices' clerks to have increased powers to manage cases, while limiting their administrative functions. These reforms could be taken further by appointing them to the Bench, making them legally qualified chairpersons, or giving them formal powers to rule on all points of law, while leaving the determination of the facts to the lay justices. The academic Penny Darbyshire has, however, sounded a note of caution to such developments. In an article in 1999 she argues that case management is not an administrative activity but a judicial one. She considers that such powers should not be delegated to justices' clerks unless they are selected and screened in the same way as judges and given the same protection as judges to ensure their independence.

In its submission to the Auld Review of the Criminal Courts (discussed on p. 178), the Association of Magisterial Officers, which represents staff in magistrates' courts, called for a major transfer of powers from lay magistrates to court clerks. The union argued that the role of lay magistrates should be restricted to arbiters of fact. Court clerks would take on full responsibility for all pre-trial issues apart from the grant or removal of bail. Where lay magistrates were involved, they would act as 'wingers' in three-person tribunals chaired by court clerks. The clerks' decision on points of law would be final, but any decision on the facts would be by simple majority. Sir Robin Auld rejected this submission and essentially recommended that the role of the court clerk should remain unchanged.

The selection process

The *Review of the Criminal Courts* (2001) recommended that steps should be taken to make magistrates reflect more broadly than at present the communities they serve. Increased loss of earnings allowances and creche facilities at courts (to help young parents) are all ways of attracting a more varied range of candidates. Legislation preventing employers from discriminating against magistrates would be difficult to enforce, but might at least make employers more wary about being seen to discriminate, and thus encourage more working-class and younger applicants.

Membership of local advisory committees could be broadened to include members of the ethnic minorities and the working class, perhaps drawn from community organizations and trade unions.

The Auld Review (2001) recommended that local advisory committees should be equipped with the information they need to enable them to submit for consideration for appointment candidates that will produce and maintain Benches broadly reflective of the communities they serve. This would include the establishment and maintenance of national and local databases of information on the make-up of the local community and on the composition of the local magistracy.

At the moment the Lord Chancellor's Department seeks to achieve a social balance on the Bench by taking into account a person's political affiliation when making appointments. This stems from the time when people tended to vote along class lines, with people from the working class voting predominantly for the Labour Party. Political opinion is no longer a reliable gauge of a person's social background and the Lord Chancellor has therefore investigated the possibility of replacing the gauge of political affiliation with a new geo-demographic system. An initial proposal would have classified people in social groups according to age, sex, ethnic origin, and whether they owned a home or car, using statistics from the national census. On consultation in 1999 this proposal was not well received and the Lord Chancellor abandoned the project, stating:

> I remain committed to finding an alternative to political balance as a measure of social background, but I have reluctantly concluded that for now it remains the most practical measure. I have asked only officials to look at other options for the future.

The Lord Chancellor's Department is now developing a new approach looking at occupational categories, alongside factors such as age, sex and regional spread.

Improvements in consistency

Achieving precise uniformity in sentencing and the granting of bail throughout the country is probably impossible, given the number of cases handled by magistrates' courts; but more detailed guidelines, regularly updated, more training, and some supervision by the higher courts could at least curb the more significant variations.

▶ ANSWERING QUESTIONS

As well as the following examples, the role of magistrates may also be considered as part of a question on lay involvement in the criminal justice system generally (see p. 202), and in questions on the criminal justice system itself.

1 'Magistrates' courts are cheap, but it is wrong that matters of vital concern to the citizen should be decided by amateurs.' In your opinion, how far is this statement true?

You need to address the three points made by this question in turn. First, are magistrates cheap? This is covered in the first point under Advantages of lay magistrates on p. 192. Secondly, can they be fairly described as amateurs? You could mention here that lay magistrates do not have legal qualifications, but do have some training – you might refer to the extra training given to magistrates dealing with family and juvenile cases and to those acting as the chairperson. You should also mention the role of the clerk, who can guide them on the law.

You then need to point out what matters of vital concern they decide – these will mainly be criminal, and you should note that some summary and either way offences can be serious, and even those which appear minor, such as driving offences, can have serious consequences for individuals. You could also draw attention to the fact that the criminal jurisdiction of the magistrates' court has been increased with more offences being made summary only. In civil cases, the magistrates' family jurisdiction can be seen as being of vital importance for the citizen.

The main emphasis in your essay should be on the next part: do you think it is right that amateur magistrates should decide such important cases? Do not be tempted simply to list the advantages and disadvantages of magistrates – although that is the information you will use, you must relate it to the idea of magistrates as amateurs. Obvious points to make would be those about inconsistency, and possibly about bias towards the police.

You might then go on to state any advantages of magistrates which could outweigh, or balance out, the problems of being amateurs – their local knowledge, and the fact that they involve the community, for example. You could make a brief comparison between trial by magistrates and trial by jury, drawing attention to the fact that juries too are lay people who have also been accused of providing amateur justice. You could also compare trial by magistrates with the other alternatives – those listed as alternatives to juries (pp. 177–79) are also alternatives to magistrates. You might point out that one of the allegations made against magistrates – that they come from a narrow social background – is even more true of professional judges. If you have time, run through some of the suggested reforms to magistrates, such as better training.

Your conclusion should state your opinion – you might say that magistrates are amateur and should not be given such vital matters to deal with, or that their advantages outweigh their amateur status. You could conclude that if reforms were made, the position would be improved, or even suggest that amateur status is a positive advantage – it all depends what the rest of your answer has argued – but you should give some opinion.

2 **Recent reforms have increased the powers of magistrates in the criminal justice system. Are their powers now too great – or too small?**

You need to start by outlining the criminal powers of magistrates, and particularly those powers which have come about as a result of recent changes – these are described in the section on criminal jurisdiction in this chapter. You could point out that there are also areas where magistrates have lost powers – the abolition of committal proceedings, and the decreased use of magistrates' warrants (see chapter 9). You could point to the recent reforms discussed at p. 190 allowing justices to exercise certain case management powers on their own. The main part of your essay should concentrate on whether the powers should be increased or decreased.

You need to go through any reasons why it might be seen as a good idea to increase the powers of magistrates – cost is obviously one, and you might also consider some of the other advantages of magistrates, such as local knowledge or community involvement, which also justify increased powers.

Then consider any reasons why magistrates' powers should not be increased, or should even be decreased. The problems of bias towards the police and inconsistency are clearly relevant here.

If you have time, you could run through any of the relevant reforms mentioned in this chapter, and if you have been arguing that magistrates' powers are too great, say whether you think those powers would be acceptable, or could be increased, if these reforms were carried out.

3 Study the extract below and then answer the questions which follow.
Over 95 per cent of criminal trials take place in a magistrates' court. A bench of usually three justices of the peace will hear the evidence, decide whether the accused is innocent or guilty and, if guilty, pass sentence. They also hear committal proceedings. Yet these men and women are not trained lawyers, they are not paid for their work and they sit in court perhaps once a month. Magistrates' courts are regularly criticized for inconsistency. Sentences for the same offence vary widely from one court to another; applications for legal aid and bail are granted far more often in one court than they are in another. Even more seriously, magistrates are accused of being far too willing to accept police evidence and to convict.
(a) How are Justices of the Peace appointed? *(4 marks)*
(b) Explain what is meant by 'committal proceedings'. *(4 marks)*
(c) What are the advantages of trial in a Magistrates' Court? *(8 marks)*
(d) What changes would you recommend to improve the working of the magistrates' courts? *(9 marks) Edexcel*

(a)   It was seen at p. 185 that Justices of the Peace are appointed by the Lord Chancellor on the recommendation of local Advisory Committees. At pp. 187–89 it was mentioned that there has been criticism of the type of persons who are in practice selected.

(b)   Committal proceedings are discussed at p. 280 in the chapter on the criminal justice system. In summary, they assess the evidence for offences triable either way to see whether there is a *prima facie* case to put to a jury in a Crown Court.

(c)   Some advantages of trial by magistrates are discussed at pp. 192–93. You could also use the material in the next chapter looking generally at the advantages of lay participation in the legal system (p. 203).

(d)   Possible reforms are discussed at pp. 196–98. As the question is phrased widely to include 'the workings of the Magistrates' Courts' you could also look at whether the current trend to increase the workload of the magistrates' courts should be reversed.

Reading on the Internet

The research of Rod Morgan and Neil Russell, *The Judiciary in the Magistrates' Courts* (2000), is available on the Home Office website in the section dedicated to the Research Development and Statistics Directorate:

http://www.homeoffice.gov.uk/rds/pdfs/occ-judiciary.pdf

7 Lay participation in the legal system

As well as serving as magistrates and jurors, lay people fulfil other functions within the legal system.

Tribunal members

Tribunals are presided over by a panel, which is usually headed by a legally qualified chairperson. Other members of the panel are generally lay people chosen for their knowledge and experience in the relevant area – doctors sit on Medical Appeal Tribunals, for example, and the panel for an Employment Tribunal will include one lay member drawn from a panel approved by the Confederation of British Industry, and one from a panel approved by the Trades Union Congress.

'McKenzie friends'

Where a litigant chooses to represent themselves in court, they may take along someone to advise them, though this person may not themselves address the court. They are called a 'McKenzie friend' or 'McKenzie adviser' after the case in which the court made it clear that the attendance of a lay adviser was permissible: **McKenzie** v **McKenzie** (1971). Workers from Citizens' Advice Bureaux, Law Centres and law students' groups are among those who commonly act as 'McKenzie friends', though anyone requested by the litigant could do so.

'McKenzie friends' may in fact be legally qualified: solicitor Ole Hansen acted in this capacity in a High Court case in 1993; as a solicitor he would not at the time have been allowed to represent a client directly in that court.

Lay assessors and scientific advisers

Under the Supreme Court Act 1981, judges may appoint people with special expertise in a particular area to sit with them in certain cases – usually those involving scientific or technical evidence. Their role is to hear the evidence and give the judge whatever assistance is needed in interpreting it and forming a judgment, though the judge still makes the final decision. In the event of an appeal, the appeal court may take the reasoning of lay assessors into account when assessing the original court's decision.

In most cases, lay persons are given technical advice from lawyers to make legal decisions – for example the magistrates are advised by the legally qualified magistrates' clerk and the judge sums up the law and the facts for the benefit of the jury.

Rights of audience for lay people?

The Courts and Legal Services Act 1990 (CLSA) was intended to develop and improve legal services by making provision for new ways of providing such services, including a wider choice of persons able to provide them. The Act therefore provided for rights of audience to be extended to 'suitably qualified people'. In normal circumstances, the decision on whether people (or more commonly, professions as a whole) are 'suitably qualified' is for the Lord Chancellor's Department, but the Act allows the courts some discretion to grant rights of audience. In **D** *v* **S** (1996), the chairman of a charity representing the rights of divorced fathers sought to use this provision to gain rights of audience to represent a member of the same charity. He pointed out that both parties agreed to his acting in the case, and that his work with the charity had given him considerable knowledge of the relevant area of law, and therefore he could be considered 'suitably qualified' for the purpose of the Act.

The Court of Appeal disagreed. It held that the discretion allowed to courts under the Act was only intended to be used in exceptional circumstances, and not merely because the parties consented to it. Parliament had laid down stringent rules about the requirements for rights of audience, and these should not be bypassed.

The Access to Justice Act 1999 is designed to go further than the CLSA in widening rights of audience, and the Act is very much concerned with using the skill and experience of the voluntary sector, so it may be that certain lay people will be given rights of audience in the future.

Advantages of lay participation

- It is cheap.
- It involves the community and promotes public confidence.
- It keeps procedure simple. It has been suggested that the only reason why Crown Court procedure has had to remain intelligible to the general public is because it is necessary for the jury to understand the proceedings.

Disadvantages

- 'Amateur justice' – the alleged inconsistency of magistrates and 'perverse' verdicts of juries. The lay panels which heard supplementary benefit appeals in the 1960s and 1970s were a disaster, deciding cases on the basis of who they thought were 'the deserving poor', and had to be replaced by a panel of two lay persons with specialist knowledge of welfare problems and a legally qualified, experienced chairperson.
- Lack of procedure. The simple approach can go too far. As an example, discipline in prisons is in the hands of boards of visitors, the bulk of whose membership is drawn from magistrates; they hold hearings when prisoners are accused of offences against prison discipline, such as rioting, and may impose punishments. The courts had to intervene in the process, in **R** *v* **Board of Visitors of Hull Prison, ex parte St Germain** (1979), because boards of visitors were found to be showing complete disregard for the rules of natural justice.
- Ignoring the law. While the jury's right to find a verdict according to its conscience is seen as a strength and a safeguard, the tendency of some lay participants to ignore the law can have the opposite effect. Mental Health Review Tribunals, for example, have to decide whether to release compulsorily detained psychiatric patients, and must do so if the patient is no longer mentally ill or no longer needs to be detained. In a number of recent cases the tribunals decided not to release patients who fell into one of these categories because they felt that some of them might be dangerous, or unable to survive in the outside world. The High Court has quashed the tribunal decisions as being wholly outside their statutory power.
- Problems with bias. It is suggested that lay people may be less able than professionals to put any personal prejudices aside.

ANSWERING QUESTIONS

1 Evaluate the use of lay persons in the administration of justice. *Edexcel*

For this question you need to talk about magistrates and juries, and the other lay people mentioned in this chapter. Obviously there is quite a lot of material in this area in the book so you need to be selective. You might say a little about the long history of lay involvement in your introduction, and perhaps mention the more recent changes – the fact that juries are now very rarely used in civil cases and the extension of the magistrates' role in criminal justice.

You are asked to evaluate, so you need to assess the strengths and weaknesses of using lay people in the administration of justice. A good way of structuring your essay would be to deal with strengths common to lay participants in general, such as those listed in this chapter (cheapness, involvement of the community and simplicity), and then any benefits which are specific to particular types of lay involvement, for example the specific background knowledge possessed by some of the Employment Tribunal members, or the way in which juries are able to represent society as a whole. You can then follow the same procedure for the weaknesses of lay involvement, looking at the general points made in this chapter (amateurism, lack of procedure, ignoring the law, and problems with bias), and then discussing any weaknesses specific to particular lay participants.

Your conclusion should say how effective and useful you think lay participants are in the legal system, and on the basis of that you may want to say whether you think their role should be increased, reduced or abolished.

2 'Experience of the performance of juries and lay magistrates tends to confirm that decisions in legal cases should be left to lawyers.'
(a) Describe the qualifications, appointment and role of jurors and magistrates.
(b) Do you agree with the statement above? *AQA (AEB)*

Part (a) is self-explanatory – the only points to watch are that you should not spend so long on this part that you leave yourself insufficient time for the second part, and you must discuss both juries and magistrates. For part (b), you need to outline the evidence concerning the performance of juries and lay magistrates, from within the relevant chapters. Then you need to say whether in your view this evidence does mean that decisions should be left to lawyers, which effectively means professional judges (including district judges (magistrates' courts)). Bring in any reasons which might outweigh these problems – such as cost, or the importance of community involvement.

You should also talk about the alternatives to juries and magistrates, both those involving lawyers only, and those which mix the two – these are detailed in chapter 5: The jury system. You need to assess whether these would be a better alternative. You could also talk about any reforms which you feel would improve the performance of magistrates or juries.

Note that this question is only asking about the lay role in decision-making – so McKenzie friends and scientific advisers are not relevant here.

▶ Reading on the Internet

The Citizens' Advice Bureau website is:
http://nacab.org.uk

8 Access to justice

Since society requires that all its members keep the law, it follows that all members of society should be not only equally bound by, but also equally served by, the legal system. Legal rights are after all worthless unless they can be enforced. Yet justice may be open to all, but only in the same way as the Ritz Hotel. In other words, anyone can go there, but only if they can afford it – and just like the Ritz Hotel, legal advice and help can be very expensive. As a result, many people simply cannot afford to enforce their legal rights and are therefore denied access to justice.

What is more, cost is not the only thing which stops many ordinary people from using the legal system. Other issues such as awareness of legal rights, the elitist image of the legal profession and even its geographical situation all contribute to the problem which legal writers call 'unmet legal need'. In the following section, we look at what unmet legal need really means, and the causes of it; later in the chapter we consider the various attempts which have been made to resolve the problem, including government funded legal services, which as we will see is currently in the process of radical change.

▶ UNMET NEED FOR LEGAL SERVICES

Unmet legal need essentially describes the situation where a person has a problem that could potentially be solved through the law, but the person is unable to get whatever help he or she needs to use the legal system. Research by Richard White in 1973 suggested four situations in which this can happen:

- the person fails to recognize a problem as having legal implications and so does not seek out legal advice
- the problem is recognized as being a legal one, but the person involved does not know of the existence of a legal service that could help, or their own eligibility to use it

- the person knows the problem is a legal one, and knows of the service that could help with it, but chooses not to make use of it because of some barrier, such as cost, ignorance of state funding or the unapproach-able image of solicitors
- the person knows there is a legal problem and wants legal help, but fails to get it because they cannot find a service to deal with it.

Of these reasons, the barrier of cost has traditionally received most atten-tion, and it is an important one; a 1991 *Which?* report found one in ten people were put off seeking legal advice by cost. Simply obtaining legal advice from a private solicitor is expensive, and taking a case to court much more so – and in English law, the loser in a civil case must usually pay the costs of the winner as well as their own costs. This gives the rich three major advantages: they can hire good lawyers and pay for the time needed to do the job properly; they can afford to take the risk of losing litigation; and they can use their wealth to bully a less well-off opponent, by dragging out the case or making it more complex (and therefore more expensive). Bear in mind that 'the rich' does not just mean the millionaire in the Rolls Royce, but also the employer you might want to sue for unfair dismissal, the company whose products could make you ill or the builder who left you with a leaky roof, and you can see the problem.

However, as White's research shows, cost is not the only reason why people fail to secure help with their legal problems. This is backed up by the 1973 research of Abel-Smith *et al.*, which compared people's own perception of their need for legal help and the action they took to get it. Almost all the respondents consulted a solicitor when they felt they needed advice on buying a house (though, of course, this only includes those with sufficient means to buy their own home). For employment problems though, only 4 per cent consulted a solicitor; 34 per cent took advice from some other source and 62 per cent took no advice at all. For Social Security problems, solicitors were consulted by even fewer people: just 3 per cent saw a solicitor, while 16 per cent took other advice and 81 per cent took none at all. Yet in all these cases, the people surveyed realized that they did need some legal advice.

Similarly, Zander has pointed out that even the poorest members of society consult solicitors about divorce, while the middle classes seem no more likely than working class people to consult solicitors about employ-ment or consumer problems.

American sociologists Mayhew and Reiss put forward a 'social organiza-tion' theory to explain why solicitors are consulted in some cases and not others. This theory suggests that certain types of work are related to social contact – most people know people who have used solicitors for conveyancing and divorce, and it becomes an obvious step to take. As

Zander points out, lawyers adjust the services they offer to demand and so it becomes a self-fulfilling prophecy.

Research carried out by Professor Hazel Genn in 1998 categorized the different types of people who are confronted by a legal problem. Five per cent were labelled as 'lumpers'. This group had low incomes, low education levels and were frequently unemployed. They were unable to see any way out of their money and employment problems and therefore did absolutely nothing. This could lead to a 'cluster' of problems where the person was increasingly incapable of helping him or herself. The next group were described as 'self-helpers' and only had a 50 per cent chance of resolving their legal problems. They often believed until the last minute that nothing could be done to help them and when they tried to take action they found they had gone, or been sent, to the wrong place; or were confronted by queues, unanswered telephones and restricted opening times. Professor Genn found that social distress could be caused where legal problems were left unresolved. By contrast, if people got good quality early advice they could help themselves.

Another problem, identified by the Royal Commission on Legal Services, is the uneven geographical distribution of solicitors throughout the country. The Commission highlighted research showing that while there was one solicitor's office for every 4,700 people in England and Wales, their distribution varied enormously, from one office for every 2,000 people in prosperous owner-occupier areas such as Bournemouth and Guildford, to one for every 66,000 in working-class areas such as Huyton in Liverpool. The Commission concluded that the low rates for state-funded work had much to do with this; most private firms need to subsidize such work with privately funded work, and the poorer areas may not provide enough of this to keep more than a few solicitors in each area in business. Other advice agencies, such as law centres and Citizens' Advice Bureaux may also be thin on the ground in some, particularly rural, areas. The image of lawyers as predominantly white, male and from privileged backgrounds may also contribute to the problem, making them unapproachable to many people.

In its 1999 report *A Balancing Act; Surviving the Risk Society*, the National Association of Citizens' Advice Bureaux (NACAB) suggested that the problem of unmet legal need may still be growing. It pointed out that changes in society are forcing more and more people to take on responsibility for their own welfare in areas where the state would once have made provision, while insecurity in work, housing and family relationships is increasing. This means more and more people are placed in situations where they need to assert their legal rights – divorce, homelessness, debt or employment problems, for example – but are unable to do so because there is too little access to free, independent legal advice.

In the following sections, we look at the attempts that successive governments have made to ease the problem of unmet legal need by providing state-funded legal help, and then at a range of other approaches to the problem.

STATE-FUNDED LEGAL SERVICES

The system of state-funded legal help in this country goes back almost half a century. After the Second World War, the Labour Government introduced a range of measures designed to address the huge inequalities between rich and poor. These included the National Health Service, the beginnings of today's Social Security system and, in 1949, the first state-funded legal aid scheme. The legal aid scheme was designed to allow poorer people access to legal advice and representation in court: this would be provided by solicitors in private practice, but the state, rather than the client, would pay all or part of the fees. By the 1980s, the system had developed into six different schemes, covering most kinds of legal case, and administered by the Legal Aid Board. But the growing cost of these schemes was causing concern. In the 1990s the Conservative Government sought to keep the escalating costs down by reducing financial eligibility for the schemes, which in turn led to criticisms that they were also reducing access to justice. As a result of all this, the Labour Government passed the Access to Justice Act 1999 which made major changes to the system.

Before looking at the new system of state funding, it is useful to look at the system that it replaced, in order to consider what problems the changes are designed to address, and how successful they are likely to be.

Legal aid before the Access to Justice Act 1999

The six schemes which made up the legal aid scheme until the Access to Justice Act 1999 was brought into force were:

- the legal advice and assistance scheme (known as the 'green form' scheme because of the paperwork used)
- assistance by way of representation (ABWOR)
- civil legal aid
- criminal legal aid
- duty solicitor schemes in police stations
- duty solicitor schemes for criminal cases in magistrates' courts.

Each scheme had its own rules on eligibility and some included means and/or merits tests. A means test assesses eligibility on the basis of the applicant's disposable income, which is the money left each week after paying for certain essential living expenses; and sometimes disposable capital, which effectively means savings. Only those with disposable incomes below the limit laid down for the type of legal aid required were eligible for help. Merits tests assess whether the applicant's case is likely to succeed, and whether it is sufficiently important to justify state funding. The specific details of the means and merits tests varied according to the type of legal aid, and some imposed neither test.

Legal aid was not always free – for civil and criminal legal aid, clients whose income or savings were above a certain limit were expected to contribute towards their legal costs. And with civil legal aid, it frequently acted more like a loan, since the costs could be deducted from the damages awarded to the successful client.

The Lord Chancellor was the Government Minister responsible for the legal aid scheme, but its day-to-day administration was undertaken by the Legal Aid Board, through area directors and committees.

The six schemes that existed before the Access to Justice Act 1999 came into force will now be considered in more detail.

The Green Form scheme

This was set up to provide legal advice and assistance in any civil or criminal matter, except conveyancing and drawing up wills. The assistance given included drafting letters and other documents and advising clients who intended to represent themselves in court on what to say, but did not cover representation in court by the solicitor.

Applicants had to pass a means test. Until 1993, around 30 per cent of the population qualified under the means test. Of that 30 per cent, the poorest received free help, and the rest had to contribute towards the cost. But the rising cost of the scheme led the previous Conservative Government to cut back sharply its availability. So by 1999 only those with a disposable income of less than £75 a week were eligible for the scheme, those earning more than this were excluded completely.

Assistance by way of representation (ABWOR)

This was an extension of the Green Form scheme, which provided representation in a limited number of situations and was subject to a means test.

Civil legal aid

This covered all the work involved in bringing or defending a civil case, including representation in court by a solicitor or barrister. Eligibility for civil legal aid was subject to both a merits and a means test. To fulfil the merits test, an applicant had to satisfy the Legal Aid Board that they had a reasonable case, with a reasonable chance of success.

Where a person who had civil legal aid won their case, if the costs recovered from the other party (and any contributions made by the legally aided person) did not cover the amount spent by the legal aid fund, the fund could recover the difference from the damages won (subject to certain restrictions in matrimonial cases). This was called the statutory charge. In such cases civil legal aid acted more like a loan.

Criminal legal aid

Like civil legal aid, this covered the whole range of legal advice, assistance and representation, including the cost of a barrister if the case was heard in the Crown Court. Because decisions often needed to be made more quickly than in civil cases, an application for criminal legal aid was made to the courts, not the Legal Aid Board. Eligibility was subject to both means and merits tests.

Duty solicitor schemes in police stations

This scheme has been retained following the 1999 reforms. Duty solicitor schemes in the police station were set up in response to the provisions of the Police and Criminal Evidence Act 1984, which provides a right to legal advice for suspects detained by the police. The idea is to ensure that access to a solicitor for advice and assistance is available 24 hours a day to anyone detained by the police. Clients are not, however, obliged to use duty solicitors, and can still consult their own solicitors.

The scheme is free and available to anyone who is being questioned by the police, regardless of whether they have been arrested. There are no means or merits tests.

Duty solicitor schemes in magistrates' courts

This scheme has also been retained following the 1999 reforms. Solicitors on a rota basis are present at the courts to advise unrepresented defendants. There is no means or merits test.

Problems with the six schemes

Even by the early 1980s, it was clear that there were severe problems with the state-funded schemes. They had become extremely costly – by 1997, state-funded legal aid was costing £1.6 billion, six times higher than in 1979 – yet even the huge amounts being spent were failing to deliver real access to justice for all levels of society. There were essentially two separate sets of problems, one relating to legal aid as it applied to civil cases, and the other to its use in criminal cases, so we will look at each in turn.

Problems with legal aid in civil cases

Eligibility As explained above, eligibility levels for the means-tested schemes were drastically lowered after 1992. In 1979, 79 per cent of adults were eligible for civil legal aid, including those who would have had to pay contributions, but by 1993 this had dropped to 48 per cent, which was still the level in 1999.

The result of this was that while the very poor could get legal aid, and the rich, as ever, could afford their own legal costs, the vast majority of people on moderate incomes faced a choice between incurring severe financial burdens, or simply being unable to assert their legal rights.

Even for those who did still qualify for legal aid, eligibility for free help ran out at an extremely low level, and above that, the contributions payable could be very expensive, especially for those at the top end of the eligibility scale. Once contributions became payable throughout the duration of a case, so that litigants could not know in advance how much they would be expected to spend, they clearly had the potential to discourage many people from taking legal action at all.

Funding Lawyers constantly claimed that the system was underfunded and that lawyers working within it were badly paid, with the result that many lawyers were not interested in taking part. The underfunding risked creating a second-class service, not necessarily because of lack of quality in the lawyers themselves, but because they simply could not afford to spend the same amount of time on a case as a privately funded lawyer.

Reliance on private practice When the legal aid system was set up the Government had a choice between using the existing private practice structures or setting up a totally separate system of lawyers, who would be paid salaries from public funds (as doctors are in the NHS), rather than being paid on a case-by-case basis. They chose to give legal aid work to lawyers in private practice, who would be paid per case. Kate Markus, writing in *The Critical Lawyer's Handbook* argues that this causes five main problems.

First, rather than responding to need, state-funded practitioners in private practice are ruled by the requirements of running a business in a highly competitive marketplace. Private practitioners have to make a profit, even where they are paid by the state, and therefore often feel that they must limit the time they spend on state-funded cases. This problem severely limits the services they can offer to the clients, and is also the reason why so many lawyers have refused to do state-funded work, which given the funding problems, has never been able to compete with privately paid work in terms of the salaries paid. Secondly, private solicitors' practices are very much geared towards legal problems concerning money and property, which means that as far as general High Street solicitors are concerned, their expertise is often not developed in those areas affecting the poorer client. The third problem, which we have mentioned before, is that solicitors in private practice may be seen as intimidating by the majority of poorer clients, who are then put off bringing their problems to them, especially in areas where they are not sure whether it is appropriate to involve a lawyer. The fourth issue Markus highlights is that private practice is geared largely to litigation (bringing cases to court), which is not always the best solution to the kind of problems facing the poorer members of society. Let us say, for example, that a local council is failing to fulfil its obligations to tenants, with the result that many of them are living in unacceptable housing. Each affected family could take the council to court, but that would be expensive and time-consuming, and only solve the problem for those families who actually did so. But with access to good legal advice on their rights, the tenants could get together and put pressure on the council themselves, potentially solving a problem affecting lots of people in one action, and much more cheaply. Law centres (see below) often work this way, but the working practices of private practitioners, and the case-by-case way in which legal aid was funded, made it impossible for them to do much, if any, of this kind of work.

Finally, Markus makes the point that any system which seeks to make justice truly accessible has to address the problem of widespread ignorance of legal rights and how to assert them; after all, if a person with a legal problem is unaware that there might be a legal right which could solve it, he or she will not even think of getting legal help in the first place. That means educating people about their rights, and private practice, where every task a lawyer does has to be paid for, is simply not set up to do that kind of work.

Fraud and misuse In 1997, the Lord Chancellor's Department revealed that over the previous year, more than 25,000 individuals granted legal aid were later discovered not to have been entitled to it. Newspapers estimated that these claims were costing up to £60 million a year, and pointed out that the figure only applied to claims that had been detected, so undiscovered fraud might be running on an even bigger scale. Solicitors were also implicated in attempts to defraud the legal aid schemes, and in particular, the Green Form scheme, where it was said to be easy to claim for non-existent work – by 1995, 100 firms had been investigated by the Legal Aid Board, and a number referred to the Serious Fraud Office.

Patchy coverage The piecemeal development of the statutory schemes brought about considerable overlap between schemes, while failing to fill important gaps. One of the most significant was that legal aid was not available for cases brought before most tribunals. This was a major anomaly, given that tribunals were created to give ordinary citizens a way of asserting their rights, and in many tribunals the 'ordinary citizen' faces an opponent with ready access to the best legal advice and representation – Government departments, for example, or large companies – in the Employment Tribunal. This can put the unrepresented litigant at a serious disadvantage (see p. 393). By contrast, a business owner, so long as he or she was a sole trader and met the relevant means and merits tests, could in principle get legal aid to pursue a business dispute, which was hardly the kind of problem the scheme was designed to address.

Another gap was that legal aid was never available for defamation cases slander, which meant that only the wealthy and powerful could afford the luxury of defending their reputations. The knock-on effect of this was that unscrupulous newspapers knew that ordinary people were unlikely to sue and were therefore willing to take the risk of defaming them.

The statutory charge The statutory charge could claw back all of a claimant's damages, which, as far as the client was concerned, could make the whole action a waste of time. Although solicitors were required to explain the effect of the charge to legally aided clients, for those who went through all the stress of a court case, won it and then came away empty-handed, it looked suspiciously as though the legal aid scheme was run more for the benefit of lawyers than for people with legal problems.

Costs for non-legally aided parties Where a legally aided client lost a case, there were limits on the amount of costs that their opponent could get back from them, as would normally happen in a civil case. Clearly this could place the legally aided client at an unfair advantage, since costs could be used as a weapon to force an early settlement.

Problems with legal aid in criminal cases

Standards of work A number of problems with criminal legal aid were uncovered by the 1993 Royal Commission on Criminal Justice, which was set up to look at the whole of the criminal justice system after a number of miscarriages of justice were uncovered in the late 1980s and early 1990s. The most serious allegation, made in research by McConville and Hodgson (1993), was that the standard of legally aided criminal defence work was very low. Much of it was done by unqualified staff; there was little investigative work, and solicitors pushed clients towards pleading guilty rather than taking time to prepare an effective defence. McConville claimed that the heavy workloads and low pay of legal aid work forced solicitors to see their clients as 'economic units', to be processed as quickly as possible.

The Royal Commission highlighted particular problems with standards of work among duty solicitors at police stations. Sanders' research carried out in 1993 found that advice was often given over the telephone rather than in person, or solicitors left the station after giving advice without attending the interrogation – a solicitor was present in only 14 per cent of interrogations. Where someone was sent to the police station, in many cases they lacked sufficient knowledge and experience. The research showed that legal advisers sent under the scheme made few interventions during interrogation: in 66 per cent of cases they said nothing at all; and in only 9 per cent did they actively intervene on behalf of the suspect and object to police questions. In some cases the legal adviser seemed to identify more with the police than with the suspect. They were also ineffective in discovering vital information about the case: in 45 per cent of cases, no attempt was made to seek information from the police, and the solicitor relied completely on what clients knew. They routinely failed to discover important information, or to examine adequately the client's legal position.

In practice, firms often sent an unqualified junior member of staff rather than a solicitor, which was seen as a particular problem because an effective duty solicitor also needs sufficient confidence to stand up to the police where necessary in the client's interests, and this is likely to be difficult for young, inexperienced personnel. McConville's research found that almost half of firms studied sent employees who were former police officers.

The Commission found that although the number of people getting legal advice at police stations had increased since the duty solicitor scheme began, it was still quite low – less than 20 per cent according to Sanders' 1989 research – and varied widely between stations. Sanders' 1993 research suggested that this was partly due to the police not giving proper advice about the scheme, or discouraging suspects from using it, and partly due to suspects' own unwillingness to take up the offer when it was made, for any number of reasons: dislike of lawyers, desire to get things over with without delay, perception of the offence as trivial, confidence that their own innocence would save them, or conversely, belief that nothing could help them. However, inefficiency on the part of solicitors also contributed, in that their response to calls was often slow, especially at night, with less than 60 per cent of duty solicitors reaching police stations within an hour. This was seen as a serious problem, given that delay seemed to be a vital factor in putting suspects off asking for a duty solicitor (and a factor which the police could and did highlight when attempting to put a suspect off using the scheme). Nearly half of those respondents questioned for the Royal Commission who did not take up the offer of legal advice said they would have done so if a solicitor had been already available at the police station, rather than having to be called in from elsewhere. However, the Royal Commission saw little prospect of such a scheme being introduced.

Funding Just as with civil legal aid, solicitors claimed that underfunding of criminal legal aid made it impossible for them to deliver the best service to defendants, and discouraged many good lawyers from undertaking legally aided work at all. This was a particular problem for the duty solicitor scheme: the pay for duty solicitors is higher than that for most legal aid work, but still low considering the irregular hours, with the result that few solicitors wanted to take part, and the burden on the rest could at times become intolerable. Some local schemes collapsed as a result, and in 1992 the Law Society expressed its 'grave concern' at the drop in the number of solicitors involved.

The problem of solicitors' fees was – from the solicitors' point of view at least – made worse with the introduction of fixed fees. Originally, all legal aid was paid for on the basis of the amount of work done on each individual case, paid by the hour. In 1987, the Lord Chancellor announced that this arrangement would be changed for criminal cases, and fixed fees would by payable, assessed by the type of case and remaining the same regardless of the amount of work done on a particular case. As far as the Government was concerned, this was merely a 'swings and roundabouts' approach: lawyers would lose out on cases which took more work than usual, but gain on cases which were simpler and quicker than usual, and overall the fees would balance out. The Law Society saw it differently, pointing out that cases which could be processed without much work were in a definite minority. They claimed that standard fees would penalize solicitors who prepared their cases thoroughly, and reward those who cut corners. In addition, it was clear that fixed fees were to be used to keep costs down, and that meant the Lord Chancellor could choose to keep annual increases in the fees below the level of inflation, in effect forcing solicitors to take annual pay cuts.

Problems with the means test Before 1984, the courts had only limited powers to order contributions in criminal cases, and few orders were made. In 1984, new rules were introduced, which critics said gave a higher priority to saving money than to ensuring justice, and certainly after the rules came into force, many more contribution orders began to be made. The Royal Commission on Criminal Justice acknowledged the need to keep public expenditure down, but stressed that it would be 'very seriously concerned' if it transpired that the changes meant an increase in the number of defendants without legal representation, especially in the Crown Court.

Ironically, critics claimed that the system also suffered from the opposite problem: failure to collect contributions from those who could afford them. In 1994, the National Audit Office reported that the information supplied on means test forms was rarely checked, so that it was easy to avoid contributions being ordered at all by lying about one's income. In addition, where contributions were ordered, experienced defendants avoided paying them before the trial began, knowing that once it started, the judge would not want to withdraw legal aid and end up with the delay and inconvenience of an unrepresented defendant, and once it was over, they were likely either to be in prison, with no income to pay the contributions, or acquitted, in which case the state would pay.

Furthermore, the system of means testing was expensive in itself; in 1997–98 contributions made by defendants to the cost of their legal aid amounted to £6.2 million, but the direct cost of administering means testing and enforcing contributions was around £5 million.

Problems with the merits test In concentrating on the seriousness of the charge and possible penalty, the merits test made it more difficult for defendants to get legal aid for minor offences. These may be the least important ones, but the effects of a conviction on the individual may be profound – and if society does not want its members to see minor offences as trivial, the criminal justice system should not be seen to treat them as such. A further problem was that it could be difficult to know whether the merits criteria applied until after a trial had started, and even if legal aid was then granted, the defendant might already have been disadvantaged.

State funding of legal services today

With the passing of the Access to Justice Act 1999 the Labour Government introduced some major reforms to the provision of state-funded legal services. Through these reforms the Government hoped to improve the quality and accessibility of the legal services on offer, while keeping a tighter control on their budget. On 1 April 2001 the Legal Aid Board was abolished and replaced by the Legal Services Commission. It currently has a budget of £1.6 billion a year. The Commission is guided in its work by the Lord Chancellor (who must make any such guidance public) but the Lord Chancellor is not allowed to give guidance about the handling of any individual case.

In order to develop the standard and accessibility of legal services the Legal Services Commission has established a quality mark, is building partnerships with the different suppliers of legal services and has set up a website.

Quality mark

The Commission has created a new quality mark to help people make more informed choices about the legal service providers they use. The mark is applied to all kinds of legal services, from information leaflets and general advice agencies to specialist solicitors. To be awarded a quality mark, the service providers have to meet set quality standards, so that users of their services know when they see the mark that those standards have been met.

Community Legal Service Partnerships

The Legal Services Commission has a duty to liaise with other funders of legal services (such as local councils, who help fund local advice centres) in order to develop a network of legal service providers. The idea is to develop local, national and regional plans which will match the services available in a particular area to the needs of the people living there. To do this, the Commission is setting up Community Legal Service Partnerships (CLSPs) in each local authority area, involving the Commission, the local authority and other significant funders of legal services to coordinate funding and planning. Partnerships can provide a forum for sharing expertise, developing and improving services and for monitoring what is happening locally. The partnerships should facilitate the creation of effective local referral networks in every area and ensure that funding is appropriately targeted. The Government intends that 90 per cent of the population of England and Wales will be covered by a partnership by April 2002, and 70 are currently underway.

As we have seen, gaps in the geographical distribution of legal services increases unmet legal need. The Commission and the Community Legal Service Partnerships are encouraging the voluntary sector to use the Internet and mobile services to reach more remote communities.

Website

The Legal Services Commission website can be found at www.justask.org.uk. The website provides basic advice and information for members of the public.

The schemes

The Legal Services Commission administers two schemes: the Community Legal Service which is concerned with civil matters and the Criminal Defence Service which is concerned with criminal matters. These two schemes will be considered in turn.

The Community Legal Service

Funding
Whereas previously legal aid in civil cases was available on a demand-led basis (meaning that all cases which met the merits and means tests would be funded), there is now a Community Legal Service Fund, containing a fixed amount of money, set each year as part of the normal round of Government spending plans.

The detailed way in which the Fund is to be spent is decided by a Funding Code, drawn up by the Legal Services Commission and approved by the Lord Chancellor, which sets out the criteria and procedures to be used when deciding whether a particular case should be funded. The Commission has a duty to obtain the best value for money, which the explanatory notes to the Access to Justice Act 1999 defines as taking into account 'a combination of price and quality'. In other words, the Commission is not obliged to choose the cheapest possible service, but it is not obliged to choose the best quality one either; it has to find the best balance between the two.

Levels of funded legal services

Only solicitors or advice agencies holding a contract with the Legal Services Commission are able to provide advice or representation directly funded by the Commission. For specialist areas of law such as family law, immigration, mental health and clinical negligence only specialist firms are funded to do the work. The merits test for civil legal aid has been replaced by the new Funding Code discussed on p. 218. This Code lays down the rules as to which cases should receive funding. Direct funding is provided for different categories of legal service, as follows:

- *Legal Help.* Legal Help provides initial advice and assistance with any legal problem. A means test is applied. This level of service covers work previously carried out under the 'Green Form' scheme.
- *Legal Representation.* Funding is available for a person to be represented in court proceedings. Both a means and a merits test are applied. This scheme replaces civil legal aid.
- *Help at Court.* Help at Court allows somebody (a solicitor or adviser) to speak on another's behalf at certain court hearings, without formally acting for them in the whole proceedings. A means test is applied.
- *Approved Family Help.* Approved Family Help provides help in relation to a family dispute, including assistance in resolving that dispute through negotiation or otherwise. This overlaps with the services covered by Legal Help, but also includes issuing proceedings and representation where necessary to obtain disclosure of information from another party, or to obtain a consent order where the parties have reached an agreement.
- *Family Mediation.* This level of service covers mediation for a family dispute, including finding out whether mediation appears suitable or not.

Coverage

Certain types of case have been removed from the state funded system altogether. These are:

- Personal injury cases (with the exception of clinical negligence cases). Instead these are funded by conditional fee agreements which are discussed later in this chapter.
- Cases of defamation and malicious falsehood. Legal aid was never available for defamation, but in some cases, behaviour which would normally be classed as defamation could be categorized as the related tort of malicious falsehood, for which legal aid was available. Now neither is eligible for state funding, because the Government believes that these cases are not sufficiently important to justify it, and they may in any case be suitable for funding by conditional fee agreements.
- Disputes arising in the course of a business. Business traders can insure against the cost of having to bring or defend a legal action, and the

Government believes that taxpayers should not be required to meet the legal costs of those who fail to do so.

- Matters concerning the law relating to companies, partnerships, trusts (trusts are a way of holding property, and as such, tend mainly to affect wealthier people) or boundary disputes (for example, disputes between neighbours as to where each party's garden begins and ends).

The Government considers that none of these types of case are sufficiently important to justify public funding. Approximately 80,000 people are injured each year at work, on the road or during a leisure activity. It has been estimated that personal injury cases accounted for around 60 per cent of cases previously funded by legal aid, most of which would have been personal injury cases. However, the Access to Justice Act 1999 provides that the Lord Chancellor can direct the Commission to provide services for excluded categories in exceptional circumstances.

Eligibility

There will continue to be both merits and means tests for some forms of state funding of civil legal services. The Government has made no major changes to the previous eligibility limits. Eventually it intends to extend the availability of advice and assistance (as provided under the old system by the Green Form scheme) to those who can afford to pay contributions towards the cost.

The old merits test has been replaced by the criteria set out in the Funding Code, and this is intended to be more flexible than the previous test, in that different criteria can be applied to different types of case, depending on their priority. For example, the chances of success might be relevant in many types of case, but would not be in cases about whether a child should be taken into local authority care.

Suppliers

In the past, a person who wanted help with a problem covered by legal aid could go to any lawyer and, providing the client met the relevant means and merits tests, that lawyer would be paid by the Government for the help given in that particular case. This situation was beginning to change even before the 1999 Act was passed. In 1994 the Legal Aid Board began a quality assurance scheme called franchising. Law firms could apply for a franchise in particular areas of work, and would have to pass quality control tests in order to get one, but would then be able to attract more work in that area. Similar agreements were made, on a pilot basis, with advice agencies, so that they could provide advice and assistance in specific areas. The Act takes this idea further, so that only solicitors and advice agencies holding contracts with the Legal Services Commission are able to get state funding.

The 1999 Act also gives the Commission power to make grants to service providers, such as advice centres, and to employ staff directly to deliver legal services to the public. This latter point means that the Commission could, if it wished, create a system of lawyers employed by the state to provide legal help to the public, though there appear to be no plans to do so with regard to civil cases at the moment.

Future changes

The Act allows for a new way of funding legal help for individuals, which at present the Government has no plans to use. It provides for a scheme in which people could be given state funding, but required to agree that if they win their case, they will pay back the state funding (which they would presumably claim from the losing party), plus a further sum. This would make it possible to fund certain types of case on a self-financing basis, with the extra sums paid by winning litigants funding the costs of those who lose their cases.

The Criminal Defence Service

In April 2001 a Criminal Defence Service was introduced, replacing the old system of criminal legal aid. This Criminal Defence Service is administered by the Legal Services Commission.

Funding

Unlike legal aid in civil cases, state-funded criminal defence will continue to be given on a demand-led basis; there will be no set budget and all cases which fit the merits criteria will be funded.

Levels of funded legal services

As part of this service the Commission directly funds the provision of criminal legal services, employs public defenders and pays for duty solicitor schemes. Thus under the Criminal Defence Service, legal services are provided by both lawyers in private practice and employed lawyers. The Government believes that a mixed system of public and private lawyers will provide the best value for money for the taxpayer. The salaried service is intended to provide a benchmark to assess whether prices charged by private practice lawyers are reasonable, as well as filling in gaps in the system.

Direct funding Only solicitor firms having a contract with the Legal Services Commission are able to offer state funded criminal defence work. Unlike the contracts for civil matters, the contracts for criminal defence matters do not limit the number of cases that can be taken on, nor the total value of the payments that may be made. Contracted solicitors will be paid for all work actually undertaken in accordance with the contract.

Solicitors with a contract should be able to provide the full range of criminal defence services, from the time of arrest until the end of the case (unlike with the previous system, where defendants could receive assistance relating to the same alleged offence under several different schemes, each resulting in a separate payment for the lawyers involved). In certain cases – such as serious fraud trials – there are panels of firms or individual lawyers who specialize in the relevant type of case, and defendants will be required to choose from that panel. State funding can support three types of service.

- *Advice and assistance.* Funding is available for the provision of advice and assistance from a solicitor, including giving general advice, writing letters, negotiating, getting a barrister's opinion and preparing a written case. A means test is applied but people who are eligible do not have to make any contribution to the legal costs. It does not cover representation in court.

    When a person is questioned by the police they have a right to free legal advice from a contracted solicitor and no means test is applied.
- *Advocacy assistance.* Advocacy assistance covers the costs of a solicitor preparing a client's case and their initial representation in certain proceedings in both the magistrates' court and the Crown Court and in certain other circumstances. There is no means test but there is a merits test.
- *Representation.* When a person has been charged with a criminal offence, representation covers the cost of a solicitor to prepare their defence and to represent them in court. It may also be available for a bail application. It will sometimes pay for a barrister, particularly for the Crown Court and for the cost of an appeal.

Decisions to grant representation in individual cases are made by the magistrates' courts. Representation will be granted when it is in the 'interests of justice'. The court may decide that it is in the interests of justice to grant representation where, for example, the case is so serious that on conviction a person is likely to be sent to prison or to lose their job, where there are substantial questions of law to be argued, or where the defendant is unable to follow the proceedings and explain their case because they do not speak English well enough or are suffering from a psychiatric illness.

Before criminal legal aid was means tested. Under the new scheme the means test has been abolished. Instead, for cases heard in the Crown Court orders can be issued at the end of a trial to recover the defence costs against wealthy people who have been convicted of an offence. This reform reflected the fact that in most cases the defendants are too poor to pay for their own legal services – in the past only 1 per cent of applicants were refused legal aid. The hope is that by abolishing the means test altogether the criminal process will be speeded up.

Criminal defenders Since May 2001 the Legal Services Commission directly employs a number of criminal defence lawyers, known as public defenders. The plans envisage a start-up phase for the salaried service of four years, to run alongside a research programme. The research is looking into a range of issues, including the cost-effectiveness and the quality of the service provided by the pilot projects. There are six regional offices being piloted at the moment. The public defenders can provide the same services as lawyers in private practice and have to compete for work. The Government has promised that clients will not be forced to choose a public defender, but public defenders will be allocated slots on duty solicitor schemes in police stations and magistrates' courts where they will meet potential clients. It is then anticipated that, because there are many repeat offenders, there will be an expanding client base.

There has been strong opposition to the introduction of public defenders. The explanatory notes to the Access to Justice Act 1999 state that the idea is to provide flexibility, so that employed lawyers could be used if, for example, there is a shortage of suitable private lawyers in remoter areas. The notes point out that using salaried lawyers will also give the Commission better information about the real costs of providing the services. Commission lawyers are required to follow a code of conduct guaranteeing certain standards of professional behaviour, including duties to avoid discrimination, to protect the interests of those who they are defending, to avoid conflicts of interest and to maintain confidentiality.

At the moment public defenders are only employed in six pilot areas, but the intention is for them to be available nationally in the future. People suspected of crime will therefore have a choice only between these public defenders and lawyers who have a contract with the Commission, though within that limited range it is intended that there should be some choice in all but the most exceptional circumstances.

Duty solicitor schemes The duty solicitor schemes have remained unchanged by the reforms. Duty solicitors are available at police stations and magistrates' courts and offer free legal advice.

Coverage
The aim of the Criminal Defence Service, according to the explanatory notes to the Access to Justice Act 1999, is to ensure that individuals involved in criminal investigations or criminal proceedings 'have access to such advice, assistance and representation as the interests of justice require'.

Eligibility
State funding for criminal cases is no longer subject to a means test. Instead, it is automatically granted if the merits test is satisfied. The merits

test has remained unchanged with the 1999 Act. Where cases are tried in the Crown Court (which is substantially more costly than the magistrates' courts), at the end of the case the judge will have the power to order a defendant to pay some or all of the costs of his or her defence. The Commission is able to investigate the financial position of defendants in such cases, in order to help the judge decide whether to make such an order.

Other participants in the Community Legal Service

There are a number of non-profit making agencies which give legal advice and sometimes representation, and initiatives by the legal profession and other commercial organizations also address the issue of access to justice.

Law centres

Law centres offer a free, non-means-tested service to people who live or work in their area. They aim to be accessible to anyone who needs legal help, and in order to achieve this they usually operate from ground floor, high street premises, stay open beyond office hours, employ a high proportion of lay people as well as lawyers and generally encourage a more relaxed atmosphere than that found in most private solicitors' offices. Most law centres are run by a management committee drawn from the local area, so that they have direct links with the community.

The first law centres were established in 1969 and by 1984 there were around 50 of them. The Law Society allowed them to advertise (before the restriction on advertising was lifted for solicitors in general) in exchange for the centres not undertaking certain areas of work which were the mainstay of the average high street solicitor – small personal injury cases, wills and conveyancing. Their main areas of work are housing, welfare, immigration and employment.

Law centres are largely funded by grants from central and local government, though a few have also managed to secure some financial support from large local private firms. This method of funding means that they do not have to work on a case-by-case basis but can allocate funding according to community priorities.

Because they do not depend on case-by-case funding, law centres have developed innovative ways of solving legal problems. As well as dealing with individual cases, they run campaigns designed to make local people aware of their legal rights, act as a pressure group on local issues such as bad housing, and take action where appropriate on behalf of groups as well as individuals. The reasoning behind this approach is that resources and time are better used tackling problems as a whole, rather than aspects of those problems as they appear case by case. For example, if a council has failed to replace lead piping or asbestos in its council houses, it would seem more efficient to approach the council about all the properties rather than take out individual cases for each tenant as they become aware that they have a problem.

Law centres also provide valuable services in areas not covered by the statutory schemes, such as inquests, and several have set up duty solicitor schemes to deal with housing cases in the county court and help prevent evictions. They may offer a 24-hour general emergency service.

Most law centres face long-term problems with funding; several have closed, and others go through periodic struggles for survival. It is hoped that the Access to Justice Act 1999, with its emphasis on making the most of voluntary advice services, will mean better funding in future. The danger is that local authorities will withdraw funding as funding becomes available from the Legal Services Commission.

Citizens' Advice Bureaux

There are around 700 Citizens' Advice Bureaux across the country, offering free advice and help with a whole range of problems, though the most common areas at the moment are social security and debt. They are largely staffed by trained volunteers, who can become expert in the areas they most frequently deal with. Where professional legal help is required, some Bureaux employ solicitors, some have regular help from solicitor volunteers and others refer individuals to local solicitors who undertake state funded work. The Bureaux are overseen by the National Association of Citizens' Advice Bureaux and must conform to its standards and codes of practice.

One of their major advantages is a very high level of public awareness – because they are frequently mentioned in the press and have easily recognizable high street offices, most people know where they are and what they do.

Like law centres, they have come under considerable financial pressure in recent years, with the result that many can only open for a very limited number of hours a week. The Access to Justice Act may mean better funding in future.

Other sources of legal help

Some local authorities run money, welfare, consumer and housing advice centres to provide both advice and a mechanism for dealing with complaints, while charities such as Shelter, the Child Poverty Action Group and MIND often offer legal help in their specialist areas. Other organizations, such as trade unions, motoring organizations, such as the AA and RAC, and the Consumers' Association give free or inexpensive legal help to their members. Some university law faculties run 'law clinics', where students, supervised by their tutors, give free help and advice to members of the public.

There are a number of Internet sites giving basic legal advice for free, and some magazines publish legal advice lines, which charge a premium rate for readers to phone and get one-to-one legal advice from qualified solicitors. It is also possible to insure against legal expenses, either as a stand-alone policy, or more usually, as part of household, credit card or motor insurance.

As we saw earlier, cost is not the only cause of unmet legal need; a reluctance among many ordinary people to bring problems to lawyers is also recognized. In recent years the profession has taken steps to address the issue, including the use of advertising and public relations campaigns. Many high street firms now advertise their services locally, while some of the firms currently involved in suing cigarette manufacturers for illnesses caused by smoking attracted potential clients by advertising specifically for people with smoking-related diseases. In 1994, the Law Society set up Accident Line, under which accident victims can get a free initial interview with a solicitor specializing in personal injury.

The Access to Justice Act: an assessment

The Access to Justice Act 1999 was the subject of much opposition during the legislative process, and though some of the criticisms were addressed during the passing of the Act, some of this opposition remains. Below we detail the main criticisms, but first we look at some of the advantages claimed for the new system.

Advantages of the Access to Justice Act reforms

Increased access to justice
By opening up the availability of conditional fee agreements (which was done before the Act was passed) and then making them easier to use by allowing both the solicitor's uplift and any insurance premiums to be claimed as costs, the Government claims it has made it possible for people of moderate means to enforce their legal rights, when they could previously not afford to do so. Furthermore, taking out of the system those cases which previously would have been funded by legal aid means more money can be spent in other areas, so further increasing access to justice.

In addition, the new system specifically addresses the problem of lack of awareness of legal rights, with its emphasis on funding basic advice and information. The quality assurance mark should help those who have no prior experience of the legal system to make more informed choices about getting the help they need.

The new system allows sufficient flexibility to address the problem of uneven geographical distribution of lawyers. The contracting system will allow the Commission, if it chooses to do so, to pay extra to lawyers and firms willing to work in more remote areas.

Control of costs
As we have seen, the cost of the previous legal aid system was a major problem. The Government claims that the issuing of contracts, the fixed budget for state funding in civil cases and the fact that the Funding Code will set out clear criteria which reflect agreed priorities, will now mean that costs can be kept under control.

Better allocation of resources
The Funding Code for civil matters will be designed to reflect agreed priorities, so money can be channelled into those areas which the Government considers to reflect best the needs of society, whereas the demand-led approach of the past could not do this.

Higher standards of work
By limiting state funding to contracted lawyers and firms who have passed quality control standards, the Government claims that standards of work should be consistently high. The quality assurance mark will be used to spread high standards beyond law firms, to any organization which might offer legal advice to the public. In addition, the Lord Chancellor has suggested (*The Times*, 7 September 1999) that the creation of defence lawyers employed by the Commission would create a 'healthy rivalry' with private criminal lawyers and so stimulate them to give a better service.

Disadvantages of the reforms

Problems with conditional fee agreements
As we have seen, the 1999 Act has removed personal injury cases from the state-funded system, with the intention that they should instead be funded privately under conditional fee agreements. Many of the criticisms of the legislation centre around the drawbacks of such agreements, which are discussed in the next section of this chapter.

Cost-cutting
Critics, including the legal professions and some MPs, have accused the Government of putting cost-cutting before access to justice. The Legal Aid Practitioners Group chairman Richard Miller told *The Lawyer* newspaper in December 1998 that he believed the fixed budget for civil matters was designed to make it easy for the Government to cut the amount spent in later years: 'The Legal Services Commission will simply be able to say, this is the budget and if there are any more cases, tough luck.'

There are particular concerns that civil cases will suffer from the priority given to criminal defence work. In order to meet its obligations to guarantee a fair trial under human rights legislation, the Government has had to continue to allow the funding for criminal defence to be demand-led. The Lord Chancellor has admitted, however, that there is a fixed overall budget for legal services, which means that the budget for civil cases is effectively whatever is left over once criminal defence work is paid for.

Problems with Commission-employed defenders

The legal profession has fiercely opposed the idea of the Commission employing its own lawyers to do criminal defence work. Both the Bar Council and the Criminal Law Solicitors Association have expressed concern that lawyers who are wholly dependent on the state for their income cannot be sufficiently independent to defend properly people suspected of crime – people who, by definition, are on the opposite side to the state. Interviewed by *The Lawyer* newspaper in December 1998, Bar Council chairperson, Heather Hallett QC, pointed to the example of the US, where public defenders have been used for some years, arguing that as a result, the justice system there has become geared towards administrative convenience and cost-cutting, leading to an emphasis on plea bargaining and uncontested cases.

The experience of foreign jurisdictions such as the US and Canada shows that any system of public defenders must be properly funded and staffed if it is to retain the confidence of providers, users and the courts. Unfortunately they are frequently underfunded in practice, relying as a result on inexperienced lawyers with excessive caseloads and who are not respected by their clients, opponents or the court.

Restrictions on choice of lawyer

The idea of limiting state funding to firms and individuals with contracts is criticized by the legal profession, who maintain that it will severely restrict client choice. A 1999 survey conducted among legal aid firms by the Legal Aid Practitioners Group found that 95 per cent believed that exclusive contracting would lead to a reduction in access to legal services.

Part of the problem is that many firms have in the past done a small amount of legal aid work out of a sense of social duty, and could afford to do so because of the money they earned from private work. Such firms have not wanted to bid for block contracts because they have not wanted to increase the amount of comparatively poorly paid state-funded work they take on. There are now only 5,000 solicitor firms offering state-funded legal services, compared with 11,000 under the old legal aid system. The result, many fear, will be the creation of a two-tier legal profession, with one set of firms doing poorly paid state-funded work and another doing exclusively private work.

Small businesses
Research has been carried out at the Institute of Advanced Legal Studies into the impact of the Access to Justice Act 1999 funding reforms (*Breaking the code: the impact of legal aid reforms on general civil litigation* (2000)). It highlights problems resulting from the removal of state funding for legal services relating to business disputes. The removal of state funding in this area has attracted little attention which has led the researchers to comment:

> The problem with any discussion of 'businessmen' is that the phrase is laden with overtones. It conjures up an image of a man in a 'business suit', possibly flying 'business class' to a 'business meeting'.

While this is an accurate picture of some businessmen, it is far from accurate for many others. The Government justified excluding business disputes from state funding on the basis that such cases did not lead to social exclusion and, according to the Lord Chancellor's Department, 'it is not thought justified to spend public money helping businessmen, who fail to insure against the risk of facing legal costs'.

In fact, the research has found that the withdrawal of state funding for business disputes is leaving low-paid workers, such as self-employed cleaners and taxi drivers, with no means of redress if their businesses run into legal difficulties. The researcher, Ms Goriely, found that 'Business failure is a fast track to social exclusion'. When small businesses fail, the impact on a person's life can be enormous. People often end up losing 'their homes, their savings, their marriages, their health and their self-esteem'. Legal expenses insurance is often too expensive and specifically excludes the kinds of difficulties that failing small businesses face. Many policies have clearly been developed for businesses with million-pound turnovers, not for self-employed builders and taxi drivers.

Lack of independence from Government
State-funded work is likely to become the most important source of income for those firms which hold contracts – in some cases, even the only source of income. There are therefore concerns that the threat of losing their contract if they make themselves unpopular with the Government might lead firms to shy away from taking on cases that challenge Government action, or might in any other way embarrass or annoy the Government.

Poorer standards of work
The survey carried out in 1999 for the Legal Aid Practitioners Group found that 84 per cent of legal aid firms believed the Act's reliance on exclusive contracts would reduce the quality of legal services.

The Consumer's Association undertook in 2001 research into the experiences of people seeking help from the Community Legal Service. The research consisted of in-depth interviews of people who had sought help from the service, particularly those from vulnerable groups in society. It found that community centres and law centres provided the best help and advice, but many people felt that the legal system gave them a second-rate service. The research criticized the apparent lack of commitment and poor communication of some solicitors. There were still not enough solicitors and advisers specialising in areas like Social Security, housing, disability discrimination, employment and immigration law. People with disabilities complained of poor physical access to buildings.

The Legal Services Commission has paid for some research into the impact of different funding arrangements on the quality of the provision of legal services (*Quality and Cost: Final report on the contracting of civil, non-family advice and assistance pilot* (2001)). A study was undertaken over two years of 80,000 cases handled by 43 not-for-profit agencies and 100 solicitors' firms. The solicitors' firms were randomly allocated to one of three payment groups: those who continued to be paid as under the old Green Form system; those paid a fixed sum and left to determine how many cases it was reasonable for them to do for the money; and those paid a fixed sum and given a specific number of cases which had to be undertaken. The research concluded that where the payment system gave firms an incentive to do work cheaply, the quality of work suffered. Thus firms in the third group performed worst on most indicators, with 20 per cent of the contracted advisers doing poor quality work. Group 2 in general, performed better than Group 1.

In his *Review of the Criminal Justice Courts* (2001) Sir Robin Auld has recommended that changes should be made to the arrangements for the payment of defence lawyers so that they are rewarded for carrying out adequate case preparation.

▶ CONDITIONAL FEE AGREEMENTS

In the US, a great many cases brought by ordinary individuals are funded by what are called contingency fees, or 'no win, no fee' agreements. Lawyers can agree with clients that no fee will be charged if they lose the case, but if they win, the fee will be an agreed percentage of the damages won. This obviously gives the lawyer a direct personal interest in the level of damages, and there have been suggestions that this is partly responsible for the soaring levels of damages seen in the US courts.

In the English legal system, contingency fees are banned, but in 1991 the Courts and Legal Services Act (CLSA) made provision for the introduction of conditional fee agreements. Under a conditional fee agreement, solicitors can agree to take no fee or a reduced fee if they lose, and raise their fee by an agreed percentage if they win, up to a maximum of double the usual fee. The solicitor calculates the extra fee (usually called the 'uplift' or 'success fee') on the basis of the size of the risk involved – if the client seems very likely to win, the uplift will generally be lower than in a case where the outcome is more difficult to predict. The rule that the losing party must pay the winner's costs remains, so a party using a conditional fee agreement will usually take out insurance to cover this if he or she should lose.

The change made by the CLSA came into effect in 1995, but only applied to cases involving personal injury, insolvency and applications to the European Court of Human Rights. After consulting with the legal profession and other interested parties, in 1998 the Government extended them to all other areas of civil law, except family matters. Now the Access to Justice Act 1999 means conditional fees are set to become a very important method of funding legal cases, since the Act removes state funding from all personal injury cases (except clinical negligence), with the intention that these should be funded by conditional fee agreements.

The 1999 Act also makes some changes to the arrangements for conditional fee agreements in order to promote their use. Where a person who has made a conditional fee agreement wins his or her case, it will be possible for the court to order the losing party to pay the success fee, as well as the normal legal costs. Thus the success fee is now only ever payable by the losing party, which is a complete reversal of the previous situation. This provision is designed to meet the criticism that damages are calculated to compensate the litigant for the damage done to him or her, so if the 'uplift' has to come out of the client's damages, the amount left will be less than the court calculated as necessary for the purpose of full compensation.

Similarly, where a winning litigant has taken out insurance to provide for payment of the other side's costs if he or she loses, the court can order that the other side also pays the cost of the insurance premium. As a result, people who are bringing actions for remedies other than the payment of money can use a conditional fee arrangement.

The Government is currently considering introducing collective conditional fee agreements. These are designed for bulk users of legal services such as trade unions and insurers.

Advantages of conditional fee agreements

Cost to the state

Conditional fee agreements cost the state nothing – the costs are entirely borne by the solicitor or the losing party, depending on the outcome. By removing the huge number of personal injury cases from state funding and promoting conditional fee agreements for them instead, the Government claims it can devote more resources to those cases which still need state funding, such as tenants' claims against landlords, and direct more money towards suppliers of free legal advice, such as Citizens' Advice Bureaux.

Wider access to justice

The Government believes that conditional fee agreements will allow many people to bring or defend cases who would not have been eligible for state funding and who could not previously have afforded to bring cases at their own expense. As long as they can afford to insure against losing, and can persuade a solicitor that the case is worth the risk, anyone will be able to bring or defend a case for damages. Critics point out that there are a number of problems with this argument (see below).

Performance incentives

Supporters claim conditional fees encourage solicitors to perform better, since they have a financial interest in winning cases funded this way.

Wider coverage

Conditional fee agreements are allowed for defamation actions, and cases brought before tribunals, two major gaps in the provision of state funding.

Public acceptance

The Law Society suggests that clients have readily accepted conditional fee agreements in those areas where they have been permitted in the past. Within two years of the agreements being introduced, almost 30,000 conditional fee agreements had been signed, and by 1999 around 25,000 were in operation.

Fairness to opponents

There are restrictions on the costs state-funded clients can be made to pay to the other side, which can give them an unfair advantage, particularly in cases where both sides are ordinary individuals but only one has qualified for state funding. The requirement for insurance in conditional fee cases solves this problem.

Disadvantages of conditional fee agreements

Uncertain cases

Most of those who have criticized the legislation on conditional fee agreements accept that they are a good addition to the state-funded system, but are concerned that they may not be adequate as a substitute. In particular, critics – including the Bar, the Law Society, the Legal Action Group and the Vice-Chancellor of the Supreme Court, Sir Richard Scott – have expressed strong concerns that certain types of case will lose out under the new rules. They suggest that solicitors will only want to take on cases under conditional fee agreements where there is a very high chance of winning.

It was for this reason that clinical negligence cases have been kept within the state-funded system. These cases are generally very difficult for claimants to win – the success rate is around 17 per cent, compared with 85 per cent for other personal injury claims. It can often cost between £2,000 and £5,000 simply to do the initial investigations necessary to assess accurately whether the case is worth pursuing. As a result, solicitors would be very unlikely to want to take on such cases on a conditional fee basis, and even if they did, the uncertainty of outcome means that insurance against losing would be extremely expensive, possibly amounting to thousands of pounds. The Government clearly listened and took notice of the concerns in this area, but critics say there may still be other types of case where similar problems arise.

Another area which could be hit is that of cases which have enormous public importance, but which need large amounts of work, are difficult to win, and may attract relatively low levels of damages even if successful. These include some types of action against the police and Government, such as complaints by prisoners about their treatment. The Act does address these issues in that it provides for cases in excluded categories to be funded in exceptional circumstances; it remains to be seen whether this will be sufficiently flexible in practice.

Insurance costs

There are concerns that insurance against losing can be expensive. In the area of personal injury, the Law Society provides an affordable insurance scheme, but in other areas, the only suppliers are private insurance companies, who charge according to risk, so that clients with cases where the outcome is uncertain may be faced with very high premiums.

Both the Law Society and the Bar have suggested that a better idea would be the establishment of a self-financing Contingency Fund, which would pay for cases on the understanding that successful litigants would pay a proportion of their damages back to the fund. As we said earlier, this is allowed by the Act, but the Government has said it has no plans to use the power at the moment.

Financial involvement of lawyers

The Bar has criticized the idea of allowing lawyers a financial interest in the outcome of a case. In a letter to the Lord Chancellor, the Chair of the

Bar Council argued that since clients generally lack the knowledge to assess their chances of winning their case, lawyers will be able to charge whatever they think they can get away with (within the set limits). This seems a rather strange argument for a representative of the legal profession to put forward, and critics have widely suggested that the real reason behind this and the other criticisms made by the legal profession is that lawyers were reluctant to lose the no-risk income that state-funded legal aid allowed them.

The evidence on solicitors' approach to the uplift on fees is currently rather inconclusive. A 1997 report by the Policy Studies Institute on the effects of the changes made under the Courts and Legal Services Act 1990 found that the average uplift was 43 per cent, less than half the 100 per cent maximum allowed – but within that average, one in ten solicitors were charging between 90 and 100 per cent. The author of the study, Stella Yarrow, commented that the number of cases assessed as having a low chance of success was surprisingly large, suggesting that solicitors might be under-estimating the chances of winning, in order to increase the uplift.

In 1999, the Forum of Insurance Lawyers (Foil) suggested that the chance to make extra money was encouraging solicitors to push clients into conditional fee agreements, even where the clients did not need such an agreement. Around 17 million people in Britain have some form of legal expenses insurance attached to their home, car or credit card insurance, and in many cases this will pay their legal costs for them. However, Foil points out, many people have this insurance without realizing it, and it claims that instead of suggesting that clients check whether they have it, solicitors are persuading them into unnecessary conditional fee agreements.

A further problem was highlighted by members of the Bar in an article on the subject in *The Lawyer* newspaper in 1999. The piece gave as an example one barrister who had lost three conditional fee cases in a row, thus earning nothing at all for his work on them. This is clearly a risk that lawyers choose to face, but human nature being what it is, the article points out, the temptation for that barrister next time would be to settle the case early, even if that means accepting compensation lower than the client might get in court, with the guarantee of some financial reward, rather than going to court and risking the fee again. The result is that there will be cases where the lawyer's financial interest is in direct opposition to the client's.

Insurance pressures

There may also be pressure to settle from insurance companies, some of whom have been known to threaten to withdraw their cover if a client refuses to accept an offer of settlement that the insurance company considers reasonable. Clearly the insurance company's primary interest will be to avoid having to pay out, so it is not difficult to see that their idea of a reasonable settlement might be very different from the client's – or from what the client could expect to get if the case continued.

ARE LAWYERS ALWAYS NECESSARY?

As we have seen, many of the non-statutory advice schemes use advisers who are not legally qualified. Some of these lay advisers appear as advocates in tribunals and in some cases have been granted discretionary rights of audience in the county courts, as well as giving legal advice. In particular, advisers for charities such as MIND have shown themselves to be more than a match for most solicitors in their knowledge of the law in their fields. Many solicitor firms also employ non-qualified workers to do legal work.

The skills of a good adviser are not always the same as those of a good lawyer; what the client needs is someone who can interview sympathetically, ascertain the pertinent facts from what may be a long, rambling and in some cases emotional story, analyse the problem and suggest a course of action. The preliminary skills are just as likely to be possessed by a lay person as by a lawyer, even if a lawyer may be needed to advise on the course of action.

Nor are lawyers considered to be the best advocates in every situation. The National Consumer Council advised against allowing them to represent clients in the Small Claims Court, on the grounds that they could make the procedure unnecessarily long-winded and legalistic.

However, critics identify two possible problems in the growing use of lay advisers. First, although most organizations are scrupulous in training their advisers, some may be more casual, and there is no obligatory check on advisers before they are allowed to deal with cases. The general public may not always be in a position to assess the quality of the advice they are given. Secondly, the large number of overlapping agencies means it can be difficult for consumers of legal advice to find the best provider for them and can be wasteful of scarce resources. The Government hopes that the development of Community Legal Service Partnerships will help to tackle this problem.

ALTERNATIVE PROPOSALS FOR REFORM

With the Access to Justice Act 1999 the Government introduced major reforms to the provision of state funding of legal services. The following are some additional proposals that have been made, addressing not just cost, but many of the other problems associated with unmet legal need.

A national legal service?

Perhaps the most radical reform would be to take the statutory scheme entirely out of the hands of private practice and establish a nationwide network of salaried lawyers on the law centre model. All funding could be given on a block rather than case-by-case basis, for centres to use in whatever ways best met the needs of their own locality, in consultation with management committees representing the community.

This would deal with some of the criticisms of the current schemes made by Kate Markus and discussed above (p. 212). In particular the advantages of this idea include:

- state-funded work would no longer have to compete with private work for lawyers' time;
- state funding would no longer have to include an element of profit for the lawyer;
- resources could be more flexibly employed, on a combination of individual casework and litigation, education and campaigning, or any other approach that suited particular problems;
- this more flexible approach to dealing with problems would get away from the over-emphasis on litigation of solicitors in private practice;
- the ability to run educative campaigns would help deal with public ignorance of legal rights;
- law centres appear not to suffer from the unapproachable image of the legal profession in general;
- law centres have been successful in attracting problems not previously brought to lawyers, especially welfare and employment cases;
- a nationwide network of such centres would help overcome the uneven distribution of solicitors' firms.

The 1979 Royal Commission on Legal Services did suggest the establishment of a nationwide network of centrally financed Citizens Law Centres, but felt that these should be restricted to individual casework only and not get involved in general work for the community. This idea would fail to take advantage of one of the real strengths of the law centre movement, and the fact that solicitors in private practice would still be allowed to undertake state-funded work would limit the improvements to be made in cost-efficiency. The Law Centres Federation rejected the idea.

In a 1995 article for the *Guardian* newspaper barrister Daniel Stilitz argued for a similar scheme, though not necessarily based on law centres. Under his National Justice Service, anyone seeking to bring a legal action would need to show a reasonable cause. If the case had a reasonable prospect of success, the National Justice Service would decide what services were needed, fix a budget and allocate a lawyer on the basis of suitability and availability. Stilitz points out that for such a scheme to equalize access to justice, it would have to be compulsory – if one side was allowed to 'go private', the scales might be tipped unfairly in their favour. So, both sides would be obliged to use National Justice Service lawyers. The service would be means-tested, with contributions of up to 100 per cent, ensuring that those who could afford to pay the whole cost did so, but could not use that wealth to secure an advantage in the justice system. Those who could not afford to pay would receive free or subsidized help. The result, says Stilitz, would be a level playing field, with cases decided on merits and wasteful tactics designed to drive up costs eliminated.

Stilitz acknowledges that the plan would remove client choice, but argues that improving access to justice is more important. He also points out that while many might object to the loss of independence involved in tying lawyers so closely to the state, this cannot have a worse effect on individual rights than the current system, under which financial pressures mean that for many citizens, their rights are useless because they cannot afford to enforce them.

No-fault compensation

Instead of looking to conditional fee agreements to secure justice for those injured in accidents, such cases could be removed from the litigation arena by the establishment of a system of no-fault compensation for personal injury cases, as in New Zealand.

ANSWERING QUESTIONS

1 **Critically evaluate the Access to Justice Act 1999 with regard to the problem of unmet legal need.**

You should begin your answer by explaining what unmet legal need is, and discussing its causes. You should then briefly describe the changes made by the Access to Justice Act, and then in the main part of your answer, talk about how the provisions of the Act are designed to meet the problem of unmet legal need. The material you need for this is mainly to be found in the section on the advantages of the Act, but remember to direct it towards the question asked. You could either do this by taking each of the causes of unmet legal need in turn, and explaining which provisions address each problem and how, or you could take the relevant provisions in turn and talk about what aspects of the problem of unmet legal need they address and how (which of these approaches you take is not really important, so long as you do choose one that gives your essay a good, well-organized structure and shows you are using the material you have to really answer the question). You should then talk about the drawbacks of the Access to Justice Act, pointing out how these will compromise its ability to deal with the problem of unmet legal need. Finally, you could set your answer in a broader context (always a good way of showing the examiners that you really know the subject) by pointing out that the Access to Justice Act, although clearly aimed at dealing with the problem of unmet legal need, also had to address other issues, such as cost, and the need to get value for money, and so never intended to solve the problem of unmet legal need at any cost, but to do what it could with limited resources. Your conclusion can then state whether, in view of this broader context, you feel the Act does provide a satisfactory – if not perfect – solution to the problem.

▶ Reading on the Internet

The report of the National Association of Citizens' Advice Bureaux, *A Balancing Act; Surviving the Risk Society* (1999) is available on their website at:

http://www.nacab.org.uk/poldocs.ihtml?polcode=LE&zone=6

The website of the Legal Services Commission is:
http://www.legalservices.gov.uk/

The website of the Community Legal Service is:
http://www.justask.org.uk

9 The criminal justice system

The criminal justice system is one of the most important tools available to society for the control of anti-social behaviour. It is also the area of the English legal system which has most potential for controversy, given that through the criminal justice system, the state has the means to interfere with individual freedom in the strongest way: by sending people to prison.

An effective criminal justice system needs to strike a balance between punishing the guilty and protecting the innocent; our systems of investigating crime need safeguards which prevent the innocent being found guilty, but those safeguards must not make it impossible to convict those who are guilty. This balance has been the subject of much debate in recent years: a large number of miscarriages of justice, where innocent people were sent to prison, suggested the system was weighted too heavily towards proving guilt, yet shortly after these cases had been uncovered, there were claims, particularly from the police, that the balance had tipped too far in the other direction. It may be that the incorporation of the European Convention on Human Rights into British law will lead to a further shift in the balance, as the British courts interpret such rights as the right to a 'fair trial' contained in Art. 6 of the Convention.

Review of the Criminal Courts

The Government commissioned a full-scale review of the criminal courts, headed by a senior Court of Appeal judge, Sir Robin Auld. The Lord Chancellor, in announcing his appointment, said:

> The Government's aim is to provide criminal courts which are, and are seen to be:
> - Modern and in touch with the communities they serve;
> - Efficient;
> - Fair and responsive to the needs of all their users;
> - Co-operative in their relations with other criminal justice agencies; and
> - With modern and effective case management to remove unnecessary delays from the system.

Sir Robin Auld commenced his work in January 2000 and his report was published in 2001. The key proposals of his report are mentioned at the relevant points in this chapter and in the chapters on juries and appeals. Sir Robin Auld's main concern was to remove the unnecessary complexities in the system that were slowing it down and making it inefficient. The central plank of his proposal was the creation of a middle-ranking court, called a District Division where cases would be heard by a professional judge and two lay magistrates (discussed on p. 166). The Government is now considering his proposals and legislation introducing some, but not all, of his recommendations is expected in 2002 or 2003, depending on parliamentary time.

The miscarriages of justice

Before looking in detail at the criminal justice system, it is useful to understand what happened to cause the miscarriages of justice which hit the headlines in the 1990s, leading to a crisis of confidence in the system. The following are just some examples of those miscarriages.

The Guildford Four

In October 1974, the IRA bombed a pub in Guildford. A year later, Patrick Armstrong, Paul Hill, Carole Richardson, Gerard Conlon and two others were convicted of the five murders arising from the bombing. Mr Armstrong and Mr Hill were also convicted of two murders arising from an explosion in November 1974 at a pub in Woolwich. All were sentenced to life imprisonment.

The prosecution case was based almost entirely on confessions which were alleged to have been made while the four were in police custody. There was no other evidence that any of the four were members of the IRA, and they were certainly not the type of people that an effective terrorist organization would choose to carry out such an important part of its campaign – Patrick Armstrong and Carole Richardson, for example, took drugs, lived in a squat and were involved in petty crime.

Like the other victims of miscarriages of justice, they tried to get their convictions referred to the Court of Appeal under s. 17 of the Criminal Appeal Act 1968 (since repealed), but were initially unsuccessful. In 1987, a Home Office memorandum recognized that the Four were unlikely terrorists, but the Home Office concluded that this could not be considered to be new evidence justifying referral to the Court of Appeal.

Then, in 1989, a police detective looking into the case found a set of typed notes of interviews with Patrick Armstrong, which contained deletions and additions, both typed and handwritten, as well as some rearrangements of material. At their original trial the police evidence had consisted of a set of handwritten notes which they said were made at the time of the interview, and a typed version of these notes; both incorporated the corrections made on the newly discovered typewritten set, suggesting that the handwritten version was actually made after the interviews had been conducted. The implication was that the notes had been constructed so as to fit in with the case the police wished to present.

Patrick Armstrong's confession was central to the prosecution case. Anything which cast doubt on it would undermine all four convictions. The Director of Public Prosecutions, Alan Green, decided that he should not oppose a further appeal, and this took place in 1989. Giving judgment, the Lord Chief Justice said there were two possible explanations. The first was that the typescripts were a complete fabrication, amended to make them more effective and then written out by hand to appear as if they were contemporaneous. Alternatively, the police had started with a contemporaneous note, typed it up to improve legibility, amended it to make it read better and then converted it back to a manuscript note. Either way, the police officers had not told the truth. The Lord Chief Justice concluded: 'If they were prepared to tell this sort of lie then the whole of their evidence became suspect.' As a result, the Guildford Four were released, after having spent 15 years in prison for crimes which they did not commit.

The Maguires

In March 1976, the Maguire family, including Patrick Conlon, were convicted of unlawfully possessing the explosive nitroglycerine in December 1974. They were sentenced to between four and fourteen years' imprisonment.

The family came under investigation because Gerard Conlon, one of the Guildford Four, allegedly told the police while being questioned about the Guildford bombings, that Mrs Maguire (his aunt) had shown him how to make bombs at her home in London. The police raided Mrs Maguire's house; no explosives were found but the family were arrested. The prosecution case was largely based on forensic tests which apparently showed minute traces of explosives on their hands (or, in Mrs Maguire's case, on her gloves). The Maguire family always maintained their innocence, but in the face of the test results, it was difficult to put forward a successful defence. An appeal was eventually allowed when new scientific evidence showed that the forensic tests were far from conclusive. A positive result in these tests could have been produced by the soap or detergent used to wash laboratory dishes, or in some cases, even from smoking cigarettes. Patrick Conlon died in custody.

The Birmingham Six

In November 1974, 21 people died and 162 were injured when IRA bombs exploded in two crowded pubs in the centre of Birmingham. The bombs caused outrage in Britain, and led to a wave of anti-Irish feeling.

The six Irishmen who became known as the Birmingham Six were arrested after police kept a watch on ports immediately after the bombings. The police asked them to undergo forensic tests in order to eliminate them from their inquiries. The men had told the police that they were travelling to Northern Ireland to see relatives; this was partly true, but their main reason for travelling was to attend the funeral of James McDade, an IRA man. Although some of the Six may well have had Republican sympathies, none were actually members of the IRA. They were unaware, until McDade was killed, that he was involved in terrorism. Nevertheless, they all knew his family, and intended to go to the funeral as a mark of respect, a normal practice in Northern Ireland which would not necessarily suggest support for the dead person's political views.

Perhaps not surprisingly given the situation at the time, the men did not mention the funeral when the police asked why they were travelling and, equally unsurprisingly, when the police searched their luggage and found evidence of the real reason for their journey, they became extremely suspicious. When the forensic tests, conducted by a Dr Skuse, indicated that the men had been handling explosives, the police were convinced their suspicions were right.

At their trial, the case rested on two main pieces of evidence: the forensic tests and confessions which the men had made to the police. The Six claimed that while at the police station, they had been beaten, kicked and threatened with death; they were also told that their families were in danger and would only be protected if the men confessed. There was clear evidence that the Six were beaten up; photos taken three days after their admission on remand to Winston Green prison show serious scars. However, the men were also beaten up by prison officers once they were remanded in custody, and the prosecution used this beating to explain the photographic evidence, stating that there had been no physical abuse by the police and that, therefore, the confessions were valid. Yet a close examination of the confessions would have made it obvious that they were made by people who knew nothing about the bombings: they contradicted each other, none of them revealed anything about the way the terrorist attacks were carried out that the police did not know already, and some of the 'revelations' proved to be untrue – for example, three of the men said the bombs were left in carrier bags, when forensic evidence later showed them to have been in holdalls. The men were never put on identity parades, even though at least one person who had been present in one of the bombed pubs felt he could have identified the bombers. Nevertheless, the Six were convicted and sentenced to life imprisonment, the judge commenting: 'You have been convicted on the clearest and most overwhelming evidence I have ever heard in a case of murder.' On appeal, the judges reprimanded the trial judge for aspects of his summing up and a character attack on a defence witness; they acknowledged the weaknesses in the forensic evidence, yet concluded that this evidence would have played a small part in the jury's decision; and as far as the confession evidence was concerned, a judge mentioned the black eye on one of the defendants, 'the origin of which I have forgotten', but said 'I do not think it matters much anyway'. The appeal was dismissed.

Fourteen prison officers were subsequently tried for assaulting the Six; their victims were not allowed to appear as witnesses, and they were all acquitted. Evidence given suggested that the men had already been injured when they arrived at the prison. The Six then brought a civil action for assault against the police force. This claim was struck out. Lord Denning's judgment summed up the legal system's attitude to the case, pointing out that if the Six won, and proved they had been assaulted in order to secure their confessions, this would mean the police had lied, used violence and threats, and that the convictions were false; the Home Secretary would have to recommend a pardon or send the case back to the Court of Appeal. The general feeling seemed to be that such serious miscarriages were simply unthinkable, and so the system for a long time turned its back on the growing claims that the unthinkable had actually happened.

In January 1987, the Home Secretary referred the case back to the Court of Appeal. The appeal took a year; the convictions were upheld. The Lord Chief Justice Lord Lane ended the court's judgment with remarks which were to become notorious: 'The longer this hearing has gone on, the more convinced this court has become that the verdict of the jury was correct. We have no doubt that these convictions were both safe and satisfactory.'

In the end, it took 16 years for the Six to get their convictions quashed. In 1990, another Home Secretary referred the case back to the Court of Appeal. A new technique had been developed, known as Electrostatic Document Analysis (ESDA) which could examine the indentations made on paper by writing on the sheets above. The test suggested that notes of a police interview with one of the Six had not been recorded contemporaneously, as West Midlands detectives had claimed in court. The scientific findings in the Maguire case also meant that the nitroglycerine tests could no longer be relied on. The prosecution decided not to seek to sustain the convictions and the Six were finally freed in 1991.

Judith Ward

Judith Ward was given a life sentence in 1974 for offences including the murder of 12 people, who died when a bomb exploded in a coach on the M62 motorway. During her trial she made admissions and confessions, some of which could be shown to be clearly untrue, and part of the scientific evidence against her was given by Dr Frank Skuse, the Home Office forensic scientist who also gave evidence against the Birmingham

Six. In addition, the prosecution had in its possession over 5,000 items of evidence which would have pointed to her innocence, but failed to disclose them. She was finally released and her conviction quashed after 18 years in prison. The Court of Appeal said that a grave miscarriage of justice had occurred because: 'in failing to disclose evidence [to the defence] . . . one or more members of the West Yorkshire police, the scientists who gave evidence at the trial, and some of those members of the staff of the DPP and counsel who advised them . . . failed to carry out . . . their basic duty to seek to ensure a trial which is fair to both the prosecution . . . and the accused.'

The Tottenham Three

Engin Raghip, Winston Silcott and Mark Braithwaite were convicted of murdering PC Keith Blakelock in 1985 during rioting at the Broadwater Farm Estate in North London. As with the Irish miscarriages of justice, the crime was one which evoked strong feelings, among both police and ordinary people. Newspapers carried graphic details of the savage way in which PC Blakelock was killed, and exhorted the police to find the killer.

Again, confession evidence and statements given to the police proved unreliable. One apparent witness allegedly gave a 55-page statement, describing the murder in full detail, and incriminating himself and 27 others. The whole confession was later discovered to be complete fiction; the 'witness' had not even been at Broadwater Farm that night. The statement was obtained after the man had been held incommunicado for two days in Barnet police station.

There were hundreds of police photos of the scene, yet the three men appeared in none of them, and nor was there any scientific evidence. Winston Silcott never signed his alleged confession, which was the only evidence against him. Mark Braithwaite was suffering from claustrophobia and was detained for long hours in a police cell when he gave his 'confession'. Mr Raghip was of low intelligence and would have been abnormally suggestible under the pressure of a police interview.

Finally, the ESDA test, described above, satisfied the Court of Appeal that vital parts of the notes were inserted after other parts of Mr Silcott's interview were completed. As there was no other evidence against him, the conviction was quashed. The other two were cleared due to alleged misconduct by the police in the course of the original police investigation.

The Bridgewater Four

In 1979 Vincent Hickey, Michael Hickey, Jimmy Robertson and Pat Molloy were convicted of the murder of a 13-year-old boy, Carl Bridgewater. Appeals against their convictions were twice rejected by the Court of

Appeal, following seven different police investigations into their case. Pat Molloy died in custody in 1981. Their convictions were quashed in April 1997. The Crown conceded that the case against the men was 'flawed' due to the questioning of Mr Molloy for ten days without access to a solicitor, and the use of a fabricated statement from Vincent Hickey to persuade Mr Molloy to confess to the crime. In addition, fingerprint evidence had come to light which was not disclosed by the prosecution to the defence and which would have been very useful to the defendants' case. The former police officers alleged to have falsified the evidence are now under investigation.

The response to the miscarriages of justice

The miscarriages of justice described above, and others, showed that there was something seriously wrong with the criminal justice system. On 14 March 1991, when the Court of Appeal quashed the convictions of the Birmingham Six, the Home Secretary announced that a Royal Commission on Criminal Justice (RCCJ) would be set up to examine the penal process from start to finish – from the time the police first investigate to the final appeal. The RCCJ (sometimes called the Runciman Commission, after its chairperson) considered these issues for two years, during which they received evidence from over 600 organizations and asked academics to carry out 22 research studies on how the system works in practice. In July 1993 they published their final report. In examining the criminal justice system, some of the research presented to the RCCJ, its recommendations and some changes that have subsequently been made, will be considered.

Human Rights Act 1998

The passing of the Human Rights Act 1998, incorporating the European Convention on Human Rights into domestic law (see p. 456) will have a significant impact on all stages of the criminal justice system. The provisions of the European Convention could potentially provide an important safeguard against abuses and excesses within the system. Of particular relevance in this field are Art. 3 prohibiting torture and inhuman or degrading treatment; Art. 5 protecting the right to liberty including the right not to be arrested or detained by the police without lawful authority; Art. 6 guaranteeing a fair trial; and Art. 8 which recognizes the right to respect of an individual's right to private and family life. The powers of arrest, stop and search and the refusal of bail are all likely to be the subject of legal challenges on the basis that their exercise has breached the Convention. For example, in **Caballero** *v* **UK** (2000) the UK Government accepted that the law on bail breached Art. 5 of the Convention and the domestic law was reformed as a result.

The adversarial process

The English system of criminal justice can be described as adversarial. This means each side is responsible for putting their own case: collecting evidence, interviewing witnesses and retaining experts. In court they will present their own evidence and attack their opponent's evidence by cross-examining their adversary's witnesses. Both parties only call those witnesses likely to advance their cause and both parties are permitted to attack the credibility and reliability of the witnesses testifying for the other side. The role of the judge is limited to that of a referee ensuring fair play, making sure that the rules on procedure and evidence are followed. It is often compared with a battle with each side fighting their own corner. The adversarial system is typical of common law countries. The alternative is an inquisitorial system, which exists in most of the rest of Europe. Under that system, a judge (known in France as the *juge d'instruction*) plays the dominant role in collecting evidence before the trial. During the course of a lengthy investigation, the judge will interview witnesses and inspect documents, and the final trial is often just to rubber stamp the investigating judge's findings.

In the light of the recent miscarriages of justice, some people suggested that we should introduce an inquisitorial system into England. Arguments were put forward that the inquisitorial system provides a properly organized and regulated pre-trial phase, with an independent figure supervising the whole investigation. The RCCJ ordered research into the French and German criminal justice system (Leigh and Zedner, 1992). The researchers rejected the idea of introducing the inquisitorial system into England. They did not think that the *juge d'instruction* was a real protection against overbearing police practices, except in rare cases where physical brutality was involved. Furthermore, despite the fact that only 10 per cent of cases go before the *juge d'instruction* in France, the system is overburdened and works slowly. In Germany and Italy the powers of the investigating judge have been transferred to the public prosecutor, to avoid potential conflict between the functions of investigator and judge.

The organization of the police

In the UK the tradition is to have local police forces, rather than one single national police force. This decentralization is considered to help build the links between the police and the local community that is being policed, and to reduce the risk of the police behaving oppressively. However, a step towards centralization was taken when the Police and Magistrates' Courts Act 1994 provided that the Home Secretary was allowed to 'determine objectives for the policing of the areas of all police authorities'. Then, in 1997, the Police Act created a new National Crime Squad to tackle serious and organized crime. Pointing to its limited remit, the Home Secretary made it clear that it was not intended to be a British version of the FBI.

Within the regional policing structure it is important to coordinate the information and activities available to the different local forces. The Police Act 1997 makes provision for a Police Information Technology Organization and a National Criminal Intelligence Service (NCIS). The NCIS has no police role as such, but gathers and processes intelligence relating to offences that concern more than one police area, usually organized crime such as drug dealing, car theft and football hooliganism.

Police powers

Most people's first contact with the criminal justice system involves the police, and because they have responsibility for investigating crimes, gathering evidence and deciding whether to charge a suspect, they play an important part in its overall operation. They also have wide powers over suspects, which may be used to help convict the guilty or, as the miscarriages of justice have shown, abused to convict the innocent.

The main piece of legislation regulating police powers is the Police and Criminal Evidence Act 1984 (PACE). The Act was the product of a Royal Commission set up following an earlier miscarriage of justice, concerning the murder in 1977 of a man called Maxwell Confait. Confait was found strangled with electric flex in a burning house, and three boys, aged 14, 15 and 18, one of whom was educationally subnormal, were arrested, interrogated and, as a result of their confessions, charged with murder. Three years later, they were all released after an official report into the case (the Fisher Report) concluded that they had nothing to do with the killing.

In the light of concern over the police conduct of this case, and in particular the interrogation process, the then Labour Government set up the Royal Commission on Criminal Procedure (RCCP), sometimes known as the Philips Commission, to examine police procedures. It concluded in its report of 1981 that a balance needed to be reached between 'the interests of the community in bringing offenders to justice and the rights and liberties of persons suspected or accused of crime'. For a criminal justice system that achieved this balance would reach the standards of fairness, openness and accountability. However, the Commission, and the subsequent Act (PACE), were criticized by some as unjustifiably extending police powers, especially in the areas of stop and search, arrest and detention at the police station.

PACE was intended to replace a confusing mixture of common law, legislation and local bye-laws on pre-trial procedure with a single coherent statute. The Act provides a comprehensive code of police powers to stop, search, arrest, detain and interrogate members of the public. It also lays down the suspects' rights. The Criminal Justice and Public

Order Act 1994 (CJPOA) extended police powers significantly. It introduced some of the recommendations of the RCCJ, and other changes that the RCCJ was opposed to, for example, the abolition of the right to silence.

As well as the statutory rules on police powers, contained in PACE and the CJPOA, there are Codes of Practice, drawn up by the Home Office under s. 66 of PACE and revised in 1995, which do not form part of the law, but which provide extra detail on the provisions of the legislation. Breach of these Codes cannot be the ground for a legal action, but can give rise to disciplinary procedures, and if they are breached in very serious ways, evidence obtained as a result of such a breach may be excluded in a criminal trial. It has been argued that some of the Code provisions should be legally enforceable and form part of PACE itself.

Pre-arrest powers

Police officers are always free to ask members of the public questions in order to prevent and detect crime, but members of the public are not obliged to answer such questions, nor to go to a police station or be detained at a police station unless they are lawfully arrested. In **Rice** *v* **Connolly** (1966), the appellant was spotted by police officers in the early hours of the morning, behaving suspiciously in an area where burglaries had taken place that night. The officers asked where he was going and where he had come from; he refused to answer, or to give his full name and address, though he did give a name and the name of a road, which were not untrue. The officers asked him to go with them to a police box for identification purposes, but he refused, saying, 'If you want me, you will have to arrest me'. He was arrested and eventually convicted of obstructing a police officer in the execution of his duty. His conviction was quashed on appeal on the basis that nobody is obliged to answer police questions.

The line between maintaining the freedom not to answer questions and actually obstructing the police would appear to be a thin one. In **Ricketts** *v* **Cox** (1982), two police officers, who were looking for youths responsible for a serious assault, approached the defendant and another man in the early hours of the morning. The defendant was said to have been abusive, uncooperative and hostile to the officers, using obscene language which was designed to provoke and antagonize the officers and eventually trying to walk away from them. The magistrates found that the police acted in a proper manner and were entitled to put questions to the two men; the defendant's behaviour and attitude amounted to an obstruction of the police officers in the execution of their duty. An appeal was dismissed, and the implication appears to be that while merely refusing to answer questions is lawful, rudely refusing to do so may amount to the offence of obstruction.

An even more problematic area is the question of how far the police are allowed to detain a person without arresting them. The courts appear to have concluded that under common law the police cannot actually prevent a person from moving away, though they can touch them to attract their attention (they also have some statutory powers in this area, discussed below). Two schoolboys, in **Kenlin** *v* **Gardiner** (1967), were going from house to house to remind members of their rugby team about a game. Two plain-clothed police officers became suspicious and, producing a warrant card, asked what they were doing. The boys did not believe the men were police officers, and one of them appeared to try to run away. A police officer caught hold of his arm, and the boy responded by struggling violently, punching and kicking the officer, at which point the second boy got involved and struck the other officer. Both boys were convicted of assaulting a police constable in the execution of his duty in the magistrates' court, but an appeal was allowed, on the ground that the police did not have the power to detain the boys prior to arrest, and so the boys were merely acting in self-defence.

In **Donnelly** *v* **Jackman** (1970), the appellant was walking along a road one Saturday evening at about 11.15 pm, when a uniformed police officer came up to him, intending to make inquiries about an offence which the officer had reason to believe the appellant might have committed. The officer asked the appellant if he could have a word with him, but the appellant ignored him and walked on. The officer followed close behind him, repeated the request and, on being ignored, tapped him on the shoulder. The appellant turned round and tapped the officer on the chest saying 'Now we are even, copper'. When the officer tapped him on the shoulder a second time, the appellant turned round again, and this time hit him with force. He was convicted of assaulting an officer in the execution of his duty, and argued in his defence that in tapping him on the shoulder the officer had acted outside his duty. The Court of Appeal held that what the officer had done was not unlawful detention but merely 'a trivial interference with liberty', and the conviction was upheld.

Stop and search under PACE

PACE repealed a variety of often obscure and unsatisfactory statutory provisions on stop and search; the main powers in this area are now contained in s. 1 of PACE. Under s. 1 a constable may search a person or vehicle in public for stolen or prohibited articles (defined as offensive weapons or articles used for the purpose of burglary or related crimes). This power can only be used where the police have 'reasonable grounds for suspecting that they will find stolen or prohibited articles' (s. 1(3)).

The requirement of reasonable suspicion is intended to protect individuals from being subject to stop and search on a random basis, or on grounds that the law rightly finds unacceptable, such as age or racial background. Code of Practice A (concerning the exercise of statutory powers of stop and search) provides guidance on the meaning of 'reasonable grounds for suspecting'. Paragraph 1.7 of the Code states:

> Reasonable suspicion can never be supported on the basis of personal factors alone. For example, a person's colour, age, hairstyle or manner of dress, or the fact that he is known to have a previous conviction for possession of an unlawful article, cannot be used alone or in combination with each other as the sole basis on which to search that person. Nor may it be found on the basis of stereotyped images of certain persons or groups as more likely to be committing offences.

Paragraph 1.7A of the Code makes it clear that even if the police think that the particular individual is innocent of the relevant crime, they may still search if there are reasonable grounds for suspecting that person to be carrying the items concerned – so for example, they may search someone reasonably suspected of being in possession of stolen goods, even if they do not suspect that person of stealing them.

Research by Sanders ('Controlling the Discretion of the Individual Officer', 1993) has found that in practice, one of the main factors which prompts the police to search someone is knowledge that the person has previous convictions. Pre-PACE research by Smith and Gray (1983) observed that in carrying out a stop and search, the police often relied on instinct; this could lead to class and race bias, and in turn to those groups which were commonly stopped feeling that they were suffering from police harassment.

Before searching under these powers, police officers must, among other things, identify themselves and the station where they are based, and tell the person to be searched the grounds for the search. If not in uniform, police officers must provide documentary identification (s. 2(3)). Reasonable force may be used (s. 117), but the suspect cannot be required to remove any clothing in public, except for an outer coat, jacket or gloves (s. 2(9)).

Any stolen or prohibited articles discovered by the police during the search may be seized (s. 1(6)). Details of the search must be recorded, and if requested a copy must be supplied to the person searched (s. 3), unless the suspect submitted to the search voluntarily.

Other powers to stop and search

Various statutes give specific stop and search powers regarding particular offences. For example, the Misuse of Drugs Act 1971, s. 23, allows the police to stop and search anyone who is suspected on reasonable grounds to be in unlawful possession of a controlled drug; and the Sporting Events Act 1985 contains a power to stop and search people before entry into certain sporting events such as a football match. Section 60 of the Criminal Justice and Public Order Act 1994 provides that where a senior police officer reasonably believes that serious violence may take place in an area, they may, in order to prevent its occurrence, give written authorization for officers to stop and search persons and vehicles in that area for up to 24 hours. This can be extended by a further 30 hours. When such authorization is in place, police officers can stop and search any pedestrian or vehicle for offensive weapons or dangerous instruments. Offensive weapon bears the same meaning as in s. 1 of PACE; a dangerous instrument refers to an object which has a blade or is sharply pointed (s. 60(11)). Unlike s. 1 of PACE, these powers do not require reasonable grounds for suspicion. The police can also be authorized to stop and search randomly any pedestrian or vehicle in an area where it is suspected that knives or offensive weapons are being carried without good reason.

In addition, under s. 65 of the Criminal Justice and Public Order Act 1994, an officer can stop anyone on their way to a 'rave' and direct them not to proceed. Similar powers exist under s. 71, in relation to trespassory assemblies (defined on p. 477). These rather draconian powers can be exercised within five miles of the rave or assembly.

There are clearly potential dangers in granting wide stop and search powers to the police if there is a possibility that the powers will be abused, with harassment of ethnic minority groups being a particular concern. A police operation against street robberies in Lambeth in 1981, codenamed SWAMP 81, involved 943 stops, mostly of black youths, over a period of two weeks. Of these, only 118 led to arrests and 75 to charges, one of which was for robbery. The operation, which had no noticeable effect on the crime figures, shattered relations between the police and the ethnic community, and was one of the triggers of the Brixton riots that occurred soon afterwards. Nevertheless, in his report on the Brixton disorders, Lord Scarman thought such powers necessary to combat street crime, provided that the safeguard of 'reasonable suspicion' was properly and objectively applied.

Powers of arrest

Powers of arrest allow people to be detained against their will. Such detention is only lawful if the arrest is carried out in accordance with the law. An arrest can take place either with or without a warrant.

Arrest with a warrant
Under s. 1 of the Magistrates' Courts Act 1980, criminal proceedings may be initiated either by the issue of a summons requiring the accused to attend court on a particular day or, in more serious cases, by a warrant of arrest issued by the magistrates' court. The police obtain a warrant by applying in writing to a magistrate, and backing up the application with

an oral statement made on oath. The warrant issued must specify the name of the person to be arrested and general particulars of the offence. When an arrest warrant has been granted, a constable may enter and search premises to make the arrest, using such reasonable force as is necessary (PACE, s. 117).

Arrest without a warrant

There are now four main categories of arrest without warrant, which will be considered in turn.

Reasonable suspicion concerning an arrestable offence. Under s. 24 of PACE, a police officer can arrest without a warrant a person whom they reasonably suspect has committed or is committing, or is about to commit an arrestable offence.

Arrestable offences comprise:

- offences with a sentence fixed by law (for example, life imprisonment in the case of murder);
- offences for which the maximum sentence for an adult is five years' imprisonment or longer;
- certain other specified offences (for example, kerb-crawling, offences contained in the Official Secrets Acts 1911–89, the Sexual Offences Act 1956 and the Theft Act 1968).

The same rules apply to the concept of reasonable suspicion for arrest as were discussed for stop and search powers. Its meaning in the context of an arrest was considered by the House of Lords in **O'Hara** *v* **Chief Constable of the Royal Ulster Constabulary** (1996). Lord Steyn stated that reasonable suspicion did not require a belief in evidence that amounted to a *prima facie* case, as one was merely concerned with the preliminary stages in an investigation. However, the mere fact that a senior officer told a junior officer to arrest a particular person could not, in itself, constitute reasonable suspicion.

General arrest conditions. Section 25 of PACE gives the police a power to arrest anyone who they reasonably suspect has committed or attempted, or is committing or attempting, any offence if serving a summons appears inappropriate or impracticable because of the existence of specified circumstances. Known as the 'general arrest conditions', these circumstances are:

- that the suspect will not give their name and address, or the police officer reasonably suspects that the name or address given is false, or the address is unsatisfactory for service of a summons; or
- that arrest is necessary to prevent physical harm and damage to property, to prevent obstruction of the highway, to protect a child or other

vulnerable person from the suspect, or to protect the suspect from harming themselves or suffering physical injury.

In **G** *v* **Director of Public Prosecutions** (1989), it was held that a belief by the police officer concerned that 'suspects generally give false names' was not sufficient to satisfy the general arrest conditions.

Other statutory powers of arrest. Certain other statutes provide powers of arrest. For example, s. 5 of the Public Order Act 1986 permits a police officer to arrest without a warrant anyone who commits the offence of disorderly conduct, provided the officer has warned the person in question to stop the disorderly conduct, and the person has continued; and the CJPOA gives a constable in uniform the power to arrest without a warrant a person reasonably suspected of attending or preparing for a rave.

Arrest for breach of the peace. Section 26 of PACE preserves the old common law power of arrest for breach of the peace recognized in the important case of **R** *v* **Howell** (1982). This area of common law was strictly applied in **Nicol** *v* **DPP** (1996). During an angling competition animal rights activists blew horns, threw twigs into the water and tried to persuade the anglers to stop fishing. This provoked the anglers so that they were on the verge of using force to remove the protesters, at which point the activists were arrested for breach of the peace. The court found that the protesters were lawfully arrested as, while their behaviour was in itself lawful, it was not reasonable.

The police have a power to arrest not just where a breach of the peace has occurred, but also where they fear that such a breach will occur and in order to prevent it from doing so. In **Foulkes** *v* **Chief Constable for the Merseyside Police** (1998), the claimant was locked out of his house during a domestic dispute. He called the police who suggested that he leave the vicinity of the house since his wife and children did not want him to enter. He refused and was arrested on the ground that the police feared a breach of the peace if he attempted to enter the property or remained outside it. The claimant's subsequent claim for damages for unlawful arrest was successful. The Court of Appeal ruled that the police could only arrest where no breach of the peace had actually occurred but where they feared it would occur, if the threat of a breach of the peace was sufficiently serious and imminent. This was not the case on these facts.

Citizen's arrest

An ordinary citizen can arrest someone who is reasonably suspected to be committing an arrestable offence and, where such an offence has been committed, anyone who is reasonably suspected of being guilty of it. If the offence has not actually been committed by anyone, the citizen may be liable for damages (**Walters** *v* **WH Smith** (1914)).

Manner of arrest

PACE requires that at the time of, or as soon as practicable after the arrest, the person arrested must be informed that they are under arrest, and given the grounds for that arrest, even if it is perfectly obvious that they are being arrested and why (s. 28). This is in line with the pre-existing case law, where in **Christie** *v* **Leachinsky** (1947) Viscount Simon said: 'No one, I think, would approve a situation in which when the person arrested asked for the reason, the policeman replied "that has nothing to do with you: come along with me" . . .'

There is no set form of words that must be used, and colloquial language such as 'You're nicked for mugging' may be acceptable.

Police detention

Apart from powers given by anti-terrorist legislation, before 1984 the police in England and Wales had no express power to detain suspects for further investigations to be carried out, nor did they have a general power to detain individuals for questioning, whether as suspects or potential witnesses. In practice, the police often acted as if they had these powers.

The 1981 Royal Commission on Criminal Procedure recommended that the police should be given express powers to detain suspects for questioning, with safeguards to ensure that those powers were not abused. These express powers were granted by PACE. Before PACE, it was generally thought that the police were obliged to bring a suspect before a court within 24 hours, or release them; the Act allows suspects to be detained without charge for up to four days, although there are some safeguards designed to prevent abuse of this power. PACE provides that an arrested person must be brought to a police station as soon as practicable after the arrest, though this may be delayed if their presence elsewhere is necessary for an immediate investigation (s. 30). On arrival at the police station, they should usually be taken to the custody officer, who has to decide whether sufficient evidence exists to charge the person. If, on arrest, there is already sufficient evidence to charge the suspect, they must be charged and then released on bail unless there are reasons why this is not appropriate. Such reasons include the fact that the defendant's name and address are not known, there are reasonable grounds for believing that the address given is false, or that the suspect may commit an offence while on bail (s. 38(1)). A person who has been charged and is being held in custody must be brought before magistrates as soon as practicable, and in any event not later than the first sitting after being charged with the offence (s. 46).

If there is not sufficient evidence to charge the suspect, then the person can be detained for the purpose of securing or obtaining such evidence – often through questioning (s. 37). Where a person is being detained and has not been charged, a review officer should assess whether there are grounds for continued detention after the first six hours and then at intervals of not more than nine hours (s. 40). As a basic rule, the police can detain a person for up to 24 hours from the time of arrival at the police station, after which the suspect should generally be either released or charged (s. 41). However, there are major exceptions to this. Continued detention for a further 12 hours can be authorized by the police themselves, if the detention is necessary to secure or preserve evidence and the offence is a 'serious arrestable offence'. This category includes such offences as murder, manslaughter, rape, kidnap, drug-trafficking, hostage-taking and some sexual offences (PACE s. 117), plus any arrestable offence which has led or is intended to lead to serious harm to the security of the state or public order; serious interference with administration of justice or investigation of offences; death or injury; or substantial financial gain or loss to a person.

Further periods of continued detention, up to 96 hours, are possible with approval from the magistrates' court. After 96 hours the suspect must be charged or released. In fact prolonged detention is rare, with only 5 per cent of suspects detained for more than 18 hours, and 1 per cent for more than 24 hours.

The custody officer is responsible for keeping the custody record (which records the various stages of detention) and checks that the provisions of PACE in relation to the detention are complied with. These theoretical safeguards for the suspect have proved weak in practice. PACE seems to contemplate that custody officers will be quasi-judicial figures, who can distance themselves from the needs of the investigation and put the rights of the suspect first. In practice this has never been realistic; custody officers are ordinary members of the station staff, and likely to share their view of the investigation. In addition, they will often be of a more junior rank than the investigating officer. They are therefore highly unlikely to refuse to allow the detention of a suspect, or to prevent breaches of PACE and its codes during the detention.

Police interrogation
The usual reason for detaining a suspect is so that the police can question them, in the hope of securing a confession. This has come to be a very important investigative tool, since it is cheap (compared, for example, with scientific evidence) and the end result, a confession, is seen as reliable and convincing evidence by judges and juries alike. Research by Mitchell (1983) suggests that a high proportion of suspects do make either partial or complete confessions.

Unfortunately, as the miscarriages of justice show, relying too much on confession evidence can have severe drawbacks. Instances of police completely falsifying confessions, or threatening or beating suspects so that they confess even when they are innocent, may be rare but the miscarriages show that police have been willing to use these techniques where they think they can get away with it. In addition, there are less dramatic, but probably more widespread problems. The 1993 Royal Commission raised questions about the poor standard of police interviewing; research by John Baldwin (*Video Taping Police Interviews with Suspects: an Evaluation* (1992)) suggested that police officers went into the interview situation not with the aim of finding out whether the person was guilty, but on the assumption that they were and with the intention of securing a confession to that effect. Interviews were often rambling and repetitious; police officers dismissed the suspect's explanations and asked the same questions over and over again until they were given the answer they wanted. In some cases the researchers felt this treatment amounted to bullying or harassment and in several cases the 'admissions' were one-word answers given in response to leading questions. Suspects were also offered inducements to confess, such as lighter sentences.

Obviously the implication here is that, under this kind of pressure, suspects might confess to crimes they did not commit – as many of the miscarriage of justice victims did. But such false confessions do not only occur where the suspects are physically threatened. A study by psychologist G.H. Gudjonsson (*The Psychology of Interrogations, Confessions and Testimony*, 1992) found that there were four situations in which people were likely to confess to crimes they did not commit. First, a minority may make confessions quite voluntarily, out of a disturbed desire for publicity, to relieve general feelings of guilt or because they cannot distinguish between reality and fantasy – it has been suggested that this was partly the case with Judith Ward. Secondly, they may want to protect someone else, perhaps a friend or relative, from interrogation and prosecution. Thirdly, they may be unable to see further than a desire to put the questioning to an end and get away from the police station, which can, after all, be a frightening place for those who are not accustomed to it. A psychologist giving evidence to the 1993 Royal Commission commented that: 'Some children are brought up in such a way that confession always seems to produce forgiveness, in which case a false confession may be one way of bringing an unpleasant situation [the interrogation] to an end.' Among this group there may also be a feeling that, once they get out of the police station, they will be able to make everyone see sense, and realize their innocence: Judith Ward has commented that she frequently felt that sooner or later someone would realize there had been a mistake.

Finally, the pressure of questioning, and the fact that the police seem convinced of their case, may temporarily persuade the suspect that they must have done the act in question. Obviously the young, as in the Confait case, the disturbed (such as Judith Ward) and the mentally subnormal are likely to be particularly vulnerable to this last situation, but Gudjonsson's research found that its effects were not confined to those who might be considered abnormally suggestible. Their subjects included people of reasonable intelligence who scored highly in tests on suggestibility, showing that they were particularly prepared to go along with what someone in authority was saying. Under hostile interrogation in the psychologically intimidating environment of a police station, even non-vulnerable people are likely to make admissions which are not true, failing to realize that once a statement has been made, it will be extremely difficult to retract.

The RCCJ recommended that police training should be improved to recognize the dangers of bad interviewing, and the need to listen to what the suspect says and, where practicable, to follow up and check their story.

Safeguards for the suspect

Certain safeguards are contained in PACE to try to protect the suspect in the police station. Some of these – the custody officer, the custody record, and the time limits for detention – have already been mentioned, and we will now look at the rest. It has been claimed that these safeguards would prevent miscarriages of justice in the future, yet the police station where Winston Silcott was questioned was meant to be following the PACE guidelines on a pilot basis. PACE officially came into force in January 1986 and Mark Braithwaite was arrested in February of that year, yet he was denied access to the legal advice guaranteed by the Act.

The caution
Under Code C, a person must normally be cautioned on arrest, and a person of whom there are grounds to suspect of an offence must be cautioned before being asked any questions regarding involvement, or suspected involvement, in that offence. Until recently, the caution was: 'You do not have to say anything unless you wish to do so but what you say may be given in evidence.' Since the abolition of the right to silence (see p. 262), the correct wording is: 'You do not have to say anything. But it may harm your defence if you do not mention when questioned something which you later rely on in court. Anything you do say may be given in evidence.'

Tape-recording
Section 60 of PACE states that interviews must be tape-recorded. This measure was designed to ensure that oppressive treatment and threats could not be used, nor confessions made up by the police. Sadly, it has proved a weaker safeguard than it might seem. In the first place, research presented to the RCCJ showed that police routinely got round the provision by beginning their questioning outside the interview room – in the car on the way to the police station, for example. In addition, they appeared quite willing to use oppressive questioning methods even once the tape-recorder was running – the RCCJ listened to tapes of interviews

with the Cardiff Three, victims of another miscarriage of justice whose convictions were quashed in December 1992, and expressed concern at the continuous repetitive questioning that the tapes revealed. The Home Office is carrying out pilot schemes for the use of video recordings in interviews. However, video recording is unlikely to be introduced at a national level in the near future as the the cost of establishing such a scheme would be about £100 million.

The right to inform someone of the detention

Section 56 of PACE provides that on arrival at a police station, a suspect is entitled to have someone, such as a relative, informed of their arrest. The person who the suspect chooses must be told of the arrest, and where the suspect is being held, without delay.

This right may be suspended for up to 36 hours if the detention is in connection with a serious arrestable offence, as defined at p. 255, and the authorizing officer reasonably believes that informing the person chosen by the suspect would lead to interference with, or harm to, evidence connected with a serious arrestable offence; the alerting of other suspects; interference with or injury to others; hindrance in recovering any property gained as a result of a serious arrestable offence, or in drug-trafficking offences; hindrance in recovering the profits of that offence.

The right to consult a legal adviser

Under s. 58 of PACE, a person held in custody is entitled to consult a legal adviser privately and free of charge. The House of Lords ruled in **R v Chief Constable of the RUC, ex parte Begley** (1998) that there was no equivalent right under common law. The legal adviser will either be a solicitor or, since 1995, an 'accredited representative'. To become an accredited representative a person must register with the Legal Aid Board with a signed undertaking from a solicitor that they are 'suitable' for this work. Once registered they can attend police stations on behalf of their solicitor and deal with summary or either way offences, but not indictable only offences. Within six months the representative must complete and submit a portfolio of work undertaken. This will include two police station visits where they observed their instructing solicitor, two visits where the solicitor observed them and five visits which they completed on their own. If they pass the portfolio stage they then have to take a written and an oral examination, at which point they are fully qualified to represent clients in the police station for any criminal matters.

The right to see a legal adviser may be suspended for up to 36 hours on the same grounds as the right to have another person informed. In **R v Samuel** (1988) the appellant was detained for six hours on suspicion of armed robbery and then refused lawyers because the police claimed there was a danger that other suspects might be warned. He was interviewed on two further occasions, and denied the suspected offence but admitted carrying out two burglaries. After 48 hours, a lawyer sent by Samuel's mother arrived at the police station, but was refused access to Samuel for a further three hours, during which time he confessed to the armed robbery. The Court of Appeal said that the denial of access to legal advice was unjustified and the confession obtained as a result was inadmissible. They stated that a police officer who sought to justify refusal of legal advice had to do so by reference to the specific circumstances of the case. It was not enough to believe that giving access to a solicitor might generally lead to the alerting of accomplices; there had to be a belief that in the specific case it probably would, and such cases would be very rare – especially where the lawyer called was the duty solicitor.

On the other hand, in **R** *v* **Alladice** (1988), a suspect was refused access to a lawyer. Despite this clear breach of PACE, the court held that the interview was in fact conducted with propriety, and that legal advice would have added nothing to the defendant's knowledge of his rights, so the suspect's confession was allowed in evidence.

Research by Sanders in 1989 showed that only about a quarter of all those arrested asked to see a legal adviser (*Advice and Assistance at Police Stations and the 24-hour Duty Solicitors Scheme*). It appeared that part of the reason for this was a range of ploys used by the police to dissuade suspects from seeing a lawyer. The most common – and most successful – ploy was to suggest that asking for a solicitor would lead to delay, so that the suspect, who is generally keen to leave the police station as soon as possible, decides to go ahead without legal advice. In addition, defendants were not always given the leaflet advising them of their rights, were asked to sign at a particular point on their custody record without being told that in doing so they were waiving their right to see a solicitor, or were not told that the service was free. This last ploy was addressed in April 1991, when a change in the relevant Code required the police to tell suspects that they were entitled to free legal advice, and research by Brown in 1993 found that after this the proportion of suspects requesting legal advice went up to 32 per cent. For cases ending up in the Crown Court, around half of defendants (53 per cent) had a solicitor present during questioning.

In the past there has been concern as to the quality of the legal advice given in the police station. Research by McConville and Hodgson (1993) found that only a quarter of those attending police stations were qualified solicitors; the rest were articled clerks, unqualified clerks or even former police officers. Firms tended to give this area of work very low priority, sending those employees who could most easily be spared from other work, rather than those who were most likely to have relevant skills and experience. Research by Baldwin (1992) found that in 66 per cent of interviews the legal representative said nothing at all, and in only 9 per cent of cases did they actively intervene on behalf of the suspect or object to police questions. Baldwin comments:

The interview takes place on police territory and it is police officers who are in charge of it . . . Passivity and compliance on the part of lawyers are therefore the normal, the expected, almost the required responses at the police station. Solicitors are conditioned by their history, their experience, even their professional training and guidance, to be passive in the police interview room, and the existing rules reinforce this by giving police officers the upper hand. The junior staff who mainly turn up to police stations are more inclined to facilitate police questioning than they are to challenge it.

McConville and Hodgson (1993) found that legal advisers often lacked adequate legal knowledge or confidence, and sometimes appeared to identify more with the police than with the suspect. They were usually told very little about the case by the police, and had only minimal discussions with their client beforehand (around half spent less than ten minutes alone with the client). They were therefore rarely in a position to give useful advice.

In the light of concerns about the quality of advice given by solicitors' representatives, the accreditation scheme was introduced in 1995 to raise the standard of legal advice offered at this vital stage in the criminal system. This scheme seems to have led to significant improvements in the quality of advice given. Research carried out by Lee Bridges and Satnam Choongh (*Improving Police Station Legal Advice* (1998)), found that accredited representatives performed as well as duty solicitors and other solicitors, though there were still high rates of non-compliance with the Law Society's standards of performance. In particular, they observed failures to ask suspects about their treatment by the police, to inform them of their right to break interviews for further advice and to intervene to object to inappropriate police questioning.

There remains a danger that the police may have questioned the suspect before the official interview, and may continue to do so after a lawyer has visited. In some situations, legal advisers have proved reluctant to visit the police station at all, preferring to speak to suspects on the telephone instead (Sanders (1989)).

Taking into account these problems, the RCCJ recommended that the police should ask suspects for reasons if they chose to waive their rights; and these communications should be videoed (along with the interview itself). Police training should include formal instruction in the role that solicitors are properly expected to play in the criminal justice system. The Law Society should take appropriate action to ensure that its advice becomes more widely known, better understood, and more consistently acted upon.

An 'appropriate adult'

PACE and Code C provide that young people and mentally disordered or mentally handicapped adults must have an 'appropriate adult' with them during a police interview, as well as having the usual right to legal advice.

This may be a parent, but is often a social worker. Surprisingly, Evans's 1993 research for the RCCJ found that parents were not necessarily a protection for the suspect, since they often took the side of the police and helped them to produce a confession.

With more and more patients of psychiatric institutions being released into so-called 'community care', higher numbers of mentally vulnerable adults are finding themselves in police stations. Unlike children, they may be difficult to identify, making it likely that the required safeguards will not be in place when they are interviewed. Research by the psychologist Gudjonsson (1992) calculated that between 15 and 20 per cent of suspects may need an appropriate adult present – considerably more than the 4 per cent whom the police currently identify. The RCCJ recommended that the police ought to be given clearer guidelines and special training in identifying vulnerable individuals, and that there should be a full review of who should be considered an 'appropriate adult', and what their role in the police station should be.

They also raised the possibility of establishing duty psychiatrist schemes at busy police stations in city centres, and felt that in any event, all police stations should have arrangements for calling in psychiatric help where necessary.

Treatment of suspects
PACE codes stipulate that interview rooms must be adequately lit, heated and ventilated, that suspects must be allowed to sit during questioning, and that adequate breaks for meals, refreshments and sleep must be given.

Record of the interview
After the interview is over, the police must make a record of it, which is kept on file. Baldwin's 1993 research checked a sample of such records against the taped recordings, and concluded that even those police forces considered to be more progressive were often failing to produce good quality records of interviews. Half the records were faulty or misleading, and the longer the interview, the more likely the record was to be inaccurate. These findings were backed up by a separate study carried out by Roger Evans (1993). He found that in some summaries, the police stated that suspects had confessed during the interview, but, on listening to the tape recordings the researchers could find no evidence of this, and felt that the suspects were in fact denying the offence.

Baldwin points out that the job of police officers is to catch criminals, and their temperament, aptitude and training are focused on this; the skills required for making careful summaries of complex material are not among those generally thought to be required in the job. Since police officers would inevitably summarize interviews from the point of view of a prosecution, defence lawyers should be prepared to take this into account and, rather than taking the summaries on trust, needed to listen to the interview tapes themselves. In practice, solicitors request interview tapes in only 10 per cent of cases.

Exclusion of evidence

One of the most important safeguards in PACE is the possibility for the courts to refuse to admit evidence which has been improperly obtained. Given that the reason why police officers bend or break the rules is to secure a conviction, preventing them from using the evidence obtained in this way is likely to constitute an effective deterrent.

PACE contains two provisions on the admissibility of evidence. Section 76(2) requires the prosecution to prove beyond reasonable doubt that a confession was not obtained by oppression (which is defined in s. 76(8) as torture, inhuman or degrading treatment or the use or threat of violence), or otherwise in circumstances likely to render the confession unreliable. Section 78 allows the court to refuse evidence (of any kind) if it appears to the court that the admission of such evidence would have such an adverse effect on the fairness of the proceedings that the court ought not to admit it.

These provisions have been used to render evidence inadmissible when the police have breached PACE or its Codes, although breaches of the Codes alone must be 'serious and substantial' in order to make evidence inadmissible. Such breaches were found in **R** v **Canale** (1990), where the court refused to accept evidence of interviews which were not contemporaneously written up, describing this breach of a Code as 'flagrant, deliberate and cynical'. In **R** v **Latif and Shahzad** (1996) the House of Lords took a very narrow approach to s. 78. The appellants had been convicted of being knowingly concerned in the importation of heroin into the UK from Pakistan. An undercover police officer had assisted in the importation in order to trick Shahzad into entering the UK so that he could be prosecuted here, there being no extradition treaty with Pakistan. Despite the fact that the court found that the police officer's conduct had been criminal and had involved trickery and deception, the House of Lords refused to exclude his evidence under s. 78.

The right to silence

Until 1994, the law provided a further safeguard for those suspected of criminal conduct, in the form of the traditional 'right to silence'. This essentially meant that suspects were free to say nothing at all in response to police questioning, and the prosecution could not suggest in court that this silence implied guilt (with some very limited exceptions).

Once PACE was introduced, the police argued that its safeguards, especially the right of access to legal advice, had tipped the balance too far in favour of suspects, so that the right to silence was no longer needed. Despite the fact that the RCCJ opposed this view, the Government agreed with the police, and the right to silence was abolished by the CJPOA. This does not mean that subjects can be forced to speak, but it provides four situations in which, if the suspect chooses not to speak, the court will be entitled to draw such inferences from that silence as appear proper. The four situations are where suspects:

- when questioned under caution or charge, fail to mention facts which they later rely on as part of their defence and which it is reasonable to expect them to have mentioned (s. 34);
- are silent during the trial, including choosing not to give evidence or to answer any question without good cause (s. 35);
- following arrest, fail to account for objects, substances or marks on clothing when requested to do so (s. 36);
- following arrest, fail to account for their presence at a particular place when requested to do so (s. 37).

Section 55 of the Youth Justice and Criminal Evidence Act 1999 provides that no inferences from silence can be drawn where a suspect has been denied access to legal advice. The European Court of Human Rights stated in **Murray** v **United Kingdom** (1996) that, in the context of the anti-terrorist legislation, the abolition of the right to silence was not in breach of the European Convention, because of the existence of a range of other safeguards ensuring that the defendant had a fair trial.

Adverse inferences cannot always be drawn from silence. Where the statute does not apply, the judge should explicitly direct the jury that they should not draw adverse inferences from the defendant's silence, as the old common law applies. In **R** v **McGarry** (1998) the defendant, on leaving a club, had punched a man in the face. When questioned by the police about the incident after being cautioned, he had provided a short written statement that he had acted in self-defence and then had answered 'no comment' to all subsequent questions. At his trial he relied on the defence of self-defence and the jury heard the tape of his interview when he had refused to answer questions. The Court of Appeal ruled that he fell outside s. 34 as he had not failed to mention facts that he later relied on at his trial in his defence. The judge should therefore have directed the jury not to draw adverse inferences from his refusal to answer questions.

In **R** v **N** (1998) the defendant was prosecuted for indecent assault. At his trial the judge informed the jury that they could draw an adverse inference from the appellant's failure in the police interview to provide the explanation for the presence of semen on the victim's night-dress that he had given at his trial. The appellant was convicted and appealed. The Court of Appeal ruled that the trial judge had made a mistake since, at the time of the interview, it was not known that there were semen stains on the night-dress, and so the appellant was not asked to explain them. Section 34 of the CJPOA had to be limited to its express terms: an adverse inference could only be drawn from a failure to mention a fact when being questioned in relation to it. Merely failing to mention a fact during the police interview was not sufficient.

In **Condron** *v* **UK** (2000) the applicants were heroin addicts accused of being involved in the supply and possession of heroin. The prosecution case was that the applicants kept the wholesale heroin in their flat, and passed retail packets to the adjacent flat, where another person made the actual sales. Modest support was given to this theory by surveillance videos which showed small objects (such as a cigarette packet) being passed from the balcony of the applicants' flat to the window of the adjacent flat.

In the police station their solicitor had concluded that they were unfit to be interviewed because they were suffering from withdrawal symptoms, and therefore advised them not to answer questions. At their trial the applicants gave various innocent explanations for the transactions on the balcony. The trial judge directed the jury that they could draw adverse inferences of guilt from the applicants' silence in the police station.

The applicants took their case to the European Court of Human Rights, claiming that their right to a fair trial guaranteed under article 6(1) of the European Convention on Human Rights had been violated by the judge's direction to the jury. Their application was successful as the Court held that the judge's direction had been inadequate. The jury should have been required to consider the explanation for silence offered, and to draw adverse inferences from the silence only if satisfied that the explanation could not sensibly be accepted. The jury should have been told that if they were satisfied with the explanation given, it was inappropriate to draw an adverse inference from the applicants' silence in the police station.

Interviews outside the station

PACE states that, where practicable, interviews with arrested suspects should always take place at a police station. However, evidence obtained by questioning or voluntary statements outside the police station may still be admissible. Since such interviews are not subject to most of the safeguards explained above, the obvious danger is that police may evade PACE requirements by conducting 'unofficial' interviews – such as the practice known as taking the 'scenic route' to the station, in which suspects are questioned in the police car. The RCCJ found that about 30 per cent of suspects report being questioned prior to arrest.

Even at the police station, research by McConville ('Videotaping Interrogations: Police Behaviour On and Off Camera' (1992)) shows that illegal, informal and unrecorded visits were made to suspects in cells to prepare the ground for an interview and to persuade them not to raise a defence. Sometimes suspects themselves ask to see police officers informally, in the hope of doing some kind of deal. In some cases the formal interview that followed was little more than a set piece, scripted by the police. Yet defence lawyers often accepted the police version of these events as the truth. Despite the obvious dangers of these practices, the RCCJ did not recommend excluding evidence obtained in this way, but merely discussed the possibility of requiring tape-recording of all contact between a suspect and the police.

Search of the person after arrest

Section 32 of PACE provides that the police may search an arrested person at a place other than a police station if there are reasonable grounds for believing they are in possession of evidence, or anything that might assist escape or present a danger.

The police have the power to search arrested persons on arrival at the police station, and to seize anything which they reasonably believe the suspect might use to injure anyone, or use to make an escape, or that is evidence of an offence or has been obtained as the result of an offence (s. 54).

Intimate searches and fingerprinting

Section 55 of PACE gives police the power to conduct intimate searches of a suspect, which means searches of the body's orifices. Such a search must be authorized by a superintendent, who must have reasonable grounds for believing that a weapon or drug is concealed, and must be carried out by a qualified doctor or nurse.

The safeguards on the use of this power caused problems for the police when confronted with drug dealers. The dealers frequently stored drugs in their mouths, knowing that search of the mouth was regarded as an intimate search needing to be carried out by a member of the medical profession with special authorization. To address this problem, s. 65 of PACE, as amended by the CJPOA 1994, now provides that a search of the mouth is not an intimate search.

Section 62 of PACE states that intimate samples, including blood, saliva or semen, can be taken from a suspect, but in some cases their written consent is required, though this is becoming increasingly rare following the Criminal Evidence (Amendment) Act 1997. Non-intimate samples, such as hair or nail clippings, can be taken from a suspect without their consent, under s. 63, although this procedure must be authorized by an officer at the level of inspector or above. The authorization must be in writing and recorded on the custody record. Section 61 of PACE permits the police to take fingerprints from suspects.

These powers have been extended by the CJPOA, which allows what the Act calls 'speculative searches', whereby fingerprints, samples or information drawn from them can be checked against other similar data available to the police. These changes broadly reflect the recommendations of the RCCJ. The powers of the police to take and retain DNA samples are contained in the Criminal Justice and Police Act 2001.

The Criminal Justice and Court Services Act 2000 allows the compulsory drug testing of alleged offenders.

Powers to search premises

The police can always search premises if the occupier consents to this. In addition, Part II of PACE (ss. 8–18) provides the police with statutory powers to enter and search premises for evidence. These powers can be executed either with or without a warrant.

Search with a warrant

A number of statutes allow the granting of search warrants, but the main provisions are to be found in PACE. The police apply for the warrant to a magistrate, who must be satisfied that the police reasonably believe a serious arrestable offence has been committed, and that the premises concerned contain relevant evidence or material likely to be of substantial use to the investigation. In addition, it must be impractical to make the search without a warrant (which means with the consent of the person entitled to grant entry or access to evidence), because it is not practicable to communicate with that person, because entry would not be granted without a warrant, or because the purpose of the search would be frustrated or seriously prejudiced if immediate entry could not be obtained on arrival.

In practice, research by Lidstone (1984) indicates that magistrates rarely refuse to grant a warrant; if certain magistrates were known to refuse applications, the police would simply stop applying to them and go to another magistrate instead. About 12 per cent of searches are made with a warrant.

There are certain classes of material for which these basic powers cannot be used: privileged material (communications between lawyers and their clients); excluded material (medical records and journalistic material held in confidence); and special procedure material (other journalistic material and material acquired through business and held in confidence).

Once the warrant is issued, entry and search must take place within one month, and must be undertaken at a reasonable hour, unless that would frustrate the search. Reasonable force may be used (PACE, s. 117). The officers concerned should provide documentary evidence of their status, plus a copy of the warrant, unless it is impracticable to do so. The Codes also require that police hand out a notice giving information about the grounds for and powers of search, and the rights of the occupier, including rights to compensation for any damage done.

Search without a warrant

PACE provides a range of powers of search which can be exercised without a warrant. Section 17 allows the police to enter and search to execute a warrant of arrest; to make an arrest without warrant; to capture a person unlawfully at large; or to protect people from serious injury or prevent serious damage to property.

Under s. 18, after an arrest for an arrestable offence, the police can search premises occupied or controlled by the suspect if they reasonably suspect that there is evidence of the immediate offence or other offences on the premises.

Section 32 provides that, after an arrest for an arrestable offence, an officer can lawfully enter and search premises where the person was when arrested or immediately before they were arrested, if the constable reasonably suspects that there is evidence relating to the offence in question on the premises.

There is also a common law power to enter and remain on premises 'to deal with or prevent a breach of the peace'. This is based on **Thomas** *v* **Sawkins** (1935), where it was held to be lawful for police to enter and insist on remaining in a hall where a political meeting was taking place, because their past experience of such meetings gave them reasonable grounds to apprehend a breach of the peace.

In **McLeod** *v* **UK** (1998), Mrs McLeod was ordered by the county court to deliver certain property to her ex-husband. Mr McLeod mistakenly believed he had the right to collect the property from her home. His solicitors asked two police officers to escort him to prevent a breach of the peace. Mrs McLeod was not actually at home when he arrived and he entered her house escorted by two police officers. The Court of Appeal found that the police entry was lawful. Lord Neill commented:

> I am satisfied that Parliament in s. 17(6) has now recognised that there is a power to enter premises to prevent a breach of the peace as a form of preventive justice. I can see no satisfactory basis for restricting that power to particular classes of premises such as those where public meetings are held. If the police reasonably believe that a breach of the peace is likely to take place on private premises, they have power to enter those premises to prevent it. The apprehension must, of course be genuine and it must relate to the near future.

Mrs McLeod took her case to the European Court of Human Rights. That court ruled that Art. 8 of the European Convention on Human Rights, which protects the right to privacy, had been violated. While the breach of the peace doctrine could in certain circumstances justify an interference with a person's privacy, on the facts of the case there was almost no grounds to apprehend that a breach of the peace would occur, and so it provided no justification for the interference with Mrs McLeod's privacy. As soon as it became apparent that she was away from home, the officers should not have entered her house since it should have been clear that there was no risk of a breach of the peace.

Searches of premises are governed by Code B, which states that searches should be made at a reasonable time, that only reasonable force should be used and that the police should show due consideration and courtesy towards the property and privacy of the occupier. How far this is observed in practice might be doubted by anyone who watched television news coverage of the anti-burglary campaign Operation Bumblebee, in which police broke down suspects' doors with sledgehammers at 6 am. The fact that in high-profile cases, such searches are often accompanied by TV cameras suggests that the media may be tipped off by the police, which, whether such tip-offs are official or not, suggests little regard for the suspects' privacy.

Once the police are lawfully on premises, then under s. 19 of PACE they may seize and retain any item that is evidence of a crime.

Surveillance

In recent years a combination of developing technology, concern about confession evidence and the changing nature of financial and drug-related crime, has led the police to adopt increasingly sophisticated and intrusive methods of investigation. Surveillance operations can include the placing of bugging devices on private property, the interception of communications, including mobile phones and e-mails, and the use of undercover police officers. Such surveillance activities were in the past unregulated which may have been in breach of the European Convention on Human Rights which protects the right to privacy (Art. 8). Legislation was therefore required. The relevant legislative provisions are now contained in the Police Act 1997 and the Regulation of Investigatory Powers Act 2000. Except in the case of an emergency, the police have to obtain the authorization of an independent Commissioner before they can use intrusive surveillance techniques.

Cautions

Rather than prosecuting an offence, the police may decide to issue a caution. This is a formal warning to offenders about what they have done, and their conduct in the future. Home Office guidelines lay down the criteria on which the decision to caution should be made. A caution can only be given where the offender admits guilt, and there would be a realistic prospect of a successful prosecution. In the case of a juvenile, the parents or guardian must consent to a caution being given. If these criteria are met, other factors to be taken into account are the seriousness of the offence and the extent of the damage done; the interests and desires of the victim; the previous conduct of the offender; the family background of the offender; and the offender's conduct after the offence, such as a willingness to make reparation to the victim.

Formal cautions are recorded and if the person is convicted of another offence afterwards, can be cited as part of their criminal record. The 1980s saw a substantial increase in the use of cautioning with the number of cautions given doubling between 1983 to 1993, peaking at 311,300 cautions for that year, primarily to juveniles. There has subsequently been a slight decline in their use with the figures for 1995 showing a 6 per cent reduction in the use of cautions.

Cautioning appears to be effective in terms of preventing reoffending: 87 per cent of those cautioned in 1985 were not convicted of a standard list offence within two years of the caution. However, this may reflect the kind of individuals and offences that are seen as suitable for a caution: for example, 80 per cent of those cautioned had no previous cautions or convictions, but for those who had been previously convicted there was a much greater likelihood that they would reoffend. Prosecution is the most expensive method of dealing with offenders. The RCCJ recognized the value of diversionary schemes, stating that there could safely be more cautioning of petty offenders. They were concerned, though, that rates of cautioning varied widely across the country, and recommended the introduction of statutory guidelines. The initial decision on whether to caution should remain with the police, but the Crown Prosecution Service (CPS) should be able to require the police to caution instead of bringing a prosecution.

Despite the RCCJ's recommendations for more cautioning, the national guidelines that were subsequently introduced are more restrictive than previous practice, removing any presumption that juveniles should be cautioned, and discouraging repeat cautions and cautions for serious offences. Problems with variations in the use of cautioning continues – the Criminal Statistics 1995 showed that there were big differences in police caution rates between different police forces with Gloucestershire, Suffolk and Warwickshire having a rate of over 54 per cent, while Merseyside, Durham, Dorset, South Wales and Cumbria had a rate of 30 per cent or less. The current Labour Government has expressed its concern that cautions have been overused, and are proposing to restrict the use of cautions further. Their Crime and Disorder Bill would replace repeat cautions with a single final warning.

The Crown Prosecution Service

Until 1986, criminal prosecutions were officially brought by private citizens rather than by the state; in practice most prosecutions were brought by the police (though technically they were prosecuting as private citizens). Although the police obviously employed solicitors to help them in this task, their relationship with those solicitors was a normal client relationship, and so the police were not obliged to act on the solicitors' advice. Cases in the magistrates' court were sometimes actually presented by the police themselves.

In 1970, a report by the law reform pressure group, JUSTICE, criticized the role of the police in the prosecution process (*The Prosecution in England and Wales*, 1970). It argued that it was not in the interests of justice for the same body to be responsible for the two very different functions of investigation and prosecution. This dual role prevented the prosecution from being independent and impartial: the police had become concerned with winning or losing, when the aim of the prosecution should be the discovery of the truth. As a result, there was a danger of the police withholding from the defence information that might make a conviction less likely. The report pointed out that public policy and the circumstances of the individual were relevant considerations in the decision to prosecute, and that the English system was unique in Europe in allowing the whole process, from interrogation to prosecution, to be effectively under the control of the police in the majority of cases. In addition, it noted, police officers were not trained as lawyers or advocates.

The prosecution process was reviewed by the Royal Commission on Criminal Procedure (RCCP) in 1981. Their report highlighted a range of problems. There was a lack of uniformity, with differing procedures and standards applied across the country on such matters as whether to prosecute or caution, and the system prevented a consistent national prosecution policy. The process was inefficient, with inadequate preparation of cases; research by McConville and Baldwin (1981) found many cases of defendants being acquitted due to judges stopping the trial at the end of the prosecution case, or directing the jury to acquit, because the prosecution evidence was insufficient. The failure of prosecution witnesses at trial accounted for many of these cases, but there were clearly some where it should have been foreseen that the evidence would be inadequate.

The RCCP agreed with JUSTICE that, in principle, investigation and prosecution should be separate processes, conducted by different people. The goals of investigation and of prosecution were incompatible, although a total separation was thought to be impossible in practice. There was also no executive or democratic accountability or control over the existing system.

As a result of these findings, the RCCP recommended the establishment of a Crown Prosecution Service, divided into separate sections for each police force area, with a Chief Crown Prosecutor responsible locally to a supervisory body and nationally to the Director of Public Prosecutions.

The Government followed the main recommendations, though it opposed the establishment of separate local services. The Crown Prosecution Service (CPS) was set up under the Prosecution of Offences Act 1985, as a national prosecution service for England and Wales. The service as a whole is headed by the Director of Public Prosecutions (DPP). The DPP reports on the running of the service to the Attorney-General, who is responsible in Parliament for general policy but not for individual cases. The only formal mechanism for accountability of the CPS is the requirement that an annual report must be presented to the Attorney-General, who is obliged to lay it before Parliament.

The establishment of the CPS means that the prosecution of offences is now separated from their detection and investigation, which is undertaken by the police. The CPS has no involvement in cases where the police decide not to prosecute, including those where the offender is given a caution. If the police decide the offender should be prosecuted, a file on the case will be sent to the CPS. They then review that decision, on the basis of criteria set out in the Code for Crown Prosecutors, issued by the DPP under s. 10 of the Prosecution of Offences Act 1985. The latest edition of this Code (published in June 1994) explains that this decision is taken in two stages. First, they must ask whether there is enough evidence to provide a 'realistic prospect of conviction', that is to say that a court is more likely than not to convict. If the case does not pass this evidential test, the prosecution must not go ahead, no matter how important or serious the case may be.

If the case does pass the evidential test, the CPS must then consider whether the public interest requires a prosecution. For example, a prosecution is more likely to be in the public interest if a conviction is likely to result in a significant sentence, if the offence was committed against a person serving the public (such as a police officer) or if the offence, although not serious in itself, is widespread in the area where it was committed. On the other hand, a prosecution is less likely to be in the public interest where the defendant is elderly, or suffering from significant mental or physical ill-health. A long delay between the offence taking place and the date of the trial may be a public interest reason not to prosecute, except where the offence is serious, the delay is partly the defendant's fault, the offence has only recently been discovered, or its complexity has made a long investigation necessary.

At the end of this two-stage test, the CPS may decide to go ahead with prosecution, send the case back to the police for a caution instead of a prosecution, or take no further action. The decision is theirs, and the police need not be consulted.

The clear distinction that was initially drawn between the police and the CPS is weakened by recent reforms. Following the Narey Report, *Review of Delay in the Criminal Justice System* (1997), some CPS staff now work alongside police officers in criminal justice units to prepare cases for court. This is an attempt to improve efficiency as well as police-CPS relations.

The Glidewell Report

When the CPS first started to operate in 1986, it was organized into 31 areas, each with a Chief Crown Prosecutor. These were subsequently increased to 38, but in 1993, in an effort to improve efficiency, the areas were enlarged into just 13 across the country and the administration was centralized around headquarters in London, with the DPP playing an increased role in the direct administration of the CPS. In the light of continuing concern over the functioning of the CPS, a review was carried out by a body chaired by Sir Ian Glidewell which reported in 1998. The *Review of the Crown Prosecution Service* (also known as the Glidewell Report) heavily criticized the CPS. It concluded that the 1993 reform had been a mistake, as it made the organization too centralized and excessively bureaucratic. It found that there was a problem with judge-ordered acquittals (where the case is too weak to be left to the jury), which constituted over 20 per cent of acquittals in 1996. Not all of these were due to poor case preparation by the CPS, as some involved errors in witness warnings by the police. But many were due to inadequate compilation of case papers between committal and trial by non-qualified staff who lacked supervision; the drafting of inadequate or erroneous indictments; and counsel being briefed too late to put things right.

Glidewell concluded that the CPS 'has the potential to become a lively, successful and esteemed part of the criminal justice system, but . . . sadly none of these adjectives applies to the service as a whole at present'.

The key recommendation of the Report was that there should be a devolution of powers from the centre to the regions, with the London headquarters playing a more limited role. This would involve replacing the existing 13 CPS areas with 42 areas corresponding to police force areas (the Metropolitan Police and City of London Police, which are two separate forces, would count as one for this purpose). Each area would be headed by a Chief Crown Prosecutor with considerable autonomy and an independent budget. In addition, it proposed that the CPS should take over the conduct of prosecutions immediately after the police charge a defendant. The CPS would then organize the initial hearing in the magistrates' court and make all the arrangements for witnesses to attend court proceedings. It proposed that teams of CPS lawyers, police and administrative caseworkers (together known as a Criminal Justice Unit), should be established to prepare and deal with many straightforward cases in their entirety (in other words both the case preparation and the court advocacy); the section which dealt with the most serious cases, called Central Casework, needed more staff, with more training and closer monitoring; there should be at least one full-time CPS lawyer in each Crown Court; CPS lawyers should be allowed to concentrate more on court work rather than paperwork; the DPP ought to play less of a role in the administration of the CPS and concentrate largely on the prosecution and legal process.

The Government accepted the main recommendations of the Glidewell Report and the new 42 areas of the CPS came into effect on 22 April 1999.

Powers of CPS employees

In the past, barristers from the independent Bar had to be paid by the CPS to carry out the advocacy required for prosecutions in the Crown Court, because lawyers employed in the CPS, including qualified barristers, did not have rights of audience in the Crown Court. The Access to Justice Act 1999 allows CPS lawyers to carry out this work themselves, with the aim of achieving greater efficiency while saving money. This was heavily criticized, particularly by the Bar Council and Professor Michael Zander, on the basis that, as full-time salaried employees with performance targets, CPS lawyers will sometimes be tempted to get convictions using dubious tactics because their jobs and prospects of promotion will depend on conviction success rates. To reduce this risk, s. 37 of the Act states that every advocate 'has a duty to the court to act in the interests of justice', which overrides any inconsistent duty, for example, to an employer. Professor Michael Zander has dismissed these as 'mere words' writing in a letter to *The Times*, that:

> The CPS as an organisation is constantly under pressure in regard to proportion of discontinuances, acquittal and conviction rates. These are factors in the day to day work of any CPS lawyer. It is disingenuous to imagine they will not have a powerful effect on decision making. (*The Times*, 29 December 1998)

Section 53 of the Crime and Disorder Act 1998 confers certain powers on employees of the CPS who are not qualified lawyers. Such employees can now present straightforward guilty plea cases in magistrates' courts and the DPP can confer on lay staff the power of a Crown Prosecutor to review files.

Private prosecutions

Private prosecutions can still be brought, and although statistically these are few, they can play an important role, particularly in highlighting or encouraging public concern over relevant issues.

In 1974, a PC Joy stopped a motorist and reported him for a motoring offence. The motorist was a Member of Parliament and PC Joy's superiors refused to pursue the case; PC Joy thought this unjust and successfully brought a private prosecution. Mary Whitehouse has also brought important private prosecutions in the past. More recently, the family of Stephen Lawrence, a teenager murdered in south London, took out a private prosecution against three men suspected of the killing, after the CPS dropped the case because it said there was insufficient evidence. Unfortunately, the private prosecution was unsuccessful for lack of evidence. The case primarily relied on the identification evidence of Duwayne Brooks. This was weak because the attack had lasted only for a matter of seconds. He was unable to be specific about the number of attackers, saying that it was a 'group of 4 to 6'. In his initial statement to the police, he said that, 'Of the group of 6 youths, I can only really describe one of them'. At one identification parade, he identified a member of the public. At another he identified no one although there was a suspect present. He had originally said Stephen had been hit on the head with an iron bar although he was later found to have sustained no head injuries. The judge summed up by saying: 'Where recognition or identification is concerned, [Brooks] simply does not know whether he is on his head or his heels . . . Adding one injustice to another does not cure the first injustice done to the Lawrence family.' The judge withdrew the case from the jury and ordered an acquittal. The decision to bring the private prosecution has been criticized as their acquittal prevents the suspects from being prosecuted for the same offence in the future when stronger evidence might have been available.

Historical powers of the Attorney-General and Director of Public Prosecutions

We have noted that with the creation of the CPS, the Director of Public Prosecutions (DPP) was placed at its head. However, before the creation of this body the DPP and the Attorney-General had certain powers to control the bringing of prosecutions and both have kept these powers despite the existence of the CPS.

For certain offences prosecutions can only be brought if the Attorney-General or the DPP has given their consent. The Law Commission reviewed this area of law in a report of 1998. It recommended that the need for consent to prosecutions be abolished except in three categories of offences. The first category is where the defendant is very likely to contend that a prosecution for a particular offence would infringe a right bestowed by the European Convention on Human Rights. The second category is the prosecution of offences involving national security or some international element. The third category is where there is a high risk that the right of private prosecution will be abused and the institution of proceedings will cause irreparable harm to the defendant, for example, the institution of proceedings for misfeasance of public office instituted by a private prosecution shortly before an election is held where the defendant is a candidate. Where consent to a prosecution is required by reference to national security or some international element, the consent should be given by a law officer; otherwise consents should be given by the DPP.

The Attorney-General has the power to stop proceedings that would be brought before the Crown Court. This is known as granting a *nolle prosequi* and is not actually an acquittal, so a prosecution can be brought in the future on the same charge. Controversy was caused in 1998 when the

Attorney-General entered a *nolle prosequi* in the trial of Justice Richard Gee who had been accused of a £1 million fraud.

When a private prosecution is brought, the DPP may choose to take over the case. Those powers are exercised in practice on his or her behalf by the CPS. Although the CPS has so far been reluctant to interfere in the individual's right to prosecute, it could take over such a case only to discontinue it, on either evidential or public interest grounds.

Following the Hillsborough football disaster, a private prosecution was brought by the Hillsborough Family Support Group against two of the senior police officers on duty at the stadium. The DPP refused to intervene to terminate this prosecution and his decision was challenged by the police officers in **R** *v* **DPP, ex parte Duckenfield** and **R** *v* **South Yorkshire Police Authority, ex parte Chief Constable of the South Yorkshire Police** (1999). This challenge was only partially successful.

Criminal Defence Service

The Access to Justice Act 1999 provides for the creation of a Criminal Defence Service. For a discussion of this body see p. 221.

Appearance in court

Persons charged with an offence can be called to court by means of a summons, or by a charge following arrest without a warrant. Arrest under a warrant signed by a magistrate under s. 1(1) of the Magistrates' Courts Act 1980 is not common today, and its main use is to arrest those who, having been granted bail, do not turn up for trial.

In order to have a summons served, the prosecutor must give a short account of the alleged offence, usually in writing, to the magistrates or their clerk (a process called laying an information). The information may be substantiated by an oral statement from the police, given on oath before a magistrate; such a statement must be given if the information is to be used as the basis for a warrant for arrest. A summons setting out the offence is then issued and served, either in person or, for minor offences, through Recorded Delivery or Registered post.

The defendant is entitled to plead guilty by post for any summary offence for which the maximum penalty does not exceed three months' imprisonment (s. 12 of the Magistrates' Courts Act 1980). In this situation the defendant does not need to attend court, and the procedure is frequently used for traffic offences. In the past, delays were caused when people failed to respond to the summons in which they were given the opportunity to plead guilty by post: neither pleading guilty by post nor turning up for the court hearing. This led to the case being adjourned while witness statements were prepared or arrangements made for witnesses to attend. To avoid such adjournments in future, the Magistrates'

Courts (Procedure) Act 1998 was passed which allows witness statements to be served with the original correspondence, so that if the defendant fails to respond the case can be tried at the first hearing.

Under s. 57 of the Crime and Disorder Act 1998, if an accused is being held in custody, all pre-trial hearings can take place using a live TV link between the court and the prison. The accused will be treated as if he or she is present at the court.

Bail

A person accused, convicted or under arrest for an offence may be granted bail, which means they are released under a duty to attend court or the police station at a given time. The criteria for granting or refusing bail are contained in the Bail Act 1976. There is a general presumption in favour of bail for unconvicted defendants, but there are some important exceptions. Bail need not be granted where there are substantial grounds for believing that, unless kept in custody, the accused would fail to surrender to bail, or would commit an offence, interfere with witnesses or otherwise obstruct the course of justice. In assessing these risks, the court may take account of the nature and seriousness of the offence and the probable sentence, along with the character, antecedents, associations and community ties of the defendant. Following the Criminal Justice and Court Services Act 2000 a court considering the question of bail must take into account any drug misuse by the defendant.

The courts need not grant bail when the magistrates think the accused should be kept in custody for their own protection, where the accused is already serving a prison sentence or where there has been insufficient time to obtain information as to the criteria for bail. If the court does choose to grant bail in such cases, its reasons for doing so must be included in the bail record. The presumption in favour of bail is reversed where someone is charged with a further indictable offence which appears to have been committed while on bail.

The Criminal Justice and Public Order Act 1994, following concern at offences being committed by accused while on bail, provided that a person charged or convicted of murder, manslaughter, rape, attempted murder or attempted rape could never be granted bail if they had a previous conviction for such an offence. This complete ban was found to be in breach of the European Convention on Human Rights by the European Commission of Human Rights in the case of Mr C, who was charged with attempted rape. The matter has been referred to the European Court of Human Rights. The law has now been reformed by the Crime and Disorder Act 1998, under which such a person may only be granted bail where there are exceptional circumstances which justify doing so. Thus Sion Jenkins, who was convicted of the murder of his foster-daughter Billy-Jo, was on bail throughout most of the proceedings.

When bail is refused for any of the stated reasons, other than insufficient information, the accused will usually be allowed only one further bail application; the court does not have to hear further applications unless there has been a change in circumstances. Where the remand in custody is on the basis of insufficient information, this is not technically a refusal of bail, so the accused may still make two applications. The Law Commission reported in 1999 that the rules on bail probably still breached the European Convention (*Bail and the Human Rights Act 1998*, Law Commission Report No. 157).

Bail can be granted subject to conditions, such as that the accused obtain legal advice before their next court appearance or that they give a security (which is a payment into court that will be forfeited if they fail to attend a court hearing), or the payment of a surety by a third party. Section 55 of the Crime and Disorder Act amends the Magistrates' Courts Act 1980 so that a magistrates' court must declare a recognizance to be forfeited immediately upon the non-appearance of a defendant released on bail and issue a summons to each surety to show cause why the court should not order full payment of the recognizance. A defendant refused bail, or who objects to the conditions under which it is offered, must be told the reasons for the decision, and informed of the right to apply to the Crown Court or a High Court judge, who have power to grant bail or vary the conditions under which it has been offered. The prosecution also have limited rights to appeal against a decision to grant bail.

In 1992 the average proportion of unconvicted and unsentenced prisoners was 22 per cent of the average prison population. Many of these remand prisoners, who have not been convicted of any offence, are kept in prison for between six months and a year before being tried, despite the fact that 60 per cent of them go on to be acquitted or given a non-custodial sentence.

The Government is currently preparing a Criminal Justice Bill which would further restrict the use of bail.

Classification of offences

There are three different categories of criminal offence.

Summary offences

These are the most minor crimes, and are only triable summarily in the magistrates' court. 'Summary' refers to the process of ordering the defendant to attend the court by summons, a written order usually delivered by post which is the most frequent procedure adopted in the magistrates' courts. There has been some criticism of the fact that more and more offences have been made summary only, reducing the right to trial by jury.

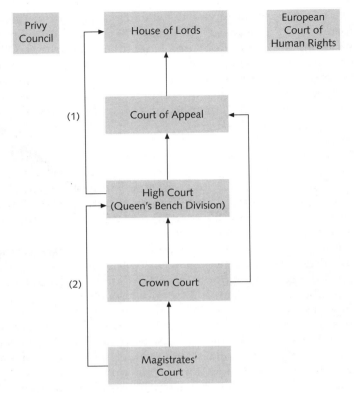

Figure 9.1 The Criminal Court System

[1] Leap frog procedure
[2] Appeal by way of case stated

Indictable offences

These are the more serious offences, such as rape and murder. They can only be heard by the Crown Court. The indictment is a formal document containing the alleged offences against the accused, supported by brief facts.

Offences triable either way

These offences may be tried in either the magistrates' court or the Crown Court. Common examples are theft and burglary.

Mode of trial

Where a person is charged with a triable either way offence, they can insist on a trial by jury, otherwise the decision is for the magistrates.

In reaching this decision the magistrates will take into account the seriousness of the case and whether they are likely to have sufficient sentencing powers to deal with it. Since 1996 the magistrates are also able to take into account the defendant's plea of guilty or not guilty, which will be given, for triable either way offences, before the mode of trial decision. If the defendant indicates a guilty plea, the court proceeds to sentence or commit to the Crown Court for sentence. If the defendant pleads not guilty, or fails to indicate a plea, the court decides the mode of trial.

It was hoped that the early plea procedure would increase the number of cases retained in the magistrates' courts with predicted savings for the CPS alone of up to £7.5 million. In fact, the new system of plea before venue has meant that there are many more people being sent to the Crown Court for sentencing, though fewer are being sent to the Crown Court for trial.

Research undertaken prior to the 1996 amendment (Hedderman and Moxon, 1992) showed that most offences tried in the Crown Court were 'either way' offences. Just 18 per cent were indictable only. There are three main reasons why defendants may choose to be dealt with by the Crown Court. First, it automatically puts off the day of trial. This has particular benefits to those who are remanded in custody and believe they will be found guilty and sent back to prison, because remand prisoners are entitled to privileges which are not available to sentenced prisoners (and time spent on remand is included in the time the prisoner eventually serves).

Secondly, many defendants believe they stand a better chance of acquittal in the Crown Court. A study by Vennard ('The Outcome of Contested Trials') suggests that they may be right: acquittal rates were significantly higher in the Crown Court (57 per cent) than in magistrates' courts (30 per cent). However, most of those who choose to be tried in the Crown Court then proceed to plead guilty. Hedderman and Moxon's 1992 study found that 27 per cent of defendants who elected Crown Court trial intended from the outset to plead guilty, and on the day of trial, many more did so, with 70 per cent pleading guilty to all charges and a further 13 per cent pleading guilty to some of them.

Thirdly, around a half of defendants are under the mistaken impression that they will get lighter sentences in the Crown Court. The RCCJ noted that, in fact, judges were three times more likely to impose prison sentences, and their sentences were, on average, two-and-a-half times longer than those imposed by magistrates. Perhaps not surprisingly, a third of the defendants who chose Crown Court trial thought that they had made a mistake, and would have been better off being dealt with by magistrates.

There are now serious moves to remove the right to elect a jury trial. These developments are discussed in Chapter 5 at p. 165.

Committal proceedings

Triable either way offences begin with an initial hearing in the magistrates' court, called the committal proceedings. These proceedings are designed to allow the magistrates to check that there is sufficient evidence to proceed to a full Crown Court trial, and to filter the weak cases. The Criminal Procedure and Investigation Act 1996 has introduced some amendments to the committal procedures in order to improve their efficiency and protect witnesses. Sections 51 and 52 of the Crime and Disorder Act 1998 will abolish committal proceedings for all purely indictable offences.

There are two types of committal procedures, known as the old style committal contained in s. 6(1) of the Magistrates' Courts Act 1980, and the new style committal contained in s. 6(2). The old style committal was the more lengthy, traditional procedure which included the hearing of oral evidence, while the new style committal was much more brief, concentrating on the documentation.

While the new style committals remain essentially unchanged by the 1996 Act, the main reform introduced by the Act concerns the old style committal. A committal under s. 6(1) will involve the reading aloud of sections of written statements by the prosecution and then the defence may make a submission that there is insufficient evidence with which to put the defendant on trial.

All oral evidence will now be excluded from s. 6(2) committals. The only evidence which may be tendered will be written statements, depositions and other documents and exhibits submitted by the prosecution. Thus, normally, no live evidence will be heard and prosecution witnesses will not have to give oral evidence unless the court accepts an application from the defence that they should do so. No defence evidence will be allowed at committal hearings and the examining magistrate will merely be testing the quality of the prosecution case on paper. While the abolition of oral evidence from witnesses will save time for both the court and the witnesses, it will also mean that the defendant will have no opportunity to test the strength of the prosecution evidence before the trial. The defendant must be present but the hearing involves no consideration of the evidence tendered by or on behalf of the prosecution. The new style committal is the type that is most frequently used. Research carried out by the Home Office in 1981 found that over 90 per cent of Crown Court trials were preceded by a s. 6(2) committal and this percentage may subsequently have increased.

Sending for trial

The 'sending for trial' is a new procedure created by ss. 51 and 52 of the Crime and Disorder Act 1998, and replaces committal procedures for indictable only offences (about 20,000 cases a year). The new procedure has been described as a 'fast track' for indictable only cases. After being piloted, the system was introduced nationally in 2001. Until this reform was introduced, a case might have given rise to half a dozen hearings in a magistrates' court before being sent up to the Crown Court for trial. Under the new system, every adult charged with an indictable only offence has to appear only once in a magistrates' court to determine issues concerning funding from the Legal Services Commission, bail, and the use of statements and exhibits. The magistrates' court then provides defendants with a statement of the evidence against them as well as a notice setting out the offence(s) for which they are to be sent for trial and the place where they are to be tried. They are then sent immediately for trial in the Crown Court. The Crown Court has taken over from the magistrates' court all remaining case-management duties. For this purpose, plea and directions hearings and preparatory hearings (discussed below) are held at a much earlier stage for indictable only offences. The first hearing in the Crown Court has to take place within eight days when a defendant is being held in custody on remand, and within 28 days when the defendant is on bail. The first opportunity for a defendant to assert that there is no case to answer is at the Crown Court.

The purpose of the new procedure is to cut costs and delays. It is hoped that trials will be heard a month earlier than in the past. The pilots for these changes suggested that the likely annual savings to the criminal justice system as a whole were just under £16 million.

Plea and direction hearings

The courts have the power to lay down their own rules as to how they should function. They sometimes do this by means of an official announcement known as a 'practice direction'. This procedure was used in 1995 to set up a new procedure known as a 'plea and direction hearing' (PDH) which was introduced into the Crown Court by the Supreme Court of Judicature Practice Direction (Crown Court: Plea and Directions Hearing) (1995).

The PDH takes place in the Crown Court after committal proceedings or the new sending for trial procedure and aims to encourage early preparation of cases and to reduce the number of 'cracked' trials. These hearings are normally held in open court with the defendants present, who are required to plead guilty or not guilty to the charges against them. This process is known as the 'arraignment'. If the defendants plead guilty, the judge will proceed to sentence the defendants wherever possible. Where they plead not guilty the prosecution and defence will have to identify the key issues, and provide any additional information required to organize the actual trial, such as which witnesses will be required to attend, facts that are admitted by both sides and issues of law that are likely to arise.

The original value of these hearings was limited by the lack of judicial power to make binding rulings. Section 40 of the Criminal Procedure and Investigation Act 1996 has now introduced the power to make such rulings on both the admissibility of evidence and questions of law. These provisions enable effective directions to be given at a much earlier stage and without the need for a jury.

A similar procedure for the magistrates' courts was introduced by ss. 49 and 50 of the Crime and Disorder Act 1998. These provide for optional pre-trial reviews and early administrative hearings conducted by single lay justices or justices' clerks. They aim to ensure more efficient pre-trial preparation and, after the successful results of six pilot schemes, they were introduced nationally in November 1999.

Preparatory hearings

A system of preparatory hearings was introduced by s. 29 of the Criminal Procedure and Investigation Act 1996. Crown Court judges have a general power to order preparatory hearings for complex or potentially lengthy cases. The hearing is treated as the start of the trial, though it takes place before the jury has been sworn in. The judge can then make binding rulings on the admissibility of evidence and questions of law. Appeals may be taken from any ruling of a judge at a preparatory hearing to the Court of Appeal.

Preparatory hearings are only available for complex or potentially lengthy cases. The purpose of these hearings is to allow a more detailed investigation of the issues than is possible at a PDH so as to assist the trial judge in the management of the trial, to reduce the length of the hearing before a jury and to make the case easier for the jury to understand.

Disclosure

The issue of disclosure is concerned with the responsibility of the prosecution and defence to reveal information related to the case prior to the trial. Until the introduction of the Criminal Procedure and Investigation Act 1996 the rules concerning disclosure were primarily covered by the common law. Following judicial concern over the serious miscarriages of justice that had come to light, the prosecution had a duty to reveal virtually all information in their possession (**R** *v* **Judith Ward** (1993)), while the defence had only a very limited duty of disclosure, for example to inform the court in advance that they intended to call an alibi or expert witness. These rules were imposing a heavy administrative burden on the Crown Prosecution Service and the Director of Public Prosecutions expressed concern that there was insufficient protection of sensitive information, such as the names of informants.

The Criminal Procedure and Investigation Act 1996 radically reformed this area of the law, introducing a statutory scheme for prosecution and defence disclosure which allows the prosecution considerable discretion about what is disclosed to defence solicitors. First, the prosecution must give to the defence all relevant unused material which might undermine the prosecution case (known as 'primary prosecution disclosure'). At the same time as primary disclosure is given, the prosecution must provide a list of any remaining material held by the prosecution which they consider is not sensitive.

In Crown Court proceedings, the defence must in response (usually within 14 days) provide the prosecution with a defence statement. This discloses, in general terms, the case for the defence, the matters on which it takes issue with the prosecution, and the reasons for this. If the defence wish to rely on an alibi they must provide relevant details including the names and addresses of witnesses supporting the particulars of the alibi. This is a much broader duty of disclosure on the defence than existed before. Inferences can be drawn from certain failures in relation to disclosure by the defendant, though such an inference cannot provide the sole ground for a conviction. It has been suggested that this tips the scales of justice too far in favour of the prosecution, and in magistrates' court proceedings the defence only have to give voluntary disclosure.

After defence disclosure, the prosecution is obliged to disclose any additional unused material which might reasonably be expected to assist the defence case (known as 'secondary prosecution disclosure'). At any stage the defence can apply for disclosure of specific unused prosecution material. Prosecution material must not be disclosed where the court, on application by the prosecution, orders that it is not in the public interest to do so.

A Code of Practice has been drawn up to support the disclosure regime. It lays down guidelines as to the recording and preservation by police of information obtained during an investigation and its disclosure to the prosecution. If the police could simply destroy evidence that favoured the defence the process of disclosure would clearly be undermined. The Code also contains guidance on the handling of sensitive material, such as names of informants. These guidelines were revised in 2001 following concern that the prosecutors were not disclosing all the material required by the defence. Under the new guidelines prosecutors should provide the defence with all the evidence they propose to rely on at trial. They should also provide the defence with material seized by investigators but not examined because it appeared to be irrelevant.

The Sexual Offences (Protected Material) Act 1997 regulates access by the defendant to prosecution evidence, particularly victim statements, in cases concerned with certain sexual offences. This legislation was passed due to concern that some defendants were gaining further pleasure from their offence by seeing and keeping this material.

▶ Plea bargaining

Plea bargaining is the name given to negotiations between the prosecution and defence lawyers over the outcome of a case; for example, where a defendant is choosing to plead not guilty, the prosecution may offer to reduce the charge to a similar offence with a smaller maximum sentence, in return for the defendant pleading guilty. Although plea bargaining is well known in the US criminal justice system, for many years the official view was that it did not happen here, although those involved in the system knew quite well that in fact it happened all the time. Its existence in the English penal system was confirmed in a 1977 study by McConville and Baldwin, and it is now recognized to be a widespread phenomenon.

Effective plea bargaining requires the active cooperation of the judge, but the Court of Appeal has consistently set itself against any such involvement. In **R** *v* **Turner** (1970), the defendant was indicted for theft and pleaded not guilty. He had been advised by his counsel to change his plea, on the grounds that a guilty plea normally reduces the sentence, so that if he pleaded guilty he was likely to receive a non-custodial sentence, whereas if he stuck with his plea of not guilty, he was likely to end up in prison. This advice was repeated after the defence counsel had a meeting with the judge, and Turner then changed his plea. The Court of Appeal held that although there should be freedom of access between the judge and counsel and that counsel could advise a client in strong terms, any such discussion should involve both prosecution and defence, and should be restricted to matters that counsel could not mention in open court. The Court also stressed that judges should never indicate what sentence they had in mind in a particular case, except to say that, regardless of plea, the sentence would not take a particular form.

Section 152 of the Powers of Criminal Courts (Sentencing) Act 2000 allows the courts, when sentencing offenders, to take into account the stage at which they indicate an intention to plead guilty and the circumstances in which that indication was given. If the court imposes a less severe punishment as a result of this, it must state in open court that it has done so. In time, this will lead to case law regarding the level of discounts for late or early guilty pleas. Since defence counsel and the court will need to make defendants aware of these discounts, plea bargaining is likely to become more overt in the future. Research carried out by Flood-Page and Mackie ('Sentencing during the Nineties', 1998) found that offenders who pleaded guilty had their sentences reduced by around a third at the Crown Court.

In 2001 the Attorney-General issued guidelines on plea bargaining which make it clear that any negotiations must take place in public. Only in the most exceptional circumstances can discussions about plea and sentence take place in private, and then an independent written record of the discussions must be made. Where the prosecution decide to participate in plea bargaining, they should inform the victim or their family and take into account their views. These guidelines were issued after a headmaster was only given an 18-month suspended sentence on being convicted of sexual misconduct at his school in South London. There was public uproar at the low sentence, but it had been the product of plea bargaining that had taken place in private.

Should plea bargaining be allowed?

It can be argued that plea bargaining offers benefits on all sides: for the defendant, there is obviously a shorter sentence; for the courts, the police, and ultimately the taxpayers, there are the financial savings made by drastically shortening trials. In fact without a high proportion of guilty pleas, the courts would be seriously overloaded, causing severe delays which in turn would raise costs still further, especially given the number of prisoners remanded in custody awaiting trial.

Despite this, plea bargaining has been widely criticized as being against the interests of justice. Several studies have shown that the practice may persuade innocent people to plead guilty: Zander and Henderson (1993) concluded that each year there were some 1,400 possibly innocent persons whose counsel felt they had pleaded guilty in order to achieve a reduction in the charges faced or in the sentence. Critics also point out that the judge should be, and be seen to be, an impartial referee, acting in accordance with the law rather than the dictates of cost-efficiency. In addition, plea bargaining goes against the principle that offenders should be punished for what they have actually done. As well as leading to cases where people are punished more leniently than their conduct would seem to demand, it may lead to quite inappropriate punishments. For example, the high rate of acquittals in rape trials frequently leads to the prosecution reducing the charge to an ordinary offence against the person, in exchange for a guilty plea; this means that offenders who might usefully be given psychiatric help never receive it.

These criticisms are backed up by the fact that, in practice, plea bargaining does not necessarily save time or money because, in many cases, it occurs at the last moment, so there is no time to arrange for another case to slot into the court timetable. Such cases are often known as 'cracked trials', and Zander and Henderson's study found that 43 per cent of those cases listed as not guilty pleas 'cracked', which represented 26 per cent of listed cases overall.

▶ The trial

Apart from the role played by the jury in the Crown Court, the law and procedure in the Crown Court and magistrates' court are essentially the same. The burden of proof is on the prosecution, which means that they must prove, beyond reasonable doubt, that the accused is guilty; the defendant is not required to prove his or her innocence.

The trial will normally begin with the prosecution outlining the case against the accused, and then producing evidence to prove its case. The prosecution calls its witnesses, who will give their evidence in response to questions from the prosecution (called examination-in-chief). These witnesses can then be questioned by the defence (called cross-examination), and then if required, re-examined by the prosecution to address any points brought up in cross-examination.

When the prosecution has presented all its evidence, the defence can submit that there is no case to answer, which means that on the prosecution evidence, no reasonable jury (or bench of magistrates) could convict. If the submission is successful, a verdict of not guilty will be given straight away. If no such submission is made, or if the submission is unsuccessful, the defence then puts forward its case, using the same procedure for examining witnesses as the prosecution did. The accused is the only witness who cannot be forced to give evidence.

The Youth Justice and Criminal Evidence Act 1999 contains a range of measures to make it easier for disabled and vulnerable witnesses to give evidence, including children under 17 and victims of sexual offences. The special arrangements that can be made for such witnesses include the use of screens, the giving of evidence by live television link, the abandoning of formal court dress and the use of pre-recorded video evidence.

Once the defence has presented all its evidence, each side makes a closing speech, outlining their case and seeking to persuade the magistrates or jury of it. In the Crown Court, this is followed by the judge's summing up to the jury. The judge should review the evidence, draw the jury's attention to the important points of the case, and direct them on the law if necessary, but must not trespass on the jury's function of deciding the true facts of the case. At the end of the summing up the judge reminds the jury that the prosecution must prove its case beyond reasonable doubt, and tries to explain in simple terms what this means.

Models of criminal justice systems

In order to judge the effectiveness of a criminal justice system (or anything else for that matter), you need first to know what that system sets out to do. The academic Herbert Packer has identified two quite different potential aims for criminal justice systems: the 'due process' model; and the 'crime control' model. The former gives priority to fairness of procedure and to protecting the innocent from wrongful conviction, accepting that a high level of protection for suspects makes it more difficult to convict the guilty, and that some guilty people will therefore go free. The latter places most importance on convicting the guilty, taking the risk that occasionally some innocent people will be convicted.

Obviously, criminal justice systems tend not to fall completely within one model or the other: most seek to strike a balance between the two. This is not always easy: imagine for a moment that you are put in charge of our criminal justice system, and you have to decide the balance at which it should aim. How many innocent people do you believe it is acceptable to convict? Bear in mind that if you answer 'none', the chances are that protections against this may have to be so strong that very few guilty people will be convicted either. Would it be acceptable for 10 per cent of innocent people to be convicted if that means 50 per cent of the guilty were also convicted? If that 10 per cent seems totally unacceptable, does it become more reasonable if it means that 90 per cent of the guilty are convicted? It is not an easy choice to make.

Looking at the balance which a criminal justice system seeks to strike, and how well that balance is in fact struck, is a useful way to assess the system's effectiveness. As mentioned at the beginning of this chapter, in recent years this balance has been the subject of much debate and dis-agreement as regards our criminal justice system, with the police, magis-trates and the Government claiming that the balance has been tipped too far in favour of suspects' rights, at the expense of convicting the guilty. On the other hand, civil liberties organizations, many academics and the lawyers involved in the well-known miscarriages of justice feel that the system has not learned from those miscarriages, and that the protections for suspects are still inadequate.

The latter group have particularly criticized the findings of the RCCJ. Sean Enright (1993) has written: 'One would not guess from a reading of the Commission's proposals that this Royal Commission was set up in response to some astonishing miscarriages of justice. Rather, the abiding impression is that this Commission was primarily concerned with a ruthlessly efficient and cost effective disposal of criminal business.' The barrister Michael Mansfield, who represented Judith Ward, some of the Birmingham Six and the Tottenham Three, among others, agrees, pointing out that the RCCJ proposals and the subsequent changes made to the criminal justice system are 'a complete denial of the basic principle of the presumption of innocence . . . the position has deteriorated to such an extent that further wrongful convictions are guaranteed' (*Presumed Guilty* (1993)).

Criticism and reform

Criticisms and suggestions for reform have been made throughout this chapter, but the following have been the subject of particular debate.

Racism

Britain is a multicultural and ethnically diverse community. Successful policing requires that all members of British society must have confidence in the police force. Following the fatal stabbing of Stephen Lawrence, a black teenager who was an A-level student from south London, by a group of racist youths in 1993, defects in several aspects of the English legal system failed to bring his killers to justice. Following concern at the handling of the police investigation into the killing, a judicial inquiry headed by a former High Court judge, Sir William Macpherson, was set up by the Government in 1997 and its report was published in February 1999. It found that the Metropolitan police suffered from institutional racism. This is defined as existing where there is a 'collective failure of an organisation to provide an appropriate and professional service to people because of their colour, culture and ethnic origin. It can be seen or detected in processes, attitudes and behaviour which amount to discrimination through unwitting prejudice, ignorance, thoughtlessness and racist stereotypical behaviour.'

The presence of institutional racism was reflected in the fact that the first senior officer at the scene of the crime assumed that what had occurred had been a fight; it was also expressed in the absence of adequate family liaison and the 'patronising and thoughtless approach' of some officers to Mr and Mrs Lawrence; and it could be seen in the side-lining of Stephen Lawrence's friend, the surviving victim of the attack. There was, furthermore, a refusal to accept, by at least five officers involved in the case, that this was a racist murder. Finally, there was the use of inappropriate and offensive language by police officers, including, on occasion, during their appearance before the Inquiry itself. It found that racism awareness training was 'almost non-existent at every level', and concluded that institutional racism could only be tackled effectively if there was an 'unequivocal acceptance that the problem actually exists'.

The Inquiry, however, concluded that institutional racism was not 'universally the cause of the failure of this investigation'. The investigation by the Metropolitan Police was 'marred by a combination of professional incompetence, institutional racism and a failure of leadership by senior officers'.

The Report contained 20 recommendations for reform. In March 1999, the Government issued its Action Plan in response to the Macpherson Report. A steering group, chaired by the Home Secretary, has been established to oversee the programme of reform. In the past the Race Relations Act 1976 did not apply to the police, so that there was no legal remedy if a black person thought they had been stopped by the police because of racial prejudice. Now the Race Relations (Amendment) Act 2000 has been passed. This Act amends the 1976 Act, making it unlawful for a public authority, including the police, to discriminate in carrying out any of their functions. This legislation is discussed in more detail at p. 488. Over a three-year period, police forces are to review their provision of racism awareness training. Research is to be carried out into the use of stop and search powers (where it is recognized that there is a danger of racism) and consideration is to be given to the recording of stops beyond those covered by the Police and Criminal Evidence Act 1984 (PACE). Targets have been set for the recruitment and retention of ethnic minority police officers. The recommendation that the use of racist language in private should be criminalized has been rejected.

While the Macpherson Report is one step towards tackling institutional racism in the police, it is worrying that Lord Scarman's report into the Brixton riots of 1981 had already identified this problem, and though some progress was subsequently made, this has clearly not been sufficient. In 1999/2000 the British Crime Survey suggested that there were 143,000 racially motivated crimes committed and yet only 1,832 defendants were prosecuted for such offences.

Police corruption

The police exercise an extremely delicate role in society and, as criminals are able to generate large sums of money from their criminal conduct, the danger of corruption is real. High risk areas include the handling of informers and positions within drug, vice and crime squads where constant vigilance is required. Where corruption is rife, one can no longer fall back on the idea of a few rotten apples and accept that the system itself must be corrupting its members.

Sir Paul Condon made anti-corruption a touchstone of his tenure as Commissioner of the Metropolitan Police. He has estimated that there may be as many as 250 corrupt officers in his force, some of whom are directly involved in very serious criminal activity, and has dedicated resources to their detection. A more proactive approach can be expected at a national level, as New Scotland Yard has established a special squad concentrating on corruption in the police and the Association of Chief Police Officers established in 1998 a Taskforce on Corruption. During the course of that year, 28 police officers were convicted of corruption-related offences, and at the end of the year, 153 police officers were suspended for alleged corruption and similar matters.

'Bobbies on the beat'

Four billion pounds is spent each year on police patrols, but the reality is that at any one time only 5 per cent of police officers are out on patrol. The Audit Commission report, *Streetwise – Effective Police Patrol* (1996), notes that the public are keen to see more 'bobbies on the beat' and that this provides the public with a feeling of security. A review of research in 1998 found that random patrols are ineffective in reducing crime but that targeted patrols on crime hot spots can be effective (Nuttall, Goldblatt and Lewis, *Reducing Offending: An Assessment of Research Evidence on Ways of Dealing with Offending Behaviour* (1998)).

Police conduct

During 1997, well over 6,000 complaints of alleged rudeness and incivility by police officers were recorded. Her Majesty's Inspectorate of Constabulary undertook a wide-ranging exploration of the level of integrity in the police because it was recognized that 'public confidence was becoming seriously affected by the bad behaviour of a small minority of police'. In *Police Integrity: Securing and Maintaining Public Confidence* (1999) the Inspectorate reported that: 'Numerous examples were found in all forces visited of poor behaviour towards members of the public and colleagues alike, including rudeness, arrogance and discriminatory comment.' In the Inspectorate's view, one consequence of tolerating bullying, rudeness and racist or sexist behaviour is that 'corruption and other wrongdoing will flourish'.

The right to silence

The abolition of the right to silence has been one of the most severely criticized changes to the criminal justice system in recent years. As the academic John Fitzpatrick has written, the basis of the right to silence is the presumption of innocence, which places the burden of proof on the prosecution: 'this burden begins to shift, and the presumption of innocence to dwindle, as soon as we are obliged to explain or justify our actions in any way' (*Legal Action*, May 1994).

Those who objected to the right to silence claimed that only the guilty would have anything to hide and that the innocent should therefore have no objection to answering questions. It was suggested that the calculated use of this right by professional criminals was leading to serious cases being dropped for lack of evidence, and that 'ambush' defences (in which defendants remain silent till the last moment and then produce an unexpected defence) were leading to acquittals because the prosecution had no time to prepare for the defence.

These arguments were put to the RCCJ, by a Home Office Working Group among others, but, after commissioning its own research into the subject the RCCJ rejected the idea of abolishing the right to silence. This research, by Leng, McConville and Hodgson (1993), showed that in fact only 5 per cent of suspects exercised their right to silence, and there was no evidence of an unacceptable acquittal rate for these defendants. Nor was there any serious problem with ambush defences.

As we have seen, the Conservative Government decided to ignore the RCCJ recommendations and abolish the right to silence – a somewhat strange decision considering that it was the same Government which set up the Commission in the first place. The law reform body, JUSTICE, has claimed that this decision will lead to increased pressure on suspects and, in turn, to more miscarriages of justice. It studied the effects of removing the right to silence in Northern Ireland (which took place five years before removal of the right in England and Wales). Apparently, suspects frequently failed to understand the new caution and were put under unfair pressure to speak, while lawyers found it difficult to advise suspects when they did not know the full case against them. Most importantly, JUSTICE claims that while at first trial judges were cautious about drawing inferences of guilt from a suspect's silence, five years on, they were giving such silence considerable weight, and in some cases treating it almost as a presumption of guilt.

The Crown Prosecution Service

The CPS ran into problems from the very beginning. Because the Home Office had apparently underestimated the cost of the new service, the salaries offered were low, making it impossible to find sufficient numbers of good lawyers. As a result, the CPS gained a reputation for incompetence and delay. In 1996 a MORI poll found that 70 per cent of CPS lawyers responding to a questionnaire considered that the CPS was either below average or one of the worst places to work. In 1990 the House of Commons Public Accounts Committee noted that the CPS appeared to be costing almost twice as much as the previous prosecution arrangements, and the number of staff required was practically double that originally envisaged.

Relations between the police and the CPS have not been good: the police resented the new service and its demands for a higher standard of case preparation from police. While the CPS saw a high rate of discontinued cases as a success story, the police saw this as letting offenders off the hook. Reforms introduced following the Glidewell Report aim to improve police/CPS relations with police and CPS staff working in integrated teams and the creation of 42 prosecuting authorities which correlate with the 42 police forces. Following the 1997 Narey Report into delay in the criminal justice system, CPS staff now work alongside police officers in police stations to prepare cases for court. However, it may be that these reforms could go to the opposite extreme. The CPS was created to put an end to the close and often cosy relations between police officers and the lawyers who used to prosecute their cases, as this could lead to malpractice.

Some of the teething problems have now been ironed out, but problems still remain. There is doubt as to how far the CPS provides an independent perspective on deciding whether or not to prosecute. Since the police still take the initial decision on whether to pass the file to the CPS, such decisions are taken without the CPS being able to exercise any control, which leads to wide variations in cautioning rates. Where the police do refer a case for prosecution, the CPS makes up its mind on the basis of information with which it is provided – it cannot ask for further inquiries to be made. Given that the police, once satisfied that the suspect is guilty, will tend to look for evidence that supports this conclusion, and see any material that points in another direction as mistaken or irrelevant, the file may paint a very partial picture of the true situation.

One solution would be to give prosecutors some powers of direction over investigations, and to remove altogether from the police the decision to prosecute. In their research for the RCCJ, Leigh and Zedner (1992) comment:

> It is remarkable that such procedures as application for search warrants need not be made by the CPS. It is surely remarkable, also, that applications to a magistrates' court for extended detention under PACE are made by the police, and not by the prosecutor. Prosecutorial involvement in such procedures would seem axiomatic in France and Germany. It enables the prosecutor both to review the file and to determine the necessity for a police procedure which affects the liberty of the subject. It can also serve to guard against error.

Leigh and Zedner suggest that in some types of case, police interrogations should be attended by a duty prosecutor. This would help overcome the problem of defence solicitors being reluctant to attend interviews, and would reinforce the status of the CPS. Baldwin and Moloney's research (*Supervision of police investigations in serious criminal cases*, 1993) found that the police were actually keen on the idea of early legal advice, and could see considerable benefits in involving the CPS early on in the investigative process. The researchers concluded that in complex cases the CPS should see all the evidence the police have collected and suggest any further inquiries that they feel should be made.

The general feeling of the researchers for the RCCJ seems to have been that the CPS should be given a greater role in the English criminal system, but that this should not go as far as giving them the functions of the French 'juge d'instruction'. Unfortunately, the RCCJ failed to take this opportunity to clarify the future relationship between the CPS and the police; their Report merely suggests that the police should seek CPS advice in a greater number of cases. We will have to wait and see how far the involvement of the CPS from the time of charge following the 1999 reforms will satisfy these concerns.

In his *Review of the Criminal Courts* (2001) Sir Robin Auld has recommended that the CPS should be involved in criminal cases at an earlier stage. He considers that the CPS and not the police should normally decide the appropriate charge. The police would only retain this power to decide the charge for very minor or urgent cases.

Decisions by the CPS not to prosecute

In the three years from October 1986, the CPS discontinued over 250,000 cases. The Service claims that this is evidence of its success, demonstrating that it 'has been effective in filtering a considerable number of unmeritorious cases out of the judicial system'. However, there are wide variations across the country, with some areas discontinuing 4 per cent of cases, while others discontinue 19 per cent. In 1990 the Home Affairs Committee expressed concern at the large proportion of discontinued cases which were not dropped until the court hearing, and was surprised that the CPS undertook no systematic analysis of the reasons for discontinuance.

In 1993 the RCCJ found that the CPS did exercise the power to discontinue appropriately, citing one study (Moxon and Crisp, 1994) which suggested that nearly a third of discontinuances were dropped on public interest grounds. Of these, nearly half were discontinued because the offence was trivial and/or the likely penalty was nominal. Only 5 per cent of the cases were discontinued before any court appearance, and where cases were terminated at the court, the decision to discontinue was often taken before the hearing but not communicated to the defendant in time to save a court appearance – either because the decision had been taken too late in the day or because the CPS did not know where the defendant was.

In assessing the incidence of weak cases in the Crown Court (which may be cases that should have been discontinued), the numbers of ordered and directed acquittals are relevant. According to the 1996 Judicial Statistics, in one in every five cases a judge ordered an acquittal.

New arrangements are being piloted in which the CPS will offer to meet victims of certain crimes, including racially aggravated crimes, to explain its decisions not to prosecute or to substantially alter charges. This is part of a much wider plan to improve victim and witness care across the whole of the criminal justice system.

Crown Prosecution Service Inspectorate

A Crown Prosecution Service Inspectorate was established under the Crown Prosecution Service Inspectorate Act 2000. This is an independent inspectorate which investigates alleged miscarriages of justice and accusations of incompetence. It is hoped that the Inspectorate will help to improve the working practices within the CPS.

Committal proceedings

This area of criminal procedure has attracted much political and academic attention in recent years. There has been a broad consensus that committal proceedings were not an effective filter process. Research by Block, Corbett and Peay (1993), *Ordered and Directed Acquittals in the Crown Court*, reported that of 100 ordered and directed Crown Court acquittals studied, 11 resulted from the absence of an essential legal element which could have been, but was not, detected at the committal stage.

The Runciman Commission recommended the abolition of committals and their replacement with a simple transfer procedure. This proposal was essentially adopted in the Criminal Justice and Public Order Act 1994. Section 44 of that Act would have abolished committals and replaced them with transfer for trial procedures giving a predicted saving of £10 million. The new procedure would have automatically transferred cases to the Crown Court that were due to be tried there by giving the defendant a written notice to this effect at the end of the mode of trial hearing or through the post. The notice would have informed defendants that they could apply to the court to dismiss the whole or part of the case against them. This application would usually have been determined in the absence of the defendant on the basis of primarily written evidence. The process was to be subject to statutory time limits. The transfer to the court would normally have been an administrative act and would not have involved any appearance in court.

In fact, these provisions were never brought into force for practical reasons. No consensus could be reached as to what the time limits should be for the procedure. The Law Society expressed the view that the system would be 'bureaucratic and cumbersome' and 'likely to collapse under the strain unto everyone who will have to operate it'. The CPS advised the Government that court appearances for ancillary matters, such as bail applications and custodial time limits, would still be necessary in the majority of cases. The Criminal Procedure and Investigation Act 1996 therefore repealed the relevant legislation on transfer for trial proceedings and instead introduced amendments to the existing committal procedures. With the new sending for trial procedures introduced by the Crime and Disorder Act 1998, committal proceedings are now restricted to either way offences.

Sir Robin Auld's *Review of the Criminal Courts* (2001) again recommends that commital proceedings should be abolished altogether.

Disclosure

The intention of the Criminal Procedure and Investigation Act 1996 was to redress the balance between the prosecution and defence, but there is a danger that it has gone too far in favour of the prosecution. The new rules allow considerable discretion to the prosecution to decide what should be disclosed to the defence solicitor. There is a risk that they will not disclose information highlighting weaknesses in the prosecution case. Such a failure was one of the main causes of the high-profile miscarriages of justice. For example, Judith Ward's conviction was quashed after 18 years of incarceration when medical evidence came to light which ought to have been disclosed by the prosecution at the time of her original trial. The Law Society fears that the changes in prosecution disclosure may leave future miscarriages of justice undetected.

Prosecution disclosure does not have to take place until after the defendant has pleaded not guilty, and many have argued that the defendant needs to see this information before they can sensibly decide their plea.

The new rules for defence disclosure have given rise to considerable controversy, as many feel that they further undermine the right to silence. According to the Consultation Paper that preceded the Act, the reforms are intended to prevent defendants 'ambushing' the trial by producing an unexpected defence at the last moment which the prosecution is unprepared for, and therefore enabling the defendant to be wrongly acquitted. In fact, research prepared for the RCCJ suggested that there was little evidence of this happening in practice. Sir Robin Auld has recommended some limited changes to the existing system of disclosure. These include that prosecutors should be made responsible for identifying all potentially disclosable material and automatic prosecution disclosure of certain documents.

Cracked trials

The Government has been concerned by the problem of 'cracked trials' – those cases in which public money and administration is wasted because, once the courtroom is booked and the parties ready to proceed with a full trial, the defendant pleads guilty at arraignment, leaving no time to arrange for another case to slot into the court timetable. Zander and Henderson's study in 1993 of the Crown Court found that 43 per cent of those cases listed as not guilty pleas 'cracked', which represented 26 per cent of listed cases overall.

One of the reasons why defendants plead guilty at the last minute is that this change of plea tends to be made on the advice of their barrister, and often barristers only become involved in the case at this stage. The *Crown Court Study* found that in over half of contested Crown Court trials defendants did not see their barrister until the morning of the hearing.

The report of Her Majesty's Inspectors of the Magistrates' Court Service (1995–96) has observed that the problem of cracked trials is not limited to the Crown Court but also occurs in the magistrates' court. The report observes: 'Where monitoring data is available, the incidence of cracked trials is commonly found to be at least 50 per cent of all trials listed, with even higher rates in some areas.'

However, following the introduction of the plea before venue procedure (discussed at p. 279) and the reduction in sentence for early pleas (see p. 311) the number of cracked trials has been halved.

A corroboration rule?

The major role played by confession evidence in the miscarriages of justice has led to suggestions that confession evidence alone should be regarded as insufficient to secure a conviction; in other words, the prosecution would be required to produce other evidence (such as witnesses, or forensic evidence) to support the confession.

Research by McConville for the RCCJ suggests that in 95 per cent of cases where confession evidence played a part, supporting evidence was available, indicating that a requirement for such extra evidence would only lead to automatic acquittals in a handful of cases. He calculated that, even without changes in police investigative practices, only 8 per cent of prosecutions would be affected, and these would mostly be less serious cases: a reasonable price to pay for avoiding more miscarriages of justice.

Three members of the RCCJ agreed that there should be a requirement for corroborating evidence of confessions. However, the majority merely recommended that judges should warn juries that care was needed in convicting on the basis of the confession alone, and explain the reasons why people might confess to crimes that they did not commit.

Confession evidence usually consists of confessions given to the police, but the case of Michael Stone also highlighted the danger of courts relying on uncorroborated evidence of confessions given to other prisoners. Michael Stone was convicted in 1998 of the murder of Lin Russell and her daughter Megan. They had been walking home from school through a cornfield with the other daughter Josie, when they were brutally attacked. Josie had been left for dead but had survived. While Josie had regained some memory of the incident, she was not able to pick out Stone from the identity parade. Apart from circumstantial evidence, the main evidence against Michael Stone were statements that Stone had allegedly made to three other prisoners while in prison on remand. One of these prisoners subsequently told the *Mirror* newspaper that he had lied to the court. Confessions made to fellow prisoners have none of the protections surrounding confessions made to the police that are laid down in PACE. As the defence lawyer pointed out to the jury in Michael Stone's trial: 'In an unconscious way you may think that everyone desperately wants Michael Stone to be guilty. If he's guilty the police guessed right and if he's guilty then the killer's caught and if he's guilty then all of us can sleep a little sounder in our beds tonight.' Confession evidence may be attractive but it does not necessarily do justice.

Conviction rates

Recent years have seen a large rise in reported crime but falling conviction rates. For example, for sexual offences there were 21,107 cases reported in 1980 and 31,284 by 1993. By contrast, the convictions in those years were 8,000 in 1980 and only 4,300 in 1993. However, in 1998 convictions overall rose by 6 per cent.

Criminal appeals

A reluctance to refer cases back to appeal has been a major feature of most of the high-profile miscarriages of justice. This is discussed in chapter 14.

Victims

There is a growing awareness that the criminal justice system pays insufficient attention to the needs of the victims of crime. For many years, victims of crime had virtually no rights. In English legal theory and practice, victims are not parties to the prosecution, but are only witnesses. Traditionally, victims have had no legal right to participation, consultation, or even information about their cases. By comparison, suspects and defendants do have rights, even if not all of them are enforceable in practice. Organizations such as Victim Support have campaigned for many years to persuade the Government to recognize that victims are not simply witnesses, and that they should have distinct rights.

One attempt to redress the balance has been the establishment of a Victim's Charter in 1990. This was revised in 1996 and the Government intends to improve it further in the near future. The Criminal Injuries Compensation Scheme provides limited financial compensation to the victims of some forms of crime.

The Home Secretary has now pledged to introduce a national system of victim statements. These will enable victims to make formal statements about the effects they have suffered as a result of the crime. The statement will be included in the case papers and taken into account at all stages of the criminal process, including appeal and parole review. In homicide cases, the statement can be made by a next of kin, or by parents or carers where the victims are children.

Victims have repeatedly complained of the lack of information they receive from the criminal justice system about the progress of their case. The Witness Satisfaction Survey in 2000 showed that more than half of prosecution witnesses were not kept informed about the progress of the case and over 40 per cent were not told the verdict but had to find out for themselves. Under the Criminal Justice and Court Services Act 2000 victims of certain types of offence have a right to information about the case and can make representations about the offender's release. The offences giving rise to these rights are sexual and violent offences where the offender has been sentenced to prison for 12 months or more.

From October 2002 the CPS will have a responsibility to inform victims of key casework decisions such as the dropping of charges and, in serious cases, the victim will have the opportunity of a face-to-face meeting with a senior prosecutor.

The Macpherson Report which followed the failure to convict the murderers of Stephen Lawrence suggested that the Government should consider allowing victims or their families to become 'civil parties' to criminal proceedings. This is the approach taken in countries such as France and ensures the provision of all relevant information to victims and their families.

The role of the media and public opinion

It is noticeable that all the serious miscarriages of justice occurred in cases where a particular crime had outraged public opinion, and led to enormous pressure on the police to find the culprits. In the case of the Birmingham Six, feelings ran so high that the trial judge consented to the case being heard away from Birmingham, on the ground that a Birmingham jury might be 'unable to bring to the trial that degree of detachment that is necessary to reach a dispassionate and objective verdict'. Given the graphic media descriptions of the carnage the real bombers had left behind them, it was in fact debatable whether any jury, anywhere, would have found it easy to summon up such detachment. The chances of a fair trial must have decreased even further when, halfway through the trial, the *Daily Mirror* devoted an entire front page to photographs of the Six, boasting that they were the 'first pictures' (implying that they were the first pictures of the bombers).

Fears that the media are prejudicing the course of justice have led the Lord Chancellor's Department to issue a consultation document on proposals to ban payments by the media to witnesses in criminal trials. The issue was highlighted by breaches of the Press Complaints Commission's Code of Practice during Rosemary West's trial.

On the other hand, in the case of Stephen Lawrence, a young black student murdered at a bus stop in South London in an apparently racially motivated attack, one branch of the media saw itself as a vital tool in fighting for justice: the refusal of five youths, who many suspected to be the murderers, to give evidence at the coroner's court led to the *Daily Mail* labelling them as the killers on its front pages, despite the fact that they had already been acquitted by a criminal court.

The miscarriages of justice were characterized by a reluctance to refer cases back to appeal. While campaigning by some newspapers and television programmes was eventually to help bring about the successful appeals, other sections of the media, and in particular the tabloid newspapers, were keen to dismiss the idea that miscarriages of justice might have occurred. Nor was there a great amount of public interest in the alleged plight of the Birmingham Six or the other victims – in stark contrast to the petitioning on behalf of Private Lee Clegg during 1995. There was a common feeling of satisfaction that someone had been punished for such terrible crimes, and the public did not want to hear that the system had punished the wrong people.

Even when the miscarriages of justice were finally uncovered, a lingering 'whispering campaign' suggested that the victims of those miscarriages had been let off on some kind of technicality – that there had been police misbehaviour, but that those accused of the bombings and so on were really guilty. Again, tabloid newspapers were only too pleased to contribute to this view. On the day that the report of the RCCJ was published, the *Daily Mail* printed an article entitled 'The true victims of injustice'. In it, victims of the bombings expressed anger that the Guildford Four and the Birmingham Six had been released – as though justice for those wrongly convicted of a crime somehow meant less justice for the victims of that crime – and raised doubts as to their innocence. The newspaper commented that 'the decent majority' were more concerned to see measures designed to convict criminals than to prevent further miscarriages of justice.

The implications of all this for the criminal justice system are important. Clearly such a system does not operate in a vacuum, and in jury trials in particular, public opinion can never really be kept out of the courtroom. That does not mean that juries should not be used in emotive cases, nor that the media should be gagged. What it does mean is that, in those cases which arouse strong public opinion, the police, the prosecution, judges and defence lawyers must all be extra vigilant to ensure that the natural desire to find a culprit does not take the place of the need to find the truth – and to make clear to juries that they must do the same. In addition, measures must be taken to prevent 'trial by newspaper' – the Contempt of Court Act 1981 already provides powers in this respect, but in using these powers, the courts must be able to take into account the profits to be made from crime 'scoops' by newspapers, and punish breaches of the law accordingly. Rather than impose fines, which can be paid from the increased profits, preventing newspapers from publishing for a day or more might be a greater deterrent. The law of contempt relating to payments to witnesses in criminal cases and the publication of information before trials is currently being reviewed by the Government. It is considering proposals to legislate against payments and to control trial publicity.

Recommendations of Sir Robin Auld

In his *Review of the Criminal Courts* (2001) Sir Robin Auld made a wide range of recommendations, some of which have already been considered at relevant points in this book. Other interesting recommendations have included codification, reform of the management structures, increased use of information technology and the introduction of standard timetables.

Codification
Sir Robin Auld recommended that the law covering offences, court procedures, evidence and sentencing should be codified. This would make the law simpler and more accessible for the legal professions and members of the public to whom these rules can be applied. The Government seems committed to doing this at some point in the future.

Management structures

The Review recommended that a Criminal Justice Board should be established as part of the central management of the criminal justice system, and replace all the existing national planning and operational bodies. It would provide the overall direction for the criminal justice departments and agencies in the criminal justice system. National and local committees would also be restructured to provide a simpler and clearer management framework.

A Criminal Justice Council, chaired by a senior judge would be established to replace existing advisory and consultative bodies. It would have statutory power and a duty to keep the criminal justice system under review, to advise the Government on all proposed reforms, to make proposals for reform and to exercise general oversight over the codification of the criminal law.

The Government's response to these proposals has been that it has already made some adjustments to the present administrative arrangements and wants to see how effective these are before making further changes.

Information technology

Sir Robin Auld has emphasized the need for much greater use to be made of information technology in the criminal justice system. In particular, he is particularly keen to see the introduction of single electronic case files, managed by a new criminal Case Management Agency. The Government is currently investing in information technology for the criminal justice system.

Standard timetables

The Review proposes that there should be a move away from all forms of pre-trial hearings. Instead, standard timetables would be issued and the parties would be required to cooperate with each other in order to comply with these timetables. There would then be a written or electronic 'pretrial assessment' by the court (discretionary for the magistrates' court) of the parties' readiness for trial. Only if the court or the parties are unable to resolve all matters in this way would there be a pretrial hearing.

▶ ANSWERING QUESTIONS

1 **(a) What are the powers of the police to detain and question suspects following arrest?** *(13 marks)*
(b) Do you consider these powers to be sufficient and appropriately exercised? *(12 marks) AQA (NEAB)*

(a) Most of the material you need to answer this part of the question is found under the heading 'Police detention' at p. 254 and 'Police interrogation' at p. 255.

(b) Your answer to this section of the question should be divided into two, looking first of all at how far the powers of detention and questioning are 'sufficient' and secondly whether they are 'appropriately exercised'. On the question of whether they are sufficient, you could point to the fact that the police rarely detain individuals for the full statutory maximum length of time, suggesting that the police normally find the time available to them sufficient. You could draw attention to the fact that, if anything, PACE extended the time available for detention. On interrogation, the restrictions contained in the codes about the need for breaks and time to sleep are not unreasonable. However, the fact that the police cannot normally question someone once they have been charged can cause practical difficulties for a police investigation.

On whether the powers are 'appropriately exercised', you could look at the material discussed under the heading 'Safeguards for the suspect' at p. 257 which are supposed to make sure that these powers are not abused. But then you could mention the high-profile miscarriages of justice, some of which occurred after the PACE provisions had been introduced and which included misrepresenting confession statements. Such miscarriages of justice throw doubt as to whether the powers are in practice being used appropriately. You could consider whether the right to silence should be re-introduced.

2 **Outline the reasons for the creation of the Crown Prosecution Service. Describe its functions and assess its effectiveness.** *WJEC*

You should briefly define what the CPS is, and then divide your answer into the two parts suggested by the question. First, discuss why the CPS was felt to be needed, including the points made by the Justice Report. Then go on to describe what the CPS does and, in assessing its effectiveness, state how you think the creation of the CPS has improved the criminal justice system, if at all, and point out the problems with it, including a discussion of the Glidewell reforms.

3 **How far can miscarriages of justice be avoided in the future?**

There are a range of approaches that could be taken to answering this question. You could start by discussing the information contained under the subheading 'Models of criminal justice systems' at p. 286 and the material in the introduction to this chapter. This highlights the fact that the law has to draw a balance between the desire to convict the guilty and the need to prevent innocent people being wrongly convicted.

You could then move on to mention briefly some of the high-profile miscarriage of justice cases, such as the Birmingham Six, the Tottenham Three and the Stephen Lawrence investigation. You could point to ways these wrongful convictions could have been avoided by, for example, the introduction of a corroboration rule for confession evidence, stricter controls of the activities of the police in the police station and more money for the defence to challenge forensic evidence. The material contained in the section headed 'Safeguards for the suspect' at p. 257 could be considered which are all means of preventing miscarriages of justice.

In your conclusion, you could return to the concept of a balance and discuss the fact that a miscarriage of justice occurs not only when an innocent person is convicted but also when a guilty person is not convicted. It is impossible to create a system where no miscarriages of justice could ever occur, but the aim should be to minimize them. You could question how far such developments as the abolition of the right to silence are likely to achieve this.

Reading on the Internet

The Auld Report is available on:
http://www.criminal-courts-review.org.uk

The *Criminal Statistics England and Wales 1999* is published at:
http://www.official-documents.co.uk/document/cm50/5001/5001.htm

The *2000 British Crime Survey* is published at:
http://www.homeoffice.gov.uk/rds/pdfs/hosb1800.pdf

Information on the criminal justice system is available at:
http://www.criminal-justice-system.gov.uk/

The website of the Crown Prosecution Service is:
http://www.cps.gov.uk

10 Sentencing

This chapter is concerned with the punishment of those convicted of crimes, including the types of punishment available, and how the choice between them is made by the sentencer. But first, we need to consider why people are punished at all – what is it supposed to achieve? This will vary with the situation, but there are four main aims which may be present, alone or in combination: retribution; deterrence; rehabilitation; and public protection.

AIMS OF PUNISHMENT

Retribution

Retribution is concerned with recognizing that the criminal has done something wrong and taking revenge on behalf of both the victim and society as a whole. Making punishments achieve retribution was a high priority during the last years of the Conservative Government with Michael Howard as the Home Secretary. In the White Paper of 1990, *Crime, Justice and Protecting the Public*, reference was made to the need for sentences to achieve 'just deserts', stating that punishments should match the harm done, and show society's disapproval of that harm. The problem with this is that other factors all too often intervene: for example, those whose crime is deemed to 'fit' a fine may end up in prison because they are too poor to pay it, while the choice of punishment is also affected by whether the offender is a 'good risk' – those from stable homes, with jobs, are more likely to get non-custodial sentences than those without, who may be sent to prison even though their crime more properly fits a non-custodial sentence.

Deterrence

Deterrence is concerned with preventing the commission of future crimes; the idea is that the prospect of an unpleasant punishment will put people who might otherwise commit crime off the idea. Punishments may aim at individual deterrence (dissuading the offender in question from committing crime again), or general deterrence (showing other people what is likely to happen to them if they commit crime).

One problem with the use of punishment as a deterrent is that its effectiveness depends on the chances of detection: a serious punishment for a particular crime will not deter people from committing that offence if there is very little chance of being caught and prosecuted for it. This was shown when Denmark was occupied during the Second World War. All the Danish police were interned, drastically cutting the risk for ordinary criminals of being arrested. Despite increases in punishment, the number of property offences soared.

Linked with this problem is the fact that a deterrent effect requires the offender to stop and think about the consequences of what they are about to do, and, as the previous Government's 1990 White Paper pointed out, this is often unrealistic:

> Deterrence is a principle with much immediate appeal . . . But much crime is committed on impulse, given the opportunity presented by an open window or unlocked door, and it is committed by offenders who live from moment to moment; their crimes are as impulsive as the rest of their feckless, sad or pathetic lives. It is unrealistic to construct sentencing arrangements on the assumption that most offenders will weigh up the possibilities in advance and base their conduct on rational calculation. Often they do not.

The deterrent effect of punishment on individuals becomes weaker each time they are punished. The more deeply a person becomes involved with a criminal way of life, the harder it is to reform and, at the same time, the fear of punishment becomes less because they have been through it all before.

It has been argued that, to deal with this problem, offenders should be given a severe sentence at an early stage – which politicians like to call a 'short, sharp, shock' – rather than having gradually increased sentences which are counterbalanced by the progressive hardening of the offender to the effects of punishment. Successive attempts at the 'short, sharp, shock' treatment have, however, shown themselves to have no meaningful effect on reconviction rates. The approach was introduced under the Detention Centre Order, created by the Criminal Justice Act 1982; it was abolished in the Criminal Justice Act 1988.

Where a specific crime is thought to be on the increase, the courts will sometimes try to deter such conduct by passing what is called an exemplary sentence. This is a sentence higher than that which would normally be imposed to show people that the problem is being treated seriously, and make potential offenders aware that they may be severely punished. There is some debate as to whether exemplary sentences actually work; their effectiveness depends on publicity, yet British newspapers tend to highlight only those sentences which seem too low for an offence which concerns society, or which seem too high for a trivial offence. In addition, even where there is publicity, the results may be negligible – Smith and Hogan (1999) point to an exemplary sentence passed for street robbery at a time when mugging was the subject of great social concern. The sentence was publicized by newspapers and television, yet there was no apparent effect on rates of street robbery even in the area where the case in question took place. We should also question whether exemplary sentences are in the interests of justice, which demands that like cases be treated alike; the person who mugs someone in the street when there has not been a public outcry about that offence is no better than one who mugs when there has.

Rehabilitation

The aim of rehabilitation is to reform the offender, so that they are less likely to commit offences in the future – either because they learn to see the harm they are causing, or because, through education, training and other help, they find other ways to make a living or spend their leisure time. During the 1960s, a great deal of emphasis was placed on the need for rehabilitation, but the results were felt by many to be disappointing. By 1974 the American researcher Robert Martinson was denouncing rehabilitation programmes for prisoners in his paper *What Works*, in which he came to the conclusion that 'nothing works'.

Although rehabilitation sounds like a sensible aim, Bottoms and Preston argue in *The Coming Penal Crisis* (1980) that rehabilitative sentences are fundamentally flawed. First, such sentences assume that all crime is the result of some deficiency or fault in the individual offender; Marxist academics argue that crime is actually a result of the way society is organized. Secondly, they discriminate against the less advantaged in society, who are seen as in need of reform, whereas when an offender comes from a more privileged background, their offence tends to be seen as a one-off, temporary slip. This means that punishment is dictated not by the harm caused, but by the background of the offender. Thirdly, in some cases the pursuit of reform can encourage inexcusable interference with the dignity and privacy of individuals. This has included, in some countries, implanting electrodes in the brain, and in the UK in the 1970s experiments were carried out involving hormone drug treatment for sex offenders.

Faced with a growing prison population, there seems to be a renewed interest in the idea of rehabilitation. Over the past five years, offending behaviour programmes have been developed in many of the prisons of England and Wales. From an initial fragmented range of courses on such matters as anger management, alcohol and drug abuse, domestic violence and victim awareness, the emphasis is now on programmes aimed at changing the way the prisoners think, such as 'Reasoning and Rehabilitation' and 'Enhanced Thinking Skills'. Reasoning and Rehabilitation courses do not look directly at the prisoners' offending; instead, over a 35-session course run by prison probation officers and psychologists, they focus on six key areas – impulse control, flexible thinking (learning from experience), means-end testing (predicting probable outcomes of behaviour), perspective taking (seeing other people's points of view), problem solving and social skills. Enhanced Thinking Skills courses follow a similar pattern, but over 20 sessions. Attendance on the courses is voluntary – but a long-term prisoner is unlikely to be released early without having completed one.

In 1998–99, 3,000 prisoners successfully completed one of these programmes, but this still represents only a very small proportion of the prison population. This is expected to be doubled by 2002. Whether a prisoner has the opportunity to undertake a course depends on the establishment in which he or she is being held. Not all prisons run these courses and in most of the ones that do, priority is given to prisoners serving four years or more, in other words, those who have to apply for early release. Yet many persistent offenders are in prison for less than four years. It is common to find people who have had a series of successive two and three-year sentences, separated by mere weeks and often only days of freedom before they have reoffended and returned to prison. The senior judge, Lord Bingham, would like to see offending behaviour programmes made a legal requirement for all prisoners.

But how far will efforts to change the way a prisoner thinks reduce reoffending? One of the main problems faced by prisoners on release is a lack of work and consequent lack of an honest income or legitimate ways to spend their time. Many prisoners come out with the best of intentions but faced with empty days and even emptier pockets, they soon succumb to their old temptations. There is a danger that prisoners released into their old environment without having acquired any practical or vocational skills to help them on their way will fall back into a life of crime.

A recent report of the Parliamentary Penal Affairs Group, *Changing Offending Behaviour – Some Things Work* (1999) found that 'cognitive behavioural' programmes did work. But in addition, they argued that there is increasing evidence that programmes focused directly on the needs of the offender in relation to the offending behaviour are successful in reducing the risk of reoffending. The types of needs that can be tackled include the need for employment, education, improved social skills and a break from negative peer groups. The need to tackle alcohol and drug problems is also highlighted.

Public protection

By placing an offender in custody, you prevent them from committing further offences and the public are thereby protected. While this has its merits where highly dangerous offenders are concerned, it is an extremely expensive way of dealing with crime prevention and, since prison is often the place where criminals pick up new ideas and techniques, may be ultimately counter-productive.

SENTENCING PRACTICE

In recent years there has been a considerable amount of legislation trying to control and regulate the sentencing practices of the judges. Important pieces of legislation have included the Criminal Justice Act 1991, the Crime (Sentences) Act 1997 and the Crime and Disorder Act 1998. Most of the key legislative provisions have now been consolidated in the Powers of Criminal Courts (Sentencing) Act 2000. The Act will be referred to in this chapter as the PCC(S)A 2000. While it was intended that this consolidating Act would simplify the legislation in its field by grouping the key provisions together, it has already been amended by the Criminal Justice and Court Services Act 2000.

On conviction in the Crown Court, it is the trial judge alone (without the help of the jury) who determines the appropriate sentence. On conviction in the magistrates' court, the magistrates can determine the sentence themselves or, under s. 3 of the PCC(S)A 2000, the defendant can be committed to the Crown Court for sentence. If sentenced by the magistrates' court, the maximum sentence that can be imposed for a summary offence is usually six months' imprisonment (s. 78 PCC(S)A 2000) and the minimum is five days' (s. 132 of the Magistrates' Courts Act 1980).

Once the defendant has been found guilty, it must be decided first what category of sentence is appropriate and then the amount, duration and form of that sentence. The legislature has increasingly sought to reduce the discretion available to the judiciary in selecting the sentence. We will first look at the legislative provisions and then the common law practice known as the tariff system.

Legislation

Parliamentary legislation has for a minority of offences fixed the sentence that must be imposed for certain offences. Since 1997 it has imposed minimum sentences for some repeat offenders. Some rules have also been laid down restricting the judiciary's choice of sentence.

Mandatory sentences

Certain offences have a mandatory sentence when committed for the first time. The most notable example of this is murder, which has a mandatory sentence of life imprisonment.

Minimum sentences

Following the White Paper, *Protecting the Public: the Government's Strategy on Crime in England and Wales* (1996), the Crime (Sentences) Act 1997 was passed. This Act marked a significant change in the Conservative Government's policy towards sentencing. It swung away from the principle of just deserts and towards an emphasis on deterrence. The Act focused on the problems caused by serious, dangerous and persistent offenders. Its main innovation was to impose minimum sentences on certain repeat offenders. Its key provisions are now contained in the PCC(S)A 2000.

An automatic life sentence is imposed on a person aged 18 or over convicted of committing a second serious sexual or violent offence, unless there are exceptional circumstances which justify an alternative sentence (PCC(S)A 2000, s. 109). A third conviction of a class A drug trafficking offence attracts a minimum sentence of at least seven years' imprisonment unless the court believes that this would be unjust (PCC(S)A 2000, s. 110). A minimum sentence of at least three years' is imposed on the third conviction of a domestic burglary unless the court believes this would be unjust (PCC(S)A 2000, s. 111).

The concept of 'exceptional circumstances' under s. 109 enabling the court to avoid applying a life sentence has been the subject of much recent litigation. The leading case is now **R *v* Offen** (2001) where the legislation was interpreted extremely leniently in the light of the Human Rights Act 1998. All the previous cases must now be read in the light of this case. The appellants had been given automatic life sentences after having committed two serious offences. The Court of Appeal held that the purpose behind the legislation was the protection of the public. The fact that an offender did not pose a considerable risk to the public constituted an 'exceptional circumstance' under s. 2 and the court was not, therefore, compelled to impose a life sentence. If the two offences were of a different kind, or if there was a long period which had elapsed between the offences during which the offender had not committed other offences, that could be a very relevant indicator as to the degree of risk to the public posed by the offender. Where an offender did pose a considerable risk to the public, an automatic life sentence would not, in the opinion of the court, contravene Convention rights.

Before this case the Court of Appeal had taken a very tough approach to the legislation. In **R *v* Turner** (2000), Turner had been convicted of manslaughter in 1967 at the age of 22 and sentenced to three years' imprisonment. Thirty-three years later he was convicted of causing grievous bodily harm and sentenced to life imprisonment. He appealed to the Court of Appeal, contending that the passage of time since his first offence and the fact that he was provoked into committing the second offence constituted 'exceptional circumstances' within the meaning of the legislation.

The Court of Appeal dismissed his application. It held that the phrase 'exceptional circumstances' was to be construed restrictively, as an ordinary adjective. In the present case there were no such exceptional circumstances so the court was obliged to uphold the life sentence, much to its distaste. The court commented that it was remarkable that Parliament intended the legislation to compel judges to impose mandatory sentences which might offend their sense of justice. This case now appears to be bad law in the light of **R** v **Offen**.

General restrictions on sentences

The legislator has divided sentences into four categories: custodial sentences, community sentences, fines and certain miscellaneous sentences. Except where the sentence is fixed by law (such as life imprisonment for murder), the judge starts from the presumption that the sentence will be a fine. A custodial or community sentence can only be ordered where certain statutory conditions are satisfied.

Custodial sentences

A custodial sentence is defined by s. 76 of the PCC(S)A 2000. For a person aged 18 or over it is a sentence of imprisonment or a suspended sentence. For a person under 18 a custodial sentence includes detention in a young offender's institution or a sentence of custody for life.

Where a custodial sentence is imposed (whatever the offence, unless the sentence is fixed by law), a pre-sentence report must be prepared by the probation service, containing background information about the defendant, and the courts must give reasons for giving a custodial sentence.

In defining when a custodial sentence is appropriate, the 1991 Act divides offences between offences which are not violent or sexual, and those which are.

Non-violent and non-sexual offences The majority of these are property offences and a court should not pass a custodial sentence for these unless it considers that the crime was so serious that only a custodial sentence is justified (PCC(S)A 2000, s. 79).

In considering the seriousness of any offence the court may take into account previous convictions, failure to respond to previous sentences and the commission of an offence while on bail (PCC(S)A 2000, s. 151).

The legislation does not define seriousness, and so case law is likely to become important on this issue. In **R** v **Cox** (1993) an 18-year-old defendant pleaded guilty to theft of some tools and reckless driving, and was sentenced to four months' custody. The Court of Appeal said that the phrase 'so serious that only a custodial sentence is justified' means:

The kind of offence which when committed by a young person would make all right-thinking members of the public, knowing all the facts, feel that justice had not been done by the passing of any sentence other than a custodial one.

Violent and sexual offences Where an offence is violent and/or sexual, the PCC(S)A 2000 requires the court to take into account the need to protect the public. A custodial sentence may be imposed where it is necessary to protect the public from 'serious harm' (PCC(S)A 2000, s. 80(2)(b)). Serious harm is defined as 'death or serious injury, whether physical or psychological occasioned by further offences' (PCC(S)A 2000, s. 161).

In such cases, the court can take into account not only the circumstances of the offence, but also any information about the offender which is before it. Therefore, even where the seriousness of the offence committed does not necessarily require custody, the court may decide custody is necessary because of what the defendant might do if let free.

In exceptional circumstances, a court may impose a custodial sentence where it has proposed a community sentence which requires the defendant's consent, and the defendant refuses to give that consent.

Under s. 85 of the PCC(S)A 2000 a court can impose extended sentences for a sexual or violent offence. This is allowed where a court proposes to impose a custodial sentence but considers that the ordinary licence arrangements (discussed at p. 315) would not be adequate to prevent the commission of further offences or secure a person's rehabilitation. The sentence will consist of the main sentence and the extension period. During the extension period the offender is subject to a licence. The extension period will be for the length of time necessary to prevent offending or to secure the offender's rehabilitation, up to a maximum of ten years for sex offenders and five years for violent offenders.

Community sentences

A community sentence means a sentence of one or more community orders. These include community rehabilitation orders, community punishment orders, community punishment and rehabilitation orders, curfew orders, supervision orders and attendance centre orders.

Section 35 of the PCC(S)A 2000 states that a community sentence can only be imposed if the offence(s) was 'serious enough to warrant such a sentence'. Once this is established, the court must decide which order is the most suitable for the offender. The restrictions on liberty imposed by the order must be such as in the opinion of the court are 'commensurate with the seriousness of the offence, or the combination of the offence and one or more offences associated with it'.

In a few cases, particularly where young offenders are concerned, a pre-sentence report may be required before a community sentence is imposed.

The tariff system

The legislation regulates the type of sentence imposed and, in its focus on seriousness, clearly has implications for the length of a custodial or community sentence or the amount of a fine. In deciding the latter issues, judges also rely on what has been called the tariff principle, first recognized by Dr David Thomas in his book *Principles of Sentencing* (1970).

The tariff system is based on treating like cases alike: people with similar backgrounds who commit similar offences in similar circumstances should receive similar sentences. That does not mean that judges apply a rigid scale of penalties, but that for most types of criminal offence it is possible to identify a range within which the sentences for different factual situations will fall. The system works in two stages: calculation of the initial tariff sentence, and then the application of secondary tariff principles. To begin with, the judge will take the tariff sentence that is generally thought appropriate for the offence. This may then be lowered by taking into account secondary tariff principles such as mitigating factors – reasons why the defendant should be punished less severely than the facts of the case might suggest. These include youth or old age; previous good character; the 'jump effect' (a requirement that sentences for repeat offenders should increase steadily rather than by large jumps); provocation; domestic or financial problems; drink, drugs or ill-health; and any special hardship offenders may have to undergo in prison, such as the fact that sex offenders and police informers may have to be held in solitary confinement for their own protection. In some cases, where an offender has already been held on remand, the courts may reduce the tariff sentence on the basis that the shock of being locked up has already constituted a severe punishment. The offender's behaviour after committing the offence may also be a factor, including efforts to help the police and/or compensate the victim; a plea of guilty is usually taken as a sign of remorse and according to Thomas the initial tariff placement can be reduced by between one-quarter and one-third for this reason alone. This process has been given formal recognition by s. 157 of the PCC(S)A 2000, which allows the courts, when sentencing offenders, to take into account the stage at which they indicate an intention to plead guilty and the circumstances in which that indication was given. As far as the offence itself is concerned, the fact that it was committed on impulse and not premeditated may be a mitigating factor.

There may also be aggravating factors, as a result of which the court may want to pass an exemplary sentence. The Court of Appeal has stated that the correct way to deal with this is to ignore mitigating factors and not to increase the initial tariff. Under PCC(S)A 2000, s. 153, a court must treat the fact that an offence was racially motivated as an aggravating factor that increased the seriousness of the offence.

The Court of Appeal plays a central role in developing the tariff system by providing guidance to the judges of first instance as to the appropriate sentence for certain types of offences and offenders. Section 80 of the Crime and Disorder Act 1998 now states that the Court of Appeal has a duty to provide and revise such guidance. Section 81 of the 1998 Act created a Sentencing Advisory Panel to assist in the development of a fair sentencing practice. The Court of Appeal is required to consider the views of the Panel in framing its sentencing guidelines, the need to promote consistency in sentencing, sentences already imposed in England and Wales for offences in the relevant category, the cost of different sentences and their relative effectiveness in preventing reoffending, and the need to promote public confidence in the criminal justice system.

In its first year the Sentencing Advisory Panel issued guidance on sentencing practice in three areas of law: environmental offences, offences involving the possession of offensive weapons and offences of importation and possession of opium. The initial response of the Court of Appeal has been disappointing. In **R** *v* **Milford Haven Port Authority** (2000), which concerned the pollution to the environment caused by the *Sea Empress* ship, the Court of Appeal expressed its gratitude for the Panel's advice, but went on to conclude that the Court could not usefully frame guidelines for future environmental offences. If the Court of Appeal continues to take this approach to the Panel's reports, then the Panel will prove ineffective.

Individualized sentences

In some cases, the courts prefer not to use the tariff system, but to impose a sentence aimed at dealing with the individual needs of the offender. There are four main types of offender for whom individualized sentencing is used: young offenders; intermediate recidivists; inadequate recidivists; and those who need psychiatric treatment. Individualized sentences are often given to young offenders in the hope of steering them away from a life of crime. Intermediate recidivists are offenders in their late twenties or early thirties, with a criminal record dating back to their childhood; rather than simply ordering steadily increased tariff sentences for them, the courts may give an individualized sentence if there is evidence that a new approach may work. Inadequate recidivists are middle-aged or elderly offenders who have a long history of committing relatively minor crimes, which have resulted in imprisonment and most other types of sentence; individualized sentences may be ordered for them on the simple basis that their record shows increasing tariff sentences to have been ineffective in stopping their offending. Finally, offenders who need psychiatric treatment are given individualized sentences within which such treatment can be undertaken.

▶ TYPES OF SENTENCE

It was mentioned above (p. 309) that there are four main categories of sentence: custodial sentences; community sentences; fines; and other miscellaneous sentences. The death penalty has been abolished. We will now look at the particular forms that the four existing sentences can take.

▶ Fines

A fine may be imposed for almost any offence other than murder. Offences tried in the magistrates' court carry a set maximum, depending on the offence; the highest is £5,000. There is no maximum in the Crown Court. The courts must ensure that the amount of the fine reflects the seriousness of the offence, and also takes account of the offender's means, reducing or increasing it as a result (PCC(S)A 2000, s. 128). Magistrates' courts can arrange for the automatic deduction of a fine from the offender's earnings, known as an 'attachment of earnings order' when imposing the fine or following a failure to pay.

Advantages

Evidence suggests that people are less likely to reoffend after being sentenced to a fine than following other sentences, though this can be partly explained by the type of offenders that are given fines in the first place. Fines also bring income into the system, and they do not have the long-term disruptive effects of imprisonment.

Disadvantages

There are high rates of non-payment. This not only makes the sentence ineffective, but repeated non-payment of a fine can, and often does, lead to a custodial sentence, with the result that a high proportion of the inmates of English prisons are there for very minor offences, such as failure to pay for a television licence.

Research carried out for the Home Office, *Enforcing Financial Penalties* (1997), found that the majority of fine defaulters were out of work (only 22 per cent of the men and 11 per cent of the women had any paid employment, even part-time). Predominant among reasons for non-payment were changes in circumstances through illness or job loss, and financial difficulties brought on by other debts. There was evidence that courts were 'writing off' more fines partly because performance indicators (p. 184) encouraged writing off rather than lengthy attempts to obtain payment.

The study highlighted practical difficulties in trying to arrange the deduction of fines from social security benefits. In any case, some magistrates and justices' clerks were reluctant to make such an order, on the ground that the maximum deduction of £2.40 a week permitted by the Department of Social Security was 'too small to be experienced as a punishment'. This may reflect a failure of the middle-classes to appreciate the problems faced by many unwaged people. Some magistrates also felt that attachment of earnings orders removed the responsibility from the defaulter for ensuring that the fine was paid, which was seen as part of the punishment.

Fines can be unfair, since the same fine may be a very severe punishment to a poor defendant, but make little impact on one who is well-off. In an attempt to address this problem, the Criminal Justice Act 1991 originally laid down a system of unit fines for the magistrates' courts. A maximum number of units was allocated to each offence, up to a total of 50. Within that maximum, the court had to determine the number of units which was commensurate with the seriousness of the case. The value of the unit depended on the offender's disposable weekly income (their income after having deducted any regular household expenses), with the minimum value of a unit being £4, and the maximum £100. The unit fines system aimed to even out the effects of fines so that, although the sums to be paid were different, the impact on the offender would be similar. The pilot schemes for the unit fines suggested that fines were paid more quickly and there was a drop in debtors ending up in prison, because of the more realistic assessment of the fines.

Unfortunately, the idea aroused huge public opposition after press coverage of what seemed to be high fines for relatively minor offences and very low fines for the unemployed – despite the fact that even if some of these were unfair, they were less unfair than the previous system. As a result, unit fines were abolished, and the courts reverted to their previous practice, except that they are now required to take into account ability to pay when setting fines.

Fixed penalty fines

In order to clamp down on loutish behaviour the police have been given the power to impose fixed penalty fines by the Criminal Justice and Police Act 2001. These fines can be imposed for such offences as being drunk in a public place and being drunk and disorderly. A police officer may give a person over the age of 18 a penalty notice if there is reason to believe that the person has committed a penalty offence (s. 2). The fine for each offence is fixed by the Home Secretary and can be for up to a quarter of the maximum fine applicable to the offence. Recipients must either pay the fine within 21 days or opt for trial (they will not be marched off to the cashpoint by the police officer, as was originally suggested). If they fail to do either then a sum which is one and a half times the penalty will be registered against them for enforcement as a fine. If the person pays the fixed penalty fine there is no criminal conviction or admission of guilt associated with the payment of the penalty.

Advantages
In the past much minor offending escaped sanction because of the need to focus police and court resources on more important matters. It is hoped that fixed penalty fines will provide a quick and efficient way of dealing with low-level, but disruptive, criminal behaviour.

Disadvantages
Fixed penalty fines take place outside the protective framework of the court system, and there is therefore a danger of abuse and corruption.

Custodial sentences

For adult defendants, a custodial sentence means prison. Most of those given custodial sentences do not serve the full sentence. In the past, they could be released early on parole, which essentially meant that they could be taken back into prison if they reoffended, or given remission, which shortened the length of the sentence to be served if they were of good behaviour while in custody. The Criminal Justice Act 1991 abolished remission and parole for most offenders, and put in its place the single concept of early release. Offenders serving sentences of up to four years' are now automatically released after half the sentence has been served. Where the sentence is more than 12 months', they are released on licence under the supervision of the probation service. Breaching their licence is an offence punishable by a fine or recall to prison.

Those serving more than four years' may be released at a point somewhere between one-half and two-thirds of the sentence; the decision in each case is made on the basis of a recommendation made by the Parole Board. Such offenders are on licence until the three-quarter point of the sentence. Breach of the licence can only be dealt with by recall to prison. An offender released early who commits a new offence during the duration of the original sentence may have to go back to prison and serve the complete sentence.

The Crime (Sentences) Act 1997 contained provisions to abolish automatic release for all but life sentence prisoners. Instead there were to be small reductions in sentences for good behaviour. The logic behind the legislation was that 'five years should mean five years', but the prison governors expressed their concern that it might lead to greater difficulties in maintaining discipline in the prisons. With the arrival of a new Government these provisions were repealed before ever being brought into force.

Home detention curfews were introduced by the Crime and Disorder Act 1998, ss. 99 and 100. Prisoners sentenced to between three months' and four years' imprisonment can be released early (usually 60 days early) on a licence that includes a curfew condition. This requires the released prisoners to remain at a certain address at set times, during which period they will be subjected to electronic monitoring. Most curfews are set for 12 hours between 7 pm and 7 am. The person can be recalled to prison if there is a failure to comply with the conditions of the curfew condition or in order to protect the public from serious harm. Private contractors fit the tag to a person's ankle, install monitoring equipment which plugs into the telephone system in their home and connects with a central computer system, and notify breaches of curfew to the Prison Service. There are concerns that curfew arrangements may increase the problem of prisoners being reintegrated into their families after their release. By 2001 only 4 per cent of those released on home detention curfew were returned to prison for breach of the curfew.

An area that has caused considerable controversy and litigation in recent years is the question of the release of prisoners sentenced to life imprisonment, and in particular the Home Secretary's involvement in this decision. Those sentenced to a discretionary life sentence are now dealt with by the courts and the Parole Board and the Home Secretary plays no role in the decision making. The Home Secretary still plays a role in the decision to release offenders given a mandatory life sentence. The danger is that Home Secretaries might be influenced by issues of political popularity rather than the justice in the particular case. The matter has been highlighted in the case of Myra Hindley who was convicted for life in 1966 for the murder of two children and for her involvement in the killing of a third. In 1985, the then Home Secretary provisionally decided that the appropriate tariff was 30 years', but did not communicate this to Myra Hindley. In 1987, she confessed that she had in fact been involved, with her co-accused, in five murders, and in 1990, the Home Secretary decided to set the tariff as her whole life, rather than a fixed number of years. In 1997, the new Home Secretary, Jack Straw, confirmed the whole life tariff in her case, though he stated that he would keep the tariff under review. Myra Hindley sought judicial review of these decisions in **R** *v* **Secretary of State for the Home Department, ex parte Hindley** (2000). The House of Lords ruled that the decision had been lawful. While normally extending a fixed tariff to a whole life tariff would be unlawful, it would be allowed in exceptional circumstances. Here the applicant's confession to killing five children would have amounted to such a circumstance justifying an increase in the tariff. The Home Secretary, however, had to keep the tariff under regular review. There are apparently currently 23 prisoners subject to a whole life tariff.

Advantages
The previous Conservative Government claimed that prison 'works', in the sense that offenders cannot commit crime while they are in prison,

and so the public is protected. The current Government claims that prison can be made to work both by protecting the public and by making use of the opportunity for rehabilitation.

Disadvantages

In her book, *Bricks of Shame* (1987), Vivienne Stern highlights several reasons why imprisonment lacks any great reformative power, and may even make people more, rather than less, likely to reoffend. Prisoners spend time with other criminals, from whom they frequently acquire new ideas for criminal enterprises; budget cuts have meant there is now little effective training and education in prisons, while the stigma of having been in prison means their opportunities for employment are fewer when they are released; and families often break down, so that the ex-prisoner may become homeless. The result, says Stern, is that 'going straight can present the quite unattractive option of a boring, lonely existence in a hostel or rented room, eking out the Income Support'. All this can also mean that prison punishes the innocent as well as the guilty, with the prisoner's family suffering stigma, financial difficulties, the misery of being parted from the prisoner, and often family break-down in the end.

Short prison sentences make little sense from the standpoint of public protection and the prevention of reoffending. Such sentences combine the maximum disruption of offenders' lives in terms of loss of jobs, homes and community ties, with minimum scope for rehabilitative work.

Stern rejects the idea that prison works because it protects the public. She points out that although it may prevent the individual offending for a while, the percentage of crime that is actually detected and prosecuted is so small that imprisonment has little effect on the crime rate.

Prisons are also extremely expensive – at £24,000 a year per prisoner, three weeks in prison costs more than a whole community punishment order, or a year on a community rehabilitation order. To this must be added the costs associated with the family breakdown and unemployment that imprisonment frequently causes. As well as those who find them-selves in prison through non-payment of fines, many of those actually sentenced to prison have committed relatively minor offences and could be dealt with just as effectively, and far more cheaply, in the community.

The conditions within prisons continue to cause concern. While all prisoners are now supposed to have 24-hour access to toilet facilities, with the practice of 'slopping out' ended in 1996, other problems remain. A continuing area of concern that has been highlighted in the Prison Ombudsman's report for 1998 is the failure of the Prison Service's internal complaints system to investigate complaints adequately. Lord Woolf in his inquiry into the prison disturbances that took place in 1990 found that one of the root causes of the riots was that prisoners believed they had no other effective method of airing their grievances.

Where prison conditions are poor there is an increased risk of suicide. Between 1990 and 1997, 436 people committed suicide in prison and 88 of them were under the age of 21.

The number of people in prison has been growing at an alarming rate over recent years. By 1997 the prison population hit a record high of 60,000 inmates. This represented an increase of over a third in only five years. While some people believe this is the result of growing criminal activity, others argue that in times of social discontent, sentencers simply perceive a danger of increased lawlessness and impose more prison sentences to counter it. A Home Office bulletin issued in 2000 showed the courts in England and Wales to be among the toughest in western Europe in terms of numbers imprisoned, while a Council of Europe study revealed that defendants in English courts get longer sentences for assault, robbery or theft than they do elsewhere in Europe. Average prison populations in Europe are approximately a third lower as a proportion of the population to that of the UK.

Sir David Ramsbotham, Chief Inspector of Prisons, claimed in an interview for the *Guardian* in 2001 that the prison population could be cut to 40,000 if you took away 'the kids, the elderly, the mentally ill, the asylum seekers, those inside for trivial shoplifting or drug offences'.

Research carried out for the Home Office (White and Power, *Revised Projections of Long Term Trends in the Prison Population to 2005* (1998)), predicts that there will be 82,800 people in prison by the year 2005. The inevitable result is prison overcrowding. In 1996 matters reached crisis point and this led to a controversial scheme whereby a converted ship was used as a floating prison. In *Prison Sardines* (1996), a Howard League report, it was noted that at the end of February 1996, 46 prisons were overcrowded, with Usk Prison in Gwent being 75 per cent overcrowded.

The passing of the Crime (Sentences) Act 1997 to introduce minimum custodial sentences was heavily criticized by Lord Taylor, the previous Lord Chief Justice. Speaking to newspapers at the time, he argued that they took away sentencing discretion from the judges and that money would be better channelled into policing than sentencing:

> I make no criticism of the police, who do their best within the limited resources they are given. But does anyone believe that a professional burglar who knows he has at most only three chances in 20 of being caught will be deterred by the possible addition of 6 months or even 2 years to his sentence?

This view is supported by recent research in the field carried out by Cambridge University: *Criminal deterrence and sentence severity, an analysis of recent research* (1998). This shows that criminals are deterred by the fear of detection rather than the actual punishment. There was little evidence of a substantial statistical link between the severity of sentencing and crime rates.

Paul Cavadino, a spokesperson for NACRO, has commented:

If the money needed to pay for minimum sentences were used to extend preventive measures to more households it would prevent several times more burglary than longer prison terms. Home Office research into the Safer Cities programme showed that every pound spent on burglary prevention saved twice that amount in reduced burglaries. Even on the most optimistic estimates of the effect of containing persistent burglars, every pound spent would prevent no more than 34 pence worth of burglary... Repeat burglars range from persistent professional burglars to inadequate young people whose amateurish burglary attempts arise from problems which would best be tackled by intensive probation programmes. Courts should have the discretion to choose sentences which fit the widely varying circumstances of each case.

The philosophy behind the Crime (Sentences) Act 1997 can be traced back to the US and in particular California, where in their attempt to 'get tough on crime' a system known as 'three strikes and you're out' has been introduced. Under this system a person convicted of committing a third offence classified as a 'felony' will receive an automatic life sentence. The result of this has been a rapid surge in the prison population and 11 new prisons have had to be built in California in the last decade to cope with the increase. In the US as a whole, there are now over 2 million people in prison, compared with 220,000 in 1974. As a proportion of its population, this is five times higher than in the UK. This means that 25 per cent of the worlds' total prison population is now in US jails. Many of them are serving long sentences for drug possession. The annual bill for keeping prisoners behind bars is $35 billion, which is more than is spent on education.

The scheme is also over-burdening the court system, with defendants becoming reluctant to agree to a plea bargain and demanding a jury trial more often. As a result, in Los Angeles alone there is a backlog of 1,500 cases. Some juries are refusing to convict people of offences, even though there is strong evidence against the person, because of a reluctance to be responsible for sending them to a life in prison. There are suggestions that suspects are more likely to resist arrest, with sometimes dangerous gunfights ensuing.

The general experience in the US is that the mandatory minimum sentences have the greatest impact on the petty offenders, where the courts have in the past exercised their sentencing discretion in a sensible manner. The possible injustice that can arise was illustrated by the case of Jerry Williams, a 27-year-old man who was sentenced to life on conviction of his third offence, which was the stealing of a piece of pizza from a group of children when he was drunk.

Resort to mandatory minimum sentences raises an issue of principle as to where discretion should reside in individual cases. As noted by a leading American expert (Michael Tonry, *Sentencing Matters* (1996)), this

Thousands

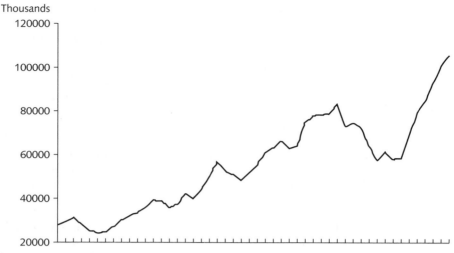

Figure 10.1 Persons sentenced to immediate custody, 1950–99
Source: *Criminal Statistics England and Wales 1999*

is a popular sentencing innovation in the US because it appears to shift that discretion to the elected legislature: if judges cannot be relied upon to be severe, the people's representatives will tie their hands. The reality is rather different: discretion moves away from the judiciary to be exercised by other participants in the criminal justice process, in particular the prosecutor. As a result, plea bargaining, combined with devious means to circumvent the legislation, becomes the norm, without the protection of the judicial controls of the courtroom being available.

On the other hand, in the first six months of the introduction of the scheme in California, robberies dropped by 12.7 per cent, rapes by 10.8 per cent, murders by 10.6 per cent and burglaries by 6.3 per cent. But these statistics must be handled with care as there is apparently a general fall in the crime rate across the US, which some have linked with the drop in the number of young people in the country, since young people are among those who are most likely to be convicted of crimes.

A major factor in the dramatic increase in the US prison population has been the expansion of the private prison sector. The US prison industry is the second largest employer in the US (second only to General Motors). Critics say that such is the level of vested economic interest that politicians will not wish to upset their financial backers by introducing policies that divert people away from custody.

Suspended sentence

Where a court passes a sentence of up to two years' imprisonment, it may order that the sentence will not take effect unless the offender commits another imprisonable offence during a period fixed by the court, which must be between one and two years.

Suspended sentences were introduced in 1967, with the aim of reducing the number of people sent to prison. In fact, they turned out to have the opposite effect. This might not have been the case if the courts had confined suspended sentences to those cases where they would otherwise have sent the offenders to prison, but the courts failed to do this. Instead, suspended sentences were frequently used as an alternative to a community sentence. If the offender committed another offence, the suspended sentence was often activated, so that the offender ended up in prison, even though the original offence had not demanded a prison sentence.

The Criminal Justice Act 1991 addressed this problem by requiring the court to satisfy itself that exceptional circumstances of the case justify use of the power to suspend (PCC(S)A 2000, s. 118). The case of **Okinikan** (1993) indicates that circumstances must be out of the ordinary; in that case, good character, youth and an early plea were held not to be sufficiently exceptional, either by themselves or together. An offender should not receive a suspended sentence of imprisonment unless imprisonment would have been appropriate if the power to suspend had not existed. Where courts seek to impose a suspended sentence, they are required to state in open court why the defendant requires a custodial sentence within the terms of the Act.

Community sentences

Recent governments have been anxious to emphasize that community sentences impose substantial restrictions on the offender's freedom and should not be seen as 'soft options'. Over the last 20 years there has been a shift towards using community sentences instead of fines as these are seen to be a more constructive form of punishment. Sadly, there is no evidence that this switch has achieved anything by way of crime reduction (Nuttall, Goldblatt and Lewis (1998)).

National Standards were introduced in 1992 to apply to the Probation Service to try and promote consistency in their application as this was felt to be a weakness in the system. The current National Standards were published in 2000. Research carried out for the Home Office, *Enforcing Community Sentences: Supervisors' Perspectives on Ensuring Compliance and Dealing with Breach* (1996), found wide divergence in the enforcement of community rehabilitation orders despite the introduction of National Standards. This inconsistency could be seen from the decision whether to register a failure to attend, and whether to pursue breach proceedings. The study highlighted the practice in some probation areas, when there was pressure on officers' workloads, of ending orders early and of transferring troublesome offenders to 'low grade reporting' (mere signing-up) rather than regular reporting to the supervisor in person.

The Criminal Justice and Court Services Act 2000 creates a statutory warning to reinforce the National Standards. Offenders are now issued with a maximum of one warning for an unacceptable failure to comply with a community sentence in any 12-month period, rather than, as previously, two warnings. Offenders are warned that if they again fail to comply with any requirement of the order during the next 12 months they will be returned to court. Where a further breach of the order occurs, the court has to determine whether the offender is likely to comply with the requirements of the order if it remains in force. If the court does not consider this likely, then it must impose a custodial sentence as punishment for breach of the community order, even where the original offence was not imprisonable, unless there are exceptional circumstances. Otherwise the court must impose a further community penalty. Electronic monitoring (discussed at p. 325) can be used to monitor compliance with the community sentence.

Following the Criminal Justice and Court Services Act 2000, in certain circumstances a court can be required to impose a drug abstinence requirement as part of a community sentence.

There are a range of different community sentences available to the courts. The names of some of these sentences were changed by the Criminal Justice and Court Services Act 2000 in order to make them more easily understood by the public.

Community rehabilitation orders

Probation orders have been renamed as community rehabilitation orders by the Criminal Justice and Court Services Act 2000. They place the offender under the supervision of a probation officer for a fixed period of between six months and three years. After consulting with a probation officer, the court may impose conditions as part of the community rehabilitation order. These commonly require the offender to attend a specified place and engage in certain activities for a maximum of 60 days (longer if the convict is a sex offender), or not to undertake specified activities for either the whole or part of the period covered by the order. Other possible conditions include requiring the offender to live in a specified place, such as a probation hostel, to receive psychiatric treatment or to undergo medical treatment for drug or alcohol problems. Following the Criminal Justice and Court Services Act the sentence can include a curfew requirement ordering an offender to remain in a certain place, usually their home, at set times.

A community rehabilitation order can be made for any offender aged 16 or over. The court must be satisfied that supervision is desirable in the interests of rehabilitating the offender, or preventing them from committing further offences or harming the public.

Where conditions are imposed and the offender breaks one of them, the probation officer may decide that the offender should be brought before the court again. In that case the court can fine the offender, or pass a new sentence for the original offence. An offender who commits another crime while under a community rehabilitation order may be dealt with for both the subsequent offence and the original one.

Advantages
Community rehabilitation orders have fewer disruptive effects than prison and, sensibly applied, conditions may help keep the offender away from criminal influences. Home Office research into the probation service (Mair and May, *Offenders on Probation* (1997)) found that 90 per cent of the people supervised thought that their community rehabilitation order had been useful. The most common reason given for this view was that it offered them someone independent to talk to about problems. A third mentioned getting practical help or advice with specific problems and about 20 per cent mentioned being helped to keep out of trouble and avoid offending. The research concluded:

> The message contained in this report is a good one for the probation service; it is viewed favourably by most of those it supervises, and seems to work hard at trying to achieve its formal aims and objectives as stated in the National Standards. However, this should not lead to any sense of complacency. It is arguable that any agency which provided similar help to that provided by the probation service to the poor and unemployed would be seen in an equally positive light.

Disadvantages
Reconviction rates are disappointing. Recent research shows that, with the exceptions of juveniles and adult males with between one and four previous convictions, offenders are more likely to reoffend after being placed under a community rehabilitation order than if they had been given any other non-custodial sentence.

Community punishment orders

'Community punishment order' is the new name given to community service orders by the Criminal Justice and Court Services Act 2000. These orders were introduced in 1972 as an alternative way of dealing with offenders who would otherwise have been sentenced to a short term of imprisonment. The order requires the offender to perform, over a period of 12 months, a specified number of hours of unpaid work for the benefit of the community. The number of hours must be between 40 and 240. The kind of work done includes tasks on conservation projects, archaeological sites and canal clearance.

The general conditions for making such an order are much the same as for a community rehabilitation order and it is in fact supervised by a probation officer. The offender must be 16 or over and have been convicted of an imprisonable offence. They must keep in touch with the probation officer, and notify them of any change of address.

Advantages
Community punishment orders are less disruptive than prison; allow useful community work to be done; and may give offenders a sense of achievement which helps them stay out of trouble afterwards.

Disadvantages
These orders were designed to be an alternative to imprisonment, but there is evidence that they have frequently been made for offenders who would otherwise have been given another non-custodial sentence. Reconviction rates are unimpressive: in one Home Office study, they were even higher for young adult men than for those released from detention centres. Community punishment orders have also suffered from being seen as a 'soft option', giving them little deterrent value.

Community punishment and rehabilitation orders

Community punishment and rehabilitation orders were known as combination orders before the Criminal Justice and Court Services Act 2000. A community rehabilitation order of between one and three years can be combined with between 40 and 100 hours' community punishment.

Advantages
This sentence provides greater flexibility to the sentencer to individualize the sentence to the offender.

Disadvantages
The research carried out in 1996 for the Home Office (*Enforcing Community Sentences: Supervisors' Perspectives on Ensuring Compliance and Dealing with Breach*) noted that magistrates have tended to impose community punishment and rehabilitation orders in more cases than expected. Sometimes these were imposed on offenders unequal to their demands, and some tangles have occurred because of the involvement of probation officers and community punishment officers in enforcing the different component parts of the sentence.

Curfew orders

Curfew orders were introduced in 1991 and the relevant legislative provisions are now contained in ss. 37 and 59 of the PCC(S)A 2000. Under a curfew order an offender can be required to remain in a specified place or places for periods of not less than two hours or more than 12 hours in any one day for up to six months. The court should avoid imposing conditions which would interfere with the offender's work or education, or cause conflict with their religious beliefs or the requirements of any other community order. A specified person must be made responsible for monitoring the offender's whereabouts. Courts can require offenders to wear electronic tags, in order to monitor that they are conforming to their curfew order.

Advantages

Tagging will cost about £4,000 a year compared with £24,000 for a prison place. Curfew orders have the potential to keep offenders out of trouble and protect the public, without the disruptive effects of imprisonment. In the US city of Atlanta, a night curfew has been imposed on anyone under 16. This was introduced to protect children, but has also had the effect of considerably reducing juvenile crime. While such use of curfew orders on those who have not been convicted of crimes intrudes on the right to freedom of movement, the results show that, as a sentence, it could prove very useful.

Disadvantages

The Penal Affairs Consortium have argued that the money spent on electronic tagging would be better spent on constructive options such as community rehabilitation orders, which work to change offenders' long-term attitudes towards offending. Opponents to electronic tagging claim they are degrading to the person concerned, but their supporters – including one or two well-known former prisoners – point out that it is far less degrading than imprisonment. This argument applies only where tagging is used as an alternative to imprisonment: its opponents claim that it is likely to be used in practice to replace other non-custodial measures. Existing research suggests, however, that curfew orders with tagging are being seen as a genuine alternative to custody (Nuttall, Goldblatt and Lewis (1998)).

Exclusion orders

This is a new sentence introduced by the Criminal Justice and Court Services Act 2000. It requires an offender to stay away from a certain place or places at set times. Electronic tags can be used to monitor compliance with this order. It is aimed at people, such as stalkers, who present a particular danger or nuisance to a victim. An exclusion order is similar in many respects to a curfew order. However, whereas a curfew order requires an offender to remain at a specified place, an exclusion order prohibits an offender from entering a specific place.

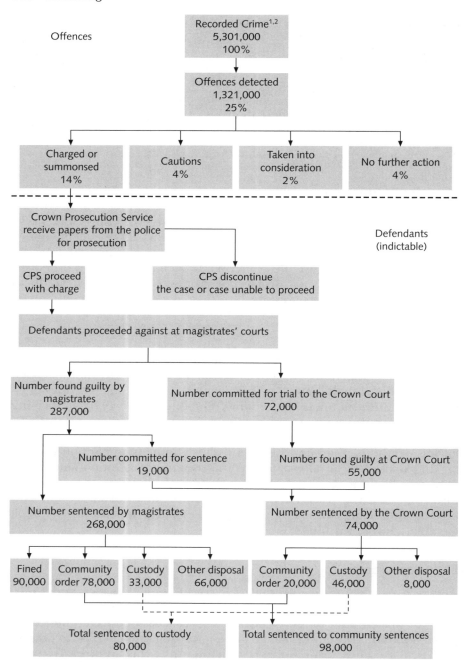

Offences

Recorded Crime[1,2]
5,301,000
100%

Offences detected
1,321,000
25%

Charged or
summonsed
14%

Cautions
4%

Taken into
consideration
2%

No further action
4%

Crown Prosecution Service
receive papers from the police
for prosecution

Defendants
(indictable)

CPS proceed
with charge

CPS discontinue
the case or case unable to proceed

Defendants proceeded against at magistrates' courts

Number found guilty by
magistrates
287,000

Number committed for trial to the Crown Court
72,000

Number committed for sentence
19,000

Number found guilty at Crown Court
55,000

Number sentenced by magistrates
268,000

Number sentenced by the Crown Court
74,000

Fined
90,000

Community
order 78,000

Custody
33,000

Other disposal
66,000

Community
order 20,000

Custody
46,000

Other disposal
8,000

Total sentenced to custody
80,000

Total sentenced to community sentences
98,000

Figure 10.2 Flows through the Criminal Justice System, 1999

[1] Covers all indictable, including triable either way, offences plus a few closely associated summary offences
[2] In the financial year 1999/00
Source: *Criminal Statistics England and Wales 1999*

Drug treatment and testing orders

The drug treatment and testing order is the latest attempt to direct drug users away from criminality and into treatment. This order can be made where an offender aged 16 or over is dependent on, or has a propensity to misuse, drugs and their condition requires and is susceptible to treatment. It places the offender under the supervision of a probation officer and requires them to submit to treatment and regular testing with a view to the reduction or elimination of their drug problem (PCC(S)A 2000, ss. 52–58). The order can be made for between six months and three years.

Drug abstinence orders

This punishment was introduced by the Criminal Justice and Court Services Act 2000. It requires the offender to abstain from misusing certain serious drugs and to undertake a drug test when requested. The order can be for a minimum of six months and a maximum of three years.

Miscellaneous sentences

Compensation orders

Where an offence causes personal injury, loss or damage (unless it arises from a road accident), the courts may order the offender to pay compensation. This may be up to £1,000 in a magistrates' court and is unlimited in the Crown Court. Orders can also be made for the return of stolen property to its owner, or, where stolen property has been disposed of, for compensation to be paid to the victim from any money taken from the offender when arrested.

Confiscation orders

Under the Criminal Justice Act 1988 and the Drug Trafficking Act 1994, a confiscation order may be imposed on the conviction of an individual for a criminal offence. The order seeks to confiscate from the criminal the illegal profits of their trade. This area of the law was examined by a Home Office working party which issued a report in 1998 called *Criminal Assets*. It found that the existing confiscation arrangements have fallen short of original expectations. During 1996, only 1,500 confiscation orders were made in England and Wales for drug trafficking offences when there were 45,000 convictions for the supply of drugs. Between January 1987 and December 1996, about 40 per cent of the assets subjected to these orders were successfully confiscated. The total sums recovered during this period were estimated to be £37 million and £4.5 million for drug and non-drug offences respectively. This was praised as 'commendable' given the difficulties associated with the enforcement process. But the report concluded that the total amount recovered was a 'tiny proportion of the sums by which criminals are benefiting from crime'.

The working group was advised by the police and customs authorities that they regularly encountered cases:

> where there is strong circumstantial evidence of the criminal origins of property, but insufficient evidence for a criminal prosecution of the owner. Cases are known where individuals are enjoying great wealth and a lavish lifestyle, in circumstances where if civil forfeiture were available a court would be very likely to conclude that the assets are of criminal origin. The working group believes that the inability of the authorities to intervene in cases of this kind, some of which become known locally, can be damaging to public confidence in our system of justice.

The working group therefore recommended that the police should have the power to confiscate property even where there have been no criminal proceedings. This would be possible if it had been proved on the civil burden of proof that the assets represented the proceeds of criminal conduct. The Home Secretary announced that he intended to introduce legislation containing these reforms. The proposed legislation would create a Criminal Assets Recovery Agency which would have an array of investigative powers. The development is contentious as it violates the ordinary principle that a penalty can only be imposed after a criminal conviction and may therefore breach the European Convention on Human Rights.

Mental health orders

Under the Mental Health Act 1983, the Crown Court can order the detention of offenders in hospital on conviction for an imprisonable offence if they are suffering from a mental disorder, the nature or degree of which makes detention in hospital for medical treatment appropriate; and, if psychopathic disorder or mental impairment is present, the court is satisfied that the treatment is likely to help the condition or stop it getting worse. The order can only be made if the court considers such an order to be the most suitable way of dealing with the case. Alternatively, the court may place the offender under the guardianship of a local authority.

Where detention in hospital is ordered by the Crown Court, and it believes the public needs to be protected from the offender, it can make an order restricting their discharge either for a specified period or without limit.

A magistrates' court can make an order for detention in a hospital when an offender has been convicted of an imprisonable offence, or even if the offender has not been convicted, if the court is satisfied as to guilt.

There has been growing concern about offences committed by paedo-philes and by persons benefiting from care in the community. The case of Michael Stone was particularly distressing. He was accused of killing Lin and Megan Russell in a brutal attack in the countryside. It appears that he suffers from a severe personality disorder but could not be detained under the current legislation because his condition was not treatable. The Home Secretary therefore announced plans in 1999 to introduce new powers to detain individuals. These would allow indefinite detention without trial of dangerous persons with severe and untreatable personal-ity disorders. A court could make a care and treatment order where a person posed a significant risk of serious harm to others as a result of their severe personality disorder.

Binding over to be of good behaviour

This order dates back to the thirteenth century and the relevant legislat-ive provisions can be found in the Justices of the Peace Act 1361 and the Magistrates' Courts Act 1980. It can be made against any person who is before the court and has 'breached the peace' – not just the defendant, but also any witness. People who are bound over have to put up a sum of money and/or find someone else to do so, which will be forfeited if the undertaking is broken. A person who refuses to be bound over can be imprisoned, despite the fact that they may not have been convicted of any offence. The order usually lasts for a year.

This area of the law was considered by the European Court of Human Rights in **Steel and Others** *v* **UK** (1998). The first applicant, Ms Steel, was arrested in 1992 when she walked in front of an armed member of a grouse shoot, preventing him from shooting. She was charged with causing a breach of the peace and was detained for 44 hours. At her trial the complaint of breach of the peace was proved true and she was bound over to keep the peace for 12 months. Her appeal to the Crown Court was dismissed and when she refused to be bound over she was imprisoned for 28 days.

The second applicant was arrested while demonstrating against the building of a motorway. She had stood in front of a digging machine to stop it being used, and was charged with conduct likely to cause a breach of the peace. She was found to have committed a breach of the peace and was bound over for 12 months. She refused, and was sent to prison for seven days.

The other three applicants were all arrested for handing out leaflets and displaying banners against the sale of weapons at the 'Fighter Heli-copter II Conference' in London in 1994.

The applicants claimed that their arrests and detention had not been 'prescribed by law' as required by Art. 5 of the Convention and had amounted to a disproportionate interference with their freedom of expression in breach of Art. 10. The European Court of Human Rights found that the powers to bind over were compatible with the European Convention on Human Rights. It was satisfied that the concept of breach of the peace was clear and that it had been established in English law that it was committed only when a person caused harm to persons or property, or acted in a manner the natural consequence of which was to provoke others to violence.

The court accepted that in the case of the first and second applicants the police had been justified in fearing that their behaviour might provoke others to violence. Bearing in mind the aim of deterrence, and also the importance in a democratic society of maintaining the rule of law and the authority of the judiciary, the court did not find it disproportionate that they were sent to prison.

However, concerning the three protesters at the arms fair, the court found that their behaviour had been entirely peaceful and could not have justified the police in fearing that a breach of the peace was likely to occur. For that reason, it found that their arrest and detention had been unlawful, under both the English law on breach of the peace and under Arts. 5 and 10 of the Convention. The arrest and detention of these protesters had been disproportionate to the aim of preventing disorder or of protecting the rights of others.

Absolute and conditional discharges

If the court finds an offender guilty of any offence (except one for which the penalty is fixed by law), but believes that in the circumstances it is unnecessary to punish the person and a community rehabilitation order is inappropriate, it may discharge the defendant either absolutely or conditionally.

An absolute discharge effectively means that no action is taken at all, and is generally made where the defendant's conduct is wrong in law, but no reasonable person would blame them for doing what they did. A conditional discharge means that no further action will be taken unless the offender commits another offence within a specified period of up to three years. This order is commonly made where the court accepts that the offender's conduct was wrong as well as illegal but the mitigating circumstances are very strong. If an offender who has received a conditional discharge is convicted of another offence during the specified period, they may, in addition to any other punishment imposed, be sentenced for the original offence. A discharge does not count as a conviction unless it is conditional and the offender reoffends within the specified period.

Deferred sentences

Section 1 of the PCC(S)A 2000 allows the courts to defer passing sentence for a period of up to six months after conviction. The Act contains few guidelines on the use of this power, but does state that it can be exercised only with the consent of the offender, and where deferring sentence is in the interests of justice. Deferred sentences are intended for situations where the sentencer has reason to believe that within the deferral period, the offender's circumstances will materially change, with the result that no punishment will be necessary, or that the punishment imposed should be less than it would have been if imposed at the time of conviction. For example, offenders may make reparation to the victim, settle down to employment or otherwise demonstrate that they have changed for the better.

Disqualification

This is most common as a punishment for motoring offences when offenders can be disqualified from driving. Under ss. 146–147 of the PCC(S)A 2000 a court may disqualify a person from driving as a punishment for a non-motoring offence. A conviction for offences concerning cruelty to animals may also lead to disqualification from keeping pets or livestock.

Anti-social behaviour orders

Section 1 of the Crime and Disorder Act 1998 provides that a local authority or the police in a local government area may apply to the magistrates' court for an anti-social behaviour order. The order will be made against a person aged ten or over who has acted in an anti-social manner, that is, a manner which is likely to cause harassment, alarm or distress to someone not in the same household as the person describ[ed] in the order, and who is likely to do so again. Guidance on the legisla[tion] provided by the Home Office suggests that typical behaviour which m[ay] fall within this provision includes 'serious vandalism or persistent [intim]idation of elderly people'. The court has power to prohibit that [person] from doing anything described in the order for a period of not [less than] two years.

Sex offender orders

Section 2 of the Crime and Disorder Act 1998 [...] officer of police may apply to the magistrates' cou[rt ...] order. Under this order restrictions can be placed on [...] they have been released from prison in order to protect [...] serious harm.

Appeals against sentence

The defence may appeal against a sentence considered too harsh, while the prosecution can appeal if they feel the sentence was too low. In addition, ss. 35 and 36 of the Criminal Justice Act 1988 give the Attorney-General the power to refer a case to the Court of Appeal where the sentence is believed to have been too lenient.

Problems with sentencing

The role of the judge

We have seen that the sentence in England is traditionally a decision for the judge, which can lead to inconsistent punishments, especially among magistrates' courts. This situation clearly offends against the principle of justice that requires like cases to be treated alike.

The Government has tried to restrict judicial discretion through legislative guidelines and has also set up a Sentencing Advisory Panel and a Judicial Studies Board for Crown Court judges. Overseen by the Lord Chancellor's Department, the functions of the Judicial Studies Board include running seminars on sentencing, which seek to reduce inconsistencies; courses for newly appointed judges; and refresher courses for more experienced members of the judiciary. The Board also publishes a regular bulletin summarizing recent legislation, sentencing decisions, research findings and developments in other countries, while the Magistrates' Association issues a *Sentencing Guide for Criminal Offences* to its members.

Other jurisdictions generally allow judges less discretion in sentencing. In the US, for example, many states use 'indeterminate' sentencing by which a conviction automatically means a punishment of, say, one to five years' imprisonment, and the exact length of the sentence is decided by prison authorities. However, in this country, control of sentencing is as an important aspect of judicial independence, and provisions in 97 Act for more legislative control have been criticized as inter- with the judiciary's constitutional position.

tencing practice in England have frequently alleged that ic minorities are treated more harshly than white ple, black men form 1.9 per cent of the population of et, according to Home Office figures for June 1997, er cent of the male prison population. This difference ess if only UK nationals are considered, because one in ople in prison is a foreign national, often imprisoned for illegally importing drugs. Whether these figures actually point to racial discrimination in sentencing is the subject of much debate, but research has strongly suggested that there are differences in the way black and white people are treated by sentencers.

In 1985, David Martin of the South East London Probation Service conducted a survey of 117 young men who were either in youth custody or had been released on licence. At that time, 29 per cent of the service's youth custody cases concerned black people, compared with 4.7 per cent of the total population. Of the young men studied, those who were black were less likely than white men to be offered supervision or community rehabilitation orders before being sentenced to youth custody, and were sentenced to youth custody with fewer previous convictions than white men, even though they generally came from more stable backgrounds than the white subjects, which would normally make them a 'better risk' for non-custodial sentences.

In 1986, a study by the West Midlands Probation Service looked into the role of Social Inquiry Reports (since replaced by the pre-sentence report) in sentencing differences between white and black people. The study showed that where the defendant was black, sentencers were less likely to follow the sentencing recommendations than they were if the defendant was white, and the result of not following recommendations was more likely to be a custodial sentence where defendants were black, than if they were white. In cases where the Social Inquiry Report made no sentencing recommendation, all the black defendants were given custodial sentences, compared with only 57 per cent of the white defendants.

The study then looked at the offences committed, to see if this could explain the sentencing differences. It found that, on balance, the white defendants had committed a higher proportion of the more serious offences than the black defendants and that, where the offence was the same, black people were more likely to receive custodial sentences: for example, 79 per cent of black defendants for burglary received custody, compared with 25 per cent of white defendants. Nor were the difference explained by previous records of sentencing: of those receiving a cus dial sentence, 58 per cent of the white defendants had already bee custody, compared with 37 per cent of the black defendants.

In addition to any racism in the system, the legal and procedur tors which affect sentencing may account for some of the diff in the punishment of black and white offenders. More black elect for Crown Court trial and plead not guilty, which convicted they would probably receive harsher senten sentences in the Crown Court are higher than those in th court and they would not benefit from a discount for a gu Research by Flood-Page and Mackie in 1998 found that there w evidence that black or Asian offenders were more likely than wh offenders to receive a custodial sentence when all relevant factors were taken into account.

The experience of black people when in the prison system has also given rise to concern. An internal report commissioned by the prison service in 2000 found a blatantly racist regime at Brixton prison, where black staff as well as inmates suffered from bullying and harassment. The head of the prison service, Martin Narey, has acknowledged that the prison service is 'institutionally racist' and that 'pockets of malicious racism exist'. He has promised to sack all prison officers found to be members of extreme right-wing groups such as the British National Party. Prison officers' training now includes classes on race relations.

Sexism

There is enormous controversy over the treatment of women by sentencers. On the one hand, many claim that women are treated more leniently than men. In 1998, there were only 3,000 female prisoners, which was 5 per cent of the prison population. A Home Office study carried out by Hedderman and Hough in 1994 reported that, regardless of their previous records, women were far less likely than men to receive a custodial sentence for virtually all indictable offences except those concerning drugs, and that when they do receive prison sentences these tend to be shorter than those imposed on men. Flood-Page and Mackie also found in 1998 that women were less likely to receive a prison sentence or be fined when all relevant factors were taken into account. This has been variously attributed to the fact that women are less likely to be tried in the Crown Court; chivalry on the part of sentencers; assumptions that women are not really bad, but offend only as a result of mental illness or medical problems; and reluctance to harm children by sending their mothers to prison.

On the other hand, some surveys have suggested that women are actually treated less leniently than men. A 1990 study by the National Association for the Care and Resettlement of Offenders found that one-third of sentenced female prisoners had no previous convictions, compared with per cent of men, and most of them were in prison for minor, non- offences. Because they are usually on lower incomes than men, are thought more likely to end up in prison for non-payment of

critics have suggested that women who step outside traditional are treated more harshly than both men and other women. arlen (1983) studied the sentencing of a large group of und that judges were more likely to imprison those who as failing in their female role as wife and mother – those who ingle or divorced, or had children in care. This was reflected in the ments made by sentencers, including 'It may not be necessary to send her to prison if she has a husband. He may tell her to stop it' and 'If she's a good mother we don't want to take her away. If she's not, it doesn't really matter.'

Today women represent the fastest growing sector of the prison population, their numbers have more than doubled in the six years from 1,300 in 1992 to over 3,000 in 1998. About one-fifth of the total female prison population have been sentenced as drugs couriers and, of these, some seven out of every ten are foreign nationals (Penny Green, *Drug Couriers: A New Perspective* (1996)). HM Chief Inspector of Prisons, Sir David Ramsbotham, has commented 'There is considerable doubt whether all the women in custody [at Holloway] really needed to be there in order for the public to be protected' (*Report on Holloway Prison* (1997)). Helen Edwards, the Chief Executive of NACRO has observed that 'the vast majority of women in prison do not commit violent offences and much of their offending relates to addiction and poverty. Prison is not an appropriate, necessary or cost-effective way of dealing with these problems.'

The needs of women prisoners have wrongly been assumed to be the same as men. The Chief Inspector of Prisons has emphasized that female prisoners have different social and criminal profiles, as well as different health care, dietary and other needs. In 1997 the Home Office published a study of women in prison: *Women in Prison: A Thematic Review*. Their survey revealed that the great majority of women in prison come from deprived backgrounds. Over half had spent time in local authority care, had attended a special school or had been in an institution as a child. A third had had a period of being homeless, half had run away from home, half reported having suffered violence at home (from a parent or a partner) and a third had been sexually abused. Forty per cent of sentenced women prisoners had a drug dependency, and alcohol problems were also found to be very common. Almost 20 per cent had spent time in a psychiatric hospital prior to being imprisoned and 40 per cent reported receiving help or treatment for a psychiatric, nervous or emotional problem in the year before coming into prison. Nearly two in five reported having attempted suicide.

Privatization

Criminal justice has, historically, been regarded as a matter for the state. Recently, however, first under the Conservative Government in the early 1990s, and now under Labour, various parts of the system have been privatized, including ten prisons. The Home Secretary said in 1998 that all new prisons would be privately built and run. Such moves have not generally been seen as runaway successes. Privatized prison escort services have come in for severe criticism, with prisoners managing to escape or not being brought to the court on time.

Reform

The Home Office undertook a review of sentencing that was carried out by John Halliday and published in 2001. A wide range of recommendations are contained in his report, *Making Punishment Work, Report of the Review of the Sentencing Framework for England and Wales*. The Government is now considering the Report and it is clear that it does not intend to accept all of its recommendations.

Central to the approach of the Halliday Review is that the courts should have a greater role in the implementation of sentences and that offenders should spend more time under supervision after their release from custody. He also wanted to see a greater predictability in sentencing so that the sentencing practice would have a greater deterrent effect on potential offenders. He was particularly concerned by the approach of the courts to persistent offenders, who he thought committed a disproportionate amount of crime.

At present, judges and magistrates are required to take a single decision on sentence after a person has been found guilty of an offence. Having done so, the court may not hear of the matter again. John Halliday considers that the court could learn more and do more good by remaining involved in the sentencing process after the initial sentence has been handed down. The courts would become involved in the implementation of the sentence through a sentence review procedure. In practice this sentencing review could not always take place before the same judge or magistrates. Sentencing matters would be returned to the courts in four situations. These situations would be when:

- a community sentence has been breached;
- an appeal has been launched against a recall to prison;
- a plan is being prepared prior to a person's release from custody; and
- a review is held on the progress of a person being supervised in the community.

Sir Robin Auld, in his *Review of the Criminal Courts*, supports the idea of a sentence review. The Government's initial response is to accept that the courts should be involved in sentence management, but it is concerned that sentence reviews could clog up the courts unnecessarily, causing additional delays. The introduction of sentence reviews would also be expensive, costing the country around £28 million every year.

John Halliday recommended that new guidelines should be introduced for the use of judicial discretion to make sentencing more predictable. These could be set out in a separate Code and would apply to all criminal courts. The guidelines would:

- specify graded levels of seriousness of offence;
- provide 'entry points' of sentence severity in relation to each level of seriousness;

- set out how severity of sentence should increase in relation to numbers and types of previous convictions;
- explain other possible grounds for mitigation and aggravation.

The report argues that prison sentences of less than 12 months have little meaningful impact on criminal behaviour, because only half of the sentence time is actually served in prison, and the person is then released without conditions. The Prison Service has little opportunity to tackle criminal behaviour as the period served in custody is so short. In addition, such sentences can have long-term adverse effects on family cohesion, employment and training prospects – all of which are key to the rehabilitation of offenders. This is regrettable as these sentences are used for large numbers of persistent offenders who are likely to reoffend.

The review proposed that a new sentence of 'custody plus' should be introduced. Under this a person would be under supervision on their release from a short prison sentence up until the end of their sentence. Offenders would be required to undertake supervised programmes after release, under conditions, which – if breached – could result in a swift return to custody. The initial period in custody could be between two and three months, and the period of supervision could last between six and ten months. For those small numbers of offenders for whom post-custody supervision is not needed, a sentence of ordinary custody, of up to three months, would be available.

For sentences of over 12 months Halliday recommends that after serving half the sentence in custody, the remainder should be served under strict supervision in the community right up until the end of the sentence.

John Halliday also favoured the introduction of a new sentence: 'intermittent custody'. This would allow offenders to spend part of a custodial sentence out of prison, but have to return to prison at night or at the weekend. At the moment the prison facilities are not suitable for such arrangements but the Home Secretary wants consideration to be given to this matter.

The Review recommended that in order to achieve crime reduction, sentencing should do more to target persistent offenders. Thus, the existing 'just deserts' philosophy should be modified by incorporating a new presumption that severity of sentence should increase when an offender has sufficiently recent and relevant previous convictions.

The danger of John Halliday's recommendations is that they could lead to yet another increase in the prison population. The early experience of suspended sentences, which bears some resemblance to some of the key proposals, was that individuals committed offences during the period of the suspended sentence and then found themselves in prison, when if the suspended sentence had not existed the judge would have given a non-custodial sentence. As well as increasing the prison population the recommendations could put unrealistic demands on the available resources in the criminal justice system. For example, if the recommendations were introduced, the probation service could be working at any one time with up to 80,000 more offenders.

▶ ANSWERING QUESTIONS

1 Margaret, aged 26, is charged with manslaughter and has appeared before Hattown magistrates.
(i) What are the powers of Hattown magistrates to deal with Margaret?
(ii) How may Margaret obtain funding from the Legal Services Commission?
(iii) If Margaret is convicted what sentences might be passed upon her?

Part (i): the information needed for this part is covered fully in chapter 9 but essentially the powers of the magistrates concern bail and sending the case to the Crown Court for trial, since manslaughter is a crime triable only on indictment.

Part (ii): these issues are covered in chapter 8 at p. 221.

Part (iii): as we are given no details about the form of manslaughter or the circumstances, and as Margaret is an adult offender, in theory any of the sentencing options described above could be relevant. You need to outline what these options are and the criteria that would be used to decide which of these is imposed on Margaret.

2 How do judges arrive at decisions as to what sentences should be imposed on persons convicted of offences? *Edexcel*

You could start your answer to this question by pointing out the important role that judges have traditionally played in sentencing in our system, highlighting the fact that although there are some mandatory sentences and now greater statutory guidance for judges, they still maintain a wide discretion in sentencing. You could then point out that there are a number of principles which are officially accepted as guiding such judicial decisions but that it is alleged that these decisions may also be affected by certain unadmitted factors, such as racism and sexism.

You can then proceed to look at the official factors that determine how judges choose a sentence first, discussing the four key principles that can underlie the sentence (retribution, deterrence, rehabilitation and public protection) and the process of sentencing (the statutory guidance, the tariff system and individualized sentences). After this you could examine some of the allegations that racism and sexism also influence judges in arriving at sentencing decisions, mentioning the research studies detailed in the relevant sections above.

3 Describe the main aims of sentencing and explain how these are implemented by judges in imposing sentences on offenders. *Edexcel*

Divide your essay into two parts to reflect the structure of the question. First look at the four main aims of sentencing that are discussed at pp. 303–307: retribution, deterrence, rehabilitation and public protection. Secondly, look at how these aims are implemented in practice by the judges. One way of approaching this part of the question would be to consider each type of sentence in turn and look at how far they seek to achieve one or more of the four aims. For example, a community sentence tends to place a greater emphasis on rehabilitation and deterrence while a custodial sentence prioritizes retribution and public protection. You could also consider the legislative controls of judicial discretion in sentencing and discuss which aims these seek to achieve. For example, the mandatory minimum sentences are focusing on deterrence.

▶ Reading on the Internet

The report of John Halliday on sentencing is available at:
http://www.homeoffice.gov.uk/cpg/halliday.htm

A webpage set up by the Home Office to consider the issue of sentence reform following the report of John Halliday is:
http://www.fairer-sentencing.co.uk

The Powers of Criminal Courts (Sentencing) Act 2000 is available on Her Majesty's Stationery Office website at:
http://www.hmso.gov.uk/acts/acts2000/20000006.htm

The explanatory notes to the Criminal Justice and Court Services Act 2000 can be found on Her Majesty's Stationery Office website at:
http://www.legislation.hmso.gov.uk/acts/en/2000en43.htm

11 Young offenders

Offenders who are under 18 years old are dealt with differently from adults by the criminal justice system. There have in the past been a number of reasons for this, including a belief that children are less responsible for their actions than adults, a wish to steer children away from any further involvement in crime, and the feeling that sentencing can be used to reform as well as, or instead of, punishing them. However, in recent years the mood towards young offenders has become more severe due to a widespread public perception of mounting youth crime and the killing of the toddler James Bulger by two ten-year-old boys. The Audit Commission found that in some neighbourhoods 26 per cent of known offenders were aged under 18 (*Misspent Youth: Young People and Crime* (1997)). At present one in three young men are found guilty of a criminal offence by the age of 22 and nine out of ten under-17s are reconvicted within two years of release from a custodial sentence. Youth crime costs the public services £1 billion a year. In fact, some of the public's fears are exaggerated. The Home Office British Crime Survey for 1998 found that two-thirds of the people questioned for the survey believed young people were becoming increasingly involved in crime between 1995 and 1997, while official statistics showed the numbers remaining constant, or declining. Only 17 per cent of known offenders are aged between ten and 17.

The Government stated in its 1998 White Paper, *No More Excuses – A New Approach to Tackling Youth Crime in England and Wales* (1998) that it wanted to reverse the 'excuse culture' that had developed within the youth justice system. A change in approach was signalled by the passing of the Crime and Disorder Act 1998. This piece of legislation was central to the current Government's approach to youth crime. The Act sought to reduce offending by young people in two ways. First, by promoting strategies for the prevention of youth crime and, secondly, by creating a range of extended powers available to the police and the courts to deal with young offenders and their parents. Many of its key provisions are now contained in the Powers of Criminal Courts (Sentencing) Act 2000.

Section 37 of the Act specifies that the aim of the youth justice system is to prevent offending by young people. A Youth Justice Board for

England and Wales has been established under s. 41 of the 1998 Act. Its principal functions are to monitor, set standards and promote good practice for the youth justice system. Its main focus to date has been to try and speed up the youth justice system, encourage the creation of programmes aimed at preventing youth crime and assist in the implementation of the provisions in the 1998 Act concerning young offenders.

Local authorities must formulate and implement a youth justice plan setting out how youth justice services are to be provided and funded (s. 40). They must, acting in cooperation with police authorities, probation committees and health authorities, establish one or more youth offending teams whose duty it is to coordinate the provision of youth justice services and to carry out their functions under the youth justice plan (s. 39).

Criminal liability

Under criminal law children under ten cannot be liable for a criminal offence at all. In the past there was also a well-established presumption that children between the ages of ten and 14 were not criminally liable. This presumption could be rebutted by the prosecution successfully adducing evidence that the child knew right from wrong and knew that what they were doing was more than just naughty. In 1998 this rebuttable presumption was repealed by the Crime and Disorder Act 1998. In this respect children aged ten and above are now treated like adults. British children are almost alone in Europe in being regarded as criminals at the age of 10.

Young people and the police

Most of the police powers concerning adults also apply to young suspects, but because they are thought to be more vulnerable, some extra rules apply. For example, Code C of the Police and Criminal Evidence Act 1984 (PACE) states that young suspects should not be arrested or interviewed at school and, when brought to a police station, they should not be held in a cell. The police must find out who is responsible for the young person's welfare as quickly as possible and then inform that person of the arrest, stating where and why the suspect is being held. If the person responsible for their welfare chooses not to come to the police station, the police must find another 'appropriate adult', who should be present during the various stages of cautioning, identification, intimate searches and questioning. Where the suspect's parent is not present the appropriate adult will often be a social worker, though it may be anyone defined as a responsible adult, except someone involved in the offence, a person of low intelligence, someone hostile to the young person or a solicitor acting in a professional capacity.

The role of the adult is to ensure that the young person is aware of their rights, particularly to legal advice. The adult should be told that their function is not just that of observer, but also of adviser to the young person, ensuring that the interview is conducted properly and facilitating communication between suspect and interviewer. Unfortunately, research by Brown (1992) suggests that some adults are so overawed by the whole process that they are of little use as advisers; they may even side with the interviewer.

Remand and bail

A young person charged with an offence has the right to bail under the Bail Act 1976 (see chapter 9). Where the police refuse bail, children under 17 are usually remanded to local authority accommodation, which can range from remand fostering schemes to accommodation with high levels of supervision. Those under 17 should not be held in police custody before being brought to court, unless the custody officer certifies that it is impracticable to transfer them to local authority accommodation or, so long as they are over 12, that no local authority secure accommodation is available and that other accommodation would be inadequate to protect the public from serious harm.

Children under 15 should not be held on remand in adult prisons or remand centres. Following the Crime and Disorder Act 1998, s. 98, young people who are 15 and 16 can be remanded to an adult prison or remand centre. In other respects defendants aged 17 and over are subject to the same rules as adults with regard to conditions in police custody, bail and remand.

Reprimands and warnings

People involved in administering the criminal justice system have, in the past, been concerned to try and stop a young offender from a cycle of court appearances, punishments and further offending, often aggravated by contact with other offenders during the process. The police therefore tried to divert the young offenders from the criminal justice system by issuing them with a caution rather than bringing a prosecution. A caution was an official warning about what the person had done, designed to make them see that they had done wrong and deter them from further offending (it is quite separate from the caution administered before questioning, concerning the right to silence).

However, there was growing concern that the caution procedure was being overused in practice, so that young repeat offenders were acting with a sense of impunity. Section 65 of the Crime and Disorder Act 1998 therefore abolished the system of cautions for young offenders aged between ten and 17, and replaced them with a new system of reprimands and warnings.

Section 65 of the Crime and Disorder Act 1998 provides that a first offence can be met with a reprimand, a final warning or a criminal charge, depending on its seriousness. The usual sequence will be a reprimand for a first offence, followed by a warning for a subsequent offence, followed by a charge on a third occasion (or a warning where the offender has not received a warning for at least two years and the offence is not serious enough for a charge).

Before the police can issue a reprimand or warning, four conditions must be satisfied:

1 there must be sufficient evidence;
2 the young person must admit the crime;
3 they must have no previous convictions; and
4 it is not in the public interest to bring a prosecution.

The reprimand or warning will be given in the presence of an 'appropriate' adult. Where a warning has been given, the officer must refer the offender to a youth offending team as soon as practicable. The youth offending team will assess the offender to determine whether a rehabilitation scheme aimed at preventing the person from reoffending is appropriate. Where it is appropriate, a scheme should be established for the offender.

Sir Robin Auld in his *Review of the Criminal Courts* (2001) has recommended that a system of 'caution-plus' should be introduced. This would allow the prosecutor, with the consent of the offender, to impose a caution combined with a condition as to their future conduct where a minor offence is alleged to have been committed. Offenders could be brought before a court if they breached one of the conditions. If introduced this recommendation would represent a dangerous shift whereby cautions would actually take on the form of a punishment administered outside the court system. As such it might well breach the European Convention on Human Rights.

Trial

Young offenders are usually tried in youth courts (formerly called juvenile courts), which are a branch of the magistrates' court. Other than those involved in the proceedings, the parents and the press, nobody may be present unless authorized by the court. Parents or guardians of children under 16 must attend court at all stages of the proceedings, and the court has the power to order parents of older children to attend.

Young persons can only be tried in a Crown Court if the offence charged is murder, manslaughter or causing death by dangerous driving, or if they are at least 14 and are likely, if convicted, to be detained under s. 90 of the Police and Criminal Courts (Sentencing) Act 2000 (PCC(S)A) (in practice this means that they are charged with a very serious offence, usually involving violence). They may also sometimes be tried in an adult magistrates' court or the Crown Court if there is a co-defendant in the case who is an adult. Following a Practice Direction, discussed below, a separate trial should be ordered unless it is in the interests of justice to do otherwise. If a joint trial is ordered, the ordinary procedures apply 'subject to such modifications (if any) as the court might see fit to order'.

The trial procedures for young offenders have been reformed in the light of a recent ruling of the European Court of Human Rights. This found that Jon Venables and Robert Thompson who were convicted by a Crown Court of murdering the two-year-old James Bulger in 1993, did not have a fair trial in accordance with Art. 6 of the European Convention on Human Rights. It concluded that the criminal procedures adopted in the trial prevented their participation:

> The public trial process in an adult court with attendant publicity was a severely intimidating procedure for eleven year old children . . . The way in which the trial placed the accused in a raised dock as the focus of intense public attention over a period of three weeks, had impinged on their ability to participate in the proceedings in any meaningful manner.

Following this decision, a Practice Direction has been issued by the Lord Chief Justice laying down guidance on how young offenders should be tried when their case is to be heard in the Crown Court. The language used by the Practice Direction follows closely that used in the European decision. It does not lay down fixed rules but states that the individual trial judge must decide what special measures are required by the particular case taking into account 'the age, maturity and development (intellectual and emotional) of the young defendant on trial'. The trial process should not expose that defendant to avoidable intimidation, humiliation or distress. All possible steps should be taken to assist the defendant to understand and participate in the proceedings. It recommends that young defendants should be brought into the court out of hours in order to become accustomed to its layout. Jon Venables and Robert Thompson had both benefited from these familiarization visits. The police should make every effort to avoid exposure of the defendant to intimidation, vilification or abuse.

As regards the trial, it is recommended that wigs and gowns should not be worn and public access should be limited. The courtroom should be adapted so that, ordinarily, everyone sits on the same level. In the Bulger trial, the two defendants sat in a specially raised dock. The decision to raise the dock had been taken so that the defendants could view the proceedings, but the European Court of Human Rights noted that whilst it did accomplish this, it also made the defendants aware that everyone was looking at them. Placing everyone on the same level should alleviate this problem. In addition, the Practice Direction states that young defendants should sit next to their families or an appropriate adult and near their lawyers.

The Practice Direction suggests that only those with a direct interest in the outcome of the trial should be permitted inside the court room. Where the press are restricted, provision should be made for the trial to be viewed through a CCTV link to another court area.

It seems that in most other European countries, children aged under 14 who commit offences do not appear before criminal courts, but are dealt with by civil family courts as children in need of compulsory measures of care.

Sentencing

Sentencing for young offenders has always posed a dilemma: should such offenders be seen as a product of their upbringing and have their problems treated, or are they to be regarded as bad, and have their actions punished? Over the past couple of decades, sentencing policy has swung between these two views. In 1969, the Labour Government took the approach that delinquency was a result of deprivation, which could be 'treated', and one of the aims of the Children and Young Persons Act of that year was to decriminalize the offending of young people. Instead of going through criminal proceedings, they would be handed over to the social services, under either a supervision order or a care order, the latter giving the social services the power to take the young person into some form of custody. The magistracy constantly fought against this approach and, when a Conservative Government was elected in 1970, they declined to bring much of the Act into force and the care order provisions have now been repealed.

The opposite approach introduced by the Conservatives led to the UK having a higher number of young people locked up than any other west European country, but reconviction rates of 75–80 per cent suggested that this was benefiting neither the young offenders themselves, nor the country as a whole.

The philosophy behind the Criminal Justice Act 1982 was that the sentencing of young people should be based on the offence committed and not on the offender's personal or social circumstances, or the consequent chances of reform. This succeeded in lowering the level of detention for young offenders, and the Criminal Justice Act 1991 continued this approach for young persons, and extended it to adults.

Custodial sentences

Currently, the courts may not pass a sentence of imprisonment on an offender under the age of 18. Such offenders may be detained in other places, such as a young offenders' institute or local authority accommodation or a secure training centre, but in order to pass a sentence of this kind, the court must satisfy the same conditions as for adults (discussed in chapter 10) and in some cases additional criteria as well.

There has been a rapid increase in the number of people under the age of 18 sentenced or remanded to custody. Between June 1993 and February 1997 this number almost doubled, from 1,304 to 2,518, a trend which is in dramatic contrast to the pattern of the previous ten years.

Near the end of 1999, a scheme was announced to release young offenders from prison directly into the army, rather than on licence to the probation service. It appears that the driving force behind the plan is a 6,000 shortfall in soldiers as the army faces acute recruitment difficulties.

The quality of the custodial accommodation has on occasion given rise to concern. For example, large sums of money have been spent developing the Feltham young offenders institution near Heathrow Airport. It is now the largest such institution in the UK with places for 900 young offenders. In 1999 Sir David Ramsbotham was Her Majesty's Chief Inspector of Prisons. He reported that the conditions in Feltham 'were unacceptable in a civilised society'. As the inspector makes clear in a blistering report, the problem was not one of lack of resources, but of staff attitudes and management. This is exemplified by the Inspectorate finding two cases of appalling bedding conditions while there were new and unused mattresses being held in storage. Cell and common areas were dilapidated, dirty and cold. Bedding and linen were unwashed and in a poor state of repair. Despite ample stocks of available clothing in the central stores, the personal clothing provision was pitifully inadequate. All meals had to be taken not in dining rooms but in dirty cells with filthy toilets. Most of the youngsters were locked up for 22 hours a day. A 16-year-old boy who had been on the unit for three months told the inspector: 'I have nothing to do. I get hungry and there's nothing to distract me. If I get depressed, I talk to the chaplain and ask him to pray for me. Most of the time I sleep. My mum's not home during the day and I'm not allowed to phone her in the evening.' The report concluded that 'there were too many examples of distant and disinterested staff throughout the institution who were palpably failing to meet the health and welfare needs of the young people in their charge'. Sir David Ramsbotham has gone as far as describing the conditions in some institutions as 'institutionalised child abuse'.

In response to such criticism the Prison Service is currently seeking to produce a discrete juvenile secure estate within the Prison Service. This approach has already been criticized by the Youth Justice Board in *Creating a Vision for the Secure Juvenile Estate* (1999). It considers that, in order to create a caring, safe and secure environment for young people in custody, institutions should have no more than 150 inmates, while the Prison Service has in mind large facilities with up to 400 places.

England and Wales
Thousands

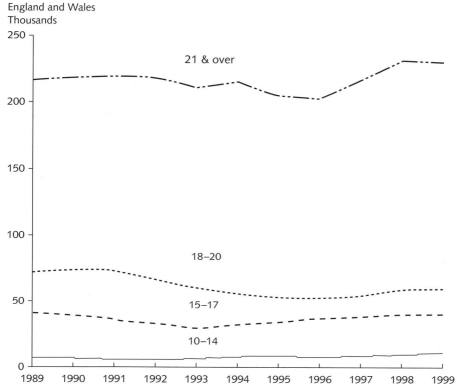

Figure 11.1 Persons sentenced for indictable offences to immediate custody in England and Wales, by age

Source: *Criminal Statistics England and Wales 1999*

Detention 'during Her Majesty's pleasure'

Under the PCC(S)A 2000, s. 90 an offender convicted of murder who was under 18 when the offence was committed must be sentenced to be detained indefinitely, known as 'during Her Majesty's pleasure'.

This form of sentence was considered by the House of Lords in **R** *v* **Secretary of State, ex parte Venables and Thompson** (1997). The two applicants had been convicted of the murder of James Bulger. They had been ten years old at the time of the offence and were given a sentence of detention during Her Majesty's pleasure. The Home Secretary received several petitions signed by thousands of people demanding that the boys serve at least 25 years in custody. In 1994 the Home Secretary, applying the same procedures to children detained at Her Majesty's pleasure as to adults given a mandatory life sentence, decided that the minimum sentence that they should serve was 15 years. The case was taken to the European Court of Human Rights. In **T** *v* **UK** and **V** *v* **UK** the court held that it was not compatible with the Convention for the Home Secretary to set tariffs in the case of detention during Her Majesty's pleasure. In response to this finding the Criminal Justice and Court Services Act 2000 makes provision for the sentencing court to set the tariff in these cases.

Detention under s. 91 PCC(S)A 2000

The PCC(S)A s. 91 provides that where a person aged ten or over has been convicted in the Crown Court of an offence with a maximum sentence of 14 years' imprisonment or more, the court may pass a sentence not exceeding that maximum.

Under the Crime (Sentences) Act 1997, s. 28 the Home Secretary must release on licence a life prisoner who was under 18 at the time of the offence when directed to do so by the Parole Board.

Detention and training orders

The use of custody against young children is particularly controversial as, by definition, this involves their removal from their family. Under s. 100 of the PCC(S)A 2000 the courts can make a detention and training order. Such an order must be for a term of between four and 24 months. Half this period will be spent in detention and the other half under supervision. The detention period can be served in any secure accommodation deemed suitable by the Home Secretary, for example, a Young Offenders' Institution, Secure Training Centre, Youth Treatment Centre or local authority secure unit. The order will be available initially for offenders aged at least 12 years, but the Home Secretary has power to extend it to ten- and 11-year-olds. The sentence of detention in a Young Offender Institution will remain available for offenders aged 18 to 20 years.

The privately run Medway Secure Training Centre in Kent was completed in 1998 in order to detain 12 to 14-year-olds. This has places for 40 trainees. As the children detained are very young, it is important that they can maintain links with their families during their detention. Many will be detained far away from home and there will be an assisted visits scheme financed by the Home Office for visits on a weekly basis and arrangements for contact through letters and telephone calls. The training and education programmes will include education for 25 hours a week based on the national curriculum, one hour daily for tackling offending behaviour and crime avoidance, regular practical tuition in social skills and domestic training. There will also be the opportunity to acquire and develop interests to occupy leisure time while in custody and after release.

It is debatable whether it is necessary to impose custodial sentences on children by means of a detention and training order. The vast majority of crime committed by this age group are minor property offences, and for more serious cases s. 91 of the PCC(S)A 2000 applies. Given the problems associated with custodial sentences, putting young persons at risk of custody for more minor offences may not be effective in crime reduction in the long term.

The tariff

Because the maximum custodial sentences for young offenders are usually quite short, the tariff approach described in the chapter on sentencing is of limited application to the sentencing of young offenders, except in the sense that young offenders can usually rely on their youth as strong mitigation.

Community sentences

A range of community sentences have been developed to tackle the problem of young offenders.

Referral orders

Most young offenders appearing before a youth court for the first time will be given a mandatory referral to a youth offender panel if they plead guilty. This order was created by the Youth Justice and Criminal Evidence Act 1999, and the relevant legislative provisions are now contained in PCC(S)A 2000, s. 16. Referral orders are only available for first-time convictions where the sentence is not fixed by law and where a custodial sentence is not appropriate. The youth offender panel agrees a 'programme of behaviour' with the young offender, the primary aims of which are the prevention of reoffending and restorative justice (in other words, that the offender pays back the victim or society in some way). Once agreed the terms of the programme of behaviour are written in a youth offender contract. This may require the offender, among other things, to compensate financially or otherwise victims or other people whom the panel consider to have been affected by the offence; to attend mediation sessions with victims; to carry out unpaid work in the community or to observe prescribed curfews. The order is administered by the local youth offending team (mentioned at p. 341). Subsequent meetings will be arranged with the panel to review compliance with the contract and a final meeting will determine whether the contract has been satisfactorily completed.

It is hoped that this procedure will prove more effective than the traditional court sentencing process, which the Home Secretary has criticized in Parliament, saying:

> [T]he young offender is, at best, a spectator in a theatre where other people are the actors. At worst, the young offender is wholly detached and contemptuous of what is going on . . . never asked to engage his brain as to what he has done, or why he hurt the victim.

Referral orders are likely to be introduced nationally in 2002.

Supervision orders

These are applied to offenders aged between 10 and 16, and require a probation officer or social services department to supervise the offender for up to three years. The order is basically a junior version of probation, except that a stronger emphasis is placed on assisting the personal development of the young person; it was introduced by the CYPA 1969 to replace community rehabilitation orders for young offenders. The consent of a young person to a basic supervision order is not required.

As with community rehabilitation orders, the supervisor must assist, advise and befriend the offender. Schedule 6 to the PCC(S)A 2000 lays down certain requirements that can be included as part of a supervision order. The young offender can be ordered to live in specified accommodation, attend a particular place, take part in set activities, or any combination of the three, for up to 90 days. The purpose of such requirements is to remove the young person from their home environment and make them take part in challenging activities – these might include rock climbing, pot-holing or even simply attending a local youth club. Youth court magistrates, after consultation with the supervisors, can also specify activities which the offender should not participate in; for this, consent must be obtained from the young person and a parent or guardian. A young offender of compulsory school age can be ordered to comply with arrangements for their education.

If an offender breaches a requirement in a supervision order and the supervisor brings this to the court's attention, the court may change the order, fine the offender up to £100, or make an attendance centre order. If they have reached the age of 17, the court may discharge the order and pass a new sentence for the original offence.

Young offenders over 16 may be made subject to a community rehabilitation order.

Attendance centre orders

Under s. 60 of the PCC(S)A 2000 an offender under 21 convicted of an imprisonable offence may be ordered to go to an attendance centre for a specified number of hours spread over a certain period of time. The number of hours of attendance that may be ordered is not less than 12 (unless the offender is under 14 and 12 hours seems excessive), and not more than 24 in the case of those under 16, and 36 for those aged 16 to 20. Breach of an attendance centre order may result in the offender being sentenced again for the original offence. The centres are normally run by the police, and tend to involve attendance on Saturday afternoons for physical education classes or practical courses. Unless there are special circumstances, such an order should not be made if the offender has previously been sentenced to detention in a young offenders' institute.

Curfew orders

Section 37 of the PCC(S)A 2000 enables a court to impose a curfew order with electronic monitoring of up to three months on an offender under the age of 16 years.

Local authorities may set up local child curfew schemes for the purpose of maintaining order (Crime and Disorder Act 1998, s. 14). This can ban for a specified period children under ten from being in a public place during certain hours between 9 pm and 6 am unless they are accompanied by an adult. A police officer who has reasonable cause to believe a child to be in contravention of the ban may inform the local authority of the contravention and take the child home (Crime and Disorder Act 1998, s. 15).

Compliance with the curfew order can be monitored through the use of an electronic tag. The use of electronic tagging on young offenders was piloted in two schemes, the results of which were not particularly promising. In Manchester 39 per cent of young offenders breached the curfew order. The majority of the offenders spent their time at home watching more television or sleeping. There is also a danger that some children will wear their tags with pride, seeing them as trophies to be shown off to their peers.

Reparation orders

Under s. 73 of the PCC(S)A 2000 a court can hand down a reparation order requiring an offender under the age of 18 to make reparation commensurate with the seriousness of the offence, to the victim or to the community at large. Before making such an order, the court must obtain a report as to what type of work is suitable for the offender and the attitude of the victim or victims to the proposed requirements (s. 74 PCC(S)A 2000). Guidance from the Home Office indicates that the order may, for example, require the writing of a letter of apology to the victim, help to be given in repairing damage caused by the offending conduct, the cleaning of graffiti, weeding a garden, collecting litter or doing other work to help the community. The work required must not exceed 24 hours over a period of three months. The order may be combined with a compensation order if the court considers that financial compensation would also be appropriate. These orders are being piloted in specified areas.

In the 1998 British Crime Survey, 60 per cent of respondents approved of the concept of reparation orders, though only 40 per cent would be prepared to meet the offender.

Action plan orders

Action plan orders were introduced in 1998 and are now contained in s. 69 of the PCC(S)A 2000. They are tailored to address the cause of the young person's offending behaviour with the aim of securing the rehabilitation of the offender or the prevention of further offending. Under such an order, a young offender under the age of 18 who is convicted of an offence will be placed under supervision for a maximum of three months and obliged to comply with a series of requirements with respect to their actions and whereabouts for a specified period. The Home Office guidance lists examples of requirements to include attendance at anger management classes, motor education projects, drug or alcohol misuse programmes or specified remedial educational classes. The action plan order cannot be combined with a custodial sentence or any other community sentence.

Parents of young offenders

Where a young offender is under 16, a parent or guardian must be required to attend the court hearing, unless the court considers that this would be unreasonable. If the offender is convicted, the court is required to bind over the parents to take proper care and exercise proper control over their child; the courts also have discretion to do this in the case of 16 or 17-year-olds. Although the consent of the parents is required, an unreasonable refusal can attract a fine of up to £1,000. Parents or guardians can also be bound over to ensure that the young offender complies with a community sentence (PCC(S)A 2000, s. 150).

Where an offender under 16 is sentenced to a fine, the parents are required to pay it. The court may also order parents to pay in the case of 16 and 17-year-old children. The fine will be assessed taking into account the financial situation of the parent, rather than the young offender. Where a local authority has parental responsibility for a young person who is in their care, or has provided accommodation for them, it is to be treated as the young person's parent for these purposes.

In 1997 the Home Office published a study *Women in Prison: A Thematic Review*. It noted that when fines for juvenile offences are imposed on the parent or guardian, this is usually in practice the mother, often alone, and coping in difficult circumstances. If she does not (or cannot) pay the fine, she runs the risk of imprisonment. The report gives the example of Margaret, aged 46 and on income support. She had to pay fines imposed as a result of her son's criminal offences (he was then 16). Magistrates sentenced her to 27 days' imprisonment for a remaining debt of £170.50, despite the fact that she had not personally committed any crime.

In specified areas and during specified periods, a constable is empowered by s. 16 of the Crime and Disorder Act 1998 to remove truants found in a public place to premises designated by the local authority, or to the school from which the truant is absent.

Child safety orders

A local authority can commence civil proceedings for a child safety order to be made by a magistrates' court under ss. 11–13 of the Crime and Disorder Act 1998. It can require a child under the age of ten to be at home at specified times or to avoid certain people or places to limit the risk of their involvement in crime. The order can be made if the child has committed or risks committing an act which would have constituted an offence if they had been older, they have breached a curfew notice, or have behaved in an anti-social manner. The aim of this order is to divert children below the age of ten from behaviour that would bring them into conflict with the criminal law. The child will be placed under the supervision of a social worker or member of a youth offending team for up to three months (and exceptionally 12 months), and the child will be required to comply with the requirements in the order. These requirements are not specified in the Act and are whatever the court considers desirable in the interests of securing that the child receives appropriate care, protection and support and is subject to proper control, and to prevent the repetition of the offending behaviour. It is targeting those children who are 'running wild' but are too young to be the subject of criminal proceedings. Where longer-term intervention is required, care proceedings will be brought by the local authority instead, with a care order continuing until the child becomes an adult. If the child safety order is breached care proceedings may also be brought.

Parenting orders

Under s. 8 of the Crime and Disorder Act 1998, a court may make a parenting order. The order is designed to help and support parents (or guardians) in addressing their child's anti-social behaviour. It is available in five situations:

1 a court makes a child safety order;
2 a court makes a sex-offender order against a young person;
3 a court makes an anti-social behaviour order against a young person;
4 a young person has been convicted of an offence;
5 a parent has been convicted for failing to secure their child's attendance at school.

The order can be for a maximum of 12 months and consists of two elements. First, the parent will have to attend counselling or guidance sessions for up to three months. Secondly, the parent must comply with certain specific requirements aimed at ensuring that they exercise control over their child.

Time limits

In 1998 the criminal justice system took, on average, four-and-a-half months to process a young offender from the time of arrest to sentence. The Audit Commission found that in 1997 cases were generally adjourned on four occasions before completion. The Crime and Disorder Act 1998 aims to reduce this period as there is concern that delays in the system are undermining the impact of the sentence on the offender. In cases involving persons under the age of 18, s. 44 provides that time limits may be applied from arrest to the commencement of proceedings and from conviction to sentence. The Government's target was for half of cases involving persistent offenders to be dealt with within 71 days. The Home Secretary commented:

> Young people must be made to recognise and accept responsibility for their crimes – at the time, not many months later. Only when this happens will there be serious pressure on young offenders to change their behaviour rather than settle into a life of crime.

In order to assist practitioners in delivering the current target, the Government has provided guidelines on the length of time each stage of the youth justice process should take in a straightforward case involving a persistent young offender. These are as follows:

- arrest to charge: 2 days
- charge to first appearance at court: 7 days
- first appearance to start of trial: 28 days
- verdict to sentence: 14 days.

Arrest to sentence times for persistent young offenders have been declining steadily since 1996, when the average time stood at 142 days. The average time from arrest to sentence dropped to 96 days in the first three months of 2000, compared with 117 days at the beginning of 1999. Magistrates' court cases took an average of 85 days from arrest to sentence, compared with 206 days in the Crown Court. There were also significant regional variations.

Zero tolerance

The Labour Party described its approach to young offenders as being one of 'zero tolerance'. This is a concept that developed in the US during Ronald Reagan's time in office, and has come to mean that the law will be strictly enforced in order to reduce crime. The idea was first seen in the context of the war against drugs. A recent use of 'zero tolerance' policy has been by the police in Los Angeles in an attempt to curtail the activities of gang members. Concern had developed that gangs in Los Angeles were disrupting neighbourhoods by dealing in drugs, painting graffiti on walls, urinating on private property, having all-night parties and committing violence and murder. The Los Angeles police, in conjunction with local prosecutors, strictly applied existing law by issuing civil court injunctions against gang members which prevented them from, for example, 'standing, sitting, walking, driving, gathering or appearing anywhere in public view' in a four-block area where their activities were disruptive. Since the imposition of the zero tolerance policy some local residents say that the injunctions have returned their neighbourhoods to normal, allowing their children once again to play outside. Opponents to the policy claim that it breaches individuals' rights to freedom of association and speech.

One of the main forms of implementation of the zero tolerance policy by the Labour Government is through the introduction of anti-social behaviour orders discussed at p. 331. Zero tolerance policing was spearheaded in the UK in Cleveland. Home Office statistics suggest that the policing method was successful in reducing offences targeted by the policy. Between January and December 1997 reported burglary in Cleveland dropped by 26.1 per cent, robbery by 25.2 per cent and overall reported crime by 18 per cent. This was the highest reported reduction in England and Wales. Crime in the Middlesbrough area is at a six-year low, with a total of 20,312 reports compared with 25,876 in 1991. At the same time, the area has seen a threefold increase in the incidence of stop and searches. Its clear-up rate had also declined from 27 per cent in 1993 to 25 per cent in 1997, a figure that is 3 per cent below the British average.

▶ ANSWERING QUESTIONS

1 Deborah, aged 15, has been seen by a police officer attacking an old man. He arrests her and takes her to the police station.
(i) Explain the rules concerning the police powers to question Deborah about the offence.
(ii) If Deborah is charged and prosecuted, which courts are likely to deal with her case (excluding possible appeals)?
(iii) What sentencing powers do the courts have in respect of her offence?

(i) Note that because of Deborah's age, you are talking about a young offender and not an adult. The general rules concerning a suspect in the police station are explained in chapter 9, but you also need to include the particular rules that apply to Deborah because of her age, which are detailed at p. 341.
(ii) Special rules apply to the trial of young offenders, which are discussed in this chapter at p. 343.
(iii) If the legislation on referral orders has been brought into force then it will be important to know whether this is Deborah's first conviction. If it is Deborah's first conviction then she will automatically get a referral order (discussed at p. 349). If she is a repeat offender the other sentencing powers will be important. The material in chapter 10 covering the statutory guidance on sentencing is relevant here. Note that this is a crime of violence. As to the specific sentences that could be passed, starting with the most serious, custodial sentences, note that Deborah cannot be sent to prison – if custody is felt to be appropriate she would be given a detention and training order. As regards a community sentence, supervision orders and attendance centre orders are specific to young offenders, but the other forms of community sentences discussed in chapter 10 are also relevant here. She

might be given a reparation order, action plan order or be referred to a youth offender panel. The maximum length of sentences is often shorter for young offenders. A fine is a possibility, and if imposed, will have to be paid by Deborah's parents. You might also want to mention the fact that her parents may themselves be subject to sanctions, such as being bound over or receiving a parenting order.

Reading on the Internet

Research carried out for the Home Office on referral orders (*Youth Justice: the Introduction of Referral Orders into the Youth Justice System* (2001), RDS Occasional Paper No. 70) is available on the Home Office website:

http://www.homeoffice.gov.uk/rds/pdfs/occ70-youth.pdf

12 The civil justice system

The civil justice system is designed to sort out disputes between individuals or organizations. One party, known as the claimant, sues the other, called the defendant, usually for money they claim is owed or for compensation for a harm to their interests. Typical examples might be the victim of a car accident suing the driver of the car for compensation, or one business suing another for payment due on goods supplied. The burden of proof is usually on the claimant, who must prove their case on a balance of probabilities – that it is more likely than not. This is a lower standard of proof than the 'beyond reasonable doubt' test used by the criminal courts and, for this reason, it is possible to be acquitted of a criminal charge yet still be found to have breached the civil law. This happened to the celebrity O.J. Simpson in the US who, having been acquitted of murdering his ex-wife and her friend by the criminal courts, was successfully sued in the civil courts for damages by the victim's family.

Major changes have been made to the civil justice system in recent years. After the Civil Justice Review of 1988, reforms were made by the Courts and Legal Services Act 1990. Following continued criticism of the civil justice system, the previous Conservative Government ten years later appointed Lord Woolf to carry out a far-reaching review of the civil justice system. Lord Woolf's inquiry is the 63rd such review in 100 years. Lord Woolf made far-reaching recommendations in his report, *Access to Justice*, which was published in 1996. As with the Civil Justice Review, his aim was to reduce the cost, delay and complexity of the system and increase access to justice. Most of his recommendations were implemented in April 1999.

▶ HISTORY

The legal process for civil cases developed in a rather piecemeal fashion, responding to different needs at different times with the result that, at the end of the eighteenth century, civil matters were being dealt with by

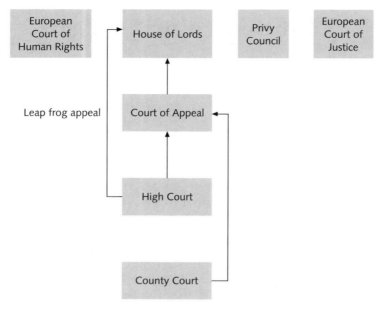

Figure 12.1 The Civil Court System

several different series of courts. Three common law courts, supplemented by the Court of Chancery, did most of the work, but there was also a Court of Admiralty and the ecclesiastical (church) courts. They had separate, but often overlapping, jurisdictions and between them administered three different 'systems' of law: civilian law (based on Roman law), common law and equity. The courts were also largely centralized in London, making access difficult for those in the provinces.

With no coordination of the increasingly complex court system, inefficiency, incompetence and delays were common and the courts acquired a reputation for binding themselves up in cumbersome procedural rules. Until well into the nineteenth century, litigation in the higher courts was an extravagance which could be afforded only by the very rich and, in many respects, the system benefited the judges and the legal professions far more than litigants. Reform began in 1846, with the creation of a nationwide system of county courts, designed to provide cheaper, quicker justice at a local level for businessmen. This was followed, in the early 1870s, by the creation of one Supreme Court consisting of the High Court, the Court of Appeal and the Crown Court, although the High Court was still divided into five divisions. In 1881, these were reduced to three: Queen's Bench, Chancery, and what is now known as the Family Division.

The civil courts

There are currently around 300 county courts concerned exclusively with civil work. About 170 of them are designated as divorce county courts and, thereby, have jurisdiction to hear undefended divorces and cases concerning adoption and guardianship.

In the High Court, the three divisions mentioned above remain today – they act as separate courts, with judges usually working within one division only. Lord Woolf recommended that these divisions should remain. The Family Division hears cases concerning marriage, children and the family, such as divorce, adoption and wills. The Chancery Division deals with matters of finance and property, such as tax and bankruptcy. The Queen's Bench Division is the biggest of the three, with the most varied jurisdiction. The major part of its work is handling those contract and tort cases which are unsuitable for the county courts (see below). Sitting as the Divisional Court of the Queen's Bench, its judges also hear certain criminal appeals (originating primarily from the magistrates' courts) and applications for judicial review – for details see chapter 14. High Court judges usually sit alone, but the Divisional Court is so important that two or three judges sit together.

Trials in the High Court are heard either in London or in one of the 26 provincial trial centres. In theory, they are all presided over by High Court judges, but in fact there are not enough High Court judges to cope with the case load. Some cases, therefore, have to be dealt with by circuit judges and others by barristers sitting as part-time, temporary, deputy judges.

Following the Woolf reforms, trial centres have been identified, headed by a Designated Civil Justice. They report to the Head of Civil Justice, a position currently held by Sir Richard Scott.

Although most civil cases are dealt with by either the county courts or the High Court, magistrates' courts have a limited civil jurisdiction, and some types of cases are tried by tribunals.

The civil justice system before April 1999

Before the implementation of the Woolf reforms, there were two separate sets of civil procedure rules: the Rules of the Supreme Court in the 'White Book' for the High Court and the Court of Appeal, and the County Court Rules in the 'Green Book' for the county courts. High Court actions were started with a writ, county court ones by a summons, but there were also specialized procedures which required specific documents and formalities to be used. These documents were served on the defendant to a case, and informed the person that an action was being brought against them. The rules on serving documents were fairly restrictive and ignored modern modes of communication. Defendants had to acknowledge service. The claimant served a statement of claim if bringing an action in the High Court, or the particulars of a claim in the county court. Both were formal pleadings which outlined the facts and legal basis of the action and the remedy sought. The defendant responded with a defence. Either party could request more details from the other, in a document known as 'a request for further and better particulars'. These would then be supplied. Each party provided the other with a list of the documents which they had in relation to the action. The parties could ask to see some or all of this material, a process known as discovery. The trial was conducted along adversarial lines, with each side calling its own witnesses and cross-examining those of the other. As in a criminal hearing, judges relied on the parties to present the evidence, rather than making their own investigations.

The case could be settled out of court at any point in the civil process. The defendant could at any time during the process make a payment into court, which the claimant could accept as settlement of the claim. If they did not accept it, the process continued as before, but if the case continued to trial and the claimant won but was awarded less than the sum paid in, they had to pay the defendant's costs from the time of the payment in.

The Civil Justice Review was set up in 1985 by the Lord Chancellor in response to public criticism of the delay, cost and complexity of the civil court system. Unusually, it was chaired by a non-lawyer, Maurice Hodgson, the Chairman of Bhs, and only a minority of its members were lawyers. They therefore tended to be less pro-lawyer than previous committees that had been dominated by judges and barristers, which may explain why many of the Review's more innovative suggestions were ignored or only partially implemented. Some important changes were made to the division of work between the county courts and High Court by the Courts and Legal Services Act 1990 in response to some of the proposals of the 1985 Review.

One of the Review's main findings was that too many cases were being heard in the High Court rather than the cheaper and quicker county courts, often for relatively small amounts of money: in 1987, half of all money claims started in the Queen's Bench Division were for less than £3,000. Consequently, the Review aimed to increase the number of cases heard in the county courts, thereby freeing High Court time for public law cases, specialist litigation and trials considered to be of importance, complexity and substance.

As a result, following the Courts and Legal Services Act 1990, claims worth under £3,000 were automatically dealt with by the Small Claims procedure of the county court, the amount having been increased at the beginning of 1996 from £1,000. All personal injury cases worth less than £50,000 had to be brought in the county court. Both the county court and the High Court had jurisdiction over any other tort or contract case. There was no longer a fixed maximum limit for cases heard in the county court, nor a minimum one for the High Court. In general though, cases worth less than £25,000 would be commenced in the county court, and cases worth more than £50,000 in the High Court; for actions falling between £25,000 and £50,000, the proper court would depend on the complexity and importance of the case.

Problems with the civil justice system before April 1999

Lord Woolf was appointed by the previous Conservative Government to carry out a far reaching review of the civil justice system. In *Access to Justice: Final Report*, published in 1996, he stated that a civil justice system should:

• be just in the results it delivers;
• be fair in the way it treats litigants;
• offer appropriate procedures at a reasonable cost;
• deal with cases with reasonable speed;
• be understandable to those who use it;
• be responsive to the needs of those who use it;
• provide as much certainty as the nature of particular cases allows;
• be effective, adequately resourced and organized.

Lord Woolf concluded that the system at the time failed to achieve all those goals. It is possible that this failure is inevitable, as some of the aims conflict with others. A system based on cost-efficiency alone would make it difficult to justify claims for comparatively small sums, yet these cases are very important to the parties involved, and wide access to justice is vital. Promoting efficiency in terms of speed can also conflict with the need for fairness. Making the courts more accessible could lead to a flood of cases which would make it impossible to provide a speedy resolution and keep costs down. One practical example of the conflict between different aims is that the availability of legal aid to one party, one of the aims of widening access to justice, can put pressure on the other side if they are funding themselves, and so clash with the need for fairness.

In addition, changes made to the civil justice system may have effects outside it – making it easier to bring personal injury actions, for example, could push up the costs of insurance, and it has been suggested that in the US this has led to unwillingness on the part of doctors to perform any risky medical treatment.

It is impossible to resolve all of these conflicts and a successful legal system must simply aim for the best possible balance. Lord Scarman has commented:

> To be acceptable to ordinary people, I believe [the] legal process in litigation must be designed to encourage, first, settlement by agreement; secondly, open and speedy trial if agreement is not forthcoming. In other words, justice, not truth is its purpose. It is against the criteria of justice and fairness that the system must be assessed.

In the final analysis, it is for the Government to decide the balance they wish to strike, and how much they are prepared to spend on it. While conflicting interests may mean it is impossible to achieve a civil justice system that satisfies everyone, there were serious concerns that the civil justice system before April 1999 was giving satisfaction to only a small minority of users for a range of reasons which will be considered in turn.

Too expensive

Research carried out for Lord Woolf's review found that one side's costs exceeded the amount in dispute in over 40 per cent of cases where the claim was for under £12,500. Where the claim was for between £12,500 and £25,000 average costs were between 40 per cent and 95 per cent of the claim. The bill for one claim of just £2,000 came to £69,295; that for another of £1,000 was £26,398. The survey concluded that the simplest cases often incurred the highest costs in proportion to the value of the claim.

Because of the complexity of the process, lawyers were usually needed and High Court litigation especially is not a game for the inexperienced, so barristers often draft the pleadings and advise on the evidence. This is expensive. The sheer length of civil proceedings also affected the size of the bill at the end.

Lord Woolf has said that, 15 years ago, his report would not have been necessary, because most lawyers made their money from other work, such as conveyancing, seeing litigation as a loss-maker that they would only undertake reluctantly. But, with the huge increase in the number of lawyers combined with the recession in the property market at the end of the 1980s, lawyers suddenly found that litigation could generate a steady income. He found that costs were now so high that even big companies were wary, with some preferring to fight cases in New York.

Delays

The Civil Justice Review observed that the system was overstretched, and the time between the incident giving rise to the claim and the trial could be up to three years for the county courts and five for the High Court. Research carried out for Lord Woolf found the worst delays in personal injury and medical negligence cases, with these actions taking a median time of 54 and 61 months respectively. The average waiting time for a county court claim was 79 weeks. Time limits were laid down for every stage of an action but both lawyers and the courts disregarded them. Often time limits were waived by the lawyers to create an opportunity to negotiate, which was reasonable, but the problem was that there was no effective control of when and why it was done. The High Court's long vacation (the two months during the summer when the judges do not sit) also contributed to delay.

According to the Civil Justice Review, long delays placed intolerable psychological and financial burdens on accident victims and undermined the justice of the trial, by making it more difficult to gather evidence which was then unreliable because witnesses had to remember the events of several years before. The overall result was to lower public estimation of the legal system as a whole.

The reforms made by the Courts and Legal Services Act 1990 had done little to ease delays. The main complaints were that county courts had not been given enough administrators to cope with their new workload, so High Court delays had simply been transferred to the county courts; the county courts were understaffed and underfunded to cope with the increase in business.

Injustice

Usually an out-of-court settlement is negotiated before the litigants ever reach the trial stage. For every 9,000 personal injury cases commenced, only 300 are submitted for judgment. Outside personal injuries, for every 100,000 writs issued before 1999, fewer than 300 actually came for trial. An out-of-court settlement can have the advantage of providing a quick end to the dispute, and a reduction in costs – although these start to build up from the time each side consults a lawyer – the trial itself is by far the most expensive part. For the claimant, a settlement means they are sure of getting something, and do not have to risk losing the case altogether and probably having to pay the other side's costs as well as their own; but they must weigh this up against the chances of being awarded a better settlement if the case goes to trial and they win. The defendant risks the possibility that they might have won and therefore had to pay nothing, or that they may be paying more than the judge would have awarded if the claimant had won the case, against the chance that the claimant wins and is awarded more than the settlement would have cost.

The high number of out-of-court settlements created injustice, because the parties usually held very unequal bargaining positions. In the first place, one party might be in a better financial position than the other, and therefore under less pressure to keep costs down by settling quickly.

Secondly, as Galanter's 1974 study revealed, litigants could often be divided into 'one-shotters' and 'repeat players'. One-shotters are individuals involved in litigation for probably the only time in their life, for whom the procedure is unfamiliar and traumatic; the case is very important to them and tends to occupy most of their thoughts while it continues. Repeat players, on the other hand, include companies and businesses (particularly insurance companies), for whom litigation is routine. They are used to working with the law and lawyers and, while they obviously want to win the case for financial reasons, they do not have the same emotional investment in it as the individual one-shotter. Where a repeat player and a one-shotter are on opposing sides – as is often the case in personal injury litigation, where an individual is fighting an insurance company – the repeat player is likely to have the upper hand in out-of-court bargaining.

A third factor was highlighted by Hazel Genn's 1987 study of negotiated settlements of accident claims. She found that having a non-specialist lawyer could seriously prejudice a client's interests when an out-of-court settlement is made. A non-specialist may be unfamiliar with court procedure and reluctant to fight the case in court. They may, therefore, not encourage their client to hold out against an unsatisfactory settlement. Specialist lawyers on the other side may take advantage of this inexperience, putting on pressure for the acceptance of a low settlement. Repeat players are more likely to have access to their own specialist lawyers, whereas, for the one-shotter, finding a suitable lawyer can be something of a lottery, since they have little information on which to base their choice.

Clearly, these factors did affect the fairness of out-of-court settlements. In court, the judge would treat the parties as equals, but for out-of-court negotiations one party often had a very obvious advantage.

The rules on payments into court increased the unfairness of the pre-trial procedures. As Zander (1988) observed, the rule was 'highly favourable' to the defendant, putting extra pressure on the claimant to accept an offer.

Pressures of time caused injustice. Special continuous trial centres were set up, in which most of the business was heard very quickly, thus allowing the court to hear a number of cases each day. This could lead to an emphasis on processing people through the system at speed, rather than examining the evidence and making a judicial decision. One research report put the average court time spent on local authority repossession cases at 90 seconds, and one judge described the judicial role in such cases as 'purely administrative, somebody independent of the local authority to rubber-stamp the document'.

The adversarial process

Many problems resulted from the adversarial process which encouraged tactical manoeuvring rather than cooperation. It would be far simpler and cheaper for each side to state precisely what it alleged in the pleadings, disclose all the documents they held, and give the other side copies of their witness statements. Attitudes did appear to be slowly changing, with a growing appreciation that the public interest demanded justice be provided as quickly and economically as possible. Some of the procedural rules, for example on expert witnesses, were changed and there was less scope for tactical manoeuvring.

Emphasis on oral evidence

Too much emphasis was placed on oral evidence at trial. This may have been appropriate when juries were commonly used in civil proceedings, but in the twentieth century much of the information the judge needed could be provided on paper and read before the trial. Oral evidence slowed down proceedings, adding to cost and delays.

There were also doubts about the usefulness of oral evidence. In particular, there was a danger that the ordinary witness, often giving evidence years after the events occurred, would be so intimidated by the nature of the questioning and the formality of the proceedings that their evidence would appear far less credible than should be the case; while the evidence of an expert witness familiar with courtroom antics might well have an aura of authority which it did not deserve.

There had been a limited move away from oral evidence – for example, a 1995 Practice Direction provided that witness statements would be accepted as the evidence-in-chief of that witness.

Enforcement

It was sometimes difficult to enforce judgments against debtors; responsibility for this was largely left to the parties.

Changes in jurisdiction

Though designed to ease the problems of the civil system, the reforms implemented by the 1990 Courts and Legal Services Act to the jurisdiction rules of the High Court and county court had created some new ones of their own. The changes had caused delay in the county courts (see p. 362). There was also a suggestion that the High Court had been preserved as a small, elite court hearing only a few public and commercial cases, while smaller cases, such as accidents at work or on the roads, wrongful arrests, contracts of employment or tenancies and housing conditions – in other words, the problems of the average citizen – were getting second-class justice in the county court.

Lawyers specializing in personal injury litigation (most of whom would previously have been dealing with the High Court) said problems in county courts were considerable: papers lost, letters and phone calls unanswered, inadequate pre-trial procedures, too few administrators and a shortage of experienced, informed judges.

Specialist personal injury firms also regretted the loss of direct control over the running of cases they enjoyed in the High Court. While solicitors could, with the court's permission, prepare and serve their own documents in county court actions, it was not always possible to do so, and there were long delays in some cities as summonses were sent to typing centres. Even if solicitors took on the work themselves, they had to keep in touch with the court; telephones were often busy and correspondence went unanswered. Many solicitors reported that contact by letter or telephone was so difficult that they sent employees to the county court in person several times a week to check on progress with cases.

Not all county courts had the same procedural practices and differing procedures created confusion for firms dealing with a number of different county courts. Some solicitors avoided problematic county courts and, as the news spread about courts to avoid, delays could build up in the more popular courts. There was also concern that the quality of judges would be lower, and that the damages awarded would be smaller than in the High Court.

The civil justice system after April 1999

On 26 April 1999 new Civil Procedure Rules and accompanying Practice Directions came into force. The new rules apply to any proceedings commenced after that date. They constitute the most fundamental reform of the civil justice system of the twentieth century, introducing the main recommendations of Lord Woolf in his final report, *Access to Justice*. He described his proposals as providing 'a new landscape for civil justice for the twenty-first century'.

The Woolf Report was the product of two years' intensive consultation, and was written with the help of expert working parties of experienced practitioners and academics. The recommendations of the Report received universal support from the senior judiciary, the Bar, the Law Society, consumer organizations and the media. In 1996, Sir Richard Scott was appointed as Head of Civil Justice with responsibility for implementing the reforms. The Civil Procedure Act 1997 was passed to implement the first stages of the Woolf Report. Following their election into office, the Labour Government set up their own review of the civil justice system and of Lord Woolf's proposed reforms. They quite reasonably wanted a second opinion before adopting the policies of their predecessors on those issues. The review was chaired by Sir Peter Middleton and took four months to complete. The final report was essentially in favour of implementation of Lord Woolf's proposals. His report placed an emphasis on the financial implications of the proposals and in particular the opportunities for cost-cutting. In November 1998, an intensive period of training for judges and court staff began to prepare them for the changes, whilst the Treasury made available an additional £2 million to implement the reforms.

The reforms aim to eliminate unnecessary cost, delay and complexity in the civil justice system. The general approach of Lord Woolf is reflected in his statement: 'If "time and money are no object" was the right approach in the past, then it certainly is not today. Both lawyers and judges, in making decisions as to the conduct of litigation, must take into account more than they do at present, questions of cost and time and the means of the parties.' Lord Woolf has suggested that the reforms should lead to a reduction in legal bills by as much as 75 per cent, though it might also mean some lawyers would lose their livelihoods.

The ultimate goal is to change fundamentally the litigation culture. Thus, the first rule of the new Civil Procedure Rules lays down an overriding objective which is to underpin the whole system. This overriding objective is that the rules should enable the courts to deal with cases 'justly'. This objective prevails over all other rules in case of a conflict. The parties and their legal representatives are expected to assist the judges in achieving this objective. The Woolf report had heavily criticized practitioners, who were accused of manipulating the old system for their own convenience and causing delay and expense to both their clients and the users of the system as a whole. Lord Woolf felt that a change in attitude among the lawyers was vital for the new rules to succeed. According to r. 1.1(2):

Dealing with a case justly includes, so far as is practicable –
a. ensuring that the parties are on an equal footing;
b. saving expense;
c. dealing with the case in ways which are proportionate –
    i.   to the amount of money involved;
    ii. to the importance of the case;
    iii. to the complexity of the issues; and
    iv. to the financial position of each party;
d. ensuring that it is dealt with expeditiously and fairly; and
e. allotting to it an appropriate share of the Court's resources, while taking into account the need to allot resources to other cases.

The emphasis of the new rules is on avoiding litigation through pre-trial settlements. Litigation is to be viewed as a last resort, with the court having a continuing obligation to encourage and facilitate settlement. Lord Woolf had observed that it was strange that, although the majority of disputes ended in settlement, the old rules had been mainly directed towards preparation for trial. Thus the new rules put a greater emphasis on preparing cases for settlement rather than a trial.

The new approach to civil procedure will now be examined in more detail.

Civil Procedure Rules

The Lord Chancellor appointed the Civil Procedure Rules Committee to produce and maintain one unified procedural code for both the county court and the High Court. This produced the new Civil Procedure Rules which came into force in April 1999 and replaced the Rules of the Supreme Court and the County Court Rules. The new rules are simpler than their predecessors, providing a broad framework of general application rather than detailed rules covering every contingency. These framework rules are then fleshed out by a number of Practice Directions. There has been an attempt to write the rules in plain English, replacing old-fashioned terminology with more accessible terms. Lord Woolf hoped that the change in language would help to support a change in attitude, away from a legalistic, technical interpretation of words designed to give one party an advantage over their opponent, towards an attitude which was open and fair according to the overriding objective of the new rules.

While the new rules introduce some radical changes to the civil justice system, they also inherit much from the old system. In outline the procedure is as follows. Almost all proceedings start with the same document called a claim form. This replaces the writ for the High Court and the summons for the County Court, and other specialist documents. The procedure for starting an action is thus undoubtedly simpler than under the old system. The claim form informs the defendant that an action is being brought against them. When claimants are making a claim for money, they must provide a statement as to the value of the claim in the claim form.

The Practice Direction supplementing Part 7 of the new Civil Procedure Rules (*How to start proceedings – the Claim Form*) specifies in which court proceedings should be started. For non-personal injury actions, a claim may be started in the High Court where the claimant expects to recover more than £15,000. For personal injury actions, a claim can only be started in the High Court where the claimant expects to recover at least £50,000 for pain, suffering and loss of amenity.

The claim form is served on the defendant to a case. The methods of service have been liberalized to reflect modern modes of communication, including the use of fax and e-mails. Service will normally be carried out by the court through postage by first class post, unless a party notifies the court that they will serve the documents. Defendants must acknowledge service. The claimant (known before 1999 as the plaintiff) must then serve on the defendant the particulars of claim (previously called the statement of claim in the High Court).

The defendant should respond within 14 days by either filing an acknowledgement of service or a defence with the court. If the defendant fails to do either of these within that period of time, the claimant can enter judgment in default against the defendant (r. 12.3). The mechanics of pleading a defence are now regulated more strictly. Defendants may

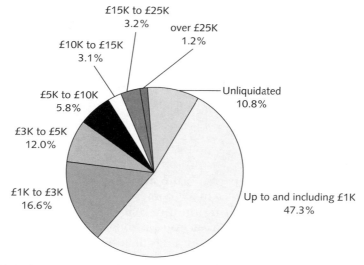

£15K to £25K
3.2%

over £25K
1.2%

£10K to £15K
3.1%

£5K to £10K
5.8%

£3K to £5K
12.0%

£1K to £3K
16.6%

Unliquidated
10.8%

Up to and including £1K
47.3%

Figure 12.2 County courts: Claims issued by amount of claim, 1999[1]

[1] Figures based on three months' sample data from selected county courts
Source: *Judicial Statistics 1999*

no longer simply deny an allegation, but must state their reasons for the denial and, if they intend to put forward a different version of events from that given by the claimant, then they must state their own version.

If the defendant files a defence, the court will serve an allocation questionnaire on each party (r. 24.4(1)). This is designed to enable the court to allocate each claim to one of the three tracks discussed at p. 372.

The disclosure procedures (previously known as discovery) are then followed, as discussed below. Either party may seek more details from the other, through a 'request for information'. This procedure merges the old system of interrogatories and requests for further and better particulars. The new rules adopt an amended version of the payment into court procedures discussed at p. 360, which are now called 'Part 36 payments'. If the case is not settled out of court, the case proceeds to trial.

The different formal documents are described as the statement of case, while in the past they were called the pleadings. All statements of case must be verified by a statement of truth. This is a statement signed by the claimant (or their legal representative), in the following words: 'I believe that the facts stated in these particulars of claim are true.' The purpose of such a statement is to prevent a party from putting in facts for purely tactical purposes which they have no intention of relying upon. If a party makes a false statement in a statement of case verified by a statement of truth, the party will be guilty of contempt of court (r. 28.14).

Either party can apply for a summary judgment on the ground that the claim or defence has no real prospect of success. The court can also reach this conclusion on its own initiative.

The emphasis of the new procedural rules is to encourage an early settlement of proceedings. A MORI poll of 100 solicitors carried out in 2000 found that 76 per cent of solicitors believed that the reforms had increased the chances of an early settlement. The majority felt that the reforms had cut the amount of litigation. Between May 1999 and January 2000 there was a 25 per cent reduction in the number of cases issued in the county courts compared with the same period the previous year.

Pre-action protocols

The pre-trial procedure is, perhaps, the most important area of the civil process, since few civil cases actually come to trial. To push the parties into behaving reasonably during the pre-trial stage, Lord Woolf recommended the development of pre-action protocols to lay down a code of conduct for this stage of the proceedings. The pre-action protocols that have been produced to date cover such areas of practice as personal injury, medical negligence and housing cases. They were developed in consultation with most of the key players in the relevant fields, including legal, health and insurance professionals. They are a major innovation and aim to encourage:

- more pre-action contact between the parties;
- an earlier and fuller exchange of information;
- improved pre-action investigation;
- a settlement before proceedings have commenced.

They strive to achieve this through establishing a timetable for the exchange of information, by setting standards for the content of correspondence, providing schedules of documents that should be disclosed along with a mechanism for agreeing a single joint expert. This should lead to the parties being better informed as to the merits of their case so that they will be in a position to settle cases fairly, so reducing the need for litigation. If settlement is not reached the parties should be able to proceed to litigation on a more informed basis. Pre-action protocols should also enable proceedings to run to timetable, and efficiently, if litigation proves to be necessary.

As regards the clinical disputes pre-action protocol, which is concerned with medical negligence litigation, Lord Woolf identified that the major cause of delay and escalating costs in such cases occurred at the pre-action stage. This pre-action protocol seeks to reduce delay and costs by encouraging a culture of 'openness' when something has gone wrong with a patient's treatment and by providing general guidance on how 'openness' can be achieved.

Compliance with a pre-action protocol is not compulsory, but if a party unreasonably refuses to comply, then this can be taken into account when the court makes orders for costs. It may be that these protocols will need 'sharper teeth' in order to be effective.

Alternative Dispute Resolution

At various stages in a dispute's history, the court will actively promote settlement by Alternative Dispute Resolution (ADR). For a detailed discussion of ADR in the English legal system see p. 441. There is a general statement in the new rules that the court's duty to further the overriding objective by active case management includes both encouraging the parties to use an alternative dispute resolution procedure (if the court considers that appropriate) and facilitating the use of that procedure (r. 1.4(2)(e)). Also, when filling in the allocation questionnaire, the parties can request a one-month stay of proceedings while they try to settle the case by ADR or other means (r. 26.4). The parties will have to show that they genuinely attempted to resolve their dispute through ADR and have not just paid lip service to the ideal, as has been the tendency in the past.

Case management

This is the most significant innovation of the 1999 reforms. Case management means that the court will be the active manager of the litigation. The main aim of this approach is to bring cases to trial quickly and efficiently. Traditionally it has been left to the parties and their lawyers to manage the cases. In 1995, the courts had made a move towards case management following a Practice Direction encouraging such methods, but it was only with the new Civil Procedure Rules that case management came fully into force. The new Rules firmly place the management of a case in the hands of the judges, with r. 1.4 emphasizing that the court's duty is to take a proactive role in the management of each case. The judges are given considerable discretion in the exercise of their case management role. Lord Woolf does not feel that this will undermine the adversarial tradition, but he sees the legal professions fulfilling their adversarial functions in a more controlled environment.

Once proceedings have commenced, the court's powers of case management will be triggered by the filing of a defence. When the defence has been filed and case management has started, the parties are on a moving train, trial dates will be fixed and will be difficult to postpone, and litigants will not normally be able to slow down or stop unless they settle. The court first needs to allocate the case to one of the three tracks: the small claims track, the fast-track or the multi-track (r. 24.6(1)), which will determine the future conduct of the proceedings. To determine which is the appropriate track the court will serve an allocation questionnaire on each party. The answers to this questionnaire will form the basis for deciding the appropriate track. When considering the allocation questionnaire, the judge will determine whether a case should be subject to summary judgment, or whether a stay of proceedings should be given for alternative dispute resolution; and if neither of these matters apply, whether there should be an allocation hearing called or whether the matter can be the subject of a paper determination of the allocation to a particular track.

The three tracks

The court allocates the case to the most appropriate track depending primarily on the financial value of the claim, but other factors that can be taken into account include the case's importance and complexity (r. 26.6). Normally:

- small claims track cases deal with actions with a value of less than £5,000;
- fast-track cases deal with actions of a value between £5,000 and £15,000;
- multi-track cases deal with actions with a value higher than £15,000.

The three tracks will now be considered in turn.

The small claims track. The handling of small claims is largely unchanged by the Woolf reforms. In the small claims track, directions will be issued for each case providing a date for the hearing and an estimate of the hearing time, unless the case requires a preliminary hearing appointment to assist the parties in the conduct of the case. This track was previously known as the small claims court, though it was never actually a separate court, but a procedure used by county courts to deal with relatively small claims. It was introduced in response to a report from the Consumers Association in 1967 claiming that county courts were being used primarily as a debt collection agency for businesses: 89.2 per cent of the summonses were taken out by firms and only 9 per cent by individuals, who were put off by costs and complexity.

Established in 1973, this special procedure aims to provide a cheap, simple mechanism for resolving small-scale consumer disputes. Disclosure is dispensed with and if the litigation continues to trial, it is usually held in private rather than in open court. The hearing is simple and informal, with few rules about the admissibility or presentation of evidence. No experts may be used without leave. It is usually a very quick process, with 60 per cent of hearings taking less than 30 minutes. Costs are limited except where, by consent, a case with a financial value such that it would normally be allocated to the fast track was allocated to the small claims track. The procedure is designed to make it easy for parties to represent themselves without the aid of a lawyer, and legal aid for representation is not available. Under the Lay Representatives (Rights of Audience) Order 1992 made under s. 11 of the Courts and Legal Services Act 1990, a party can choose to be represented by a lay person, though the party must also attend.

There is little right of appeal: the judge's decision can be set aside but only on the ground that there has been a serious irregularity affecting the proceedings or the court made a mistake of law. As the court records of arbitrations are concise and do not usually state the reason for the award, the proceedings rarely give rise to an appeal. Approximately 5,000 cases are appealed each year, but there is a possibility that these limited grounds of appeal may breach the Human Rights Act 1998. The Lord Chancellor's Department has now published a consultation paper on small claims appeals. The plan is to remove the limitation on the appeal grounds; introduce a requirement for permission to appeal; give the parties the right to an oral hearing on the substantive appeal; and treat the appeal as a review rather than a rehearing.

There are around 80,000 small claim actions each year. The procedure is quicker, simpler and cheaper than the full county court process, which is helpful to both litigants and the overworked court system. It gives individuals and small businesses a useful lever against creditors or for consumer complaints. Without it, threats to sue over small amounts would be ignored on the basis that going to court would cost more than the value of the debt or compensation claimed. Public confidence is also increased, by proving that the legal system is not only accessible to the rich and powerful.

The fast-track. Fast-track cases will normally be dealt with by the county court. Upon allocation to the fast track the court gives directions for the management of the case, and sets a timetable for the disclosure of documents, the exchange of witness statements, the exchange (and number) of expert reports, and the trial date or a period within which the trial will take place, which will be no more than 30 weeks later (compared to an average of 80 weeks before 1999).

A Practice Direction gives an example of a typical timetable that a court may give:

- disclosure: 4 weeks;
- exchange of witness statements: 10 weeks;
- exchange of experts' reports: 14 weeks;
- hearing: 30 weeks.

Although the parties can vary certain matters by agreement, such as disclosure or the exchange of witness statements, the rules are quite clear than an application must be made to court if a party wishes to vary the date for the trial.

Under this track the maximum length of the trial is normally one day. The relevant Practice Direction states that the judge will normally have read the papers in the trial bundle and may dispense with an opening address. Witness statements will usually stand as evidence in chief. Oral expert evidence will be limited to one expert per party in relation to any expert field and expert evidence will be limited to two expert fields.

In an attempt to keep lawyers' bills down, fixed costs for 'fast-track' trials have been introduced, but the introduction of pre-trial fixed costs has been delayed until additional information is available to inform the development of the revised costs regime. Lord Woolf had recommended that there should be a £2,500 limit on costs for fast-track cases (though clients could enter into a written agreement to pay more to their solicitors). Apart from the trial itself, litigants are still committing themselves to open-ended payment by the hour, which Lord Woolf described as being equivalent to handing out a blank cheque. He observed: 'If you and I are having our house repaired, we don't do it on a time and materials basis, because we know it will be a disaster. There is no incentive for the builder to do it in the least time and do it with the most economical materials.'

The multi-track. Upon allocation to the multi-track, the court can give directions for the management of the case and set a timetable for those steps to be taken. Alternatively, for heavier cases, the court may fix a case management conference or a pre-trial review or both. Unlike the fast-track, the court does not at this stage automatically set a trial date or a period within which the trial will take place. Instead it will fix this as soon as it is practicable to do so. Thus, this track offers individual case management with tailor-made directions according to the needs of the case. The High Court only hears multi-track cases.

A proactive approach
Gone are the days when the court waited for the lawyers to bring the case back before it or allowed the lawyers to dictate without question the number of witnesses or the amount of costs incurred. In managing litigation the court must have regard to the overriding objective, set out in Part 1, which is to deal with cases justly. To fulfil this key objective of the reformed civil justice system, the court is required to:

- identify the issues at an early stage;
- decide promptly which issues require full investigation and dispose summarily of the others;
- encourage the parties to seek alternative dispute resolution where appropriate;
- encourage the parties to cooperate with each other in the conduct of the procedures;
- help the parties to settle the whole or part of the case;
- decide the order in which issues are to be resolved;
- fix timetables or otherwise control the progress of the case;

- consider whether the likely benefits of taking a particular step will justify the cost of taking it;
- deal with a case without the parties' attendance at court if this is possible;
- make appropriate use of technology;
- give directions to ensure that the trial of a case proceeds quickly and efficiently.

Disclosure

Before the 1999 reforms, disclosure was known as 'discovery'. The procedure used to involve each party providing the other with a list of all the documents which they had in relation to the action. The parties could then ask to see some or all of this material. The process could be time-consuming and costly. Pre-action disclosure was also available in claims for personal injury and death. Lord Woolf recommended that disclosure should generally be limited to documents which were readily available and which to a 'material extent' adversely affected or supported a party's case, though this could be extended for multi-track cases. This change would have altered significantly the disclosure process and risked going against the philosophy of openness between the parties generally advocated by Lord Woolf. He also favoured extending pre-action disclosure to be available for all proceedings and against people who would not have been parties to the future proceedings. However, the new Civil Procedure Rules are actually very similar to the old rules. These require the disclosure of documents on which they rely or which adversely affected or supported a party's case. It is not necessary for this impact to be to a 'material extent'. As under the old rules, additional disclosure will be ordered where it is 'necessary in order to dispose fairly of the claim or to save costs'. The availability of pre-action disclosure was not extended despite the fact that the Civil Procedure Act 1997 provided for its extension. The pre-action protocols are designed to ensure voluntary disclosure is made between likely parties. It seems that the Government wishes to see how the pre-action protocols operate in practice before implementing such changes.

Sanctions

Tough rules on sanctions give the courts stringent powers to enforce the new rules on civil procedure to ensure that litigation is pursued diligently. The two main sanctions are an adverse award of costs and an order for a case or part of a case to be struck out. These sanctions were available under the old rules, but the novelty of the new regime lies in the commitment to enforce strict compliance. There is an increasing willingness of the courts to manage cases with a stick rather than a carrot. The courts can treat the standards set in the pre-action protocols as the normal approach to pre-action conduct and have the power to penalize parties for non-compliance.

One of the most significant changes to the civil system made by the Woolf reforms concerned the approach to legal costs. Under the old system there was a basic principle that the loser paid the winner's costs. This principle was only departed from in exceptional circumstances. Although this principle still exists under the new system, it is now treated only as a starting point which the court can readily depart from. Where a party has not complied with court directions, particularly as to time, they can be penalized by being ordered to pay heavier costs, or by losing the right to have some or all of their costs paid.

A party who fails to comply with the case timetable or court orders may be struck out. The court has power to strike out a party's statement of case, or part of it where there has been a failure to comply with a rule, Practice Direction or court order (r. 3.4). This power can be exercised on an application from a party, or on the court's own initiative. Mere delay will be enough in itself to deprive a party of the power to bring or defend an action.

It is up to the defaulting party to apply for relief from sanctions using the procedure contained in r. 3.9. This is dramatically different to the previous state of affairs where a party in default of a court order was not the subject of any sanction unless the innocent party brought the matter to the court's attention.

Where, during the trial, any representative of a party incurs costs as a result of their own improper, unreasonable or negligent conduct they will not receive payment for those wasted costs. A wasted costs order is essentially a power to 'fine' practitioners who incur the disapproval of the court.

Some guidance as to the court's approach to the use of sanctions was provided by the Court of Appeal in **Biguzzi** *v* **Rank Leisure Plc** (1999). Giving the court's judgment, Lord Woolf commented:

> The fact that the judge has [the power to strike out a claim] does not mean that in applying the overriding objective the initial approach will be to strike out the statement of case. The advantage of the CPR over the previous rules is that the court's powers are much broader than they were. In many cases there will be alternatives which enable a case to be dealt with justly without taking the draconian step of striking the case out.

Lord Woolf warned against a lax approach since this could lead to a return to the previous culture of regarding time limits as being unimportant. However he went on to state:

> There are alternative powers which the courts have which they can exercise to make it clear that the courts will not tolerate delays other than striking out the case. In a great many situations those other powers will be the appropriate ones to adopt because they produce a more just result.

This judgment was considered by the Court of Appeal in **UCB Corporate Services** *v* **Halifax (SW) Ltd** (1999) where it stated:

> It would indeed be ironic if as a result of the new rules coming into force and the judgment of this court in the **Biguzzi** case, judges were required to treat cases of delay with greater leniency than they would have done under the old procedure. I feel sure that that cannot have been the intention of the Master of the Rolls in giving judgment in the **Biguzzi** case. What he was concerned to point out was that there are now additional powers which the court may and should use in the less serious cases. But in the more serious cases, striking out remains the appropriate remedy where that is what justice requires.

Court fees

Court fees have been increased significantly in the last few years. First they were increased by 150 per cent by the Conservative Government in 1997. The aim was to make the court self-financing and managed according to business principles. Initially the 1997 change to court fees also removed the right to exemptions for those on income support or suffering financial hardship. This was challenged in **R** *v* **Lord Chancellor, ex parte Witham** (1997). The abolition was condemned as illegal since it effectively removed a constitutional right of access to the courts, without express legislative authority. The action had been brought with the support of the Law Society by a man on income support. He was unable to afford the £500 fee required to bring an action for libel to clear his name following an insinuation that he had been involved in a fraudulent activity. In the light of this judgment the exemptions were reinstated.

The court fees were increased again by the Labour Government in 1999 and 2000. They introduced a 'pay-as-you-go' system, which requires parties to pay for each stage of a civil action, with the costs obviously mounting if a party chooses to proceed all the way to a trial. The aim is both that the courts should be self-financing and that people should be encouraged to settle. The minimum county court commencement fee was raised from £10 to £20 (on a claim not exceeding £200). Multi-track proceedings require a fee of £300 for actions worth up to £50,000. New fees are now payable at two later stages. On the filing of the allocation questionnaire, all claimants have to pay £80. On the filing of the listing questionnaire £200 has to be paid on the fast-track and £300–400 on the multi-track. This is refundable if the case is settled sufficiently early before trial. There is a power to strike out a claim for failure to pay the relevant court fee.

The increased court fees have been criticized on the ground that they will deter many lower-income households from pursuing reasonable claims for justice. Some observers point out that payments are not made by members of the public at the point of use in the education and health systems and that justice can be seen as being just as important as those services. The head of the civil justice system, Sir Richard Scott has warned that justice should be accessible and that:

> The policy fails to recognise that the civil justice system is, like the criminal justice system, the bulwark of a civilised state and the maintenance of order within that state. People have to use the civil courts. They can't engage in self-help in a way which would lead to chaos.

Computerization

The civil courts are in the process of introducing, at vast expense, a new computer system. Once up and running it is intended that the courts will move from a paper-based system to one where many communications take place electronically. For example, evidence and statements will be exchanged by e-mail. The first part of the system should be functioning by September 2002.

▶ Criticism of the 1999 reforms

The 1999 reforms have generally been very well received, though the immediate transition obviously caused some tensions. There had been fears that the 'big bang' of the implementation would explode into chaos. Sir Richard Scott VC admitted to the Association of Personal Injury Lawyers that the start date was 'too soon' and was causing something 'approaching panic stations'. There is concern that particularly the small firms, who are going to be most concerned by the fast-track system, were not able to master the new rules before their implementation as they were only available in December 1999 and amendments continued to be made in the subsequent months. But the explosion never happened; instead there has been a rather eerie silence as many lawyers have delayed bringing litigation, preferring to wait until others have taken the plunge. There was a huge upsurge of work before 'Woolf day' on 26 April with 360 old-style writs being issued in the High Court on the last Friday of the old system and then a dramatic drop afterwards, with only four claim forms being issued on 26 April. According to the judicial statistics issued by the Lord Chancellor's Department, there has been an 11 per cent drop in county court proceedings since the introduction of the Woolf reforms, while actions in the High Court have dropped by 37 per cent.

A pilot simulation carried out by civil litigators on behalf of the Lord Chancellor's Department to try and predict the impact of the Woolf reforms on the civil justice system was not encouraging (*Report of the Fast Track Simulation Pilot*, Lord Chancellor's Department Research Secretariat (1998)). Those involved expressed the fear that pressures on practitioners in terms of both time and costs might lead to corner-cutting, devolution of cases to less experienced fee earners, insufficient time for proper investigation of the claim, and the incurring of irrecoverable costs. They worried too that the openness that Lord Woolf was so keen to encourage as a fundamental principle underlying his reforms might be prejudiced by the 'fear factor'. In other words solicitors might be secretive during the early stages of the litigation so as to avoid client criticism and potential negligence claims; and be reluctant to tell a client about the weakness of a case.

A major irritation for practitioners has been the fact that since the launch of the new Civil Procedure Rules they have been continually amended and extended. A large number of new Practice Directions have been issued and practitioners are finding it difficult to keep up with the pace of change.

The Government's first evaluation of the new Civil Procedure Rules has found that overall the reforms have been beneficial: *Emerging Findings: an early evaluation of the Civil Justice Reforms* (2001). It seems that cases are settling earlier, rather than at the door of the court. Lawyers and clients are now regarding litigation as a last resort, and making more use of alternative methods of dispute resolution. The pre-action protocols have been a success. Their effect has been to concentrate the minds of defendants and make them deal properly with a claim at the early stages rather than months after the issue of proceedings (conditional fee agreements could also be an explanation for this). While generally cases are being heard more quickly after the issue of the claim, small claims are taking longer. But the picture is not quite as straightforward as it looks. Lawyers know that as soon as they issue the claim form they will lose control of the pace of the negotiations and are going to be locked into timetables and procedures which they may find burdensome as well as costly. There is evidence that lawyers are therefore delaying issuing the claim. It is not yet clear whether litigation has become cheaper. The report quotes practitioners who believe the front-end loading of costs caused by the pre-action protocols means that overall costs have actually gone up.

Professor Zander, a leading academic, felt that the reforms were fundamentally flawed, rather than prone to temporary hiccups, and was very vociferous in expressing his opposition to the reforms prior to their implementation. He is reported to have said that they amounted to taking a sledgehammer to crack a nut. Below is an analysis of the main concerns he has expressed.

The causes of delay

Lord Woolf's view was that the chief cause of delay was the way the adversarial system was played by the lawyers. Zander has criticized this analysis, pointing out that it is only supported by 'unsubstantiated opinion' rather than real evidence, despite the fact that it forms the basis for most of the subsequent proposals. By contrast, Zander has drawn attention to research carried out for the Lord Chancellor's Department in 1994 into the causes of delay. It identified seven causes: the type of case; the parties; the judiciary; court procedures; court administration; the lawyers (mainly due to pressure of work, inexperience or inefficiency); and external factors such as the difficulty of getting experts' reports, including medical reports. Of these seven factors, the last two factors were felt to be the most significant. Not all the reasons for the delay were the fault of the system, for example, in some cases it may be necessary to wait for an accident victim's medical condition to stabilize in order to assess the long-term prognosis. Accident victims in particular often do not seek legal advice until some time after the accident has occurred.

Clearly, if Lord Woolf has wrongly diagnosed the causes of delay it is unlikely that his reforms will resolve these problems.

Case management

Zander feels that court management is appropriate for only a minority of cases and that the key is to identify these. He has remarked that judges do not have the time, skills or inclination to undertake the task of case management. The court does not know enough about the workings of a solicitor's office to be able to set appropriate time-tables. In addition, litigants on the fast-track may feel that the brisk way in which a three-hour hearing deals with the dispute is inadequate. Most will not feel that justice has been done by a short, sharp trial with restricted oral evidence and an interventionist judge chivvying the parties to a resolution of their dispute.

A move towards judicial management has already been seen in the US, Australia and Canada. A major official study was published by the Institute of Civil Justice at the Rand Corporation in California. This research was not available to Lord Woolf while he was compiling his report. The study was based on a five-year survey of 10,000 cases looking at the effect of the American Civil Justice Reform Act 1990. This Act required certain federal courts to practise case management. Judicial case management has been part of the US system for many years so that, compared with this country, the procedural innovations being studied operated from a different starting point.

The study found that judicial case management did lead to a reduced time to disposition. Its early use yielded a reduction of one-and-a-half or two months to resolution for cases that lasted at least nine months. Also, having a discovery time-table and reducing the time within which discovery took place both significantly reduced time to disposition and significantly reduced the amount of hours spent on the case by a lawyer. These benefits were achieved without any significant change in the lawyers' or litigants' satisfaction or views of fairness.

On the other hand, case management led to an approximate 20-hour increase in lawyer work hours overall. Their work increased with the need to respond to the court's management directions. In addition, once judicial case management had begun, a discovery cut-off date had usually been established and lawyers felt an obligation to begin discovery on a case which might be settled.

Thus, the Rand Report found that case management, by generating more work for lawyers, tended to increase rather than reduce costs. If the fixed costs did not reflect the extra cost then this would be unjust to the lawyers and their clients. The danger is that case management will front-load costs onto cases which would have settled anyway before reaching court, and which therefore did not need judicial management.

The Rand Report noted that the effectiveness of implementation depended on judicial attitudes. Some judges viewed these procedural innovations as an attack on judicial independence and felt that it emphasized speed and efficiency at the possible expense of justice. The Report concluded, among other things, that judicial management should wait a month after the defence has been entered in case the action settles.

Sanctions

Procedural time-tables for the fast-track are, according to Professor Zander, doomed to failure because a huge proportion of firms, for a range of reasons, will fail to keep to the prescribed time-tables. This will necessitate enforcement procedures and sanctions on a vast scale which, in turn, will lead to innumerable appeals. Sanctions will be imposed that are disproportionate and therefore unjust, and will cause injustice to clients for the failings of the lawyers. Furthermore, if the judges did impose severe sanctions when lawyers failed to comply with time-table deadlines, it would usually be the litigants rather than the lawyers who would be penalized.

Professor Zander has pointed to the courts' experience of Ord. 17 under the old County Court Rules as evidence that lawyers are not good at time limits and sanctions were unlikely to change that. Under that order an action would be automatically struck out if the claimant failed to take certain steps within the time limits set by the rule. From its introduction in 1990 until 1998, roughly 20,000 cases had been struck out on this basis, leaving 20,000 people either to sue their lawyers for negligence or to start all over again. In relation to Ord. 17, the Court of Appeal stated in **Bannister** (1997):

> This rule has given rise to great difficulties and has generated an immense amount of litigation devoted to the question whether a particular action has been struck out and if so, whether it should be reinstated. In short, the rule has in a large number of cases achieved the opposite of its object, which was to speed up the litigation process in the county courts.

There is the danger that, if the court does not exercise its power temperately and judiciously, then in its eagerness to dispose of litigation, it will actually generate more litigation. This danger is particularly acute where the court exercises powers on its own initiative. If, for example, the court moves to strike out a statement of case on its own initiative, the likely result is that the party affected will apply to have its case reinstated; and if, in fact, it was not a suitable case for striking out, unnecessary cost and delay will be the result.

There is a risk that unrealistic trial dates and time-tables will be set, particularly in heavy litigation, at an early stage, and of the judges insisting on their being adhered to thereafter, regardless of the consequences.

Costs

Litigation can be very costly and legal aid is often not available (see chapter 8). In many cases, especially those involving personal injury, the defendant's costs, and sometimes those of the claimant, will be paid by an insurance company – for example, the parties in a car accident are likely to have been insured and professionals such as doctors are insured against negligence claims. As Hazel Genn's 1987 study showed, where only one party is insured, this can place great pressure on the other, unless they have been granted legal aid. The insured side may try to drag out the proceedings for as long as possible, in the hope of exhausting the other party's financial reserves and forcing a low settlement.

Professor Zander has argued that in many civil cases the claimant wins and the defendant is an insurance company who currently pays the claimant's costs. If, in future, the court can only order the loser to pay fixed and fairly low costs, then the claimant's lawyers will not be able to claim back everything that it was in fact necessary to spend on the case in order to win. He predicts that, as a result, either the work will not be done or the client will have to pay for it out of their damages. Either way, justice will not have been served.

Court appointed experts

Court appointed experts may tend to increase cost in that the parties will often still employ their own experts.

Small claims track

There are long standing concerns about the small claims procedure, which have not been tackled by the 1999 reforms. Small claims are not necessarily simple claims; they may involve complex and unusual points of law. Is the small claimant entitled to be judged by the law of the land or by speedier, more rough-and-ready concepts of fairness?

The procedure is not simple enough. The Consumers' Association magazine *Which?* reported in 1986 that the process was still 'quite an ordeal', and the level of formality varied widely. The submissions of both the National Consumer Council and the National Association of Citizens' Advice Bureaux to the Civil Justice Review echoed this feeling. The Civil Justice Review recommended that court forms and leaflets should be simplified. The system is still largely used by small businesses chasing debtors, rather than by the individual consumer for whom it was set up. A consultation paper was issued in 1995 suggesting that, in limited cases, the judge might be given the power to award an additional sum of up to £135 to cover the cost of legal advice and assistance in the preparation of the case. If this reform is introduced it might assist individual consumers to bring their cases.

There are also problems with enforcement. A survey by the Lord Chancellor's Department in 1986 found that 25 per cent of parties were failing to get the payment owed to them from the defendant following a successful application.

The financial limit needs regular updating – the Consumers' Association has suggested replacing it with a list of the type of goods and services covered by the procedure, and establishing an annual review of average expenditure on these in order to ensure the financial limit keeps pace with inflation.

A Report by the Consumers' Association (November 1997) suggests that many people using the small claims procedure are being denied justice because of slow and inefficient enforcement procedures. The court is not responsible for enforcement, which is left to the winning party to secure. The Report found that only a minority of defendants paid up on time and that after six months a substantial minority of people still had not paid their debts. The Report's author, Professor John Baldwin of Birmingham University, concluded that the enforcement problem was so serious that it threatened to undermine the small claims procedure itself by deterring people from using it.

▶ REFORM

Clearly the civil justice system underwent significant reforms in 1999, but further reforms could be made.

▶ More efficient enforcement of judgments

In 1969 the Payne Committee recommended the establishment of an Enforcements Office which would select the most appropriate method of enforcing a judgment. The proposal has not been implemented, mainly because of cost – the Civil Justice Review considered the idea to be expensive and inefficient.

▶ Integration

A proposal to integrate the High Court and the county court to produce a simpler system was considered by the Gorell Committee on county court procedure, but rejected, mainly on the grounds that hearing big cases in the county courts would prejudice the handling of smaller ones.

The proposal was also considered by the Civil Justice Review, which pointed out that the two-court system was inflexible, making it difficult to make rational allocations of judges' and administrators' time between the different courts. Consequently, some courts have much longer delays than others. In a unified court, all cases would start in the same way and be allocated to different sorts of judges on the basis of their complexity. The Lord Chancellor's Department could send judges where they were needed most, and some higher level judges could be based outside London.

The recommendation was supported by solicitors, advice centres and consumer organizations but strongly opposed by barristers and judges, for rather unattractive reasons. Barristers feared that solicitors would have greater rights of audience in the unified court and that the London Bar would lose business to provincial solicitors; High Court judges thought that the proposals would reduce their standing and destroy their special way of life, especially if they were expected to be based for long periods of time in the provinces.

In the end the Review rejected the idea of a unified court, on the grounds that there was no general support for it, the financial implications were uncertain, a unified court would require major legislation and a lengthy implementation period and it might have adverse effects on the standing of the High Court judiciary. But the Head of Civil Justice, Sir Richard Scott VC has predicted that ultimately the High Court and county courts will merge.

An inquisitorial system

In theory, the civil justice system could move to an inquisitorial system, in which the judge would take a more investigative role and the two parties would be required to cooperate by revealing all their evidence to each other. Tactics would become less important, and since delay is often a part of these tactics, the whole process could be speeded up. Some would suggest that this system might also be fairer, since being able to afford the best lawyer would be less important.

In fact, a full change away from the adversarial system seems extremely unlikely, but there have been proposals for such movement in certain areas: the Civil Justice Review suggested that a paper adjudication scheme might be considered for handling certain claims, which would move to an oral hearing only if the adjudicator felt there were difficulties which made one necessary. The procedure would be compulsory for road accidents and claims under £5,000 and could also be used in other cases where the parties agreed. This idea has been opposed by both the National Consumer Council and the National Association of Citizens' Advice Bureaux, on the grounds that those who could afford a skilled lawyer to draft their papers would have too much of an advantage. Some of the Woolf proposals also favour a move towards an inquisitorial approach and a less aggressive form of litigation.

Progress towards full pre-trial disclosure of evidence, and the fact that Small Claims Court arbitrators now take a more interventionist approach, can be seen as moves towards a more inquisitorial system.

Reform of compensation for personal injury

Tort law dictates that the victims of an accident (other than industrial accidents, which are covered by a compensation scheme) can get compensation only if they can prove that the harm caused to them was somebody else's fault. The result of this is that individuals with identical injuries may receive hundreds of thousands of pounds in compensation, or nothing more than state benefits, depending not on their needs but on whether they can prove fault – often very difficult to do conclusively. In many cases, the state has to spend money, in the form of legal aid, but if the case is lost, the only person to benefit from that expenditure is the lawyer. Because of this, it is often suggested that the tort action for personal injury should be abolished and the financial savings should be used to provide improved welfare benefits for all those injured by accidents. New Zealand has adopted such an approach and established a no fault system of compensation.

Modernization

The Government has issued a consultation paper, *Modernizing the Civil Courts* (2001). This looks at the possibility of applying the same developments in technology to the Court Service that have been applied to the private sector, such as retail banking. Some court appointments will remain face-to-face, some face-to-video and others will be electronic. Through new means of access the Government hopes to give people who currently do not have easy access to a court building easy access to court services.

It seems that as part of the modernization process, the Lord Chancellor thinks that wigs should no longer be worn in civil courts (though he thinks they still have a role in criminal courts).

A modern court system should place more emphasis on customer care. At the moment the county courts list all morning business as starting at 10.30 am, so that everybody has to wait until their case is called, rather than giving specific appointments.

▶ ANSWERING QUESTIONS

1 **(a) What are the major strengths and weaknesses of resolution of disputes in civil matters through the traditional court structure?** *(15 marks)*
(b) What reforms, if any, might it be desirable to introduce? *(10 marks) AQA (AEB)*

(a) The capacity of the traditional civil courts to resolve disputes in a manner that is efficient, economic and speedy, is an issue of enduring concern. While the question talks about the 'traditional court structure', you could point out that while the courts themselves have remained the same in recent years, the procedures practised within them have changed dramatically. With the recent introduction of the Woolf reforms it is difficult to assess at the moment how successful these reforms have been. You could discuss the weaknesses that had existed (see p. 361) and you could mention Zander's concerns that these reforms will not put an end to these problems (see p. 379). When looking at the strengths of the current system, you could mention the status of the judiciary in our society, the general belief in judicial impartiality, the certainty provided by the use of precedent (discussed at p. 22) and the structure of appeals to remedy mistakes (see p. 401).

(b) You could point out that major reforms have only just been introduced in April 1999, and it might be wise to wait and see how far these reforms will prove to be effective before giving judgement on what should be done next. But possible reforms are discussed at p. 383. You could also consider whether a reversion to the pre-1999 position might be desirable. Using material from chapter 16, you might discuss how far alternative methods of dispute resolution should replace the civil system.

2 **How satisfactory are the current arrangements for the resolution of the civil law disputes through the courts? Suggest what improvements may be necessary.** *AQA (AEB)*

You could begin this essay by discussing some of the possible aims of a civil justice system described above (pp. 359–61) and pointing out that, as they may conflict, it is not always possible to fulfil them all – so a balance needs to be struck. You might give some examples of such aims being in conflict. You could introduce a discussion on justice (see p. 562) but as applied to the context of the civil justice system. Consideration could then be given to how the different aims are approached in practice, by looking at the reforms introduced following Lord Woolf's report. How far will the new system prove to be more satisfactory than the old one? In this context you can look closely at the criticisms and concerns raised by Zander, that are discussed at p. 379. You could then discuss whether any of the additional reform suggestions mentioned at p. 383 would improve the situation. You could mention that in real life, less noble principles may play a part – as the vested interests of lawyers and judges did in their response to proposals in the Civil Justice Review. How have reforms aimed at making the system quicker, cheaper and simpler affected the overall balance?

3 Study the extract below and then answer the questions which follow.
One of the major divisions in law is between criminal and civil. In reality, the distinction is not always so clear cut. Consider a person attacked and injured by another. Is this a civil matter or criminal? The answer is that it may be either or both. It all depends on what action the victim decides to take. The victim may complain to the police who may bring criminal charges against the assailant. If the police, or the Crown Prosecution Service, are unwilling to prosecute, then the aggrieved victim may take out a private action against the assailant. The victim would do this by contacting a solicitor and then sue the assailant. It is therefore possible for the same conduct to be prosecuted and also to be followed through the civil courts. This frequently happens in cases of road traffic accidents.

(a) What are the aims of sentencing in a criminal case? *(4 marks)*

(b) What is the burden of proof:

   (i) in a criminal trial?

   (ii) in a civil trial? *(4 marks)*

(c) Explain how a criminal trial will differ from a civil action. *(8 marks)*

(d) In what circumstances might a victim prefer to pursue a civil case as an alternative to a criminal prosecution? *(9 marks) Edexcel*

This question mixes issues from this chapter and from chapters 9 and 10.

(a) At p. 303 it was mentioned that the four main aims of sentencing are retribution, deterrence, rehabilitation and public protection.

(b)(i) At p. 285 it was stated that the burden of proof is on the prosecution to prove guilt beyond all reasonable doubt.

(ii) At p. 357 it was noted that in civil cases the claimant has to prove their case on the balance of probabilities.

(c) Criminal trials are brought by the state unless it is a private prosecution, while civil cases are brought by individuals. The focus of a criminal trial is whether the defendant committed a crime while civil trials are concerned with civil wrongs. Criminal trials have a higher burden of proof and take place in the Crown Court or the magistrates' court. Civil trials normally take place in the High Court or the county court, though some civil procedures are heard by magistrates. A criminal case will be decided either by a lay jury sitting with a professional judge or magistrates. Civil cases are normally decided by professional judges, though rare cases can be heard by a jury or magistrates. A successful criminal prosecution will result in a sentence for punishment, including potentially a custodial sentence. The main remedy in civil cases is damages for compensation.

You could also point to the different procedures, for example, a defendant is either arrested or summoned to attend a criminal court while civil proceedings commence with the issue of a claim form.

(d) Victims have more control in civil cases, the burden of proof is lower and it is therefore easier to win the case. You could illustrate this with the example of O.J. Simpson that was mentioned at p. 357. The victims will usually be awarded damages after a successful civil case, while it is rare for the criminal courts to make reparation or compensation orders. You could look at the problems that arose from the unsuccessful private prosecution brought by Stephen Lawrence's family which is discussed at pp. 273–74.

Reading on the Internet

The consultation paper, *Modernising Civil Courts* (2001) is available on the court service website at:

http://www.courtservice.gov.uk/notices/mcc_consultation_paper.pdf

The research *Emerging Findings: an early evaluation of the Civil Justice Reforms* (2001) is available on the Lord Chancellor's website at:

http://www.lcd.gov.uk/civil/emerge/emerge.htm

Lord Woolf's final report, *Access to Justice* is available on the Lord Chancellor's Department website at:

http://www.lcd.gov.uk/civil/finalfr.htm

13 Tribunals

Many claims and disputes are settled not by the courts, but by tribunals, each specializing in a particular area. Tribunals decide almost half a million cases every year. Employment (formally called Industrial) Tribunals are probably the best-known example, but there are many others, dealing with subjects ranging from Social Security and tax to forestry and patents. Not all are actually called tribunals – the category includes, for example, the Education Appeal Committee, which hears appeals concerning the allocation of school places, and the Criminal Injuries Compensation Board, which assesses applications for compensation for victims of violent crime. The majority deal with disputes between the citizen and the state, though the Employment Tribunal is an obvious exception.

Tribunals are generally distinguished from the other courts by less formal procedures, and by the fact that they specialize. However, they are all expected to conduct themselves according to the same principles of natural justice used by the courts: a fair hearing for both sides and open and impartial decision-making.

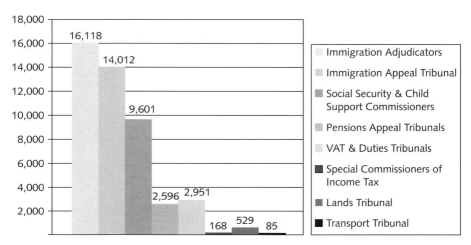

Figure 13.1 Tribunals: Cases received, 1999

Source: *Judicial Statistics 1999*

Individual tribunals may differ quite markedly from each other in terms of procedure, workload and membership. For example, Employment Tribunals operate on an adversarial model, whereas procedure in the Social Security tribunals is much more inquisitorial.

History

Tribunals were in existence as long ago as 1799, but the present system has really grown up since the Second World War. The main reason for this was the growth of legislation in areas which were previously considered private, and therefore rarely addressed by the state, such as Social Security benefits, housing, town and country planning, education and employment.

This legislation gave people rights – to a school place, to unemployment benefit, or not to be unfairly sacked, for example – but its rules also placed limits on these rights. Naturally, this leads to disputes: employer and employee disagree on whether the latter's dismissal was unfair under the terms of the legislation; a Social Security claimant believes he or she has been wrongly denied benefit; a landowner disputes the right of the local authority to purchase her field compulsorily.

Given the potentially vast number of disputes likely to arise, and the detailed nature of the legislation concerning them, it was felt that the ordinary court system would neither have been able to cope with the workload, nor be the best forum for sorting out such problems, hence the growth of tribunals.

As well as the administrative tribunals dealing with this kind of dispute, there are domestic tribunals, which deal with disputes and matters of discipline within particular professions – trade unions and the medical and legal professions all have tribunals like this, the Solicitors Complaints Tribunal being an example. The decisions of these tribunals are based on the particular rules of the organization concerned, but they are still required to subscribe to the same standards of justice as the ordinary courts and in the case of those set up by statute, their decisions can be appealed to the ordinary courts – as can those of most administrative tribunals.

The Franks Report

In 1957, the Franks Committee investigated the workings of tribunals. It reported that the tribunal system was likely to become an increasingly important part of the legal system, and recommended that tribunal procedures should be marked by 'openness, fairness and impartiality'. Openness required, where possible, hearings in public and explanations of the reasoning behind decisions. Fairness entailed the adoption of clear procedures, which allowed parties to know their rights, present their case fully, and be aware of the case against them. Impartiality meant that tribunals should be free of undue influence from any Government departments concerned with their subject area. The Committee was particularly concerned that tribunals were often on Ministry premises, with Ministry staff.

The Committee also recommended the establishment of two permanent Councils on Tribunals, one for England and Wales and one for Scotland, to supervise procedures. Although a Council was set up (with a Scottish committee), its functions are only advisory – it has little real power, and cannot reverse or even direct further consideration of individual tribunal decisions. In 1980, it put forward a report asking for further powers, but these were not granted.

Tribunals today

Composition

Most tribunals consist of a legally trained chairperson, and two lay people who have some particular expertise in the relevant subject area – doctors in the Medical Appeal Tribunal, for example, and representatives of both employees' and employers' organizations in the Employment Tribunal. The lay members take an active part in decision-making.

Tribunals composed entirely of lay people are considered to have been less effective than those with a legally qualified chairperson.

Status

Tribunals are regarded as inferior to the ordinary courts, even though they are largely independent from them in their own jurisdictions. This was confirmed in the case of **Peach Grey & Co** *v* **Sommers** (1995), which concerned a claim of wrongful dismissal against a firm of solicitors, heard by an Industrial Tribunal. The person dismissed had tried to influence a witness due to appear before the Tribunal, and his former employers claimed that this was contempt of court. The Divisional Court agreed, and in accepting that it had jurisdiction to punish this contempt, it confirmed that the Tribunal is an inferior court.

Workload

The 1979 Royal Commission on Legal Services found that in 1978, tribunals heard six times as many contested cases as the High Court and county courts. Although they have often been seen as an unimportant part of the legal system, this caseload clearly shows that they are now playing a major role.

Appeals from tribunals

There is no uniform appeals procedure from tribunals, though most do allow some right of appeal. The Tribunals and Inquiries Act 1992 provides for appeals to the High Court on points of law from some of the most important tribunals. These appeals are heard by the Queen's Bench Division.

In addition to appeal rights, decisions of tribunals are always subject to judicial review by the High Court on the grounds that they have not been made in accordance with the rules of natural justice or were not within the powers of the tribunal to make (see p. 422).

Controls over tribunals

Aside from the judicial review procedure, which supervises the actual decisions of tribunals, the workings of tribunals are overseen by the Council on Tribunals. This consists of ten to 15 members appointed by the Lord Chancellor. It reviews and reports on the constitution and workings of certain specified tribunals, and is consulted before any changes to their procedural rules are made; it also considers and reports on matters referred to it concerning any tribunal. However, it has no firm say in any of these matters, and cannot overrule any decisions.

Advantages of tribunals

Speed

Tribunal cases come to court fairly quickly, and many are dealt with within a day. Many tribunals are able to specify the exact date and time at which a case will be heard, so minimizing time-wasting for the parties.

Cost

Tribunals usually do not charge fees, and each party usually pays their own costs, rather than the loser having to pay all. The simpler procedures of tribunals should mean that legal representation is unnecessary, so reducing cost, but that is not always the case (see below).

Informality

This varies between different tribunals, but as a general rule, wigs are not worn, the strict rules of evidence do not apply, and attempts are made to create an unintimidating atmosphere. This is obviously a help where individuals are representing themselves.

Flexibility

Although they obviously aim to apply fairly consistent principles, tribunals do not operate strict rules of precedent, so are able to respond more flexibly than courts.

Specialization

Tribunal members already have expertise in the relevant subject area, and through sitting on tribunals are able to build up a depth of knowledge of that area that judges in ordinary courts could not hope to match.

Relief of congestion in the ordinary courts

If the volume of cases heard by tribunals was transferred to the ordinary courts, the system would be completely overloaded.

Awareness of policy

The expertise of tribunal members means they are likely to understand the policy behind legislation in their area, and they often have wide discretionary powers which allow them to put this into practice.

Privacy

Tribunals may, in some circumstances, meet in private, so that the individual is not obliged to have their circumstances broadcast to the general public (but see the first disadvantage below).

Disadvantages of tribunals

Lack of openness

The fact that some tribunals are held in private can lead to suspicion about the fairness of their decisions.

Unavailability of state funding

Full funding from the Legal Services Commission is available for only a small number of minor tribunals. Tribunals are of course designed to do away with the need for representation, but the fact is that in many of them, the ordinary individual will be facing an opponent with access to the very best representation – an employer, for example, or a Government department – and this clearly places them at a serious disadvantage.

Even though the procedures are generally informal compared with those in ordinary courts, the average person is likely to be very much out of their depth, and research by Genn and Genn in 1989 found that much of the law with which tribunals was concerned was complex, and their adjudicative process sometimes highly technical; individuals who were represented had a much better chance of winning their case.

There is however some dispute as to the desirability of such representation necessarily involving lawyers; although in some cases this will be the more appropriate form of representation, there are fears that introducing lawyers could detract from the aims of speed and informality. If money for tribunal representation were available, it may be better spent on developing lay representation, such as that offered by specialist agencies such as the UK Immigration Advisory Service, or the Child Poverty Action Group, who can develop real expertise in specific areas, as well as general agencies such as the Citizens' Advice Bureaux.

Reasons for decisions not always given

Although the majority of tribunals are obliged to explain their reasoning if requested, a few are not.

Lack of accessibility

The Franks Committee recommendation that tribunals should be 'open' requires more than just a rule that hearings should usually be held in public; it also demands that citizens should be aware of tribunals and their right to use them. In cases where the dispute is between a citizen and the Government, the citizen will usually be notified of procedures to deal with disputes, but in other cases more thought needs to be given to publicizing citizens' rights.

Lack of coherence

Each tribunal has evolved as a solution to a particular problem, adapted to one particular area of law. As a result most tribunals are entirely self-contained, and operate separately from each other, using different practices and procedures. The result is a system that lacks coherence and which is not providing a uniformly high standard of service.

Not user-friendly

The tribunals were originally intended to be user-friendly, providing easy access to justice. Over time many have become increasingly like courts and it is difficult as a result for claimants without professional legal help to take their case to a tribunal.

Dependent

At the moment the relevant Ministry frequently provides the administrative support for the tribunal, selects the tribunal members, pays their fees and expenses and lays down the tribunal procedures. This means that tribunals neither appear to be, nor are in fact, independent. Responsibility for tribunals and their administration should not lie with those whose policies or decisions it is the tribunals' duty to consider. Otherwise, for users every case is an 'away game'. The current arrangements in this respect could be the subject of a successful challenge under Art. 6 of the European Convention on Human Rights, which guarantees the right to a fair trial.

Problems with controls over tribunals

Diversity

Although they are often considered together, tribunals vary widely, in procedure and the subjects with which they deal, and they make thousands of decisions every year in very different types of case. This great diversity makes it difficult to establish mechanisms of supervision that are appropriate to them all.

The Council on Tribunals

The Council is a watchdog with no teeth. It can advise the Government of problems, but has no real power to ensure they are dealt with.

Rights of appeal

There is no absolute right of appeal from a tribunal: such rights exist only where they are laid down in statute with regard to a particular tribunal. Consequently there is no uniform appeals system, and some tribunals offer no appeal rights at all. An example is the Vaccine Damage Tribunals, set up under the Vaccine Damage Payments Act 1971 to assess claimants' rights to damages for disabilities caused by vaccination. Some tribunal appeals can only be made to the relevant Minister, who can hardly be seen as a disinterested party. Others have appeal rights to the High Court, which is expensive, complex and time-consuming, and therefore seems inconsistent with the basic aims of tribunals.

Judicial review

As always, the controlling effect of the potential for judicial review is limited by the fact that it cannot consider the merits of decisions, and that where wide discretionary powers are given to a Minister, Government department or local authority, the court will find it difficult to prove that many decisions are outside those powers (see p. 426).

Reform

In 2000/2001 the tribunals were the subject of a major Review undertaken at the request of the Lord Chancellor by Sir Andrew Leggatt, a retired Lord Justice of Appeal. This was the first systematic examination of tribunals since the Franks Report in 1957. The review was asked to look at the funding and management of tribunals, their structure and standards, and whether they complied with the Human Rights Act 1998.

The Review issued a consultation document in which it agreed with the Franks' Committee that the main characteristics required of tribunals are fairness, openness and impartiality, though it saw openness and impartiality as components of the overarching requirement of fairness. The Review proposed certain benchmarks against which the achievement of fairness could be tested. These benchmarks included the following:

- independence from sponsoring departments;
- an accessible and supportive system;
- tribunals exercising a jurisdiction suitable for the area that each is intended to cover;
- simple procedures;
- effective decision-making;
- ensuring that the decision-making process is suitable for the type of dispute;
- providing proportionate remedies;
- speed in reaching finality;
- authority and expertise appropriate for their task; and
- cost effectiveness.

The report of the Review, *Tribunals for Users: One System, One Service*, was published in 2001. Of the 70 different administrative tribunals in England and Wales, it found that their quality varied 'from excellent to inadequate'. It identified some significant weaknesses in the current system. In particular, it was concerned by the lack of coherence in the existing tribunal system, the fact that they were not always user-friendly and the absence of independence of the tribunals from the Ministries whose decisions were the subject of the tribunal work. These criticisms have been discussed at p. 394.

Proposals

The review concluded that the tribunals had to be rationalized and modernized, and that a radical approach was both necessary and justified. Its proposals have four main aims:

- to make the 70 tribunals into one Tribunal System;
- to render the tribunals independent of their sponsoring departments by having them administered by one Tribunal Service;
- to improve the training of chairpersons and members in the interpersonal skills particularly required by tribunals; and

- to enable unrepresented users to participate effectively and without apprehension in tribunal proceedings.

The precise proposals of the tribunal were as follows.

Tribunal Service

The main proposal of the Review was that a single Tribunal Service should be established which would be responsible for the administration of all the tribunals. According to the Review, this would achieve efficiency, coherence and independence.

Any citizen who wished to apply to a tribunal would simply have to submit their case to the Tribunal Service and the case would be allocated to the appropriate tribunal. This would be a considerable advance in clarity and simplicity for users and their advisers. The single system would enable a coherent, user-focused approach to the provision of information which would enable tribunals to meet the claim that they operate in ways which enable citizens to participate directly in preparing and presenting their own cases.

It is hoped that a Tribunal Service would raise the status of tribunals, while preserving their distinctness from the courts. In the medium term it would yield considerable economies of scale, particularly in relation to the provision of premises for all tribunals, common basic training and the use of information technology. It would provide a single point of contact for users, improved geographical distribution of tribunal centres, common standards, an enhanced corporate image, and a greater prospect of job satisfaction for employees on account of the size and coherence of the Tribunal Service.

The Tribunal Service should be an executive agency of the Lord Chancellor's Department. The Review considers that the independence of tribunals would best be safeguarded by having their administrative support provided by the Lord Chancellor's Department. This Ministry has extensive experience of managing courts.

Structure of the tribunal system

The review proposes that the tribunals should be organized into Divisions grouping together coherent areas of work. The first-tier tribunals would be grouped into eight Divisions:

- education
- financial
- health and social services
- immigration
- land and valuation
- social security and pensions
- transport
- regulatory and employment.

Tribunal procedure

At the moment the tribunals all have their own rules of procedure. The Review proposes the establishment of a unified set of procedural rules. Its proposals are heavily influenced by the reforms introduced to the rules of civil procedure following the Woolf Report. It considers that at the moment cases take too long and are often ill-prepared. To deal with this problem it favours the increased use of case management, with the imposition of vigorous time constraints supported by sanctions. Each Division would have at least one registrar to assist the tribunal members with case management duties. Registrars would have the power to order the production of documents and attendance of witnesses and to issue directions. They would seek to minimize the length of oral hearings by ordering the exchange of documentary evidence before the hearing, and by directing that written arguments from the department whose decision is challenged be sent before the hearing to the tribunal and to the other party. The registrar would consider during pre-hearing procedures (with advice, as needed from the tribunal chairperson) whether the case was suitable for some alternative method of dispute resolution. Where a department fails without reasonable excuse to comply with an order or direction, the tribunal would have the power to allow the application against the department. Tribunals would not have the power to award costs against a party.

The same overarching principle would apply to tribunals as is now enshrined in the Civil Procedure Rules. The tribunals would be under a duty to ensure, so far as practical, that procedures were as speedy, proportionate and cheap as the nature of each case allowed.

Suitable information technology would be provided for workflow management and tracking.

A user-friendly system

The Review considered that tribunal users should be able to prepare and present their cases themselves. The tribunals should give the parties confidence in their ability to participate regardless of their skills or knowledge. Working where possible with user groups, tribunals should do all they can to render themselves understandable, unthreatening and useful to users. Information about venues, time-tables, and sources of professional advice should be easily accessible. All judgments should contain reasons written in plain English.

Appeals

The current arrangements for appeals against tribunal decisions have developed haphazardly so that there are a confusing and illogical variety of routes of appeal from tribunal decisions. The Review proposes that the existing appeal system should be replaced by a simple, clear structure which would be capable of developing the law consistently. There would be a single route of appeal for all tribunals. Each new Division would have a corresponding appellate tribunal. There would be a right of appeal on a point of law, by permission, on the ground that the decision of the tribunal was unlawful. The appeal route would be from first-tier tribunal to second-tier tribunal and from second-tier tribunal to the Court of Appeal. The appellate body would have the power to quash the decision, to remit it for reconsideration, to grant declaratory relief or (if there was no substantial prejudice) to give no relief. There would be specific provision for certain appeals direct to the Court of Appeal.

The Council on Tribunals
The Review recommends that the Council on Tribunals should continue to exist, with extended powers. It would monitor progress in the implementation of the Tribunal System. It would also check that the practices and procedures of the Government departments were compliant with the European Convention on Human Rights.

▶ ANSWERING QUESTIONS

1 Consider the role of tribunals in the administration of justice. *Edexcel*

You can begin by considering the role of tribunals. You should point out that they do vary widely, but broadly their job in the legal system can be said to include providing justice in a quick, inexpensive and accessible way, making independent decisions in disputes between the citizen and the state, putting into effect the policy behind legislation, and taking pressure off the courts. You then need to assess how well tribunals do these jobs.

The following are points you might mention:

- Speed – they are quicker than courts, but since the Franks Committee have adopted more court-like procedures, which may slow things down.
- Cost – some charge no fees, and costs are not usually awarded against a losing party as they would be in a court. However, the need for representation, and the fact that legal aid is not available may eradicate these advantages for some.
- Accessibility – procedures are usually simpler than in courts, but again, the fact that representation is allowed means that powerful litigants will have it, so less powerful ones are disadvantaged by representing themselves.
- Independence – though this has improved, there are still criticisms (see above).
- Helping the citizen to assert rights against the state – this may be compromised by lack of independence, and also the problems with legal aid, putting the individual at a disadvantage.
- Effecting policy – tribunals do often have wider discretionary powers than courts.
- Taking pressure off the courts – you could point out the vast numbers of cases which arise in the kinds of matters dealt with by tribunals.

2 Analyse the role played by tribunals in the English legal system. How far are the methods of supervising and reviewing their judgments adequate?

The role of tribunals is described above – if you have time, it is worth mentioning some of the assessment points, since you are being asked what role is actually played, rather than just what role tribunals aim to play.

For the second part of the question, you need to outline what methods of supervising tribunals and reviewing their decisions are available. The problems with these methods are outlined above, and you should also refer to the section on judicial review in general (p. 422), and to any relevant points made by chapter 14. You should make express reference to the review undertaken by Sir Andrew Leggatt. One of the concerns of this review is the conformity of the tribunal system with the Human Rights Act 1998.

▶ Reading on the Internet

The Report of the Review of tribunals by Sir Andrew Leggatt is available on:
http://www.tribunals-review.org.uk/

The website of the Council on Tribunals is:
http://www.council-on-tribunals.gov.uk/

14 Appeals and judicial review

APPEALS

The appeals system provides a way of overseeing the lower courts, and has two basic functions:

- Putting right any unjust or incorrect decisions, whether caused by errors of fact, law or procedure. An error of fact might be that a victim was stabbed with a knife rather than a broken bottle; an error of law might be that the judge has wrongly defined an offence when explaining to the jury what needs to be proved; and an error of procedure means that the trial has not been conducted as it should have been.
- Promoting a consistent development of the law.

Judicial review is not technically an appeal, though it is a way of reviewing the decisions of courts and tribunals. It will be considered after the appeals system.

Appeals in civil law cases

Civil appeals may be made by either party to a dispute. The Government has been concerned at the increasing number of appeals being brought in civil proceedings. In 1990 there were 954 appeals heard and 573 applications outstanding. By 1996, 1,825 appeals were heard and 1,288 applications were outstanding. It expects that additional appeals will result from the Human Rights Act 1998. A review of the Civil Division of the Court of Appeal was undertaken by a Committee chaired by Sir Jeffrey Bowman. It produced a report in the spring of 1998. A number of problems were identified as besetting the Court of Appeal. In particular, the court was being asked to consider numerous appeals which were not of sufficient weight or complexity for two or three of the country's most senior judges, and which had sometimes already been through one or more levels of appeal. Additionally, existing provisions concerning the constitution of the court were too inflexible to deal appropriately with its workload. Recommendations were made designed to reduce the delays in the hearing of civil appeals and the Lord Chancellor accepted many of its proposals.

The Access to Justice Act 1999 introduced some significant reforms to the civil appeal process.

In the past permission was required for most cases going to the Civil Division of the Court of Appeal, but not elsewhere. Following the Access to Justice Act 1999, court rules require permission to appeal to be obtained for all appeals to the county courts, High Court and the Civil Division of the Court of Appeal. This permission will be obtained either from the court of first instance or from the appellate court itself. Leave will be given where the appeal has a realistic prospect of success or where there is some other compelling reason why the appeal should be heard. More stringent conditions are applied for the granting of permission to appeal case management decisions. The main situation where permission to appeal is not required is where the liberty of the subject is at stake, for example, following the rejection of a *habeas corpus* application. The general rule is that appeal lies to the next level of judge in the court hierarchy.

The Access to Justice Act 1999 provides that in normal circumstances there will be only one level of appeal to the courts. Where the county court or High Court has already reached a decision in a case brought on appeal, there will be no further possibility for the case to be considered by the Court of Appeal, unless it considers that the appeal would raise an important point of principle or practice, or there is some other compelling reason for the Court of Appeal to hear it. Thus in future second appeals will become a rarity. Only the Court of Appeal can grant permission for this second appeal.

In the Court of Appeal cases are normally heard by three judges, but following the Access to Justice Act 1999 the Master of the Rolls can issue directions allowing smaller cases to be heard by a single judge.

Civil appeals will normally simply be a review of the decision of the lower court, rather than a full rehearing, unless the appeal court considers that it is in the interests of justice to hold a rehearing. The appeal will only be allowed where the decision of the lower court was wrong, or where it was unjust because of a serious procedural or other irregularity in the proceedings of the lower court.

From the county court

Appeals based on alleged errors of law or fact are made to the Civil Division of the Court of Appeal. Appeals from a district judge's decision normally go first to a circuit judge and then to the High Court (though exceptionally they will go to the Court of Appeal instead of the High Court).

The Court of Appeal does not hear all the evidence again, calling witnesses and so forth, but considers the appeal on the basis of the notes made by the trial judge, and/or other documentary evidence of the proceedings. Written skeleton arguments should normally be provided to the court so that oral submissions can be kept brief to save time and costs.

The Court of Appeal may affirm, vary (for example, by altering the amount of damages) or reverse the judgment of the county court. It is generally reluctant to overturn the trial judge's finding of fact because it does not hold a complete rehearing. As the trial judge will have had the advantage of observing the demeanour of witnesses giving their evidence, the Court of Appeal will hardly ever question his or her findings about their veracity and reliability as witnesses. From the Court of Appeal, there may be a further appeal to the House of Lords, for which leave must be granted.

Judicial review by the High Court is also possible.

From the High Court

Cases started in the High Court may be appealed to the Civil Division of the Court of Appeal. The case is examined through transcripts rather than being reheard, as above. From there, a further appeal on questions of law or fact may be made, with leave, to the House of Lords.

The exception to this process is the 'leap frog' procedure, provided for in the Administration of Justice Act 1969. Under this procedure, an appeal can go directly from the High Court to the House of Lords, missing out the Court of Appeal. The underlying rationale is that the Court of Appeal may be bound by a decision of the House of Lords, so that money and time would be wasted by going to the Court of Appeal when the only court that could look at the issue afresh is the House of Lords. In order to use this procedure, all the parties must consent to it and the High Court judge who heard the original trial must certify that the appeal is on a point of law that either:

(a) relates wholly or mainly to the construction of an enactment or of a statutory instrument, and has been fully argued in the proceedings and fully considered in the judgment of the judge in the proceedings; or

(b) is one in respect of which the judge is bound by a decision of the Court of Appeal or of the House of Lords in previous proceedings, and was fully considered in the judgments given by the Court of Appeal or the House of Lords (as the case may be) in those previous proceedings (s. 12(3)).

The trial judge has a discretion whether or not to grant this certificate, and there is no right of appeal against this decision. Even if a certificate is granted, leave will still need to be obtained from the House of Lords.

From the civil jurisdiction of the magistrates' court

Appeals concerning family proceedings go to the Family Division of the High Court. From there, appeal with leave lies to the Court of Appeal and the House of Lords. Appeals on licensing matters are heard by the Crown Court.

It is also possible for the magistrates to state a case (see point 3 on p. 405) and for judicial review to be applied.

From tribunals

These may have their own appeal system – the Employment Appeal Tribunal, for example, hears cases from employment tribunals. Otherwise appeals from tribunals tend to be limited to points of law, which are usually referred to the High Court. They are also subject to judicial review.

Appeals in criminal law cases

Significant reforms have been introduced to the criminal appeal system in the light of heavy criticism following some high-profile miscarriages of justice. The appeal process is supposed to spot cases where there have been wrongful convictions at an early stage so that the injustice can be promptly remedied. A wrongful conviction could arise because of police or prosecution malpractice, a misdirection by a judge, judicial bias, or because expert evidence, such as forensic evidence, was misleading. Sadly, the Court of Appeal in particular failed in the past to detect such problems and this led to demands for reform. The Criminal Appeal Act 1995 was therefore passed to make major amendments to the criminal appeal procedure.

From the magistrates' court (criminal jurisdiction)

There are four routes of appeal:

1 The magistrates can rectify an error they have made under s. 142 of the Magistrates' Courts Act 1980, as amended by the Criminal Appeals Act 1995. The case is retried before a different bench where it would be in the interests of justice to do so and the sentence can be varied.

2 A defendant who has pleaded not guilty may appeal as of right to the Crown Court on the grounds of being wrongly convicted or too harshly sentenced. Only appeals against sentence are allowed if the defendant pleaded guilty. The appeal has to be made within 28 days of the conviction. These appeals are normally heard by a circuit judge sitting with between two and four magistrates (not those who heard the original trial). Each person's vote has the same weight except where the court is equally divided when the circuit judge has the casting vote.

The court will rehear the facts of the case and either confirm the verdict and/or sentence of the original magistrates, or substitute its own decision for that of the lower court. It can impose any sentence that the magistrates might have imposed – which can occasionally result in the accused's sentence being increased. In 1994 there were 22,600 appeals heard by the Crown Court, of which 43 per cent were successful.

3 Alternatively, either the prosecution or the accused may appeal on the grounds that the magistrates have made an error of law, or acted outside their jurisdiction. The magistrates (or the Crown Court when hearing an appeal from the magistrates) are asked to 'state the case' for their decision to be considered by the High Court. This is, therefore, known as an appeal by way of case stated. In **R** *v* **Mildenhall Magistrates' Court, ex parte Forest Heath DC** (1997) the Court of Appeal held that magistrates could refuse to state a case if they feel that the application is frivolous, which they defined as 'futile, misconceived, hopeless or academic'. They must inform the defendant why they have reached this conclusion.

Appeals by way of case stated are heard by up to three judges of the Queen's Bench Division and the sitting is known as a Divisional Court. The court can confirm, reverse or vary the decision; give the magistrates their opinion on the relevant point of law; or make such other order as it sees fit, which may include ordering a rehearing before a different bench.

4 The Criminal Cases Review Commission can refer appeals from the magistrates' court to the Crown Court. This body is discussed in more detail from p. 412 onwards. In fact, only 5 per cent of new cases received by the Commission since 1997 have been against convictions by the magistrates.

If an appeal has been made to the Crown Court, either side may then appeal against the Crown Court's decision by way of case stated. If a party has already appealed to the High Court by way of case stated they may not afterwards appeal to the Crown Court. In 1993 there were 199 appeals from magistrates' courts and 37 appeals from Crown Courts under this procedure, of which 39 per cent were allowed.

From the Divisional Court there may be a further appeal, by either party, to the House of Lords, but only if the Divisional Court certifies that the question of law is one of public importance and the House of Lords or the Divisional Court gives permission for the appeal to be heard.

Criminal cases tried by magistrates are also subject to judicial review.

In practice, appeals from the decisions of magistrates are taken in only 1 per cent of cases. This may be because most accused plead guilty, and since the offences are relatively minor and the punishment usually a fine, many of those who pleaded not guilty may prefer just to pay up and put the case behind them, avoiding the expense, publicity and embarrassment involved in an appeal.

A Home Office report (R. Taylor, *Cautions, Court Proceedings and Sentencing in England and Wales* (1996)) found that the introduction of the right of magistrates to reopen cases to rectify their own mistakes by the Criminal

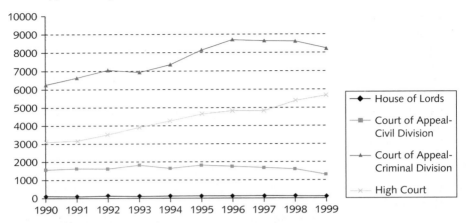

Figure 14.1 Appellate Courts: Appeals entered 1990–99

Figures for the House of Lords include those for the Judicial Committee of the Privy Council
Source: *Judicial Statistics 1999*

Appeals Act 1995 had led to a significant reduction in both the number of appeals and the proportion of successful appeals. The number of appeals against conviction had fallen by 28 per cent from 14,100 in 1995 to 10,100 in 1996. The proportion of successful appeals – in other words, where the conviction was quashed or a retrial ordered – had fallen during the same period from a success rate of 41 per cent to 33 per cent.

From the Crown Court

There are three types of appeal for cases tried in the Crown Court.

1 An appeal on grounds that involve the facts, the law, or the length of the sentence can be made to the Court of Appeal. The accused must get leave to appeal from the trial judge or the Court of Appeal. A sentence cannot be imposed that is more severe than that ordered by the Crown Court. An appeal against sentence will only be successful where the sentence is wrong in principle or manifestly severe; the court will not interfere merely because it might have passed a different sanction.

   While only the accused can appeal to the Court of Appeal, from there either the accused or the prosecution may appeal on a point of law to the House of Lords, provided that either the Court of Appeal or the House of Lords grant leave for the appeal and that the Court of Appeal certifies that the case involves a matter of law of general public importance. The Royal Commission on Criminal Justice 1993 (set up after the release of the Birmingham Six) recommended that this latter requirement should be abolished.

2 The Criminal Appeal Act 1995 established the Criminal Cases Review Commission (CCRC), following a proposal made by the RCCJ. This body is not a court deciding appeals, rather it is responsible for bringing

cases, where there may have been a miscarriage of justice, to the attention of the Court of Appeal if the case was originally heard by the Crown Court (or the Crown Court if the case was originally heard by a magistrates' court). Either a person can apply to the Commission to consider their case or the Commission can consider it on their own initiative if an ordinary appeal is time barred. The Commission can carry out an investigation into the case, which may involve asking the police to re-investigate a crime. Before making a reference the Commission is able to seek the Court of Appeal's opinion on any matter.

The decision as to whether or not to refer a case will be taken by a committee consisting of at least three members of the Commission. It can make such a reference in relation to a conviction where it appears to them that any argument or evidence, which was not raised in any relevant court proceedings, gives rise to a real possibility that the conviction would not be upheld were the reference to be made. A reference in relation to a sentence will be possible if 'any argument on a point of law, or any information' was not so raised and, again, there is a real possibility that the conviction might not be upheld. Where the Commission refers a conviction or sentence to the Court of Appeal it is treated as a fresh appeal and the Commission has no further involvement in the case.

The Commission is based in Birmingham and consists of no fewer than 11 members, at least a third of whom will be lawyers and one will have knowledge of the criminal justice system in Northern Ireland. They are appointed by the Queen on the advice of the Prime Minister. The current Chairperson of the the Commission is Sir Frederick Crawford, formerly Vice Chancellor of Aston University. It has about 60 support staff and it is anticipated that it will receive about six cases a day.

3 Following the Access to Justice Act 1999, appeals by way of case stated have been introduced from the Crown Court to the High Court. Before these were only available from the magistrates' court.

Procedure before the Court of Appeal

Whichever appeal route is taken to reach the Court of Appeal, once the case is before the court it is dealt with under the same procedure which will now be considered.

Admission of fresh evidence

Unlike an appeal from the magistrates' court to the Crown Court, the Court of Appeal in criminal cases does not rehear the whole case with all its evidence. Instead, it aims merely to review the lower court's decision. This is at least partly because the Court of Appeal is reluctant to overturn the verdict of a jury, apparently fearing that to do so might undermine the public's respect for juries in general.

The Court of Appeal can admit fresh evidence 'if they think it necessary or expedient in the interests of justice' (Criminal Appeal Act 1968, s. 23(1)). In deciding whether to admit fresh evidence they must consider whether:

- the evidence is capable of belief;
- the evidence could afford a ground for allowing the appeal;
- the evidence would have been admissible at the trial; and
- there is a reasonable explanation why it was not so adduced.

In addition, under the 1995 Act, the Court of Appeal can direct the Criminal Cases Review Commission to investigate and report on any matter relevant to the determination of a case being considered by the court. Thus, the Court of Appeal has a radical new power to seek out new evidence themselves, something that no other criminal court in England currently has been able to do, due to our traditional adversarial procedures.

At one time, the Court of Appeal considered new evidence in the light of the effect it might have had on the decision of the jury; but, in **Stafford** v **DPP** (1974), Viscount Dilhourne said that if the court was satisfied that there was no reasonable doubt about the guilt of the accused, the conviction should not be quashed even though the jury might have come to a different view; the court was not bound to ask whether the evidence might have led to the jury returning a verdict of not guilty. The judges are, therefore, replacing the jury's opinion with their own, which is viewed by some as weakening the right to trial by jury. This approach of second-guessing the outcome of jury deliberations has been criticized by the European Court of Human Rights in **Condron** v **United Kingdom** (2000).

Outcome of the appeal

The appellate court can allow the appeal, dismiss it or order a new trial. Under s. 2 of the Criminal Appeal Act 1968 (as amended by the 1995 Act) an appeal should be allowed if the court thinks that the conviction 'is unsafe'. The Court of Appeal may order a retrial where it feels this is required by the interests of justice. It will only do so if it accepts that the additional evidence is true but is not convinced that it is conclusive – in other words, that it would have led to a different verdict.

Powers of the prosecution following acquittal

The general rule is that once a person has been tried and acquitted they cannot be retried for the same offence, under the principle of double jeopardy. The rule aims to prevent the oppressive use of the criminal justice system by public authorities. Following the unsuccessful private prosecution of three men suspected of killing Stephen Lawrence, the judicial inquiry into the affair recommended that the principle of double jeopardy should be abolished. It proposed that the Court of Appeal should have the power to permit prosecution after acquittal 'where fresh and viable evidence is presented'. The Home Secretary referred the matter to the Law Commission. This body has recommended that the double jeopardy rule should be limited. Under this recommendation it would be possible to retry someone acquitted of murder if new evidence is later discovered which makes the prosecution case substantially stronger and the new evidence could not have been obtained before the first trial. The Government is proposing to introduce this reform in its Criminal Justice Bill outlined in the Queen's speech in 2001. Sir Robin Auld's *Review of the Criminal Courts* (2001) has subsequently recommended that the double jeopardy rule should be abolished for all grave offences punishable with life or a long term of imprisonment.

The Law Commission also provisionally recommended in 2001 that the prosecution should have a right to appeal against a legal ruling by a judge which would otherwise bring an end to the case and result in the release of the defendant. This right would only apply to rulings made up to the end of the prosecution case. It would not apply to a ruling that the defendant had no case to answer. For example, if a judge rules that evidence is inadmissible which effectively deprives the prosecution of a central part of their case, this could be subject to an early appeal.

Certain exceptions to the principle of double jeopardy already exist:

- The prosecution can state a case for consideration of the High Court following the acquittal of a defendant by the magistrates' court. This is restricted to a point of law or a dispute on jurisdiction.
- The prosecution can also, with leave, appeal to the House of Lords against a decision of the Court of Appeal.
- The Criminal Justice Act 1972 gives the Attorney-General powers to refer any point of law which has arisen in a case for the opinion of the Court of Appeal, even where the defendant was acquitted. Defendants are not identified (though they may be represented) and their acquittal remains unaffected even if the point of law goes against them – so this procedure is not, strictly speaking, an appeal. The purpose of this power is to enable the Court of Appeal to review a potentially incorrect legal ruling before it gains too wide a circulation in the trial courts.
- The Criminal Justice Act 1988 enables the Attorney-General to refer to the Court of Appeal cases of apparently too lenient sentencing, including cases where it appears the judge has erred in law as to their powers of sentencing. Leave from the Court of Appeal is required. The Court of Appeal may quash the sentence and pass a more appropriate one. This is the first time that the prosecution is involved in the sentencing process. The provision was enacted in response to the Government's view that public confidence in the criminal justice system was being

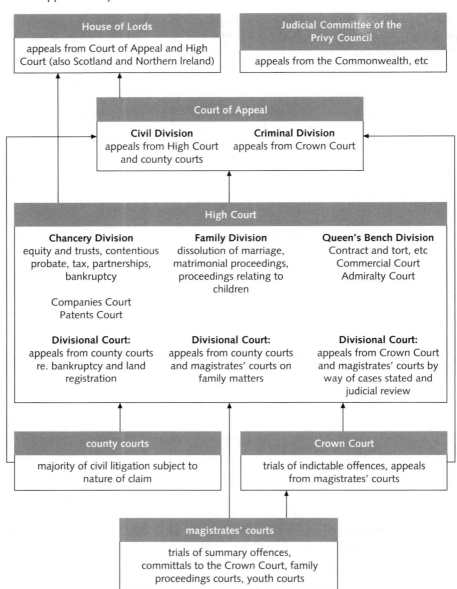

Figure 14.2 An outline of the court structure in England and Wales

This diagram is, of necessity, much simplified and should not be taken as a comprehensive statement on the jurisdiction of any specific court

Source: *Judicial Statistics 1999*

undermined by unduly lenient sentences, which had been given much publicity by the tabloid press.
* The Criminal Procedure and Investigation Act 1996 created a power to order a retrial where a person has been convicted of an offence involving interference with, or intimidation of a juror, witness or potential witness, in any proceedings which led to an acquittal.

Criticism and reform of the appeal system

Lord Woolf on appeals

With regard to civil appeals, Lord Woolf has recommended the introduction of a system where cases could be referred to the Court of Appeal or House of Lords in order to ensure proper development of the law. This would be appropriate where the lower court has reached an unsatisfactory decision but where no appeal has been brought or is possible.

Sir Robin Auld on appeals

In his *Review of the Criminal Courts* (2001), Sir Robin Auld wanted to see a simplification of the appeal process. He recommended that all appeals should apply the same test, and favoured the adoption of the Court of Appeal test. He thought that there should be a single line of appeal from the magistrates' courts to the Court of Appeal. He would therefore abolish appeals from magistrates' courts to the Crown Court by way of re-hearing and replace it with an appeal to the Crown Court without a jury. He would also abolish appeals from the magistrates' court and the Crown Court to the High Court by way of a case stated and judicial review.

He thought that the Court of Appeal should be variously constituted according to the nature, legal importance and complexity of its work. In straightforward appeals only two judges would sit. In cases of exceptional legal importance and complexity, a distinguished academic could either be appointed to act as a judge in the case or be invited to submit a written brief to the court on the points in issue.

He thought the Court of Appeal needed to slow down so that appeal hearings were less rushed. More time needed to be allocated for the judges to prepare for cases and to write their judgments.

On points of law of general public importance, where there are conflicting decisions of the Court of Appeal or where the law is in such an unsatisfactory state that only the House of Lords can resolve it, he favoured the introduction of a 'leap-frog' appeal from the Crown Court to the House of Lords, similar to that which exists for civil appeals.

He also favoured giving the prosecution a new right to appeal what they considered to be a perverse acquittal by a jury, a reform which has been criticized by the Bar Council as containing 'grave dangers'.

The Privy Council

The Judicial Committee of the Privy Council hears appeals from Commonwealth countries, such as the Bahamas, Barbados, Bermuda, the Channel Islands, the Falkland Islands, Gibraltar, Jamaica, New Zealand and Trinidad and Tobago. Certain independent Commonwealth countries, including Australia, India, Malaysia, Nigeria, Pakistan and Singapore, have chosen to stop sending their final appeals to London. The Privy Council also hears appeals from, for example, disciplinary proceedings by professional bodies and the courts of the Church of England.

In recent years there has been much debate about the future of appeals to the Judicial Committee of the Privy Council from independent Caribbean countries. All of these countries have retained the mandatory death penalty by hanging for the crime of murder. The Privy Council is seen locally as an obstacle in the desire to execute those on death row. One proposal is to abolish the criminal jurisdiction of the Privy Council.

The Criminal Cases Review Commission

The CCRC was established to replace the old section 17 procedure contained in the Criminal Appeal Act 1968 and repealed in 1995. Under the old procedure, the Home Secretary could refer a case that had been previously heard in the Crown Court to the Court of Appeal, despite the fact that the normal time limit for appeals had expired or an unsuccessful appeal had already been heard. The Home Secretary had considerable discretion whether or not to make this referral: the statute simply required a reference to be made 'if he thinks fit'.

There were serious difficulties with the section 17 procedure. The Home Secretary only usually referred cases where new evidence had come to light, and which were continuing to attract media comment and public concern long after the trial had taken place. Each year there were about 730 applications to the Home Office and its equivalent in Northern Ireland, but only ten to 12 of those cases were actually referred to the Court of Appeal.

Problems with the process were highlighted by such cases as the Birmingham Six and the Tottenham Three, where references were only ordered after years of persuasion and publicity. The original appeal of the Birmingham Six was rejected in 1976. It was not until 1987 that the Home Secretary referred their case back to the Court of Appeal, though that appeal was rejected. Three years later, he again referred the case to the Court of Appeal and this time the Director of Public Prosecutions did not resist the application so that the court had little choice but to allow the appeal and quash the convictions.

The Court of Appeal showed a general reluctance to allow section 17 appeals in cases where it had already dismissed an appeal, and in fact appeared to dislike section 17 referrals generally: in the first (unsuccessful) section 17 appeal from the Birmingham Six, the court stated that: 'As has happened before in references by the Home Secretary to this court, the longer the hearing has gone on the more convinced this court has become that the verdict of the jury was correct.' As MP Chris Mullins's book on the Birmingham Six points out, this seemed to be a thinly-veiled message to the Home Secretary that referring such cases was a waste of time.

A further problem was that, once the reference was made, the appeal was governed by the Criminal Appeal Act 1968, and the expense and responsibility of preparing the appeal lay with the defendant, who would probably be in prison and have been there for quite some time. Legal aid might be available but investigation in these circumstances would be difficult.

It has been hoped that the CCRC will mark a considerable improvement on the old section 17 procedure, but concerns have already been expressed about the new arrangements. One problem with the Commission is that, while it is predicted more cases will reach the Court of Appeal than they did under the section 17 procedure, one of the weaknesses with that procedure was that even when the case was referred to the Court of Appeal the convictions were often upheld, even though later it was acknowledged that there had been a miscarriage of justice. Thus, cases such as the Birmingham Six had to be repeatedly referred back to the Court of Appeal before they would eventually overturn the original conviction. In that case the appeal was allowed on the basis that there was 'fresh' evidence as to the police interrogation techniques and the forensic evidence. In reality this evidence had, in essence, been before the Court of Appeal in 1987; the difference was that the court was forced to accept that the evidence raised a lurking doubt in 1991. Only if the other provisions are adequate to improve the Court of Appeal process will the same problems be avoided. An alternative solution would have been to give the Commission the power to decide appeals themselves.

The pressure group, JUSTICE, has criticized the fact that the CCRC has no power to assign in-house staff as investigating officers. It has argued that without this power the Commission could not guarantee the independence of an inquiry. The CCRC has no independent powers to carry out searches of premises, to check criminal records, to use police computers, or to make an arrest. To do this they would have to appoint someone who had these powers, usually a police officer. The fact that investigations carried out on behalf of the CCRC will be by the police has caused concern. Many allegations of a miscarriage of justice involve accusations of malpractice by the police. Experience of police investigations into the high-profile miscarriages of justice suggest that these are not always effective, with a tendency for the police to close ranks and try to protect each other. JUSTICE has also questioned the independence of the organization as its members are government appointees.

The CCRC issued its third annual report in June 2000. This states that it received a total of 13,193 applications in its first three years. Eighty of these were referred to the courts; all were appeals following conviction in the Crown Court apart from one which was an appeal from the magistrates' court. Twenty-seven of these referrals have resulted in convictions being quashed or sentences modified. One of the first referrals made by the CCRC concerned Derek Bentley. He had been involved with a friend in an unsuccessful burglary. This had resulted in a police chase when his friend had pointed a gun at a police officer and Derek Bentley had said 'let him have it', at which point the friend shot and killed the officer. Derek Bentley was convicted as an accomplice to the murder. He appealed but his appeal was rejected and he was hanged in January 1953.

The circumstances of his conviction gave rise to a long campaign by his family and numerous representations were made to the Home Office. He was given a royal pardon in 1993 but this was in respect of the sentence only. The family continued their campaign for the conviction itself to be quashed and in 1998 the CCRC referred the case to the Court of Appeal which quashed the conviction. They found that the conviction was unsafe because of a defective summing-up by the trial judge to the jury, which had included such prejudicial comments about the defence case that Bentley had been denied a fair trial. This was a notable high-profile success for the CCRC, but it remains to be seen whether the Commission will have success with lower-profile referrals.

The CCRC has found the main reasons for it to refer cases back to the courts are:

- Prosecution failings (such as breach of identification and interview procedures or the use of questionable witnesses).
- Scientific evidence (such as DNA and fingerprint evidence).
- Non-disclosure of evidence.
- New evidence (such as alibis, eye-witnesses or confessions).

The biggest problem facing the CCRC since its instalment is a substantial backlog of cases waiting to be considered. This issue was considered by a Home Affairs Select Committee Report in 1999. It considered that the Commission could reduce the amount of detailed work done on each case without reducing its effectiveness, as its approach was currently 'meticulous to a fault'. It also suggested that the Commission should refer more cases to the Court of Appeal, rather than trying to second-guess the Court of Appeal and only referring cases that are highly likely to be overturned. In its annual report for 1999/2000 the Commission has responded:

> Some external commentators have advocated that the Commission should review cases faster by being less thorough, and should refer them more

readily to the appropriate courts of appeal. Not referring cases that should be referred, for lack of thoroughness, would perpetuate the very miscarriages of justice that the Commission was set up to review, and would be likely to result in resubmission of cases and judicial review. Referring unmeritorious cases would impose a costly burden on the courts of appeal. Such behaviour would rapidly diminish public confidence in the competence of the Commission, and in the wider criminal justice system.

The CCRC has improved its procedures and been given increased resoures to try and deal more speedily with its workload.

There is also a problem of funding submissions to the Commission. At the moment the Legal Services Commission only pays for two hours of a solicitor's time, which is insufficient for the preparation of such an application. As a result, more than 90 per cent of applicants are not represented by a solicitor.

Reluctance to overturn jury verdicts

The Court of Appeal seems to feel that overturning jury verdicts weakens public confidence in the jury system, and it is therefore very reluctant to do it. This view was spelt out during the final, successful appeal of the Birmingham Six in 1991, in which the Court of Appeal stated:

> Nothing in s. 2 of the Act, or anywhere else obliges or entitles us to say whether we think that the appellant is innocent. This is a point of great constitutional importance. The task of deciding whether a man is innocent or guilty falls on the jury. We are concerned solely with the question whether the verdict of the jury can stand.
>
> Rightly or wrongly (we think rightly) trial by jury is the foundation of our criminal justice system . . . The primacy of the jury in the criminal justice system is well illustrated by the difference between the Criminal and Civil Divisions of the Court of Appeal . . . A civil appeal is by way of rehearing of the whole of the case. So the court is concerned with fact as well as law . . . It follows that in a civil case the Court of Appeal may take a different view of the facts from the court below. In a criminal case this is not possible . . . the Criminal Division is perhaps more accurately described as a court of review.

The case of Winston Silcott (discussed on p. 244) illustrates the dangers. He had been convicted in 1985 of murdering PC Blakelock during the Tottenham riots. The offence had been committed by a group of 30 people. Six had gone on trial and only three were convicted, including Silcott. The only evidence against Silcott was a statement he was alleged to have made: 'You won't pin this on me . . . nobody will talk', which he had not signed. Despite these obvious weaknesses in the case, conviction was initially upheld by the Court of Appeal and was only overturned in 1991.

The major problem with the Appeal Court's approach is that in many cases, the fault lies not with the decision-making powers of the jury, but in the evidence presented to them. Where a jury has not seen all the evidence, or where the evidence it has heard has been falsified by the police (as was alleged in some of the well-known miscarriages of justice), or where the jury has in any other way failed to have the case properly presented to it, overturning the verdict should not automatically be viewed as a criticism of its ability to make correct decisions. A better way to demonstrate confidence in the jury system might be to order a retrial with a new jury.

The Runciman Commission concluded that the Court of Appeal should show greater willingness to substitute its judgment for that of the jury. They pointed out that in gauging the evidence juries could make errors, particularly in a high-profile case in which emotions run high. The trial of Winston Silcott is a classic case in point. We will have to wait and see whether the Criminal Appeal Act 1995 might instigate a change of philosophy in this regard, particularly in the light of the changes to the rules on the admissibility of fresh evidence.

Up to 1995 the Court of Appeal was able to conclude that even if there was found to have been a material irregularity in the trial they could still uphold the conviction if they felt that no miscarriage of justice had occurred. This was known as 'applying the proviso' but the relevant statutory provision has now been repealed which may lead to a greater willingness to overturn a jury verdict.

Admission of fresh evidence

Until 1995, s. 23 of the 1968 Act, as well as giving the court a discretion to admit new evidence, imposed a duty on the court to receive fresh evidence where it was 'likely to be credible'. In practice, the Court of Appeal was very reluctant to admit fresh evidence, despite the apparently broad drafting of the legislation. One of the reasons for the court's approach was that they were unwilling to turn what was supposed to be a process of review into a full rehearing. But, in effect, defendants could be punished and denied the right to a fair hearing for omissions caused by their lawyers' incompetence, the underfunding of the legal aid system, or the prosecution's obstructiveness. The RCCJ concluded that the statutory powers to admit fresh evidence were sufficient, the problem was that in practice they were being given too narrow an interpretation. Thus, they encouraged the Court of Appeal to take a more flexible approach.

Now the appeal court merely have a discretion to receive fresh evidence where 'it is capable of belief'. At the time of the amendment it was suggested this provided a wider discretion for the court in the interests of justice. Unfortunately, this does not seem to be reflected in the Court of Appeal's interpretation of the provision. In **R** *v* **Jones (Steven Martin)**

(1996) the appellant had been convicted of his wife's murder and, on appeal, he had applied for the court to receive fresh expert evidence from three forensic pathologists. While on the facts of the case the evidence was allowed, the court stated that in general only new factual evidence as opposed to expert evidence would normally be admitted, noting that the test for admissibility was more appropriate to such evidence as one could rarely consider expert evidence as 'incapable of belief'. This case shows that the legislative amendment to s. 23 may have actually accentuated the problems of the Court of Appeal refusing to admit fresh evidence.

Lord Devlin, in his book *The Judge* (1979), criticized the Court of Appeal's decision in **Stafford** *v* **DPP** to follow their own view of whether new evidence makes a conviction unsafe (or unsatisfactory), rather than assessing the effect such evidence might have had on the trial jury. He felt that this involves judges in findings of fact, a function that properly belongs to the jury. The jury ends up playing a subordinate part in the verdict, since it has not heard all the evidence. He believes the change from assessing the possible effect of new evidence on the trial jury has not been sanctioned by Parliament and is an attack on the jury system.

Unwillingness to order retrials

Many have argued that the Court of Appeal should use its power to order retrials more often. The number of such retrials has been growing from three in 1990 to 23 in 1992, though they remain rare.

Lord Devlin has argued, as stated above, that a retrial should be ordered wherever fresh evidence could have made a difference to the verdict – the original verdict being clearly unsatisfactory since it was given without the jury hearing all the evidence.

Opponents argue that it may be unfair to the accused to reopen a decided case, and that a second trial cannot be a fair one, especially if some time has passed and/or the case has received a lot of publicity. But, as Lord Devlin argues, this does not stop retrials being ordered where the jury has failed to agree a verdict, nor are prosecutions necessarily stifled because witnesses have to speak of events many years before. In fact, at the same time as the Birmingham Six were told that a retrial 13 years after the original one was inappropriate, the Government was debating the prosecution of war criminals, some 44 years after the end of the Second World War. Shortly after the Six's unsuccessful appeal, an IRA man was brought to trial on charges dating back 13 years.

As far as publicity is concerned, the second jury may well know of the defendant's record and have noted other adverse publicity, as well as knowing that the defendant has already been convicted on a previous occasion for the crime. On the other hand, in all the high-profile miscarriages of justice, no further publicity could have affected the attitudes of potential jurors more than that surrounding the original offences and trials – in fact prejudicial media reporting was one reason given for finding the convictions of the Taylor sisters unsafe and unsatisfactory in 1995.

Many wrongful convictions result from mistaken identity, and it is difficult for the Court of Appeal, which does not usually re-examine witnesses, to assess the strength of such evidence. Retrials might be the best way of dealing with this problem. A general power to order a retrial could also be a way of convicting offenders who escape on a technicality first time round, and might be a more obviously just solution than applying the old proviso, or letting such defendants go free, which has a negative effect on the public, the jury and the victim. However, it could also subject genuinely innocent defendants to a second ordeal.

It has been suggested that wider use of retrials would 'open the flood-gates' to a deluge of appeals, yet this does not appear to be a problem in other countries with wider powers of retrial, including Scotland. In any case, Lord Atkin has pointed out, 'Finality is a good thing but justice is better'.

The Runciman Commission considered the issue and concluded that the Court of Appeal should use the power to order a retrial more extensively.

The single test for quashing convictions

Before the 1995 Act, there used to be three grounds on which the Criminal Division of the Court of Appeal could allow an appeal. These were where the Court thought that:

- the jury's verdict was unsafe and unsatisfactory; or
- there was an error of law; or
- there was a material irregularity in the course of the trial.

The old law was criticized by the Runciman Commission on the basis that it was unnecessarily complex and that the different grounds for quashing a conviction overlapped. For example, it felt that there was no real difference between the words 'unsafe' and 'unsatisfactory'. In the light of this criticism the law has been reduced by the Criminal Appeals Act 1995 to a single test that the court thinks the conviction is unsafe. This is narrower than that recommended by the Runciman Commission as it had favoured a retrial where the conviction 'may' be unsafe. The Law Society, the Bar, Liberty and JUSTICE all unsuccessfully called on the Government to follow the RCCJ's proposal. The Government's expressed view was that any such doubt implied by the concept of 'may be unsafe' was already implicit in the idea of a conviction being 'unsafe'.

Government Ministers insisted that the effect of the new law was simply to restate or consolidate the existing practice of the Court of Appeal. However, the leading criminal law academic, Professor J.C. Smith, and the Director of the pressure group JUSTICE, Anne Owens (1995) have both criticized the new single test on the basis that there is a danger it will be interpreted more narrowly than the previous tests.

Michael Zander (one of the Commissioners and a leading academic on the English legal system) along with one other Commissioner disagreed with the final proposal. They took the view that where there had been serious police malpractice then the conviction should always be quashed to discourage such conduct, and to prevent the police believing that they could benefit in terms of getting convictions by such behaviour. This is a situation where, under the old law, the Court of Appeal might have stated that the conviction was safe but it would be quashed because it was unsatisfactory. This route is no longer open to the Court.

Legal advice

Legal advice should be available immediately after the conviction, including advice on the possibility of an appeal. Research carried out for the Runciman Commission by Plotnikoff and Wilson – *Information and Advice for Prisoners about Grounds for Appeal and the Appeal Process* (1993) – found serious defects in the provision of such legal advice. Nine per cent of those convicted were not visited afterwards in the cells in order to be given legal advice, 23 per cent not advised about appeal and nearly 90 per cent received nothing in writing about an appeal. Malleson, in his research for the Runciman Commission – *A Review of the Appeal Process* (1993) – found that lawyers themselves were often ill-informed about the powers of the Court of Appeal, some believing that they had the power to increase sentences on appeal by defendants. Not surprisingly those applicants who sought to appeal without legal advice were less successful. In the light of this evidence, the Runciman Commission argued that appellants needed to receive more legal advice.

General unwillingness to address faults in the system

The problems outlined above can be seen as symptomatic of a more general reluctance to uncover the extent of miscarriages of justice in our system. This attitude was typified by Lord Denning's speech in **McIlkenny** *v* **Chief Constable of the West Midlands** (1980), the case in which the police successfully appealed against a civil action, brought against them by the Birmingham Six, in respect of injuries sustained after their arrest. Lord Denning said:

> If the six men win, it will mean that the police were guilty of perjury, that they were guilty of violence and threats . . . and that the convictions were erroneous . . . the Home Secretary would have either to recommend that they be pardoned or he would have to remit the case to the Court of Appeal . . . This is such an appalling vista that every sensible person in the land would say 'It cannot be right that these actions should go any further'.

The implication was that, even if the men were innocent, the damage such a revelation could do to confidence in the justice system meant it was better not known.

The acquitted

There are two situations where the victim of an injustice has little or no possibility of appeal or redress:

- Acquittals – 55 per cent of defendants who pleaded not guilty to all charges in the Crown Court in 1989 were acquitted. Many of these people will have spent time on remand. Clearly, not all of these are victims of injustice but those that are have no legal remedy except a civil action against the police for malicious prosecution, which is notoriously difficult to prove.
- Where a person has been kept in custody and released without charge – again there is no remedy except a civil action for false imprisonment.

The role of the House of Lords

From time to time the question is asked whether we need two courts with purely appellate jurisdiction. For those who consider that we do not, the answer is usually to abolish the House of Lords (as a court) – the Court of Appeal could not be abolished because its much larger caseload cannot be absorbed by the House of Lords. Efforts to abolish the appellate jurisdiction of the House of Lords date back over 100 years – in fact the Judicature Act of 1873 contained a section which did just that, but was never brought into force. The following are some of the arguments on both sides.

For abolition

- The Court of Appeal should be sufficient; a third tier is unnecessary and illogical. A.P. Herbert points out that giving appellants the chance to get their case decided by two appellate courts is like having your appendix taken out by a distinguished surgeon and then being referred to another who might confirm the first surgeon's decision, but might just as easily recommend the appendix be replaced! Reversing legal decisions might not pose the same practical problems as medical ones but, nevertheless, it may seem odd that the decisions of the eminent judges in the Court of Appeal can be completely overturned by the House of Lords.
- It allows a litigant with the support of a minority of judges to win. Take the example of a litigant losing a civil case, appealing to the Court of Appeal and losing, but finally winning in the House of Lords. Counting all the judges involved together, they may have had six against them

(the original trial judge, the three judges hearing the case in the Court of Appeal, and two out of five in the House of Lords). Yet, if three judges in the House of Lords are in their favour they win the case overall, even though twice as many judges supported their opponent.

- It adds cost and delay to achieving a decision. Usually QCs are instructed in appeals to the House of Lords, substantially increasing costs, and extra time is taken up. This can add to emotional stress and financial hardship for one or both litigants.
- It has failed to make any adequate contribution to development of the criminal law. This point is made by the eminent criminal law specialists J.C. Smith and Glanville Williams. Unlike the Court of Appeal, the House of Lords has no specialist divisions, and criticisms of the quality of their decisions in criminal appeals may stem from this. Glanville Williams points out that: 'It is particularly inapt that a Chancery judge should have the casting vote in the House of Lords in a criminal case, as Lord Cross did in **Hyam**.' He also suggests that the age of judges in the House of Lords is a problem, since old men are 'often fixed in their opinions' and 'tend to ignore the opinions of others'; this may be true, but the judges of the Court of Appeal are hardly in the first flush of youth either.

  Part of the problem may be due to the strict conditions for appealing to the House of Lords, which mean that few criminal cases get there, and the Law Lords actually have very little chance to make notable contributions to this area of the law.
- It tends to side with the establishment, and usually the Government. This is the argument advanced by Griffiths (see p. 112), but there is little evidence to suggest that the Court of Appeal would be very different in this respect if it became the highest court.
- The House of Lords offers nothing beyond finality, and that could be more efficiently achieved without it. Jackson, an academic in the field, examined the 15 appeals made to the House of Lords in 1972, and found that eight involved Government departments or national authorities and, five were disputes between commercial concerns. He deduced that, in the case of both Government departments and commercial concerns, the reason for taking the case to the House of Lords was nothing more than the fact that it is the final court.

  In the case of Government departments, where judicial decisions appear to obstruct them, their object is to remove that obstruction; appeal to the House of Lords may achieve this, but if not, the matter can be put right by legislation. However, they must have the final decision of the judiciary before this can happen, and must therefore go to the House of Lords – not because of any innate quality of its decision-making, but simply because it is the final court. Jackson felt that the commercial cases were also likely to be based on the pursuit of finality. If this is correct, abolishing the House of Lords would enable finality to be achieved more quickly and cheaply.

Against abolition

- Its small membership allows the House of Lords to give a consistent leadership that the Court of Appeal, with its much greater number of judges, could not, and therefore to guide the harmonious development of the law. Louis Blom-Cooper QC has argued that, especially since the Practice Direction of 1966 allowing the House of Lords to overrule its own decisions, the Law Lords are in a unique position to be able to re-form the law from the top. The much larger size of the Court of Appeal, and its division into different courts, means there would always be a danger of different courts within it applying different views of the law.
- The combination of the two appellate courts allows the majority of appeals to be dealt with more quickly than the House of Lords could hope to deal with them, while still retaining the smaller court for those matters which require further consideration, and for promoting consistent development of the law.
- The House of Lords plays a valuable role in correcting decisions by the Court of Appeal – in 1988 it reversed nearly 40 per cent of civil and 33 per cent of criminal appeals that were referred to it.
- It has made some important contributions to the development of our law, including making marital rape a crime – in **R** *v* **R** (1991) – and confirming the restricted scope of parental rights in a modern society in **Gillick** (1985).

▶ JUDICIAL REVIEW

The system of judicial review by the High Court oversees the decisions of public bodies and officials, such as inferior courts and tribunals, local councils, and members of the executive including police officers and Government Ministers. Cases are heard by the Queen's Bench Division. Certain public bodies are exempt from judicial review. For example, in **R** *v* **Parliamentary Commissioner for Standards, ex parte Al Fayed** (1998) the Court of Appeal ruled that the Parliamentary Commissioner for Standards could not be subjected to judicial review. One of the functions of the Commissioner is to receive and, where appropriate, investigate complaints from the public in relation to the conduct of Members of Parliament. Mohammed Al Fayed, the owner of Harrods, had made such a complaint that Michael Howard, while Home Secretary, had received a corrupt payment. The complaint had been investigated and then rejected and Al Fayed had sought judicial review of this decision. The Court of Appeal ruled that the Parliamentary Commissioner for Standards operated as part of the proceedings of Parliament and its activities were non-justiciable. This is because of the principles of the separation of power discussed at p. 2.

Unlike the appeal process, judicial review does not examine the merits of the decision. It can only quash a decision if the public body had no power to make it, known as *ultra vires* (*ultra* is latin for 'beyond' and *vires* is latin for 'powers'). There are two forms of *ultra vires*: procedural *ultra vires* and substantive *ultra vires*.

Procedural *ultra vires*

Where there has been procedural *ultra vires* it is often said that there has been a breach of natural justice. This means either that the body reaching the particular decision complained of was biased, or that the applicant was not given a fair opportunity to be heard. In **Dimes *v* Grand Junction Canal Proprietors** (1852), a dispute about land, Lord Chancellor Cottenham found in favour of the canal company. It was then discovered that he owned several thousand pounds worth of shares in Grand Junction Canal Proprietors, and the decision was set aside. This was the principle that was applied in the litigation concerning the extradition of Pinochet, the former dictator of Chile. In those proceedings the House of Lords had handed down a judgment that Pinochet could be extradited to Spain. It was subsequently discovered that one of the judges, Lord Hoffmann, had links with Amnesty International, a human rights organization that was involved in the proceedings. Because the process could, as a result, be viewed as unfair the House of Lords reopened the case and gave a fresh judgment several months later. Note, there is no need to prove the decision was in fact biased, only that there is a financial interest or some other reason why bias is likely – this is on the grounds that justice must be seen to be done as well as actually be done – **R *v* Bow Street Metropolitan Stipendiary Magistrate, ex parte Pinochet Ugarte (No. 2)** (1999).

Following the **Pinochet** case a series of cases have arisen where a litigant has challenged the impartiality of the judge. In **Locabail (UK) Ltd *v* Bayfield Properties Ltd** (2000) the Court of Appeal laid down guidance as to when a judge should be disqualified from hearing a case. This is where there is a 'real danger or possibility' of bias. Bias will be presumed where a judge has a personal interest in the outcome of a trial. Following the **Pinochet** case this interest may be of either a financial or non-financial nature. Any matter that the judge was unaware of will be irrelevant to the issue. Matters that might give rise to a real danger of bias include personal friendship or animosity between the judge and any member of the public in the case. Matters which could not ground a successful objection were the judge's religion, ethnic or national origin, gender, age, class, means or sexual orientation. Matters which would not ordinarily ground a successful objection were the judge's social, educational or employment background, political affiliation, membership of bodies, including Masonic associations, or any extra-judicial academic or professional activity.

Substantive *ultra vires*

This occurs where the content of the decision was outside the power of the public body that made it. Sometimes legislation may make it clear what the limits on the public body's powers are. Thus, the limits on the magistrates' jurisdiction are clearly laid down in legislation. If a magistrates' court decides to hear a case which is indictable only, and should therefore have been heard in the Crown Court, the magistrates' decision can be ruled *ultra vires* and quashed.

Often, however, the legislation does not lay down clear limits on the public body's powers. For example, the legislation might simply say that the Minister can appoint 'who he thinks fit'. If the Minister then appoints someone who is totally unqualified for the job, it is very difficult for the court to prove that the Minister did not think he was fit for the job. To get round some of the problems caused by broadly drafted powers such as these, the courts are prepared to imply certain limitations on the official's power even where they are not laid down by the relevant legislation.

Wednesbury unreasonable

A decision will be held to be outside the public body's power if it was so unreasonable that no reasonable public body could have reached the decision. This is known as the Wednesbury principle and was laid down in **Associated Picture Houses Ltd** *v* **Wednesbury Corporation** (1948). Lord Diplock described such a decision in **Council of Civil Service Unions** *v* **Minister for the Civil Service** (1984) as 'a decision which is so outrageous in its defiance of logic or of accepted moral standards that no sensible person . . . could have arrived at it'.

In **R** *v* **Chief Constable of Sussex, ex parte International Traders Ferry Ltd** (1998) lorries carrying livestock for export required police protection from animal rights protesters in order to gain access to the ferries. The Chief Constable decided to reduce the protection to certain days of the week due to insufficient police resources. The ferry company sought judicial review of this decision but it was held by the Court of Appeal and the House of Lords that the decision was not unreasonable.

If a decision interferes with fundamental human rights then the court applies a more stringent test in determining whether the decision was reasonable. The relevant test is whether a reasonable body could, on the material before it, have reasonably concluded that such interference was justifiable. The more substantial the interference with human rights, the more the courts require by way of justification before they are satisfied that a decision is reasonable. **R** *v* **Lord Saville and Others, ex parte B** (1999) arose from the events of 'Bloody Sunday' when 13 people were killed and many others injured when British soldiers opened fire on a demonstration in Northern Ireland. In 1972 the Widgery tribunal was set up to inquire into the incident. The majority of soldiers giving evidence in that inquiry were allowed to remain anonymous. The subsequent report was criticized and eventually in 1998 a further inquiry was set up presided over by Lord Saville. In May 1999 the Ministry of Defence asked the tribunal to permit military witnesses to give their evidence again without disclosing their names, primarily on the grounds that such disclosure would endanger their lives as they would be exposed to the threat of revenge attacks by terrorist organizations. While the tribunal accepted that anonymity would not prevent it from discovering the truth, it refused to grant this request. An application was then made to the High Court by soldiers who had fired live bullets on 'Bloody Sunday' for judicial review of the tribunal's decisions, contending that it was unreasonable. The High Court accepted that the tribunal's decision potentially interfered with fundamental human rights, those rights being the rights to life, safety and to live free of fear. The question for the court was, given the tribunal's clear finding that anonymity would not impede it in its fundamental task of discovering the truth, could a reasonable tribunal conclude that the additional degree of openness to be gained by disclosure of the names of the 17 soldiers who fired the shots amount to so compelling a public interest as to justify subjecting the soldiers and their families to a significant danger to their lives. The authorities established that where fundamental human rights might be affected by a decision of a public authority, the law gave those rights precedence. The law was that such rights were to prevail unless either the threat that they would be infringed was slight or there was a compelling reason why they should yield. The High Court found that the tribunal had not accorded the applicants' fundamental human rights the required weight. The tribunal's decision was quashed and a subsequent appeal to the Court of Appeal was dismissed.

Irrelevant considerations

If the court concludes that a public body took into account irrelevant considerations then its decision may be quashed. For example, in **R v Somerset County Council, ex parte Fewings** (1995) Somerset County Council passed a resolution prohibiting stag hunting on its land. The ban was challenged on the ground that it was acting outside its statutory authority; the power under s. 120(1)(b) of the Local Government Act 1972, to manage its land for the benefit of the authority's area, did not extend to banning stag hunting on the ground that it was cruel or unethical. The Court of Appeal held that the ban was illegal. It found that, while the assertion that hunting was cruel was not a completely irrelevant consideration when exercising its discretion, the council may have given undue weight to the moral question concerning the desirability of hunting, at the expense of the statutory requirement to manage the land for the benefit of the authority's area.

Improper purpose

The idea of a body acting outside its powers has been extended to include abusing those powers by using them for an improper purpose. In **R v Derbyshire County Council, ex parte The Times Supplements** (1990), *The Times* challenged Derbyshire County Council's decision to withdraw its advertising for educational appointments from *Times* publications, after the *Sunday Times* had printed two articles accusing the council of improper and legally doubtful behaviour. The Divisional Court held that the Council's decision had been motivated by bad faith and vindictiveness, and was therefore an abuse of power.

Fettered discretion

Where the public body does have a discretion, that is to say a choice, they must exercise that choice. In **British Oxygen Co v Board of Trade** (1971) a scheme had been set up where grants towards capital expenditure (the purchase of large pieces of machinery, etc.) by industry could be awarded from the Ministry of Trade at the Ministry's discretion. The Ministry developed a rule that grants would not be given for machinery costing less than £25. The British Oxygen Company had spent over £4 million on gas cylinders which cost £20 each. They applied for a grant to assist with the expenditure and applying this blanket rule the Ministry rejected their application. On appeal, the House of Lords concluded that a public body with a general legislative discretion was only allowed to develop such internal policies if it was prepared to listen to arguments for the exercise of individual discretion in particular cases.

In **R v Southwark London Borough Council, ex parte Udu** (1995) the applicant had obtained a law degree from South Bank University. The applicant applied to his local authority for a discretionary maintenance award in order to study the Legal Practice Course at the College of Law to qualify as a solicitor. The authority rejected the application in accordance with its policy of not providing grants for study at private institutions. The application for judicial review was dismissed. The authority could have a policy on the award of postgraduate grants provided it was rational and flexible and rejected the argument that the result of the policy was that only children of wealthy parents could enter the legal profession.

Error on the face of the record

Where the decision-making body's own record of the proceedings reveals it has made a mistake concerning the law, the decision may be quashed.

Remedies

In addition to any of the ordinary civil law remedies of damages, an injunction, or a declaration, the High Court may order a public law remedy only available through the judicial review proceedings. These remedies are often called prerogative orders, and three such remedies exist:

Certiorari

This order quashes (nullifies) an *ultra vires* decision. For example, it might be used to quash the refusal to award a mandatory student grant. It is not available against the Crown, but usually a declaration in that situation will be sufficient.

Mandamus

This is an order to do something and might be used, for example, to force a local authority to produce its accounts for inspection by a local resident, or to compel a tribunal to hear a previously refused appeal. *Mandamus* is not available against the Crown. Often an applicant will seek both an order of *certiorari* and a *mandamus* order. *Certiorari* could quash an *ultra vires* decision and *mandamus* could compel the public body to decide the case according to their legal powers.

Prohibition

This can order a body not to act unlawfully in the future. Thus while *certiorari* quashes decisions already made, a prohibition prevents a decision being made which, if made, would be subject to a *certiorari* order. For example, it can prohibit an inferior court or tribunal from starting or continuing proceedings which are, or threaten to be, outside their jurisdiction, or in breach of natural justice.

The former Labour leader Michael Foot made an unsuccessful application for a prohibition order in **R _v_ Boundary Commission for England, ex parte Foot** (1983). He had challenged the recommendations of the Boundary Commission on amendments to the boundaries of electoral constituencies, as he thought they were unjust. His application was rejected.

Discretion

All the prerogative remedies are discretionary, so even if an applicant proves that the public body behaved illegally, the court can still refuse a remedy. Thus in deciding whether to grant a remedy the court should take into account whether it would be detrimental to good administration. If an alternative remedy is available such as through the appeals process or a specialized tribunal, the court is unlikely to grant a prerogative order. Examples of other factors that might influence their use are consistency with other cases, the nature of the remedy sought, delay, and the motive of the applicant.

Procedure

Part 54 of the Civil Procedure Rules lays down the procedures to be followed for judicial review. The rules contain safeguards to protect public authorities from unreasonable or frivolous complaints and to prevent abuse of the legal process.

Time limit

An application should normally be made within three months of the date when the grounds for the application arose. Even where the application is made within this time, if the court concludes that it was not made promptly it may still not be allowed. On the other hand, the court has a discretion to allow applications made outside the three-month time limit if there was good reason for the delay.

Leave

Before the case can be heard, leave must be obtained from a single judge in the High Court. To obtain leave, the applicants must prove that they have an arguable case. This is quite a low threshold, but the aim is to sift out very weak cases at an early stage to avoid too much unnecessary inconvenience to the administration.

Locus standi

The applicant must have 'a sufficient interest in the matter to which the application relates'. They must, therefore, have a close connection with the subject of the action. This is known as *locus standi*. Again, this rule aims to prevent time being wasted by vexatious litigants or unworthy cases. The issue can be considered both when leave is sought and at the main hearing.

An important case in the field is **R v Inland Revenue Commissioners, ex parte National Federation of Self-Employed and Small Businesses** (1982), often called the Fleet Street Casuals case. An application for judicial review had been made by a taxpayers' association. They wanted to challenge an agreement that had been made by the Inland Revenue to waive the income tax arrears for 6,000 freelance workers in the newspaper printing industry, based at the time in Fleet Street, if they declared their earnings fully in the future. The House of Lords held that the applicant lacked *locus standi*. In deciding whether there was *locus standi* the merits of the case could be taken into account and the case had no merit as the Inland Revenue had no duty to collect every penny of tax due. The tax-payers' association did not have a sufficient interest in other taxpayers' affairs.

Since that case the concept of *locus standi* has been broadened to include some interest and pressure groups. The Attorney-General always has *locus standi*. If a party has failed to prove *locus standi* the Attorney-General can choose to permit the action through a proceeding known as a 'relator action'. Under this mechanism the action officially proceeds under the Attorney-General's name.

There is limited discovery of documents and cross-examination is only allowed in certain circumstances.

Where an application for judicial review is refused by the Divisional Court, application may be made to the Court of Appeal, which, if it accepts that the case should be heard, may refer it back to the Divisional Court, or conduct the hearing itself. Decisions made in a judicial review case may be appealed to the Court of Appeal, and from there to the House of Lords.

Criticisms of judicial review

Problems with control of wide discretionary powers

While the courts have been prepared to imply certain limits to apparently broad discretionary powers of public bodies, it is still very difficult for such powers to be controlled. The Housing Act 1980, for example, empowers the Secretary of State for the Environment to 'do all such things as appear to him necessary or expedient' to enable council tenants to buy their council houses. In 1982, the then Secretary of State decided that this allowed him to take the sale of council houses out of the hands of local authorities who were not proceeding with such sales as quickly as he wished, and in **R** *v* **Secretary of State for the Environment, ex parte Norwich City Council** (1982), the courts had to agree. The powers granted were so wide that very little could be considered *ultra vires*.

Strictness of 'Wednesbury principles'

As Geoffrey Robertson points out in his book *Freedom, the Individual and the Law* (1993), the very narrow test of unreasonableness severely limits the court's power to supervise the executive. For example, in **R** *v* **Ministry of Defence, ex parte Smith** (1995) the applicants had been dismissed from the armed forces because they were homosexuals and sought judicial review of the Ministry of Defence's policy of banning homosexuals. The ban was held to be legal as it was not Wednesbury unreasonable; the decision was not completely irrational even if the reasons for the ban did not appear convincing. This illustrates how weak the test renders judicial review for protecting fundamental human rights.

From time to time the courts have toyed with the idea of adopting the principle of proportionality as a ground for judicial review. This principle, which is recognized by the administrative law of many European countries, would allow a decision to be struck down on the grounds that although not irrational on Wednesbury terms, it is out of proportion to the benefit it seeks to obtain, or the harm it wishes to avoid – in other words, where a sledgehammer is being used to crack a nut. Clearly, this would provide a wider test than the Wednesbury principle and could lead to more decisions being struck down.

The idea of proportionality as a criteria for judicial review has been mentioned in **Council of Civil Service Unions** v **Minister for the Civil Service** (1984). It was also raised in **R** v **Secretary of State for the Home Department, ex parte Brind** (1991), where journalists unsuccessfully sought to challenge the Home Secretary's ban on broadcasting direct interviews with members of the IRA and other groups from Northern Ireland. In both cases the courts felt it was not open to them to accept it as a criteria at the time, but indicated that case-by-case development might eventually bring it into consideration.

When the courts are considering European law in the domestic context they are prepared to take into account the issue of proportionality. In **R** v **Chief Constable of Sussex, ex parte International Traders Ferry Ltd** (1997) – discussed at p. 424 – the House of Lords made direct reference to the concept of proportionality. One of the basic precepts of Europe is free movement of goods. But this free movement can be restricted on the grounds of public policy. To fall within this concept the authority's conduct must have been proportionate to the risk involved. This required a balance to be reached between the restriction on the fundamental freedom, the right of local residents to protection from crime and disorder and the right to hold lawful demonstrations. On the facts the House of Lords held the particular decision to have been lawful.

Political nature of decisions

The nature of cases brought under judicial review means they inevitably become political at times. Critics, notably Griffith (1985), have noted that the judiciary seem more reluctant to interfere in decisions made by the executive where the executive concerned is a Conservative one. Cases such as **R** v **Boundary Commission for England, ex parte Foot** mentioned at p. 427 would support this argument.

Restrictions on applications

The procedural limitations on applications for judicial review can be seen as necessary to safeguard good administration from unnecessary distractions, vexatious litigants and busybodies. One of the advantages of the judicial review procedure is that it is relatively quick and if the volume of cases were increased this would cease to be true. On the other hand, they can also be seen as ways to discourage ordinary people from seeking to challenge Government or other authorities. There is no leave requirement for ordinary civil proceedings. It could be argued that the current time limits are too short and the courts' discretion is too vague so that sometimes justice is not done.

The concept of national security

Some have criticized reliance on the requirements of national security to inhibit judicial review of Government decisions. In **Council of Civil Service Unions** *v* **Minister for the Civil Service** (1985), the Civil Service union challenged the Government's decision to ban employees of Government Communications Headquarters (GCHQ, the Government intelligence centre, which monitors communications from abroad and ensures security for UK military and official communications) from membership of trade unions. The Divisional Court upheld the complaint on the ground that the decision had been made unfairly, since the unions had not even been consulted. On appeal, the Government argued that its decision had been motivated by considerations of national security, because the centre had been disrupted by industrial action some years earlier. Despite the fact that this argument had not been advanced in the initial proceedings, and that a no-strike agreement was offered by the union, the House of Lords overturned the original decision and upheld the ban. The Government was not required to prove that the ban was necessary, or even justifiable in the interests of security; only that the decision had been motivated by national security concerns.

Similarly, in **R** *v* **Secretary of State for Home Affairs, ex parte Hosenball** (1977), Mark Hosenball, an American journalist, was made the subject of a deportation order on the ground that his presence in the UK was not conducive to the public good. He challenged the order on the basis that he had been given no details of the case against him so that the rules of natural justice had not been followed. The Court of Appeal held that although the proceedings had been unjust, the rules of natural justice were not to be applied to deportation decisions made on grounds of national security.

As Geoffrey Robertson points out, where national security is invoked, the courts are reluctant to assess the strength of evidence presented, even to assert whether decisions made on such grounds were made rationally.

He alleges that, so long as there appears to be some evidence of national security concerns, however slight or dubious, the courts will take a 'hands-off' approach. Obviously this problem occurs in only a minority of cases, but as the above examples show, they may be those which affect fundamental civil liberties.

ANSWERING QUESTIONS

1 **Assess the impact of the Criminal Cases Review Commission on the appeal process.**

This is a very topical area, and therefore one which you would be wise to study carefully. You could start your essay by stating what the Commission is, and looking at the reasons for its creation – what were the problems with criminal appeals? You could mention the role that these problems played in the well-known miscarriages of justice – these are highlighted in the section on criticisms in this chapter, while the stories of some of the miscarriages of justice are told in more detail in chapter 9.

Then move on to look in detail at the Commission itself; its membership, function and powers. One of the points you might want to make is that it is not an appeal court as such, but can merely refer cases for appeal, and that it replaces the old section 17 procedure under which the Home Secretary referred cases back to appeal. You are asked to assess its impact; this essentially means considering how far it is solving the problems it was set up to address. In answering this, you should highlight ways in which it is an improvement on the previous situation – the problems with the section 17 procedure are relevant here for example – and also any criticisms which can be made of it. You could point to the successful appeal in Derek Bentley's case (see p. 414), but that there is now a serious backlog of cases that is rapidly growing.

2 **Gavin is due to be tried at Amcaster Crown Court for robbery of £7,000 from a bank.**
(a) If he is found guilty what appeal routes are open to him? *(10 marks)*
(b) What appeal rights are available to the prosecution? *(15 marks)*
(c) Is this system of appeals satisfactory? *(25 marks) OCR*

(a) The appeal route is first to the Court of Appeal. The information required for this part of the answer is contained under the heading 'From the Crown Court' at p. 406. Note that reaching the Court of Appeal via the Criminal Cases Review Commission is an exceptional procedure. There is then a further appeal possible to the House of Lords. Following the Access to Justice Act 1999, he could also make an appeal by way of case stated to the High Court.

(b) Here you should discuss the material contained under the sub-heading 'Powers of the prosecution following acquittal', at p. 408.

(c) The material contained in the section 'Criticism and reform of the appeals system' at p. 411 is relevant to this part of the answer. In particular, you would want to discuss how far the Criminal Cases Review Commission is more satisfactory than the old section 17 procedure, the new rules on the admission of fresh evidence and the whole debate surrounding the House of Lords.

3 An Act of Parliament gave power to local councils to pass laws for purposes of (among other things), 'ensuring the safety and well-being of all pedestrians and other authorised users of pedestrianised areas', but required the local authority to consult with representatives of all interested parties before any laws were made. The local authority passed a law requiring all street entertainers to be in possession of a licence and to perform only in the area designated in the licence. Before doing so, officials of the local authority sought the views of town centre traders, the pedestrian society and a small number of street musicians. In the six months after the law was passed, no licences were granted to any jugglers or fire-eaters. When H, a juggler who had always previously given performances in the area, enquired why he had been refused a licence, he was told that juggling and fire-eating were too dangerous. After his appeal against the refusal to grant a licence had been turned down by a committee established by the local authority to hear complaints, H discovered that the chairman of the committee was the brother of a street entertainer who had been granted a licence and whose earnings were reputed to have risen dramatically since the introduction of the licensing system. Explain whether there is any way in which H may challenge the actions and decisions by which he has been deprived of his chance to earn money by juggling in the street. *Edexcel*

The Act of Parliament was a parent Act which gave the local authority the power to make delegated legislation. H can challenge the actions and decisions by which he has been deprived of his chance to earn money through the system of judicial review. In order to bring such proceedings, H would have to satisfy the strict procedural rules discussed from p. 428 onwards, and in particular the rule on *locus standi*. As H has lost his livelihood due to the local government's conduct, a court would rule that he did have *locus standi* to bring the proceedings.

H can found his challenge on two grounds: that the delegated legislation was made in breach of the law and that the decision of the committee had breached the law. Looking first at the delegated legislation, the relevant material on this issue can be found at p. 53. The delegated legislation could be challenged as invalid on the basis of procedural *ultra vires*. It would be claimed that the proper procedures were not followed in its creation. The parent Act required that the local authority consult representatives of all interested parties before making the delegated legislation. H could argue that though representatives of traders and pedestrians were consulted, the consultation of street musicians was not representative of all the street entertainers.

Looking secondly at the decision of the committee, H could argue that there was substantive *ultra vires*. In particular he could argue that it had been made for an improper purpose as there is a suggestion that the decision may have been taken to favour certain kinds of entertainers, perhaps from personal motives. Another line of argument would be that a policy appears to have been adopted to exclude jugglers and fire-eaters. Thus, it may be that the local authority has fettered its discretion to grant licences.

He could also point to procedural *ultra vires* on the basis that the rules of natural justice had been violated. There is a strong possibility of bias in the decision-making process, as the chairman of the committee either has a personal financial interest (through his brother) or is likely to favour the local authority decision because of his concern for his brother's livelihood.

Finally you could point to the different remedies available under these procedures, especially *certiorari* (to quash the decision), *mandamus* (to compel further decision-making that is free of the illegality) and damages.

Reading on the Internet

The third annual report of the Criminal Cases Review Commission has been released on the Commission's website at:

http://www.ccrc.gov.uk/report/report.html

15 Ombudsmen

The rights and duties of the state, and the limits of its powers over individuals form what is called administrative law. In some countries, such as France, this forms a comprehensive branch of law, with its own courts and case law. In this country, however, such issues are dealt with by various unrelated systems, the most important being administrative tribunals and judicial review (discussed on pp. 389 and 422), and the two Ombudsmen empowered to investigate complaints against central and local government respectively.

The Parliamentary Commissioner for Administration and Health Service Commissioner

The Parliamentary Commissioner Act 1967 established the office of Parliamentary Commissioner for Administration, popularly called the Ombudsman. The Ombudsman is appointed by the Crown (on the advice of the Prime Minister), and remains in office until reaching the age of 65. No qualifications for the position are specified, and the office has been held by lawyers and civil servants. The role of the Ombudsman is to investigate complaints by individuals who claim to have suffered injustice as a result of maladministration by Government departments. Following the Courts and Legal Services Act 1990 jurisdiction has been extended to cover complaints of maladministration by administrative staff of courts and tribunals, but does not include the judiciary or tribunal members.

Examples of the kind of complaints dealt with include general inattention or delay; rudeness, bias, discrimination or inconsistency; misleading or inaccurate advice; and failure to follow, or properly follow, administrative rules or procedures. Around 1,000 complaints are dealt with every year, with around 90 per cent proving wholly or partly justified.

The Ombudsman will not consider complaints if alternative remedies exist through courts or administrative tribunals, unless it is unreasonable to expect the complainant to use these, and may not deal with complaints concerning any of the following matters:

- nationalized industries;
- relations with other Governments or international organizations;
- actions taken by Crown officials outside the UK;
- the administration of Governments of the dependencies;
- extradition proceedings;
- investigation of crime;
- security of the state;
- contractual or commercial transactions by Government departments (other than those relating to compulsory purchase of land);
- conduct of legal proceedings, whether civil or criminal;
- conditions of service in the Civil Service or Armed Forces;
- granting of awards, honours and royal charters.

The Ombudsman cannot act on his or her own initiative, not even on a complaint direct from a citizen. Complaints must initially be made, in writing, to an MP, who can refer them to the Ombudsman. On receiving a complaint the Ombudsman assesses whether it is within his or her jurisdiction and, if so, conducts a private investigation, giving the head of the relevant department the opportunity to comment on the allegations. The Ombudsman has full powers to examine departmental documents (though not Cabinet papers) and take written or oral evidence, and wilful obstruction of an investigation is punishable as if it were contempt of court. Under the Act of 1967 the Parliamentary Commissioner has a discretion whether to investigate a complaint or not. It was held in **R** *v* **Parliamentary Commissioner, ex parte Dyer** (1994) that the exercise of this discretion could be controlled by judicial review.

The results of an investigation are reported to the MP who referred the complaint, and to the heads of the departments concerned, and the Ombudsman may request that the causes of any injustice be put right, but has no power to alter administrative decisions. The Ombudsman reports annually to Parliament, and may in this report draw attention to any problems that have been revealed and not remedied by the department concerned. These are then considered by a House of Commons Committee.

The **Sachsenhausen** case was the first occasion on which the Commissioner found a department to be seriously at fault. Under the Anglo-German Agreement of 1964 the German Government provided £1 million to compensate UK citizens who suffered from Nazi persecution during the Second World War. Its distribution was at the discretion of the British Government. The UK Foreign Secretary approved rules for its distribution, and under these rules 12 people who had been detained in the Sachsenhausen concentration camp were refused compensation. The Commissioner investigated their case and found that there were serious defects in the Foreign Office's procedures. By this time all of the £1 million had been distributed. The Foreign Secretary maintained that the decisions were correct but none the less made an additional £25,000 available in order that the claimants might receive the same rate of compensation as successful claimants on the fund.

The most elaborate investigation ever undertaken by the Ombudsman concerned the Barlow Clowes affair, which 159 MPs had referred to him. The Barlow Clowes investment business had collapsed in 1988, leaving millions of pounds owing to investors, many of whom were elderly persons of modest means. The Department of Trade and Industry had licensed the business under the Prevention of Fraud (Investments) Act 1958 (since repealed), despite indications that the business was not properly conducted. The Parliamentary Commissioner found that there had been maladministration on the part of civil servants. The Government rejected the findings of maladministration, but none the less undertook *ex gratia* to provide £150 million to compensate investors for up to 90 per cent of their loss. An action in negligence against the Department of Trade and Industry would almost certainly have failed (because the investors would have been owed no duty of care).

Commissioners for Local Administration

This office was established under the Local Government Act 1974, and deals with the same sort of complaints as the Parliamentary Commissioner, but with regard to local authorities, including planning boards and police authorities. Local commissioners will not deal with complaints on the following:

- anything that affects all or most of the local inhabitants (such as the size of its Council Tax);
- conduct of court proceedings;
- investigation or prevention of crime;
- conduct of police officers;
- personnel matters;
- internal affairs of schools and colleges;
- contractual and commercial transactions (unless relating to land);
- public transport;
- docks and harbours;
- industrial establishments and markets.

The relevant authority must have been given a chance to solve the problem before a complaint is accepted, and complaints must usually be referred by a local councillor. The Commissioners consider whether it is within their jurisdiction, then investigate and finally send a report to the authority, which must be available to the public for at least three weeks. Like the Parliamentary Commissioner, Local Commissioners cannot interfere with a decision, only make a report – which the local authority is under no obligation to heed. If they do not, the Commissioners may make further reports, which, especially if given press coverage, may well be persuasive. There are, however, no provisions for enforcing recommendations if a council is really obstinate.

Miscellaneous ombudsmen

In recent times more specialist Ombudsmen have been created. In 1994 a Prison Ombudsman was created. The Courts and Legal Services Act 1990 created the office of Legal Ombudsman whose function is to help people who have a genuine cause for complaint against members of the legal profession but have not been able to find an alternative remedy. The Legal Ombudsman can investigate the handling of complaints by the Law Society, the Bar and the Council for Licensed Conveyancers, reinvestigate complaints and recommend remedies, including the payment of compensation, and reports annually to the Lord Chancellor and Parliament. His or her powers have been increased by the Access to Justice Act 1999. The 1990 Act also created a Conveyancing Ombudsman. The Pension Schemes Act 1993 provides for a Pensions Ombudsman to adjudicate disputes concerning pension schemes. There is now a European Ombudsman under a new Art. 138e of the EEC Treaty, appointed by the European Parliament to investigate maladministration by Community institutions including the non-judicial functions of the EC courts. The European Ombudsman can be approached directly or through an MEP, or may carry out an investigation on his or her own initiative. The European Ombudsman holds office for the duration of the Parliament and can only be dismissed by the European Court at the request of Parliament. Following the report of Sir Leonard Peach into the appointment of judges and Queen's Counsel a commissioner is to be appointed to act as an ombudsman for judicial appointments (see p. 100).

Strengths of Parliamentary and Local Commissioners

Access to Government

The Parliamentary Commissioner in particular can help the ordinary citizen penetrate the maze of secrecy in which Government departments habitually conduct their business.

Publicity

Both Commissioners can draw attention to problems. This can be very persuasive, especially in investigations conducted by local commissioners where the local press take up the story.

Authority

They both provide some means of redress when other avenues fail. The Parliamentary Commissioner has been known to persuade the Inland Revenue to modify or waive tax demands which, while legal, are likely to cause major hardship, and in the **Sachsenhausen** case, uncovered maladministration in the Foreign Office's dealings with compensation claims by former prisoners of war.

Cost

Their services are free and therefore available to all, regardless of means.

Weaknesses of Parliamentary and Local Commissioners

Lack of power

Neither has the power to change decisions and practices, or to compel redress of grievances. Local councils have fairly frequently ignored the recommendations of Local Commissioners.

Narrow jurisdiction

They can only deal with maladministration, which means they have no way of questioning a decision taken in accordance with proper procedures, even if the decision itself seems unfair or wrong. Both also have a long list of areas with which they will not deal, which include some areas of potential concern for citizens.

Access by individuals

Neither will handle complaints submitted directly from citizens, and complainants must therefore find a sympathetic MP or councillor, who must then find time to look at the complaint, before the process can even start. This seems an unnecessary waste of everybody's time, and may prevent problems from being dealt with. A possible improvement in the system would be to allow the Parliamentary Commissioner to receive complaints directly, after pointing out that 150 MPs, almost a quarter of the House, have not referred a single complaint from their constituents; either their constituents are unusually content, or the complaints are not getting through.

Delay

Complaints can take a long time to deal with – around a year is usual for complaints to the Parliamentary Commissioner.

Lack of awareness

The services of the ombudsmen are not well publicized – even the literature of Community Health Councils gives the addresses of Local Commissioners for complaints about the NHS, which should go to the Parliamentary Commissioner.

▶ ANSWERING QUESTIONS

Ombudsmen rarely merit an examination question in their own right, but they are often relevant to answering general questions about the remedies available if, for example, a person's civil liberties have been breached.

▶ Reading on the Internet

The website for the Parliamentary Ombudsman is:
http://www.ombudsman.org.uk/

The website of the Legal Services Ombudsman is:
http://www.olso.org/index2.html

On the website of the British and Irish Ombudsmen Association there are links to the websites of all the main Ombudsman schemes:
http://www.bioa.org.uk/

16 Alternative methods of dispute resolution

Court hearings are not always the best methods of resolving a dispute, and their disadvantages mean that for some types of problem, alternative mechanisms may be more suitable. The main uses of these at present are in family, consumer, commercial, construction and employment cases, but following Lord Woolf's reforms of the civil justice system, these alternative mechanisms should play a more important role in solving all types of civil disputes.

Problems with court hearings

Alternative methods of dispute resolution have become increasingly popular because of the difficulties of trying to resolve disputes through court hearings. Below are some of the specific problems posed by court hearings.

The adversarial process

A trial necessarily involves a winner and a loser, and the adversarial procedure combined with the often aggressive atmosphere of court proceedings divides the parties, making them end up enemies even where they did not start out that way. This can be a disadvantage where there is some reason for the parties to sustain a relationship after the problem under discussion is sorted out – child custody cases are the obvious example, but in business too, there may be advantages in resolving a dispute in a way which does not make enemies of the parties. The court system is often said to be best suited to areas where the parties are strangers and happy to remain so – it is interesting to note that in small-scale societies with close kinship links, court-type procedures are rarely used, and disputes are usually settled by negotiation processes that aim to satisfy both parties, and thus maintain the harmony of the group.

Technical cases

Some types of dispute rest on detailed technical points, such as the way in which a machine should be made, or the details of a medical problem, rather than on points of law. The significance of such technical details may not be readily understandable by an ordinary judge. Expert witnesses or advisers may be brought in to advise on these points, but this takes time, and so raises costs. Where detailed technical evidence is at issue, alternative methods of dispute resolution can employ experts in a particular field to take the place of a judge.

Inflexibility

In a court hearing, the rules of procedure lay down a fixed framework for the way in which problems are addressed. This may be inappropriate in areas which are of largely private concern to the parties involved. Alternative methods can allow the parties themselves to take more control of the process.

Imposed solutions

Court hearings impose a solution on the parties, which since it does not involve their consent, may need to be enforced. If the parties are able to negotiate a settlement between them, to which they both agree, this should be less of a problem.

Publicity

The majority of court hearings are public. This may be undesirable in some business disputes, where one or both of the parties may prefer not to make public the details of their financial situation or business practices because of competition.

▶ ALTERNATIVE DISPUTE RESOLUTION MECHANISMS

Where, for one or more of the reasons explained above, court action is not the best way of solving a dispute, a wide range of alternative methods of dispute resolution (often known as ADR) may be used. Three main forms of ADR can be identified: arbitration, mediation and conciliation:

- **Arbitration** is a procedure whereby both sides to a dispute agree to let a third party, the arbitrator, decide. The arbitrator may be a lawyer, or may be an expert in the field of the dispute. He or she will make a decision according to the law and the decision is legally binding.
- **Mediation** involves the appointment of a mediator to help the parties to a dispute reach an agreement which each considers acceptable.

Mediation can be 'evaluative', where the mediator gives an assessment of the legal strength of a case, or 'facilitative', where the mediator concentrates on assisting the parties to define the issues. When a mediation is successful and an agreement is reached, it is written down and forms a legally binding contract unless the parties state otherwise.

- **Conciliation** is similar to mediation but the conciliator takes a more interventionist role than the mediator in bringing the two parties together and in suggesting possible solutions to help achieve an agreed settlement. The term conciliation is gradually falling into disuse and the process is regarded as a form of mediation.

One of the simplest forms of ADR is, of course, informal negotiation between the parties themselves, with or without the help of lawyers – the high number of civil cases settled out of court are examples of this. Formal schemes include the Advisory, Conciliation and Arbitration Service (ACAS) which mediates in many industrial disputes and unfair dismissal cases; the role of Ombudsmen in dealing with disputes in the fields of insurance and banking, and in complaints against central and local government and public services; the pre-hearing arbitration sometimes used in the Small Claims Court; the work done by trade organizations such as the Association of British Travel Agents (ABTA) in settling consumer complaints; inquiries into such areas as objections concerning compulsory purchase or town and country planning; the conciliation schemes offered by courts and voluntary organizations to divorcing couples; and the arbitration schemes run by the Institute of Arbitrators for business disputes. We will look at some of these in more detail below. Though procedural details vary widely, what they all have in common is that they are attempting to provide a method of settling disagreements that avoids some or all of the disadvantages listed above.

The Lord Chancellor is keen to promote ADR. He has set up a working party to draw up plans to increase awareness of the availability of ADR and intends to launch a wide-ranging awareness campaign. He has also announced that as part of the Government's commitment to promote alternative dispute resolution, Government legal disputes will be settled by mediation or arbitration whenever possible. Government departments will only go to court as a last resort.

Conciliation in unfair dismissal cases

A statutory conciliation scheme administered by ACAS operates before cases of unfair dismissal can be taken to an Employment Tribunal. ACAS conciliation officers talk to both sides with the aim of settling the dispute without a tribunal hearing; they are supposed to procure reinstatement of the employee where possible, but in practice most settlements are only for damages.

A conciliation officer contacts each party or their representatives to discuss the case and advise each side on the strength or weakness of their position. They may tell each side what the other has said, but if the case does eventually go to a tribunal, none of this information is admissible without the consent of the party who gave it.

Evaluation

The success of the scheme is sometimes measured by the fact that two-thirds of cases are either withdrawn or settled by the conciliation process. However, this ignores the imbalance in power between the employer and the employee, especially where the employee has no legal representation – the fact that there has been a settlement does not necessarily mean it is a fair one, when one party is under far more pressure to agree than the other. Dickens's 1985 study of unfair dismissal cases found that awards after a hearing were generally higher than those achieved by conciliation, implying that employees may feel under pressure to agree to any settlement. The study suggested that the scheme would be more effective in promoting fair settlements – rather than settlement at any price – if conciliation officers had a less neutral stance and instead tried to help enforce the worker's rights.

Mediation in divorce cases

In many ways, the court system is an undesirable forum for divorce and its attendant disputes over property and children, since the adversarial nature of the system can aggravate the differences between the parties. This makes the whole process more traumatic for those involved, and clearly is especially harmful where there are children. Consequently conciliation has for some time been made available to divorcing couples, not necessarily to get them back together (though this can happen), but to try to ensure that any arrangements between them can be made as amicably as possible, reducing the strain on the parties themselves as well as their children.

The Family Law Act 1996 makes changes to the divorce laws and places a greater emphasis on mediation. The Act requires those seeking public funds for representation in family proceedings to attend a meeting with a mediator to consider whether mediation might be suitable in their case.

Evaluation

In divorce cases generally, success depends on the parties themselves and their willingness to cooperate. The parties may find that meeting in a neutral environment, with the help of an experienced, impartial professional helps them communicate calmly, and can make the process of divorce less painful for the couple and their children, by avoiding the need for a court battle in which each feels obliged to accuse the other of being unfit to look after their children – a battle which can be as expensive as it is unpleasant, at a time when one or both parties may be under considerable financial strain.

A three-year study undertaken as a pilot scheme for the new reforms found that eight out of ten couples reached agreement on some issues through mediation, and four in ten reached a complete settlement. However, the Solicitors' Family Law Association point out that because men are usually the main earners in a family, and women's earning abilities may be limited by the demands of childcare, women may need lawyers to get a fair deal financially; in fact the Association says the reforms may well turn out to be 'a rogue's charter for unscrupulous husbands'.

Trade association arbitration schemes

The Fair Trading Act 1973 provides that the Director-General of Fair Trading has a duty to promote codes of practice for trade associations, which include arrangements for handling complaints. So far, more than 20 codes have received approval from the Office of Fair Trading (OFT), and there are many other voluntary schemes not yet approved. Many include provisions for an initial conciliation procedure between consumers and retailers or suppliers in case of complaints, often followed by independent arbitration if conciliation fails.

One of the best-known examples is that set up by The Association of British Travel Agents (ABTA), which in the case of disputes between tour operators and consumers, offers impartial conciliation. If this fails, disputes may be referred to a special arbitration scheme – about half of all claims referred to it succeed, though not always winning the amount originally claimed.

A less well-known scheme is that run by the footwear industry, which offers an independent testing scheme for complaints involving faulty footwear. Where a retailer disputes that the product is faulty – blaming damage on inappropriate use by the consumer, for example – an expert opinion can be obtained from the independent Footwear Testing Centre in Kettering. A small test fee is shared by retailer and consumer, with the consumer's share (as well as the cost of the shoes) refunded if testing proves the complaint.

Evaluation

The best of the schemes offer quick, simple dispute resolution procedures, but standards do vary – the National Consumer Council has reported that some are very slow, and there is some concern about the impartiality of arbitrators. These problems could be addressed relatively easily, but the main drawback is the diversity of the codes, and widespread ignorance of their existence, not only among consumers but even among some of the retailers covered by them! Tighter controls by the OFT and better publicity could make them much more useful mechanisms.

Commercial arbitration

Many commercial contracts contain an arbitration agreement, requiring any dispute to be referred to arbitration before any court proceedings are undertaken – the aim being to do away with the need for going to court. Arbitrators usually have some expertise in the relevant field, and lists of suitable individuals are kept by the Institute of Arbitration. The parties themselves choose their arbitrator, ensuring that the person has the necessary expertise in their area and is not connected to either of them. Once appointed, the arbitrator is required to act in an impartial, judicial manner just as a judge would, but the difference is that they will not usually need to have technical points explained to them, so there is less need for expert witnesses.

Disputes may involve disagreement over the quality of goods supplied, interpretation of a trade clause or point of law, or a mixture of the two. Where points of law are involved the arbitrator may be a lawyer. The Arbitration Act 1996 aims to promote commercial arbitration by providing a clear framework for its use. It sets out the powers of the parties to shape the process according to their needs, and provides that they must each do everything necessary to allow the arbitration to proceed properly and without delay. It also spells out the powers of arbitrators, which include limiting the costs to be recoverable by either party and making orders which are equivalent to High Court injunctions if the parties agree. Arbitrators are also authorized to play an inquisitorial role, investigating the facts of the case – many of them are, after all, experts in the relevant fields.

Arbitration hearings must be conducted in a judicial manner, in accordance with the rules of natural justice, but proceedings are informal and held in private, with the time and place decided by the parties. The arbitrator's decision, known as the award, is often delivered immediately, and is as binding on the parties as a High Court judgment would be, and if necessary can be enforced as one.

The award is usually to be considered as final, but appeal may be made to the High Court on a question of law, with the consent of all the parties, or leave from the court. Leave will only be given if determination of the question could substantially affect the rights of one of the parties, and provided (with some exceptions) that they had not initially agreed to restrict rights of appeal. The High Court may confirm, vary or reverse the award, or send it back to the arbitrator for reconsideration.

Evaluation

Arbitration fees can be high, but for companies this may be outweighed by the money they save through being able to get the problem solved as soon as it arises, rather than having to wait months for a court hearing. The arbitration hearing itself tends to be quicker than a court case, because of the expertise of the arbitrator – in a court hearing time and therefore money can be wasted in explanation of technical points to the judge.

The ability of the parties to choose their arbitrator promotes mutual trust in and respect for the decision, and arbitration is conducted with a view to compromise rather than combat, which avoids destroying the business relationship between the parties. Privacy ensures that business secrets are not made known to competitors. Around 10,000 commercial cases a year go to arbitration, which tends to suggest that business people are fairly happy with the system and the more detailed framework set out by the 1996 Act is thought likely to increase use even further.

▶ Advantages of alternative methods of dispute resolution

Cost

Many procedures try to work without any need for legal representation, and even those that do involve lawyers may be quicker and therefore cheaper than going to court.

In 1998, Professor Hazel Genn carried out research into a mediation scheme at Central London County Court. The scheme's objective was to offer virtually cost-free, court-annexed mediation to disputing parties at an early stage in litigation. This involved a three-hour session with a trained mediator assisting parties to reach a settlement, with or without legal representation. The scheme's purpose was to promote swift dispute settlement and a reduction in legal costs through an informal process that parties might prefer to court proceedings. Professor Genn's research did not find clear evidence that mediation saved costs. The overall cost of cases which were settled through mediation was significantly less than those which were litigated; but where mediation was used and the parties failed to reach an agreement, and then went on to litigate, it was possible for costs to be increased.

Accessibility

Alternative methods tend to be more informal than court procedures, without complicated rules of evidence. The process can therefore be less intimidating and less stressful than court proceedings.

Speed

The delays in the civil court system are well known, and waiting for a case to come to court may, especially in commercial cases, add considerably to the overall cost, and adversely affect business.

The research carried out by Professor Genn (1998) found that mediation was able to promote and speed up settlement. The majority (62 per cent) of mediated cases settled at the mediation appointment.

Expertise

Those who run alternative dispute resolution schemes often have specialist knowledge of the relevant areas, which can promote a fairer as well as a quicker settlement.

Conciliation of the parties

Most alternative methods of dispute resolution aim to avoid irrevocably dividing the parties, so enabling business or family relationships to be maintained.

Disadvantages of alternative methods of dispute resolution

Imbalances of power

As the unfair dismissal conciliation scheme shows, the benefits of voluntarily negotiating agreement may be undermined where there is a serious imbalance of power between the parties – in effect, one party is acting less voluntarily than the other.

Lack of legal expertise

Where a dispute hinges on difficult points of law, an arbitrator may not have the required legal expertise to judge.

No system of precedent

There is no doctrine of precedent, and each case is judged on its merits, providing no real guidelines for future cases.

Enforceability

Decisions not made by courts may be difficult to enforce.

The future for ADR

Although ADR appears to meet many of the principles for effective civil justice, the proportion of people with legal problems who choose to use ADR has remained very low, even when there are convenient and free schemes available. It is not altogether clear why this is so. Professor Genn's research (1998) found that in only 5 per cent of cases did the parties agree to try mediation, despite vigorous attempts to stimulate demand. It was least likely to be used where both parties had legal representation.

At present, many of those contemplating litigation will go first to a solicitor and Professor Genn's research shows widespread misunderstanding about mediation processes amongst solicitors. Many did not know what was involved and were therefore not able to advise clients on whether their case was suitable for any form of ADR, or the benefits that might flow from seeking to use it. Solicitors were apprehensive about showing weakness through accepting mediation in the context of traditional adversarial litigation. Litigants were also hostile to the idea of compromise, particularly in the early stages of litigation.

It is likely that in the future ADR will play an increasingly important role in the resolution of disputes. It is already widely used in the US where the law frequently requires parties to try mediation before their case can be set down for trial. It is generally accepted that the UK will see a similar expansion in the use of ADR, as both the courts and the legal profession begin to take ADR more seriously than they once did. Following Lord Woolf's reforms of the civil justice system, the new rules of procedure in the civil courts impose on the judges a duty to encourage parties in appropriate cases to use ADR and to facilitate its use. Parties can request that court proceedings be postponed while they try ADR and the court can also order a postponement for this reason. Backing up this position is the fact that the Government has said, in the explanatory notes to the Access to Justice Act 1999, that in time they hope to extend public funding increasingly to cover the use of ADR.

ANSWERING QUESTIONS

1 Do you think that the courts offer the best means of solving disputes?

Your introduction might mention the fact that although courts are accepted as a means of resolving disputes, there are some types of dispute where they are not helpful, and so other methods of dispute resolution have developed. You can then examine the disadvantages of courts as means of dispute resolution, and then relate these disadvantages to the types of dispute where courts have not been found to offer the best solution.

You could then go through the four types of alternative dispute resolution we have examined, pointing out why they have advantages over the court system for those types of dispute. In this essay you could also look at tribunals (see chapter 13), and examine how and why they provide a useful alternative to courts.

You might then discuss some of the disadvantages of alternative methods of dispute resolution, pointing out the kinds of case for which these disadvantages might make them unsuitable. Your conclusion might simply point out that courts may provide the best way of solving some disputes, but be unhelpful in others.

2 **'Courts and tribunals do not provide the only means of resolving disputes.' What other existing methods provide alternatives? How satisfactory are they?**
Edexcel

This question uses much the same material as the previous one, but you are required to evaluate the alternative methods of dispute resolution. Also note that you could not bring tribunals into this answer.

▌ Reading on the Internet

The research carried out by Professor Genn in 1998 on the mediation scheme at Central London County Court is available on the Lord Chancellor's Department website:

http://www.lcd.gov.uk/research/1998/598esfr.htm

A consultation paper, *Alternative Dispute Resolution – A Discussion Paper* (1999), has been published on the Lord Chancellor's Department website:

www.open.gov.uk/lcd/consult/civ-just/adr/section1.htm

17 The administration of justice

The English legal system is currently administered by a range of Government departments, with the Lord Chancellor's Department (LCD) and the Home Office taking the most important roles. The LCD has responsibility for the appointment of judges, judicial salaries and the disciplining of the lower judiciary. It administers the courts, oversees legal aid and advice and contributes to the work on law reform. The Home Office is responsible for the police, national security, reform of the criminal law, prisons, immigration, elections and civil rights.

There is also a small Law Officers' Department. The Law Officers are the Attorney-General and the Solicitor-General, who are both Ministers, though not members of the Cabinet. The Attorney-General is the Government's main legal adviser and is responsible for major domestic and international litigation involving the Government. Other functions of the post include giving consent to certain categories of prosecution, granting immunities from prosecution and terminating prosecutions where appropriate, through a process known as *nolle prosequi*. The Director of Public Prosecutions answers to the Attorney-General in relation to the running of the Crown Prosecution Service. The Solicitor-General used to carry out such functions as the Attorney-General delegated to that office. Following the Law Officers Act 1997, the Law Officers can agree a general division of labour between them, as the Act specifically empowers the Solicitor-General to perform all the functions of the Attorney-General. This formal authorization for any delegation is no longer required.

In addition, Ministers from other departments play a role in legal matters through their responsibility for law reform in their particular area. There is, therefore, no single Minister with responsibility for legal affairs, but a range of Ministers who might be involved at any one time.

This situation has been subject to a number of criticisms. First, the division of most of the important legal work between the Home Office and the LCD seems illogical. Why should two different departments each play a leading role in the same area?

Secondly, the different functions of the Home Office give rise to a potential conflict of interests, given that it is responsible both for protecting civil liberties and for maintaining public order. Since public order requirements frequently clash with those of civil liberties, it is a tall order to ask one department to balance the two, and chances are that one or other will suffer – especially if, as over the past decade or so, the Government has been elected with law and order highlighted in its manifesto. In such situations, there is little political advantage for the Home Secretary who argues for the enlargement of civil rights, and since such enlargement is often inconvenient for Governments, the temptation is to give much less attention to this aspect of the department's job.

A further problem is that legal matters may be easily ignored when the Government is unenthusiastic about them, since there is no single Minister who can be pressurized in Parliament. An example is the issue of funding for law centres: while the Department of the Environment has given grants to set up centres, their continued funding appears not to be the responsibility of any department, and so they have been forced to rely on local authorities – themselves under severe financial restraints – and any other sources of funding they can drum up themselves. The Lord Chancellor's Advisory Committee on Legal Aid has described the lack of clear ministerial responsibility for legal services in general as a chronic problem and has criticized the Government's failure to decide on future funding for law centres.

The position of the Lord Chancellor has caused particular concern. Despite being the Minister at the head of the LCD, the Lord Chancellor does not sit in the House of Commons, but is the Speaker of the House of Lords. This means that MPs are not able to ask direct questions in the House of Commons about the work of the LCD, and that the department's democratic accountability is limited. In addition, neither the LCD nor the Law Officers' Department are subject to the select committee system, which is another way in which MPs can question the running of departments. Instead, the Attorney-General takes parliamentary questions about every four weeks, which can include questions about the LCD. However, in most cases such questions are merely referred back to the Lord Chancellor, rather than being answered by the Attorney-General, and replies are not always forthcoming after such referrals.

It is sometimes claimed that the Lord Chancellor is accountable through the House of Lords but, while such accountability may be possible in theory, in practice it is ineffective. For example, during Lord Hailsham's Chancellorship there were incidents such as the removal of a circuit judge in 1983, and refusals to renew temporary judicial posts, which would certainly have provoked challenges to a Minister sitting in the House of Commons. Yet, despite many opportunities for peers to inquire into these matters and other issues relating to the judiciary, there were no questions or debate in the Lords about any of these matters.

This overall lack of accountability is important, not only because of the importance of the issues with which the LCD deals, but also because it is responsible for spending a great deal of public money.

A Ministry of Justice?

The situation described above is unusual: most countries with a developed legal system have a Ministry of Justice to take responsibility for the legal matters which in Britain are spread over many different departments. Given the criticisms detailed above, and the problems listed in the chapter on law reform (which also suffers from the lack of a single, responsible department), it has frequently been suggested that England should introduce such a ministry.

If this were to take place, there is some debate as to what form the new ministry should take. The simplest option would be to merge the Home Office and the LCD. However, this would produce a huge department which might be too large to work efficiently, and it would not avoid the problem of concentrating the functions of public order and protection of civil liberties in the same department.

A leading public law expert, Rodney Brazier, has argued that we should keep two separate ministries, by retaining the Home Office and substituting a new Law Department (simply another name for a Ministry of Justice) for the LCD, but dividing functions between them logically, with the Law Department responsible for all issues of law reform, administration of the courts and protection of civil liberties.

Opponents of a Ministry of Justice argue that the political pressure a Minister in the House of Commons would be under would endanger the independence of the judiciary, which should be completely free of political involvement. This fear seems to be somewhat overcautious, given that the vast majority of the work performed by a Ministry of Justice (like that carried out by the LCD now) has nothing to do with matters of judicial service – and, as Brazier points out, the current system does not avoid the danger of political decisions being made in relation to judges, since the Lord Chancellor is both head of the judiciary and a member of the Government. If there is a choice to be made between political decisions based on pressure from Government, or political decisions based on pressure from Parliament, the second would seem to be the more attractive option. In any case, the problem could be avoided if, as Brazier suggests, the creation of a Ministry of Justice was accompanied by a new Judicial Service Commission, responsible for judicial appointments, promotions and the disciplining of judges. It would not be a ministry and would therefore avoid difficulties with political patronage.

Another possibility would be to have one large Ministry of Justice, with a Minister in the House of Commons and, in addition, keep the Lord Chancellor's responsibility for the judiciary and his function as Speaker of the House of Lords. In such a situation, the Lord Chancellor could cease to be a party politician and a member of the Cabinet, and so the problem of political pressure would be removed altogether.

A small-scale reform was proposed by the Royal Commission on Legal Services in 1979, which noted the heavy workload of the Lord Chancellor and suggested that the Prime Minister appoint a junior Minister in the House of Commons to help with the administrative and parliamentary work. This suggestion has not been taken up.

▶ ANSWERING QUESTIONS

1 Would the English legal system be improved by the creation of a Ministry of Justice?

Your answer could start by briefly describing what a Ministry of Justice is, and pointing out that most other countries have one. You could then explain how the normal functions of such a Ministry are currently distributed in this country, and detail the criticisms of this system. You can go on to describe the possible forms a Ministry of Justice might take in the UK, and point out the objections to it. Your conclusion should state, drawing on the points you have made, whether you think such a reform would be justified.

▶ Reading on the Internet

The Lord Chancellor's Department website is at:
http://www.lcd.gov.uk

The Home Office website is at:
http://www.homeoffice.gov.uk/

18 Introduction to civil liberties

In democratic societies, it is usually felt that there are certain basic rights – often called civil liberties, civil rights or human rights – which should be available to everyone. Exactly what these rights are vary in different legal systems, but they generally include such freedoms as the right to say, think and believe what you like (freedom of expression, thought and conscience), to form groups with others, such as trade unions and pressure groups (freedom of assembly), to protest peacefully and to be imprisoned or otherwise punished only for breaking the law and after a fair trial. Part of the reason why these freedoms are considered important is the nature of democracy: citizens can only make the kind of free choice of government required by a democratic system if there is open discussion and debate.

Most democratic countries have a written Bill of Rights, which lays down the rights which, by law, can be enjoyed by citizens of that country. These rights have to be respected by the courts, Parliament, the police and private citizens, unless the Bill of Rights allows otherwise (for example, some rights may be suspended in times of war or when it is necessary in the interests of national security). Such a Bill may form part of a written constitution or sit alongside such a constitution: either way, it will usually have a status which is superior to that of ordinary law, in that it can only be changed by a special procedure. This will vary from country to country, but might involve holding a referendum, or securing a larger than usual majority in Parliament. Legislation which is protected in this way is said to be entrenched.

Britain is unusual among democratic countries in having, to date, neither a Bill of Rights nor a written constitution. In this country, our rights and freedoms are traditionally considered to be protected by a presumption that we are free to do whatever is not specifically forbidden by either legislation or the common law. Anyone prevented by the state from doing something which they are legally entitled to do should have a remedy against the state – an example is that a person wrongly detained in a police station can sue for false imprisonment. Citizens' rights in the UK were described as residual, in that they consisted of what was left after taking into account the lawful limitations.

The system of residual freedoms had shown itself to be seriously flawed over the past couple of decades. The idea that a person is free to do anything not specifically prohibited by law also applies to the state, so that the Government may violate individual freedom even though it is not formally empowered to do so, on the ground that it is doing nothing which is prohibited. An example of this is **Malone** *v* **Metropolitan Police Commissioner** (1979). Mr Malone's telephone had been tapped, and he was able to prove that this was done without any lawful authority – that is, there was no law which allowed the Government or its agencies to tap his phone. But equally, there was no law which forbade them to do so as English law gives no general right to privacy. Therefore, Mr Malone's action failed.

A significant change in the British position was made by the Human Rights Act 1998. This came into force in October 2000. The Act makes the European Convention on Human Rights (ECHR) part of the law of the UK. While the Convention had been part of the international law that is recognized by the UK, it had never been integrated as part of our domestic law. While the Human Rights Act represents a major shift in approach to civil liberties it still fails to give the UK a Bill of Rights, because the Act is not entrenched and can be repealed like any other Act.

The European Convention on Human Rights

The ECHR was drawn up by the Council of Europe, which was established after the Second World War when countries tried to unite to prevent such horrors ever happening again. The Council now has 25 members, including the 15 members of the EU. Signed in Rome in 1950, the Convention was ratified by the UK in 1951 and became binding on those states which had ratified it in 1953.

A special court, known as the European Court of Human Rights, was set up to deal with claims concerning breaches of the ECHR. The Court sits in Strasbourg, and handles claims made by one state against another and by individuals against a state. It only hears individual claims where the relevant state has accepted the right of individuals to bring such cases; not all states accept this right of individual petition, though the UK Government agreed to this in 1966.

The fact that a state has ratified the Convention does not mean it has to incorporate Convention provisions into its domestic law: each state can choose whether or not to do this, and about half have done so. In these cases, citizens can claim their rights under the Convention through domestic courts and the national parliaments cannot usually legislate in conflict with the Convention.

The UK refused for many years to incorporate the Convention and so it was not recognized by the national courts as part of English law. UK citizens who believed that their rights under the Convention had been breached could not bring their claim through the normal domestic courts, but had to take their case to the European Court of Human Rights; if they succeeded there, the UK Government was expected to amend whatever aspect of domestic law caused the problem. But such litigation is slow and expensive and the eventual remedies often inadequate. As with any other international treaty, British courts could take the Convention into account when interpreting UK legislation, and presume that Parliament did not intend to legislate inconsistently with it. Where a statute was ambiguous, they could use the Convention as a guide to its correct interpretation; an example of this is provided by **Waddington** *v* **Miah** (1974), where the House of Lords referred to Art. 7 of the Convention to support its view that s. 34 of the Immigration Act 1971 could not be interpreted as having retrospective effect. Where the words of a statute were clear, domestic courts have to apply them, even if they obviously conflict with the Convention. This position has changed radically with the passing of the Human Rights Act 1998 incorporating the Convention into domestic law.

The Human Rights Act 1998

The Human Rights Act 1998 came into force in October 2000. In **R** *v* **Lambert** (2001) the House of Lords ruled that the Act did not have retrospective effect. This Act incorporated the ECHR (and its first protocol) into domestic law. The effect of this is to strengthen the protection of individual rights by UK courts and provide improved remedies where these are violated. The Convention is now applicable directly in the UK courts, so that it is no longer necessary to go all the way to Strasbourg (s. 7), though it is skill possible. Under s. 2 of the Human Rights Act, the domestic judiciary 'must take into account' any relevant Strasbourg jurisprudence, although they are not bound by it. This is quite a weak obligation, since it is open to the judiciary to consider but disapply a particular decision.

The UK courts are required to interpret all legislation in a way which is compatible with Convention rights 'so far as it is possible to do so' (s. 3). This goes much further than the previous position of allowing ambiguities to be interpreted in favour of the Convention.

It is unlawful for public authorities to act in a way which is incompatible with Convention rights (s. 6). A public authority includes central and local government, the police and the NHS. The specific meaning of a public authority was considered in **Donoghue** *v* **Poplar Housing and Regeneration Community Association Ltd** (2001). The Court of Appeal relied heavily on the case law that had been developed on the issue in the context of judicial review. It concluded that a public authority could include a housing association for these purposes, as by providing accommodation it was fulfilling the local authority's statutory obligation.

There has been some debate as to whether the Act allows individual citizens to enforce Convention rights in proceedings against other individuals (known as 'horizontal effect'). Section 6 states that public authorities cannot breach Convention rights. It is therefore clear from s. 6 that citizens can rely on their Convention rights against the state (known as 'vertical effect'). The reference only to 'public authorities' would suggest that individual citizens can breach the Convention with impunity. But the courts are public authorities. It is therefore arguable that if a civil court failed to apply a Convention right in legal proceedings between private parties it would be in breach of the Human Rights Act. Academic opinion on this issue is sharply divided.

Under s. 19 Government Ministers have to publish a written statement as to whether or not a Bill is compatible with the Convention.

While the Human Rights Act represents an important advance for civil liberties in the UK, there are still significant limitations on the impact that the Act will have. In particular, legislation which is incompatible with the Convention are still valid; judges do not have the power to strike down offending statutes as unconstitutional. Thus, the principle of parliamentary sovereignty remains intact. If a higher court does find that legislation is incompatible with the Convention, then it can choose to make a declaration to this effect (Art. 4) and a Minister can subsequently amend the offending legislation by a fast-track procedure which avoids the full parliamentary process. An early example of a declaration of incompatibility is provided by the case of **Wilson** *v* **First County Trust** (2001) where the Court of Appeal declared that a provision of the Consumer Credit Act 1974 violated the Convention.

The judiciary has a lot of power in determining the impact and success of the Human Rights Act 1998. The Convention rights are very loosely drafted and through their interpretation the judges could easily dilute them and render them ineffective. The Government is clearly aware of the central role of the judges in the success or failure of the Act. It spent £4.5 million training the judges, magistrates and tribunal chairpersons ready for the implementation of the Act. The Lord Chancellor wrote directly to all the judges pointing out their vital role. The letter stated:

> With proper training and planning, I am confident that all courts and tribunals will be able to give full effect to the rights recognised by the Convention and to make their distinctive contribution to fostering a culture of awareness of, and respect for, human rights throughout the whole of society. I hope you look forward to playing your part in making those rights real, as do I.

There had been fears that the courts would be overrun with speculative human rights claims, but this has not in fact happened. One of the first cases to seek to rely on the Human Rights Act 1998 was **Procurator Fiscal** *v* **Brown** (2000), which started in the Scottish courts. Under the road traffic legislation, Ms Brown had been required to inform the police of the identity of the person driving her car on the evening she was questioned. It would have been a criminal offence for her not to have answered the question. She admitted that she had been driving her car and was prosecuted for drink-driving. She claimed at her trial that her confession should not be admissible as evidence as she had been forced to incriminate herself in breach of her right to a fair trial in Art. 6 of the European Convention. The High Court in Scotland accepted this argument. This decision was highly controversial as it threatened the credibility of the Human Rights Act. It appeared to justify fears that the Act would create a large amount of litigation and give people rights that went against the general interests of society. However, on appeal the Privy Council ruled that the road traffic legislation did not breach the European Convention and the evidence was admissible at her trial. Reviewing the case law of the European Court of Human Rights, Lord Bingham concluded:

> The jurisprudence of the European Court very clearly established that while the overall fairness of a criminal trial cannot be compromised, the constituent rights comprised, whether expressly or implicitly, within Art. 6 [such as freedom from self-incrimination] are not themselves absolute.

The privilege against self-incrimination was not absolute, but had to be balanced against the wider interests of the community, in particular public safety. The Privy Council found that the obligation to state who was driving the vehicle represented a proportionate response to the serious social problem of death and injury on the roads. The case was distinguished from **Saunders** *v* **UK** (1996) (discussed at p. 460) where the UK legislation had allowed prolonged questioning, as opposed to the answering of a single question in this case. The decision shows that the courts will not tolerate attempts to misuse provisions of the Convention in ways which are contrary to the public interest.

Advantages of incorporation

Improved access

Bringing a case to Strasbourg can take up to six years and can be very expensive. Through incorporation, UK citizens are now able to enforce their rights under the Convention directly before the domestic courts (though applications to Strasbourg are still possible as a last resort).

Remedies

The remedies available from the European Court of Human Rights are inadequate. Also, the long delays mean that the remedies awarded can be too late to be effective. The national courts are able to provide quicker and more effective remedies.

Tried and tested

The ECHR has already been tried and tested over the last 30 years. The UK courts have developed some knowledge of its provisions as their decisions have been challenged in Strasbourg. The Privy Council has also developed case law in relation to similar provisions to be found in the written constitutions of Commonwealth countries, which were often drafted with the Convention in mind. It is therefore likely to prove easier to incorporate the Convention into domestic law than a completely new Bill of Rights.

Avoid conflict between domestic and international law

Problems with the current arrangements were highlighted by recent litigation. In **R** v **Saunders** (1996) evidence obtained by Government inspectors under s. 177 of the Financial Services Act 1986 was used against Saunders in criminal proceedings for insider dealing. The English courts ruled that in English law this evidence was admissible at a criminal trial. The court in Strasbourg ruled that this evidence had been obtained by an unfair procedure and should have been excluded from the trial – **Saunders** v **UK** (1997). Evidence obtained in the same way was accepted by the trial court in **R** v **Morrissey** and **R** v **Staines** (1997). The Court of Appeal stated that it was 'an unsatisfactory position' that it was obliged to follow the domestic decision, which had held Saunders' evidence was admissible, despite the fact that the European Court had subsequently ruled that this breached the Convention.

Encouraging conformity

While there are many instances of UK Governments changing the law as a result of losing cases in the European Court of Human Rights, they are not always keen to do so. In **Brogan** v **United Kingdom** (1988) the provisions of the Prevention of Terrorism (Temporary Provisions) Act 1984, allowing detention of suspects for up to seven days without judicial authority, were found to violate Art. 5, protecting freedom of the person. The Government responded by declaring that the power was necessary on security grounds and by depositing at Strasbourg a limited derogation under Art. 15 from the Convention to the extent that the legislation violated Art. 5.

In **Abdulaziz** v **United Kingdom** (1985) the Government technically complied with the European Court of Human Rights' decision, but in such a way as to decrease rather than increase rights. The case alleged that British immigration rules discriminated against women, because men permanently settled in the UK were allowed to bring their wives and fiancées to live with them here, but women in the same position could not bring their husbands and fiancés into the country. The European Court agreed, but the Government was determined not to increase immigration rights. Instead of allowing husbands and fiancés to settle here, they removed the right of wives and fiancées to do so, thereby ending the sexual discrimination but making the immigration laws even more restrictive.

Incorporation has reduced the problem of bringing domestic law into line with the ECHR. The courts are contributing to this process in every case where a conflict arises between the Convention and domestic law.

International image

It is not good for the UK's image abroad frequently to be found in error by a 'foreign' court, as it has been many times.

Clarity and accessibility

The law on civil rights has been complex and disorderly. For example, there has been no clear definition of the right to freedom of expression, only a collection of statutes and cases which state when and how such a freedom can be restricted. The ECHR provides a comprehensive and easily accessible statement of rights and freedoms enforceable in the UK.

Education

The ECHR sets out for citizens, Government and the judiciary the basic rights and freedoms we are all entitled to expect. This should lead to better awareness by citizens of their legal rights, and to legislation and judicial decisions which take those rights as their starting point, rather than just one of many things to be considered.

Disadvantages of incorporation

Legal status

Incorporation of the ECHR would have had more impact if it had been entrenched. Any legislation which did not comply with it would have been struck down by the courts, and the ECHR itself could only have been changed in domestic law by special procedures, such as a referendum or an increased parliamentary majority. The Human Rights Act 1998 does not give UK citizens a Bill of Rights.

Many experts believe it would be constitutionally impossible to make the ECHR an entrenched Bill of Rights. This is because the doctrine of parliamentary sovereignty provides that no sitting Parliament can bind a future one: in other words, every Parliament is free to unmake laws made by their predecessors. This means that a future Parliament could simply abolish a Bill of Rights and any arrangements for entrenchment could be legislated away.

Not everybody agrees that such entrenchment would be impossible. Many Commonwealth countries which have inherited ideas of parliamentary sovereignty from the UK have enacted entrenched Bills of Rights without any constitutional problems arising. Alternatively, the ECHR could have been partially entrenched so that it was treated in the same way as EU law is today.

As the Labour Government has decided not to entrench or partly entrench the ECHR into domestic law, so the legal protections provided by it are limited. Real weight would be given to the Convention if it was both entrenched and a constitutional court were created.

Limited scope

The Convention is enforceable against the state and not against private individuals. This is not the case, for example, in relation to the rights provided under the new Constitution in South Africa.

The ECHR is over 30 years old and, since its creation, new rights have become important – for example, the Convention makes limited provision for preventing racial discrimination and none at all for preventing discrimination on the basis of disability or sexual orientation. Some people feel that a UK Bill of Rights should be broader, including environmental, economic and social rights.

There is also the question of whether the same protection is appropriate for all parts of the UK. Northern Ireland may require special treatment given the intensity of religious and political animosity.

Drafting style

The ECHR follows the more general, looser European style of legislative drafting, in contrast to the more tightly worded legislation our courts are used to applying – though as EU law has grown in importance, British courts are gaining more experience of this approach.

A Human Rights Commission

The Labour Government considered establishing a Human Rights Commission but no provision is made for its establishment in the Human Rights Act 1998. The functions of such a Commission could have included:

- providing advice and guidance to people wishing to assert their rights;
- instituting and supporting litigation;
- conducting inquiries;
- monitoring the operation of the ECHR in domestic law;
- scrutinizing new legislation;
- ensuring the conformity of EU law with human rights obligations under international treaties.

In the absence of such a Commission there is a danger that the rights given in theory by the Human Rights Act will not, in practice, be effectively enforced.

The scope of the Convention

The rights protected by the ECHR include the right to life (Art. 2); freedom from torture, inhuman or degrading treatment (Art. 3); freedom from slavery or forced labour (Art. 4); the right to liberty and security of the person (Art. 5); the right to a fair trial (Art. 6); the prohibition of retrospective criminal laws (Art. 7); the right to respect for a person's private and family life, home and correspondence (Art. 8); freedom of thought, conscience and religion (Art. 9); freedom of expression (Art. 10); freedom of peaceful assembly and association, including the right to join a trade union (Art. 11); and the right to marry and have a family (Art. 12).

The Convention provides that people should be able to enjoy these rights without discrimination (Art. 14). Some additions, known as Protocols, have been made to the ECHR since it was first drawn up. The First Protocol was written in 1952 and provides three new rights: the right to peaceful enjoyment of one's possessions (Art. 1); the right to education (Art. 2); and the right to take part in free elections by secret ballot (Art. 3). The other important Protocol is the fourth, concluded in 1963, which guarantees freedom of movement within a state and freedom to leave any country; it precludes a country from expelling or refusing to admit its own nationals. This Protocol has not been ratified by the UK and, in the past, some citizens from Northern Ireland have been excluded from mainland Britain.

Many of the rights provided under the Convention contain specific restrictions and exemptions. For example, Art. 10 allows restrictions on freedom of expression where they are:

> necessary in a democratic society, in the interests of national security, territorial integrity or public safety, for the prevention of disorder or crime, for the protection of health or morals, for the protection of the reputation or rights of others, for preventing the disclosure of information received in confidence, or for maintaining the authority and impartiality of the judiciary.

Member states may decline to carry out most of their obligations under the Convention in time of war or some other national emergency. The UK has done so in respect of Northern Ireland. In such cases a state must inform the Secretary-General of the Council of Europe with its reasons (Art. 15). There are some rights, most importantly freedom from torture, inhuman or degrading treatment, from which states are never permitted to derogate. The Convention does not cover the whole field of human rights. It omits general economic and social rights, such as a right to housing, a minimum income and free health care, which some would argue should be guaranteed in a civilized society. This is because there is less agreement between different countries on such issues than there is on the traditional freedoms currently protected by the ECHR.

The administration

The European Court of Human Rights has the same number of judges as contracting states, which is currently 41. The court is divided into four Sections, there are Committees of three judges and Chambers of seven judges. There is also a Grand Chamber of 17 judges. Any contracting state or individual claiming to be a victim of a violation of the Convention by a contracting state may lodge an application directly with the court in Strasbourg. Each individual application is assigned to a Section and a judge, called a rapporteur, makes a preliminary examination of the case and decides whether it should be dealt with by a three-member Committee or by a Chamber. A Committee may decide, by unanimous vote, to declare an application inadmissible or strike it out. Cases are admissible only after the applicant has exhausted all available domestic remedies and makes the application no more than six months after the final national decision (Art. 26). The Committee will also reject as inadmissible any petition which is outside the scope of the Convention or manifestly ill-founded (Art. 27). Apart from those cases that are struck out by a Committee, all the other cases are heard by a Chamber. Chambers may at any time relinquish jurisdiction in favour of a Grand Chamber where a case raises a serious question of interpretation of the Convention or where there is a risk of departing from existing case law, unless one of the parties objects to this transfer.

Within three months of delivery of the judgment of a Chamber, any party may request that a case be referred to the Grand Chamber if it raises a serious question of interpretation or application or a serious issue of general importance. Such requests are examined by a Grand Chamber panel of five judges. If the panel accepts the request the decision of the Grand Chamber is final. As well as deciding whether a state is in breach of the Convention, the court can award compensation or other 'just satisfaction' of the complaint (Art. 50). Responsibility for supervising the execution of judgments lies with the Committee of Ministers of the Council of Europe.

Cases brought against the United Kingdom

Since 1966, over 60 individual petitions have been brought against the UK Government, and there have also been inter-state references to the Commission by the Republic of Ireland. Of the 49 individual cases decided by September 1994, the UK lost 31 and won 18. This figure is often quoted as suggesting the UK has one of the worst records of breaching the Convention – only Italy has lost more cases. While it is certainly true that our record is open to criticism, the figures must be read in the light of the fact that many states have not recognized the right of individual petition for as long as the UK, and therefore have had less time to build up a record of individual petitions. In addition, those countries which have incorporated the Convention into domestic law will obviously have a lower rate of petitions, successful or otherwise, because most cases will be dealt with in their domestic courts.

The first individual petition from a UK citizen to be considered by the European Court of Human Rights was **Golder** *v* **United Kingdom** (1975), which alleged breaches of the right to privacy for private correspondence (Art. 8) and to a fair hearing (Art. 6). Golder was a prisoner who was contemplating bringing an action for defamation against a prison officer and who had been refused access to a solicitor under the Prison Rules. The court held that the Prison Rules were inconsistent with the ECHR. This resulted in the rules being changed.

The law on contempt of court, and its relationship with the right to free expression, was considered in **Sunday Times** *v* **United Kingdom** (1991). One of the purposes of contempt of court legislation is to prevent the publication of any information which is likely to prejudice the result of a court case. This action arose out of the thalidomide scandal, when thousands of expectant mothers were prescribed a drug, thalidomide. During the parents' long drawn-out struggle for compensation, the *Sunday Times* published an article on the subject which, among other things, urged the drug manufacturers, Distillers, to pay generous compensation. The common law of contempt was used to obtain an injunction against the paper, preventing any further publication of such articles. The paper challenged this order in the European Court of Human Rights, alleging breach of Art. 10, the right to freedom of information. The court ruled, by a majority of eleven votes to nine, that the injunction was inconsistent with the ECHR. The Contempt of Court Act 1981 changed the law on contempt to avoid the conflict highlighted by the case.

In **Chahal** *v* **United Kingdom** (1996) Mr Chahal illegally entered the UK in 1971 and was granted indefinite leave to remain in 1974. When visiting Punjab ten years later to attend a family wedding he became involved in organizing passive resistance in support of an independent Sikh homeland to be carved out of India, leading to his arrest and torture by the Indian police. On his return to the UK he became a prominent figure in British Sikh affairs, establishing the International Sikh Youth Federation. The Home Secretary decided, in 1990, to deport Mr Chahal on the grounds of 'national security and the fight against terrorism'. Pending his deportation he was held in prison. On the basis that he would face torture if he returned to India, he applied for political asylum but his application was rejected. He took his case to the European Court of Human Rights arguing that his deportation would be in breach of Art. 3 of the ECHR which forbids the use of torture, inhuman or degrading treatment. The court found that the protection provided by Art. 3 was absolute: not even people suspected of terrorism should be exposed to such malpractice. Therefore the issue was not whether Mr Chahal was involved in terrorist activities, but whether there were substantial grounds for believing he would be ill-treated in India. As there was evidence of serious human rights violations in that country and the court was not convinced by assurances given by the Indian Government, his deportation would constitute a breach of Art. 3. Therefore, after six years of detention, Mr Chahal was released.

Article 3 was also the subject of the application in **D** *v* **UK** (1997). The applicant had been arrested on his arrival into the UK from St Kitts and subsequently convicted for importing the controlled drug, cocaine. In prison he was diagnosed as having AIDS. After three years in custody, and shortly before his release on licence, the immigration authorities ordered his removal to St Kitts. The court in Strasbourg again took a very strict approach to Art. 3. As the applicant had been in the UK for over three years he was protected by the Convention. The authorities in St Kitts were unable to provide the necessary treatment for the applicant's condition. Therefore, his deportation was likely to cause his death and would amount to inhuman treatment in breach of Art. 3 of the Convention.

The case of **Benham** *v* **United Kingdom** (1995) concerned an applicant who had been ordered to serve 30 days' imprisonment for failure to pay his Community Charge. The European Court of Human Rights held that there had been a contravention of Art. 5, which protects the right to liberty, as the magistrates had failed to conduct an adequate inquiry into why he had failed to pay. The right to a fair hearing under Art. 6 had also been breached as he had not been provided with legal representation.

McCann and Others *v* **United Kingdom** (1995) arose from the killing of IRA terrorists by members of the SAS in Gibraltar in March 1986. They were killed while they were in the process of executing a plan to conduct a terrorist attack on British Army personnel in Gibraltar. The SAS soldiers had believed that their action was necessary to prevent the suspects from remotely detonating a car bomb, with subsequent loss of life on a large scale. The applications were made by the parents of the victims, who alleged that there had been a violation of Art. 2 of the Convention laying down the right to life. The Article itself provides that this right is not breached if a person is deprived of their life in order to defend another from unlawful violence and no more force was used than was absolutely necessary. On the facts of the case, the European Court of Human Rights found that there was no evidence to support the allegation that the killings were premeditated, or that the British authorities had encouraged the execution of the terrorists. The action of the SAS soldiers, given the information they had received, did not in itself amount to a breach of the Convention. However, the British authorities had acted with insufficient care in their control of the operation, so that more force had been used than was absolutely necessary to protect others. In particular, the suspects could have been detained when they entered Gibraltar and there was a series of subsequent misjudgments. Despite this finding, no damages were awarded to the families in compensation, as this was felt to be inappropriate in the circumstances given that the victims had been in the act of planting a bomb.

As was mentioned above, the UK has also been the subject of inter-state actions brought by the Republic of Ireland. In 1971, Ireland lodged complaints with the Commission alleging that the security forces had failed to protect life, as required under Art. 2, that detained suspects were subject to treatment which amounted to torture, inhuman and degrading treatment contrary to Art. 3, and that internment without trial violated Arts. 5, 6 and 14. Finally the allegation was made that the UK Government had failed to honour the rights and freedoms contained in Art. 1 of the ECHR. The court held that Art. 3 had been breached. As a result of the court's decision, the UK Government sought to incorporate the substance of Art. 3 into the domestic law in Northern Ireland; it enacted the Northern Ireland (Emergency Provisions) Act 1987 which allows the courts in Northern Ireland to exclude evidence where there is *prima facie* evidence that the accused was subject to 'torture, to inhuman or degrading treatment, or to any violence or threat of violence'.

Many petitions against the UK have been withdrawn when the Government has agreed to take action in particular cases, or to change the general law.

▶ The European Court of Human Rights and the ECJ

The European Court of Human Rights is often confused with the European Court of Justice (ECJ), but these are quite separate institutions, as are the Commission of Human Rights and the Commission of the European Community. The phrase 'taking your case to Europe' tends to be used broadly, but the process and grounds for bringing an action to the ECJ is quite distinct from that for the European Court of Human Rights.

There are, however, growing links between the ECHR and European Union law. Article 164 of the Treaty of Rome provides that one of the functions of the ECJ is to ensure observance of the general principles of law contained in that Treaty. In recent cases the ECJ has suggested that respect for human rights is one of these principles, and that for guidance in understanding the scope of this principle they can look to the Convention. For example in **P v S and Cornwall CC** (1996) P was dismissed from her employment because she was a transsexual. Her application to the UK courts for sex discrimination was rejected. When the case was heard by the ECJ the Court referred to the European Court of Human Rights' judgment in **Rees** (1986). It concluded that the European Equal Treatment Directive had been breached, as this directive encapsulated the fundamental principle of equality.

In addition, the preamble to the Single European Act 1986 pledges members to 'work together to promote democracy on the basis of the fundamental rights recognized in the Convention'. Similar commitments to respect for fundamental human rights are included in the Maastricht Treaty.

There have been moves recently towards the European Union acceding to the ECHR which would effectively make its provisions part of European law. With this in mind, the Council of Ministers requested an opinion from the ECJ to confirm whether or not the EU, as it now stands, could accede to the Convention. The ECJ concluded (**Re Accession of the Community to the European Human Rights Convention** (1997)) that the EU currently had no competence to accede to the ECHR and that therefore the EC Treaty would have to be amended in order for this to happen.

A Bill of Rights for the UK?

It has been observed that the ECHR does not constitute a Bill of Rights for the UK because it has not been entrenched. Many people feel that while the Human Rights Act 1998 is a first step in the right direction, ultimately the UK needs a properly entrenched Bill of Rights to protect its citizens. Among developed Western countries, Israel and the UK are the only ones without such a Bill.

Arguments in favour of a Bill of Rights

Curbs on the executive

A Bill of Rights provides an important check on the enormous powers of the executive (the Government of the day and its agencies, such as the police, the army and Government departments). Constitutional writers of the nineteenth century, such as Dicey, made much of the role of Parliament as a watchdog over the executive, ensuring that oppressive legislation could not be passed. Since Dicey's time, the growth of a strong party system has fundamentally altered the nature of Parliament; in the vast majority of cases, a Government can expect its own members to obey party discipline, so that Government proposals will almost invariably be passed – during the 1980s, for example, only one Government Bill was defeated. Not only do those in opposition lack the numbers to prevent this, but the pressures of parliamentary time may even curtail a detailed scrutiny of proposed legislation. This can result in Governments being able to legislate against individual rights and freedoms almost at will.

The movement in favour of a Bill of Rights gained considerable support during the later years of the Thatcher regime, when the Government showed itself willing to compromise many important civil liberties. Many commentators were alarmed as they watched the banning of trade unions at Government Communications Headquarters (GCHQ), the attempts to ban the publication of *Spycatcher* (the memoirs of a retired security service agent) and the use of the Official Secrets Act 1911 to prosecute civil servants Sarah Tisdall and Clive Ponting who leaked official information the Government had wished to keep secret.

The fact that, given a decent majority in Parliament, Governments can make whatever law they like, means that they can simply legislate freedoms away, secure in the knowledge that the courts cannot refuse to apply their legislation, as they can in countries which have a Bill of Rights or written constitution. The Public Order Act 1986 and the Criminal Justice and Public Order Act 1994, for example, severely restrict rights of peaceful protest, of assembly and of movement, but English courts must apply this legislation nevertheless.

Supporters of a Bill of Rights claim it would curb executive powers, since the courts could simply refuse to apply laws which conflicted with it. This in turn would be a powerful incentive for a Government to avoid introducing such legislative provisions in the first place.

While the provision in s. 19 of the Human Rights Act 1998, requiring Ministers to state whether a Bill conforms with the 1998 Act, will discourage the executive in some circumstances from introducing legislation that breaches the ECHR, they are still able to do so.

Attitude of the judiciary
Even where the constitution does allow for judicial protection of civil rights, British judges have frequently proved themselves unequal to the task. As Griffith (1985) has famously pointed out, they show a tendency to view the public interest as the maintenance of established authority and traditional values. Though exceptions can always be found, the overall result has been that the maintenance of 'order' and the suppression of challenges to established authority – whether of trade unions or terrorists – have taken precedence over the kind of liberties a Bill of Rights might seek to protect. For example, in **R** *v* **Secretary of State for the Home Department, ex parte Brind** (1989), the judiciary upheld a broadcasting ban on members of a legitimate political party in Northern Ireland; in **Council of Civil Service Unions** *v* **Minister for the Civil Service** (1984),

the ban on trade unions at GCHQ was accepted; and in **Kent v Metropolitan Police Commissioner** (1981) a blanket ban on protest marches through an area of London was allowed.

The numerous miscarriages of justice suggest there is little protection of the right to a fair trial, nor, given the treatment of some of those involved while in police custody, to freedom from torture and inhuman treatment. The wide powers of surveillance permitted under statute to the police and security services prove the right to privacy a fallacy.

The Human Rights Act 1998 only requires the UK courts to interpret legislation in a way which is compatible with Convention rights 'so far as it is possible to do so' (s. 3). If a judge decides that the Act breaches a Convention right, the Act prevails.

Arguments against a Bill of Rights

Unnecessary
The previous Conservative Government was among those who asserted that civil liberties were already adequately protected in this country.

Increased power for the judiciary
Among those who oppose a Bill of Rights, mistrust of the judiciary, and constitutional objections to taking power from Parliament and giving it to judges, are perhaps the most frequent reasons given. There is no doubt that such a Bill would considerably increase judicial power. Unlike British statutes, the language of a Bill of Rights is typically open and imprecise, setting out broad principles rather than detailed provisions. This gives judges a wide discretion in interpretation – so wide that in the US, for example, the provisions against racial discrimination in the American Bill of Rights were once held to allow a form of apartheid, yet since 1954 such a system has been held to violate the Bill. Even within the last decade, the US Bill of Rights has been interpreted to allow discrimination against minorities. Thus, in the Supreme Court's decision in **Bowers v Hardwick** (1986), the constitutional right of privacy was effectively denied to homosexuals.

A Bill of Rights also calls upon judges to decide the relative importance of protected rights where two of them clash. Should, for example, the right to free expression of members of the British National Party override or give way to that of ethnic minorities to be free of racial harassment? Does a foetus have a right to life which overrides its mother's right to liberty and security of the person? There are no obvious right or wrong answers to questions like these and nor are there always obvious legal answers, even where there is a Bill of Rights. In many such cases the real problem is not what the law is, but what the law should be. Many people believe that is not a question which should be answered by judges who are not elected, but appointed from a narrow social elite by a secretive procedure. As Griffith (1985) has pointed out, these questions are political and political questions should, as far as possible, be answered by politicians elected to do so.

Supporters of such a Bill argue that the problems associated with greater judicial power could be dealt with by reforming judicial selection and drawing judges from a wider spread of the population. While this is clearly desirable in itself, it would not remove the fundamental objection that judges are not elected and nor, whatever the reforms, is it likely to avoid the fact that, by virtue of their education and their lifestyle, judges would be unrepresentative of the mass of the population. Those like Griffiths, who oppose a Bill of Rights, argue that what is needed is not so much reform of the judiciary, but political reforms that would allow a democratically elected legislature genuinely to supervise the acts of the executive and to fetter the exercise of executive discretion. The protection of fundamental freedoms and rights should not be for the individual to establish in court, but for the legislature to safeguard as part of their job.

Inflexibility
Supporters of our current constitutional arrangements argue that without a written constitution, our system can adapt over time, meeting new needs as they arise. They contend that a Bill of Rights would lack this flexibility. Two responses to this are that first, the open and imprecise language of a Bill of Rights allows flexibility, and secondly, the Bills can be changed when necessary: the arrangements for entrenchment will usually set down a special procedure that can be used to make amendments. The fact that these procedures may be long and difficult simply protects those rights originally laid down from rash or unpopular change; it does not set them in stone.

Too much flexibility
Ironically, it is also argued that the imprecise language typical of a Bill of Rights would lead to uncertainty about the law, leading to increased litigation with no clear objectives as to how general principles might emerge and policies be interpreted. This is clearly linked to the problem of mistrust of the judiciary.

Rights are not powers
A more fundamental problem is the idea that merely granting rights is not enough to secure individual freedom and empowerment. It is all very well to grant rights but, unless they are underpinned by economic and social provision, they may prove to be useless. Freedom of labour is effectively useless in times of high unemployment, when it becomes nothing more than the freedom to live in poverty. Freedom of movement fails to

help disabled people who cannot use public transport or afford their own. Freedom of association offers little advantage if employers refuse to recognize trade unions, and liberty of the person means nothing for the battered wife or abused child who has neither the personal nor the practical resources to escape.

Where there are huge imbalances in power in society, giving equal rights to all may be of limited use because those who have the most power can use it to find a way round the rights of those who are less powerful. For example, recent compensation payments made to women sacked for being pregnant have led to speculation that as a result employers may simply become even less keen than before to employ women; cases on racial discrimination may have had similar effects on the employment prospects of members of ethnic minorities. While it should not be denied that this kind of provision helps people, it can be argued that in focusing on individual rights, rather than social duties, a Bill of Rights might detract attention from any real commitment to a just society. The point is not that a Bill of Rights is undesirable but that, on its own, it cannot make the kind of changes sought by its supporters.

There is also the question of whether the same Bill of Rights would be appropriate for all parts of the UK. Northern Ireland may require special treatment given the intensity of religious and political animosity.

Drafting style
The ECHR follows the more general, looser European style of legislative drafting, in contrast to the more tightly worded legislation our courts are used to applying – though as European law has grown in importance, British courts are gaining more experience of this approach.

▶ ANSWERING QUESTIONS

1 **Assess the impact of the European Convention on Human Rights on UK law.** *WJEC*

You should begin your essay by stating what the Convention is, briefly outlining its origins and stating some of the rights and freedoms which it protects – remember to point out that states can depart from these principles under certain circumstances.

Then discuss the relationship of the Convention to UK law prior to the Human Rights Act 1998 coming into force, pointing out first of all that the Convention did not give directly enforceable rights in the UK. Explain how UK citizens who believed that their rights under the Convention had been breached had to bring a claim in the European Court of Human Rights, and the expectation that the UK Government would change the law if they were found in breach. You could talk about some of the cases in which this has happened, emphasizing the important changes in the law that have been made as a result of them. You could mention at this point that such cases did not always lead to better protection for the rights of UK citizens and cite the cases of **Brogan** v **United Kingdom** and **Abdulaziz** v **United Kingdom**.

You should then discuss what the position is today now that the Human Rights Act 1998 (HRA) has come into force. Your conclusion could be that the Convention has a much greater impact on UK law following the passing of the HRA 1998, but this impact would have been even greater if the Act had been entrenched.

2 **(a) Explain and illustrate the approach of English law to the protection of fundamental rights and freedoms.** *(15 marks)*
(b) Discuss what changes to that approach might be desirable. *(10 marks)* AQA *(AEB)*

Part (a): Define first of all what fundamental rights and freedoms are, giving examples of the kinds of rights and freedoms generally considered fundamental in modern, democratic societies. Then explain the traditional English approach to these rights – the idea of residual freedoms, giving examples of this approach from case law, such as **Malone**. In order to explain the approach fully, you might want briefly to contrast it with the Bill of Rights approach. You could also point out the problems which spring from this approach to fundamental rights: the complexity, and the way in which freedoms can be legislated away, for example. You could then discuss how a change of approach has been signalled by the passing of the Human Rights Act 1998, but that this change does not amount to a revolution because the Act is not entrenched.

Part (b): the main change which could be made to this approach would be through the passing of an entrenched Bill of Rights. Explain how this would work and in what way it would improve the situation; you could also highlight any drawbacks to it.

3 Explaining the approach currently adopted, consider whether English law provides adequate protection for fundamental rights and freedoms. AQA *(AEB)*

This question would require the same type of answer as that for question 2.

▌ Reading on the Internet

The Human Rights Act 1998 is available on Her Majesty's Stationery Office website at:

http://www.hmso.gov.uk/acts/acts1998/19980042.htm

The website of the European Court of Human Rights is:

http://www.echr.coe.int/

19 Freedom of assembly

Freedom of assembly means the right to meet together with other people. The relevant provision of the European Convention on Human Rights is Art. 11 which states:

1. Everyone has the right to freedom of peaceful assembly and to freedom of association with others, including the right to form and to join trade unions for the protection of his interests.
2. No restrictions shall be placed on the exercise of these rights other than such as are prescribed by law and are necessary in a democratic society in the interests of national security or public safety, for the prevention of disorder or crime, for the protection of health or morals or for the protection of the rights and freedoms of others. This article shall not prevent the imposition of lawful restrictions on the exercise of these rights by members of the armed forces, of the police or the administration of the State.

The aspect of freedom of assembly which has most relevance to civil rights law is the right to meet for a public protest, whether in a static assembly, or a march. The danger of such meetings leading to public disorder – especially where rival groups hold demonstrations in the same area – has led to a number of provisions restricting rights of assembly.

The legislation

The Public Order Act 1986 was passed after over a decade of periodic public order problems. During the 1970s, there were a number of incidents arising from confrontations between rival processions organized by the National Front and anti-fascist groups. These came to a head on a Saturday afternoon in June 1974, when a march to Red Lion Square by the National Front antagonized many people. A counter march was organized and despite police efforts public order broke down. In clashes that ensued one student was killed and many other people were injured.

The Home Secretary appointed Lord Scarman to conduct an inquiry into the incident. In his report on the disorders he considered the relationship between public protest and public order, concluding that the law needed to reach a balance between these often conflicting interests. The early 1980s saw further breakdowns in public order, beginning with inner city riots – apparently sparked off by heavy-handed policing among the ethnic minorities – followed by violent scenes on picket lines during the Wapping newspaper dispute and later the miners' strike – when around 140 charges of riot and over 500 of unlawful assembly were brought. Finally, there was an increase in violence at football matches, culminating in the Heysel stadium tragedy.

All these incidents were the subject of a massive media outcry, and right-wing papers in particular suggested that law and order was breaking down. The Government responded by passing the Public Order Act 1986 which, building on the provisions of the 1936 Public Order Act, establishes potentially severe limits on freedom of assembly. Further restrictions were added by the Criminal Justice and Public Order Act 1994 – a highly controversial piece of legislation which was opposed by a wide variety of groups. The civil rights pressure group, Liberty, has stated that many of its provisions may violate the European Convention on Human Rights.

There are also common law offences concerning freedom of assembly, and torts which may be committed when attending an assembly. These will be considered in detail below, along with the statutory restrictions.

Powers to control assemblies

The common law

Under common law, public authorities traditionally had very little power to prevent the holding of assemblies. This can be seen in the case of **Beatty** v **Gillbanks** (1882), which concerned regular Sunday marches held by the Salvation Army in Weston-super-Mare. These marches antagonized some inhabitants of the town, who set up a rival group, called the Skeleton Army, and attempted to disrupt Salvation Army marches. To try and prevent breaches of the peace occurring, the Salvation Army were banned from holding their marches. When they ignored the ban, this was held to be an offence and they were bound over to keep the peace. This order was set aside on appeal: they could not be prohibited from assembling merely because their lawful conduct might induce others to act unlawfully.

More recently, the common law has increased the powers of the police to deal with assemblies. In **Moss** v **McLachlan** (1985), which arose during the miners' strike, the four defendants were stopped at a motorway exit by police officers. The police suspected they were travelling to attend a picket line and told them to turn back. The men refused and were arrested, on the basis that there were reasonable grounds to suspect a breach of the peace would occur if the men were allowed to proceed. Despite the fact that the men were some miles away from the nearest picket line, the arrests were found to be justified. The court held that, if the police reasonably apprehend that the holding of a gathering in a public place will give rise to a breach of the peace, they are under a common law duty to take reasonable steps to prevent that gathering from taking place or to break it up. Questions of public order outweighed strong restrictions on both freedom of assembly and freedom of movement.

Statutory controls

These are contained in the Public Order Act 1986 and the Criminal Justice and Public Order Act 1994. The fuel protests that took place in 2000 fell within this legislation, but the police initially chose not to make use of these powers. Different provisions apply to static assemblies (such as public meetings or rallies) and moving ones (marches and processions).

Static assemblies

The Public Order Act 1986 defines a public assembly as a gathering of 20 or more people in a public place which is wholly or partly open to the air (s. 16). It does not, therefore, include assemblies in buildings, including public buildings.

Section 14 of the Act allows conditions to be imposed by the police on static assemblies, either before an assembly takes place, or during it. This power allows the police to limit the number of people attending, the duration and the place of the assembly. The police can impose these conditions where they reasonably believe the assembly may result in serious public disorder, damage to property, or disruption to the life of the community, or that the purpose of organizing the assembly is to intimidate others.

Such powers can be very draconian, contributing a major restriction on the right to hold an assembly. Take the example of a meeting held outside a town hall to demonstrate opposition to council policies, or outside a foreign embassy to highlight the relevant country's bad record on human rights. The whole point of such a demonstration is to draw attention to a cause. By moving the demonstration to a local park or a side street, where nobody will notice it, or limiting it to a handful of people, the police have the power to make the demonstration all but useless. In addition, the conditions under which those powers can be exercised show how far the Act tips the balance in favour of public order and against freedom of assembly; in the White Paper preceding the 1986 statute, an example given of disruption to the life of the community was that of marches held on Saturdays in shopping centres. As far as the Act is concerned, it appears that getting your shopping done is more important than being able to exercise a fundamental civil right.

The police tried to exercise their powers under s. 14 in **DPP** *v* **Baillie** (1995). Baillie was involved in promoting festivals and social events. He had distributed free news-sheets and provided a telephone information service, which gave vague details of when and where events would take place. The police issued the respondent with a s. 14 notice ordering him to comply with certain conditions regarding a particular gathering, and in due course he was convicted for failing to comply with the order. The Queen's Bench Division ruled that the police had not had the power to issue the order because they had not known enough about the proposed event (such as the time, location and number of people involved) to know whether the conditions for the exercise of s. 14 had been satisfied.

Further controls over static assemblies were introduced in the Criminal Justice and Public Order Act 1994, which inserts a new s. 14A (covering trespassory assemblies as opposed to public assemblies), into the Public Order Act 1986. Where an assembly is intended to be held on land to which the public has no or only limited access, the chief constable for the area may apply to the local council for a banning order. This order can be granted, with the Home Secretary's approval, if (a) the assembly is likely to be held without the owner's permission or to exceed that permission, and there is a risk of serious disruption to the life of the community, or (b) the land is of historical, architectural, archaeological or scientific interest, and serious damage may result. An order may ban all assemblies within a five-mile radius for up to four days. Once the banning order is in place, people may be turned back from attempting to attend the proposed assembly. Under s. 14B it is an arrestable offence to organize, participate in, or incite an assembly which you know breaches a banning order.

The potential coverage of s. 14A is vast. It would now apply to many of the demonstrations that occurred during the miners' strike, as they often took place on National Coal Board land. Sit-ins and worker occupations would also be covered. But the dividing line between private and public property is nowhere near as clear cut as is presumed by the legislation. What about, for example, protests in a shopping-mall, or at an airport? Even in a public park, access is limited by virtue of bye-laws. The precise scope of the section will only be known once it begins to be interpreted by the courts, but previous case law suggest the domestic courts will give the section a broad application. Contrast, for example, the following two cases, the first from Canada and the second from England. In both cases, airport authorities tried to prevent a group of individuals carrying placards and distributing pamphlets inside the airport. In **Committee for the Commonwealth of Canada** *v* **The Queen in Right of Canada** (1986) the court held that the airport's action breached the Canadian Charter; while, in **British Airports Authority** *v* **Ashton** (1983) the British court held that the airport authority was entitled to prevent the demonstration.

The first case interpreting s. 14A was **DPP** *v* **Jones** (1998). The police had obtained an order from the local authority under s. 14A prohibiting for four days the holding of assemblies within a four-mile radius of Stonehenge. The respondents had taken part in a peaceful, non-obstructive gathering of about 20 people on the grass verge of a road running along the perimeter fence of the historical site as part of a demonstration for the right to access to the monument. This gathering contravened the order and, on failing to disperse at the request of the police, the demonstrators were arrested. The defendants in the case were convicted in the magistrates' court of being party to a trespassory assembly contrary to s. 14B of the 1986 Act. Their appeal was allowed by the Crown Court which stated that any assembly on the highway is lawful providing it is peaceful and non-obstructive. The DPP appealed by way of case stated to the Queen's Bench Division which held that the Crown Court had misstated the law and the respondents had committed an offence in breaching the banning order. On a further appeal to the House of Lords, this was reversed, and the Crown Court judgment approved.

In **Windle** *v* **DPP** (1996) it was found that an offence had been committed under s. 14B when the respondents had run after a hunt intending to disrupt it when they were sufficiently close. The case therefore confirmed the fears of many that the 1994 Act constitutes a significant erosion of an already limited freedom.

Public processions
Under the Public Order Act 1986 the organizers of a public procession must give advance notice to the police, unless it is not reasonably practicable to do so (s. 11). At least six days before the planned procession (or as soon as reasonably practical) notice must be given of the route and time of the proposed march, and the name and address of the organizer(s). Failure to do so incurs criminal liability.

Police can impose on the assembly such conditions as appear necessary if one of the same grounds required for static assemblies is satisfied (s. 12). If a chief constable reasonably believes that their powers to impose conditions on the procession would be inadequate to prevent serious public disorder, they may obtain from the council, with the consent of the Home Secretary, a ban of up to three months on all public processions or a specified class of procession (s. 13). It is an offence knowingly to organize, participate in or incite someone to participate in a procession which violates a banning order.

Miscellaneous powers

Bye-laws and regulations restricting the use of public areas for meetings, and requiring advance notice of processions are in effect in many areas of Britain. Public rallies in Trafalgar Square in London, for example, must be authorized by the Secretary of State for the Environment at his discretion (Trafalgar Square Regulations 1952, reg. 3).

In many other countries, there is a right to hold meetings in public areas and publicly owned buildings, but this is not the case here. There are, however, some positive rights. Meetings organized as part of a candidate's election campaign are entitled to be held in a state school or in other publicly owned rooms (Representation of the People Act 1983), and universities and colleges have a general duty to make their halls available to all groups, whether popular or unpopular, without discriminating between them on political or other grounds, under the Education (No. 2) Act 1986. By s. 43, the governing bodies of such establishments must 'take such steps as are reasonably practicable to ensure that freedom of speech within the law is secured for members, students and employees of the establishment and for visiting speakers'.

This section was invoked in **R** *v* **University of Liverpool, ex parte Caesar-Gordon** (1990). The student Conservative Association had sparked considerable controversy by inviting two representatives of the South African Embassy to address a meeting. South Africa, at the time, was still living under apartheid. Fearing that this event could antagonize local residents in Toxteth, an area which had already suffered from race riots, the university authorities banned the meeting. The chairman of the Conservative Association applied for judical review, and the court held that, when deciding whether to permit a meeting, governing bodies of Universities should only consider the reactions of those within the University and not those residents outside its boundaries. The decision to deny permission was therefore *ultra vires*.

Animal rights activists seeking to prevent laboratory experiments being carried out on animals have picketed the homes of employees of companies (such as Huntingdon Life Sciences) involved in such experiments. To combat this behaviour, s. 42 of the Criminal Justice and Police Act 2000 provides the police with new powers. A police officer can direct persons to leave the vicinity of a person's home, or issue other directions, in order to prevent harassment, alarm or distress to persons in the home. The explanatory notes to the legislation state that a peaceful protest could still take place away from the vicinity of the home.

Offences committed during assemblies and marches

As well as the crimes detailed above, there are a number of other criminal offences which are specific to public order situations, some of the most important of which are detailed in Part I of the Public Order Act 1986.

Riot

Riot is the most serious public order offence. It is committed when 12 or more people, who are present together, use or threaten unlawful violence for a common purpose. Their conduct (taken together) must be such as would cause a person of reasonable firmness present at the scene to fear for their personal safety (s. 1). It can take place in public or private and nobody else need actually be present. The crime carries a maximum penalty of ten years' imprisonment and a fine.

Violent disorder

Violent disorder is committed when three or more persons who are present together use or threaten unlawful violence. Their conduct (taken together) must be such as would cause a person of reasonable firmness present at the scene to fear for their personal safety (s. 2). Again, the offence can take place in a public or private place, and no person of reasonable firmness need actually be present. The defendant must intend to use or threaten violence, or be aware that their conduct may be violent or threaten violence. The maximum sentence on indictment is a five-year prison sentence and a fine, or on summary conviction six months' imprisonment or a fine of up to £5,000.

Affray

Affray is committed by using or threatening unlawful violence towards another, such as to cause a person of reasonable firmness present at the scene to fear for their personal safety (s. 3). The threat must come from more than just words and, again, the offence can be committed in a public or private place, and no person of reasonable firmness need actually be present. On indictment the maximum sentence is three years' imprisonment and a fine; summarily it is three months' imprisonment and a fine of up to £5,000.

Threatening behaviour

The offence of threatening behaviour occurs when a person uses towards another threatening, abusive or insulting words or conduct. It is also committed where someone distributes or displays material which is threatening, abusive or insulting with intent to make another believe that unlawful violence is going to be used or provoked (s. 4). The crime can be committed in a public or private place, apart from where both involved are in a dwelling. There is a maximum sentence of six months' imprisonment and a fine of £5,000.

The case of **R v Horseferry Road Magistrates, ex parte Siadatan** (1991) considered the scope of this offence. It concerned the publication of the book *The Satanic Verses*, by Salman Rushdie, which many devout Muslims found offensive. The applicant alleged that publication and distribution of the book was an offence under s. 4(1), on the ground that the book contained abusive and insulting writing which was likely to provoke unlawful violence. On a strict construction of the legislation, the Divisional Court held that the magistrate was correct in refusing to issue a summons. In the view of the court, the requirement in the Act that the insulted person should be 'likely to believe that such violence will be used' should be restricted to where the victim is likely to believe that the violence will be used immediately.

Intentional harassment, alarm or distress

Under s. 4A of the Public Order Act 1986 a person commits this offence where, with intent to cause harassment, alarm or distress, they use threatening, abusive or insulting words or behaviour, display such material or behave in a disorderly manner. Their conduct must have caused harassment, alarm or distress. The crime is not committed if the people concerned are in a dwelling. A person found guilty can be liable to six months' imprisonment or a fine of £5,000.

Disorderly conduct

A person is guilty of this offence if they use threatening, abusive or insulting words or behaviour, display such material or behave in a disorderly manner. This conduct must have been within hearing or sight of anyone likely to be caused harassment, alarm or distress (s. 5). The crime can be committed in public or private places, but not where the people concerned are in a dwelling. The maximum penalty is a £1,000 fine.

Incitement to racial hatred

This offence is defined in the Public Order Act 1986, ss. 17–23. 'Racial hatred' means 'hatred against a group of persons in Great Britain defined by reference to colour, race, nationality (including citizenship) or ethnic or national origins' (s. 17).

Section 18 of the Act makes it an offence to use threatening, abusive or insulting words or behaviour, or to display any such material, if done with intent or likelihood of stirring up racial hatred. The offence applies to theatrical performances (s. 20), cinemas (s. 21) and television and radio broadcasts (s. 22). Under s. 23 it is an offence to possess material which if published or displayed would amount to an offence under s. 18.

The Home Office is considering extending criminal liability to include the stirring up of hatred because of a person's religion. The Commission for Racial Equality has observed that 'it cannot be any more acceptable to stir up hatred against people because they are seen to be Muslims, than to do so because they are seen to be Pakistanis'.

Obstruction of the police

Obstructing the police in the execution of their duty is a statutory offence under the Police Act 1996, s. 89. The courts have shown themselves very willing to uphold a wide use of this offence, even where its use severely restricts freedom of assembly. In **Duncan** v **Jones** (1936), a speaker addressing a crowd from a box on the highway was told to stop, because the police feared a breach of peace. Despite the fact that the only ground for this fear was that a disturbance had occurred in the same place a year earlier, the courts upheld the arrest of the speaker for obstruction, after she refused to stop speaking.

Obstruction of the highway

This is another offence with very wide application. Under the Highways Act 1980, s. 137, it is an offence 'if a person without lawful authority or excuse in any way wilfully obstructs the free passage along a highway'. For the purposes of this crime, the highway includes the pavement as well as the road. If a police officer orders a speaker, distributor, vendor or audience to 'move along', and they refuse to do so, they are likely to be arrested for obstruction of the highway or obstruction of a constable in the execution of his duty.

Public nuisance

A procession or public meeting may amount to a public nuisance if it entails an unreasonable use of the highway, causing obstruction or excessive noise. There may be a difference in the degrees of obstruction needed to obtain convictions for a public nuisance and for wilful obstruction under the Highways Act 1980.

▌ Torts

Assemblies held without permission on land which is in private ownership constitute trespass. If they are held on a highway, they often constitute a trespass at common law against the person or body in whom the highway is vested, unless the owner has given his or her consent. This is because the primary purpose of a highway is for passage and repassage. Thus public processions are *prima facie* lawful, since they simply involve collective exercise of the right to passage along the highway. But the use of the highway must still be reasonable; a procession becomes a nuisance if the right is exercised unreasonably or with reckless disregard of the rights of others. This might cover, for example, demonstrators linking arms so as to block the highway as they walked.

▌ ANSWERING QUESTIONS

1 The Government published proposals to abandon the practice of preventing the spread of rabies by quarantining animals being brought into the country and replacing it with a system of vaccination. These proposals aroused widespread support and opposition and led to the formation of 'pro' and 'anti' vaccination groups (P and A groups). When the P group organized a march and demonstration

to express its support, members of the A group marched along opposite them, shouting and jeering, holding up placards showing animals suffering from rabies and depicting members of the P group as animal killers. Scuffles broke out along the length of the march and A group members frequently banded together to threaten both P group members and any bystanders who indicated any support for them. Subsequently, there was a great deal of public criticism of police tactics at the march and also of the behaviour of the A group. Nevertheless, the P group announced that it would be holding another march followed by a meeting in church grounds adjacent to privately owned playing fields (onto which, it was immediately objected, the meeting would spill). The A group then made it clear that it would be present to demonstrate its opposition once again.

Explain what liability arises out of the incidents at the first march and demonstration and consider how the police should deal with the plans by the P group to hold a second march and meeting. *Edexcel*

Your answer should be divided into two halves looking first at the liability arising from the first march and demonstration and secondly at how the police should deal with the plans for a second march and meeting. In the first half, the conduct of members of the A group is likely to amount to threatening behaviour within s. 4 of the Public Order Act 1986. They are using threatening, abusive and insulting words and behaviour directed at the members of the P group and at bystanders and displaying abusive or insulting signs to the members of the P group. Similarly, the offences under s. 4A (intentional harassment, alarm and distress) and s. 5 (disorderly conduct) are also likely to have been committed.

The scuffles may amount to the offence of affray under s. 3 of the Public Order Act 1986. The tendency of members of the A group to band together to threaten P group members and bystanders raises the possibility of the more serious offence of violent disorder, for which there must be at least three persons present together using or threatening unlawful violence. It seems unlikely that the most serious offence, riot, will have occurred in view of the requirement for proof of 12 people acting together.

There may well have been instances of obstruction of the highway under s. 137 of the Highways Act 1980 and significant breaches of the peace will have occurred. The police will have had powers of arrest and dispersal in consequence of the commission of the offences and the occurrences of breaches of the peace.

In relation to the second half of the question note that we are both concerned with the law on static assemblies and public processions. The police must be careful not to restrict the freedom of expression of the P group merely because another group intends to be disruptive and to behave in an unlawful manner. The case of **Beatty v Gillbanks** (1882) is particularly relevant to these facts. Thus, while taking account of the need to preserve public order, the police should try to apply measures designed to minimize the threat from the A group, rather than to constrain the P group. Even so, the police might wish to consider activating the trespassory assembly provisions (a general ban) under the Public Order Act 1986, s. 14A to prevent the meeting spilling over into private grounds.

The police should receive a notice of the march from the organizers. They will then decide whether the proposed route poses any particular problems and whether to impose conditions. It may be useful for a police superintendent in the locality to authorize random stop and search for offensive weapons and dangerous instruments under s. 60 of the Criminal Justice and Public Order Act 1994, which may be aimed at forestalling trouble from the A group.

If trouble develops at the march, this can be dealt with by using the general powers conferred by the preventive provisions of the Public Order Act 1986, and by powers associated with obstruction (Police Act 1996, s. 89(2)) and breach of the peace.

You could conclude with a discussion of any possible impact of Art. 11 of the European Convention on Human Rights on the UK law in this field.

2 **'A tension clearly exists between the legitimate interest of the state in maintaining order on the one hand and, on the other, the protection of the freedom of assembly.' (Fenwick, *Civil Liberties*, 1998)**
Consider whether this tension is adequately accommodated in the UK.

This essay requires you to reflect on the protection of freedom of assembly in the UK. One approach would be to argue that during the 1980s and the first half of the 1990s legislation failed to achieve a balance between the public order interest and the freedom to assemble, moving too far towards the desire to maintain order while showing too little respect for the protection of the freedom to assemble. Whatever your line of argument, you must provide detailed examples from the existing law on the current limits on freedom of assembly, including common law cases such as **Moss v McLachlan** (1985) and statutory provisions such as the Public Order Act 1986 and the Criminal Justice and Public Order Act 1994. The passing of the Human Rights Act 1998 may suggest a shift back in favour of freedom of assembly, as Art. 11 of the European Convention protects this right, though the European Court of Human Rights has not, under its existing powers, tried to contain the restrictions in the UK on freedom of assembly.

Your conclusion could be that if one attempts to restrict the freedom to assemble too far this can actually create a threat to public order rather than prevent it. This view could be supported by reference to the demonstration against capitalism that took place in the summer of 1999 in the City of London. This was organized as an underground movement outside the controls of the state and by a movement that had learnt from the repression of 'raves' to use the Internet as an effective means of communication to like-minded people.

▶ Reading on the Internet

The Criminal Justice and Public Order Act 1994 is available on Her Majesty's Stationery Office website at:

http://www.hmso.gov.uk/acts/acts1994/Ukpga_19940033_en_1.htm

20 Freedom of association

Freedom of association is concerned with the right to meet with other people, and to form organizations, such as trade unions and pressure groups. This right is an essential part of a democratic system, allowing the formation of political groups opposed to Government policies. The relevant provision of the European Convention on Human Rights is Art. 11 which is quoted at p. 474.

In general, English law imposes no restrictions upon the freedom of individuals to associate together for political purposes; in less democratic countries, political parties, action groups, campaign committees and so on have to be officially registered, and in some cases may be forbidden altogether. However, freedom of association in this country is not entirely unrestricted. The following are some of its important limitations.

Terrorist organizations

The situation in Northern Ireland has led to special restrictions on membership of organizations viewed as terrorist groups. The Terrorism Act 2000 makes it an offence to belong to a proscribed organization which includes the Irish Republican Army (IRA) and the Irish National Liberation Army (INLA).

The Public Order Act 1936

The Public Order Act 1936 was passed largely in response to problems caused by a Fascist organization known as the 'Blackshirts'. Against the background of growing Nazi influence in Germany, this organization held provocative marches wearing their uniform of a black shirt, through the East End of London – an area which then, as now, had a high ethnic minority population.

The Public Order Act 1936, s. 1 made it an offence to wear a political uniform in a public place or at a public meeting (except with the permission of the Home Secretary). The offence was used against IRA members in the case of **O'Moran** v **Director of Public Prosecutions** (1975). Individuals who attended the funeral of an IRA member in London, wearing the recognized IRA uniform of black berets and dark glasses, were prosecuted for the section 1 offence.

Section 2 of the Public Order Act 1936 makes it an offence to organize or train a body to usurp the functions of the police or the armed forces, or to promote a political object. In 1963, the leaders of a neo-Nazi movement known as Spearhead, whose members wore uniforms and exchanged Nazi salutes, were convicted under this section. During the same decade, the offence was successfully used against leaders of the Free Wales Army.

Measures against subversion

Subversion is defined as conduct intended to undermine or overthrow parliamentary democracy in the UK by political, industrial or violent means. While membership of subversive organizations is not banned in the UK, members of such groups are prohibited from holding certain kinds of civil service jobs.

Trade union membership

With the exception of certain Government posts, workers in the UK are free to join trade unions if they wish. The benefit of this freedom has been compromised by the strict anti-union laws introduced since 1979, which make it very difficult to take industrial action that is both effective and within the law. Secondary action, in which union members not directly affected by a particular employment dispute take action in support of their fellow union members, has been made illegal. There is no requirement for UK employers to negotiate with unions, even where a high proportion of their employees are union members. This situation shows how the presence of formal rights can conceal the fact that such rights may have little force in practice.

In the 1980s trade union membership was banned at Government Communications Headquarters (GCHQ). This was not imposed because of the risk of infiltration by extremist organizations, but because the Government argued that the possibility of industrial action by union members threatened national security, even though the relevant union had offered a no-strike deal. Union membership was reviewed following the election of a Labour Government.

ANSWERING QUESTIONS

Examination questions are rarely devoted to freedom of association alone, but you could use the material in this chapter as part of a general discussion of civil liberties.

Reading on the Internet

The Terrorism Act 2000 is available on Her Majesty's Stationery Office website at:

http://www.hmso.gov.uk/acts/acts2000/20000011.htm

The explanatory notes to the Terrorism Act 2000 are available at:

http://www.legislation.hmso.gov.uk/acts/en/2000en11.htm

21 Freedom from discrimination

At common law, no restrictions existed against discrimination but, over the past couple of decades, legislation has introduced protection from both sexual and racial discrimination and, to a limited extent, discrimination on the basis of disability. Campaigners are currently trying to extend this to cover discrimination due to a person's age or sexuality.

The need for protection from discrimination actually stems from the basic freedom of British law, that a person may do anything not prohibited by the law. In the past, this meant that, for example, landlords were free not to accept black tenants, and employers not to employ female workers. The law itself did not discriminate – it did not state positively that women or black people should have fewer rights than others – but by not specifically preventing discrimination on these grounds, it allowed those with power in society to discriminate against those without.

Race discrimination

Provisions against race discrimination are now contained in both national and European legislation and each will be considered in turn.

National legislation

The issue of race discrimination was first addressed in the Race Relations Act 1965 and is now covered by the Race Relations Act 1976. Some changes were made to this Act by the Race Relations (Amendment) Act 2000. Under English law, racial discrimination is defined as treating someone less favourably than you would treat other people, on racial grounds: the question to be asked is not whether the person's treatment was good or bad, fair or unfair, but simply whether it would have been different but for his or her racial background. The 1976 Act makes it an offence to discriminate on racial grounds, or to incite, instruct or induce someone else to do so.

The Act prohibits both direct and indirect discrimination. Direct discrimination occurs where a person treats another less favourably due to their race – examples would include excluding black people from membership of a club or refusing to employ Irish people. Indirect discrimination can be less easy to spot. It occurs where a condition imposed – on employees or potential tenants, for example – are such that the proportion of persons of a particular racial group who can comply with it is considerably smaller than for those from other racial groups, and such a condition is not justifiable for any reason that does not concern racial considerations, and have a detrimental effect on those who are unable to comply.

Where indirect discrimination is alleged, it is a defence to an action for damages for the alleged discriminator to prove that there was no intention to discriminate against the claimant on racial grounds (s. 57(3)). This kind of discrimination was examined in **Mandla** *v* **Dowell Lee** (1983). The case concerned the application of a Sikh schoolboy to a school which forbade the wearing of any kind of headgear. The Sikh religion requires that men wear turbans, and so the boy's father alleged that the school rule indirectly discriminated against Sikhs. The school did not say it would not accept Sikh pupils (which would have been direct discrimination) but by enforcing a rule with which Sikhs could not comply and other people could, it treated Sikhs differently on the basis of their race alone. The House of Lords upheld this argument.

It is illegal to discriminate when offering employment, except where the work is in a private household or where membership of a particular racial group is a genuine qualification for a stated job (for example, a role in the theatre). Discrimination is unlawful in education and in the provision of goods, services and facilities to the public or a section of the public (s. 20). There are exceptions for residential accommodation in small premises and for the fostering or care of children in a person's home (s. 23(2)). In **Farah** *v* **Commissioner of Police of the Metropolis** (1996) it was held that 'services' included those provided by the police. Farah was a 17-year-old girl who was a refugee from Somali. A group of white teenagers attacked her and her ten-year-old cousin and let loose a dog on her causing her injury. She telephoned the police but, when they arrived, they made no attempt to arrest her attackers; instead she was arrested and charged with affray, assault and causing unnecessary suffering to a dog. At her trial she was acquitted when the prosecution offered no evidence. She subsequently brought an action for damages, and the Court of Appeal made it clear that a police officer fell within s. 20 of the Race Relations Act 1976. This is important as a survey carried out by the Runnymede Trust in 1996 (*This is Where I Live*) found that two out of five Asian respondents felt they could not rely on police protection from racial harassment. To illustrate the problem of negative stereotyping by the police the report quoted a young black man saying: 'Getting hassled by the police is part of life. If you're black, you look suspicious; if you've got a mobile phone, you're a drug dealer.'

Clubs which have more than 25 members may not discriminate in their selection of members (s. 25) but a club whose main aim is to provide benefits to persons of a particular racial group may discriminate on grounds of race, nationality or ethnic origin, but not as regards colour (s. 26).

Following the changes introduced to the 1976 Act by the Race Relations (Amendment) Act 2000, it is now unlawful for a public authority to do any act constituting discrimination while carrying out its functions. The notion of a 'public authority' is given a wide definition and includes the police, national and local government and the NHS. Public bodies also now have a statutory duty to promote race equality. They will be expected to consider the implications for race equality of everything they do; for example, allocating council housing and school places, closing a hospital or managing prisons.

The need for this extension in the fight against racism has been highlighted by the race riots that took place in the north of England in the summer of 2001 and the media's coverage of asylum seekers coming to the UK.

Allegations of discrimination in relation to employment are brought before an employment tribunal. Other types of discrimination may be brought before designated county courts, which can award damages, including compensation for injury to feelings.

The Commission for Racial Equality consists of a chairperson and up to 14 members. The members are appointed by the Home Secretary, though the Commission is formally independent of the Government. One of its main functions is to conduct investigations into alleged discriminatory practices where there is reasonable suspicion that acts of discrimination have occurred. It may order the organization or person concerned to supply information and produce documents, and hold a hearing. If the investigation finds discrimination, the Commission may issue a non-discrimination notice requiring the prejudicial conduct to stop. There is a right of appeal to the county court, or to an employment tribunal in the case of employment discrimination. The Commission can follow up a notice within five years of it being issued, to ensure that it has been complied with. In the case of non-compliance, an application for an injunction can be made to the county court.

Following the Race Relations (Amendment) Act 2000 the Commission for Racial Equality is given the power to issue Codes of Practice to provide guidance to public authorities on how to fulfil their general and specific duties to promote race equality. A critical feature of the new duty to promote race equality is that it is enforceable. If the Commission finds that a public authority is not complying with its specific duties, it will be able to serve a compliance notice. This will require the authority to comply with its duties and inform the Commission of the measures it has taken. If necessary, the Commission can ask the county court to order the authority to comply.

Some forms of racist behaviour are made a criminal offence under the Public Order Act 1986 (see p. 481). In addition, the Crime and Disorder

Act 1998 created new racially aggravated offences (ss. 28–32). These offences are racially aggravated assault, grievous bodily harm, criminal damage, public order and harassment. They carry heavier sentences than the simple offence, for example, an ordinary assault carries a maximum sentence of six months' imprisonment, while a racially aggravated assault has a maximum of two years'. An offence is racially aggravated if:

> at the time of committing the offence, or immediately before or after doing so, the offender demonstrates towards the victim of the offence hostility based on the victim's membership (or presumed membership) of a racial group; or . . . the offence is motivated (wholly or partly) by hostility towards members of a racial group . . . (s. 28).

The Act also lays down that for other offences that were racially motivated, this motive must be treated as an aggravating factor when sentencing (s. 82(2)).

European legislation

With the Treaty of Amsterdam that came into force in 1999, Europe adopted a new social policy agenda with the aim of making Europe a more competitive market-place with economic growth and greater social cohesion. Part of the reason for this is the fact that a number of Eastern European countries are due to become members of the European Union. Some of these countries have an appalling record of race discrimination, particularly in relation to the Romany Gypsies who live, for example, in Slovakia. At the same time, right-wing extremist groups are growing in popularity in some parts of Europe, such as Austria, Germany and Italy, with the risk of political upheaval and unrest. European policy advisers have recognized that economic prosperity is linked to a mobile and young migrant community. Minority communities in Europe require protection from racial discrimination and better integration to prevent them becoming a volatile underclass undermining a more inclusive Europe.

Article 13 of the EU Treaty now empowers the Council of Ministers to take action to combat race discrimination. A directive has been produced which outlaws race discrimination within employment and specific non-employment areas and is due to be implemented in July 2003. Some of the provisions of the Race Relations (Amendment) Act 2000 seek to bring the UK law into compliance with the EU directive.

Sex discrimination

Although the cause of equality for women had been a major issue since the beginning of the century, Britain did not create laws against sex discrimination until 1976. The field is now covered by two interrelated Acts, the Equal Pay Act 1970 and the Sex Discrimination Act 1975, as well as

European law. Following a European Directive in 1998 the burden of proof in proceedings arising under this legislation falls upon the defendant.

The Equal Pay Act 1970

In Britain in 1970 women only earned 63 per cent of the average male wage. The Equal Pay Act 1970 tried to redress the balance, stating that women are to have the same pay and conditions of employment as men where they are doing the same work (a man who believes he is paid less than a woman doing like work has the same rights, but in practice the victim of lower pay is usually a woman). This does not mean that their jobs must be identical in order to draw the comparison: different jobs done by men and women will be considered as 'like work' where the differences in job content are not significant or, though significant, do not occur frequently. An official job evaluation study can also be carried out to see whether different jobs performed by men are equivalent to those performed by women. In **Hayward** *v* **Cammell Laird Shipbuilders Ltd** (1988), a female cook was held to be entitled to the same wage as carpenters, joiners and thermal insulation engineers employed by her company because her work and theirs were of equal value to their employer.

A woman who believes she is not receiving equal pay and conditions can bring her claim before an Employment Tribunal. As well as gaining equal pay, an employee who succeeds in her claim may win compensation. Where a collective bargaining agreement between employer and trade union provides different rates for men and women, it can be referred to the Industrial Arbitration Board so that any offending clauses may be removed.

The Sex Discrimination Act 1975

The 1975 Act has a broader application than the Equal Pay Act 1970, and is similar in scope to the Race Relations Act 1976. Four types of discrimination are covered: treating a woman less favourably than a man on account of sex; treating a man less favourably than a woman (maternity provisions excepted); treating a married person less favourably, on grounds of their marital status, than a single person; and victimization because someone has invoked either the 1970 or 1975 Act. Like the Race Relations Act 1976, it prohibits both direct and indirect discrimination: an example of indirect sex discrimination might be a requirement that all plumbers employed by a company should be at least 6 ft tall, since this is a requirement that is likely to be satisfied by more men than women.

Part II of the 1975 Act prohibits discrimination in employment, covering terms and conditions of employment, access to training and promotion. There is an exemption for employment which involves work in a private house and where the work can genuinely only be performed by someone of a particular sex. Complaints about discrimination in employment and training are made to an Employment Tribunal, which may award compensation.

The Act established the Equal Opportunities Commission, which has similar powers to the Commission for Racial Equality.

European law

Article 119 of the EC Treaty prohibits discrimination between men and women as regards pay and employment conditions. The leading case on equal pay under Art. 119 is **Defrenne** *v* **Sabena (No. 2)**. Defrenne was an air hostess who received a lower rate of pay than her male counterparts, cabin stewards performing the same tasks for the same employer. The European Court found that this was a case of direct discrimination.

Discrimination against disabled people

The Disability Discrimination Act 1995 aims to outlaw discrimination of disabled people in the field of employment and in the provision of services, goods and facilities. Section 1 defines disability for the purposes of the Act as 'a physical or mental impairment which has a substantial and long term adverse effect on his ability to carry out normal day-to-day activities'. Schedule 1 of the Act states that a 'long term effect' is one which has lasted or is likely to last 12 months or more. Guidance on the interpretation of s. 1 and a Code of Practice have been prepared. The Employment Appeal Tribunal (EAT) has now had the opportunity to consider the meaning of 'disability'. In **Goodwin** *v* **The Patent Office** (1998) Mr Goodwin had been employed in the Patent Office for eight months when he was dismissed following complaints from fellow employees about his behaviour. He suffered from schizophrenia and during his period of employment he had not been on proper medication. He suffered from paranoia, imagined that other people could access his thoughts and had hallucinations which would occur at random and would often cause him to leave his office or the building. He was therefore unable to concentrate for any sustained period. However, Mr Goodwin cared for himself at home and was able to do his shopping and cooking, and to attend to his own personal hygiene. Since he had been dismissed he had been put on appropriate medication, and his disturbing symptoms had ceased.

The tribunal at first instance concluded that Mr Goodwin's impairment affected his day-to-day activities, in that his concentration was adversely affected by his illness, but the impact was not substantial as he was able to perform his domestic activities on his own, to get to his office and carry out his work to a satisfactory standard. Accordingly, the tribunal concluded that he was not disabled within the meaning of the 1995 Act and dismissed his application.

He appealed to the EAT and his appeal was allowed. The EAT said that s. 1 could be seen as laying down four conditions in order for someone to be found to be suffering from a disability:

The impairment condition If there is doubt as to whether the impairment condition is fulfilled in an alleged mental illness case, it advised that the tribunal should check whether the condition was referred to in the WHO's International Classification of Diseases, if this was likely to be decisive on the matter.

The adverse effect condition The EAT warned that disabled persons often 'play down' the effect that their disabilities have on their daily lives. Thus, if asked whether they were able to cope at home the answer might well be 'yes' even though, on proper analysis, many of the ordinary day-to-day tasks were done with great difficulty due to an impaired ability to carry them out.

The substantial condition Minor impairments should be considered together in determining whether they had a substantial adverse effect on the person's ability to carry out day-to-day activities. A progressive condition which has begun to have an effect on the person's health, is deemed to have a substantial effect if it is likely to have such an effect in the future.

The long-term effect condition An adverse effect is long-term if it has or will last longer than 12 months, or for the rest of the person's life.

The EAT concluded that Mr Goodwin was suffering from a disability, but sent the case back to a fresh tribunal to consider whether the employer could show that its treatment of the applicant had been justified under s. 5 of the Disability Discrimination Act 1995 (discussed below).

It is unlawful to treat disabled people less favourably than others because of their disability, in relation to offering employment and the terms of that employment: promotion, transfer, training and other benefits and the decision to dismiss or impose some other disadvantage (s. 4). The employment provisions of the Act only apply where 15 or more people are employed.

Section 5(1) states that a person discriminates against a disabled person if:

(a) for a reason which relates to the disabled person's disability, he treats him less favourably than he treats or would treat others to whom that reason does not or would not apply; and
(b) he cannot show that the treatment in question is justified.

Under s. 5(3) '. . . treatment is justified if, but only if, the reason . . . is both material to the circumstances of the particular case and substantial'.

Clark *v* TDG Limited (trading as Novacold) (1999) was the first case to reach the Court of Appeal under the Act. Mr Clark had suffered an injury at work in August 1996 and was unable to return to work before he was dismissed in January 1997. He brought a claim that he had been unlawfully discriminated against by reason of his disability. In the Court of Appeal it was accepted that he was disabled. Section 4(2)(d) specifically states that it is 'unlawful for an employer to discriminate against a disabled person whom he employs by dismissing him or subjecting him to any other detriment'. The employment tribunal had rejected his complaint, finding that a person who was not disabled but had been absent from work for the same length of time would have been treated in the same way. On appeal, the Court of Appeal observed that it was not helpful to look at the sex and race discrimination legislation in determining whether there had been discrimination under the Disability Act. The correct comparator was a person who had been able to attend work as normal. Mr Clark was found to have been discriminated against because of his disability, but the case was returned to an Employment Tribunal to decide whether this discrimination had been justified within the meaning of s. 5(1)(b).

The Act makes it illegal to refuse to provide disabled people with goods, facilities or services, or to fail to amend a practice or procedure which makes it impossible or unreasonably difficult for a disabled person to use them. Thus, automatic ticket machines at a car park will have to be at a height accessible to disabled people. Less favourable treatment will be justified if the service provider reasonably believes that it is necessary so as not to endanger the health or safety of any person; or the disabled person (with sufficient mental capacity) has given their agreement to less favourable treatment; or it is necessary if the service is to be provided to other members of the public (s. 14). A disabled person can be required to pay more for a service if this reflects the greater cost to the provider. The Act excludes protection against discrimination in the fields of education or transport.

An action under the Act in employment matters is heard by an Employment Tribunal and in other matters by the county court. A Disability Discrimination Commission was established in 2000. It has the power to provide assistance or advice to complainants, to conduct formal investigations into suspected acts or patterns of discrimination or to bring proceedings on behalf of complainants or on its own initiative. It also has the power to set up its own independent conciliation service to handle cases where discrimination has been alleged in relation to access to goods, facilities, services and premises.

The Disability Discrimination Act 1995 has been criticized for containing too many exceptions and being very narrowly drafted. The Law Society has pointed out that the definition of a disabled person excludes those who have recovered from a psychiatric illness, such as a nervous breakdown, but are perceived as not having recovered by, for example, a potential employer. Richard Light, from the Policies Studies Institute, considers that the provisions which justify an employer's choice to employ an able-bodied person in preference to a disabled one in certain circumstances are 'obscene' and many are amazed at how such clauses could be allowed in what is supposed to be anti-discrimination legislation.

More than 2,600 claims have been lodged with tribunals since the Act came into force in 1996.

Discrimination against people because of their sexuality

Recent cases have highlighted the problem of discrimination of homosexuals and transsexuals. Under European law there was in the past no specific legislation aimed at protecting people from discrimination due to their sexuality. Instead, employees who are homosexuals or transsexuals and have suffered discrimination due to their sexuality, have tried to bring actions for breach of the legislation which seeks to protect people from discrimination due to their sex. In **P v S and Cornwall County Council** (1996) an employee successfully claimed unlawful sex discrimination after they had undergone gender re-orientation and were consequently dismissed. The European Court of Justice (ECJ) took the view that since the applicant had been dismissed as a result of a sex change, it was obvious that the reason for the dismissal was because of the sex of the employee, and therefore constituted unlawful sex discrimination. The worker, according to the ECJ's argument, had been dismissed because of her new sex, thus sex was the reason for the dismissal and so was unlawful.

Following this decision, the Equal Treatment Directive 76/207 was passed which includes protection for those who have, or are undergoing, gender reassignment. In **Chessington World of Adventures Ltd v Reed** (1997) the Employment Appeal Tribunal interpreted the Sex Discrimination Act 1975 as extending to cover discrimination at work against transsexuals. This approach has now received express legislative recognition by the Sex Discrimination (Gender Reassignment) Regulations 1999 which inserted s. 2A into the Sex Discrimination Act. This provides that it is unlawful to discriminate against a person for the purpose of employment on the grounds that that person intends to undergo, is undergoing or has undergone, gender reassignment.

The limits to the equality available to transsexuals under the European Convention on Human Rights were conspicuous in the case of **XYZ v UK** (1997). X was a female-to-male transsexual who had undergone sex reassignment surgery over 20 years earlier. He had been in a stable relationship with a woman, Y, for 18 years. Z was the first of four children born to Y by way of artificial insemination by a donor (AID). The applicant was involved in the treatment process and acted as the child's father in every respect following the birth. The UK authorities refused to register X as the father of Z, on the ground that the UK legislation envisaged that only a biological man could be regarded as a father for the purposes of the registration of births. An application was lodged with the European Court of Human Rights on the basis that this refusal amounted to a breach of Art. 8 of the Convention (protecting the right to 'family life') and Art. 14 (prohibiting discrimination). In deciding whether the Convention had been breached the European Court of Human Rights stated that it would put the interests of the child at the forefront. As it was not clear that such registration was to the advantage of the child, the UK was justified in being cautious in changing the law, as this might have undesirable and unforeseen consequences for children in Z's position. The court pointed out that many of the disadvantages suffered by Z could be avoided, for example, by X making a will; not telling others why X's name was not on the birth certificate; and applying under the Children Act 1989 for a residence order which would give X full parental responsibility. The application was therefore dismissed.

As regards homosexuals, their vulnerability to discrimination was highlighted in **R** *v* **The Secretary of State for Defence, ex parte Perkins** (1998). Mr Perkins had applied for judicial review of the Navy's decision to discharge him on the grounds of his homosexuality. It was submitted that this decision contravened Art. 2(1) of the European Equal Treatment Directive but this claim was rejected. The judge did however state that future proceedings might be successful once the Human Rights Act 1998 had come into force.

The judgment in **P** *v* **S and Cornwall County Council** gave rise to a hope that discrimination because of someone's sexual orientation could fall within the general umbrella of sex discrimination law. The test case of **Grant** *v* **South West Trains Ltd** (1998) was a gross disappointment. The applicant, Ms Grant, claimed unlawful sex discrimination under the equal pay directive. The terms of employees' contracts entitled common law spouses of at least two years and of the opposite sex to claim travel concessions. Ms Grant was a lesbian and so her partner was not entitled to the benefit under the terms of the contract. In the proceedings it was argued that Ms Grant was denied the perk simply because she was a woman rather than a man. This argument was rejected by the European Court of Justice. The Court stated that discrimination on the ground of sexual orientation did not amount to sex discrimination since lesbian women and gay men were treated equally and 'Community law as it stands at present does not cover discrimination based on sexual orientation'. But this decision of the European Court can now be contrasted with the House of Lords' judgment in **Fitzpatrick** *v* **Sterling Housing Association Ltd** (2000) which is discussed at p. 17. In that case a piece of UK legislation was interpreted as applying to homosexual couples as well as heterosexual couples.

Another recent case on the subject is **Pearce** *v* **Governing Body of Mayfield School** (2000). The applicant was a schoolteacher. She was a lesbian, and claimed that pupils had been subjecting her to homophobic taunts for some years. She brought proceedings against the school claiming that she had been discriminated against in breach of the Sex Discrimination Act 1975. The Employment Appeal Tribunal held that the correct question was whether the applicant had been treated any less favourably than a male homosexual teacher and, if so, whether this was on the grounds of her sex. It concluded that the only discrimination was on the ground of her sexual orientation and her claim was rejected.

The European Court of Human Rights ruled in **Smith** *v* **United Kingdom** (1999) that the Ministry of Defence's policy of prohibiting homosexuals from serving in the armed forces was illegal. It breached Art. 8 of the Convention, which protects the right to a private life. The court considered that the discharge from service and the investigations by the military police into the applicant's homosexuality, including interviews with the applicants and third parties on matters relating to their sexual orientation and practices, constituted a direct interference with the applicants' right to respect for their private lives. Arguments based on the hostility of serving homosexuals to sharing their careers with homosexuals were rejected. The Government subsequently decided to lift the ban.

Discrimination due to a person's age

Despite increased life expectancy, there has been a marked decline in the economic activity rate for men aged between 50 and 64 which, while it stood at 91 per cent in 1971, declined to some 73 per cent by 1996. The public is becoming increasingly aware of the difficulties faced by older people when seeking employment and advertisements for positions often state an age limit for potential applicants. The Government issued a code of practice in June 1999 called *Age Diversity in Employment – a Code of Practice*. The Code calls upon all employers to tackle age discrimination and to recognize the business benefits of an age-diverse workforce. It provides guidance on good practice in six aspects of the employment cycle – recruitment, selection, promotion, training, redundancy and retirement. The Code is merely voluntary and many fear that it will be ineffective. In the US the Age Discrimination in Employment Act 1967 has been in force since 1967.

Positive discrimination

As many people have obviously suffered discrimination in the past without receiving any remedy, some experts argue that what is needed is positive discrimination or reverse discrimination: measures which aim to compensate for the disadvantages caused by discrimination, by making rules which discriminate in favour of ethnic minorities, women or disabled people. One way of doing this is to put in place quota systems, whereby the intake of a university, or the staff of a firm, for example, would be required to reflect the percentage of ethnic minorities in society as a whole. In a culture where we are used to the idea that treating everybody the same is fair, this can seem unjust, but the alternative view is that if people start off with unequal chances – perhaps due to racial discrimination – treating them as though they were equal will simply maintain their inequality. Positive discrimination aims to promote a 'level playing field', redressing the balance between those who have the most opportunity to succeed and those who have the least.

The practice of positive discrimination has in the past risked being in breach of the law. In **Kalanke** *v* **Freie Hansestadt Bremen** (1995) a local authority in Germany enacted a law which promoted positive discrimination in the appointment of female staff to certain public sector positions. Where two applicants of different genders had the same qualifications and experience, the woman was to be appointed to the post. The claimant applied for a position in the city's parks department, but the post was given to a woman. The European Court of Justice ruled that Community law prohibited the operation of positive discrimination programmes which had the direct effect of unconditionally discriminating against men. **Marschall** *v* **Land Nordrhein-Westfalen** (1997) allowed positive discrimination where there were built-in safeguards.

The Amsterdam Treaty has inserted a new Art. 119(4) into the EC Treaty expressly allowing positive discrimination on the grounds of gender to take place, overruling the **Kalanke** decision on this issue. The article states that:

> with a view to ensuring full equality in practice between men and women in working life, the principle of equal treatment shall not prevent any Member State from maintaining or adopting measures providing for specific advantages in order to make it easier for the under-represented sex to pursue a vocational activity or to prevent or compensate for disadvantage in professional careers.

General equality legislation

The gay rights organization Outrage! has argued that the current anti-discrimination legislation targeting the specific forms of discrimination on the basis of race, sex and disability should be replaced by a comprehensive Equal Rights Act which would seek to ensure equality for everyone, including homosexuals. It would establish a broad legal framework through which all the different aspects of discrimination could be progressively challenged and overturned. Similar laws already exist in Denmark, France, Norway and Sweden. Comprehensive equal rights legislation would encourage mutually empowering alliances between everyone suffering exclusion and discrimination. This broad-based approach would minimize the likelihood of a homophobic backlash and avoids the marginalization of lesbian and gay rights as a fringe issue.

The European Convention on Human Rights has no free-standing provision against discrimination, it merely protects a person from being discriminated against in the exercise of one of their specific rights contained in the Convention (Art. 14). To fill this gap, Protocol 12 has been prepared – a Protocol is a type of supplement to a treaty. This Protocol would create a general right not to be discriminated against. It states:

> Art. 1(1) The enjoyment of any right set forth by law shall be secured without any discrimination on any ground such as sex, race, colour, language, religion, political or other opinion, national or social origin, association with a national minority, property, birth or other status.
> (2) No one shall be discriminated against by any public authority on any ground such as those mentioned in paragraph 1.

The Protocol has been available for signature since 2000, but the British Government is currently refusing to sign up to this Protocol, arguing that the provision is too broadly drafted.

Following the implementation of the Amsterdam Treaty in 1999, Art. 13 of the EC Treaty empowers the Council of Ministers to take action to combat discrimination on the grounds of sex, race, ethnic origin, religion or belief, disability, age or sexual orientation. The European Commission is currently considering a directive which would outlaw in the employment arena discrimination on the grounds of age, sexual orientation, disability, religion or belief. Discrimination on the grounds of sex and ethnic origin are already outlawed by European directives.

▶ ANSWERING QUESTIONS

1 'Even the severest critics of the [Race Relations] Act would concede that they have broken down some barriers for individuals in their quest for jobs, housing and services and that they have driven underground those overt expressions of discrimination . . . , yet most of the reformers expected more than this from the legislation.' (B. Hepple, 'Have Twenty-Five Years of the Race Relations Acts in Britain been a Failure?' in Hepple and Szyszczak (eds) *Discrimination and the Limits of the Law* 1992)

Discuss this statement with reference to the statutes and the case law.

One line of argument for your essay could be that this quote is an accurate summary of the race relations legislation. While the laws have clearly improved the position of ethnic minorities in the UK, there is still a need for progress. You could point to the practical difficulties in dealing with racial discrimination, such as the problem of dealing with indirect discrimination, though the legislation seeks to do so. The existing powers of the Commission for Racial Equality should be examined. It could be argued that the limits in the success of the Race Relations

Acts 1965 and 1976 were partly due to the limits of the legislation itself. You could discuss the criticisms of the legislation contained at p. 490. In particular the Lawrence murder case (see p. 288) could be examined as this highlighted the fact that the Race Relations Acts did not apply to the police. The improvements introduced by the Race Relations (Amendment) Act 2001 need to be considered.

You could discuss the fact that since this statement was made in 1992, more legislation has been passed to improve race relations, in particular the Race Relations (Amendment) Act 2001, the Crime and Disorder Act 1994 and the European directive on race discrimination. You could point out that the race relations legislation has been the model for anti-discrimination legislation on the grounds of sex and more recently on the grounds of disability. Thus, your conclusion could be that, while the race relations legislation has not been a resounding success it has been a step in the right direction and was a significant step for the direction of our society as a multi-cultural nation.

2 **Assess the effectiveness of the remedies available to a person who feels that he or she has been discriminated against on the grounds of race or sex.** *WJEC*

The relevant legislation and case law is discussed at pp. 488–93. You could also discuss how the sex discrimination legislation has been applied in the context of discrimination against transsexuals discussed at p. 496. As you are asked to look at how effective the remedies have been you could examine whether the law would be more effective if it embraced the concept of positive discrimination which is examined on p. 498.

Reading on the Internet

The Macpherson Report into the police investigation into the death of the black teenager Stephen Lawrence, along with subsequent developments, is available on the Home Office website at:

http://www.homeoffice.gov.uk/ppd/oppu/slawr.htm

The website of the Commission for Racial Equality is at:

http://www.cre.gov.uk/

22 Freedom of the person

Freedom of the person refers to a person's right to go about their lawful business without interference from the state and, in particular, their freedom to go where they want, and not to be imprisoned in any way. Although this is a right which we often take for granted, it is subject to some restrictions. Freedom of movement offers one of the few examples of a positive right in English law, as opposed to a residual right, though this springs originally from Britain's membership of the European Community rather than from Parliament or the common law. European treaties spell out the rights to be enjoyed by every citizen of the European Community, and the first of these is the right to move and reside freely throughout the territory of the member states.

Deportation, extradition and unlawful immigration

In theory, freedom of the person includes the right to travel and live anywhere, but this aspect of personal liberty is severely restricted in Britain. While all British citizens have the right to enter the UK and live here, anyone who is not a British citizen can be deported. Deportation can be ordered on four basic grounds:

- the Home Secretary deems it 'conducive to the public good';
- a person is over 17 and has been convicted of an offence which is punishable by imprisonment, and the court recommends deportation;
- a person is the infant child or wife of someone against whom a deportation order is made;
- immigration entry conditions have been broken.

Only very limited rights of appeal exist against decisions involving immigration.

Restrictions on travel

It is commonly believed that British citizens can go in and out of the country as they please. In fact, there are some significant restrictions on this freedom. First, the Government can refuse to issue a passport, or insist that one is handed back where:

- it is suspected that the person intends to take children out of the jurisdiction illegally;
- travellers stranded abroad have been brought back home at the UK Government's expense, and have not repaid the cost;
- a person is suspected of intending to leave the country in order to avoid arrest;
- a person is 'so notoriously undesirable or dangerous that Parliament would be expected to support the action of the Foreign Secretary in refusing them a passport'. This category has been used to deny a passport to those travelling abroad for purposes which the UK Government finds politically unacceptable, such as scientists attempting to attend conferences in Eastern Europe during the Cold War.

It has been established that the decision to withdraw or refuse to issue a passport can be reviewed by the courts.

A significant restriction on travel by UK subjects is that of exclusion orders. These are used to prevent those suspected of terrorism from travelling to the mainland from Northern Ireland, or sometimes vice versa. Involvement in terrorism does not have to be proved, and the only possible appeal consists of making written representations to the Home Secretary, or putting the case in an interview with a Home Office adjudicator, neither of which is likely to be successful.

Most recently the Government has created powers to impose travel restrictions on drug-trafficking offenders (Criminal Justice and Police Act 2001, s. 33). It has also given itself the power to restrict the movement of football hooligans, to try and deal with their unruly and violent behaviour abroad (Football Disorder Act 2000).

Psychiatric illness

The personal liberty of those suffering from psychiatric illness can be restrained by orders requiring their detention in a hospital or a psychiatric institution. This kind of detention can be used as a sentence against those convicted of criminal offences.

Police powers

For the majority of people in England, the most important legal restrictions on personal liberty can be found in the powers of the police to stop, search and arrest those suspected of being involved in criminal activity. These are discussed from p. 247 onwards.

ANSWERING QUESTIONS

1 Mandy is 13 years old. She was stopped in the street by PC Pounce, who was investigating a report of shoplifting at a nearby sweet shop. PC Pounce searched Mandy's school bag and found several bars of chocolate. He then accompanied Mandy to her home. The house was empty, as Mandy's parents were out at work. PC Pounce searched the house and found a video recorder which he thought might be stolen property. He arrested Mandy and took her to the police station, where she was questioned about the video recorder. Her requests to contact her parents and a solicitor were refused. Mandy was held in custody until the following afternoon and is to be prosecuted for theft of the video recorder.

Advise Mandy as to the legality of the actions of the police. *WJEC*

The relevant law to answer this problem question can be found at p. 249 onwards. PC Pounce first carries out a stop and search of Mandy. The relevant legislative provisions are contained in s. 1 of PACE. Under s. 1 a police officer may search a person for stolen articles where they have 'reasonable grounds for suspecting that they will find stolen or prohibited articles' (s. 1(3)). We would need to know more about why PC Pounce selected Mandy for this search in order to decide whether he had such reasonable grounds for his suspicion. After the search, PC Pounce does not appear to have carried out a formal arrest under s. 24 of PACE as we are not told that Mandy is informed of her arrest under s. 28 of PACE (see p. 254). Mandy could not therefore be taken to her home against her will, but she could consent to going with the police officer. It will be a matter of evidence whether or not she had given her consent. The powers to search property are discussed from p. 266 onwards. We are concerned here with a search without a warrant. This search would not appear to fall within ss. 18 or 32 of PACE as no lawful arrest has taken place and he could not reasonably suspect that he would find evidence relating to the offence at her home. The unlawful search will taint with illegality all his subsequent conduct.

Under s. 56 of PACE, Mandy had the right to inform her parents of her arrest and a right to consult a solicitor under s. 58 of PACE (see p. 258). Because of her age one of her parents, acting as an 'appropriate adult', should have been present throughout her interrogation (p. 260). The legality of the length of her detention is also questionable (see pp. 254–55).

She would have a range of remedies available to her for these violations of her rights which are discussed at p. 529.

2 PC Smith and PC Jones have lawfully arrested Bert for shoplifting. After his arrest they do not get Bert to the police station for over half an hour because they stop off at a cashpoint machine in order for PC Smith to take out some money and then they stop off at a burger bar for the two police officers to buy some lunch.

Upon arriving at the station PC Smith and PC Jones attempt to search Bert. He tries to resist and during the ensuing struggle Bert hits PC Jones in the stomach. PC Smith says, 'So, we've got an awkward customer here, have we? Perhaps we should get the rubber gloves out and give him a proper search.' They then conduct an intimate body search on Bert.

After the search, PC Smith and PC Jones decide to interrogate Bert. They hand him a leaflet telling him he has a right to free legal advice but Bert does not ask to see a solicitor and they conduct the interview with no solicitor being present.

Assess the legality of PC Smith's and PC Jones's actions in this scenario.

This problem question relates to the post-arrest powers of the police and the relevant law can be found at p. 254 onwards. Under s. 30 of PACE an arrested person must be brought to a police station as soon as practicable after the arrest. This may only be delayed if their presence elsewhere is necessary for an immediate investigation to be carried out (see p. 254). Thus the police conduct of going to the cashpoint and to a burger bar was in breach of the law.

The police officers were entitled to carry out their initial search of Bert as the police have the power to search arrested persons on arrival at the police station under s. 54 of PACE (see p. 265). Section 55 of PACE (see p. 265) only gives the police the power to conduct intimate searches of a suspect if they have the authorization of a superintendent who must have reasonable grounds for believing that a weapon or drug is concealed. The search must be carried out by a qualified doctor or nurse and not by the police themselves. The grounds for the intimate search do not appear to have been satisfied here nor was the search carried out by a doctor or nurse so this search was illegal.

Bert is being detained in the police station and you could examine the rules on police detention on p. 254. The right to consult a solicitor is contained in s. 58 of PACE and is considered at p. 258. Bert has impliedly consented to not seeing a legal adviser and the police were entitled to conduct the interview without a legal representative being present.

In relation to the delay in arriving at the police station and the unlawful intimate search, you could discuss the possible remedies considered at p. 529 onwards.

▶ Reading on the Internet

The website of the Government Immigration and Nationality Directorate can be found at:

http://www.ind.homeoffice.gov.uk/

23 Freedom of expression

The right to freedom of expression in most democratic countries includes freedom to hold opinions, and to receive and impart information and ideas without interference by a public authority. This is one of the basic rights in a democratic society: democracy is based on the consent of the people to their Government, and this consent is meaningless if people cannot debate and discuss ideas without Government permission. In the absence of free speech, opposition to Government cannot be expressed, and new ideas cannot be introduced. Moreover, freedom of expression is an integral part of the artistic, cultural and intellectual freedom of an open society. This freedom is protected by Art. 10 of the European Convention on Human Rights which states:

1. Everyone has the right to freedom of expression. This right shall include freedom to hold opinions and to receive and impart information and ideas without interference by public authority and regardless of frontiers. This article shall not prevent States from requiring the licensing of broadcasting, television or cinema enterprises.
2. The exercise of these freedoms, since it carries with it duties and responsibilities, may be subject to such formalities, conditions, restrictions or penalties as are prescribed by law and are necessary in a democratic society, in the interests of national security, territorial integrity or public safety, for the prevention of disorder or crime, for the protection of health or morals, for the protection of the reputation or rights of others, for preventing the disclosure of information received in confidence or for maintaining the authority and impartiality of the judiciary.

Restrictions on this freedom take two main forms: censorship of material by state authorities before it is published; and the imposition of penalties after the event. Prior censorship is particularly controversial and tends to be associated in the public's minds with totalitarian regimes, but it is actually alive and well in Britain today.

We will look first at restrictions which are aimed at specific sections of the media, and then at those which apply across the board.

Restrictions on the press

Freedom of the press has been, in theory at least, a cornerstone of civil liberties in England for centuries. One of the most important results of this is that English law does not require publishers to obtain a Government licence, unlike some other countries. This means that anyone may publish a newspaper or magazine, though in practice economic considerations mean the biggest and most widely read publications are concentrated in the hands of a small number of companies.

Concerns that a small number of newspaper owners were monopolizing the sector led to the enactment of provisions – now contained in the Fair Trading Act 1973 – to ensure that large newspaper mergers can only take place if they are in the public interest. In reaching this decision account will be taken of the need 'for accurate presentation of news and free expression of opinion'. Despite this, no controls were imposed on Rupert Murdoch, owner of the *Sun* and the *News of the World*, when he acquired *The Times* and *Sunday Times* in 1981. By 1987, three publishers between them owned 73 per cent of national daily circulation and 81 per cent of national Sunday circulation.

Complaints about the press, which usually concern invasion of privacy or unfair or inaccurate reporting, can be made to the Press Complaints Commission. The Commission is a non-statutory body, comprising a chairperson and 15 members, one-third of whom are not associated with the press. It can request that newspapers publish corrections, apologies or statements about the complaint, but cannot enforce this request. In recent years there has been growing concern that its powers are too weak, particularly in the area of invasion of privacy, and that a fully fledged privacy law should be created (see p. 524). The problem was highlighted by the circumstances of the death of Princess Diana.

Restrictions on broadcasters

Unlike the press, all broadcasting organizations are required to be licensed by the Government: it is an offence under the Wireless Telegraphy Act 1949 to broadcast radio or television signals without a licence. The BBC receives its licence from the Government under the Wireless and Telegraphy Acts, while the ITV companies are awarded theirs by the Independent Television Commission, whose members are appointed by the Home Secretary. The licences are periodically renewed, at which point commercial organizations bid against each other; provided that certain minimum quality thresholds laid down in the 1949 Act are met, including that the applicant 'is a fit and proper person to hold' a licence, the licences must be awarded to the highest bidder. There are restrictions on licences being held by political or religious organizations and newspaper proprietors. Licences for commercial radio are awarded in the same way, but by the Radio Authority.

The BBC

The BBC, which is funded by TV licence fees, is headed by a Board of Governors, with a chairperson and deputy chairperson who are appointed by the Crown on the advice of the Prime Minister. This structure has recently been criticized as having the potential for political bias, and there have been allegations that the BBC has been too ready to respond to Government pressure in withdrawing certain programmes which the Government preferred not to be broadcast.

The operation of the BBC is regulated by the terms of its licence and an agreement between the Home Secretary and the BBC's Board of Governors, which impose a number of duties. It must broadcast a daily account of the proceedings in Parliament, and any Government Minister can require announcements to be broadcast. Where such announcements concern issues of political controversy, the opposition in Parliament has a right of reply. The Minister responsible for broadcasting may require the BBC not to show certain matters. This power has been used to prevent direct broadcasting of statements by members of certain organizations in Northern Ireland, including Sinn Fein – a recognized political party with some electoral support. The BBC is not allowed to use its programmes to express its own political views; it can issue political broadcasts on agreement with the main political parties in the country. In case of emergency, the Government has the right to take over the BBC for the duration.

As the Government is responsible for both the organization and the financing of the BBC, some people have argued that the Government may have too much influence over it. This concern has been particularly pronounced in relation to reporting of the Gulf War. It is now becoming clear that the public were only given a sanitized version of what actually happened during the conflict.

Commercial broadcasters

Commercial broadcasters are financed by revenue from advertising. They are regulated by the Independent Television Commission, under the provisions of the Broadcasting Act 1990. The Commission is obliged to ensure that a wide range of services are provided and that there is fair and effective competition in their provision.

Important restrictions on broadcasting are contained in s. 6 of the 1990 Act, which parallels regulations guiding the BBC. In addition, the Act provides detailed regulations on advertising. Advertisements directed to political ends may not be shown. In other countries, it is common to see political parties advertising on television, but here this is not allowed. Restrictions also apply to advertisements concerning industrial disputes: the Government may place such advertisements, but nobody else is allowed to.

As with the BBC, the Government has been quick to oppose programmes which criticize its role in Northern Ireland, and particular controversy was caused by a 1988 documentary made by Thames Television. Called 'Death on the Rock', it investigated the shooting of three IRA terrorists by members of the SAS in Gibraltar, reopening a previous debate about whether the security forces were operating a shoot-to-kill policy against suspected terrorists. The programme was fiercely criticized by the Government, and many believe it was no coincidence that when the time came to renew independent television licences, Thames lost theirs to another company.

Similar rules to the above apply to commercial radio, and are regulated by the Radio Authority. In **R** *v* **Radio Authority, ex parte Bull** (1995) Amnesty International (an organization founded to promote the observance of fundamental human rights) had wanted to place advertisements on the radio highlighting the plight of the citizens in Rwanda and Burundi. Permission to do so had been refused by the Radio Authority as Amnesty International was a body whose objects were 'mainly of a political nature'. Their appeal against this decision was rejected.

The Broadcasting Standards Commission

This was established by the Broadcasting Act 1996 and combines the functions of the previous Broadcasting Complaints Commission and the Broadcasting Standards Council. It adjudicates upon complaints of unjust and unfair treatment in television or radio programmes; infringement of privacy; and matters of taste and decency on radio and television. It draws up codes of practice for broadcasters, monitors the portrayal of violence and sexual conduct and commissions research into public attitudes.

Theatres

As recently as 1968, all stage performances and plays were subject to direct censorship; they could be lawfully performed only with permission from the Lord Chamberlain (an officer of the royal household), and it was a criminal offence to stage a play without such a licence. Plays dealing with controversial topics, such as homosexuality, or featuring nudity or bad language were likely to be censored.

A Private Member's Bill was introduced to abolish the Lord Chamberlain's censorship powers; it became the Theatres Act 1968. Premises still require a local authority licence if they are to be used for the public performance of a play, but this is simply in regard to such matters as public health and safety, and may not be used to impose restrictions on shows or plays to be performed.

Cinema and video

Film has the highest level of direct censorship of any media in the UK, and is subject to a two-stage process. First, all films for general release are certified by the British Board of Film Classification, a body set up and run by the film industry. It classifies films as either 'U' (universal exhibition) which are suitable for any age; 'PG' (parental guidance) where no age restriction is imposed but some scenes may be unsuitable for young children; '12', which cannot be shown to children under 12; '15', not to be shown to under-15s; '18', not to be shown to under-18s; and 18R, which means restricted distribution and over-18s only – this category would cover the kind of films shown in sex cinemas. The Board can refuse to give a film a certificate altogether, or grant one only if certain parts of the film are cut. Although these classifications have no statutory authority, and failure to receive a certificate does not mean a film cannot be shown, widespread acceptance of the system means that in practice it has a strong impact on the film's distribution. The Hollywood film *Crash* was subject to censorship in the UK.

Secondly, all cinemas have to be licensed and, in granting the licences, local authorities may impose conditions: one of these is commonly that films without British Board of Film Classification certificates should not be shown without the express permission of the licensing authority.

Concerns about 'video nasties' being too easily available to children led to the passing of the Video Recordings Act 1984. This gave the Board a statutory responsibility to classify all videos which are available for sale or hire, with the exception of music, sport, educational and religious videos. It is an offence under the Act to supply an unclassified video outside the terms of the statute. In **Wingrove v United Kingdom** (1996) the applicant had made a video called *Visions of Ecstasy* which portrayed the erotic fantasies of a sixteenth-century Carmelite nun. The British Board of Film Classification refused to grant the video a certificate on the grounds that it was blasphemous. It was contended before the European Court of Human Rights that Art. 10 of the Convention had been breached which enshrines the right to freedom of expression. The court concluded that there had been no such breach, as the applicant's freedom of expression had been restricted in pursuance of a legitimate aim of protecting freedom of thought and religion.

Provisions applying to the media in general

The Official Secrets Acts

There are quite severe restrictions on the publication, in any form, of information concerned with areas of government such as defence, the security services and foreign relations, and these are contained in the Official Secrets Acts 1911, 1920, 1939 and 1989.

The latest Official Secrets Act was passed in 1989 after long-standing criticism of s. 2 of the 1911 Act, a widely drawn section which made it an offence for any Government servant to reveal, without authorization, any information about, or gained in, their job. There was no requirement for the information to be secret, or potentially damaging to the Government; revealing the number of cups of tea drunk in the Ministry of Defence canteen, for example, would technically come within the scope of the old s. 2.

The section was the focus of several high-profile trials. Clive Ponting, an assistant secretary in the Ministry of Defence, discovered that the Government had misled the House of Commons over the sinking of the *General Belgrano*, an Argentinian battleship, during the Falklands War. Under the Official Secrets Act as it stood at the time, Ponting was banned from making such a disclosure, unless it was to someone 'to whom it is his duty in the interests of state to communicate [the information]'. Ponting admitted that he had leaked the information, but argued that he was justified in doing so because it was in the interests of the state that such information be disclosed to an MP. This argument was flatly rejected by the judge, who stated that the interests of the state simply meant the interests of the Government of the day, and directed the jury that they should not allow Ponting's defence. Nevertheless, the jury acquitted Ponting, to the enormous embarrassment of the Government.

The controversy arising from such cases led to the reform of s. 2 by the Official Secrets Act 1989 (OSA). In the new s. 2, blanket secrecy on all Government information is replaced by six categories of information. In two of these, covering primarily the work and information of the security services, any disclosure is an offence. The other four categories cover information concerned with international relations, information obtained in confidence from other Governments, information on defence and, finally, information which could impede the prevention or detection of offences. For these categories, only harmful disclosures are an offence.

The then Home Secretary called the 1989 reforms 'an essay in openness unparalleled since the Second World War', but it is difficult to see how this praise can be justified. The range of protected information may be narrower, but in practice it covers all the kinds of information ever likely to be – or to need to be – leaked. All the prosecutions brought over the last 30 years would still be restricted today. In addition, civil service disciplinary codes were redrawn to cover information not covered by the new OSA, so the commitment to openness mentioned by the Home Secretary is hard to spot.

The 1989 Act does not include a public interest defence that could have been used in a case like Ponting's. This means that even where a civil servant discovers major wrongdoing, it should not be disclosed; official secrecy is given a higher priority than good government. A further problem with the draconian nature of official secrets provisions is the climate of secrecy they create, which may make newspapers and broadcasters reluctant to touch stories concerning official wrongdoing. Just after the Ponting trial, Channel 4 withdrew a television programme in which another civil servant, Cathy Massiter, revealed that the security services were targeting members of trade unions for surveillance. The programme was eventually shown much later, but there is no way of knowing how many such stories are abandoned for fear of the OSA.

The 1989 legislation also contains wide search and seizure powers against the media. Their potential breadth was seen in 1986, when the investigative journalist Duncan Campbell produced a film for the BBC, as part of a series entitled 'Secret Society'. The programme revealed the cost and extent of a secret Defence Ministry project to put a spy satellite into orbit, and once the Government discovered this, it was banned. Using search powers derived from both PACE and the OSA, police raided Campbell's home and office, and the Glasgow offices of the BBC, removing substantial numbers of documents, even though Campbell had already published the story in the *New Statesman* before the injunction had been granted. The BBC eventually broadcast an agreed version of the programme.

'D' notices

The 'D' notice system is a little-known but powerful means of censoring broadcasters and the press. The Defence, Press and Broadcasting Committee is made up of Government representatives, permanent civil servants and representatives of the press and broadcasters. The 'D' notices it issues are requests from the Government to the media, asking them not to publish particular material on the grounds that it would have an adverse effect on national defence or security and would therefore not be in the public interest. Refusal to comply with a 'D' notice is not an offence in itself, but broadcasters and publishers who do refuse to go along with the system may find it more difficult to get access to confidential information. In addition, the arrangement is somewhat one-sided, in that gaining the Committee's approval for an item to be published does not guarantee that the publisher will not be prosecuted under the Official Secrets Act 1989. A BBC radio series, 'My Country Right or Wrong', which included interviews with former intelligence service employees, was cleared with the secretary to the Committee during its planning, yet when the BBC attempted to broadcast it, the Attorney-General secured an injunction to prevent its transmission. The series was later broadcast unamended.

In 1979–80, the 'D' notice system was reviewed by the Defence Select Committee, which heard evidence that the system was not working effectively. Chapman Pincher, an investigative journalist, pointed out that in the past there had been an unspoken agreement that if broadcasters or journalists asked whether a story was the subject of a 'D' notice before publication, and were told it was not, publication of such stories would not lead to prosecution. Once that arrangement ceased to exist, media confidence in the system had declined, and the press and broadcasters were less willing to submit to it. In addition, the growing influence of the international press was making it more difficult to keep stories within the national boundaries of the UK.

The Select Committee was divided on the issue of whether the 'D' notice system should be reformed, but agreed that some form of control over press and broadcasting activities in these areas should remain.

Contempt of court

The Contempt of Court Act 1981 prevents publication of any material which creates a substantial risk that a trial will be prejudiced. The provisions of this Act were considered in **A-G** *v* **MGN Ltd** (1997). GT was an actress in the Soap *EastEnders* and lived with GK. A criminal charge of causing grievous bodily harm to another man was brought against GK. Following his release on bail pending trial the respondents published articles concerning him, and the prosecution was dropped on the ground that the pre-trial publicity made it impossible for him to have a fair trial. The respondents were subsequently prosecuted for contempt of court committed by the publication of the various articles. It was held that the saturation publicity which had been given to the couple over the previous years, including GK's previous convictions, meant that none of the subsequent articles had created a risk of prejudice greater than that which had already been created.

Provisions against prejudicial publications apply only where court proceedings are active: criminal proceedings become active for this purpose when the suspect is arrested or charged, or an arrest warrant is issued; civil actions become active when the action is set down for trial.

The Act offers three defences against a charge of prejudicial publication:

Innocent publication. Despite taking all possible care, the publishers did not know the proceedings were active.

Fair and accurate report. Publishers are allowed to publish a contemporary report of legal proceedings held in public, if fair, accurate and produced in good faith. The court may delay such reports where necessary to prevent substantial risk of prejudice to the administration of justice.

Prejudice merely incidental. This defence applies where a discussion on public affairs contains material which is merely incidentally prejudicial to a trial. An example occurred in the case of **Attorney-General** *v* **English** (1983), which concerned an article published by the *Daily Mail* on a pro-life election candidate. The candidate's election manifesto referred to the practice of hospitals allowing newborn babies with very severe handicaps to die, and argued that this should be banned. The article was published during the trial of a doctor accused of allowing a baby to die in those circumstances. The House of Lords agreed that the article was capable of prejudicing the jury, but said that to prevent it would mean that all discussion of the subject was banned from the time that the doctor was charged, until the end of his trial, ten months later, and such a ban would prevent the election candidate from publicizing her policy.

By contrast, the journalist Sir John Junor was fined for contempt, after publishing a personal attack on the doctor which made no attempt to set the issue in a wider context.

Contempt of court powers were extended by the Court of Appeal in **Attorney-General** *v* **Newspaper Publishing plc** (1987), which concerned the *Spycatcher* saga. As part of a long series of litigation, the Government had obtained injunctions against the *Guardian* and *Observer* newspapers in relation to the writings of former MI5 officer, Peter Wright. When three other papers, who were not parties to this injunction, published details of Wright's revelations, it was held that they were guilty of contempt. The result is that where an injunction is placed on one publication, others who publish the relevant material will be in contempt, if they knew of the injunctions binding the other newspapers and, by publication, undermined the effect of those court orders with intent to impede or prejudice the administration of justice.

In the US, court proceedings are fully open to publication and are even shown on television. Trials, such as that of O.J. Simpson for the murder of his ex-wife, are watched on television by millions of US citizens. Restrictions on publication are allowed only if defendants can prove there is a real danger they will not receive a fair trial.

Contempt in the face of the court

The charge of contempt in the face of the court is the kind of contempt often referred to in TV dramas, where witnesses or the defendant are told they will be in contempt if they do not stop shouting or making impolite or inappropriate remarks, especially to the judge. However, it also covers refusal of a witness to answer questions, and it is in this context that journalists who refuse to disclose their sources may find themselves in contempt. This has implications for freedom of expression, in that those who disclose wrongdoing to journalists are often putting their own position at risk by doing so, and will only make such revelations if the journalist promises to keep the source secret. An example might be a civil servant who discloses corruption among Ministers, or an employee who spills the beans on mismanagement in their firm; both would be likely to lose their job, and quite possibly be unable to find alternative employment in a similar area, if it was discovered that they had leaked such information. Civil servants might also find themselves prosecuted under the Official Secrets Act. Clearly people in this position will be much less likely to divulge wrongdoing if they know that the courts can demand that journalists reveal their sources.

The Contempt of Court Act 1981 provides that a court can only order disclosure of sources if it is satisfied that such disclosure is necessary in the interest of justice, national security, or the prevention of disorder or crime. By giving these exceptions a wide interpretation, the courts have ensured that there are in practice very few cases in which disclosure would not be ordered. In **Secretary of State for Defence** *v* **Guardian Newspapers** (1985) Sarah Tisdall, a civil service clerk, discovered that Ministers intended to lie about the date on which cruise missiles were to arrive at Greenham Common, so as to avoid any demonstration against their arrival. Tisdall passed this information to a newspaper. The court agreed that the revelation itself posed no threat to national security, but held that the threat was not what Ms Tisdall had revealed, but what she could have revealed; the fact that someone in her position could disclose any information was in itself a threat to national security.

Breach of confidence

This doctrine prevents the revelation of any information which has been imparted under an obligation of confidence; such an obligation is implied in a contract of employment or where a confidential relationship exists. The Duke of Argyll relied on this doctrine in **Duke of Argyll** *v* **Duchess of Argyll** (1967), to prevent the publication in a newspaper of revelations by the Duchess about their marriage. In **Attorney-General** *v* **Jonathan Cape Ltd** (1976), the Government attempted to prevent the publication of the diaries of an ex-Minister, Richard Crossman. In fact the court held that publication could not be prevented because the events discussed in the diaries had taken place too long ago, making the information stale, but it accepted that Cabinet discussions could be regarded as giving rise to an obligation of confidentiality.

The doctrine of confidentiality was the subject of litigation involving the child killer Ian Brady. Brady was being held in Ashworth Special Hospital and had embarked on a hunger strike claiming that he had the right to die. An employee of the hospital obtained some of his medical records and they were sold to the *Mirror* newspaper. The newspaper was ordered by the Court of Appeal in **Ashworth Security Hospital** *v* **MGN Ltd** (2001) to reveal its source of information so that the Hospital could take action against the employee. Mr Brady enjoyed a right to confidentiality with regard to his medical records.

This doctrine has proved to be of enormous value for those who wish to suppress information and, as far as the Government is concerned, provides a more satisfactory alternative in many cases to prosecution under the OSA. First, it allows them to seek an interim injunction, preventing publication, without having actually to prove their case in a full hearing. Since the actual trial may take a long time to come to court, in many cases the issue will have become so stale by then that there is no point in publication, so the person seeking to prevent publication gets what they want even if their case was weak. In addition, they may exploit the courts' power to order discovery of evidence at this stage to vet articles and programmes before publication. When the Government objected to the BBC radio series 'My Country Right or Wrong', the courts granted an interim injunction with discovery, which allowed the Government to pre-view and vet the programmes. Finally, the civil law has a lower standard of proof than that required for criminal prosecutions, and there are no juries, who may be inclined, as in the Ponting trial, to acquit those whose revelations seem to be in the public interest.

The threat which the doctrine of confidentiality can pose for freedom of expression was shown in what has come to be known as the *Spycatcher* saga (see p. 514). *Spycatcher* was a book written by Peter Wright, an ex-member of the security services, which contained allegations that MI5 had tried to destabilize the Government when Harold Wilson was Prime Minister, and Wright and others had 'bugged and burgled our way across London at the State's behest, while pompous, bowler-hatted civil servants in Whitehall pretended to look the other way' (Peter Wright, *Spycatcher* (1987) p. 54). Despite the fact that most of the allegations had been published by other writers, in some cases years before, the British Government was determined to prevent publication. Wright had emigrated to Australia before writing the book, and it was due to be published there, putting it out of reach of the Official Secrets Act. Unable, there-fore, to bring any criminal prosecution against Wright, the Attorney-General started civil proceedings in Australia, seeking an injunction to prevent the book's publication. This action failed and, after an unsuccess-ful appeal, the book was duly published in Australia.

While the Australian litigation was in progress, the *Observer* and *Guardian* newspapers published a summary of the key allegations in the book. The Attorney-General applied for, and got, interim injunctions prevent-ing them from printing further information from either the books or the Australian court hearings, on the basis that Wright was disclosing informa-tion obtained under a duty of confidentiality. As mentioned above, the *Independent*, the *London Evening Standard* and the *Daily Mail* later pub-lished reports of the Australian hearings, and were found in contempt of the injunction on the *Observer* and the *Guardian*. In the meantime, not only were reports of the hearings, and the book's allegations, being published around the world, but the book itself had been published in the US, where the First Amendment commitment to freedom of speech meant there was no point in the UK Government even trying to prevent publica-tion; copies were being imported from there into the UK, becoming fairly freely available to anyone who could be bothered to seek them out.

When the full hearing eventually came to court, the House of Lords decided to lift the injunction stating that, as the newspapers pointed out, even if Wright's disclosures were covered by confidentiality, by now they were all in the public domain, and further publication could not be harmful.

It commented that the absolute protection of official information which the Government wanted the court to grant 'could not be achieved this side of the Iron Curtain'. The European Court of Human Rights subsequently held that the UK courts' refusal to lift the injunction after *Spycatcher* was published in the US violated Art. 10.

An important case where the doctrine of confidence was relied on concerned the killers of the toddler, James Bulger. The two killers, Venables and Thompson, were 11 years old at the time of their offence. The events were particularly shocking and distressing and the case has received intense media coverage. In 2001 the Home Office were planning to give the boys new identities on their release for their own protection. Venables and Thompson obtained from the High Court an indefinite injunction protecting their identity, whereabouts, physical appearance and other confidential information upon their release from detention: **Venables and Another _v_ News Group Newspapers and Others** (2001). The High Court ruled that in exceptional circumstances the law of confidence could be applied to protect individuals who were seriously at risk of injury or death if their identity or whereabouts became known to the public. The court looked at Art. 10 of the European Convention on Human Rights protecting freedom of expression (quoted at p. 506) and Art. 2 of the Convention which protects the right to life. The freedom of the media to publish could only be restricted if the need for restrictions could be shown to fall within the exceptions set out in Art. 10(2) of the Convention and those exceptions had to be interpreted narrowly. The court decided that it should place the right to confidence above the right of the media to publish information about the boys. For the first time an injunction was granted against the whole world: confidential information about the boys' present appearance and whereabouts could not be published, even if it was already in the public domain. In practice, particularly with the Internet, this will be exceedingly hard to enforce and was breached by a local newspaper soon after it was issued.

The doctrine of confidence has now been extended by the courts to be the basis of a right to privacy. This development occurred in the case of **Douglas and others _v_ Hello! Ltd** (2001) which concerned photographs of the marriage of the Hollywood celebrities Michael Douglas and Catherine Zeta-Jones. The litigation is discussed at p. 525.

Copyright

The *Spycatcher* case highlighted a further possibility open to a Government interested in preventing publication. The House of Lords accepted that neither the publishers nor the author had copyright in the book as copyright vested with the Crown. This suggests that in a future case, the

Crown could sue for breach of copyright, which would allow it to seek damages. Since publishers are unlikely to want to publish anything where the potential profits are at risk of being claimed by the Government this may prove a useful weapon.

Treason

The offence of treason is committed if someone owes allegiance to the monarch and conspires or incites others to kill, overthrow or levy war against him or her. This crime is still punishable by the death penalty.

Treason felony overlaps with treason and consists of inciting rebellion against the Government of the UK, or conspiring to deprive the monarch of his or her sovereignty in any of her dominions (Treason Felony Act 1858). It is punishable with life imprisonment.

Incitement to disaffection

Incitement to disaffection concerns attempts to persuade Government servants, such as police officers or members of the armed forces, to disobey their orders. The Police Act 1964, s. 53 prohibits conduct calculated to cause disaffection among police officers or to induce them to withhold their services or commit breaches of discipline. The Incitement to Disaffection Act 1934 makes it an offence maliciously and advisedly to endeavour to seduce a member of the armed forces from his duty or allegiance or to be an accomplice to this activity. The Act was used in the 1970s against campaigners for the withdrawal of British troops from Northern Ireland.

Sedition

Sedition is a common law offence, committed where a person tries to bring the monarch, the Government, the constitution or the administration of justice, into hatred or contempt. It can also be committed by inciting another to use unlawful means to bring about changes in the state or the church, to promote feelings of hostility between UK subjects, or discontent among them. In practice its scope is not as wide as it sounds; it is not a criminal offence to criticize the Queen, or the Government, or the courts, for example, nor to try to bring about changes in church or state by lawful means. Cases in this century have stressed a need to prove an intention to promote violence and disorder.

In **R v Chief Metropolitan Stipendiary Magistrate, ex parte Choudhury** (1991), an attempt was made to bring a private prosecution against Salman Rushdie, author of *The Satanic Verses*, on the grounds that the book was seditious because it had created widespread discontent and disaffection among UK subjects – publication of the book, which some Muslims claimed was blasphemous, created hostility between British Muslims who were deeply offended by it, and those who defended the book on the ground of freedom of expression, and was said to have damaged international relations between the UK and Islamic countries. The magistrate refused to issue a summons, and this decision was supported by the Divisional Court, which stated that it was not sufficient simply to create ill-will between subjects: seditious conduct must be aimed at disturbing established authority, by violent means.

Blasphemy

At common law it is a criminal offence to criticize the Christian religion in a manner that is likely to outrage the feelings of a Christian. This offence had fallen into disuse, but was revived in **Whitehouse** *v* **Gay News Ltd and Lemmon** (1978). That case was brought by the well-known anti-pornography campaigner, Mary Whitehouse. The publishers of *Gay News* were convicted of blasphemy by a jury after publishing a poem linking homosexual practices with the life and crucifixion of Christ. The conviction was upheld by the House of Lords, who stated that so long as there was proof that the defendants intended to publish the offending words, there was no need to prove an intention to blaspheme, nor that the publication was likely to cause a breach of the peace.

In **Ex parte Choudhury** (discussed above), the High Court confirmed that the offence is limited to criticism of Christianity and does not extend to other religions. This decision has been criticized on the grounds that a multi-religious society should protect all faiths or none at all, though given the existence of many small cults and sects, it might be difficult to define a religion for this purpose.

Defamation

Defamation is both a civil and a criminal wrong and we will consider each briefly in turn.

Civil liability
In civil law liability for defamation can take one of two forms: libel or slander. Libel covers statements made in some permanent form – this usually means printed or written, though it includes statues, films and the performance of plays. Slander applies to defamation made in a transitory form, such as spoken words or gestures. The main significance of this distinction is that for slander some damage must usually be proved to have resulted from the offending conduct while this is not necessary for libel: the mere fact that a libellous comment was made is sufficient to give rise to civil liability.

In order for the civil courts to find defamation claimants must prove that the defendant made a false, defamatory statement that appeared to refer to them. A statement is defamatory if it lowers the claimant's reputation in the minds of right-minded people. An insult which does not have this impact is insufficient. A statement need not directly criticize the claimant; it may do so by implication, known as an 'innuendo'. In **Tolley** *v* **JS Fry & Sons Ltd** (1931) the claimant was an amateur golfer, and his amateur status meant that he was not allowed to accept money to publicize products. Without his knowledge the defendants published an advertisement containing a cartoon of him, with a rhyme praising their product, which was chocolate. He succeeded in proving that this amounted to a defamatory statement by way of innuendo, because readers seeing it were likely to assume that he had been paid to lend his name to the product and therefore compromised his amateur status.

The requirement that the claimant be 'lowered in the estimation of right-thinking members of society generally' is illustrated by **Byrne** *v* **Deane** (1937). After the police raided a golf club and removed an illegal gambling machine, a verse appeared on the club notice board which included the words 'but he who gave the game away may he byrn in hell and rue the day', thereby hinting that Byrne was the person who had informed the police about the existence of the machine. The claimant sued the club, alleging that the statement was defamatory. It was held that, although the statement might lower him in the estimation of the club members, it would not do so in the estimation of right-thinking members of society, who would not disapprove of conduct designed to prevent crime. The action failed.

It is not possible to defame a dead person. Nor is it usually possible to defame a class of people. So, for example, if a newspaper said that all politicians were useless, no individual politician could sue. However, where the class mentioned is very small, the statement may be taken to refer to each and every member of it, and any or all of them may sue. Thus, if a defamatory statement was applied to 'all female football managers', when in fact there were only three or four in the country, any of them could bring a civil action for defamation. A remark about football managers in general would not usually allow an individual to sue because the class referred to would be too big. This law was laid down in **Knuppfer** *v* **London Express Newspapers Ltd** (1944). The defendants had published an article stating that an émigré Russian group was a fascist organization. The group had approximately 2,000 members, of which 24 were based in the UK. The claimant was a Russian immigrant living in London and he brought an action for defamation. His action was rejected by the House of Lords on the basis that the accusation of fascism was aimed at a class of people and not him.

The statement must be published. Communication of the defamation to anyone other than the claimant, or the defendant's wife, can amount to publication. The first defamation case involving use of the Internet came to the courts in 1998. In **Godfrey** *v* **Demon Internet Ltd** the defendant was an Internet Service Provider carrying on business in England and

Wales. An unknown person transmitted an article from the US which appeared on the Internet. The article was defamatory of the claimant, who was a lecturer in England. The claimant sent a fax informing the defendant's managing director that the article was a forgery, that he was not responsible for it and requesting its removal. The article was not removed and the claimant claimed damages for libel. The defendant contended that it was not at common law the publisher of the article. The High Court held that the Internet Service Provider had published the article under common law.

A range of potential defences are available of which we will mention the four most important. First, if a defamatory statement is true, the defendant will have a defence of justification. Secondly, certain statements, such as those made by MPs in Parliament and those made during judicial proceedings, enjoy a defence of 'absolute privilege'. Thirdly, the Defamation Act 1996 created a defence where a defendant has offered to make amends and is willing to pay compensation assessed by a judge, and to publish an appropriate correction and apology. Finally, a defendant will have a defence if it can be proved that the statement made was fair comment on a matter of public interest. This defence arose in defamation proceedings brought by McDonalds against two private individuals who had distributed leaflets about the fast-food chain. The leaflets included statements that McDonalds' employees worldwide did badly in terms of pay and conditions and that if one ate a lot of McDonalds' food one's diet might become high in fat with a real risk of heart disease. The trial was the longest in legal history, lasting 314 days, spaced over two-and-a-half years. At first instance McDonalds were awarded £40,000 damages. The Court of Appeal allowed part of the appeal on the ground that the above statements amounted to fair comment and the award of damages was reduced to £20,000.

A recent high-profile defamation case is **Irving** *v* **Penguin Books and Lipstadt** (2000). David Irving was a controversial historian who had been described as a 'Holocaust denier' in a book written and published by the two defendants. His action for defamation failed.

The potential for the defamation laws to be abused was highlighted by the case of the former Cabinet Minister, Jonathan Aitken. Following allegations being made about his business activities he announced that he would sue the *Guardian* and Granada TV for libel. He swore that he would take the 'simple sword of truth and the trusty shield of British fair play' to rout 'bitter and twisted journalism'. In fact, it was later discovered that he himself had been lying and was subsequently sentenced to 18 months' imprisonment for perjury, which is the offence of lying under oath in court. One potential abuse has been blocked with a decision by Mr Justice Buckley. He rejected the late Sir James Goldsmith's action, stating that political parties cannot sue for libel. (Sir James Goldsmith had been the leader of the Referendum Party.)

Criminal liability

Criminal liability is imposed under s. 5 of the Libel Act 1843 and applies only to libel and not slander. Unlike civil libel, criminal libel may apply to a class of persons or a dead person. Under the Act it is a defence to prove that the publication was both true and in the public interest.

A prosecution for criminal libel against a newspaper proprietor, publisher or editor can only be brought with leave of a judge. Leave was given for a private prosecution in 1976 by Sir James Goldsmith against the publishers of *Private Eye*. The prosecution related to allegations that Goldsmith was the ringleader of a conspiracy to obstruct the course of justice. The High Court judge said that the press was not free to publish scandalous or scurrilous articles which were wholly without foundation.

Defamatory words published in the course of a performance of a play amount to criminal libel under ss. 4 and 6 of the Theatres Act 1968.

It has been argued that defamation is not an area in which the criminal law should be involved and, in 1982, the Law Commission recommended that criminal libel at common law should be abolished and replaced by a narrower statutory offence, directed at a person who, knowing or believing it to be untrue, publishes a deliberately defamatory statement which is likely to cause the victim significant harm.

Obscenity

The Obscene Publications Act 1959 created the statutory offence of publishing obscene material, which can be used against the authors, photographers, artists, publishers, booksellers and other distributors of such material. The Criminal Law Act 1977 extended the provisions of the 1959 Act to films, and the Broadcasting Act 1990 to television and radio.

An article is obscene, under s. 1 of the 1959 Act, if it tends to deprave or corrupt a person likely to read, see or hear it; a few words or sentences are not enough. Although the Act is mainly used against pornography, it is not only concerned with sex: for example, a book which described the pleasures of drug-taking has been found to 'deprave and corrupt'.

The prosecution must prove that a significant proportion of the people likely to come into contact with the material would have their morals adversely affected, but there is no need to prove an intention to do so. It is a defence that the defendant had not examined the offending material and had no reason to believe that publication or possession would be an offence, or alternatively, that publication was for the public good in the interests of science, literature, art or learning, or other objects of public concern.

Other restrictions on indecent material include the Protection of Children Act 1978, prohibiting indecent photographs of children under 16, and the Theatre Act 1968, making it an offence to present or direct the performance of a play which is obscene.

Miscellaneous restrictions

A great number of criminal offences and torts can be committed purely by the use of spoken words or writing. For example, it is an offence to blackmail or to incite another to commit a crime, and intimidating words causing fear in the victim may amount to an assault. Several offences under the Public Order Act 1986 have implications for freedom of expression: threatening behaviour (s. 4); disorderly conduct (s. 5); and incitement to racial hatred (ss. 17–23). These are discussed in chapter 19: Freedom of assembly. Fraudulent misrepresentation and deceit are torts which can be committed by speech alone.

Freedom of information

The UK Government has in the past been extremely secretive, giving the public only very limited access to information. As we have seen, Government information is protected by Official Secrets legislation, by 'D' notices, and by the doctrine of confidentiality: state papers (often called public records) are made available to public scrutiny only after a lapse of 30 years, or longer in some cases. The Scott Report, which followed an inquiry into the sale of arms to Iraq, highlighted the lack of openness in the UK Government. The system appeared to accept unquestioningly the need to tell Parliament and the public as little as possible about subjects which were seen as politically sensitive. Until 2000 there were several Acts allowing limited public access to certain documents, such as medical records. In 1994 a *Code of Practice on Access to Government Information* was published, but again this gave only limited access and no legal rights to information.

In its manifesto for the 1997 general election, the Labour Party stated: 'Unnecessary secrecy in government leads to arrogance . . . and defective policy decisions. The Scott Report on arms to Iraq revealed Conservative abuses of power. We are pledged to a Freedom of Information Act, leading to more open government . . .' On coming to power it passed the Freedom of Information Act 2000 which provides a general right to information held by public authorities, subject to exceptions. The areas of information exempted or excluded from the legislation are significant. They include information covering national security, intelligence, the courts and policy advice from civil servants to Ministers. Confidential commercial and personal information is also exempted. Under the new regime, the current debate on the safety of GM foods might never have surfaced, because the legislation would have allowed the Government to suppress scientific evidence arising from GM food research on the ground that it was policy advice to Ministers and as such exempted information.

It is possible to appeal a refusal to provide information to a new Information Commissioner. The Commissioner has the power to recommend the discretionary disclosure of information and is empowered to enforce compliance. Public bodies have a discretion to disclose exempted information if they feel disclosure is in the public interest. But they also have the power to impose conditions restricting the use or further disclosure of the information by the person to whom it is furnished.

People requesting information can be charged up to 10 per cent of the cost to the public body. However, if it would cost more than £500 to gather the required information it can refuse the application outright. Once passed, the Bill will replace existing legislation on access to public records and will operate in tandem with the Data Protection Act 1998 which allows access to some personal information held in computerized files.

Freedom of information legislation is not entirely without its problems. For a start, it is expensive – Canada and Australia spend the equivalent of £6.6 million a year on it. On the other hand, when compared with the £200 million that is spent annually on publicizing information the British Government wants released, the cost seems comparatively low. There are also complaints that the system has ended up being used mainly by 'data brokers' who gain information in order to sell it to those with an interest and by businesses seeking commercial information; clearly taxpayers should not have to foot the bill for this.

In practice, the beneficial results of freedom of information legislation seem to outweigh these drawbacks: over the past few years, investigations made possible by the new laws have revealed radioactive contamination of water supplies, abnormal rates of cancer in nuclear plant employees, the health risks of silicone breast implants and potentially corrupt connections between public servants and big business.

▶ A right to privacy?

Closely linked to the question of freedom of expression is the right to privacy, as if a person's private life is protected this imposes restrictions on the media publishing material on the subject. In the past English law did not recognize a right to privacy: those whose privacy was invaded had no remedy, unless a specific crime or tort had been committed.

Concern over intrusive press reporting had led to much debate, particularly following the death of Princess Diana, about whether a right to privacy ought to be established by statute. Stories about the private lives of politicians and members of the royal family had highlighted the length to which some papers will go to get their story. As a result of concerns over this type of reporting, the Calcutt Committee was set up to consider whether there should be statutory powers to control media invasions of privacy. Its first report in 1990 rejected this idea, in favour of a self-regulatory system under the Press Complaints Commission. But in the second report in 1993, Calcutt concluded that the Press Complaints

Commission 'has not proved itself to be an effective regulator' and recommended tighter controls. The Committee proposed a new statutory Press Complaints Commission, to investigate allegations of unjust or unfair treatment by newspapers or magazines, with new powers to impose fines, award costs and require the printing of an apology, correction or reply. It also suggested there should be criminal offences to cover physical intrusion, such as the use of surveillance devices on private property, a tort of infringement of privacy, tightening up of the laws under the data protection legislation, and legal restrictions on press reporting empowering any court to restrict the publication of the name and address of any person by whom an offence has been alleged to have been committed. Most of these proposals have been ignored by the Government.

On the specific issue of closed-circuit TVs which have now been widely installed in public places, a Government spokesperson has stated that a Code of Practice was needed to prevent the misuse of images. Such misuse was highlighted when a film was made available that had been taken by closed-circuit TV of Princess Diana shopping in the Harvey Nichols department store.

A right to privacy in relation to public authorities has now been introduced into domestic law by incorporation of the European Convention on Human Rights. Article 8 protects the right to respect for private and family life. It states:

1. Everyone has the right to respect for his private and family life, his home and his correspondence.
2. There shall be no interference by a public authority with the exercise of this right except such as is in accordance with the law and is necessary in a democratic society in the interest of national security, public safety or the economic well-being of the country, for the prevention of disorder or crime, for the protection of health or morals, or for the protection of the rights and freedoms of others.

The common law has recently been developed by the courts to recognize a right of privacy enforceable against private individuals. This development arose in the case of **Douglas and others** *v* **Hello! Ltd** (2001). The case arose from the marriage of the Hollywood celebrities Michael Douglas and Catherine Zeta-Jones. They had sold for £1 million exclusive rights in the wedding photographs to *OK!* magazine. The rival magazine *Hello!* had obtained pictures of the event and intended to publish them. The couple objected and, at first instance, won an injunction preventing *Hello!* from publishing the photos. The Court of Appeal lifted the injunction. Its judgment is particularly significant because it recognized 'a right to privacy which we will today recognize and protect'. This right was grounded in the doctrine of breach of confidence (a concept discussed on p. 515). The judges said that if on some private occasion the claimants made it clear that no photographs were to be taken of them, then all those who were present would be bound by the obligations of confidence created by their knowledge of that restriction.

However, on the facts of the case, the position of the couple claiming a right to privacy in the photos was complicated by the fact that they had actually chosen to sell these rights to *OK!* magazine. Their contract would allow them to retain editorial control of which pictures would be published. The Court of Appeal pointed out that the couple were not seeking to have a small private wedding, instead they aimed to control the publicity. In reality the couple were more concerned with the frustration of their financial arrangement with *OK!* magazine. The court therefore decided that an award of damages at the final trial hearing would be sufficient to compensate the couple and *Hello!* magazine was allowed to publish the photographs. In allowing publication the court stated:

> although the right to freedom of expression is not in every case the ace of trumps, it is a powerful card to which the courts of this country must always pay appropriate respect.

Lord Justice Keene stated that the original concept of breach of confidence had now developed into something different from the limited area of commercial and employment relationships, which had in the past been its main concern.

The danger of any privacy law is that as well as protecting famous people from intrusion, it can also be used to prevent genuine investigative journalism from uncovering facts that the public ought to know. France has strong privacy laws and significant details about the former President Mitterrand's private life were not brought to the public's attention until after his death. To avoid such problems the law needs to develop a broad public interest defence.

▶ ANSWERING QUESTIONS

1 Many years ago, L, who was currently employed by M as a repairer of domestic appliances, had been suspected of raping a woman whom he had met at a night club, but the police decided that the evidence was too weak to support any charge. By chance, L was called to make a repair at N's house. N had formerly been a police officer and had worked at the police station where L was interviewed about the rape. He remembered L very well as a person to whom he had taken a considerable dislike to at the time, and he now telephoned M to ask if he realized that he was putting women at risk by employing L. M took the opportunity of a sudden decline in business to make L redundant. O, an investigative journalist who was working on a story about the lack of controls over engaging employees who might be a danger to members of the public, received a tip off from N about L, and described L in a newspaper article as 'an example of the worst kind of depravity lurking on everyone's doorstep'. The story was picked up by P, a Member of Parliament, who wrote to the Employment Minister demanding to know why he had not introduced measures 'to keep rapists such as L out of our homes', and repeated his question in a debate in the House of Commons.

Discuss the general issues concerning freedoms raised by L's treatment and consider whether, and against whom, he may seek redress. *Edexcel*

You could divide your answer into two main halves, first looking at the specific legal issues raised by the facts of this problem question and secondly looking at the more general issues of civil liberty highlighted by this scenario.

In the first part of your answer, you could consider whether N would have been in breach of an obligation of confidence between himself and his former employer when he revealed the information about L (see p. 515).

L might be able to bring an action for defamation (see p. 519). Though the investigation certainly took place, N's comments to M and to O appear to be an assertion that L was in fact guilty of the rape. This would be difficult for N to prove and may not be true.

The Member of Parliament, P, has made an explicit allegation against L, but he may be protected from an action in defamation by absolute parliamentary privilege. There is no doubt that his words in the debate are protected. Whether his written demand is made in the course of 'parliamentary proceedings' is rather less clear. If it is not, then the allegation is defamatory if untrue. If it is, then absolute privilege may be claimed.

On the second part of your answer, you could discuss the fact that the UK is currently developing a right to privacy (see p. 524). The facts of the case highlight the balance that needs to be achieved between the individual interest in privacy, the need to protect the public by publishing information and the importance in a democratic society of freedom of expression. The need to publish the information on L is reduced by the length of time since the offence was committed. You could point to the useful role the media can sometimes play in our society by using some of the material in Chapter 9 under the heading 'The role of the media and public opinion'.

2 Lucy won a major prize in the national lottery. Her former boyfriend, Mark, contacted the editor of the *Daily Slur* and offered to reveal intimate details of their relationship. The *Daily Slur* paid Mark £1,000 for an interview in which Mark claimed that Lucy was a compulsive liar and had frequently been arrested for shoplifting. The *Daily Slur* published the interview and a photograph of Lucy on its front page under the headline: 'My Life with Light-Fingered Lucy', without checking to find out whether Mark's claims were true. In fact, Lucy has never been arrested for shoplifting, but is presently on bail awaiting trial at the Crown Court on a charge of attempting to defraud an insurance company. Lucy is distressed by the publicity and is afraid that it may prejudice her trial.
(a) Advise Lucy as to whether she has any remedies against Mark and the *Daily Slur* (15 marks) and

(b) Consider whether the *Daily Slur* is guilty of contempt of court. *(10 marks)*
WJEC

With respect to part (a) you need to look at liability for defamation and the question of breach of confidence (p. 515). Part (b) was solely concerned with the issue of contempt of court discussed at p. 513. You needed to look at whether the defence of innocent publication would be available.

3 Maldwyn is a civil servant who works in the Welsh Office. In the course of his duties, Maldwyn has read the report of a secret enquiry into low-flying exercises carried out by the RAF over the Welsh countryside. The report concludes that such exercises serve no useful purpose as training in preparation for war and moreover pose an unacceptable threat to the safety of people living in rural Wales. Maldwyn believes that the people of Wales have a right to know of the report's findings, and has given the report to Nella, a journalist who works for *Amser*, a Welsh daily newspaper.

(a) Consider what offences, if any, have been committed by Maldwyn and Nella *(15 marks)*; **and**

(b) Consider what steps the Government may take to prevent the publication of the report by *Amser*. *(10 marks)* WJEC

(a) This part of the question requires a detailed discussion of the Official Secrets Acts (see p. 510).

(b) Here you could discuss the use of injunctions using the doctrine of breach of confidence (see p. 515) and 'D' notices (see p. 512).

4 To what extent are television services in the United Kingdom free from interference by government? *WJEC*

You could divide your answer into two halves, looking firstly at the restrictions that are specific to the television service and then, secondly, at restrictions which are of wider application but still effect the television service. On the first half of the essay the relevant information can be found from pp. 507–509. For the second half of the essay you would want to refer in particular to the Official Secrets Acts, the 'D' notices and the doctrine of breach of confidence. You need to evaluate whether these restrictions achieve a balance between freedom of information and the interests of an effective Government, which could be linked to issues raised by the debate of how far there should be a right to information (see p. 523).

▶ Reading on the Internet

The website of the Press Complaints Commission is available at:
http://www.pcc.org.uk/

24 Remedies for infringement of civil rights

Rights are only worthwhile if there are adequate remedies for their enforcement. The fact that we do not yet have a Bill of Rights, but only a collection of laws detailing what we may not do, has inevitably meant that remedies are similarly scattered. Some of the main remedies available in English law for unlawful infringement of basic rights are the subject of this section.

Judicial review

Where a public body – such as a local authority, the police, or a Government department – acts illegally, the result will often be an infringement of an individual's rights, and in some cases the remedy for this is a procedure known as judicial review. This is discussed in chapter 14.

Habeas corpus

Personal liberty is regarded as the most fundamental of all freedoms, and where individuals are wrongfully deprived of their liberty, the fact that, on release, they can sue their captor for damages under the ordinary civil law is not regarded as sufficient. *Habeas corpus* is an ancient remedy which allows a person detained to challenge the legality of detention and, if successful, get themselves quickly released. It does not punish the person responsible for the detention, but once the detainee is set free, they can still pursue any other available remedies for compensation or punishment.

Habeas corpus may be sought by, among others, convicted prisoners; those detained in custody pending trial or held by the police during criminal investigations; those awaiting extradition; psychiatric patients; and those with excessive bail conditions imposed on them. Application is made to the Divisional Court, and takes priority over all other court business.

Civil action

Where a public body breaches a person's rights in such a way as to amount to a tort, that body may be sued in the same way as a private citizen would be; since the Crown Proceedings Act 1947, this includes the Crown.

As far as civil rights are concerned, this remedy is of particular importance in relation to illegal behaviour by the police: possible actions include assault, malicious prosecution, false imprisonment, wrongful arrest and trespass to property or goods. Exemplary damages may be awarded against the police even where there has been no oppressive behaviour or other aggravating circumstances. These cases are usually heard by a jury.

In the past the police have benefited from an effective immunity from liability for negligence in their investigations. This immunity stems from the case of **Hill** *v* **Chief Constable of West Yorkshire** (1989). The case looked at whether the police owed a duty of care to a victim of Peter Sutcliffe, known as the Yorkshire Ripper. The House of Lords ruled that public policy prevented any action for negligence lying in respect of police strategies for the investigation and prevention of crime.

In **Osman** *v* **UK** (1997) the European Court of Human Rights threw into doubt the future of this immunity. In that case, a teacher had developed a fixation with a 14-year-old boy at his school. He gave him money, took photographs of him and sometimes followed him home. Graffiti of a sexual nature appeared in the neighbourhood and the parent's house and car suffered criminal damage but the teacher denied any involvement. The teacher changed his name by deed poll to include the boy's name. He was suspended from his position as a teacher and he indicated that he was thinking of 'doing a Hungerford' by which it was assumed he meant he might use firearms to kill the deputy headmaster and other victims at random. In December 1987 the police sought to interview the man in connection with allegations of criminal damage but he had disappeared. Two months later he went to the boy's home, shot and wounded him and killed his father. He also went to the home of the deputy headmaster and shot and wounded him and killed his son. He was convicted of manslaughter and placed in a psychiatric hospital.

The pupil with whom he had had an obsession and the mother brought a civil action against the Metropolitan Police for negligence. They claimed that the police had been negligent in not apprehending the man before the incident that led to the killing. Relying on **Hill** *v* **Chief Constable of West Yorkshire** the Court of Appeal upheld a ruling to strike out the case as disclosing no cause of action. The Court of Appeal treated that case as laying down a watertight defence. It was contended before the European Court of Human Rights that the rule of public policy preventing the action for negligence breached the European Convention on Human Rights. The European Court ruled that Art. 6 of the Convention, which guarantees the right to a fair trial, had been violated. It considered that the exclusionary rule formulated in the **Hill** case should not be used as a blanket immunity, but that the existence of competing public policy issues had to be considered. The approach of the Court of Appeal had amounted to an unjustifiable restriction on the right of access to a court to have a claim determined on its merits.

This interference by the European Court into the substantive law of tort has not been well received by some academics and judges in the UK. It has been argued that the right to a fair trial under Art. 6 should be restricted to looking at procedural matters rather than examining the substantive law of the country. There are some signs that the European Court may be reconsidering its approach. In **Z** v **UK** (2001) the European Court of Human Rights acknowledged that it had not fully understood the English law as laid down in the **Hill** case. It stated:

> The Court considers that its reasoning in the **Osman** judgment was based on an understanding of the law of negligence. . . . which has to be reviewed in the light of the clarifications subsequently made by the domestic courts and notably the House of Lords . . . In the present case, the Court is led to the conclusion that the inability of the applicants to sue the local authority flowed not from an immunity but from the applicable principles governing the substantive right of action in domestic law. There was no restriction on access to the court of the kind contemplated in the **Ashingdane** v **United Kingdom** (1985) judgment.

The European Court appears at least to be restricting the impact of **Osman**. In **TP and KM** v **UK** (2001) the European Court distinguished the **Osman** case and ruled that there had been no breach of Art. 6 when a case had been struck out by the UK courts because the case was doomed to fail.

The number of actions against the Metropolitan police has risen considerably in recent years from 182 in 1982 to 495 in 1995/96 with £2,014,000 being paid out in damages and settlements. 1996 saw a number of very high awards of damages in civil actions by the courts of first instance. For example, in **Goswell** v **Commissioner of Metropolitan Police** (1996) Mr Goswell was waiting in his car for his girlfriend when PC Trigg approached. Mr Goswell complained about the police failure to investigate an arson attack on his home. He was handcuffed to another officer, struck by PC Trigg (causing injuries which required stitches and left a permanent scar) and then arrested for assault and threatening behaviour. His prosecution for these charges failed and when he brought a civil action he was awarded £120,000 damages for assault, £12,000 for false imprisonment and £170,000 exemplary damages for arbitrary and oppressive behaviour.

Appeals were lodged against the more substantial payments in damages and they were reduced by the Court of Appeal. For example, Kenneth Hsu was initially awarded £220,000 damages for assault and false imprisonment. This was reduced on appeal to £35,000 and strict guidelines were laid down for future allocations of damages by a jury, including figures as a starting-point in their deliberations for different types of cases. For example, basic damages for false imprisonment should be between £500 for one hour and £3,000 for 24 hours with an upper limit of £50,000 on exemplary damages. Their Lordships claimed to be at pains to establish a proper balance between the need to add teeth to the damages paid by the defendant and the fact that this money has to be drawn from public funds. Lawyers have taken issue with the likely impact of a £50,000 award on an institution with an annual budget close to £2 billion.

Compensation

Where there has been a miscarriage of justice an award of compensation can be made by the state under s. 133 of the Criminal Justice Act 1988.

Alternatively, an *ex gratia* payment can be made in accordance with the Home Secretary's statement to the House of Commons on 29 November 1985. Such an award will be made where there has been gross misconduct by a public authority (**R** *v* **Secretary of State for the Home Department, ex parte Garner** (1999)).

Criminal proceedings

Criminal proceedings may be brought for false imprisonment or assault, if necessary by means of a private prosecution. In 1997, 218 police officers were convicted of a criminal offence, of these, 53 were for non-traffic offences. Sadly, not one police officer accused of malpractice arising from the many high-profile miscarriages of justice put right by the Court of Appeal since 1989 has been convicted of a criminal offence.

The European Court of Human Rights

A person whose rights have been breached may find that they have an eventual remedy in the European Court of Human Rights (see p. 456).

Internal police disciplinary proceedings

Under the Police Act 1996, complaints made by a member of the public about the conduct of a police officer are submitted to the chief officer of the force concerned, who should take steps to obtain or preserve relevant evidence. Complaints about officers above the rank of chief superintendent are then handled by the local police authority; complaints about other ranks by the chief officer. Minor complaints are dealt with informally, but where the problem is more serious, there may be disciplinary proceedings or a criminal prosecution. The most serious complaints must be referred to the Police Complaints Authority, which supervises the investigation itself.

The Home Office report, *Police Complaints and Discipline* (1998), found that in 1997, 22,100 complaints were made, of which 847 were substantiated, disciplinary charges against 448 officers were proven and this led to 123 officers being dismissed or required to resign.

New police disciplinary proceedings were introduced in 1997. The standard of proof was changed: the criminal standard of proof previously required in all discipline cases was replaced by the test of 'reasonableness'; the more serious the allegation the greater the weight of evidence required. Minor misconduct requires a standard of proof at the level of 'a balance of probabilities'. In exceptional circumstances such proceedings can take place before a criminal case has been heard.

The Police Complaints Authority

In the year ending 31 March 1996 the Police Complaints Authority considered 9,816 cases; supervision was undertaken in only a few hundred of these. These investigations have included high-profile cases such as police conduct at certain student demonstrations; the pickets outside the Wapping printing works in 1987; during the Broadwater Farm riots in 1985 and the miners' strike of 1984/85; and the conduct of the West Midlands Serious Crime Squad between 1986 and 1989.

There remains significant dissatisfaction amongst both public and police, with the complaints process and in particular with the practice of police investigating police. Research carried out by Maguire and Corbett (1991) found that while supervision by the Police Complaints Authority did have the effect of 'sharpening up' some police investigations, nearly 90 per cent of complainants surveyed thought the entire complaint investigation should be conducted by someone other than the police. The co-authors concluded that the creation of a completely independent investigative body could increase public confidence in the system. The Police Complaints Authority has itself called for additional powers, similar to those available to the Criminal Cases Review Commission, to be able to appoint in exceptional circumstances an *ad hoc*, non-police, investigating team.

In 2001 the Government announced in the Queen's speech that legislation would be introduced replacing the Police Complaints Authority with a new independent body using civilian investigators to undertake inquiries into serious allegations of malpractice.

The admissibility of evidence

Where police officers commit serious infringements of a suspect's rights during the investigation of an offence, the courts may hold that evidence obtained as a result of such misbehaviour is inadmissible in court, the idea being to remove any incentive for the police to break the rules.

Under s. 76(2) of PACE, confession evidence is inadmissible where it was obtained by oppression or in circumstances likely to render it unreliable and, if the defence alleges that this is the case, the onus is on the prosecution to establish otherwise (s. 76(1)). Oppression is defined as including 'torture, inhuman or degrading treatment, and the use or threat of violence (whether or not amounting to torture)' (s. 76(8)). The definition of 'oppression' was considered in **R** *v* **Fulling** (1987). In that case, the police had persuaded a woman to make a confession by telling her that her lover was being unfaithful. The court held that this did not amount to oppression, and stated that the term should carry its ordinary meaning, that of unjust treatment or cruelty, or the wrongful use of power. Excluding evidence is potentially a powerful safeguard against oppressive treatment by the police, since there is little point in pressurizing a suspect to confess if that confession cannot be used to obtain a conviction. However, the extent of this protection is diluted by s. 76(4), which states that even if a confession is excluded, any facts discovered as a result of it may still be admissible. Parts of an excluded confession may also be allowed if relevant to show that the defendant speaks or writes in a particular way. This means that the police can use oppressive treatment to secure a confession which will help them find other evidence.

Section 78 provides that in any proceedings the court may refuse to admit evidence 'if it appears to the court that, having regard to all the circumstances, including the circumstances in which the evidence was obtained, the admission of the evidence would have such an adverse effect on the fairness of the proceedings that the court ought not to admit it'. This provision covers all types of evidence, not just confessions. It is generally invoked only if the police have committed serious breaches of PACE, such as refusing a suspect access to legal advice over a long period.

The right to exercise self-defence

Any citizen may use reasonable force to prevent unlawful interference with their person or property, or to protect others from such interference. This can affect both civil and criminal liability.

Parliamentary controls

One of the basic functions of Parliament is to act as a watchdog over the rights of citizens, protecting them from undue interference by Government. A number of methods are available, from questions directed to Ministers in Parliament, to committees designed to scrutinize legislation. However, this function has suffered as a result of the strength of party discipline, which means that many MPs appear to put loyalty to their party above loyalty to the citizens they represent. The result is that even measures which clearly restrict fundamental rights can be voted through if the Government has a clear majority.

The Ombudsman

The Parliamentary Commissioner for Administration, known as the Ombudsman, has a role in protecting individual rights, and is discussed in chapter 15.

ANSWERING QUESTIONS

1 L had a long history of petty theft and burglary but had never been known to be involved in any violence. One Saturday night the police were called to investigate a stabbing in a fast food shop. Three men had run away after the stabbing and witnesses described one of them in a way which approximated to L's description. This information was relayed to Police Constable (PC) J, who was on foot patrol in the town centre some two miles away. He saw L walking down the street with K and immediately took hold of L's arm and told him to turn out all of his pockets. L refused and K sought to free him before giving up and running off. PC J then dragged L into a doorway and searched him thoroughly while a crowd gathered and laughed at L. Finding nothing on L, PC J told him that if he did not reveal K's identity and address, he could expect some rough treatment in the future. L gave PC J the information and both then went round to K's house, where L was forced to pretend that he was alone so as to get K to open the door. As soon as K did so, PC J burst in and searched the house. He found a number of car radios with their serial numbers obliterated and seized them all, despite K's protests that they were in a room which he rented out and that he knew nothing about them. L and K were then kept at the police station for 36 hours, during which they were permitted only one brief interview with the duty solicitor, and were questioned for long periods of time about the stabbing and the car radios. Eventually, both were released without charge when three men were arrested for the stabbing and K's lodger gave a satisfactory account of his possession of the car radios.

Explain whether the police were legally entitled to act as they did and consider whether L and K have any remedies. *Edexcel*

Your answer should be divided into halves, firstly looking at the police powers (see p. 247 onwards) and secondly the remedies available. On the first issue of the police powers, PC J may have had reasonable grounds to suspect that he would find offensive weapons or blades on L because of the information he had received. Thus, stop and search under s. 1 of PACE may have been justified (see p. 249). However, the search was carried out in breach of Code provisions.

It is unclear whether L was placed under arrest at any point before the discovery of the car radios. If he was, the grounds are unclear and it would almost certainly be unlawful. The entry into K's house is unlawful as it was not carried out with K's genuine consent and there are no other grounds to make it lawful (such as to arrest, consequent on arrest, or to prevent breach of the peace). Thus, seizure of the car radios is also unlawful. However, the presence of the car radios did give rise to a reasonable suspicion that an arrestable offence had been or was being committed (either theft or handling stolen goods) with the involvement of K, and possibly L. This would probably justify an arrest at this stage.

The detention and questioning of L and K may have contravened the time limits imposed by the Code of Practice requirements about breaks and refreshments, and the restricted access to the solicitor may contravene the requirements of s. 58.

On the second half of the essay concerning the remedies available, breach of the Code provisions in the carrying out of the search and questioning do not give rise to any rights under civil law, but can be the subject of a complaint to the Police Complaints Authority. The violations of PACE could give rise to civil actions for unlawful arrest, trespass to premises and false imprisonment. Criminal or disciplinary proceedings could also be brought.

2 Including in your answer an explanation of any reform(s) which you believe to be desirable, write a critical analysis of the protection of fundamental rights and freedoms within English law. *AQA (AEB)*

You could start by pointing out that civil liberties in the UK is in a period of transition with the incorporation of the European Convention on Human Rights into English law. You need to explain both what the position was before the Human Rights Act 1998 was brought into force and what it is now that it has been brought into force. You could select some material from this chapter to illustrate how far fundamental freedoms are currently being protected and you could consider how far the position has changed with the passing of the Human Rights Act 1998.

The main reform to consider is whether there should be an entrenched Bill of Rights and you would need to discuss what impact this would have on the relationship between the legislature and the judiciary. In addition, you could suggest particular reforms to individual freedoms that you have considered.

▶ Reading on the Internet

The website of the Police Complaints Authority is available at:
http://www.pca.gov.uk/

25 Law and rules

What is law? What do we mean when we say that something is the law? One answer is that a law is a type of rule, but clearly there are many rules which are not law: rules of etiquette, school or club rules, and moral rules, for example. One way to understand more about what law is, is to look at what distinguishes legal rules from other types of rules.

What is a rule?

A good starting point is the definition of a rule given by Twining and Miers in their book *How to Do Things With Rules*: 'a general norm mandating or guiding conduct or action in a given type of situation.' This definition contains several important statements about rules. Rules are general – they tend to apply to people in general or a specific class, rather than singling out individuals. They are normative, meaning that they set a standard of how things ought to be, rather than how they are – for example, 'cars should be driven on the road' is a normative statement, a rule stating how things ought to be, in contrast to 'cars are driven on the road', which is simply a factual statement. All rules – whether they are legal, moral or just customary – lay down standards of behaviour to which we ought to conform if the rule affects us.

Rules may mandate action, meaning that they say something must or must not be done, and there may be a penalty for disobedience; or they may guide behaviour, by saying what ought or ought not to be done. They tend to cover situations which have arisen in the past and are likely to arise again; if we do not know that a particular situation could arise, there will be no rules to guide behaviour in that situation. They may be written down, or simply known among those whom they affect.

Principles can be distinguished from rules; the former may have a similar form but tend to be more general, and usually have to be translated into rules before they can be put into practice. For example, the principle that if all motorists going in a particular direction drive on the same side of the road there will be fewer crashes can be put into practice as the legal rule that all cars should drive on the left.

Rules can also be contrasted with policies. Policies are broad goals at which law may aim – in our example of driving on the left, the policy behind the law is that the risk of accidents should be minimized as far as possible. Other policy aims include increasing racial harmony or sexual equality, and again, they have to be translated into rules in order to be put into effect; so, for example, the policy of increasing racial harmony has been translated into legislation against racial discrimination.

Legal rules clearly fit into the definition of rules, and are different from legal principles and from the policy behind a law. But what makes them different from other types of rule?

Austin: the command theory

The seventeenth-century writer John Austin, in his book *The Province of Jurisprudence*, argued that law differed from other rules because it was the command of a sovereign body, which the state could enforce by means of punishment. The relevant sovereign body would vary in different countries; in Britain it was the Queen in Parliament, but in other countries it might be the monarch alone, or an emperor or president.

Austin's definition has fairly clear application to some areas of law, most obviously criminal law, where we are told we must do or not do certain things, with penalties for disobedience. But there are large areas which fall outside it. Contract law, for example, details the sanctions which can be imposed when contracts are broken, but it does not command us to make contracts in the first place. The law concerning marriage does not order anyone to marry; it simply sets out the conditions under which people may do so if they wish, the procedure they should follow to make the marriage legally valid, and the legal consequences of being married. The rules about marriage and contracts could be described as rules giving power, in contrast to the rules imposing duties which comprise criminal law; they have different functions, but both types are legal rules. As Professor Hart and other legal philosophers have pointed out, there are an enormous number of legal rules which neither make commands, nor impose sanctions. The complexity and variety of legal rules make it impossible to cover them all with the proposition that laws are commands.

Hart: primary and secondary rules

In his influential book *The Concept of Law*, Professor Hart attempted to link types of rules with types of legal systems. He divided legal rules into primary rules and secondary rules, and argued that the existence of secondary rules was a mark of a developed legal system.

Primary rules were described as those which any society needs in order to survive. These rules forbid the most socially destructive forms of behaviour – typically murder, theft and fraud – and also cover areas of civil law, such as tort. According to Hart, simple societies, which generally have a high degree of social cohesion, can survive with only these basic rules but as a society becomes more complex, it will require what he described as secondary rules.

Secondary rules confer power rather than impose duties, and can be divided into three types: rules of adjudication, rules of change and rules of recognition.

Rules of adjudication

In simple societies, the primary rules can be applied and enforced by means of informal social pressures within the group; this works because the community is close-knit, and individuals rely on each other. As societies become larger and more complex, these bonds are broken, and social pressures will not be enough to shape behaviour. Therefore the community needs some means of giving authority to its rules, and the secondary rules of adjudication are designed to provide this. They enable officials (usually judges) to decide disputes, and to define the procedures to be followed and the sanctions which can be applied when rules are broken. Examples of secondary rules in our society are those which lay down what kind of issues can be decided by courts, who is qualified to be a judge and sentencing legislation for criminal cases; there are many more.

Rules of change

The second type of secondary rule is concerned with making new rules, both primary and secondary. A developed society will need these to respond to new situations – perhaps the clearest example in our society is the huge number of laws introduced over the last century as a result of the invention of motorized transport. Rules of change lay down the procedure to be followed in making new rules or changing old ones. In our system, the main rules of change are those concerning how legislation is made and how judicial decisions become part of the common law.

There are also rules of change concerning the power of individuals to produce changes in the legal relationships they have with others.

Rules of recognition

The fact that in simple forms of society rules are enforced by social pressure means that they are only binding if the community as a whole accepts them. Within a small-scale, close-knit community it will generally be obvious to all what the accepted rules are. In a more complex society, this is not the case; there may be many rules, some of them complex, and individuals cannot be expected to know them all. To minimize uncertainty, the developed society, according to Hart, develops rules of recognition, which spell out which of the many rules that govern society actually have legal force. As Hart explains, in the simpler form of society we must wait and see whether a potential rule gets accepted as a rule or not; in a system with a basic rule of recognition we can say before a rule is actually made that it will be valid if it conforms to the requirements of the rule of recognition.

Hart described the UK as having a single rule of recognition: what the Queen in Parliament enacts is law. This leaves out the issue of judge-made law; the difficulties in pinpointing exactly how precedent works mean that a rule of recognition is more difficult to specify here, but it would certainly be inaccurate to say that only what the Queen in Parliament enacts is law.

Dworkin: legal principles

Professor Dworkin rejects Hart's analysis of law as consisting purely of rules. He argues that the rich fabric of law contains not just rules, but a set of principles on which all legal rules are based. Dworkin defines rules as operating in an all or nothing manner, stating a particular answer to a particular question. Legal principles, on the other hand, are guidelines, giving a reason that argues in one direction, but does not dictate a decision. Take, for example, a hypothetical murder of a father by his son. One of the legal principles Dworkin advances is that no one should benefit from their own wrong, and this should clearly be taken into account in deciding this dispute. But it does not dictate a particular answer; there may be other aspects to the dispute which make other principles a stronger influence (perhaps the son killed in self-defence, for example). By contrast, a rule that no one can inherit property from a person they have murdered is clear-cut and straightforward in application: the son cannot inherit from his father.

Other differences between principles and rules, according to Dworkin, are that principles have a dimension of weight or importance – a suggestion of morality – that rules lack. Conflicts between principles can be weighed up by a judge, and the background guidance they give means that, even in hard cases, they should provide a fairly clear answer: if rules clash, a further rule will be needed to establish which should prevail (for example, the rule that if law and equity conflict, equity prevails). Finally, the strength of a principle can become eroded over time, whereas rules stand until they are removed.

The natural law theory

The theories of Austin and Hart attempt to define what law is, without examining what it says: they could be said to look at the outside appearance of law, rather than defining it by its content. This approach is called positivism. Another school of thought, the natural law theory, defines law by its content: only laws which conform to a particular moral code, seen as a higher form of law, can genuinely be called law. This natural law theory is discussed on p. 552.

The function of law

Some writers have taken the view that law is best understood by looking at the role it plays in society: what is it for? The following are some of the key theories in this area.

Social cohesion

The nineteenth-century French sociologist, Emile Durkheim, looked at the issue of social cohesion, searching for what keeps a society together, and concluded that law played an important role in this area. He looked at the role of law in two contrasting types of society: the first a relatively simple, technologically undeveloped society; the second highly developed in terms of technology and social structure.

Durkheim argued that in the first type of society, the whole group would have clearly identifiable common aims, and would all work to achieve them: the interests of any individual within the group would be exactly the same as those of the group as a whole. A moral and legal code based on these aims would be recognized and accepted by all, and would keep the group working together. Durkheim called this mechanical solidarity. An individual who deviated from this code would be punished, and their punishment would reinforce the code by reflecting the group's disapproval of the wrongdoing.

According to Durkheim's analysis, as social groups become larger and more complex, developing links with other social groups, the interests of individual members become less closely linked to those of the group as a whole. To take a simple example, members of a forest tribe might hunt together to provide food for everyone, whereas in a developed society individuals and families look after their own interests. Social solidarity does not disappear but becomes based on increasing interdependence, which itself stems from the division of labour. Whereas, for example, in the small-scale society, each family would make its own bread, in the developed society this task is shared between farmer, flour mill, bakery and retailer, all dependent on each other and the consumer. This interdependence means that the individual has social importance in their own right, rather than occupying a social position simply as one member of the group.

Durkheim argued that these changes would be accompanied by a corresponding change in the type of law present in the society. Penal law would become less important and would increasingly be replaced by compensatory law, where the object is not to punish but to resolve grievances by restoring the injured party to the position they were in before the dispute arose. There would be less need for resolution of disputes between the individual and society, and more for those between individuals.

Durkheim's analysis has been criticized for overestimating the extent to which criminal law would decline and give way to compensatory law in an industrialized society: if anything, industrialized societies have increased the application of criminal law and, indeed, industrialization has created new crimes, such as computer fraud and pollution. Anthropological studies have shown that he also underestimated the degree to which compensatory or civil law already exists in simple societies.

Survival

Professor Hart argues that the main function of law is simply to allow human beings to survive in a community. He suggests that there are certain truths about human existence which, without rules guiding our behaviour, would make life excessively dangerous. Each member of society has, more or less, the same physical strength and intelligence, and both our powers of self-restraint and willingness to help others are limited. We therefore all face the danger of attack from the others and competition for such resources as are available. Knowing this, any group of humans will soon recognize that it needs rules curbing individual desires and impulses. We realize that, if we attack people or take their goods when they are weak, the same could easily happen to us. To protect ourselves we must accept limitations on our behaviour. The alternative would be a degree of conflict that would make it impossible for the group to stay together, yet individual members might be even less safe if they had to face the world alone.

The realization that we are not safe in the world alone and can only be safe in a community if there are rules of self-restraint, leads to the development of such rules, protecting the property and person of others. It also leads to acceptance of the idea that observance of the rules must be guaranteed by some kind of penalty directed against the rule-breaker. Hart maintains that such rules are the minimum necessary content of law in any society.

The maintenance of order

The German sociologist, Max Weber, argues that the primary role of law is to maintain order in society. Law makes individuals accept the legitimacy of their rules, and gives them the power to make law and coerce individuals into obeying it. Without this coercive power, argues Weber, order could not be maintained.

This idea has enjoyed much political support as political parties, from either side of the spectrum, are keen to present themselves as promoting law and order. But Weber's view can be criticized as overestimating the role of law in keeping order. If he is to be believed, a relaxation of law would result in the immediate degeneration of society into chaos and disorder; but this ignores the many other factors which make our society relatively orderly. In many cases we obey the law not because it is the law, but because of social or moral pressures – we do not steal, for example, because we have been brought up to think stealing is wrong, not because we might be caught and punished for it. Similarly, we may obey moral or social rules as strictly as we obey legal ones – we are unlikely to find ourselves in court for swearing at the vicar, but few of us would do it because of strong social and moral pressures.

Critics argue that Weber's theory fails to allow for the fact that societies are not just a loose group of independent individuals; they have clear patterns of behaviour, relationships and beliefs, which differ from society to society. These are what hold society together and, while law is one aspect of them, it is not the only force for social cohesion. Other social institutions which promote cohesion include the family and schools, which transmit social standards to new generations; political institutions (Parliament, political parties); economic and commercial institutions (trade unions, manufacturers' associations, patterns of production and trade); and religious and cultural institutions (such as literature and the arts, the press, television and radio). All of these play a part in establishing social rules.

The importance of these social rules can be seen if we compare a human society to a group of animals. Like animals, we have instincts to eat, sleep and mate. But whereas animals do all these things in response only to instinct and opportunity, our behaviour is controlled, directly and indirectly, through moral standards, religious doctrines, social traditions and legal rules. For example, like animals we are born with a mating instinct but, unlike animals, human societies attempt to channel this instinct into a form of relationship which has traditionally been seen as offering benefits for society: heterosexual marriage. As we have said, there are no legal rules commanding people to marry, but there are a great many social and moral pressures upholding heterosexual marriage as the desired form of relationship; the predominant religion in our history upholds it, and alternatives, such as homosexual relationships or heterosexual couples living together without marriage, have traditionally been seen as immoral and socially unacceptable. It can be argued that these pressures have, in the past, operated just as forcefully as laws do in other areas, though they now appear to be breaking down.

Balancing different interests

The US jurist, Roscoe Pound, saw law as a social institution, created and designed to satisfy human wants, both individual and social. Pound identified different interests in society, including individual, domestic, property, social and public interests. He argued that the law's main aim was to secure and balance these different and often competing interests.

Where interests on a different level conflicted – such as individual interests conflicting with social interests – they could not be weighted against each other, but where there is a conflict between interests on the same level, they must be weighed against one another with the aim of ensuring that as many as possible are satisfied.

'Law jobs'

Karl Llewellyn was a member of the US realist school of thought which, like the positivists, is concerned with what law is, rather than what it ought to be. Working with Hoebel, an anthropologist, Llewellyn studied American Indian groups and, from this research, constructed a theory of 'law jobs' to explain the social functions of law.

Llewellyn's theory is that every social group has certain jobs which need to be done for it to survive, and law is one of the main ways in which these jobs are done. The jobs include preventing disruptive disputes within the group; providing a means of resolving disputes which do arise; allocating authority and providing mechanisms for constructing relationships between people, including ways of adjusting to change. Although these jobs are common to all societies, the ways in which the jobs are done will vary from society to society. For example, the allocation of authority in a simple society might be done by basic rules on electing or appointing a chief, while in a more complex society, this job can be done by a constitution.

Robert Summers has also looked at law in terms of the various jobs it does for society, and identified five main uses of law: putting right grievances among members of a society; prohibiting and prosecuting forbidden behaviour; promoting certain defined activities; conferring social and governmental benefits, including education and welfare; and giving effect to private arrangements, such as contracts. Although their theses are different, both Llewellyn and Summers look at law in its social context, in contrast to writers such as Austin who believe rules, including legal rules, can be analysed without reference to their settings.

Exploitation

A radical alternative to the views of writers such as Durkheim and Weber is put forward by Karl Marx. Durkheim and Weber disagreed about the precise functions of law, but they accepted the idea that law must in some way be of benefit to society as a whole. Marx, however, rejected the idea that there was a common interest in society which law could serve. He argued that society was composed of classes whose interests were fundamentally opposed to each other. Law, Marx maintained, was not made in the interests of society as a whole, but in the interests of the small group which dominates society; through law (and other social institutions, such as religion), this group is able to exploit the working class, which Marx called the proletariat.

Later Marxist writers, such as Althusser and Gramsci, have developed this thesis. They argue that the ruling class controls the ideology of society, including the beliefs and ideas which shape it. This ideology is expressed through social institutions such as the school, the family, religion and the law. By shaping the way in which people see the world around them, the ruling class is able to ensure that the working class see their exploitation as natural, as the only way things could be, rather than as the oppressive state of affairs that Marxists see. This minimizes their resistance.

Law is seen as an important part of this process. Because, for example, the law protects private property, we come to view private property and all its implications as natural and inevitable. Take, for example, the acceptance of profit. If someone pays £100 for a set of raw materials, and pays an employee £100 to turn those materials into goods which they then sell for £600, it is quite acceptable in our society for the employer to keep the profit, because they purchased both the raw materials and the employee's labour. Clearly, an acceptance of people making a profit out of another's labour is fundamental to acceptance of the capitalist system as a whole, and the legal doctrine of private property is the basis of this acceptance. But Marxists point out that the situation can be looked at in another way, as the employer stealing from the worker the added value their labour gives to the raw materials. The fact that we would not usually think to see it this way is, Marxists say, because we see it through a capitalist ideology, and law plays a fundamental role in upholding this ideology.

Marx believed that law was only needed because of the fundamental clash of interests between those of the ruling class and those of the proletariat; once society was transformed by communism, these divisions would no longer exist, and law would wither away.

Why are laws obeyed?

Austin thought laws were obeyed because of the threat of sanction and out of a habit of obedience to the state. Hart rejects this explanation, arguing that acceptance of a rule is more important than possible sanctions. As well as the external aspect of obedience – recognition of the validity of the rule, and a potential sanction – Hart argues that there is an internal process, which inclines us to obey because we consider it right and proper to do so. Hart suggests that if a law is not internalized, an individual will feel no obligation to obey it. In our system there are many examples of laws which for some reason widely fail this internalization test: parking offences, speeding, tax evasion and drug legislation are obvious examples of laws which large numbers of people apparently feel no real compulsion to follow. He suggests that in order for law to promote social cohesion in a simple society with only primary rules, members must not only obey those rules, but also consciously see them as common standards of behaviour, breaches of which can legitimately be criticized: in other words, they internalize all the rules, following them not just because they are rules, but because they consider it right to do so. But, in a more developed legal system like ours, Hart believes individuals need not internalize every rule. It is clearly desirable for them to internalize as many as possible, but, failing this, the necessary functions can be served by officials internalizing the rules and, thereby, becoming committed to their maintenance.

Fear and internalization

If we obey laws because we internalize them, what makes us internalize some rules and not others? One theory, put forward by Professor Olivercrona, suggests that fear is a strong motivation. He points out that we are all aware from childhood of the consequences of breaking rules and, as a result, we experience a tension between temptation to break rules and fear of punishment. Olivercrona suggests that the human mind cannot accommodate such tension indefinitely, and so we gradually adjust psychologically to accept conformity to rules as a means of getting rid of the fear of punishment; eventually we do not believe we are acting out of fear at all, we have just become used to keeping the rules.

Perhaps because of the efficacy of this process, many writers have suggested that law can be used to shape moral and social ideas. Aristotle suggested that law could be used to educate citizens, commenting that 'Legislators make citizens good by forming their habits'. More recently, Lord Simon of Glaisdale has observed that law still has an educative function, which it exercises when certain conduct becomes stigmatized by becoming illegal.

On the other hand, social pressures can often bring about changes in conduct which legal rules have been unable to do. A recent example is that of drink-driving. At one time this offence was seen as being in a similar category to speeding or parking offences; it was against the law, but many still saw it as acceptable. Now, as a result of social pressures, partly driven by public information campaigns, it is viewed as highly antisocial behaviour, and the law is apparently more widely obeyed.

ANSWERING QUESTIONS

1 (a) Distinguish between rules, principles and policy as they apply to law. *(10 marks)*

(b) Assess the contribution of principles and policy to the development of rules of law. *(15 marks) AQA (AEB)*

Part (a): this part of the question is fairly straightforward. You need to explain what rules, principles and policy are, highlighting the separate meanings each of them have in the context of law. Give examples of each – you might give an example of a legal rule, such as that all cars drive on the left, the principle behind it (that if all cars drive in the same direction on each side of the road, there will be fewer crashes), and the policy behind it (that accidents should be prevented as far as possible).

Part (b): Now take some areas of law which you have studied and, taking some specific rules of law, discuss how far, and in what way, principles and policies have contributed to their development. Discuss each separately – on the subject of principles, for example, the principle of no liability without fault could be explained through rules of criminal and/or civil law. Then move on to policy – you might look at the policy behind legislation, such as consumer protection or race discrimination, or the policy behind the judicial decisions which have led to the development of the law of negligence.

Whatever areas of law you choose to discuss, you should give detailed examples of the rules you are discussing, and analyse the contribution of principles and policy to them.

2 **Can society exist without law? Consider the issues involved in this question.** *Edexcel*

This type of question allows many different approaches all of which could be very successful. One approach would be to use the material under the heading 'the function of law' at pp. 541–45. You could consider each theory in turn and consider whether, if that theory is right, there would be a society without law. For example, Durkheim suggests that law achieves social cohesion, without law you could only have a primitive society and not a technologically advanced society, while Karl Marx considers that law is merely a tool for exploitation and that without law we could enjoy a much healthier society.

26 Law and morals

Morals are beliefs and values which are shared by a society, or a section of a society; they tell those who share them what is right or wrong. In our society, moral values have been heavily influenced by the dominant religion, Christianity, though this is not our only source of moral values.

Debates about morals and morality often centre around sexual issues, such as sex outside marriage, homosexuality and pornography. But moral values also shape attitudes towards money and property, gender roles, friendship, behaviour at work – in fact it is difficult to think of any area of our lives where morality has no application. Mary Warnock, an academic who has been involved in inquiries into issues of moral concern, says: 'I do not believe that there is a neat way of marking off moral issues from all others; some people, at some time, may regard things as matters of moral right or wrong, which at another time or in another place are thought to be matters of taste, or indeed to be matters of no importance at all.' However, she points out that in any society, at any time, questions relating to birth and death and to the establishing of families are regarded as morally significant. These can perhaps be regarded as core moral issues.

As Warnock has observed, moral attitudes tend to change over time. It is only within the last couple of decades, for example, that the idea of couples living together without marriage has become widely accepted; even now acceptance is not total, but a generation ago it would have been unthinkable. Similar shifts have taken place with regard to homosexuality and women's liberation.

The French sociologist, Durkheim, has highlighted the fact that in a modern, developed society it is difficult to pinpoint a set of moral values shared by all. In less developed societies, such as small tribal groups, Durkheim argued that all the members of the group are likely to share a moral code; but, in a technologically advanced society such as our own, where individuals differ widely in social status, income, occupation, ethnic background and so on, its members are unlikely to share identical moral values, even if they largely agree on some basic points. For example, most people in the UK agree that it is usually wrong to kill or steal, but there is much less consensus on whether it is wrong to take drugs, have abortions, experiment on animals or help a terminally ill person to die. Even on the basic crimes of theft and murder, some people will see these as always wrong, while others will believe there are situations in which they may be justified; among the latter, there will be disagreement as to what those situations are.

Criminologist Jock Young has pointed out that much depends on the standpoint of the observer, and how they see the norms of society. Looking at attitudes to illegal drug use, Young has observed that to those who see society's rules as based on a moral consensus, drug-taking was against that moral consensus, so those who indulged in it were therefore maladjusted and sick. But, if society's rules on deviant behaviour are seen simply as a yardstick of what that particular society considers normal, drug-taking is neither necessarily deviant nor necessarily a social problem: it is merely deviant to groups who condemn it and a problem to those who wish to eliminate it. What is being made is simply a value judgment, and values vary between people and over time.

▶ Law and morality

Both law and morals are normative; they specify what ought to be done, and aim to mark the boundaries between acceptable and unacceptable conduct. While moral rules tend not to be backed by the obvious sanctions which make some legal rules enforceable, they are often reinforced by pressures which in some cases may be as strong, if not stronger: the disapproval of family and friends, loss of status, and being shunned by the community are powerful disincentives against immoral conduct. Of course many types of undesirable behaviour offend against both moral and legal rules – serious crimes are obvious examples.

Both law and morals are often presented as if they were the only possible responses to social or political problems and crises, yet both vary widely between societies. For example, in our society, private property is such a basic doctrine that we readily condemn any infringement of our rights – legal and moral – to acquire, possess and enjoy our personal property. Stealing is seen as immoral as well as illegal. But in a society where property is held communally, any attempt by one individual to treat property as their own private possession would be regarded every bit as immoral as we would consider stealing. The idea of private property is not a basic part of human nature, as it is often presented, but a socially constructed value. Our society has for centuries been based on trade, and this requires a basis of private property.

Some areas of law are explicitly presented as raising moral issues and, when these areas arise in Parliament, MPs are allowed to vote according to their own beliefs, rather than according to party policy. This is called a vote of conscience and was used, for example, when the issue of capital punishment was debated. However, the kinds of issue on which a vote of conscience would be allowed are not the only ones to which moral values apply: when MPs vote on tax changes, the welfare state, employment or any number of issues before Parliament in every session, they are voting on moral issues, because they are voting on the way a Government treats its citizens, and the way in which citizens are allowed to treat each other.

Similarly, some areas of law, such as criminal law, have obvious moral implications, but these are also present in areas where morality is less obvious. Tort law, for example, and especially negligence, is built around the principle that those who harm others should compensate for the damage done; that, as Lord Atkin noted in the famous case of **Donoghue** *v* **Stevenson** (1932), the biblical principle of 'love thy neighbour' must include 'do not harm your neighbour'. Similarly, contract, as Atiyah has pointed out, is based around the principle that promises should be kept. Even land law which, on the surface, appears to consist of technicalities far removed from elevated questions of morality, has enormous moral importance because it is upholding the whole notion of property and ownership. Take the question of squatting: the property owner has all the rights to begin with but, if the squatting continues for long enough, the squatter can gain some rights. Is it moral that the property owner should lose rights to someone acting illegally? On the other hand, is it moral that some should be homeless while others have property they can afford to leave empty?

Changes in law and morality

As we have observed, the moral values of a society tend to change over time; the same applies to its laws. In the UK, legal changes have tended to lag behind moral ones, coming only when the process of moral acceptance is well advanced. Thus, the law was changed in 1991 to make rape within marriage a crime, the House of Lords stating that the change was necessary because marriages were now seen as equal partnerships, in which the husband could no longer enforce rights to sex. This shift in attitude had taken place long before 1991, but the time-lag between moral change and legal change was fairly typical. Often it is the possession of effective political power which finally determines which and whose definition of morality is reflected in the law.

On the other hand, law can sometimes bring about changes in social morality. Troy Duster, in *The Legislation of Morality* (1970), traced the history of drug use and its legal control in the US from the end of the nineteenth century. At that time, drug addiction was commonly restricted to the middle and upper classes, who had become dependent on morphine through the use of patented medicines; despite the fact that these contained morphine, it was perfectly legal to buy and sell them. Addiction carried no social stigma. However, when certain drugs were made illegal under the Harrison Act 1914, such drugs began to be supplied by the criminal underworld. Dependency on drugs became associated with this underworld and with the lower classes who had most contact with it. This in turn led to social stigma. Interestingly, this stigma, which was in a sense created by legal controls, was partly responsible for the calls for greater legal controls on drug-taking which have been heard over the last two decades, as more and more young people become involved in the drug culture.

Academics from the Scandinavian realist standpoint, such as Oliver-crona, argue that our morality is created by the law, rather than the law emerging from our morality. Olivercrona suggests that law has an influence on us from our earliest days, helping to mould our moral views. From the start, parents and teachers tell us what we must and must not do and we quickly learn the consequences of disobedience.

Differences between law and morality

Although law and morality are clearly closely linked, there are certain ways in which they differ. Many types of behaviour exist which may be widely considered to be immoral, yet we would be very surprised to find laws against them: telling lies, for example. Equally, some forms of behaviour are illegal, but would not usually be described as immoral, such as parking on a yellow line. Then there are areas where the law shares morality's disapproval, but not so far as to prohibit the relevant behaviour. Adultery, for example, is not illegal in this country, but it has long constituted grounds for a divorce, an important legal step for individuals.

The problem for the law in deciding whether to respond to appeals to morality is that there are very often conflicting moral views in a given situation. We can see this in the case of **Gillick** *v* **West Norfolk and Wisbech Area Health Authority** (1986). The claimant, Mrs Victoria Gillick, was a Roman Catholic. She objected to advice given to doctors from the Department of Health and Social Security that, in exceptional cases, they could offer contraceptive advice and treatment to girls under 16, without parental consent. Mrs Gillick sought a declaration that this advice was illegal because it encouraged under-age sex.

Mrs Gillick lost at first instance, won in the Court of Appeal and lost by a majority in the House of Lords. The House held that the guidelines were lawful because they concerned what were essentially medical matters. In this field, girls under 16 had the legal capacity to consent to a medical examination and treatment, including contraceptive treatment, as long as they were sufficiently mature and intelligent to understand the nature and implications of the proposed treatment. The majority, in reaching this conclusion, stressed they were merely applying the law as it stood rather than taking a moral standpoint; the minority referred to the kind of moral arguments Mrs Gillick had advanced. This does not mean that, in rejecting Mrs Gillick's view, the majority ignored morality, even though they claimed to be making an objective decision. It could be argued that if teenage girls were likely to have sexual intercourse anyway, preventing doctors from giving contraceptive help would simply increase the chances of unwanted pregnancies and it would, therefore, be moral to protect girls from that. Neither approach is objectively wrong or right; in this, as in many areas, there are opposing moral views.

Should law and morality be separate?

The view taken by Mrs Gillick would seem to suggest that if something is immoral it should also be illegal and, to the person who holds strong moral opinions, this may seem a natural conclusion. But there are problems with it. First, moral opinions, however strongly held, are just that; moral opinions. Mrs Gillick believes under-age girls should not be given contraception and many people agree with her, but many others disagree. Which group's moral opinions should be adopted by the law?

Even if there were complete consensus, the logistics of enforcing as legal rules all the moral rules of our society would present enormous problems. How would we pay for the necessary manpower, both for policing and prosecutions? What sanctions would be severe enough to compel obedience, yet not too severe for the nature of the offences? Making every immoral act also illegal seems both impossible and undesirable, yet law with no connection to morality might find it difficult to command much respect. There is still much debate as to how far law should reflect morality; the following are some of the key suggestions.

Natural law

Natural law theorists argue that law should strongly reflect morality. Though their specific theories differ, their shared premise is that there is a kind of higher law, known as the natural law, to which we can turn for a basic moral code: some, such as St Thomas Aquinas, see this higher law as coming from God, others see it as simply the foundations of a human society. The principles in this higher law should be reflected in the laws societies make for themselves; laws which do not reflect these principles cannot really be called law at all, and in some cases need not be obeyed. The campaign, during the 1980s, against payment of the Poll Tax on the grounds that it was unfair might be seen as an example of this kind of disobedience.

Different natural law theorists disagree as to the actual content of natural law, but it is usually felt to embody basic human rights which governments should respect. Bills of Rights, like that in the US Constitution, could be seen as embodying natural law principles. Professor Lon

Fuller, in *The Morality of Law*, talked about law's inner morality which he formulated in terms of eight procedural requirements of a legal system:

1 Generality: there should be rules, not *ad hoc* judgments.
2 Promulgation: the rules should be made known to all those affected by them.
3 Non-retroactivity: rules should not have retrospective effect.
4 Clarity: rules should be understandable.
5 Consistency: rules should not conflict.
6 Realism: people should not be required to do the impossible.
7 Constancy: rules should not be changed so frequently that people cannot use them to guide their behaviour.
8 Congruence: the actual administration of the rules should coincide with the information available to the public about them.

Fuller claims that a legal system which fails in any one of these areas is not just a bad system, it is not a legal system at all. As an example, he gives the legal system of Nazi Germany: although laws were made by recognized methods, in Fuller's view the system's failure to meet the above criteria meant that those laws were not really law at all.

Utilitarianism

During the nineteenth century, the rise of science and the beginning of the decline in the social importance of religion meant that natural law theories declined. In their place the theory of utilitarianism grew up, apparently offering a rational and scientific theory of law. One of the best-known exponents of this theory is John Stuart Mill. He argued that rather than society imposing morality on individuals, individuals should be free to choose their own conduct, so long as in doing so they did not harm others or, if they did, that the harm done did not outweigh the harm which would be done by interfering with individual liberty.

The view that people should be left alone to do what they like so long as they do not harm others remains influential today, but it is open to criticism. First, the fact that someone's actions do not cause another direct and physical harm, in the way Mill envisaged, does not necessarily mean they do no harm at all. For example, opponents of pornography claim that while looking at pornography may not directly inspire individual users to rape, the fact that pornography is available and, to a degree, accepted, promotes the view that women are sexual objects which, in turn, promotes sexual violence against women.

Secondly, who counts as another? This issue is clearly at the heart of debates over abortion and experimentation on embryos: does harming an unborn child count as harming another person, and from what point? The fact that abortion is legal up until a certain stage in pregnancy suggests that the law sees this as the moment at which the foetus becomes another: many people believe that point is reached earlier in pregnancy, and those opposed to abortion believe it is at the time of conception. On the other hand, many people who support the law on abortion nevertheless disapprove of experiments on embryos, even though their views of abortion might suggest that the embryo is not another at this point.

Crimes without victims

Modern theories which subscribe, at least partly, to Mill's view of individual liberty have tended to focus on what are often called victimless crimes. Using the examples of drug use, homosexuality and abortion, all of which were illegal at the time in which he was writing, in *Crimes Without Victims* (1965), the academic Schur observes that the common characteristics of such crimes are that they involve no harm to anyone except the participants; they occur through the willing participation of those involved; and, as a result, there is no victim to make a complaint, rendering the law difficult to enforce. Schur argues that there is a social demand for these activities, which continues to be met despite illegality, through such means as back street abortions and black market drug supply. There is no proof that prohibition of such activities brought greater social benefits than decriminalization, therefore there is no good reason to prohibit them.

As with John Stuart Mill, the main criticism of Schur's theory is his assertion that these activities harm no one who has not willingly taken part in them. Anti-abortionists would certainly dispute this as far as abortion is concerned. A further criticism is directed at the suggestion that participants join in these activities of their own free will; in the case of drug-taking, for example, that may be so at first, but can we really say that, once addicted, drug users take drugs of their own free will?

The Hart–Devlin Debate

The issue of whether or not law should follow morality was hotly debated during the late 1950s, when there was public concern about what was perceived to be a decline in sexual morality. The Government of the day set up a commission to look at whether the laws on homosexuality and prostitution should be changed, and much debate was triggered by publication of the commission's findings, known as the Wolfenden Report. Central to this debate were the writings of the leading judge, Lord Devlin, who opposed the report's findings, and Professor Hart who approved of them.

The Wolfenden Committee recommended that homosexuality and prostitution should be legalized, with some restrictions. Its reasoning was based on the notion that some areas of behaviour had to be left to individual morality, rather than being supervised by the law. The purpose of the criminal law, said the Report, was:

to preserve public order and decency, to protect the citizen from what is offensive and injurious and to provide sufficient safeguards against exploitation and corruption of others especially the vulnerable, that is the young, weak in body or mind, inexperienced or those in a state of physical, official or economic dependence. The law should not intervene in the private lives of citizens or seek to enforce any particular pattern of behaviour further than necessary to carry out the above purposes.

The reasoning is very like that of Mill: leave people to make their own choices, so long as they do not harm others. The Committee therefore recommended that prostitution itself should not be an offence, since the individual ought to be allowed to choose whether to take part in it, but activities associated with prostitution which could cause offence to others (such as soliciting in the street) were still to be regulated by the law.

Lord Devlin was opposed to this approach. He argued that some form of common morality, with basic agreement on good and evil, was necessary to keep society together. This being the case, the law had every right – and in fact a duty – to uphold that common morality. He compared contravention of public morality to treason, in the sense that it was something society had to protect itself against. How are we to know what this public morality consists of? Devlin argued that we can judge immorality by the standard of the right-minded person, who could perhaps be thought of as the person in the jury box. Opinions should be reached after informed and educated discussion of all relevant points of view and, if there is still debate, the majority view should prevail, as it does in the ordinary legislative process.

In addition, said Devlin, there was a set of basic principles which should be followed by the legislature. First, individuals should be allowed the maximum of freedom consistent with the integrity of society, and privacy should be respected as much as possible. Secondly, punishment should be reserved for that which creates disgust among right-minded people, and society has the right to eradicate any practice which is so abominable that its very presence is an offence. Law-makers should be slow to change laws which protect morality. Thirdly, the law should set down a minimum standard of morality; society's standards should be higher.

Reaction to Devlin's thesis was mixed. Those who felt the Wolfenden Report had gone too far agreed with him, and there were many of them – the commission's recommendations seem rather tame now, but at the time they were ground-breaking. Others felt that his approach was out of step with the times. Hart, who was influenced by John Stuart Mill and, therefore, approved of the commission's approach, led this opposition. Hart argued that using law to enforce moral values was unnecessary, undesirable and morally unacceptable: unnecessary because society was capable of containing many moral standpoints without disintegrating; undesirable because it would freeze morality at a particular point; and morally unacceptable because it infringes the liberty of the individual. Devlin's response was that individual liberty could only flourish in a stable society: disintegration of our society through lack of a shared morality would, therefore, threaten individual freedom.

Hart pointed out that the standard of the right-minded person is a tenuous one. When people object to unusual behaviour, the response is not always prompted by rational moral objections, but often by prejudice, ignorance or misunderstanding. He gave four basic reasons why moral censure should not necessarily lead to legal sanctions. First, punishing the offender involves doing some harm to them, when they may have done no harm to others. Secondly, the exercise of free choice by individuals is a moral value in itself, with which it is wrong to interfere. Thirdly, this exercise of free choice can be valuable in that it allows individuals to experiment and learn. Finally, as far as sexual morality is concerned, the suppression of sexual impulses affects the development or balance of the individual's emotional life, happiness and personality and, thus, causes them harm. He objects strongly to the idea that the law should punish behaviour which does not harm others, but merely causes them distress or disgust by its very existence, even when conducted out of their sight: recognition of individual liberty as a value involves, as a minimum, acceptance of the principle that individuals may do what they want, even if others are distressed when they learn what it is that they do, unless, of course, there are other good grounds for forbidding it.

Judicial support for Devlin's view – and perhaps reaction against liberalizing legislation – can be seen in some of the more high-profile cases which arose in its aftermath. In **Shaw** *v* **Director of Public Prosecutions** (1961), Shaw had published a booklet entitled *The Ladies' Directory*, which contained advertisements by prostitutes, featuring photographs and descriptions of the sexual practices they offered. He was convicted of the crime of conspiring to corrupt public morals, an offence which had not been prosecuted since the eighteenth century. The House of Lords upheld the conviction and, defending the court's power to uphold the recognition of such an antiquated offence, Viscount Simonds said: 'In the sphere of criminal law I entertain no doubt that there remains in the courts of law a residual power to enforce the supreme and fundamental purpose of the law, to conserve not only the safety and order but also the moral welfare of the State.' As an example of offences against this moral welfare, Viscount Simonds said:

> Let it be supposed that at some future, perhaps early, date homosexual practices between consenting adult males are no longer a crime. Would it not be an offence if, even without obscenity, such practices were publicly advocated and encouraged by pamphlet and advertisement?

This proved to be an uncannily accurate prediction: in 1967 the Sexual Offences Act was passed, which stated that homosexual acts between consenting adult males in private were no longer a criminal offence.

In **Knuller** v **Director of Public Prosecutions** (1972), the defendants were prosecuted for having published in their magazine, *International Times*, advertisements placed by readers inviting others to contact them for homosexual purposes. Once again, the charge was conspiracy to corrupt public morals and the court convicted. Lord Reid (who had dissented from the majority decision in Shaw's case, but felt that **Shaw** should still apply to avoid inconsistency) recognized that the 1967 Act legalized homosexual acts, but said:

> I find nothing in that Act to indicate that Parliament thought or intended to lay down that indulgence in these practices is not corrupting. I read the Act as saying that, even though it may be corrupting, if people choose to corrupt themselves in this way that is their affair and the law will not interfere. But no licence is given to others to encourage the practice.

More recent decisions still show judicial support for the Devlin viewpoint that some acts are intrinsically immoral, regardless of whether they harm others. In **R** v **Gibson** (1991), an artist exhibited earrings made from freeze-dried foetuses of three to four months' gestation. A conviction for the common law offence of outraging public decency was upheld. The appellants in **R** v **Brown** (1992) were homosexual men who had willingly participated in the commission of acts of sado-masochistic violence against each other, involving the use of, among other things, heated wires, mappins, stinging nettles, nails, sandpaper and safety-pins. Evidence showed that all the men involved had consented; although the activities were videotaped by the participants, this was not for any profit or gain; none of the injuries were permanent and no medical attention had been sought; the activities were carried out in private; and none of the victims had complained to the police. They were convicted of committing a range of offences against the person and appealed to the House of Lords, arguing that since all the participants had consented and the activities took place in private, the law had no reason to intervene. Their convictions were upheld; by a majority, the House held that public policy demanded such acts be treated as criminal offences. This decision was subsequently approved by the European Court of Human Rights.

The Warnock Committee

Despite the debate between Devlin and Hart, their two views are not always as opposed as they may seem, and in practice both are influential: a recent Government commission, the Warnock Committee, incorporates features of both approaches in its reasoning. The Committee was set up by the Government to consider issues relating to scientific advances concerning conception and pregnancy. With the advent of *in vitro* fertilization (the technique used to create test-tube babies) and other technological advances, new scientific possibilities have arisen. These include the possibility of creating embryos for use in medical experiments, sperm, egg and embryo donation by fertile men or women to those who are infertile, and the use of surrogate mothers – women who bear a child for another couple, using their own egg and the father's sperm. These practices raised a number of moral issues, including that of payment for surrogacy, and the parentage of children born from donated eggs and sperm.

The Committee's report, published in 1984, advised the setting up of an independent statutory body to monitor, regulate and license infertility services and embryo experiments. On the specific issues before them, they recommended that experiments on embryos up to 14 days old should be lawful; and that sperm, egg and embryo donation should be facilitated in that the babies born could be registered as the legitimate children of the non-contributing parent(s) on the birth certificate, and donors should be relieved of parental rights and duties in law. But surrogacy arrangements met with disapproval by the majority, who recommended that surrogacy agencies should be criminally prohibited, and private surrogacy arrangements between individuals should be illegal and unenforceable in the courts – although no criminal sanction would be imposed as it would be against the child's interests to be born into a family threatened by imprisonment. Many of the Committee's conclusions became law in the Human Fertilisation and Embryology Act 1990.

If we look at the reasoning behind the Committee's findings, we can see aspects of both Hart's utilitarian approach, and Devlin's upholding of common morality. In its conclusions on embryo research, it points out:

> We do not want to see a situation in which human embryos are frivolously or unnecessarily used in research but we are bound to take account of the fact that the advances in the treatment of infertility, which we have discussed in the earlier part of this report, could not have taken place without such research; and that continued research is essential, if advances in treatment and medical knowledge are to continue. A majority of us therefore agreed that research on human embryos should continue.

But this utilitarian approach is balanced against issues of morality.

> A strict utilitarian would suppose that, given procedures, it would be possible to calculate their benefits and their costs. Future advantages, therapeutic or scientific, should be weighed against present and future harm. However, even if such a calculation were possible, it could not provide a final or verifiable answer to the question whether it is right that such procedures should be carried out. There would still remain the possibility that they were unacceptable, whatever their long-term benefits were supposed to be. Moral questions, such as those with which we have been concerned are,

by definition, questions that involve not only a calculation of consequences, but also strong sentiments with regard to the nature of the proposed activities themselves.

As the report shows, issues of law and morality cannot easily be separated into distinct theoretical approaches like those of Hart and Devlin; legislators in practice have to tread an uneasy path between the two.

The Human Fertilisation and Embryology Authority

The Human Fertilisation and Embryology Act 1990 created the Human Fertilisation and Embryology Authority (HFEA). Areas of debate on morality and the need for law to prevent immorality have centred in recent years around new scientific developments. In the field of human genetics it is difficult for the law to keep up with the changes in scientific knowledge and the moral dilemmas which these can give rise to. The birth of Dolly, the cloned sheep, has caused particular concern. In January 1998 the Human Genetics Advisory Commission and the HFEA jointly published a consultation paper inviting views on various issues raised by cloning technology. The most troubling questions focused on the legality, ethics and practical consequences of human and reproductive cloning. The Authority's policy at the moment is not to license any research having reproductive cloning as its aim.

The Human Genetics Advisory Group has now recommended that controlled research using embryos (which are eggs that have been fertilized), should be allowed in order to increase understanding about human disease and disorders, and their treatment. It has recommended that reproductive cloning of human beings should remain a criminal offence. The Government has accepted these recommendations.

A case that caused some controversy is that of **R v Human Fertilisation and Embryology Authority, ex parte Blood** (1997). In that case the husband of Diane Blood contracted meningitis and lapsed into a coma. The applicant asked for samples of his sperm to be collected for future use in artificial insemination. The samples were entrusted to a research trust for storage. The husband died and the Human Fertilisation and Embryology Authority prevented the research trust from releasing the samples from storage, on the ground that the written consent of the donor to the taking of his sperm had not been obtained as required by the relevant statute. The applicant sought judicial review of the Authority's decision. The Court of Appeal ruled that the applicant could have the sperm samples and undergo treatment for an artificially assisted pregnancy. The Authority's decision had been lawful under the terms of the statute but the circumstances were exceptional and had not been foreseen by Parliament when passing the regulatory legislation. Judicial discretion was sufficiently flexible to grant the remedy which the compassionate circumstances demanded, particularly as the legal situation had never before been explored. Subsequently the Authority gave permission for Mrs Blood to export her husband's sperm provided she attended a fertility clinic abroad for treatment.

Recent issues handled by HFEA include the number of fertilized eggs that can be implanted at one time during fertilization treatment and the use of frozen eggs, which is now allowed in the UK.

It is likely that some of the future decisions of HFEA could be the subject of litigation relying on the Human Rights Act 1998. Arguments could be raised under the European Convention on Human Rights, and in particular Art. 2 (the right to life), Art. 8 (the right to respect of one's family life) and Art. 12 (the right to marry and to found a family).

▶ ANSWERING QUESTIONS

1 **To what extent are moral views significant in the development of law?** *AQA (AEB)*

A good start to this essay would be to define the meaning of morality – you could do this by contrasting moral rules with rules of law. Point out that although morality is often talked of in connection with sexual issues, it is actually a much broader concept, covering many areas of law.

If you give morality this broad definition, you can argue that moral values have influenced most, if not all, areas of law, illustrating this point with areas of law you have studied in detail. For example, if you have studied contract law, you might consider the moral view which holds that some promises should be binding and others not; in criminal law, you could discuss the idea of *mens rea* as being indicative of moral fault, and the values behind some of the defences. You need to make this part of the essay quite detailed, giving specific examples from case and statute law which back up your points.

You might then go on to make the point that some areas of law seem to have an overtly moral content, but that here again, morals are not absolute – the **Gillick** case is an example of a situation where the two sides each believed that their view represented morality.

Finally, you could discuss how far morality should influence the law, using the theoretical arguments of Devlin and Hart, and relating them to cases which you know, such as the case of **R** v **Brown** where criminal liability was imposed on homosexual sado-masochists.

2 **With reference to the role of law in modern society, consider whether there are any circumstances in which civil disobedience may be justified.** *Edexcel*

In your introduction you could explain what is meant by civil disobedience and give recent examples of where the UK has seen such behaviour, for example, during the Poll Tax riots, the animal rights protests, the Greenham Common women and demonstrations against road developments in the interests of protecting the environment.

You are asked to consider the issue of civil disobedience in the context of the role of law in a modern society, so you need to consider what that role is. The material in the previous chapter under the heading 'The function of law' will be useful to you here. If you accept Marx's theory, the role of the law is to sustain the capitalist ideology and continue the oppression of the proletariat. If this is the case then civil disobedience would always seem to be justified as a means of ending that injustice and reaching the point when the law can 'wither away'. You could draw attention to the natural law theorists who mainly accept that laws failing to reach the standards of the higher, natural law are not laws at all and can, therefore, be disobeyed.

On the other hand, academics such as Durkheim and Weber would consider that obedience of the law is very important for the cohesion of society and the maintenance of order.

Finally you could consider some of the specific areas of our substantive law, such as the Criminal Justice and Public Order Act 1994 and the absence of an entrenched Bill of Rights and consider how far in the UK civil disobedience is justified.

3 'The law ... is at its best when it is enforcing practical remedies for specific crimes; it is at its worst when it tries to enforce the morality of one group in society upon another ...' (*Clinging to the Wreckage*, John Mortimer QC)
To what extent should the law enforce morality? *Edexcel*

This is a standard question on the relationship between law and morality and the central part of your essay would discuss the Hart–Devlin debate.

▶ Reading on the Internet

The website of the Human Fertilisation and Embryology Authority is:
http://www.hfea.gov.uk/

27 Law and justice

Achieving justice is often seen as one of the most basic aims of a legal system. When areas of that system go wrong, the result is often described as injustice: for example, when people are convicted of crimes they have not committed, as in the recent cases of the Tottenham Three and the Birmingham Six, we say that a miscarriage of justice has occurred. But what is justice, and what is its relationship with law? These questions have been addressed by writers throughout the centuries, and we will look at some of the most important views in this chapter.

Aristotle

The Greek philosopher Aristotle is responsible for some of the earliest thinking on justice, and his work is still influential today. He considered that a just law was one which would allow individuals to fulfil themselves in society, and distinguished between distributive justice and corrective justice.

Distributive justice was concerned with the allocation of assets such as wealth and honour between members of the community. Here the aim of justice was to achieve proportion, but this did not mean equal shares; Aristotle thought that individuals should receive benefits in proportion to their claim on those benefits.

Corrective justice, on the other hand, applies when a situation that is distributively just, is disturbed – for example, by wrongdoing. A judge should discover what damage has been done, and then try to restore equality by imposing penalties to confiscate any gain made by the offence, and compensate for any damage caused.

Natural law theories

Natural law theories assume that there is a higher order of law, and if the laws of society follow this order they will be just. Aristotle supported this view, and believed that the higher law could be discovered from nature; others, such as the medieval scholar St Aquinas, thought that the higher law derived from God.

For Aquinas, there were two ways in which law could be unjust. First, a law which was contrary to human good, whether in its form or in its result, was, according to Aquinas, not true law at all. However, such laws might still be obeyed if to do so would avoid causing social disorder. Secondly, a law which was against God's will, and therefore a violation of the natural law, should be disregarded.

▶ Utilitarianism

The utilitarian movement, which includes such writers as Mill and Bentham, is based on the idea that society should work towards the greatest happiness for the greatest number, even if this means that some individuals lose out. Utilitarians assess the justice of rules (and therefore law) by looking at their consequences; in their view, if a rule maximized happiness or well-being or had some other desirable effect, for the majority, it was just. A law could therefore be just even if it created social inequalities, or benefited some at the expense of others, so long as the benefits to the many exceeded the loss to the minority.

The utilitarian approach can be criticized as focusing only on justice for the community as a whole, and leaving out justice for individuals.

▶ The economic analysis of law

This approach has developed mainly in the US, and attempts to offer a more sophisticated alternative to utilitarianism. While the goal of utilitarianism was to promote the greatest happiness of the greatest number, it offered no reliable way of calculating the effect of a law or policy on this goal, or measuring the relative benefits.

The economic analysis takes the view that a thing has value for a person when that person values it; its value can therefore be measured by how much the person is prepared to pay for it, or what would be required to make them give it up. As we have seen, a conflict exists between the concerns of utilitarianism and individual justice, and the same conflict exists here. Take the example of an NHS doctor with a limited budget, faced with one person who needs a life-saving operation costing £100,000, and ten others who each need more minor operations costing £10,000 each. On the face of it, doing the ten operations clearly seems to produce benefit for a greater number at the same cost, and in this sense may be the best way to spend public money. But can we say that this solution offers the first man justice?

A common criticism of the economic analysis of law is that it favours a particular ideology, that of market capitalism. It is based on the idea that the prices at which goods and services are bought and sold are the direct result of the value placed on them by buyer and seller, and therefore the result of free will; it presumes that sellers cannot exploit buyers, because nobody would pay more for something than it was worth to them. Critics of this approach point out that, in practice, power in the marketplace is frequently unequal; a seller may have the monopoly on particular goods, or sellers may collude to keep prices high. Equally, the idea that a thing has value because a person wants it ignores the question of where the desire for that thing originates; expensive advertising campaigns may produce the desire for what they sell, but can we objectively say that such publicity gives them value? In the same way, people may take low-paid jobs, not because they agree with that valuation of their labour, but because there are no other jobs and they have no power in the labour market.

Rawls: A Theory of Justice

Professor John Rawls first presented his ideas in *A Theory of Justice* which was published in 1971, and amended them slightly in his latest book, *Political Liberalism*. He approaches the question of justice through an imaginary situation in which the members of a society are to decide on a set of principles designed to make their society just, and advance the good of all its members. He describes this initial debate as the original position. The individuals involved will hold their discussions without knowing what their own position in the society is to be – whether they will be rich or poor, of high or low social status, old or young, and what will be the economic or political situation in the society. This veil of ignorance is designed to ensure that the ideas put forward really are the best for all members of society, since nobody will be willing to disadvantage a section of the community if they might find themselves a member of it.

Rawls believes that the principles which would result from such a discussion would include an equal distribution of what he calls social primary goods: these are the things which individuals are assumed to want in order to get the most out of their own lives, including rights, powers and freedoms, and, in Rawls's later work, self-respect. In addition to this, there would be two basic principles. The first involves liberty: a set of basic liberties – including freedom of thought, conscience, speech and assembly – would be available to all. Each person's freedom would be restricted only where the restriction on them was balanced out by greater liberty for the community as a whole. So, for example, the liberty of a person suspected of crime could be restricted by police powers of arrest, since these would increase the freedom from crime of society as a whole. The second basic principle is based on equality. This covers both equality of opportunity – offices and positions within society should be open to all equally – and equality of distribution. Rawls envisages an equal distribution of wealth, with inequalities allowed only where necessary to help the most disadvantaged.

If a social order is just, or nearly just, according to these principles, Rawls argues that those who accept its benefits are bound to accept its rules as well, even if they may disapprove of some of them, provided that those rules do not impose heavy burdens unequally, nor violate the basic principles. Professor Rawls would support limited disobedience, where the basic principles are violated, other means of obtaining redress fail, and no harm is done to others.

Rawls's theory has been extensively criticized. The clearest problem is simply its artificiality, particularly that of the veil of ignorance. As Dworkin has pointed out, even if we accept the scenario Rawls creates, the fact that individuals accept certain principles when they do not know what their position in society will be, does not necessarily mean they will continue to live by them if they find themselves in a position to maximize their own advantage at the expense of others. Rawls's theory appears to view human beings as rather more perfect than they have in fact shown themselves to be.

Nozick and the minimal state

Robert Nozick's provocative essay 'Anarchy, State and Utopia', argues that, for a truly just society, the state should have the minimum possible right to interfere in the affairs of individuals; its functions should be limited to the basic needs, such as protecting the individual against force, theft and fraud, and enforcing contracts. Written in 1974, the essay revives a claim traditionally associated with the seventeenth-century writer John Locke, and has strong links with eighteenth-century individualism, and nineteenth-century *laissez-faire* capitalism.

Nozick's theory emphasizes the importance of individual rights and, in particular, rights to property. He argues that the right to hold property is based on the way in which that property is obtained, either by just acquisition (such as inheritance) or just transfer (such as purchase from another), or by rectification of an unjust acquisition (for example, returning stolen property to its owner). Provided individuals have obtained their property in a just manner, the distribution of property throughout society is just; attempts to redistribute wealth are unjust because they interfere with the individual's right to hold justly obtained property. The state should, therefore, have no role in adjusting the distribution of wealth. In fact, Nozick rejects the idea that there are any goods belonging to society; goods belong only to individuals and the state has no right to interfere with them. Nozick's theories have been criticized, but they do reflect a growing disenchantment in Western society with the idea of redistributing wealth – in Britain we can see this in the emphasis placed by recent Governments on lowering taxes and expecting individuals to look after themselves, rather than taking taxes from the rich to help the poor.

Karl Marx

Marx held that it was impossible for a capitalist society to be just: such a society was organized with the aim of upholding the interests of the ruling class, rather than securing justice for all. For Marx, a just society would distribute wealth 'from each according to his capacity, to each according to his needs'; individuals should contribute what they can to society, and receive what they need in return. Marx's views are still influential, but the main criticism made of them is that so far no country has been able to put them into practice with sufficient success to bring about the fair society Marx envisaged.

Kelsen and positivism

For positivists, law can be separated from what is just or morally right. Parts of law may be based on, or incorporate ideas of, morality or justice, but this is not a necessary component of law; a law is still a law and should be obeyed even if it is completely immoral.

One of the best-known positivists is Kelsen, whose theories were first published in 1911, and further developed in his *General Theory of Law and State*, published in 1945. Kelsen tried to develop a pure theory of law, to explain what law is rather than suggesting what it ought to be. He saw justice as simply the expression of individual preferences and values and, therefore, as an irrational ideal. Because of this, argued Kelsen, it is not possible scientifically to define justice.

Justice in practice

One of the most important aspects of the British legal system is parliamentary supremacy, which essentially means that Parliament is the ultimate law-maker, and can make or unmake any law it wishes. In most other developed countries, a written constitution sets down basic principles with which law should conform, and judges can strike down any legislation which conflicts with them. That is not the case in the UK; our constitution is unwritten and judges must apply the law that Parliament makes, even if they believe it is unjust. If Parliament wanted to make laws condemning all blonde women to death, banning old men from keeping pet dogs, or obliging parents to sell their eldest child into slavery, there would probably be political obstacles to doing so, but there would be no legal ones and judges would be obliged to apply the laws.

Clearly, this situation conflicts with the natural law approach we discussed earlier, where unjust laws were considered not to be true law and, in some circumstances, not to require application by the courts or obedience by the citizen. Arguments for a Bill of Rights, a statement of basic principles against which courts could measure legislation and strike down any in conflict with them, have something in common with the natural law approach, since they assume that some values are fundamental and those given the power to make law in a society should be bound to follow them, rather than being free to make any law they want.

As with most developed legal systems, ours is based on the idea that, to achieve justice, like cases must be treated alike – thus if two people commit a crime in identical circumstances, they should be punished in a similar way. This aim requires fixed rules, so that decision-makers base their verdicts on the application of those rules to the case before them, and not on arbitrary factors such as their own mood or what they personally think of the defendant. However, the downside of this approach is that fixed rules can make it difficult to do justice in individual cases. Take the crime of murder, for example: to commit a murder, a defendant must have intended to kill or to cause serious injury; if this intention is present, the motive for killing is largely irrelevant. While this promotes the idea of like cases being treated alike, allowing judges to opt out of assessing the pros and cons of different motives, which must of necessity involve personal views, it presents problems in individual cases – can we say it is just for someone who kills a terminally ill relative to spare them from pain to be treated in the same way as someone who kills another so they can rob them? They both have intention but are they equally blameworthy? Fixed rules can sometimes promote justice in the majority of cases at the expense of justice in the individual, out-of-the-ordinary one.

The problem of fixed rules preventing justice in individual cases was one which our legal system faced early on in its life, when the common law was first becoming established. Then the answer was to develop a special branch of law, equity, with the specific aim of providing justice in cases where the ordinary rules of law failed to do so. Equity is no longer a separate branch of law, but equitable principles are still important in some areas of the civil law, and allow the courts to use their discretion in order to do justice in individual cases. In the criminal law (though not for the offence of murder) discretion over sentencing can fulfil a similar role. The challenge is to maintain a balance between too much discretion, leading to the possibility of arbitrary decisions, and too little, leading to harsh results in individual cases.

▶ ANSWERING QUESTIONS

1 **(a) To what extent should a legal system be concerned to promote justice?** *(10 marks)*
(b) How far do you believe that the English legal system does promote justice? *(15 marks) AQA (AEB)*

Part (a): a good way to start this question is to define justice, so that you can then assess the importance it should have for a legal system. We have seen that there are various theories on the nature of justice, and you could mention some of these, pointing out that they sometimes conflict. As a result, you might consider how far a system should be concerned to promote justice will depend on what you think justice is. Probably everybody would agree, for example, that a basic view of justice as fairness, is something a legal system should promote, but the meaning given to fairness often depends on a person or society's political stance, so that issues such as distributive justice may be desirable or undesirable depending on the political views of a society. You can discuss the different types of justice in this way, pointing to those which you feel a legal system should be concerned to promote. Note that this question is asking to what extent the legal system **should** be concerned to promote justice, so you need to do more than just describe how concerned it is with that issue for that part.

Part (b): This is an opportunity to apply the theories you have just discussed to areas of law which you have studied in detail. The choice of area is up to you – the important thing is that you have a detailed knowledge of both the operation of that area of law, and its background values. For example, you could talk about contract law and the capitalist values it upholds, which is linked with the kind of justice supported by Robert Nozick, and could be contrasted with the theory of distributive justice. You could also refer to any issues of law or the legal system which you feel show justice or injustice in the system – you might talk about the miscarriages of justice and their implications for the criminal justice system for example. Make sure you can make your answer detailed, mentioning specific cases or research that prove your point – it is better to choose a few areas of law you know well than to skim over the surface of everything you have learned.

28 Legal rights and duties

 One of the functions of a legal system is to define the rights owed to individuals within it, and the duties imposed upon them. The individual's relationship with the state, for example, creates a mass of both rights and duties, including rights to social security benefits, and the duty to pay tax. Rights and duties will also apply between individuals: if Anne runs Peter over in her car, she may have a duty to pay him compensation, arising from his right to claim that compensation. Similarly, parties to a contract have a duty to perform according to their agreement, and each party has a right to claim such performance.

When you study substantive branches of law – criminal, tort or contract for example – you will learn the specific rights and duties which they create, and look at how they apply to individuals. But in this chapter we are considering a more fundamental question: what exactly do we mean when we speak of a legal right or a legal duty?

An obvious answer might be that a claim is a legal right if it can be enforced; equally a legal duty might be one which you can be made to perform. But, as Professor Hart suggests, there may be many occasions where someone is physically unable to prevent their property being taken by another without authorization: the fact they could not enforce the law by preventing the property being taken would not mean they had no legal right to the property.

As well as a physical inability to enforce a legal right, there may be legal barriers to doing so. Claims in contract and tort, for example, must be brought within a certain period (usually six years); once this has expired, a court will not hear the claim. So, if Barry owes Susan money and Susan fails to bring an action within the specified period, Susan's right to a remedy is no longer available. She still has a legal right to the money, but cannot enforce that right in court.

Hohfeld's analysis of rights and duties

Clearly rights are less easy to define than they seem to be at first sight. The US legal writer, Wesley Hohfeld, has pointed out that this is because the term 'rights' actually applies to a wide range of different legal situations and relationships. It is difficult to find one meaning of rights which covers all of these.

In his book *Fundamental Legal Conceptions*, published in 1913, Hohfeld sought to clarify the different kinds of legal relationships in which rights and duties could apply. He showed that the sentence 'X has a right to R' has four different possible meanings.

The claim-right

Hohfeld's scheme started with the kind of relationship which he described as correlative: where a right gives rise to a corresponding duty. Here, the sentence 'X has a right to R' may mean that Y (or indeed everyone) has a duty to let X do R, so that X has a claim against Y. A contract is a good example of this situation: if Y has agreed to sell a CD to X for £10, and X has paid the money, X has a right to claim the CD and Y a duty to give it to X. This kind of right can be described as a claim-right.

The idea of a claim in fact pre-supposes a correlative duty, because there must be something to claim. The phrase 'X has a claim' is meaningless, but the statement 'X has a claim to the CD she has paid for' clearly has a meaning that derives from Y's duty to give X the CD. The right and the duty in this case could be described as opposite sides of the same coin.

However, not all rights have corresponding duties, nor does every duty imply a correlative claim. This area was studied by, among others, the influential nineteenth-century writer Austin. He distinguished between relative duties, which, as in our example of the sale of a CD, involve corresponding rights, and absolute duties, which are imposed by law without implying any corresponding rights. Austin's primary examples of absolute duties were those imposed by the criminal law. Clearly we are all under legal duties not to commit crimes, but it is hard to see who could gain rights against us from the creation of those duties. The same can be said of some duties created by statute; as those of you who study tort will see, these only occasionally give rise to specific correlative rights for individuals.

The function of these kinds of legal duties is primarily to regulate conduct so as to avoid what is viewed as harmful to society – that is why crimes are prosecuted by the state, rather than being regarded as an issue of rights and duties between individuals. In theory, it would be possible for the law to impose only duties, without creating corresponding rights, so that all breaches of duty were prosecuted by the state as crimes are, rather than individuals suing each other on the basis of their rights in tort or contract, for example. In practice, such a situation would demand enormous and expensive state machinery, and legal systems usually include a mixture of the kind of absolute duties discussed by Austin, where no individual correlating rights are created, and duties which do create correlating rights for individuals, and must therefore be enforced by individuals rather than the state in the event of their breach. While in some cases it will be clear which side of the line a duty falls – serious crimes such as murder, for example, will usually be dealt with by the state – other duties may be dealt with by public prosecution in one legal system, and by private legal action in another. The distinction between duties which do give rise to individual rights and those which do not can therefore be quite arbitrary, suggesting again that there is no reason why duties should necessarily give rise to rights.

The liberty/privilege-right

Hohfeld's second analysis of the sentence 'X has a right to do R' states that it may, and usually does, mean that X is free to do or not do R. It is not a statement of what Y must do (or not do) but of what X may do. Hohfeld called this type of 'right' a 'privilege'; others have preferred the term 'liberty'. Privilege can mean a special position, and encompasses situations where someone has a right to do something which would normally be a breach of a legal duty; examples include the judges' right to make slanderous remarks while acting judicially, without incurring legal responsibility, or the right to perform abortions granted to doctors in specified circumstances by the Abortion Act 1967.

Of more widespread application is the idea of a right in the sense of a liberty. What we mean here is a freedom to do something, in the sense that no one can prevent you from doing it, rather than an enforceable claim to do it. For example, when the term 'right to work' is used in our society, it refers to the fact that someone, usually trade unions, cannot prevent another working in a particular trade by denying employment to anyone who is not a member of the union. It does not mean that we all have an enforceable claim to a job. Nor does it necessarily mean that our freedom to work is unlimited – many employment contracts include terms restricting an employee's area of work on leaving that employer, by stating that they may not join a similar firm or set up a similar business within a specified distance of the previous employer. An employer can make a legal claim against any ex-employee breaking such a term. In this case the employee's liberty-right is qualified by the employer's claim-right.

Hohfeld's concept of a liberty-right includes freedom not to do something: having the right to wear a red dress by implication means also having the right to choose not to wear a red dress. The liberty-right is therefore the opposite of a duty: a duty to wear a red dress by implication means there is no liberty-right not to wear it. In the case of a liberty-right, 'X has a right' can be expressed as 'X may . . .'.

The power-right

Hohfeld's third category of right is described as a power. X has a power when X has the ability to alter a particular legal relationship by doing or not doing a particular thing. An example would be the right to foreclose on a mortgage, or to sell property.

Powers are usually based on claim-rights and privileges: thus, the owner of property has the power to sell it because of the claim-rights involved in having title to it; a police officer has the power to enter and search premises in some circumstances because of the privilege-rights granted to the police by law. But powers can exist independently of other types of right: if someone offers to sell you their property, you have a power-right to accept that offer, and thereby create a binding contract between you. Such a contract will change the seller's legal relationship with you.

Just as claim-rights give rise to correlating duties, power-rights may create correlating liabilities. So, in the case of a contract of sale the person offering to sell is generally free to withdraw that offer at any time before it is accepted: if the offer is withdrawn within this time, the power to accept, and the seller's liability to sell, both cease to exist. But, if the seller makes a binding agreement to keep the offer for sale open for a specified period, then he has a duty to do so and, if the offer is withdrawn before this period has expired, the potential buyer will have a claim against the seller for breach of their agreement.

In the case of a power-right, 'X has a right' can be expressed as 'X can'.

The immunity-right

Hohfeld's fourth, and final, type of right is an immunity. Where Y has no power to change X's legal relations, we can say that X has an immunity. An example of such an immunity occurs where a landowner gives another permission to use the land, under a licence which the law deems irrevocable. The user of the land – called the licensee – is immune from any withdrawal of the licence. The correlative of an immunity is a disability; in this example, the owner of the land is under a legal disability because he cannot withdraw the licence. Such an arrangement creates two types of right for the land user: an immunity-right preventing withdrawal of the licence, and a claim/right to use the land in accordance with the licence. The immunity-disability relationship is the basis of the claim-duty relationship.

Where an immunity-right exists, 'X has a right' can be expressed as 'You cannot do R to X'.

▶ The nature of rights

There are two main theories about the nature of rights: one emphasizes will or choice; the other interest or benefit. The will theory, expounded by Hart, among others, is based on the view that the purpose of law is to secure for individuals the greatest possible means of self-expression and self-assertion. This theory is closely related to ideas of moral individualism, in which individuals are seen as the best judge of their own interests, as opposed to society making decisions on their behalf. The effect of individuals all acting in their own best interests is assumed, by the working of the market, to produce the best outcome for society. The will theory defines the bearer of a right by the power they have over the duty created by that right: the power to choose whether to enforce it or not, to waive it or even extinguish it completely. The discretion allowed to the individual is the most important feature of this concept of rights.

By contrast, the interest (or benefit) theory argues that the purpose of rights is not to protect individual free will, but to protect interests or benefits. Originating in the work of Bentham, and expounded by modern writers such as MacCormick, this theory sees rights as benefits secured by rules which regulate relationships. The exact nature of such rights varies between different versions of the theory. One states that X has a right whenever X is in a position to benefit from the performance of a duty; another, put forward by MacCormick, argues that X can have a right whenever X's interests are recognized as being a reason for imposing obligations, whether those obligations are actually imposed or not. The latter position has the advantage of allowing us to identify where rights may lie, without needing to determine what the correlating duty may be, or on whom it should fall.

▶ ANSWERING QUESTIONS

1 **Examining the various approaches to their analysis, discuss the importance attached to rights and duties in English law.** *AQA (AEB)*

As you can see from this chapter, the terms rights and duties are capable of bearing a number of different meanings, as explained by Hohfeld. A good way to approach this question might be to start by explaining this, and then go on to discuss each different meaning as analysed by Hohfeld, relating it to areas of law which you have studied. So, for example, claim-rights and their correlative duties are obviously central to the whole notion of contract law, while absolute duties are the basis of criminal law, and liberty/privilege rights are important in the area of civil liberties. As you go through each category, you should give detailed examples of cases and other legal authority to support your points about the importance of different types of rights to different areas of the law. For example, you could look at the Criminal Justice and Public Order Act 1994 in a discussion of liberty/privilege rights or **R** v **Brown** on the imposition of criminal liability on homosexual sado-masochists.

29 Legal personality

As far as the law is concerned, it is not only human beings who can be counted as persons. In some cases, the law creates artificial persons, such as companies and corporations, which are dealt with legally as if they are people; this is called having legal personality. On the other hand, some human beings do not have full legal personality. Only when an entity has legal personality can it have legal rights and duties.

Human beings

A human being has legal personality from the beginning to the end of their life, but this is not as simple as it sounds. There is, for example, much debate over when life begins: is it at birth, at conception, or at some stage in between? This issue arose in the litigation surrounding the thalidomide tragedy during the 1960s and 1970s. Thalidomide was a drug, prescribed to pregnant women for morning sickness, which was later discovered to cause severe deformities in their unborn children. When the parents tried to sue for compensation, the issue arose of whether the drug manufacturers, Distillers, could owe a duty of care to an unborn child – in other words, whether the child could have legal personality before it was born. In the event, the litigation was settled out of court, leaving the question undecided. Later legislation, in the form of the Congenital Disabilities (Civil Liability) Act 1976, provided that if negligence caused a pre-natal injury to the mother, affecting the parents' ability to have a healthy child, then the disabled child could sue in tort after their birth for the damage caused to his or her self, but here the child's rights are derived from the parent rather than from their own possession of legal personality before birth.

Later cases have confirmed the view that an unborn child does not have legal personality of its own. In **Paton** *v* **British Pregnancy Advisory Service** (1979), a husband attempted to prevent his wife from having an abortion. Dismissing the case, the judge stated that a foetus cannot in English law have any right of its own at least until it is born. Similarly, in **Berkshire County Council** *v* **Director of Public Prosecutions** (1986), a mother addicted to drugs gave birth to a child who had severe withdrawal symptoms. Legislation allowed a child to be taken into care if its health was being avoidably impaired, and defined a child as a person under the age of 14. The court decided that an unborn baby could not fall within that definition, and so impairment to the baby's health before it was born could not justify a care order: on the other hand, impairment which happened after birth but resulted from the mother's conduct while pregnant could. Once a child has been born, it has a legal personality, but some legal rights and duties may be restricted during childhood.

Mental incapacity can also limit a person's legal rights and duties. Until the last century, married women lacked legal personality; a married couple was legally seen as one person, and that person was the man. Women could neither hold property nor make contracts.

A human being ceases to have legal personality when they die, but like the beginning of life, the end is not as straightforward as you might expect. Life-support technology and the transplanting of living organs have opened up possibilities with profound moral, social and legal implications, as can be seen in the case of Tony Bland, the football supporter injured in the Hillsborough disaster.

Although legal personality ends at death, the law still has an interest in the form of wills and inheritance, which in a sense give legal life after death, allowing the deceased to have their wishes carried out after they have passed away.

Corporate personality

As well as individuals, groups of people – such as companies, schools and councils – can have legal personality. They are broadly called corporations, and they allow the law to treat the group as separate from the individuals who operate or own it. There are three basic types of corporation.

Corporations sole

The corporation sole is a device which makes it possible to continue the official capacity of an individual beyond their lifetime, or tenure of office. The Crown is a corporation sole: its legal personality continues while individual monarchs come and go. The same can apply to holders of positions such as bishops, vicars or any office which continues to exist even though each individual only holds it for a limited time. The device of the corporation sole allows a particular occupant to acquire property or make contracts for the benefit of successors, or sue in tort for injuries to relevant property while it was in the hands of a predecessor.

Corporations aggregate

This term covers groups of people with a single legal personality, such as companies. A corporation aggregate can be created by royal charter (e.g.

universities), by statute (e.g. local authorities), or most commonly, by registration under the Companies Act 1985, s. 1.

Incorporation allows investors in a company to limit their liability if the company does not succeed. If a corporation has debts, no individual member has to pay any more than the amount outstanding, if any, on the value of their shares. By contrast, a firm which is set up as a partnership rather than a corporation has no legal personality separate from that of its individual members and the debts of the firm are, therefore, the debts of the individual members, payable in full. So, if you and two friends each invest £100 in a partnership which later incurs debts of £10,000, the three of you will be liable for the whole £10,000. But if you set up your business as a company with limited liability, your liability will be limited to the value of your shares in the company: £100. The company might go bankrupt but you would not. If, on the other hand, the company turned out to be very profitable, those profits can be paid out to shareholders in dividends. Should the company's annual profits be double the money invested in it, a £2 dividend could be paid for each £1.00 share, so for your initial £100 investment you would receive £200. The value of your shares would also increase as the high dividends attracted others to invest. Of course, if you were running the business as a partnership you would also receive profits, but you would be running the risk of losses as well.

This is of course a rather simplified account, but what you should see is that the concept of legal personality is used here to encourage investment, and so oil the wheels of commerce. Without it, investors would only put their money in the lowest-risk investments, and economic development would be slowed down.

Incorporation can also be used by individual traders, allowing them to keep business debts separate from their personal finances. This can lead to some rather bizarre and, some might say unjust, distinctions, as the case of **Salomon** *v* **Salomon** (1897) shows. Mr Salomon formed a company called Salomon & Co, in which he, his wife and their five children were the only shareholders. He had already been running a business, and sold this to the newly formed company at an exorbitant price. This new company went bankrupt shortly afterwards, still owing £10,000 of the purchase price to Salomon, and £7,000 to other creditors. Its assets only totalled £6,000, and Salomon was what is called a secured creditor, giving him a prior claim to the assets over the other, unsecured, creditors. The creditors argued that Salomon was disqualified from claiming against those assets, because he was the company and the sale was a sham. The trial judge and the Court of Appeal agreed, and gave the creditors prior claim to the assets. The House of Lords unanimously reversed the lower courts' decisions, holding that the company was in law a person distinct from Salomon and that, therefore, Salomon was preferentially entitled to the assets as secured creditor and so was entitled to be paid.

An additional reason for corporate legal personality is that it allows individuals to act in the name of the company, so that, for example, companies can make contracts and be sued.

Limited Liability Partnerships

The Limited Liability Partnerships Act 2000 created a new legal entity known as a limited liability partnership (LLP). Any business can trade as an LLP, and it is likely to be particularly popular with accountants and law firms who in the past have formed a traditional partnership which does not have legal personality. An LLP has legal personality for some purposes, for example, it can be liable in negligence.

▶ ANSWERING QUESTIONS

1 (a) Using appropriate examples, explain what is meant by legal personality. *(13 marks)*
(b) To what extent does the notion of legal personality indicate the capacity of the law to adapt to change (for instance, economic or technological)? *(12 marks)*
AQA (AEB)

Part (a): You need to distinguish between natural (human) legal personality and artificial (corporate) legal personality, and deal with each in turn. As far as natural legal personality is concerned, you should consider examples of human legal personality – for example, unborn children, newly born children (especially those who are handicapped) and comatose patients. For artificial personality, you should distinguish between corporations and other forms of business organizations, discussing the consequences for liability of different types of corporate personality.

Note that the examiners' report for this question points out that it was not intended to raise issues of status capacity (regarding children and women for example). However, the examiners say that where such discussion is combined with other more relevant material the student might gain a few extra marks.

Part (b): Again, it would be sensible to deal with natural personality and artificial personality in turn. With regard to natural personality, obvious issues to discuss might be the treatment of people in comas, mentioning the Tony Bland case, and the rights of unborn children. Although there is room to explain your own views in a question like this, an emotional outpouring about the rights or wrongs of abortion (or anything else) will not score high marks – you must anchor your points in clear legal examples.

As far as corporate personality is concerned, you could discuss the social and economic aspects of different types of corporate personality, including, for example, the growth of the limited company as a way of encouraging investment and growth.

2 Legal personality attaches both to human beings and to corporations. Discuss its meaning and importance in connection with both. *AQA (AEB)*

In looking at human personality you could use the material in the first part of this chapter and also look at the issue of gender change discussed at p. 496. As the introduction to this chapter stated, the fundamental importance of legal personality is that an entity with legal personality can have legal rights and duties. You could have shown the importance of the concept by examining the rights and duties which flow from possession of personality, for example the civil rights and freedoms under the European Convention on Human Rights.

Having explained the meaning of corporate personality, you could have shown its importance in the context of a capitalist society and note that the company structure can be used to limit liability.

❱ Reading on the Internet

The Limited Liability Partnerships Act 2000 is available on Her Majesty's Stationery Office website at:

http://www.hmso.gov.uk/acts/acts2000/20000012.htm

The explanatory notes to the Limited Liability Partnerships Act 2000 are available at:

http://www.legislation.hmso.gov.uk/acts/en/2000en12.htm

Appendix

▶ ANSWERING EXAMINATION QUESTIONS

At the end of each chapter in this book, you will find detailed guidelines for answering examination questions on the topics covered. Many of the questions are taken from actual A-Level past papers, but they are equally relevant for candidates of all law examinations, as these questions are typical of the type of questions that examiners ask in this field.

In this section, we aim to give some general guidelines for answering questions on the English legal system.

Citation of authorities

One of the most important requirements for answering questions on the law is that you must be able to back the points you make with authority, usually either a case or a statute. It is not good enough to state that the law is such and such, without stating the case or statute which says that that is the law. Some examiners are starting to suggest that the case name is not essential as long as you can remember and understand the general principle that the case laid down. However, such examiners remain in the minority and the reality is that even they are likely to give higher marks where the candidate has cited authorities; quite simply, it helps give the impression that you know your material thoroughly, rather than half-remembering something you heard once in class.

This means that you must be prepared to learn fairly long lists of cases by heart, which can be a daunting prospect. What you need to memorize is the name of the case, a brief description of the facts, and the legal principle which the case established. Once you have revised a topic well, you should find that a surprisingly high number of cases on that topic begin to stick in your mind anyway, but there will probably be some that you have trouble recalling. A good way to memorize these is to try to create a picture in your mind which links the facts, the name and the legal principle. For example, if you wanted to remember the contract law case of **Redgrave** *v* **Hurd**, you might picture the actress Vanessa Redgrave and the politician Douglas Hurd, in the situation described in the facts of the case, and imagine one of them telling the other the principle established in the case.

Knowing the names of cases makes you look more knowledgeable, and also saves writing time in the exam, but if you do forget a name, referring briefly to the facts will identify it. It is not necessary to learn the dates of cases though it is useful if you know whether it is a recent or an old case. Dates are usually required for statutes. Unless you are making a detailed comparison of the facts of a case and the facts of a problem question, in order to argue that the case should or could be distinguished, you should generally make only brief reference to facts, if at all – long descriptions of facts waste time and earn few marks.

When reading the 'Answering questions' sections at the end of each chapter in this book, bear in mind that for reasons of space, we have not highlighted every case which you should cite. The skeleton arguments outlined in those sections **must** be backed up with authority from cases and statute law.

When discussing the English legal system, as well as citing relevant cases and statutes it is particularly important to cite relevant research and reports in the field being discussed. If there are important statistics in an area, being able to quote some of them will give your answers authority.

There is no right answer

In law exams, there is not usually a right or a wrong answer. What matters is that you show you know what type of issues you are being asked about. Essay questions are likely to ask you to 'discuss', 'criticize', or 'evaluate', and you simply need to produce a good range of factual and critical material in order to do this. The answer you produce might look completely different from your friend's but both answers could be worth 'A' grades.

Breadth and depth of content

Where a question seems to raise a number of different issues – as most do – you will achieve better marks by addressing all or most of these issues than by writing at great length on just one or two. By all means spend more time on issues which you know well, but be sure to at least mention other issues which you can see are relevant, even if you can only produce a paragraph or so about them.

Civil or criminal

In some cases, a question on the English legal system will require you to confine your answer to either the civil or criminal system. This may be stated in the question – for example, 'Discuss the system of civil appeals'.

Alternatively, it may be something you are required to work out for your-self, as is often the case with problem questions. For example, a question might state:

Jane has been charged with criminal damage.
(a) How may she obtain legal aid and advice? and
(b) If convicted, to which courts may she appeal?

This question only requires you to discuss the legal aid and advice available in criminal cases, and the criminal appeals system; giving details of civil legal aid and the civil appeals system will waste time and gain you no marks, as would bringing the criminal appeals system into the previous question. Equally, where a question does not limit itself to either civil or criminal legal systems, you will lose marks if you only discuss one.

Because of this danger, it is a good idea to make a point of asking yourself before you answer any legal system question whether it covers just the civil legal system, just the criminal, or both.

The structure of the question

If a question is specifically divided into parts, for example (a), (b) and (c) then stick to those divisions and do not merge your answer into one long piece of writing.

Law examinations tend to contain a mixture of essay questions and what are known as 'problem questions'. Tackling each of these questions involves slightly different skills so we consider each in turn.

Essay questions

Answer the question asked

Over and over again, examiners complain that candidates do not answer the question they are asked – so if you can develop this skill, you will stand out from the crowd. You will get very few marks for simply writing all you know about a topic, with no attempt to address the issues raised in the question, but if you can adapt the material that you have learnt on the subject to take into account the particular emphasis given to it by the question, you will do well.

Even if you have memorized an essay which does raise the issues in the question (perhaps because those issues tend to be raised year after year), you must fit your material to the words of the question you are actually being asked. For example, suppose during your course, you wrote an essay on the advantages and disadvantages of the jury system, and then in the exam, you find yourself faced with the question 'Should juries be abolished?' The material in your coursework essay is ideally suited for the exam question, but if you begin the main part of your answer with the words 'The advantages of juries include . . .', or something similar, this is a dead giveaway to the examiner that you are merely writing down an essay you have memorized. It takes very little effort to change the words to 'Abolition of the jury system would ignore certain advantages that the current system has . . .', but it will create a much better impression, especially if you finish with a conclusion which, based on points you have made, states that abolition is a good or bad idea, the choice depending on the arguments you have made during your answer.

During your essay, you should keep referring to the words used in the question – if this seems to become repetitive, use synonyms for those words. This makes it clear to the examiner that you are keeping the question in mind as you work.

Plan your answer

Under pressure of time, it is tempting to start writing immediately, but five minutes spent planning each essay question is well worth spending – it may mean that you write less overall, but the quality of your answer will almost certainly be better. The plan need not be elaborate: just jot down everything you feel is relevant to the answer, including case names, and then organize the material into a logical order appropriate to the question asked. To put it in order, rather than wasting time copying it all out again, simply put a number next to each point according to which ones you intend to make first, second and so forth.

Provide analysis and fact

Very few essay questions require merely factual descriptions of what the law is; you will almost always be required to analyse the factual content in some way, usually highlighting any problems or gaps in the law, and suggesting possible reforms. If a question asks you to analyse whether lay magistrates should be replaced by professional judges you should not write everything you know about magistrates and judges and finish with one sentence saying magistrates should/should not be kept. Instead you should select your relevant material and your whole answer should be targeted at answering whether or not magistrates should be kept.

Where a question uses the word 'critically', as in 'critically describe' or 'critically evaluate', the examiners are merely drawing your attention to the fact that your approach should be analytical and not merely descriptive; you are not obliged to criticize every provision you describe. Having said that, even if you do not agree with particular criticisms which you have read, you should still discuss them and say why you do not think they are valid; there is very little mileage in an essay that simply describes the law and says it is perfectly satisfactory.

Structure

However good your material, you will only gain really good marks if you structure it well. Making a plan for each answer will help in this, and you should also try to learn your material in a logical order – this will make it easier to remember as well. The exact construction of your essay will obviously depend on the question, but you should aim to have an introduction, then the main discussion, and a conclusion. Where a question is divided into two or more parts, you should reflect that structure in your answer.

A word about conclusions: it is not good enough just to repeat the question, turning it into a statement, for the conclusion. So, for example, if the question is 'Is the criminal justice system satisfactory', a conclusion which simply states that the system is or is not satisfactory will gain you very little credit. Your conclusion will often summarize the arguments that you have developed during the course of your essay.

Problem questions

In problem questions, the exam paper will describe an imaginary situation, and then ask what the legal implications of the facts are – for example, 'Jane had suffered physical violence at the hands of her husband for many years. One days she lashes out and kills him. She is arrested by the police and later charged with murder. In which court will Jane be tried? If she is convicted to what court may she appeal?'

Read the question thoroughly

The first priority is to read the question thoroughly, at least a couple of times. Never start writing until you have done this, as you may well get halfway through and discover that what is said at the end makes half of what you have written irrelevant – or at worst, that the question raises issues you have no knowledge of at all.

Answer the question asked

This means paying close attention to the words printed immediately after the situation is described. In the example given above you are asked to advise about the courts and appeal procedure, so do not start discussing sentencing powers as this is not relevant to the particular question asked. Similarly, if a question asks you to advise one or other of the parties, make sure you advise the right one – the realization as you discuss the exam with your friends afterwards that you have advised the wrong party and thus rendered most of your answer irrelevant is not an experience you will enjoy.

Spot the issues

In answering a problem question in an examination you will often be short of time. One of the skills of doing well is spotting which issues are particularly relevant to the facts of the problem and spending most time on those, while skimming over more quickly those matters which are not really an issue on the facts, but which you clearly need to mention.

Apply the law to the facts

What a problem question requires you to do is to spot the issues raised by the situation, and to consider the law as it applies to those facts. It is not enough simply to describe the law without applying it to the facts. So in the example given above it is not enough to write about the appeal procedure in general for civil and criminal cases; you must apply the rules of criminal appeal to the particular case of Jane. She has committed an indictable offence that would have been tried by the Crown Court so you are primarily concerned with appeals from the Crown Court to the Court of Appeal. Nor should you start your answer by copying out all the facts. This is a complete waste of time, and will gain you no marks.

Unlike essay questions, problem questions are not usually seeking a critical analysis of the law. If you have time, it may be worth making the point that a particular area of the law you are discussing is problematic, and briefly stating why, but if you are addressing all the issues raised in the problem you are unlikely to have much time for this. What the examiner is looking for is essentially an understanding of the law and an ability to apply it to the particular facts given.

Use authority

As always, you must back up your points with authority from case or statute law.

Structure

The introduction and conclusion are much less important for problem questions than for essay questions. Your introduction can be limited to pointing out the issues raised by the question, or, where you are asked to 'advise' a person mentioned in the problem, what outcome that person will be looking for. You can also say in what order you intend to deal with the issues. Your conclusion might simply summarize the conclusions reached during the main part of the answer, for example that Jane will be tried in the Crown Court and her main route of appeal will be to the Court of Appeal.

There is no set order in which the main part of the answer must be discussed. Sometimes it will be appropriate to deal with the problem chronologically, in which case it will usually be a matter of looking at the question line by line, while in other cases it may be appropriate to group particular issues together. Problem questions on the English legal system are often broken down into clear parts – a, b, c and so on – so the answer can be broken down into the same parts. Thus with the example about Jane the question was clearly broken into two parts, and so your question should deal with first the trial court and then with the issue of appeal.

Whichever order you choose, try to deal with one issue at a time – for example, finish talking about the trial court before looking at the issue of appeal. Jumping backwards and forwards gives the impression that you have not thought about your answer. If you work through your material in a structured way, you are also less likely to leave anything out.

Glossary

Administrative law.   The body of law which deals with the rights and duties of the state and the limits of its powers over individuals.

Arraignment.   The process whereby the accused is called to the Bar of the court to plead guilty or not guilty to the charges against him.

Bill of Rights.   A statement of the basic rights which a citizen can expect to enjoy.

Case stated.   Under the proceedings, a person who was a party to a proceeding before the magistrates (or the Crown Court when it is hearing an appeal from the magistrates) may question the proceeding of the court on the ground that there was an error of law or the court had acted outside its jurisdiction. The party asks the court to state a case for the opinion of the High Court on the question of law or jurisdiction.

Caution.   1. A warning to an accused person administered on arrest or before police questioning. Since the abolition, by the Criminal Justice and Public Order Act 1994, of the right of silence, the correct wording is: 'You do not have to say anything. But it may harm your defence if you do not mention when questioned something which you later rely on in court. Anything you do say may be given in evidence.'
   2. A formal warning given to an offender about what he has done, designed to make him see that he has done wrong and deter him from further offending. This process is used instead of proceeding with the prosecution.

Certiorari.   An order quashing an *ultra vires* decision.

Chambers.   The offices of a barrister.

Community punishment order.   This order requires an offender to perform, over a period of 12 months, a specified number of hours of unpaid work for the benefit of the community, and to keep in touch with the probation officer and notify him of any change of address.

Community sentence. This means a sentence of one or more community orders (which include probation orders, community service orders, combination orders, curfew orders, supervision orders and attendance centre orders).

Constitution. A set of rules and customs which detail a country's system of government; in most cases it will be a written document but in some countries, including Britain, the constitution cannot be found written down in one document and is known as an unwritten constitution.

Contingency fee. A fee payable to a lawyer (who has taken on a case on a 'no win, no fee' basis) in the event of him winning the case.

Convention. 1. A long established tradition which tends to be followed although it does not have the force of law.
2. A treaty with a foreign power.

Corporation aggregate. This term covers groups of people with a single legal personality (e.g. a company, university or local authority).

Corporation sole. This is a device which makes it possible to continue the official capacity of an individual beyond their lifetime or tenure of office: e.g. the Crown is a corporation sole; its legal personality continues while individual monarchs come and go.

Counsel's opinion. A barrister's advice.

Custom. 'Such usage as has obtained the force of law' (**Tanistry Case (1608)**).

Delay defeats equities. Where a claimant takes an unreasonably long time to bring an action, equitable remedies will not be available.

Discovery of documents. The procedure whereby one party to an action provides the other party with a list of documents relating to the action which are or have been in his possession. The other party can then ask to see some or all of the documents.

Ejusdem generis rule. General words which follow specific ones are taken to include only things of the same kind.

Equity. In law it is a term which applies to a specific set of legal principles which were developed by the Chancery Court and add to those provided in the common law.

Expressio unius est exclusio alterius. Express mention of one thing implies the exclusion of another.

Habeas corpus. This is an ancient remedy which allows people detained to challenge the legality of their detention and, if successful, to get themselves quickly released.

He who comes to equity must come with clean hands. This means that a claimant who has been in the wrong in some way will not be granted an equitable remedy.

He who seeks equity must do equity. Anyone who seeks equitable relief must be prepared to act fairly towards their opponent.

Indictable offences. These are the more serious offences, such as rape and murder. They can only be heard by the Crown Court. The indictment is a formal document containing the alleged offences against the accused, supported by brief facts.

Law Officers. They are the Attorney-General and the Solicitor-General.

Lawyer. This is a general term which covers both branches of the legal profession, namely barristers and solicitors, as well as many people with a legal qualification.

Leapfrog procedure. This is the procedure provided for in the Administration of Justice Act 1969, whereby an appeal can go directly from the High Court to the House of Lords, missing out the Court of Appeal.

McKenzie friend. A litigant in person may take with him to the court or tribunal someone to advise him (a McKenzie friend), but that person may not usually address the court.

Mandamus. An order requiring a particular thing to be done.

Natural law. A kind of higher law, to which we can turn for a basic moral code. Some, such as Thomas Aquinas, see this higher law as coming from God, others see it simply as the basis of human society.

Noscitur a sociis. The meaning of a doubtful word may be ascertained by reference to the meaning of words associated with it.

Obiter dicta. Words in a judgment which are said 'by the way' and were not the basis on which the decision was made. They do not form part of the *ratio decidendi* and are not binding on future cases, but merely persuasive.

Parliament. Consists of the House of Commons, the House of Lords and the Monarch.

Per incuriam. Where a previous decision has been made in ignorance of a relevant law it is said to have been made *per incuriam*.

Plea bargaining. This is the name given to negotiations between the prosecution and defence lawyers over the outcome of a case: e.g. where a defendant is choosing to plead not guilty, the prosecution may offer to reduce the charge to a similar offence with a smaller maximum sentence in return for the defendant pleading guilty to that offence.

Practice Direction. An official announcement by the court laying down rules as to how it should function.

Prohibition. An order prohibiting a body from acting unlawfully in the future: e.g. it can prohibit an inferior court or tribunal from starting or continuing proceedings which are, or threaten to be, outside their jurisdiction, or in breach of natural justice.

Puisne judges. High Court judges are also known as puisne judges (pronounced puny) meaning junior judges.

Ratio decidendi. The legal principle on which a decision is based.

Relator action. A proceeding whereby a party, who has failed to prove *locus standi*, can choose to permit the action to be brought in the name of the Attorney-General.

Small Claims Court. This is not actually a separate court but a procedure used by the county courts to deal with claims under £3,000.

Sovereignty of Parliament. This has traditionally meant that the law which Parliament makes takes precedence over that from any other source, but this principle has been qualified by membership of the EU.

Stare decisis. Abiding by precedent: i.e. in deciding a case a judge must follow any decision that has been made by a higher court in a case with similar facts. As well as being bound by decisions of courts above them, some courts must follow their own previous decisions.

Summary offences. These are most minor crimes and are only triable summarily in the magistrates' courts. 'Summary' refers to the process of ordering the defendant to attend court by summons, a written order usually delivered by post, which is the most frequent procedure adopted in the magistrates' court.

Ultra vires. Outside their powers.

Wednesbury principle. This principle, which was laid down in **Associated Picture Houses Ltd** *v* **Wednesbury Corporation**, is that a decision will be held to be outside a public body's power if it is so unreasonable that no reasonable public body could have reached it.

Youth court. Young offenders are usually tried in youth courts (formerly called juvenile courts), which are a branch of the magistrates' court. Youth courts must sit in a separate courtroom, where no ordinary court proceedings have been held for at least one hour. Strict restrictions are imposed as to who may attend the sittings of the court.

Select Bibliography

Abel, R. (1988) *The Legal Profession In England and Wales*, Oxford: Basil Blackwell.

Abel-Smith, B. (1973) *Legal Problems and the Citizen*, London, Heinemann-Educational.

Alternative Dispute Resolution – A Discussion Paper (1999) London: Lord Chancellor's Department.

Aquinas, St T. (1942) *Summa Theologica*, London: Burns Oates & Washbourne.

Atiyah, P.S. (1979) *The Rise and Fall of Freedom of Contract*, Oxford: Clarendon Press.

Audit Commission (1997) *Misspent Youth: Young People and Crime*, London: Audit Commission Publications.

Auld, Sir R. (2001) *Review of the Criminal Courts*, London: H.M.S.O.

Austin, J. (1954) *The Province of Jurisprudence Determined*, London: Weidenfeld and Nicolson.

Bailey, S. and Gunn, M. (1996) *Smith and Bailey on the Modern English Legal System* (Third Edition), London: Sweet & Maxwell.

Baldwin, J. (1992) *The Role of Legal Representatives at the Police Station* (Royal Commission on Criminal Justice Research Study No. 2), London: H.M.S.O.

—— (1992) *Video Taping Police Interviews with Suspects: an Evaluation*, London: Home Office.

Baldwin, J. and McConville, M. (1979) *Jury Trials*, Oxford: Clarendon Press.

Baldwin, J. and Moloney, T. (1992) *Supervision of police investigations in serious criminal cases* (Royal Commission on Criminal Justice Research Study No. 4), London: H.M.S.O.

Bell, J. and Engle, Sir G. (eds) (1995) *Statutory Interpretation*, London: Butterworths.

Bennion, F.A.R. (1990) *Statutory Interpretation*, London: Butterworths.

Block, B.P., Corbett, C. and Peay, J. (1993) *Ordered and Directed Acquittals in the Crown Court*, London: H.M.S.O.

Bond, R.A. and Lemon, N.F. (1979) 'Changes in Magistrates: Attitudes During the First Year on the Bench' in Farrington, D.P. *et al.* (eds) (1979) *Psychology, Law and Legal Processes*, London: Macmillan.

Bottoms, A.E. and Preston, R.H. (eds) (1980) *The Coming Penal Crisis: A Criminological and Theoretical Exploration*, Edinburgh: Scottish Academic Press.

Brown, D. and Neal, D. (1988) 'Show Trials: The Media and the Gang of Twelve' in Findlay, M. and Duff, P. (eds) (1988) *The Jury under Attack*, London: Butterworths.

Brown, D. *et al.* (1992) *Changing the Code: Police Detention Under the Revised PACE Codes of Practice* (Home Office Research Study No. 129), London: H.M.S.O.

Burney, E. (1979) *Magistrates, Court and Community*, London: Hutchinson.

Carlen, P. (1983) *Women's Imprisonment: A Study in Social Control*, London: Routledge.

Consumer Council (1970) *Justice Out of Reach: A Case for Small Claims Courts: A Consumer Council Study*, London: H.M.S.O.

Cotton, J. and Povey, D. (1998) *Police Complaints and Discipline, April 1997–March 1998*, London: Home Office.

Criminal Justice: the Way Ahead (2001) Cm 5074, London: Home Office.

Denning, A. (1982) *What Next in the Law?*, London: Butterworths.

Devlin, P. (1965) *The Enforcement of Morals*, Oxford: Oxford University Press.

—— (1979) *The Judge*, Oxford: Oxford University Press.

Dicey, A. (1982) *Introduction to the Study of the Law of the Constitution*, Indianapolis: Liberty Classics.

Dickens, L. (1985) *Dismissed: A Study of Unfair Dismissal and the Industrial System*, Oxford: Blackwell.

Duster, T. (1970) *The Legislation of Morality*, New York: Free Press.

Dworkin, R. (1977) *Taking Rights Seriously*, London: Duckworth.

—— (1986) *Law's Empire*, London: Fontana Press.

Ellis, T. and Hedderman, C. (1996) *Enforcing Community Sentences: Supervisors' Perspectives on Ensuring Compliance and Dealing with Breach*, London: Home Office.

Enright, S. (1993) 'Cost effective criminal justice', *New Law Journal*.

Evans, R. (1993) *The Conduct of Police Interviews with Juveniles*, London: H.M.S.O.

Flood-Page, C. and Mackie, A. (1998) *Sentencing During the Nineties*, London: Home Office Research and Statistics Directorate.

Freeman, M.D.A. (1981) 'The Jury on Trial' 34 CLP 65.

Fuller, L. (1969) *The Morality of Law*, London: Yale University Press.

Genn, H. (1982) *Meeting Legal Needs?: An Evaluation of a Scheme for Personal Injury Victims*, Oxford: S.S.R.C. Centre for Socio-Legal Studies.

—— (1987) *Hard Bargaining: Out of Court Settlement in Personal Injury Actions*, Oxford: Clarendon Press.

—— (1998) *The Central London County Court Pilot Mediation Scheme: Evaluation Report*, London: Lord Chancellor's Department.

Genn, H. and Genn, Y. (1989) *The Effect of Representation at Tribunals*, London: Lord Chancellor's Department.

Green, P. (ed.) (1996) *Drug Couriers: A New Perspective*, London: Quartet.

Griffith, J.A.G. (1985) *Politics of the Judiciary*, London: Fontana Press.

Gudjonsson, G.H. (1992) *The Psychology of Interrogations, Confessions and Testimony*, Chichester: Wiley.

Hale, Sir M. (1979) *The History of the Common Law of England*, Chicago: University of Chicago Press.

Halliday, J. (2001) *Making Punishment Work, report of the Review of the Sentencing Framework for England and Wales*, London: Home Office.

Hart, H.L.A. (1963) *Law, Liberty and Morality*, Oxford: Oxford University Press.

—— (1994) *Concept of Law*, Oxford: Clarendon Press.

Hayek, F. (1982) *Law, Legislation and Liberty: A New Statement of the Liberal Principles of Justice and Political Economy*, London: Routledge.

Hedderman, C. and Moxon, D. (1992) *Magistrates' Court or Crown Court? Mode of Trial Decisions and Sentencing*, London: H.M.S.O.

HM Chief Inspector of Prisons (1997) *Women in Prison: A Thematic Review*, London: Home Office.

Hohfeld, W.N. and Cook, W.W. (1919) *Fundamental Legal Concepts as Applied in Judicial Reasoning*, London: Greenwood Press.

Home Office Research Development and Statistics Directorate *Jury Excusal and Deferral* (Research Findings No. 102).

Ingman, T. (1987) *English Legal Process*, London: Blackstone Press.

Jackson, R.M. (1989) *The Machinery of Justice in England*, Cambridge: Cambridge University Press.

Joseph, M. (1981) *The Conveyancing Fraud*, London: Woolwich.

—— (1985) *Lawyers Can Seriously Damage Your Health*, London: Michael Joseph.

Kelsen, H. (1949) *General Theory of Law and State*, Cambridge, Mass: Harvard University Press.

Kennedy, H. (1992) *Eve was Framed: Women and British Justice*, London: Chatto.

King, M. and May, C. (1985) *Black Magistrates: A Study of Selection and Appointment*, London: Cobden Trust.

Law Commission (1999) *Bail and the Human Rights Act 1998* (Report No. 157) London: H.M.S.O.

Lee, S. (1986) *Law and Morals*, Oxford: Oxford University Press.

Leigh, L. and Zedner, L. (1992) *A Report on the Administration of Criminal Justice in the Pretrial Phase in London, France and Germany*, London: H.M.S.O.

Leng, R. (1993) *The Right to Silence in Police Interrogation* (Royal Commission on Criminal Justice Research Study No. 10), London: H.M.S.O.

Levi, M. (1988) 'The Role of the Jury in Complex Cases' in Findlay, M. and Duff, P. (eds) (1988) *The Jury under Attack*, London: Butterworths.

—— (1992) *The Investigation, Prosecution and Trial of Serious Fraud*, London: H.M.S.O.

Locke, J. (1967) *Two Treatises of Government*, London: Cambridge University Press.

The Macpherson Report (1999) Cm 4262-I, London: H.M.S.O.

Maine, Sir H. (1917) *Ancient Law*, London: Dent.

Mair, G. and May, C. (1997) *Offenders on Probation* (Home Office Research Study No. 167) London: H.M.S.O.

Malleson, K. (1993) *A Review of the Appeal Process* (Royal Commission on Criminal Justice Research Series No. 17), London: H.M.S.O.

Mansfield, M. (1993) *Presumed Guilty: The British Legal System Exposed*, London: Heinemann.

Markus, K. (1992) 'The Politics of Legal Aid' in *The Critical Lawyer's Handbook*, London: Pluto Press.

McConville, M. (1992) 'Videotaping Interrogations: Police Behaviour On and Off Camera', *Criminal Law Review*.

McConville, M. and Baldwin, J. (1977) *Negotiated Justice: Pressures to Plead Guilty*, Oxford: Martin Robertson.

—— (1981) *Courts, Prosecution and Conviction*, Oxford: Oxford University Press.

McConville, M. and Hodgson, J. (1993) *Custodial Legal Advice and the Right to Silence* (Royal Commission on Criminal Justice Research Study No. 16), London: H.M.S.O.

McConville, M., Sanders, A. and Leng, P. (1993) *The Case for the Prosecution: Police Suspects and the Construction of Criminality*, London: Routledge.

Mitchell, B. (1983) 'Confessions and Police Interrogation of Suspects', *Criminal Law Review*.

Modernising Justice (1997) Cm 4155, London: Home Office.

Montesquieu, C. (1989) *The Spirit of the Laws*, Cambridge: Cambridge University Press.

Morgan, R. and Russell, N. (2000) *The Judiciary in the Magistrates' Courts* (Home Office RDS Occasional Paper No. 66), London: Home Office.

Moxon, D. (1985) *Managing Criminal Justice: A Collection of Papers*, London: H.M.S.O.

Moxon, D. and Crisp, D. (1994) *Case Screening by the Crown Prosecution Service: How and Why Cases are Terminated*, London: H.M.S.O.

Mullins, C. (1990) *Error of Judgement: The Truth About the Birmingham Bombings*, Dublin: Poolbeg Press.

No More Excuses – A New Approach to Tackling Youth Crime in England and Wales (1998) London: Home Office.

Nozick, R. (1975) *Anarchy, State and Utopia*, Oxford: Blackwell.

Nuttall, C., Goldblatt, P. and Lewis, C. (1998) *Reducing Offending: An Assessment of Research Evidence on Ways of Dealing with Offending Behaviour* (Home Office Research Study No. 187), London: Home Office.

Olivercrona, K. (1971) *Law as Fact*, London: Stevens.

Owens, A. (1995) 'Not Completely Appealing', *New Law Journal.*

Pannick, D. (1987) *Judges*, Oxford: Oxford University Press.

Paterson, A. (1982) *The Law Lords*, London: Macmillan.

Peach, Sir L. (1999) *Appointment Processes of Judges and Queen's Counsel in England and Wales*, London: H.M.S.O.

Pickles, J. (1988) *Straight from the Bench*, London: Coronet.

Plotnikoff, J. and Wilson, R. (1993) *Information and Advice for Prisoners about Grounds for Appeal and the Appeal Process* (Royal Commission on Criminal Justice Research Study No. 18), London: H.M.S.O.

Pound, R. (1968) *Social Control Through Law*, Hamden: Archon Books.

Rawls, J. (1972) *A Theory of Justice*, Oxford: Oxford University Press.

—— (1972) *Political Liberalism, John Dewey Essays in Philosophy*, New York: Columbia University Press.

Review of the Crown Prosecution Service (The Glidewell Report) (1998) Cm 3960, London: H.M.S.O.

Robertson, G. (1993) *Freedom, The Individual and The Law*, London: Penguin.

Royal Commission for the Reform of the House of Lords, Report of the (2000) *A House for the Future*, Cm 4534, London: H.M.S.O.

Sanders, A. (1993) 'Controlling the Discretion of the Individual Officer' in Reiner, R. and Spencer, S. (eds) *Accountable Policing.*

Sanders, A. and Bridge, L. (1982) 'Access to Legal Advice' in Walker, C. and Sturner, K. (eds) *Justice in Error.*

Sanders *et al.* (1989) 'Advice and Assistance at Police Stations and the 24 hour Duty Solicitor Scheme', London: Lord Chancellor's Department.

Schur, E. (1965) *Crimes Without Victims: Deviant Behaviour and Public Policy, Abortion, Homosexuality, Drug Addiction*, New York: Prentice Hall.

Skryme, Sir T. (1979) *The Changing Image of the Magistracy*, London: Macmillan. (Second Edition, 1983).

Smith and Bailey: see Bailey, S. and Gunn, M. (1991) *Smith and Bailey on the Modern English Legal System* (Second Edition), London: Sweet & Maxwell.

Smith, D. and Gray, J. (1983) *Police and People in London* (The Policy Studies Institute), Aldershot: Gower.

Smith, J.C. and Hogan, B. (1999) *Criminal Law*, London: Butterworths.

Stern, V. (1987) *Bricks of Shame: Britain's Prisons*, London: Penguin.

Summers, R. (1992) *Essays on the Nature of Law and Legal Reasoning*, Berlin: Duncker & Humblot.

Taylor, R. (1997) *Cautions, Court Proceedings and Sentencing in England and Wales 1996*, London: Home Office.

Thomas, D. (1970) *Principles of Sentencing: The Sentencing Policy of the Court of Appeal Criminal Division*, London: Heinemann.

Tonry, M. (1996) *Sentencing Matters*, Oxford: Oxford University Press.

Twining, W. and Miers, D. (1991) *How To Do Things With Rules*, London: Weidenfeld & Nicolson.

Vennard, J. (1985) 'The Outcome of Contested Trials' in Moxon, D. (ed.) *Managing Criminal Justice*, London: H.M.S.O.

Vennard, J. and Riley, D. (1988) *Triable Either Way Cases: Crown Court or Magistrates' Court?*, London: H.M.S.O.

Waldron, J. (1989) *The Law*, London: Routledge.

Weber, M. (1979) *Economy and Society*, Berkeley: University of California Press.

White, P. and Power, I. (1998) *Revised Projections of Long Term Trends in the Prison Population to 2005*, London: Home Office.

White, P. and Woodbridge, J. (1998) *The Prison Population in 1997*, London: Home Office.

White, R. (1973) 'Lawyers and the Enforcement of Rights' in Morris, P., White, R. and Lewis, P. (eds) *Social Needs and Legal Action*.

Whittaker, C. and Mackie, A. (1997) *Enforcing Financial Penalties*, London: Home Office.

Women in Prison: A Thematic Review (1997) London: Home Office.

Woodhead, Sir P. (1998) *The Prison Ombudsman's Annual Report*, London: Home Office.

Woolf, Lord Justice H. (1995) *Access to Justice: Interim Report to the Lord Chancellor on the Civil Justice System in England and Wales*, London: Lord Chancellor's Department.

Young, J. (1971) *The Drugtakers: The Social Meaning of Drug Use*, London: Paladin.

Your Right to Know (1997) Cm 3818, London: H.M.S.O.

Zander, M. (1988) *A Matter of Justice*, Oxford: Oxford University Press.

—— (1999) *The Law Making Process*, London: Butterworths.

—— (2001) 'Should the legal profession be shaking in its boots?', *New Law Journal* 369.

Zander, M. and Henderson, P. (1993) *Crown Court Study*, London: H.M.S.O.

Index